Family Therapy
CONCEPTS AND METHODS

FAMILY THERAPY
CONCEPTS AND METHODS

Michael P. Nichols, Ph.D.
ALBANY MEDICAL COLLEGE

With a Foreword by
Philip J. Guerin, Jr., M.D.
CENTER FOR FAMILY LEARNING

and

David R. Chabot, Ph.D.
FORDHAM UNIVERSITY AND CENTER FOR FAMILY LEARNING

GARDNER PRESS, INC.

NEW YORK LONDON

Gardner Press, Inc.
19 Union Square West
New York 10003

All foreign orders except Canada and South America to:
Gardner Press, Inc.
Chancery House
319 City Road
London N1, United Kingdom

Library of Congress Cataloging in Publication Data

Nichols, Michael P.
Family therapy, concepts and methods.

Bibliography: p.
Includes index.
1. Family psychotherapy. I. Title. [DNLM: 1. Family
therapy. WM 430.5.F2 N621f]
RC488.5.N53 1984   616.89'156   83-16492
ISBN 0-89876-093-3

Production Note
This book set in Galliard, with the display set in Quorum.
Printing and binding by Maple-Vail Press.
Typesetting by Meridian Type Service.
Book design by Raymond Solomon
PRINTED IN THE UNITED STATES OF AMERICA

To my Father who taught me kindness
and
To my Mother who taught me courage

Contents

Goals of Therapy
Conditions for Behavior Change
Techniques
Evaluating Therapy Theory and Results
Summary

Introduction
Sketches of Leading Figures
Theoretical Formulations
Goals of Therapy
Normal Family Development
Development of Behavior Disorders
Conditions for Behavior Change
Techniques
Evaluating Therapy Theory and Results
Summary

Introduction
Sketches of Leading Figures
Theoretical Formulations
Normal Family Development
Development of Behavior Disorders
Goals of Therapy
Conditions for Behavior Change
Techniques
Evaluating Therapy Theory and Results
Summary

Introduction
Theoretical Formulations
Normal Family Development
Development of Behavior Disorders
Goals of Therapy
Conditions for Behavior Change
Techniques

Context and Applicability of the Schools of Family Therapy
Selection of a Theoretical Position: Rational and Irrational Factors
Summary

Foreword

This past decade has seen a plethora of books on family therapy. Most of these publications have been anthologies of multiple authors, Guerin (1976), Gurman (1981), collections of previously published papers by a single author, Bowen (1978) or an indepth view of a single major methodology, Minuchin (1974), Hoffman (1981).

There has long been a need for a comprehensive single authored text to bring together an historical, developmental perspective with a parallel presentation of the multiple schools of family therapy. In this text Nichols has provided an impressive first attempt to fill that void.

In part one of the text an exhaustive elaboration of the historical roots and contemporary status of the family therapy field is presented.

The manner in which Nichols weaves together not only the major strands of the family therapy movement but also considers parallel efforts in other disciplines such as Lewin's work on field theory, Bion's study of group-dynamics, Moreno's psychodrama, Perls' Gestalt therapy and the contributions of Olson and Gurman is impressive. Throughout the text Nichols, a psychologist, demonstrates his discipline for detail. This discipline is used to advantage in an attempt to present as complete a picture as possible. It should be noted, however, that in spite of the magnitude of the task, the author manages to present the material in an engaging and highly readable style.

The first section provides the reader with a chronological and developmental journey through the maze of investigators, clinicians and concepts that formed what we now call Family Therapy. Nichols' refreshing perspective on the Field of Family Therapy is the closing paragraph of his 120 page overview.

"Now many axioms of family therapy are over exposed and under-examined—Family therapy has now lasted too long to be a fad; but it is still a young discipline in need of continued experimentation and study."

After a second section in which the author divides the field into different schools, considering each one in turn, he takes on the precarious task of attempting a comparative analysis of these theories and clinical methods.

Most of the family therapists whose works are reviewed in this text will probably take exception to at least some of Nichols' observations and interpretations of their work. However, what is far more important is that this text can serve as an organizing point for future generations of family therapists to define the limitations and further develop the strengths of what has gone on before them.

There continues to be a number of unresolved theoretical and practical issues within the family field itself. In fact, one could probably make a case that the general acceptance of family therapy has, in itself, contributed to some of the confusion in the field.

While there are many advantages to this diversity of activity and rapidity of developments within the field of family therapy, to date no one has been able to provide a definitive list of the elements that should be conveyed in the training of a family therapist. The following would seem to be essential: (1) an appreciation of the historical perspective to better understand the limits of present theory and technique; (2) an appreciation for the importance of clearly separating theory from the "charisma" of the founding pioneers; (3) an appreciation for the development of critical thinking about basic issues involved in family therapy in order to avoid the sterility of "cook book" mentality, and (4) a sophistication of clinical techniques that are directly related to theory.

The present text makes a major contribution to conveying these elements to future family therapists as well as helping current family therapists to more fully develop their understanding and skills. Nichols has succeeded in presenting a comprehensive survey of the field in a balanced and eclectic manner. The reader is invited to engage in critical thinking of the underlying concepts and issues without finding himself in a nihilistic state. Ultimately the reader is left with multiple suggestions on helpful clinical technique. This text should be of particular value to the applied clinician who appreciates the historical, personal and theoretical influences that have molded clinical methods.

Philip J. Guerin, Jr., MD
Center for Family Learning

David R. Chabot, Ph.D.
Fordham University Graduate School
Director of Clinical Ph.D. Program

Preface

After I set out to write this book, I discovered why no one had already done so. The spectacular growth of the family therapy movement has been matched by a vast outpouring of books on the subject. There are books on every method of treatment, books on special types of families, and edited collections of theoretical and practical papers. In short, there are books on practically every aspect of family therapy; everything, in fact, except a comprehensive description and analysis of the field written by a single author. This is understandable because the field is so large and so fast-changing that it is difficult to keep pace with.

I tried to make my presentation comprehensive but also selective. It simply isn't possible to include everything. Some readers may object that certain approaches received too little emphasis, and that other approaches received more than their due. Couples groups and multifamily groups, for example, though they continue to be popular, belong more to group than to family therapy. On the other hand, I did include psychoanalytic family therapy and sex therapy, because I do think that these are important and worthwhile approaches to the problems of families.

What makes a comprehensive presentation of family therapy even more difficult than the magnitude of the task is the rapidly changing nature of the field. Some of what was new when this project was begun is now well-accepted; some conceptual breakthroughs have become clichés. Nevertheless, there is now a significant body of well-established concepts and methods for treating families making this an opportune time for a detached assessment and integration. There will undoubtedly be important new ideas introduced after this is written, but I believe that this volume offers a useful framework within which new developments can be integrated.

The format of this book reflects my view about how best to learn family therapy. The culminating interest may lie in the methods of treatment, but they cannot be fully understood or appreciated without taking into account their context—historical and theoretical.

The book begins, as many do, with a chapter on history. In family therapy it is particularly important to know something about history, both to dispel the illusion that family therapy is, or ever was, a unitary approach, and to remind readers that the various approaches were developed to suit different patient populations with more or less unique problems. From the history I have distilled a set of enduring concepts and methods. Following that I described recent developments and how they are translated into practice on the current scene. Although there are as many theories of family therapy as there are family therapists, some concepts are so basic that everyone in the field should be familiar with them and these are discussed in the chapter on theory. These fundamental ideas include some that are familiar to most family therapists—circularity, general systems theory—and some that deserve to be better understood than they are—theories of individual development, and the family life cycle.

My selection of eight schools of family therapy was somewhat arbitrary. Although most of the schools are familiar, it is sometimes difficult to categorize individual practitioners. Some, like Virginia Satir, have clearly changed their allegiances over the years; others are just plain hard to pigeonhole. Two of the schools, family group therapy and communications family therapy, differ from the others in being more a part of family therapy's past than of its present. I included them because they were the original approaches to treating families and because some people, especially those who try to learn family therapy from books, continue to follow these models.

Each of the chapters on the systems of family therapy is organized similarly. This structure not only provides coherence among the approaches, but it also reflects a basic philosophy. I believe that before one can fully comprehend treatment it is necessary to have a clear model of disorder and a model of cure.

In describing the different approaches to family therapy I tried to give a fair and impartial description, but I also included honest appraisal and criticism. The final chapter is a comparative analysis, and this is a more personal statement representing my own attempt to pull diverse concepts and methods together, and to offer a view of what is important and lasting.

This book was written to be useful to a wide audience—from student to practitioner and from novice to expert—it is not, however, meant to be all things to all people. I tried to be inclusive, though no doubt some people will find contributions that were neglected; I tried to be fair, but I did not hold back my evaluations. I tried to consider each approach in detail, but it wasn't possible to be encyclopedic. For this reason, I have included a list of suggested readings at the back of the book for those who wish to pursue the most important original sources for each of the chapters. I also appended a glossary for additional clarification of terms.

Writing this book was enormously demanding but equally rewarding. Along the way I learned a good deal more about family therapy, and I found out that I have many friends. So many people read and commented on individual chapters that I prefer to thank them personally. I would, however, like to express my heartfelt thanks to Gardner Spungin who encouraged me to begin this project and guided me along the way. Thanks, also, to Barbara Fried who edited the text, pruning my airier clichés and pointing out when I had repeated the same idea more than three times in the same chapter. Melody Nichols, who read countless sections of the manuscript, knew when I needed criticism and when I just needed encouragement. Thank you, Melody. My kids, Sandy and Paul, know that they helped by walking on tiptoe when I was writing, and by being patient with my long absences. What they may not know is how much they taught me about loving family life. Finally, thank you Mary Shaw and Kellie Gardner for devoting so much energy to typing the manuscript.

Family Therapy
CONCEPTS AND METHODS

Part **I**

The Context of Family Therapy

1 The Historical Context of Family Therapy

INTRODUCTION

In this chapter I will discuss how family therapy emerged, and how its current concepts and methods developed. We will see that a few basic and enduring principles underlie an apparently chaotic development that incorporates conflicting and contradictory points of view.

Historical accounts necessarily blend objectivity and subjectivity. This one is no exception. Histories are written by individuals, and must be filtered through the limits of their information as well as their biases and commitments. Facts are complicated and scattered. A writer must sift through, evaluate, and edit material to give it shape and coherence. The result will naturally reflect whatever social and personal forces have shaped the writer's point of view about the material and have caused him to organize the scattered events he is describing in his own particular way. Although events themselves do have a certain objective reality, their retrospective description always reflects the outlook of the writer. Students should therefore always be alert to the dangers of this subjective bias, especially in accounts that emphasize either great men or the *Zeitgeist*.

Most previous histories of family therapy have leaned toward the "great man" theory, which is that events are shaped largely by the efforts of a few major historical figures. Pioneer family therapists tend to emphasize their own roles in the family therapy movement, and other writers have also concentrated on these major figures. For instance, Thomas Kuhn takes the position (Kuhn, 1970) that progress in science occurs in discontinuous leaps, generated by people of vision who suddenly go beyond the paradigms of normal science. The *Zeitgeist* point of view is that precedents and trends exist in the "climate of the times," which is what *Zeitgeist* means. Almost any historical development can be described as more or less due either to *Zeitgeist* or to creative individuals, and family therapy is no exception, since it is both the product of its times and of the efforts of a few significant individuals.

DISCOURAGEMENT OF CONTACT WITH FAMILIES

Before family therapy, clinicians avoided and discouraged contact with the relatives of their patients. The two most influential approaches to psychotherapy in 1950, Freud's psychoanalysis and Rogers' client-centered therapy, were both based on the premise that psychological problems arise from unhealthy interactions with others, and can best be alleviated by treatment through a private relationship between patient and therapist.

Freud was convinced that neurotic conflicts are spawned in early interactions between children and their families. He therefore sought to isolate the family as much as possible from treatment in order to liberate patients from these pathological family influences, as though the family were an infectious disease to be kept out of the psychoanalytic operating room. Furthermore, he discovered that the less he revealed of his own personality and feelings, the more his patients reacted toward him as though he were a significant figure from the patient's family. At first this "transference" reaction seemed a hindrance, but Freud soon realized that it was an invaluable method for gaining information about the ways that a patient habitually reacted to significant persons from the past. Consequently, fostering and analyzing the transference became a cornerstone of psychoanalysis and other dynamic psychotherapies. This meant that since the analyst was interested in the patient's subjective opinions and fantasies about his family members, having these relatives actually present in the sessions could add nothing to treatment, and indeed, any of the patient's current interactions with family members might even obscure information about childhood thoughts and feelings. Freud was not interested in the guarded and sublimated responses that his patients might display in the presence of the family; he was concerned with unraveling the associative chains that led to thoughts and feelings characteristic of childhood responses, and he thought absolute privacy was necessary for the patient to feel safe enough to express such raw feelings. Freud wanted to protect the special patient-therapist relationship and therefore avoided contact with family members. By doing so he safeguarded the patient's trust in the sanctity of the therapeutic relationship, and thus maximized the likelihood that the patient would repeat, in relation to the analyst, the attitudes developed early in life.

Carl Rogers also believed that psychological problems stem from destructive early interactions with other people. Each of us, Rogers said, is born with an innate tendency toward *self-actualization,* an idea that is the basic premise of all humanistic psychologies. Left to our own devices we tend to follow our own best interests. Since we are curious and intelligent, we explore and learn; since we have strong bodies, we play and exercise; and since association with others brings us pleasure, we tend to be outgoing, loving, and affectionate.

Unhappily, said Rogers, our healthy instinct toward actualization gets warped and subverted. We crave the affection and approval of other people, but these others respond to us in terms of their own needs and values. They give the approval we crave only if we do what they approve of. That is, others who are important to our feelings of worth tend to respond positively to only certain aspects of our behavior, whether or not these are the aspects that are inherently satisfying to us. Consequently children do not so much learn what is best for them as how to avoid displeasing others.

Gradually this conflict between the tendency toward self-fulfillment and the need for approval leads to denial and distortion of our inner promptings and even of the feelings which signal them. Thus we learn to deny feelings of anger when we are unfairly criticized, lest we encounter disapproval. In fact, we may spend our whole lives in vocations that were selected as a way to get approval rather than as a means of fulfilling our own inherent interests and potentials. A child whose talents and interests would be served by working out of doors at manual labor may be induced by parental pressures and social mores to seek a white-collar career, without ever fully recognizing that such a career cannot be fulfilling. The consequences of this decision may be a life of vague unhappiness, with or without more obvious psychological symptoms; but the real cause of unhappiness—the unfulfilled basic needs and feelings—may never be understood.

The therapy that Rogers developed was designed to help patients rediscover their own feelings, urges, and basic self-actualizing tendencies. Given his faith that people will find their own best interests, Rogers' view of the proper role of the therapist was that it should be passive, but supportive. The therapist doesn't do anything to the patient, but provides conditions to help the patient discover what needs to be done, primarily by providing "unconditional positive regard." The therapist listens carefully and sympathetically, communicating understanding, warmth, and respect for the patient. In the presence of such an accepting listener the patient is gradually able to discover his or her own feelings and inclinations. Although this sounds simple, it is a unique relationship. Nowhere else are we liable to encounter people who are willing to simply listen with acceptance and understanding and without imposing their own needs and values on us. Try telling somebody else about an upsetting experience, and you will find that even the most understanding listener will eventually interrupt you to tell you a similar story of his or her own, or to give you some advice about how to handle it.

The client-centered therapist, like the psychoanalyst, maintains absolute privacy in the therapeutic relationship, in order to avoid any situation in which patients' feelings and impulses might be denied and distorted to win the approval of others. Only a specially trained person can communicate the unconditional acceptance that helps patients rediscover their basic selves; therefore family members and other outsiders can have no place in the work of the client-centered therapist.

EFFECTS OF PATIENT IMPROVEMENT ON THE FAMILY AND IMPACT OF FAMILY VISITS ON HOSPITALIZED PATIENTS

Although the family's role in the etiology of psychiatric problems has always been recognized, most clinicians believed that excluding the family was a necessary condition for undoing its destructive influence. Eventually, however, therapists were forced to acknowledge the family's continuing power to influence the course of treatment, especially for patients who go mad and require hospital care. Individual psychotherapy is predicated on the patient's having a stable, dependable, and relatively constant environment, so that the therapist can take a continuing family context for granted and concentrate on the individual's personality, unconscious, and past. This approach is less reasonable when the patient's environment is itself undergoing crisis, conflict, and change. All too often the hospitalized individual is an emotional prisoner of such an environment.

Two observations indicated that reciprocal influences exist between hospitalized patients and their families. First, many therapists noticed that often when hospitalized patients improved, other members of their families developed problems. It was almost as though the family needed to have a symptomatic member, and that any member would do. In the early fifties, Don Jackson documented the effects that treating patients by psychotherapy had on their families (Jackson, 1954). In one case, Jackson was treating a woman for depression; when she began to improve, her husband called to complain that her emotional condition was getting worse. When she continued to improve, the husband lost his job. Eventually he killed himself. Apparently his stability had been predicated on having a sick wife.

In another case, a husband had urged his wife to seek psychotherapy for frigidity. When, after several months of treatment, she became less inhibited and more sexually responsive, he became impotent. Another example of a marital relationship that similarly maintains its balance only so long as one partner remains symptomatic is a marriage in which one spouse is an alcoholic and the other spouse is subtly encouraging the drinking. Apparently some people are better able to accept a needy, dependent partner than one who is a competent and capable adult, like those men who insist their wives be dependent and helpless ("feminine") to prop up their own self-esteem.

A similar pattern of shifting disturbance was discovered in families with an identified schizophrenic patient. When the patient improved, disruptions often occurred at home. The behavior of other family members changed in such a way as to push the patient back into schizophrenic behavior; or, if the patient recovered, others in the family began to show pathological stress (Bateson, 1959; Haley, 1959; Jackson 1961; Jackson and Weakland, 1959). As Otto Will (quoted in Stierlin, 1977, p. 12) noted, "Frequently it is at the first sign of progress with schizophrenics that their relatives want to take them out of treatment."

The impact of a patient's improvement on the family is not always negative. Fisher and Mendell (1958) reported a spread of positive changes from patient to other family members. However, whether the nature of the effect that patient change has on the family is productive or destructive is not the point. The fact is, change in one person changes the system.

The validity of these clinical observations was corroborated in a study conducted at the Maudsley Hospital in England, in which a group of schizophrenic patients who were discharged either to their parents' homes or to live with their spouses was compared to a similar group of patients who lived alone. A significantly higher relapse rate was observed in the group who returned to their families (Brown, 1959). At least in this sample, the disrupting effect of living with familes outweighed any positive effects from family support and nurturance. Furthermore, the fact that family visits may disturb psychiatric patients is so well known that most hospitals do not allow patients to have family visitors at least during the initial period of their hospital stay.

STUDIES OF SMALL GROUP BEHAVIOR

Those who wished to understand and treat families could readily see that there are parallels between families and small groups; the similarities between them are obvious, the differences few. This led some therapists at first to treat familes as though they were just a special type of small group; however, they found that a few significant differences limit the transfer of technologies directly from one arena to the other. Before considering the limitations of group methods as applied to family therapy, let us examine some of the principles of group dynamics and group psychotherapy.

Information about the complex and interdependent forces affecting individuals interacting in small groups has been derived from many sources, both practical and theoretical, and has been applied in social psychology, industrial psychology, sociology, social work, psychiatry, and clinical psychology.

During the 1920s social scientists began studying natural groups in society, hoping to learn how to solve social problems by coming to understand patterns of interaction in normal social groupings. They did case work with various groups and social welfare projects; they held group discussions with patients, which in the 1930s led to development of group psychotherapy; and they investigated small group dynamics. One of the most prominent and influential contributors to this field was Kurt Lewin, whose field theory (Lewin, 1951) guided a generation of researchers, industrial psychologists, group therapists, and agents of social change. In fact, Lewin, with his collaborators and students, was instrumental in developing the laboratory movement that produced first T-groups and then the encounter group movement.

Lewin's field theory describes the organic interactions between individuals and their environment. Drawing on ideas from the gestalt school of perceptual psychology, Lewin emphasized the interdependence of part-whole relationships. He developed the notion that the group is a psychologically coherent whole rather than merely a collection of individuals. The group as a whole is different from and more than the sum of its parts. This transcendent property of groups has obvious relevance to family therapists who must work not only with individuals but also with a family system. Many of Lewin's other concepts will already be familiar. They include: *life space, tension, energy, need, valence,* and *vector.* Using these concepts, people can be described (and diagrammed) as occupying more or less *life space,* experiencing varying degrees of *tension,* and being driven by fluctuating amounts of *energy* in pursuit of a variety of *needs* whose salience at the moment provides the *valence* for movement along certain *vectors.*

Another of Lewin's important discoveries is that group discussions are superior to individual instruction or lecturing as a way to change ideas and social conduct. Applied to psychotherapy, this suggests that conjoint family meetings may be more effective in changing each family member's behavior than separate meetings with individuals. Trying to coach a wife by herself to behave more assertively at home, for example, is far less likely to succeed than working with the couple. By meeting with both partners the therapist can help the wife deal better with her spouse's counterreactions, and at the same time can make the husband more aware of the need to accept the new assertiveness.

Analyzing what he called "quasi-stationary social equilibrium," Lewin pointed out that change in group behavior requires "unfreezing" and "refreezing." First something must shake up and unsettle the group members' accustomed beliefs and behaviors; only then will they be prepared to accept change. This has been confirmed by the experience of successful family therapists. In individual therapy the unfreezing process is at least begun by the disquieting experiences that lead a person to become a patient. Once he or she accepts the status of patient and meets individually with a therapist, the person has done much to unfreeze habitual group ties. When a family comes for treatment, it is quite a different matter. Many of the members may not have been sufficiently unsettled by the symptomatic member's behavior to be prepared to change their own behavior. Furthermore, family members bring their own primary reference group with them, with all its traditions, mores, and habits. Consequently much more effort is required to unfreeze, or shake up, a family than an individual before change can take place. Examples of unfreezing maneuvers include Minuchin's promotion of crises in family lunch sessions, Norman Paul's use of cross confrontations, and Peggy Papp's family choreography.

Wilfred Bion is another student of group dynamics whose influence has been far-reaching. He is best known for his description of three basic assumptions of groups (Bion, 1948). According to Bion, most groups become diverted from their primary tasks by engaging in patterns of *fight-flight, dependency,* or *pairing*. In *fight-flight* groups, members become so preoccupied with hostile conflict that battling or avoiding it, not problem-solving, becomes the real purpose of the meeting. In *dependency* groups, maintaining a dependent relationship with the leader is actually more important to the members than the content of group discussions or even the group's avowed goals. This kind of dependency is operating when students select courses in order to be entertained by witty instructors, or to be enthralled by physically attractive ones. Finally, in *pairing* groups, members are more interested in being with each other than they are in working toward the group's goals. Even in therapy groups, members may be more involved with meeting weekly to socialize than with personal exploration and change.

Bion's basic assumptions are easily extrapolated to family therapy. Some families are so afraid to face conflicts that they scrupulously avoid dealing with the issues that concern them, session after session. Others use therapy sessions just to vent their spleen, preferring to fight endlessly rather than to contemplate compromise, much less change.

Both Lewin and Bion have greatly influenced students of group dynamics. There are two major centers today devoted to analysis and change of small group behavior—the National Training Laboratory (NTL) in the United States, and the Tavistock Institute of Human Relations in Britain.

Other ideas about group dynamics also apply to family treatment. Warren Bennis, a student of Lewin's described group development as going through two main phases, each with three subphases (Bennis, 1964): Phase I *Dependence* (1)dependence-flight, (2) counterdependence-flight, and (3) resolution-catharsis; Phase II *Interdependence* (4) enchantment-flight, (5) disenchantment-flight, and (6) consensual validation. Bennis's conception of dependence and interdependence as the central problems in group life antedates similar notions among family therapists, including Minuchin's description of families as varying from enmeshment to disengagement, and Bowen's concepts of fusion and differentiation.

The *process/content* distinction in group dynamics has likewise had a major impact on family treatment. Family therapists have learned to attend more to *how* families interact than to the content of their discussions.

Strategic family therapists even go so far as to say that the ways that family members try to solve difficulties become problem-maintaining behavior and thus more troublesome than the original difficulties.

Students of small group behavior have also explored the factors involved in developing a productive atmosphere in groups, group cohesiveness; the effectiveness of high- and low-structured groups; implications of authoritarian and democratic groups; scapegoating; sociometric assessment of how friendship choices dictate channels of communication more than formal structure; leadership and power, formal and informal, autocratic, democratic, or laissez faire; and how effective leadership contributes to the emotional needs as well as to the task of the group (Luft, 1970).

The influence of roles on behavior has been an important theme in the literature of psychoanalysis, family therapy, and group dynamics. At the beginning of the century Charles Cooley, a sociologist, described differing roles in various groups as having a prepotent impact on behavior (Cooley, 1902). According to this role analysis, multiple roles and multiple group affiliations are keys to understanding individual motives. We tend to think of family members as occupying but one role (mother or son), but we need to remember that mother may also be a wife, a friend, a daughter, and an employee. Furthermore, even those roles that are not currently performed are potential and therefore important. A mother who is a single parent is also potentially a wife or lover. Her neglect of these potential roles may impoverish her life and cause her to smother her children. Failure to consider potential as well as actual roles is a form of therapeutic myopia which limits the effectiveness of family therapy.

Sherif (1948) and others have shown that multiple roles required to belong to various groups can create problems. Dutifully doing what you are told and patiently waiting for recognition and reward may work when you are in the role of son or daughter, but these attitudes do not work for a lover or employee, where more outgoing and assertive action is called for.

Roles tend to be stereotyped in most groups, and so there are characteristic behavior patterns of group members. Bales (1950) described twelve broad categories of group behavior, including: "shows solidarity" (raises others' status, gives help); "shows tension release" (jokes, laughs); "agrees" (passive accepting, compliance); "gives suggestions"; and "asks for suggestions." Similar role patterns also characterize family members, most of whom learn a particular role in the family that becomes more or less fixed. Sometimes these roles may be transferred to extrafamilial relationships, where they are generally less appropriate. Virginia Satir (1972) describes family roles, such as the placator or the disagreeable one, in her book

Peoplemaking. If you think about it, you may be able to recognize that you played a fairly regular role in your family while you were growing up. Perhaps you were "the good boy," "mother's helper," "the quiet one," "the family joker," "the counselor," "the thinker," or "the successful one." The trouble is that a role once assumed is hard to put aside. The result is often a limited range of behavior in which we continue to do what has come to be expected of us. You may have noticed that even such a simple change as growing a beard, losing weight, or changing hairstyles discomfits some people—they just aren't comfortable adapting their expectations to your change.

The encounter group movement which has had such enormous clinical and social consequences was a direct offshoot of studies of group dynamics. T-groups, forerunners of encounter groups, were begun in 1946 by Kurt Lewin and his colleagues, Leland Bradford, Kenneth Benne, and Ronald Lippit (Benne, 1964). These groups were begun as a means of using participant observation to study small group dynamics. The aim gradually shifted from simply understanding group behavior to helping members clarify their goals and learn methods by which to realize these goals in group interactions. These modest aims proved very successful in increasing effectiveness and satisfaction; as a result, T-groups evolved into encounter groups, the main purposes of which are personal growth and enrichment. Influential as the encounter group movement has been (Nichols and Zax, 1977), it came too late to have any impact on the early history of family therapy. However, the experiential school of family therapy has been influenced by the encounter group movement, and this matter will be considered further in Chapter 6.

Group therapy has also had a definite influence on the course of family therapy. Among the first to utilize the therapeutic potential of groups was Joseph Hershey Pratt, who in 1905 assembled a group of tubercular patients for encouragement and supervision. Subsequently, two psychiatrists, L. Cody Marsh and Edward Lazell, met with groups of hospitalized psychiatric patients for didactic discussions and mutual support (Nichols and Zax, 1977). Group treatment remained largely an inspirational, persuasive, and supportive technique until the psychoanalytic conceptual framework was applied by Trigant Burrows, Louis Wender, and Paul Schilder (Nichols and Zax, 1977). Their new approach, which incorporated the dynamics of small groups with the dynamics of individual personality structure, was consolidated into a coherent theory and technique by Samuel Slavson (1943).

Analytic groups focus on the unconscious strivings of group members. The patients' basic motives are considered to be dynamic equilibria between love and hate, pain and pleasure, and strictures of culture versus demands of primitive impulses. The developing ego is seen as the basic coping mechanism, and the growth and dissolution of psychological defenses the battleground on which these forces meet. Analytic groups are designed to be frustratingly unstructured in order to arouse latent unconscious conflicts. Transference reactions are enhanced and multiplied by the presence of a variety of people in addition to the therapist.

In the group dynamics approach, developed by Foulkes, Bion, and Ezriel in Great Britain, the focus shifted from individuals to the group itself, seen as a transcendent entity with its own inherent laws. These therapists studied group interaction not only for what it revealed about individual personalities, but also to discover the over-all themes or dynamics common to all patients. This *group process* was considered a fundamental characteristic of social interaction and a major vehicle for change.

The existential or experiential model was also a clear departure from psychoanalytic group therapy. Experiential group therapy, stimulated by existential psychiatrists Ludwig Binswanger, Medard Boss, and Rollo May in Europe and by Carl Rogers, Carl Whitaker, and Thomas Malone in this country, emphasizes deep personal involvement with patients as opposed to dissecting them as objects. Phenomenology replaces objective analysis, and immediate experience, especially emotional experience, is seen as the royal road to growth and change. Instead of transference, experiential therapists emphasize the profoundly real aspects of the therapeutic relationship, conceived as an authentic "I-thou" encounter.

Moreno's psychodrama, in which patients act out their conflicts instead of discussing them, was one of the earliest approaches to group treatment (Moreno, 1945). Psychodramas consist of dramatic enactments from the lives of participants, using a number of techniques to stimulate emotional expression and clarify conflicts. Because the focus is on interpersonal action, psychodrama is a direct and powerful means of exploring family relationships, and family problems are often the direct focus in psychodramatic performances. Although psychodrama has remained tangential to the mainstream of group psychotherapy, Moreno's role-playing techniques have been widely adopted by group leaders and family therapists. Minuchin, for example, conducts family treatment as though he were a theatrical director, and insists that interpersonal enactments are essential for capturing the real drama of family life. Family sculpting and choreography are even more closely derived from psychodrama.

Fritz Perls's Gestalt psychotherapy aims to enhance patients' awareness in order to increase spontaneity, creativity, and personal responsibility. Even though it is frequently used in groups, Gestalt therapy discourages other group members from interacting with the patient while he or she is working with the therapist. Although more widely used in individual than in group or family treatment, Gestalt techniques have been borrowed by encounter group leaders, such as William Schutz, to stimulate emotional interaction among group members. Some family therapists have also adopted Gestalt techniques; these will be discussed in Chapter 6.

Like Gestalt therapy, behavior therapy is aimed at individuals even when practiced in group settings. Behavioral groups are usually made up of members who share a single habit disorder; group meetings are conducted as practice sessions for trying out new forms of behavior. Assertive training groups are probably the most widespread and familiar form of behavioral group therapy.

Given these extensive and diverse procedures for exploring interpersonal relationships developed by group therapists, it was natural that some family therapists would apply group treatment models to working with families. Family group therapy was an application of small-group theory and group therapy technique to the natural group of the family. After all, what are families but collective groups with various subgroups? The first to apply group concepts to family treatment were John Elderkin Bell and Rudolph Dreikurs. Bell, whose work is well-known and influential among family therapists, first described family group therapy in 1955. Dreikurs, whose work is less well-known, began publishing his ideas in the late forties and early fifties. Family group therapy continues to be a major approach to working with families, and Bell's and Dreikurs' work will be considered at length in Chapter 5.

Before examining the question of how suitable the group treatment model is for family therapy, I must mention one more historical fact. Even before Bell and Dreikurs began to apply group psychotherapy to families, a number of workers had used the group format to enlist cooperation from family members in planning treatment for individual patients. Marsh, for instance, lectured to groups of relatives at Worcester State Hospital (Marsh, 1935); and Low also used this technique in his work (Low, 1943). Other therapists concentrated on group meetings with mothers whose children were in treatment (Amster, 1944; Burkin, Glatzer, and Hirsch, 1944; Lowrey, 1944). Some, including Ross at McGill, held weekly discussion groups for families of adult patients (Ross, 1948). In all these group meetings, relatives were treated like helpers who were not themselves in need of therapy. The "real" patients were not involved in the meetings, and the therapists who conducted the groups did not work with the patients. In this way the group sessions were kept separate from the patients' psychotherapy. This work was similar to the long tradition of group counseling with parents, especially in child welfare agencies (Grunwald and Casell, 1958).

One step closer to family therapy is family-group counseling (Freeman, Klein, Riehman, Lukoff, and Heisey, 1963). This is a sociological, problem-solving approach on the level of external interactions. Counselors facilitate communication, but de-emphasize individual goals and change. Intrapsychic conflicts are avoided. Instead, family counselors try to foster understanding at the social level of external reality by helping family members to recognize and modify interpersonal role conflicts. They aim for change in the social functioning of the whole family unit rather than in its individual members. Although changes in the social functioning of whole families can effect profound changes in individuals, Freeman and his colleagues do not try to or claim to achieve anything more than superficial support—refreshing modesty.

Family group counselors promote and guide communication in the group. They also help formulate goals and solve problems. By limiting the goals to those of whole families, rather than separate members, they seek to minimize individual strivings. A similar approach was reported by Knoblochova and Knobloch (1970), who developed and practiced what they called family therapy in Czechoslovakia from 1949 to 1953. They used a group-centered approach and conducted family meetings as a supplement to treatment of individual patients.

Kirby and Priestman (1957) described a group that went on for fourteen months with six young schizophrenic women and their mothers at Brooklyn State Hospital. When the group began, the patients were quiet and withdrawn, while the mothers talked on and on about all they tried to do for their children. This rigid complementarity is typical of psychotic families. Gradually, however, the young patients overcame their submissiveness, and began to speak up to their mothers, using words instead of symptoms. Encouraged by the support of the therapists and other patients with similar concerns, the daughters became able to voice their own feelings and complaints. Eventually another significant shift took place—the mothers gave up their defensive preoccupation with their daughters' problems, and began to discuss their own needs. This shift from the usual scapegoating pattern greatly benefitted the daughters. Even though this group closely approximated conjoint group family therapy, its focus still remained on individual expression. The daughters were encouraged to speak up, but the therapists neither sought nor sustained interaction; and though the mothers finally spoke about their own problems, no attempt was made to resolve their marital problems, nor were husbands ever invited to be present.

All these approaches to group treatment were available as models for family therapy. Some of the developments were useful, some were not. It was a short step, for instance, from observing a patient's reactions to others in a group—some of whom may be similar to siblings, parents, or children—to observing interactions with real rather than transference families.

Furthermore, from a technical point of view, group and family therapies are similar. Both involve several people. Both are more complex and amorphous and are more like everyday social reality than individual therapy. In groups and families each patient must react to a number of people, not just the therapist, and therapeutic use of this interaction is a definitive mechanism of change in both settings. Consequently, it is incumbent on group and family therapists to remain relatively inactive and decentralized, so that patients in the room will relate to each other.

In individual treatment, the therapist is a safe but somewhat artificial confidant. A patient expects a therapist to be understanding and accepting, an audience of one friendly person. It is not so with groups or families. In both, the situation is more naturalistic; more threatening perhaps, but also more like everyday experience. Transfer to life outside the consulting room is more direct.

On closer examination, however, we can see that the differences between families and groups of strangers are so many and so significant that the group therapy model has only limited application for family treatment. Families are very special groups. Family members have a long history, and —most important—a future together. Therapy groups are comprised of strangers, families of intimates. Revealing yourself to strangers is easier and safer than exposing yourself to the members of your family. In fact, great harm can be done by therapists who are so naive as to push family members to be "completely honest and open with each other." Once blurted out, there's no taking back thoughts that should have remained private—the affair, long since over, or the revelation that a woman *does* care more about her career than her children. These features of family life—continuity, commitment, and shared distortions—all mean that treatment for families has to differ from therapy for groups.

In one of the few small group studies using families, Strodtbeck (1954) tested a variety of propositions derived from groups of strangers and found major differences which he ascribed to the enduring relationship of family members. Strodtbeck (1958) later substantiated the opinion that family interactions, unlike those in ad hoc groups, can only be understood in terms of the history of the family group.

Group therapy is predicated on a few basic conditions inherent in the structure of the group (Yalom, 1970). Some of the differences between family structure and that of groups are trivial, but others are significant enough to make group therapy techniques inappropriate for families. Therapy groups are designed to provide an atmosphere of warmth and support. Being with others, patients feel less alone. They may have felt isolated before, but now they see the group as a place where they will be helped and where they can help others. This feeling of safety among sympathetic strangers cannot be part of family therapy, for instead of isolating treatment from a stressful environment, the stressful environment is actually brought into treatment. Furthermore, in group therapy, all patients have equal power and status, but this is not true of family situations. The official patient in the family, for instance, is likely to remain isolated, and to feel unique and stigmatized. After all, he or she is "the problem." The sense of protection felt in being part of therapeutic group made up of strangers, who will not have to be faced tomorrow, cannot be part of family therapy, where it isn't always safe to speak openly because no therapist will be there to protect you from retaliation on the ride home.

Another basic therapeutic mechanism of groups is that they stimulate typical patterns of social interaction which then can be analyzed and changed. This function of groups has been described as a "laboratory for social change" or a "social microcosm" (Nichols and Zax, 1977). Families, however, are less flexible and open to experimentation. They have a complex shared mythology that dictates certain roles and ways of behaving. These highly developed and patterned communications make families far less able to experiment with new social responses.

Family therapy is a less productive context for testing social reality than group therapy. Groups are specifically designed to provide opportunities for reality testing in a relatively nonthreatening atmosphere (Handlon and Parloff, 1962), so that distorted perceptions may be corrected and new ways of behaving tried out. But families share distortions of reality which must be maintained for the sake of family equilibrium. Individual members are thus unable to re-examine their perceptions as they can when they receive feedback from observers who have different points of view.

Therapy groups also provide therapeutically useful opportunities for members to display transference distortions, through the variety of the group members (Handlon and Parloff, 1962). The family therapy situation is different; the real figures are actually present. Transference still occurs, but is less amenable to exploration and correction. Parents may see their adolescent children in ways that fit the past, not the present. Children may see their parents accurately, but transfer these perceptions onto the therapists. Therapists are generally hamstrung by powerful countertransference reactions when dealing with families. Furthermore, transference distortions are often supported by family mythology. "Daddy is a monster" is a myth that pervades the thinking of many mother-child coalitions. Such distortions and misperceptions are certainly available as grist for the therapeutic mill, but they are more difficult to deal with in families.

THE CHILD GUIDANCE MOVEMENT

The child guidance movement was founded on the belief that, since emotional disorders begin in childhood, treating problems of children is the best way to prevent mental illness in the population. It was Freud who introduced the idea that psychological disorders of adulthood were the consequence of unresolved problems of childhood. Among his followers, Adler was the principal one to pursue the implication that treating the growing child might be the most effective way to prevent adult neuroses from developing. To this end, Adler organized child guidance clinics in Vienna, where not only children but also families and teachers were counseled. Adler's approach was to offer encouragement and support in an atmosphere of optimism and confidence. His technique helped to alleviate the child's feeling of isolation and *inferiority* so that he or she could work out a healthy *life style,* directed toward achieving competence and success through *social usefulness.* Adler's methods are still practiced in child guidance clinics in Europe and America.

When the child guidance movement began in the United States in the 1920s, under a grant from the Commonwealth Fund (Ginsburg, 1955), Rudolph Dreikurs, a student of Adler's, was one of its most effective proponents. American child guidance clinics provided a setting for the study and treatment of childhood psychological problems, and of the complex social and family forces contributing to these problems. Treatment was carried out by psychiatrist-psychologist-social worker teams, who focused much of their attention on the child's family environment.

Gradually, child guidance workers concluded that the real problem is not the obvious one brought to the clinic, the child's symptoms, but the tensions in the family that are their source. At first there was a tendency to see the parents, especially the mother, as a pathological influence, responsible for the child's problems. Mothers were viewed as enemies to be vanquished, and fathers were generally ignored (Burgum, 1942). The usual arrangement was for a psychiatrist to treat the child and a social worker to see the mother. Treatment of the mother was secondary to the primary goal of treating the child. The major purposes for seeing the mother were to reduce emotional pressure and anxiety, redirect hostility away from the child, and modify child-rearing attitudes. In this model, the family was viewed as an extension of the child rather than the other way around.

Although the importance of the family's influence was recognized, mothers and children were treated as separate individuals. They were not seen together, and in many clinics even discussion between their therapists was discouraged on the grounds that it might impair the privacy of the separate therapeutic relationships. Under the reigning influence of psychoanalysis, there was a tremendous emphasis on the individual psyche and its unconscious conflicts and irrational motivations. Attempts to apply a social approach to disturbances in family life were dismissed as "superficial"—the ultimate indictment from psychoanalytic clinicians.

In this climate, much was learned about individual childhood development, but clinicians often lost sight of the interpersonal context. It was assumed that resolution of the child's problems would also resolve family problems. Occasionally this happened, but more often it did not. Neurotic problems in individuals are only one problem in relationships; the others are interactional. Unfortunately, individual therapy may cause patients to increase their preoccupation with themselves, exclusive of others in the family. After analysis, the patient may be wiser, but sadder—and lonelier.

Researchers in child guidance clinics throughout the 1940s and 1950s tended to focus on parental psychopathology. David Levy (1943) was among the first to establish a relationship between pathogenic traits in parents and psychiatric disturbances in their offspring. The chief cause of childhood psychological problems, according to Levy, is *maternal over-protectiveness*. Mothers who themselves had been deprived of love while growing up became overprotective of their children. Some did so in a domineering manner, others were overly indulgent. Children with domineering mothers were submissive at home, but had difficulty making friends; children with indulgent mothers were disobedient at home, but well-behaved at school.

During this period, Frieda Fromm-Reichmann (1948) introduced her famous concept of the *schizophrenogenic mother*, a domineering, aggressive, rejecting, and insecure woman. Such women, especially when they were married to inadequate, passive, and indifferent men, were thought to provide the pathological parenting that produces schizophrenia. Adelaide

Johnson's description of the transmission of *superego lacunae* was another example of how parents were blamed for causing their children's problems (Johnson and Szurek, 1954). According to Johnson, antisocial behavior in delinquents and psychopaths was due to defects in their superegos, passed on by their parents.

Eventually, the emphasis in the child guidance movement shifted from seeing parents as noxious agents to the view that pathology was inherent in the relationships which developed among patients, parents, and significant others. This shift had profound consequences. No longer was psychopathology located within the individuals; no longer were parents villains and patients victims. Now the nature of the interaction was seen to be the problem, and this resulted in a more optimistic prognosis and changed the very nature of treatment. The goal shifted from weaning patients from their families to clarifying the relationships between parents and patients in hopes of improving them. Instead of trying—in vain—to remove patients from their families, child guidance workers began to help patients relate better to their families.

John Bowlby's work at the Tavistock Clinic exemplified the transition of the child guidance movement from an individual to a family approach. As he described his own conversion in a case study, Bowlby (1949) was treating a child using a psychoanalytic approach, and was making very little progress. Feeling frustrated he decided to see the child and his parents together for one session. During the first half of this two-hour session the child and his parents took turns complaining and blaming each other. During the second half of the session Bowlby interpreted to each of them what he thought their contributions to the problems were. Eventually, through this process, all three members of the family developed some sympathy for the others' points of view.

Although he was intrigued by the possibilities of these conjoint interviews, Bowlby was still wedded to the one-to-one format, which he believed should precede and follow joint sessions. For Bowlby, family meetings were a useful catalyst, but only an adjunct to the *real* treatment, individual psychoanalytic therapy. He rarely had joint interviews more than once or twice in a particular case. Nevertheless, by eliminating the strict separation of the child's treatment from the mother's treatment, and pioneering the use of conjoint family interviews, Bowlby began the transition from what had been individual therapy to what would become family therapy.

What Bowlby began as an experiment, Nathan Ackerman carried through —family therapy as the major form of treatment in child guidance clinics. As early as 1938, Ackerman went on record as suggesting the clinical utility of viewing the family as a single whole entity when dealing with disturbance manifest in any of its members (Ackerman, 1938). Subsequently, he (Ackerman and Sobel, 1950) recommended studying the family as a means of understanding the child, instead of the other way around. Once he saw the need to understand the family in order to diagnose problems, Ackerman soon took the next step of family treatment. Before I get to that, however, I will describe a parallel development, in research on schizophrenia, that led to the beginning of family therapy.

RESEARCH ON FAMILY DYNAMICS AND THE ETIOLOGY OF SCHIZOPHRENIA

Family therapists did not discover the role of the family in schizophrenia; recognition of family influences has existed since Freud's famous account (1911) of the case of Dr. Schreber. In this first psychoanalytic formulation of psychosis, Freud discussed some of the psychological factors involved in paranoia and schizophrenia; his view broke with the tradition that these were diseases due to cerebral defects. Although family dynamics were not central to Freud's analysis, he did discuss the part that the patient's relationships within his family had played in the development of this bizarre case.

Studies on the genetics of schizophrenia published as early as 1916 seemed to show that family played a part in the illness. Patients were interviewed with their families, and the data from these interviews led to the conclusion that there were psychological as well as genetic factors at work.

During the 1930s and 1940s efforts were made to treat schizophrenics with psychotherapy. Federn and others, noting the chaotic nature of a schizophrenic's unconscious processes, suggested that therapy should not try to probe and explore too deeply, but instead should focus on current situations and actual experience. Sullivan also focused on interpersonal relations in his brilliant work with schizophrenics. Beginning in 1927 he emphasized the importance of the hospital "family"—the physicians, nurses, and aides—as a benevolent substitute for the patient's real family. Sullivan did not, however, take the next step of directly involving real families in treatment. Frieda Fromm-Reichmann too believed that the family played a part in the dynamics of schizophrenia, and considered the hospital family important to the resolution of schizophrenic episodes; however, she also failed to recommend family treatment. Essentially, although these interpersonal psychiatrists recognized the importance of family life in schizophrenia, they continued to treat the family as a pathogenic environment from which patients must be rescued.

In the 1940s and 1950s, research on the link between family life and the development of schizophrenia led to the pioneering work of the first family therapists.

Gregory Bateson—Palo Alto. One of the groups with the strongest claim to originating family therapy was Gregory Bateson's schizophrenia project in Palo Alto, California. There were actually two Palo Alto groups; they worked closely together and shared some members, yet they had different purposes in mind. The first Palo Alto group was the "Project for the Study of Schizophrenia," under the direction of Gregory Bateson. Project members—Jay Haley and John Weakland, with Don Jackson and William Fry as principal consultants—were primarily interest in the study of communication, secondarily interested in families, and only tangentially interested in treatment. The other group was the Mental Research Institute, directed by Don Jackson, who was primarily interested in treating families. Bateson's project was thus mainly devoted to scientific study, and Jackson's group to the problems of treating families. I shall discuss Bateson's project here, and consider Jackson's work below.

A scientist in the classic mold, Gregory Bateson did research on animal behavior, learning theory, evolution, and ecology as well as in hospital psychiatry. He worked with Margaret Mead in Bali and New Guinea; then, becoming interested in cybernetics, he wrote *Naven*, and worked on synthesizing cybernetic ideas with anthropological data. He entered the psychiatric field when he worked with Jurgen Ruesch at the Langley Porter Clinic. Together they wrote *Communication: The Social Matrix of Psychiatry* (Ruesch and Bateson, 1951). In 1962, Bateson shifted to studying communication among animals, and after 1963 worked at the Oceanographic Institute in Hawaii until his death in 1980.

The Palo Alto project began in the fall of 1952 when Bateson received a grant from the Rockefeller Foundation to study the general nature of communication in terms of its levels. All communications, Bateson had written (Bateson, 1951), have two different levels or functions—"report" and "command." Each message has a stated content, as, for instance, "Wash your hands, it's time for dinner"; but in addition, the message carries how it is to be taken. In this case, the second message is that the speaker is in charge. This second message—"metacommunication"—is at a higher level and often goes unnoticed. Bateson's idea about levels of communication was derived from Bertrand Russell's *Theory of Logical Types* (Whitehead and Russell, 1910), which dealt with hierarchies in levels of abstraction, or logical types.

Russell pointed out that a class cannot be a member of itself, nor can a member of the class be the class. That is, classes and members are of different logical types. For example, the class of chairs is not a chair, but neither is it some thing other than a chair; the class of chairs is a different level of abstraction. Another illustration is that the noun *university* is a higher level, more abstract, or collective noun than the separate buildings subsumed as members of the class "university." Bateson wanted to analyze a variety of phenomena using this insight.

In early 1953, Bateson was joined by Jay Haley and John Weakland. Haley was primarily interested in social and psychological analysis of fantasy; Weakland was a chemical engineer who had become interested in cultural anthropology. Later that same year a psychiatrist, William Fry, joined them; his major interest has been the study of humor. This group of eclectic talents and catholic interests began a number of different studies: otters at play, the training of guide dogs, the meaning and uses of humor, the social and psychological significance of popular movies, and the utterances of schizophrenic patients. Jay Haley (1976) has explained that Bateson gave the project members free rein; although they investigated many kinds of complex human and animal behaviors, all their studies had to do with possible conflicts between messages and qualifying messages.

In 1954, Bateson got a two-year grant from the Macy Foundation to study schizophrenic communication. Shortly thereafter they were joined by Don Jackson, who served as a clinical consultant and supervisor of psychotherapy with schizophrenics.

The group's interests turned to developing a communication theory that might explain the origin and nature of schizophrenic behavior, particularly in the context of families. Bateson and his colleagues hypothesized that family stability is achieved by feedback that monitors the behavior of the family and its members. Whenever the family system is threatened—that is, disturbed—it moves toward balance or homeostasis. Thus, apparently puzzling behavior might become understandable if it were perceived as a homeostatic mechanism. For example, if whenever two parents argue, one of the children exhibits symptomatic behavior, the symptoms may be a way to interrupt the fighting by uniting the parents in concern for the child. In this manner the symptomatic behavior serves the cybernetic function of preserving the family's equilibrium. Unhappily, in the process, one of the family members may have to assume the role of "identified patient."

In addition to applying systems ideas to explain the over-all nature and purpose of family interaction, the group used communications theory to analyze specific sequences of family interaction. Even animals, Bateson had observed (1951), metacommunicate. Notice, for example, how two dogs or cats or monkeys play at fighting. One leaps at the other, they tussle, they nip each other, but neither fights seriously or inflicts damage. How do they know that they are playing? Clearly they must have some way of metacommunicating, of indicating that the attack is only playful. Humans achieve considerable complexity in framing and labeling messages and meaningful actions. Typically the qualifying metamessages are conveyed through nonverbal signals, including gesture, tone, posture, facial expression, and intonation. "I hate you," may be said with a grin, with tears, or with a fixed stare and clenched teeth. In each case, the metacommunication alters the message.

Hypothesizing that schizophrenia may be a result of family interaction, Bateson's group wanted to identify sequences of experience that might induce such symptomatology; they were not interested in traumatic incidents in infancy, but in characteristic family patterns of communication. Their basic premise was at this time simply conjecture; only later was it supported by observation (Bateson, Jackson, and Weakland, 1963). Once they had agreed that schizophrenic communication had to be a product of what was learned inside the family, the group looked for the kind of circumstances that could lead to such confused and confusing patterns of speech. In 1956 they published a preliminary report on their findings, "Towards a Theory of Schizophrenia," in which Bateson, Jackson, Haley, and Weakland (Fry was off doing military service) introduced the concept of the *double-bind*.

They assumed that psychotic behavior might not be the result of a collapse ("breakdown") of one's ability to deal with reality, but from having to learn to cope with a reality of confused and confusing communication. Consider someone who has an important relationship where escape is not feasible and response is necessary; when he or she receives two related but contradictory messages of different levels but finds it difficult to detect or comment on the inconsistency (Bateson, Jackson, Haley, and Weakland, 1956); that person is in a double-bind. Because this difficult concept is so often misused as a synonym for paradox or simple contradiction, it is worthwhile to review each feature of the double-bind as the authors listed them. The double-bind has six characteristics: (1) Two or more persons are involved in an important relationship; (2) The relationship is a repeated experience; (3) A primary negative injunction is given, such as, "Do not do X or I will punish you," or "If you don't do X I will punish you"; (4) A second injunction is given that conflicts with the first, but at a more abstract level; this injunction is also enforced by punishment or perceived threat. The second injunction is often nonverbal, and frequently involves one parent's negating the injunction of the other; (5) A tertiary negative injunction exists that prohibits escape from the field and also demands a response. Without this crucial factor the "victim" will not feel bound and therefore there will be no bind; (6) Finally, once the victim is conditioned to perceive the world in terms of a double-bind, the necessity for every condition to be present disappears, and almost any part is enough to precipitate panic or rage.

Most of the examples of double-binds in the literature are inadequate because they don't include all the critical elements in the definition. Skynner, for instance, cites (1976): "Boys must stand up for themselves and not be sissies"; but "Don't be rough . . . don't be rude to your mother." These two messages are confusing and may cause conflict, but they hardly constitute a double-bind; they are merely a contradiction. Faced with those two statements a child is free to choose to obey either one, to alternate, or even to say that there is a contradiction. This and many similar examples neglect the specification that the two messages exist on different levels of communication. A better example is the one given in Bateson *et al.*'s original article. A young man, recovering in the hospital from a schizophrenic episode, was visited by his mother. When he put his arm around her, she stiffened. But when he withdrew, she asked, "Don't you love me anymore?" He blushed, and she said; "Dear, you must not be so easily embarrassed and afraid of your feelings." Following this exchange, the patient became upset; after the visit with his mother was over he assaulted an aide and had to be put into seclusion. Notice that all the features of the double-bind were present in this conversation, and also that the young man was obviously caught. There is no bind if the subject is not bound. The concept is interactional.

Furthermore, we may say that this mother was made anxious by intimacy with her son, but couldn't accept her feelings; consequently she behaved overtly as a loving mother who always does the right thing. Typically, in such a family, there is no one else, such as a strong and insightful father, who can intervene and support the child. The mother tries to reduce her anxiety by controlling the closeness between herself and her child. But because she can't admit her anxiety, even to herself, she has to hide important aspects of her communication, that is, her own anxiety or hostility. In addition she forbids comments about her messages. Hence the child grows up unskilled in the ability to communicate about communication, unskilled in determining what people really mean, and unskilled in the ability to relate. Although it sounds esoteric, people need to metacommunicate in order to get along. It is often necessary to ask such questions as "What do you mean?" or "Are you serious?" But in the double-binding family such questions are not possible; comment and questioning are threatening to the parents, and the contradictory injunctions are obscure, occurring on different levels of communication.

We may all be caught in occasional double-binds, but the schizophrenic has to deal with them continually, and the effect is maddening. Unable to understand and not permitted to comment on the dilemma, the schizophrenic must respond defensively, perhaps by being concrete and literal, perhaps by speaking in disguised answers or in metaphors. Eventually the schizophrenic, like the paranoid, may come to assume that behind every statement is a concealed and hidden meaning; alternatively, he or she may gradually withdraw from the external world and grow progressively detached.

This 1956 double-bind paper has proved to be one of the most influential and controversial in the history of family therapy.

Members of the Bateson group continued to clarify the concept of double-bind and tried to document its occurrence in schizophrenic families; other researchers have created laboratory analogues of the double-bind so they might test its effects under controlled conditions. Among the laboratory situations designed to imitate the double-bind have been studies on inconsistent reward and censure (Ciotola, 1961); nonzero sum games, such as the prisoner's dilemma (Potash, 1965); the shifts and evasions that occurred when mothers of schizophrenics were asked about their feelings (Beavers, Blumberg, Timken, and Weiner, 1965); schizophrenics rating the frequency with which their mothers had used a list of double-binding verbal-nonverbal contradictions (Berger, 1965); double-binds in written communications (Ringuette and Kennedy, 1966); incongruent instructions for a task (Sojit, 1969); impossible tasks with helpers who wouldn't help (Kingsley, 1969); tasks in which anxiety was generated but denied (Schreiber, 1970); written tests of parent-to-child messages (Phillips, 1970); channel-discrepant messages and paradoxical injunctions (Guindon, 1971); training schizophrenics and neurotics to recognize double-binds (Schaeffer, 1972); punishment and contradictory material (Smith, 1972); and paradoxical alternatives in a testing situation (Ables, 1975). All of these efforts were confident attempts to bring laboratory precision to the evaluation of a highly complex construct, but most of these researchers failed to document the destructive effects of the double-bind.

The problem with these double-bind studies is that they all failed to include one or more of the essential ingredients. A genuinely crucial relationship such as child/parent or patient/therapist must be involved; otherwise the victim can simply ignore the situation and walk away from the relationship. Laboratory experiments rarely involve anything like a critical relationship; in fact, the atmosphere tends to be one of gamesmanship and skepticism. And even if all the essential conditions seem to be met, what is being studied is merely a potential bind, because a bind is not a bind unless it binds. Some studies present contradictions between verbal and nonverbal messages, paradigms of the double-bind; but this situation too is an inadequate substitute, since the levels in a true double-bind are, by definition, different *logical* levels, not simply different ways to communicate. In the final analysis, it appears that the essential features of the double-bind have eluded operationalism.

Those who have studied the double-bind have tended to look for evidence that it does or does not cause schizophrenia. But this approach is based on linear causality—A's response causes B's response. A more appropriate approach is to use the systems idea of circular causality, and ask, what's going on in schizophrenic families—A's response, then B's response, then A's response. It is more useful to think of the double-bind as a pattern of relationship than as a discrete event, and I concur with those reviewers (Ables, 1976) who have suggested that a natural history approach may be the most fruitful means of understanding the phenomenon.

The double-bind theory has undeniably offered us an enormously productive way to look at schizophrenia. Since its introduction, the concept has been extended to humor, creativity, poetry, fiction, delinquency, hypnosis, religion, art, and psychotherapy—that is, to both creative and productive behavior as well as to pathological—on the basis of the response of the person who is the victim. There are four possible ways to respond to double-binds, or indeed to disqualifying messages of any kind: comment; withdrawal from the relationship; acceptance; or counterdisqualification (Sluzki, Beavin, Tarnopolsky, and Veron, 1967). The first two avoid or offset the double-bind, and if these responses are able to circumvent the bind, they may lead to creativity (Bateson, 1978). The reason for this is that an adaptive solution to a double-bind involves stepping out of the frame, recognizing the different logical types. The ability to step back like this is a creative act, based on the rare capacity to take an objective view of one's own context. Although the double-bind was originally described as dependent on the motivation of one person (the mother's need to mask her anxiety or hostility), a comprehensive description would involve interaction with the other person's motivation. To describe interchanges between two people one must postulate functions (motives, intentions) that involve both of them.

Bateson's original paper focused on a two-person interaction, essentially between mother and child. Father was described only in a negative way, as being unable to help the child resist being caught in the bind. Family analyses limited to two persons, although frequent (notably among child behavior therapists and couples therapists), are inadequate. A mother's relationship with her child is shaped by her relationship with her husband, and in turn reshapes that relationship. So too, a therapist's relationship with a patient is mutually defined by and defines the therapist's relationship with supervisors and administrators. In 1960, Weakland attempted to extend the double-bind from two- to three-person interactions (Weakland, 1960), and discussed the fact that three people are involved in the double-bind, even though one may not be immediately apparent. However, in general, the Bateson group was more concerned with broad applications than with the intricacies of three-person systems. Thus, they suggested that the double-bind concept may be useful for analyzing three-person systems in the family, clinic, business world, government, and organized religion, but they dealt with the father's effect on the mother-child dyad in a fairly superficial fashion. Indeed, the Bateson group, as well as their communications therapy and strategic therapy offspring, have persistently failed to deal effectively with three-person systems. In a similar way, although they espoused open systems concepts, their analyses have always tended to be limited to closed systems.

The Bateson group did not stop with their work on the double-bind. In 1956 members of the project began seeing parents jointly with their schizophrenic offspring. These meetings were held to observe and explore rather than to treat, but they were nonetheless an attempt to study actual behavior rather than to speculate about it. After 1956 the project went in several directions at once. They continued to observe and try to understand double binds, and at the same time compile descriptions of communication and families. Haley began making regular visits to Phoenix to consult with Milton Erickson about the nature of hypnosis (Haley 1976). Haley was fascinated by issues of power and control, and he considered the struggle for control between people as the relationship context— that is, the motive— for double-binding. His ideas on this subject will be developed below.

In 1956 the group got a grant from the National Institute of Mental Health for a family therapy project, and another from the Foundations Fund for Research in Psychiatry for a series of experimental studies on family dynamics. A good deal of this work was done by Haley, who as a result became skeptical about the possibility of doing meaningful controlled research with families.

In 1959, Don Jackson founded the Mental Research Institute (MRI) and invited Virginia Satir to join him. Although the Bateson group and MRI staff shared the same building in downtown Palo Alto for a while, there was never any formal connection between them (Haley, 1976). Bateson, always more interested in theory than treatment, wrote: "As regards psychotherapy, all I would claim as a contribution from double-bind theory is greater insight; and I do not mean insight for the patient which some practitioners think useless or harmful. I mean that the theory gives the therapist who works with schizophrenics or with families more insight into his patients and perhaps more insight into his own actions—if that be desirable" (Bateson, 1978, p. 42). Although clinical work was never a major goal for the project, Haley and Weakland did do psychotherapy with families; so, naturally, did the psychiatrists of the group, Jackson and Fry.

All the diverse efforts of the Bateson group were united on one point, the importance of communication on the organization of families; but within this point of view there was also considerable disagreement. Bateson, for example, was most interested in pursuing the double-bind, while others were more interested in the varying patterns of communication in different types of families. They also disagree about what constitutes the central motivating force of families. Haley thought it was control; Bateson and Weakland thought it was concealment of unacceptable feelings. They all agreed that to understand families they had to use systems theory to identify the patterns of rules and stability; they also agreed that to understand interaction, they had to identify levels of messages, rules, and governing processes. All believed that schizophrenic behavior was in some way adaptive to the family context, and that family members respond in error-activated ways to each other and so govern each other's behavior. However, given the diversity of talents and interests it is not surprising that the output of this group was more a collection of ideas than an homogenous theoretical presentation. Some of their ideas are summarized in *Pragmatics of Human Communication* (Watzlawick, Beavin, and Jackson, 1967), but to get any clear idea of the full scope of their work, it is necessary to examine their papers individually. In 1962 the group disbanded.

Theodore Lidz—Yale. Theodore Lidz was an early investigator of the family dynamics of schizophrenia. His approach was grounded in psychoanalytic theory, and he sought the roots of schizophrenia in family object relationships. His investigations really were an extension of traditional psychoanalytic thinking; they were not a radical departure. Much of his work dealt with the roles which family members fulfill, and the effects of faulty parental models on identification and incorporation.

Lidz graduated from medical school at Columbia University in 1936, and subsequently studied neurology at the National Hospital in London. After completing his psychiatric residency at Johns Hopkins (from 1938 to

1941) he remained on the faculty for five years. He left Johns Hopkins to serve as a lieutenant colonel in the U.S. Army from 1946 to 1951. Like many other of the pioneers in family studies, Lidz was a psychoanalyst; he was trained at the Baltimore Institute of Psychoanalysis from 1942 to 1951. After completing his psychoanalytic training he became a professor of psychiatry at Yale, where he continued family investigations that he and his colleagues had begun at Johns Hopkins.

Lidz's studies of the families of schizophrenics took the form of clinical investigations conducted intensively on a relatively small number of cases over the course of several years. These intensive studies yielded an intimate glimpse of the environment in which young schizophrenics are reared, and his conclusions naturally reflect his clinical background, orientation, and method of study.

When Lidz began his studies of the familes of schizophrenics in 1941, while he was completing his residency at Johns Hopkins, he and his colleagues surveyed the gross features of the family environment in which schizophrenics were reared. This original study, published in 1949 (Lidz and Lidz, 1949), surveyed fifty case histories. They exhibited a prevalence of broken homes and seriously disturbed family relationships. Forty percent of the young schizophrenics patients in the sample had been deprived of at least one parent by death, divorce, or separation; 61 percent of the families exhibited serious marital strife; 48 percent of the families contained at least one extremely unstable parent (psychotic, seriously neurotic, or psychopathic); and 41 percent of the families exhibited bizarre or unusual patterns of child rearing. In all, only five of fifty randomly selected schizophrenic patients appeared to have come from stable homes, raised by two healthy and compatible parents. Lidz challenged the then current belief that maternal rejection is a major distinguishing feature of schizophrenic families, and in one of his most notable findings, observed that paternal influence was frequently as noxious as the maternal.

Lidz followed up this initial exploration with an extensive longitudinal study of a group of sixteen families each containing a schizophrenic member. The primary method of study was to periodically interview all available family members over periods ranging from six months to several years. Less immediate relatives, family friends, former teachers, and nursemaids were also interviewed; diaries as well as other productions of family members were studied; and frequent home visits were made. Additional information was gleaned from observing the interaction between families and hospital staff. Finally projective testing was done with all members of the families. Since each of the patients in the sample had been hospitalized at the Yale

Psychiatric Institute, a private hospital, they were all from middle- and upper-class families. Thus there was a bias in the sample toward a relatively high socioeconomic status, which meant there was a greater likelihood that the families were intact and better integrated than typical schizophrenic families. In the face of this bias toward better functioning, the consistent observation of severe family disruption and psychopathology is all the more striking.

Naturally when families are studied so carefully over so long a period of time, a wealth of data is amassed. Several approaches were taken to organize the voluminous material. Findings were categorized by parent-child relationships; marital interaction and its influence on the child; the dynamics of the family as a small group; the manner in which the family fosters ego integration; and the nature of family communication. And although Lidz was firmly rooted in the traditional psychoanalytic way of thinking about families, and many of his concepts focused on individuals and their roles, some of his observations went beyond one- or two-person systems and ideas about identification and incorporation to include consideration of three-person systems and the whole family as a unit. Thus Lidz bridged older theories about the impact of individual parents' personalities on their children and the more modern interest in families as systems.

Lidz believed that the major psychodynamic explanations of schizophrenia were too narrow. He rejected Freud's idea that schizophrenia is due to fixation at an early oral level and subsequent regression in the face of stress during young adulthood. Lidz did not find overt rejection of their children by any of the mothers he studied; consequently he also rejected the idea propounded by Frieda Fromm-Reichmann and John Rosen that severe rejection by mothers is a major cause of schizophrenia. Furthermore, Lidz studied the entire period of maturation, not just infancy, and tried to correct the tradition of ignoring the role of fathers.

Early in his studies, Lidz's attention was drawn to the fathers who were as frequently and as severely disturbed as the mothers (Lidz, Parker, and Cornelison, 1956). He described the fathers of schizophrenics in a landmark paper: "Intrafamilial Environment of the Schizophrenic Patient I: The Father" (Lidz, Cornelison, Fleck, and Terry, 1957a). This paper emphasized the vital role that fathers play in development. None of the fathers in the families studied was found to be effective, and their deficits were classified into five patterns.

The first group was constantly in severe conflict with their wives. These men were domineering and rigidly authoritarian. Having failed to establish intimate relationships with their wives, they sought to win their daughters over to their side. The children in these familes were simply focal points in a struggle between the parents, and young schizophrenic daughters abandoned their mothers as objects of identification and instead tried to follow their fathers' inconsistent, unrealistic demands. Consequently these youngsters failed to develop a feminine identity.

The second group of fathers were hostile toward their children rather than toward their wives. These men rivaled their sons for the mother's attention and affection, and behaved like jealous siblings rather than parents. They tended to strut about, bragging of their own accomplishments and belittling their sons' achievements. This competition seriously sabotaged the self-confidence of the sons.

The third group of fathers exhibited frankly paranoid grandiosity. They were aloof and physically distant. The sons of these men were too weak to emulate their fathers, but they continued desperately to try their best to ape some of the parent's more bizarre characteristics.

The fourth group of fathers were failures in life and nonentities in their homes. They scarcely participated in the responsibilities of childrearing. Children in these familes grew up as though fatherless. They could hardly look up to the pathetic figures who were treated with such disdain by their wives.

The fifth group of fathers were passive and submissive men who acted more like children than parents. They tended to behave in a pleasant almost motherly way toward the children, but offered weak models of identification. These submissive fathers failed to counterbalance the strong domineering influence of their wives. Lidz concluded that it may be better to grow up without a father at all, than to have one who is too aloof or too weak to serve as a healthy model for identification.

After elucidating some of the characteristics of the fathers in schizophrenic families, Lidz turned his attention to defects in the marital relationships. The theme underlying his findings was an absence of role reciprocity. The partners in these marriages did not function smoothly and harmoniously as a unit. In a successful marriage it is necessary first to fill one's own role and then to support the role of the spouse. In these families the spouses were too inadequate to fulfill their own roles and thus disinclined to support the other. Lidz followed Parsons and Bales in saying that the father's role is primarily "adaptive-instrumental" while the mother's is primarily "integrative-expressive." If each parent fulfills a version of one of these roles, then they can fit together harmoniously. However, if fathers are unsuccessful at their instrumental tasks, or mothers reject expressive nurturing, difficulties will arise in their relationship.

Lidz found the parental relationships to be highly disturbed in all cases that he studied (Lidz, Cornelison, Fleck, and Terry, 1957b). In focusing on the failure to arrive at reciprocal, interrelating roles, Lidz identified two general types of marital discord. In the first, *marital schism*, there is a chronic failure of the spouses to accommodate to each other or to achieve role reciprocity. These husbands and wives chronically undercut each other's worth to their children, and compete aggressively and blatantly for their children's loyalty and affection. Their marriages are hostile encounters in which both partners are losers. Unhappy children are then torn between conflicting loyalties to these battling adversaries. The second pattern, *marital skew*, involves serious psychopathology in one marital partner who dominates the other one. Thus one parent becomes extremely dependent while the other appears to be a strong parent figure, but is, in fact, a pathological bully. The weaker spouse, in Lidz's cases usually the father, goes along or even supports the pathological tendencies and distortions of the dominant one. In all these families the children struggle to balance their parents' precarious marriages.

In a later study, Lidz emphasized that he was not proposing simple and direct causal links between parental pathology, or marital schism or skew, and schizophrenia in the children (Lidz and Fleck, 1960); however, the impression persists that Lidz does believe that the patterns he observed are among the causes of schizophrenia, although his methodology could not prove it.

Lyman Wynne—NIMH. Like other investigators considered in this section, Lyman Wynne has examined the effects of communication and family roles on schizophrenia. What distinguishes his work is his focus on pathological thinking in the families of schizophrenics; he is also unique in being the only pioneer investigator of the fifties who still continues to study family dynamics and schizophrenia.

Wynne graduated from Harvard Medical School in 1947, and in 1949 he went to the Tavistock Clinic as a traveling fellow. The Tavistock influence is evident in Wynne's group therapy approach to family treatment. In 1952, he joined the National Institute of Mental Health (NIMH), where he remained until the early seventies, serving as a staff psychiatrist, clinical investigator, and finally as Murray Bowen's replacement as chief of the family research section. In 1972, Wynne left NIMH to become a Professor in the University of Rochester's Department of Psychiatry.

Wynne's study of families of schizophrenics, spanning three decades, began in 1954 when he started seeing the parents of his hospitalized patients in twice-weekly psychotherapy. He was fascinated by the chaos he observed in these families, and sought to make sense out of it by extending psychoanalytic concepts and role theory to the systems level. Out of this work he developed the concepts of *pseudomutuality*, the *rubber fence*, and *pseudohostility*.

Pseudomutuality was one of the most striking features in the families of schizophrenics that Wynne saw (Wynne, Ryckoff, Day, and Hirsch, 1958); it is a facade that a family develops which gives the impression that the members have good relationships. Sometimes the parents in these families had suffered from painful early separations which left them with an unnatural dread of separateness in their own families. Pseudomutual families are preoccupied with fitting together so closely that there is no room for the differentiation of separate identities, no room for recognition and appreciation of any divergence of self-interests. The family cannot tolerate either deeper, more intimate relationships, or independence. This surface togetherness masks splits and conflicts as well as deep affectionate and sexual feelings, and keeps both conflict and greater intimacy from emerging; it is especially strong in the families of acute schizophrenics, with a consequent persistent rigidity of role structure, and intense disapproval of any deviation.

In this kind of family, various mechanisms are evolved to quell any sign of separateness, either inside or outside the family. The *rubber fence* is one of these; it precludes meaningful contact outside the family. Wynne describes it as an invisible barrier which stretches to permit some essential extrafamilial involvement, such as going to school, but which springs back tightly if that involvement goes too far. The family role structure thus remains all-encompassing, and participation in the larger society is severely curtailed. The most damaging feature of the rubber fence is that precisely those who most need contact outside the family to correct family distortions of reality are the ones who are allowed it least. Instead of being a subsystem of society (Parson and Bales, 1955), the schizophrenic family becomes a complete society, with a rigid boundary and no openings.

In a context where togetherness is everything and no significant outside relationships are tolerated, recognition of personal differences may be impossible, short of the blatantly bizarre behavior seen in schizophrenic reactions. The person may thus finally achieve the status of separateness, but is then labeled schizophrenic and extruded from the family; and like mud oozing back over the place where a rock has been removed from a swamp, the family's pseudomutuality is thereupon restored. In these terms, acute schizophrenia may be considered a desperate attempt at individuation which not only fails but also costs the person membership in the family. If acute schizophrenia becomes chronic, the now defeated patient may later be re-accepted into the family.

Pseudohostility is a different guise for a similar collusion to mask the reality of real individuals with disparate needs and feelings; this concept was adduced to explain certain observations about alignments and splits in families (Wynne, 1961). Wynne believed that families could be explained in terms of alignments and splits better than in terms of roles or discrete sequences of communication. Sequences of splits and alignments may be observed during family sessions; they are used to maintain a kind of dynamic equilibrium in which change in any part of the system, either an alignment or a split, reverberates to produce change in other parts of the system. A typical situation may be an alignment between one parent and the patient, with a split between the parents. But this arrangement may be but one aspect of a shifting picture, or may be a reactive defense against an underlying split between parent and patient.

Pseudohostility is a self-rescuing operation. Although noisy and intense, it signals only a superficial split. Like pseudomutuality it blurs intimacy and affection as well as deeper hostility. And also like pseudomutuality, pseudohostility distorts communication and impairs realistic perception and rational thinking about relationships.

Psychoanalytic theory states that children identify with their parents and internalize their standards; parental codes shape the children's egos and superegos. Wynne believes that children also internalize family role structures, and that the mental chaos of schizophrenics is in part derived from their having internalized chaotic family structures. To make matters worse, family role structure is assimilated whole by preschizophrenics as an archaic superego; this directly influences behavior, rather than being evaluated by a discriminating ego (Wynne, Ryckoff, Day, and Hirsch, 1958).

Wynne also linked the newer concept of communication deviance with the older notion of thought disorder. He sees communication as the vehicle for transmitting thought disorder, which is the traditional defining characteristic of schizophrenia. Communication deviance is a more interactional concept than thought disorder, and more readily observable than doublebinds. By 1978 Wynne and his colleagues had studied over 600 families, and had gathered incontrovertible evidence that disordered styles of communication are a distinguishing feature of families with young adult schizophrenics. Similar disorders also appear in families of borderlines, neurotics, and normals, but they are progressively less severe (Singer, Wynne, and Toohey, 1978). This observation—that communication deviance is not confined solely to schizophrenic familes, but exists in a continuum with ever greater deviance with more severe pathology—is consistent with other studies that describe a spectrum of schizophrenic disorders.

Wynne's methodology has evolved from history taking, to family interviews and home visits, to progressively more sophisticated psychological testing. His use of the Rorschach inkblot test, for example, reveals not unconscious motivation and perceptual style, but how family members establish their mutual view of ambiguous reality. One family member looks at the inkblots and offers an interpretation; the others listen and comment, until a consensus is reached. In this way the *Consensus Family Rorschach* provides a standardized series of stimuli which become the subject for family interaction. Wynne thus taps styles of thinking and communicating. As the family members' responses are recorded, the experimenters score deviant communications in this "naming and explaining" task. Odd or ambiguous remarks, contradictory comments, and disqualifications are among the overt signs of thought disorder. Thirty-two categories of deviance including unintelligible remarks; inconsistent and ambiguous referents; partial disqualifications; failure to sustain a task set (forgetting, skipping around, changing the subject); unstable perceptions and thinking; extraneous, contradictory, and illogical comments; abstractness and vagueness are scored in 6 factors (Singer, Wynne, and Toohey, 1978; Wynne, 1978).

The first notable finding from this method occurred when Margaret Singer was able to match the projective responses of parents to their schizophrenic offspring. This bolstered Wynne's contention that thought disorder is transmitted from parents to their children. Subsequently, however, Wynne recognized that communication deviance is not a one-way street leading from parents to children, but instead is a reciprocal process, within and across generations.

Wynne's current procedure is to study each parent's communication with a stranger (the examiner); with each other (the Spouse Consensus Rorschach); and finally with the whole family (the Family Consensus Rorschach). Using this approach the Wynne group has achieved an impressive ability to differentiate the responses of schizophrenic family members in terms of communication deviance. Each one of their thirty-two categories of deviance differentiates (at the .01 level) parents of schizophrenics from other parents (Singer, Wynne, and Toohey, 1978). Furthermore, these findings have been replicated several times, and cross-validated at other laboratories (Hirsch and Leff, 1975).

Role Theorists. Other researchers and clinicians used role theory to explain the deviant patterns in schizophrenic families. In 1934, Kasanin, Knight, and Sage described the parent-child relationships of schizophrenics, and suggested that family relationships were an important and specific etiological factor in schizophrenia. In 45 cases of schizophrenia that they studied, they found *maternal overprotection* in 25 and *maternal rejection* in 2. Kasanin described a pair of identical twins discordant for schizophrenia, and suggested that the differences in their relationships with family members were responsible for the difference in their fates (Kasanin, Knight, and Sage, 1934). David Levy (1943) clarified the roles of *maternal overprotection* and *rejection*, and he found that maternal overprotection was much more frequently associated with schizophrenia than was maternal rejection. While the mother's overprotection was generally more obvious, Levy also found many cases of paternal overprotection. Moreover, he observed that overprotection was not simply imposed by parents on their children; children in these familes met their overprotecting parents more than halfway. Thus, Levy introduced an interactional dimension to what had previously been regarded as a monadic disposition of parents.

In 1951, the Group for the Advancement of Psychiatry (GAP) decided that families had been neglected in the field of psychiatry. They therefore appointed a committee, chaired by John Spiegel, to review the field and report their findings. The committee not only went beyond the individual patient, but also beyond the influence of individual persons on individual patients to consider the total family. When they began to think at this level, they were impressed by the degree to which families are embedded in and shaped by culture and society. This illustrates the point that individual behavior can be seen as reflecting progessively wider social influences, depending upon the focus of observation. Nevertheless, Spiegel's committee decided that limiting their observations to the level of the family would provide data that were optimally comprehensive and pragmatic.

In their report (Kluckhohn and Spiegel, 1954), the GAP committee emphasized roles as the primary structural components of families. They concluded that healthy families contained relatively few and stable roles, and that this pattern was essential to teach children a sense of status and identity. Families with stable roles were also seen to satisfy a child's need for stable and enduring relationships based on affectionate bonds to parent figures. The committee found that there are norms for every role, and that children learn these norms by imitation and identification. They also found that family roles do not exist independently from each other, but that each role is circumscribed by other, reciprocal roles. Role behavior on the part of two or more people involved in a reciprocal transaction defines and regulates their interchange. The committee explained roles as a function, not only of external social influences, but also of inner needs and drives. Thus role theory served as a link between intrapersonal and interpersonal structures.

Spiegel followed up his interests in role theory and family pathology at Harvard Medical School. He observed that symptomatic children tend to be involved in their parents' conflicts; nonsymptomatic children may also have parents in conflict, but these children do not get directly involved. Spiegel (1957) described his observations in psychoanalytic terms: the child identifies with the unconscious wishes of the parents, and acts out their unconscious emotional conflict. The child's acting out serves as a defense for the parents, who are thereby able to avoid facing their own conflicts and each other.

R.D. Laing's analysis of family dynamics has often been more polemical than scholarly, but his observations helped popularize the family's role in psychopathology. Laing (1965) borrowed Marx's concept of *mystification* (class exploitation) and applied it to the "politics of families." Mystification refers to the process of distorting children's experience by denying or relabeling it. One example of this is a parent telling a child who is feeling sad, "You must be tired." Similarly, the idea that "good" children are always quiet breeds compliant, but lifeless children.

According to Laing's analysis, labeling behavior as pathology, even "family pathology," tends to mystify it. The prime function of mystification is to maintain the status quo. Mystification contradicts perceptions and feelings—and, more ominously, reality. When parents continually mystify a child's experience, the child's existence becomes inauthentic. Because their feelings are not accepted, these children project a *false self*, while keeping the *real self* private. In mild instances this produces unassertiveness, but if the real self/false self split is carried to an extreme, the result is schizophrenic madness (Laing, 1960).

Murray Bowen at NIMH and Ivan Boszormenyi-Nagy at the Eastern Pennsylvania Psychiatric Institute also studied family dynamics and schizophrenia, but since they are better known for their contributions to family treatment, their work will be considered below.

MARRIAGE COUNSELING

The history of professional marriage counseling is a less well-known contributory to family therapy because much of it took place outside of the mainstream of psychiatry. For many years there was no apparent need for a separate profession of marriage counselors. People with marital problems are likely to discuss them with their doctors, clergy, lawyers, and teachers before they go to professional mental health workers. Some students in courses on marriage and the family stay after class to talk to their instructors about personal as well as academic problems; and many women discuss sexual problems in marriage with their gynecologists.

The first professional centers for marriage counseling were established in about 1930. Paul Popenoe opened the American Institute of Family Relations in Los Angeles, and Abraham and Hannah Stone opened a similar clinic in New York City. A third center for marriage counseling was the Marriage Council of Philadelphia, begun in 1932 by Emily Hartshorne Mudd (Broderick and Schrader, 1981). Members of this new profession started meeting annually in 1942 and formed the American Association of Marriage Counselors in 1945, in order to share ideas, establish professional standards, and foster research.

In the 1940s, the movement spread from the initial three centers to fifteen, located throughout the country. Between then and now the profession has evolved from an informal service-oriented group to an organized profession, with a code of ethics and several training centers (Nichols, 1979).

At the same time that these developments were taking place, there was a parallel trend among some psychoanalysts leading to conjoint marital therapy. Although the majority of psychoanalysts have always followed Freud's prohibition against contact with the patient's family, a few have broken the rules and experimented with concommitant and conjoint therapy for married partners.

The first report on the psychoanalysis of married couples was made by Clarence Oberndorf at the American Psychiatric Association's 1931 convention (Oberndorf, 1938). In that presentation Oberndorf advanced the theory that married couples have interlocking neuroses, and that they are best treated in concert. This view was to be the underlying point of agreement among those in the analytic community who became interested in couples. "Because of the continuous and intimate nature of marriage every neurosis in a married person is strongly anchored in the married relationship. It is a useful and at times indispensable therapeutic measure to concentrate the analytic discussions on the complementary patterns and, if necessary, to have both mates treated" (Mittleman, 1944, p. 491).

In 1948, Bela Mittleman of the New York Psychoanalytic Institute became the first to publish an account of concurrent marital therapy in the

United States. Previously, Rene LaForgue had reported in 1937 on his experience analyzing several members of the same family concurrently. Mittleman suggested that husbands and wives could be treated by the same analyst, and that by seeing both it is possible to disentangle their irrational perceptions of each other from rational ones (Mittleman, 1948). This was truly a revolutionary point of view for an analyst: that the reality of object relationships may be at least as important as their intrapsychic representations. Ackerman (1954) agreed that the concommitant treatment of married partners was a good idea, and also suggested that mothers and children could profitably be treated together.

Meanwhile in Great Britain, where object relations were the central concern of psychoanalysts, Henry Dicks and his associates at the Tavistock Clinic established a Family Psychiatric Unit. Here couples referred by the divorce courts were helped to reconcile their differences (Dicks, 1964). Subsequently, the Balints affiliated their Family Discussion Bureau with the Tavistock, adding the prestige of that clinic to their marital casework agency, and, indirectly, to the entire field of marriage counseling.

In 1956, Victor Eisenstein, Director of the New Jersey Neuropsychiatric Institute, published an edited volume, *Neurotic Interaction in Marriage*. In it were several articles describing the state of the art in marital therapy. Florence Beatman, described a casework treatment approach to marital problems (Beatman, 1956); Lawrence Kubie wrote a psychoanalytic analysis of the dynamics of marriage (Kubie, 1956); Margaret Mahler described the effects of marital conflict on child development (Mahler and Rabinovitch, 1956); and Ashley Montague added a cultural perspective to the dynamic influences on marriage (Montague, 1956). In the same volume, Mittleman (1956) wrote a more extensive description of his views on marital disorders and their treatment. He described a number of complementary marital patterns, including aggressive/submissive, and detached/demanding. These odd matches are made, according to Mittleman, because courting couples distort each other's personalities through the eyes of their illusions; she sees his independence as strength, he sees her dependency as sexy and giving. Mittleman also pointed out that the couple's reactions to each other may be shaped by their relationships to their parents. Without insight, unconscious motivation may dominate marital behavior, leading to patterns of reactive neurotic circles. For treatment, Mittleman believed that 20 percent of the time one therapist could handle all members of the family, but in other cases separate therapists may be better.

At about this time Jackson and Haley were also writing about marital therapy within the framework of communications analysis. As their ideas gained prominence among marital therapists the field of marital therapy was absorbed into the larger family therapy movement.

FROM RESEARCH TO TREATMENT: THE PIONEERS OF FAMILY THERAPY

We have seen that family therapy was preceded by clinical and research developments in several areas, including hospital psychiatry, group dynamics, interpersonal psychiatry, the child guidance movement, research on schizophrenia, and marriage counseling. But who actually started family therapy? Although there are rival claims to this honor, the distinction should probably be shared by John Elderkin Bell, Don Jackson, Nathan Ackerman, and Murray Bowen. In addition to these originators of family therapy, Jay Haley, Virginia Satir, Carl Whitaker, Lyman Wynne, Ivan Boszormenyi-Nagy, James Framo, Gerald Zuk, Christian Midelfort, and Salvador Minuchin were also significant pioneers of family treatment. Of these, Don Jackson and Jay Haley in Palo Alto, Murray Bowen in Washington, D.C., and Nathan Ackerman in New York probably had the greatest influence on the first decade of the family therapy movement. Among the others, those with the most lasting influence on the field are Carl Whitaker (Chapter 6), Salvador Minuchin (Chapter 11), and John Bell (Chapter 5).

John Bell. John Elderkin Bell occupies a unique position in the history of family therapy. Although he may have been the first family therapist, he is mentioned only tangentially in two of the most important historical accounts of the movement (Guerin, 1976; Kaslow, 1980). The reason for this is that although he began seeing families in the 1950s, he did not publish his ideas until a decade later. Moreover, unlike the other parents of family therapy, he had few offspring. He did not establish an important clinical center, develop a training program, or train well-known students. Therefore, although he was a significant early figure, his influence on the first decade of family therapy was not great.

Bell's approach (Bell 1961, 1962) to treating families is based on group therapy. In "family group therapy," Bell relies primarily on stimulating an open discussion in order to help families solve their problems. Like a group therapist, he intervenes to encourage silent participants to speak up, and he interprets the reasons for their defensiveness.

Bell has always believed that family group therapy goes through certain phases just as do groups of strangers. In his early work (Bell, 1961), he carefully structured treatment in a series of stages, each of which concentrated on a particular segment of the family. Later, he became less directive and allowed families to evolve through a naturally unfolding sequence of stages. As they did so, he would tailor his interventions to the needs of the moment. For a more complete description of Bell's family group therapy, see Chapter 5.

Palo Alto. While conducting their landmark studies of family dynamics and schizophrenia, the Bateson group stumbled into family therapy. Once the group began to meet with schizophrenic families in 1954, hoping to better understand their patterns of communication through unobtrusive, naturalistic observation, they felt a pressure to treat these obviously troubled people (Jackson and Weakland, 1961). Project members found themselves drawn into helping roles by the pain of these families. While Bateson was the undisputed scientific leader of the group, Don Jackson and Jay Haley were most influential in developing family treatment.

Jackson's work offers a rare example of the development of psychotherapy following the development of a theory—and secondary to theory. As a therapist, Jackson rejected the intrapsychic role theory and psychoanalytic concepts he had learned in training, and focused instead on the dynamics of interchange between persons. Analysis of communication was always his tool for understanding and treatment; Jackson shared Bateson's view that behavior and communication are synonymous.

Jackson's thinking about family therapy was first stimulated by encounters with patients' relatives in his private practice, and by occasional visits to the homes of individual schizophrenic patients (Jackson and Weakland, 1961). Observing the impact of families on patients—and vice versa—was not new, but Jackson's conclusions were. Since Freud, the family was understood to be the critical force in shaping personality, for better or worse. But the family was dealt with through segregation, physical and emotional, like removing a sick person from a contaminated environment. Jackson began to see the possibility of treating patients in the family as an alternative to severing the family's influence.

By 1954 Jackson had developed a rudimentary family interactional therapy, which he reported in a paper "The Question of Family Homeostasis," delivered to the American Psychiatric Association convention in St. Louis. His main emphasis was still on the effect that patients' therapy had on their families, rather that on the prospect of family treatment (Jackson, 1954). Jackson's concept of *family homeostasis* borrowed ideas from biology and systems theory. Families are described as units which maintain relative constancy of internal functioning. Consistency does not necessarily mean rigidity. Instead, family homeostasis is a nonstatic dynamic state, an equilibrium within which the family may be at point A on Monday and point B on Tuesday. Families seek to maintain or restore the status quo; family members function as governors, and the family is said to act in error-activated ways (Haley, 1963). The result is not invariance, but stability in variance, of behavior. A clinical illustration of homeostasis is to be found in families in which the symptomatic behavior of children serves to restore the status quo. Frequently, parental argument is followed by disturbed behavior from one of the children, after which the parents stop arguing, and become concerned about the now "identified patient's" symptoms.

In "Schizophrenic Symptoms and Family Interaction" (Jackson and Weakland, 1959) Jackson illustrated how patients' symptoms preserve stability in their families. In one case a young woman diagnosed as catatonic schizophrenic had as her most pronounced symptom a profound indecisiveness. However, when she did behave decisively her parents fell apart. Mother became helpless and dependent; father became, literally, impotent. In one family meeting the parents failed to hear the patient when she made a clear decision. Only after listening to a taped replay of the session *three times* did the parents finally hear their daughter's statement. The patient's indecision was neither crazy nor senseless, but protected the parents from facing their own difficulties. This case is one of the earliest published examples of how schizophrenic symptoms are meaningful in the family context. The paper also contains the shrewd observation that this patient's symptoms were often an exaggerated version of her parents' problems. The parents simply had established better social covers. In addition the case demonstrates how parents obscure and mystify feelings and conflicts. Jackson noted that often when the parents were asked to discuss their own thoughts and feelings, they quickly returned the focus to the patient, lest disagreements emerge.

In moving away from mentalistic inference to observation of behavioral (communicational) sequences among family members, Jackson found that he needed a new language of interaction. His basic assumption was that all people in continuing relationships develop patterns of interaction. This patterning he called "behavioral (or communicational) redundancy" (Jackson, 1965). The term *redundancy* not only captures an important feature of family behavior, but also reflects Jackson's phenomenological stance. More traditional psychiatric terms like *projection, defense,* and *regression* imply far more about inner states of motivation than the simple descriptive language of early family therapists. Even when using concepts that imply prescriptions, Jackson remained committed to description. Thus, his "rules hypothesis" was simply a means of summarizing the observation that within any committed unit (dyad, triad, or group) there are redundant behavior patterns. Rules (as any student of philosophy learns when studying determinism) can describe regularity, rather than regulation. A second part of the rules hypothesis is that family members use only some of the full range of behaviors available to them. This seemingly innocent fact is precisely what makes family therapy possible. One member's behavior is limited by the responses of others, and these limitations represent the rules governing what sort of relationship is to take place, and thus reflect the basic governing principles of the family. Notice that although Jackson's use of "governing" seems to imply more than description, since it rests on description it need be understood as no more than that.

By 1963 Jackson had delineated three types of family rules: (1) norms, which are covert; (2) values, which are consciously held and openly acknowledged; and (3) homeostatic mechanisms, which are rules about how norms and values are enforced (*metarules*). Many of these rules are inculcated by families of origin, but Jackson generally did not look beyond the nuclear family.

Since families operate by rules, and rules about rules, Jackson concluded that family dysfunction was due to a lack of rules for change. Therefore he sought to make explicit and to change the rules by which family transactions are governed. This is, in fact, a fancy way of describing interpretation, a technique that characterizes the treatment of communications therapists far more than their writings suggest. Although he denied that pointing out family patterns of interaction is useful (Jackson and Weakland, 1961), this technique was in practice part of his style and part of his influence.

Jackson's therapeutic strategies were based on the premise that psychiatric problems result from the way people behave with each other in a given context. He sees human problems as interactional *and* situational. Problem resolution involves shifting the context in which problems occur. Although Jackson had more to say about understanding families than treating them, many of his explanatory concepts (*homeostatic mechanisms, quid pro quo, double-bind, symmetry,* and *complementarity*) informed his strategies and tactics of therapy. He sought first to distinguish those redundant behavior patterns that are functional from those that are dysfunctional or problem-maintaining. To do this he observed routine behavior patterns and noted when problems occurred and in what context, who was present, and what the people did about the problems. Given the belief that symptoms are homeostatic mechanisms, Jackson also considered how the family might be adversely affected if the problems were alleviated. Once the sequence, context, and purpose of the problems were understood, therapy was directed at trying to change the interactional sequences that precipitated and maintained the problems. Jackson began by requiring the whole family to attend sessions, but later on he selected members who could best effect the desired changes.

One of Jackson's most popular and trenchant papers was "Family Rules: Marital Quid Pro Quo" (Jackson, 1965). In a marriage, husband and wife play a variety of different roles. Jackson denied that these roles are the result of sexual differences; instead he considered that they result from a series of *quid pro quos*, worked out in a long-term collaborative relationship. The traditional view is that marital roles stem from sex role differences. This means that behavior is ascribed to individual personalities, and ignores the fact that relationships depend in large measure upon the interactions and rules for interaction worked out between people. Jackson's view is not that sexual differences do not exist, but that they are relatively unimportant. The major differences in marriages are worked out, not given. *Quid pro quo* refers to the bargains struck between husband and wife, analogous to a legal contract. The rights and duties of each are established in a mutual exchange. Jackson cites as one of the major quid pro quos among middle-class families the arrangement in which the husband plays an instrumental role, dealing with things in a logical and practical manner, and the wife plays an emotional role, dealing more with people than with things. This division of labor is highly practical, because the dyad then contains two specialists who combine their talents. The fact that such quid pro quos are not overt or conscious is significant for family therapists, who must ferret out these agreements and help couples modify those that are not serviceable.

Another construct important to Jackson's thinking was the dichotomy (developed by Bateson) between relationships that are *complementary* and those that are *symmetrical*. *Complementary* relationships are those in which people are different in ways that fit together. If one is dominant, for instance, the other is submissive; if one is logical, the other is emotional; if one is weak, the other is strong. *Symmetrical* relationships are based on equality and similarity. Marriages between two people who both have careers and share housekeeping chores are symmetrical.

The preponderance of Jackson's descriptive concepts *(complementary/ symmetrical, quid pro quo, double-bind)* describe relationships between only two people. This is because most of his thinking concentrated on the marital dyad. Although his intent was to develop a descriptive language of whole-family interaction, his major success was in describing relationships between husband and wife. This focus on the marital dyad is one of the shortcomings of work done by the Palo Alto group. Their sophisticated interest in communication led to an adult-centered bias, and they tended to neglect the children and the various triads that make up families. As a consequence, many of their students tend to reduce family problems, even or especially where small children are presented as the patients, to marital problems.

Like the other members of the the Palo Alto group, Jay Haley's major focus was on the marital pair when dealing with families. Symptoms in a marriage partner, Haley argued, represent an incongruence between levels of communication. The symptomatic spouse does something, such as touching a doorknob six times before turning it, while at the same time indicating that he or she is not doing it, because he or she cannot help it. Haley goes on to argue the patient's symptoms are perpetuated both by the way the patient behaves and by the influence of those intimately involved with the patient. From this, his basic tactic of psychotherapy follows: to persuade the patient to change his or her behavior, and to persuade family members to change their behavior in relation to the patient.

Control in relationships is the constant theme underlying all of Haley's work. He describes everyday relationships as significantly determined by people struggling to achieve control over each other, and the therapeutic relationship as one in which patients attempt to control what is to happen with the therapist (Haley 1961). Therapists, therefore according to Haley, need to outwit and manipulate patients in such a way as to defeat their resistance and subtle uncooperativeness. Haley, who borrows many of his maneuvers from Milton Erickson, the renowned hypnotherapist, treats symptoms just as he treats resistance. Since symptoms are seen as ways of dealing with people, therapy must provide other ways of dealing with people. Thus Haley analyzes patients' manipulative and rebellious ways of dealing with family members. For example, a wife's handwashing compulsion may be seen as a means of rebelling against a tyrannical husband. A psychoanalyst would describe this as "secondary gain"; Haley sees this interpersonal payoff as the primary gain. As he puts it, "From the point of view offered here, the crucial aspect of the symptom is the advantage it gives the patient in gaining control of what is to happen in a relationship with someone else" (Haley, 1961, p. 151).

Haley's analysis of the struggle for control between therapist and patient is shrewd, as so many of his analyses are; it is also, however, simplistic. He is sharp enough to realize that the initial contact with the patient often involves subtle and not so subtle maneuvering for position. Thus when the patient says, "I work days and can only meet with you in the evening," the therapist will respond either by accepting the control or resisting it. While such struggles indeed take place—as most therapists realize—it may be simplistic to see them as the major feature of the psychotherapeutic relationship. True, if the patient gains control of what happens in therapy, he or she may lose by winning—perpetuating difficulties by continued reliance on a destructive pattern. But it does not follow that therapists can succeed merely by achieving control themselves.

Haley (1963) defined his therapy as being a directive form of treatment, and acknowledged that many of his methods were developed by Milton Erickson. There is an immediate focus on the present circumstances of the patient and the function of the patient's symptoms; and, as always, there is concern with usurping the patient's control. Thus Haley cites Erickson's device of advising the patient that since this is only the first interview there will be things that the patient may be willing to say and other things that the patient will want to withold, and that these of course should be witheld. Here Erickson is directing patients to do precisely what they will do anyway, and thus subtly gaining the upper hand.

Even while gaining initial information, the brief therapist begins to establish a context for therapeutic change. Accordingly, a history may be taken in such a way as to suggest that progressive improvement has and will continue to occur. Alternatively, with a pessimistic patient, the therapist accepts the pessimism, and says that since things have become so terribly bad, it is time for a change. In either case the therapist gathers information while at the same time encouraging a commitment to change.

The decisive technique in brief therapy (then and now) is the use of directives. As Haley put it, it is not enough to explain problems to patients; what is important is to get them to *do* something about them. However, as he points out, "One of the difficulties involved in telling patients to do something is the fact that psychiatric patients are noted for their hesitation about doing what they are told" (Haley, 1963, p. 45). The trick of course is to use directives so cleverly that patients cannot help but do what is wanted. Typical of this procedure is to prescribe symptomatic behavior, but add something in the instructions so that the symptoms come under therapeutic direction, and may slowly be modified. In one instance Haley was asked to treat a freelance photographer who compulsively made silly blunders which ruined every picture. Naturally this person became so preoccupied with avoiding mistakes that he was too tense to take satisfactory pictures. Haley instructed him to go out and take three pictures, making one deliberate error in each. While seeming to perpetuate the patient's problem, Haley was in fact paradoxically directing symptomatic behavior in such a way that the patient gained control of it. In another case, Haley prescribed that an insomniac spend his wakeful late night hours performing arduous, unpleasant tasks, like going for long walks or polishing floors. The patient reported that he dared not suffer from insomnia once he knew that if he failed to fall asleep immediately he had to spend the night polishing floors. Apparently, psychiatric patients, like the rest of us, will do almost anything to get out of certain chores—even give up their symptoms.

Central to Haley's thinking is the idea that people develop problems when they are bound by paradoxical directives from their parents, yet they can be helped to overcome these problems by a therapist's benign use of paradox. Haley cites John Rosen as a therapist who uses therapeutic paradoxes in an authoritarian manner, and Frieda Fromm-Reichmann as one who uses paradoxes in a warm, gentle manner. In one famous instance Rosen dealt with a young schizophrenic patient who claimed to be God by having the ward attendants force the patient to his knees before Rosen, thus demonstrating vividly that he, Rosen, was in charge. This patient was therefore in a paradoxical dilemma. He could not deny that he was relating to the therapist by calling himself God; yet, once on his knees he had to acknowledge either that God was subservient to the therapist, or that he was not indeed God. Frieda Fromm-Reichmann's more gentle approach is described in her book *Principles of Intensive Psychotherapy* (Fromm-Reichmann, 1950). She once treated a patient who said that everything she did occurred in relation to her own private and powerful God rather than in relation to other people. This of course provided a convenient excuse for her refusing to relate to Dr. Fromm-Reichmann. Fromm-Reichmann then instructed the patient, "Tell him that I am a doctor and you have lived with him in his kingdom now from 7 to 16—that's nine years—and he has not helped you. So now he must permit me to try and see whether you and I can do that job." This patient too was then caught in a position where she had to respond to the therapist whatever she did. She could either go to her God and repeat what she was told, thereby conceding that the doctor was in charge; or she could rebel against the doctor, which meant she was relating to her, an action which also renders questionable the existence of her God. Hence in order to acknowledge her God, she must deny him; similarly, if she defies Fromm-Reichmann, she must acknowledge her. What Haley salutes in these examples is the use of therapeutic paradox to maneuver patients into responding to their therapist. Once that happens the patients can no longer deny that they are responding to another human being; and Haley believes this is the necessary first step for treating schizophrenic patients.

Haley's conception of psychotherapy with schizophrenics is predicated on the notion that much of schizophrenic behavior is designed to avoid relating to other people. Denying relationships makes sense if you remember that double-binds pervade the schizophrenic's family. Accordingly, Haley's therapeutic tactics involve creating a paradoxical situation in which the patient cannot deny the relationship to the therapist.

Haley bases his recommendations for therapy with whole families on an amalgam of concepts from the Bateson group. As in traditional individual psychotherapy, conflict is seen as a major focus; but conflict is seen as occurring between people rather than between internal forces. The model is cybernetic; one person's behavior is seen as provoking a response in other family members; family members set limits on one another's behavior in a self-corrective process by responding in error-activated ways when any individual goes beyond the acceptable limits. This process of mutually responsive behavior defines rules in the family system. Haley relies on the metaphor of a power struggle when describing who sets the rules. The therapeutic task is to help families resolve power struggles.

Haley suggests that family therapy is formally similar to individual therapy; therapists suggest to families that they behave differently, and force them to do so by therapeutic paradoxes. While the differences between individual and family therapy are many in theory, Haley says they are few in practice; however, this observation may have been valid when he made it in 1963, but today techniques of family therapy differ in many ways from those of individual therapy. When family therapy is similar to individual therapy, the therapist is probably overly central. Today, most family therapists see their job as promoting family interaction, and then influencing it from a decentralized position. Haley apparently remained in the center of things.

In his early work Haley relied heavily on the curative effects of having family members simply sit down together and talk about their relationship. He also treated all family members as equals, rather than recognizing hierarchical distinctions—say, between parents and children. He suggested that each person have a fair turn, that minority views be expressed, and that everyone make compromises for the good of the group—which is reminiscent of the group therapy model. (Haley's current position is quite different; see Chapter 10). He considered the therapist's role one of demonstrating to family members how to handle attempts at manipulation and provocation. "By not responding on the patient's terms when the patient is exhibiting symptomatic or distressful behavior, the therapist requires the patient to deal with him in other ways, in both individual and family therapy. A difference lies in the fact that in family therapy the other members can observe, and utilize for themselves, the ways that therapists handle provocation" (Haley, 1963, p. 171). This notion of the therapist as model was then widely held; but it probably makes the therapist overly central. Instead of demonstrating to family members how to deal with each other and hoping that they will follow, a therapist is more effective when encouraging and guiding family members to deal directly with each other. Modeling effective behavior for family members also subtly conveys to them their own inadequacy, and families who have found it necessary to come for therapy need nothing less than to be reminded of their feelings of inadequacy.

Haley's discussion of psychotherapy reveals a discrepancy between what he says and what he does. He recognizes the limits of certain simple procedures, but then he often uses these procedures himself. For example, he cautions against overreliance on self-understanding, but then proceeds to encourage family members to talk openly with each other, presumably in the belief that by understanding each other, they will be able to solve many problems. The same kind of discrepancy may be seen in his advice that the therapist model for the family how to deal successfully with maneuvers. He describes how he demonstrates to families the way to avoid being drawn into symptomatic behavior, but then says that the more the therapist attempts to direct reform in a disturbed family, the more likely he or she is to induce self-corrective processes in the family and so only achieve greater rigidity. In short, he believes, a successful family therapist should not govern the family directly but should encourage typical family interactions in such a way as to maneuver the interactions so that behavior is changed. One gets the idea that at least in the early sixties Haley was better at analyzing the process of therapy than he was at describing how to actually do it.

Murray Bowen. Murray Bowen began treating families while he was directing a research project on the interaction in schizophrenic families. In the first year of this project (1954) Bowen treated each family member with individual psychotherapy. However, after concluding that the family was the unit of disorder, he began to hold therapy sessions with all family members assembled together. Thus, in 1955, Bowen became one of the founders of family therapy.

Beginning in 1955 Bowen also held large group therapy sessions open to all project staff and family members. In this early form of network therapy, Bowen assumed that togetherness and open communication would be therapeutic for problems within families, and between family members and the staff.

The history of Bowen's methods of therapy mark the evolution of his thinking. At first he used four therapists to manage the large multifamily meetings, but he became dissatisfied when he noticed that the therapists tended to pull in different directions. So he put one therapist in charge, and consigned the others to supporting roles. However, just as multiple therapists tend to pull in different directions, so do multiple families. As soon as a crucial point was being developed within one family, someone from another family became anxious and changed the subject. Finally, Bowen decided that families would have to take turns; one family became the focus for each session, while the others were silent auditors.

At first Bowen's approach to single families was the same as the one he employed with the large meetings. He did what many people do when they are new to family therapy: just brought the family members together and tried to get them talking. He reasoned that simply by being together and discussing mutual concerns families would improve. Although Bowen soon rejected this idea, many people continue to approach family treatment this way. Nondirective, participant observation has little utility beyond getting family members started talking together and perhaps resolving relatively transient problems. Bowen soon learned this, and he developed a structured and directive approach which paralleled the evolution of his theory.

When he brought family members together and encouraged them to define their problems and discuss solutions, Bowen was most struck by their intense emotional reactivity. Feelings overwhelmed thinking and tended to involve the whole group in a process whereby no one retained a separate identity. Bowen felt the family's tendency to pull him into the center of this *undifferentiated ego mass,* and he had to make a concerted effort to stay objective and detached (Bowen, 1961). He believed that if they were forced to solve their problems, the family would become more responsible and competent. So Bowen sat with them, remaining neutral and detached, while he observed the process of family interactions. His major active efforts during the sessions were to discourage scapegoating by pointing out to family members when they used the patient as an excuse for avoiding other problems. At the end of each session he summed up what he observed, emphasizing the process by which the family went about trying to solve their problems.

Parallel to the formal research project on families of schizophrenics, Bowen also conducted a larger clinical operation for families of children with a wide range of problems. Although he initially believed that the pathological mechanisms in schizophrenic families were exclusive to schizophrenic families—and were the *cause* of schizophrenia—he discovered that the same phenomena were present in all families, although to a lesser degree.

Bowen found that observing entire family units was invaluable as a source of information, but he was disappointed with the results of therapy with whole families. So beginning in 1960 he began meeting with just the parents of symptomatic children. His purpose was to block scapegoating and help the parents focus on problems in their own relationship, without being distracted by their children. He was much happier with the results of seeing the parents alone, and has continued to do so, only rarely including children. When he first began interviewing parents, Bowen analyzed the intrapsychic processes in one spouse at a time, focusing heavily on dreams for his interpretations. He soon abandoned this intrapsychic focus and shifted to explore the relationship system between spouses. Bowen experimented with different methods of working with couples until about 1964, when he developed his present method, which has not been modified much since: 1. Defining and clarifying the relationship between the spouses; 2. Keeping self detriangled; 3. Teaching the spouses about how emotional systems function; and 4. Demonstrating differentiation by taking "I-position" stands.

1. *Defining and clarifying relationships between spouses.* Bowen encourages each spouse to talk directly to the therapist, not to his or her mate. In this way the therapist, not the couple, controls the affect in the interchange. The Bowenian therapist tries to keep things calm, low-keyed, and objective. A spouse who is neither speaking nor being spoken to is less involved, less emotionally reactive, and therefore able to hear and understand better. The therapist focuses on cognition—thoughts and ideas—rather than on feelings. Only after a couple makes a great deal of progress toward understanding each other rationally, does the therapist invite them to talk about their emotional reactions and feelings. When feelings are stirred up, the therapist encourages the couple to discuss *the issues* about which they have feelings, not the feelings themselves. Emotions that do emerge from these issue-oriented discussions are probably more spontaneous than those elicited when couples are encouraged to express feelings.

2. *Keeping self detriangled.* Bowen believes that a prerequisite to avoiding emotional entanglement with client families is a mature resolution of emotional conflicts within one's own family and emotional system at work. In the absence of such personal maturity, a therapist is liable to react emotionally to family members who restimulate conflicts and blind spots. To avoid emotional entanglement, therapists should focus on process, not content, and avoid taking sides, being charmed, or getting angry. The Bowenian therapist remains calm at all times.

3. *Teaching spouses about the functioning of emotional systems.* This should only be attempted when anxiety is reduced. Otherwise whatever the therapist says is liable to be interpreted as siding with one or the other spouses. When anxiety in the couple is moderately low, Bowen may discuss progress

made in other cases, to illustrate certain points. When the anxiety between the spouses is very low he teaches them directly about functioning of emotional systems. If they are motivated he also encourages them to work on differentiating themselves in relation to their families of origin.

4. *Taking "I position" stands.* The more the therapist can define him- or herself in relationship to the family, the more family members can follow suit and define themselves in relation to the rest of the family. Defining oneself means to become clear about and express convictions, beliefs, and actions in relation to other people. By knowing what one believes and saying so in a calm, straightforward manner, one can avoid *ego-fusion* and *undifferentiation.*

The goals of Bowen's work with parents is to help them achieve a reasonable level of differentiation of self from each other and from their families of origin; to learn enough about family systems to handle future crises; and to develop the motivation to continue working toward further differentiation after therapy is terminated.

Besides treating couples Bowen has also used two other methods of treatment, couples groups and individual sessions.

When he found himself covering similar issues with different couples in session after session, Bowen decided that he might save time by working with several families at once. This seemed particularly appropriate for Bowen's therapy since it is relatively didactic. So beginning in about 1965 (Bowen, 1976), he began treating couples in groups. Bowen's use of Multiple Family Therapy was paradoxical because his major emphasis has been avoiding the fusion inherent in social and emotional togetherness. But, when he works with groups, Bowen minimizes emotional interaction between families, and forbids contact outside the group sessions. Although he found it no easier to teach families about emotional systems and much harder to remain neutral, the couples in these groups did make rapid progress. Apparently these families learned a great deal about the process of emotional systems with less anxiety as they listened to discussions of other people's problems. For several years the Multiple Family Therapy method was a major part of Bowen's practice.

In addition to couples and couples groups, Bowen also works frequently with individual family members. This is a unique approach, and it challenges facile assumptions about family therapy. Family therapy is both a method and an orientation; as an orientation it means understanding people in the context of significant emotional systems; as a method, it usually means working with whole families. Indeed some might argue that Bowen's work with separate family members is more exclusively focused on family issues, systems concepts, and emotional process than is almost any other family therapy approach.

In 1966 there was an emotional crisis in Bowen's family and his personal experience in resolving that crisis was a formative event in teaching him about changing families. Bowen himself was the oldest of five children from a tightly-knit family that for several generations had lived in the same small town in Pennsylvania. After growing up, he kept a formal distance from his parents and maintained family relationships on a comfortable but superficial basis. Like many of us, Bowen mistook avoidance for emancipation. But as he later realized, emotional tension with the family remains within us, making us vulnerable to repeat similar patterns in new relationships, as long as our family conflicts remain unresolved.

Bowen's personal resolution of emotional reactivity in his family was as significant for his work as Freud's self-analysis was for psychoanalysis. In neither case was it easy. Bowen spent twelve years trying to understand his family, using the framework of his theory, and seven or eight years of active effort to modify himself in relation to the family before the major breakthrough occurred. The going is usually slower for explorers of unknown territory than for those who come later, with maps to guide them.

In his attempt to understand and improve relationships with his own family, Bowen turned first to his nuclear family and only later to his family of origin. Although this seems a natural sequence, Bowen's experience convinced him that the most productive course is to begin with the original family. Only then is it possible to make genuine progress in reducing tension in the more significant, but more emotionally reactive, nuclear family. Differentiation of self in the family of origin begins with developing an individual, person-to-person relationship with each parent and with as many members of the family as possible. If visiting is difficult, letters and phone calls help re-establish relationships, particularly if they are personal and intimate. Differentiating one's self from the family is completed when these relationships are maintained without fusion or triangulation. Differentiated people can talk about the full range of personal issues between them without getting anxious and detouring the conversation to a third person or impersonal subject.

Bowen's most important achievement was detriangling himself from his own parents. His parents had been accustomed to complaining to him about unresolved tension and conflict between them. Most of us are flattered to receive these confidences and consider them a form of intimacy born of respect for our judgment. Bowen recognized this triangulation for what it was, and when his mother complained about his father, he told his father: "Your wife told me a story about you; I wonder why she told me instead of you." Naturally father discussed this with mother, and naturally she was annoyed. Moves to differentiate oneself violate family norms and cause emotional upheaval. If there is no upheaval then the differentiation effort is probably insignificant (Bowen, 1976). Although his mother fussed about it, Bowen's maneuver was effective in keeping his parents from trying to get him to take sides—and made it harder for them to avoid discussing things between themselves. Telling the third person what a second person says to you about him or her is one of the most effective detriangling moves.

Bowen also discovered that it is important to define self around significant issues. Since emotionally significant issues are usually dormant, the most productive visits home are during a crisis or stressful occasion, such as a death, serious illness, wedding, or birth. At these times the family's emotional reactivity is at high tide. It was at such a point that Bowen returned home for a carefully orchestrated effort to differentiate himself from a series of interlocking family triangles. The details of that venture are complex but make rewarding reading for the serious student (Anonymous, 1972).

Bowen's trip came on the heels of a family squabble over problems with the family business. He prepared the way by writing a series of intimate and provocative letters to the major players in the family drama. These letters were designed to open hidden conflicts and promote a lively confrontation. Thus he wrote to his brother, a family scapegoat, and told him all the stories and gossip about him. That did the trick.

When Bowen arrived home, the whole family was present—and hopping mad. Every segment of the family tried to engage him in an emotional tug of war. But differentiation requires thinking, instead of hasty reaction, and remaining objectively neutral about conflicts between others. Although his letters had provoked the showdown, the issues were among the family members who lived together in Pennsylvania. Bowen saw his task as stirring things up, but not taking sides. Armed by his understanding of family systems theory and knowing what to expect from the family, Bowen was able to remain absolutely neutral. This forced the feuding parties, all of whom were present, to work things out among themselves.

The trip was a great success. Bowen was able to remain in personal contact with each member of his family at a time of crisis, but without becoming triangled or emotionally reactive.

After he reported his experience with his family, many of Bowen's trainees began to return to their own families and work on differentiating themselves. They did so even though Bowen had not directly encouraged them. When he noted how productive these trainees became as therapists, as compared with those who had not returned to their own families, Bowen decided that the best way to become a family therapist is to resolve emotional problems in the family of origin. Thus, beginning in 1971, studying one's own family became the core of Bowen's approach to training. The major emphasis is on returning to the family of origin, making contact, and developing a viable working relationship with every possible member of the family, while remaining detriangled.

Nathan Ackerman. Nathan Ackerman came to family therapy from psychoanalysis, and his thinking about families continued to reflect that background. He emphasized the intrapsychic effects of families on individuals more than the behavioral sequences, communication, and interaction that systems-oriented family therapists stressed. He described families as shaping an individual's needs, security, pleasure, self-fulfillment, and belongingness through identification. Families, he said, give an appearance of unity, but underneath they are emotionally divided into competing factions. This you may recognize as similar to the psychoanalytic model of individuals who, despite apparent unity of personality, are perceived as motivated by a dynamic interplay of structural forces. Just as an individual expresses the interplay of id, ego, and superego in conscious and unconscious manifestations, so too are families dynamic coalitions, sometimes of mother and daughter against father and son, sometimes of one generation against the next. Furthermore, Ackerman perceived the conflicts among various family members as similar to the conflicts within individuals.

Ackerman was a psychoanalytically-trained child psychiatrist. After completing his residency training he worked with disturbed children at the Menninger Clinic in Topeka, Kansas. In 1937 he became chief psychiatrist of the Child Guidance Clinic. At first he followed the child guidance model of having a psychiatrist treat the child and a social worker see the mother. But by the mid-1940s he began to experiment with having the same therapist see both. Unlike Bowlby, however, Ackerman did more than use this as a temporary expedient to resolve treatment impasses. Instead, he re-evaluated his whole conception of psychopathology and began to see the family as the basic unit for diagnosis and treatment.

In 1955 Ackerman organized and led the first session on family diagnosis at a meeting of the American Orthopsychiatric Association. Two years later, in 1957, he opened the Family Mental Health Clinic of Jewish Family Services in New York City, and taught at Columbia University. From here he founded the Family Institute in 1960, which was renamed the Ackerman Institute after his death in 1971.

In addition to his clinical innovations, Ackerman also published several important articles and books. As early as 1938, he wrote "The Unity of the Family," and some consider his article, "Family Diagnosis: An Approach to the Preschool Child," (Ackerman and Sobel, 1950), as the beginning of the family therapy movement (Kaslow, 1980). In 1961 Ackerman, with Don

Jackson, co-founded the field's first journal, *Family Process*. Under the editorial leadership of first Jay Haley and later Donald Bloch, *Family Process* has continued to be a major vehicle through which family therapists communicate their ideas.

Other family therapists may focus on interactions and systems to the point where the individuals are not considered important, but Ackerman was always concerned with what goes on inside people, as well as what goes on between them. Some family therapists treat family members, particularly children, as though they were billiard balls interacting with each other. This was never true of Ackerman; he was always aware of the individual's needs, feelings, hopes, and desires (Hoffman, 1981). In fact, Ackerman's model of the family is like the psychoanalytic model of an individual writ large; instead of the conscious and unconscious, Ackerman talks about how families are aware of some issues while they avoid and deny others, particularly conflictual ones involving sex and aggression. He described his role as therapist as one of stirring up the family and bringing the family's secrets into the open.

Ackerman recommended that everyone living under the same roof be present at all family interviews. Once the family is assembled, the clinician must observe and relate to personalities as well as to the components of this system. As Ackerman put it, "It is very important at the outset to establish a meaningful emotional contact with all members of the family, to create a climate in which one really touches them and they feel they touch back" (Ackerman, 1961, p. 242). Once contact was made, Ackerman encouraged an open and honest expression of feeling. As a therapist he was always lively and ready to share his own thoughts and feelings. Because he was concerned with hidden or unconscious aspects of family functioning, Ackerman suggested that a therapist always be tuned in to nonverbal cues. Disguised feelings may be conveyed in facial expression, mood, posture, or gesture far more eloquently than in words.

Ackerman pointed out that identity has various aspects; one has identity as an individual, a member of various subsystems in the family, and as a member of the family as a whole. In order to pinpoint these various components of identity, he was alert to the coalitions revealed in family interviews. One clue to such coalitions is found in the seating arrangement; that is, as family members enter the room they tend to pair off in ways that reveal alignments. But to see these various alignments and their conflicts clearly, Ackerman recommended mobilizing spontaneous interaction among family members. Once family members interact among themselves and with the therapist, it is possible to see how the family is emotionally divided, as well as what problems and prohibitions are present. In order to promote more honest emotional interchange, Ackerman "tickled the defenses" of family members—his phrase for teasing, provoking, and stimulating members of the family to open up and say what is really on their minds. The phrase nicely reflects Ackerman's charismatic and provocative style.

What are thought to be family secrets, Ackerman said, generally turn out to be known by all family members but are simply not spoken of. Children generally know a good deal more than parents think. They also know what they are not supposed to talk about. However, as long as the therapist demonstrates he is in control, the family feels reassured that things will not get out of hand and become destructive. They therefore feel free to speak more plainly about matters that they usually avoid and submerge. Ackerman recommended that the therapist permit the family to draw him or her into the center of the family disturbance. This suggests a very active, open, free-wheeling style in which the therapist may engage in challenging discussions, dialogues, and perhaps even arguments with family members. He suggested that it is more therapeutic to use the therapist as a target for anger and hostility than other family members. According to Ackerman, the therapist's role should be neither emotionally neutral nor passive. Sometimes the therapist acts as referee, sometimes as one who supports one individual over another, and sometimes as a provocateur. In short, the therapist is spontaneous, always lively, never static or staid.

In order to encourage families to give up emotional restraint, Ackerman himself was unrestrained. He willingly sided first with one part of the family and later with another. He did not think it was necessary to be always neutral and objective; instead, he believed that an impartial balance was achieved in the long run by moving about and giving support now to one, and now to another family member. He was also unabashedly straightforward and blunt with family members. If he believed that someone was lying, he said so. To critics who suggested this bluntness might produce too much anxiety in patients, Ackerman replied that when he was direct with family members, they became more direct with him; he also believed that patients derive more protection and security from honesty than from bland support.

Ackerman also made use of psychoanalytic processes like transference, resistance, and interpretation. He used the feelings aroused in countertransference, and thought nothing happened in family therapy unless the therapist used him or herself actively and also exploited his or her own emotions for explicit ends. Ackerman's techniques do, however, require long experience and an informed awareness about which of the therapist's emotions may be shared with families and which should be kept private, as well as an ability to avoid the extremes of passivity or unchecked candor.

Ackerman explained many family events as the product of conflict. He said that conflicts within individuals, among family members, and between families and the larger community must be identified and resolved if psychological hurts are to be mended. An adaptive attempt to contain conflict is compromise, either on a rational or irrational basis. Irrational compromises are often achieved at the expense of one segment of the family, as in pathological scapegoating. Conflicts between family members and within the mind of an individual family member are related in a circular feedback system—that is, personal conflict affects intrapsychic conflict and vice versa (Ackerman, 1961). Conflicts of identity, values, and strivings may produce rifts among family members or subsystems, mobilizing one segment against another. Likewise, conflicts between segments of the family may produce subsequent disturbance within individual members. He considers symptoms to be products of the internalization of persistent pathological family conflict. To reverse symptomatic disturbances, the therapist must bring conflicts into the open and into the field of family interaction, where new solutions can be found. As long as conflicts remain locked within individuals, Ackerman believed, psychopathology remains fixed. Consequently, Ackerman described the primary diagnostic task of the family therapist as unearthing the pathogenic family conflicts that have become lodged in the intrapsychic life of a symptomatic member.

Ackerman's treatment procedure was problem-oriented rather than technique-oriented (Ackerman, 1970a). Rather than approach families with a preordained plan, he preferred to use procedures determined by the needs of the family group and its individual members. This creative flexibility makes it very difficult to describe or to teach Ackerman's approach. He was much more of a clinical artist than a systematizer. He was not even wedded to seeing any particular family unit; he might begin by seeing the nuclear family, but then subsequently meet with parents and grandparents, parents alone, or parents with their children. Unlike most family therapists, he also regularly saw individual family members. (Most family therapists will see adolescents alone during the course of family treatment, but few ever see adult family members alone).

While it may be impossible to neatly characterize Ackerman's techniques, there were clear themes. One of the major themes is the necessity for depth of commitment and involvement with families. He himself became quickly and deeply emotionally involved with the families he treated, in contrast, say, to Murray Bowen, who consistently cautioned therapists to remain uninvolved in order to avoid being triangulated. Depth also characterized the type of material on which Ackerman focused—family analogues of the kinds of conflicts, feelings, and fantasies that lie buried in the individual unconscious. Ackerman believed that there are similar currents of highly significant conflict, feeling, and fantasy excluded from the family's awareness—a kind of interpersonal unconscious of the family group. Ackerman's psychoanalytic orientation sensitized him to these hidden themes, and his flamboyant, provocative therapeutic style enabled him to help families vividly enact them.

In one very interesting paper, "The Art of Family Therapy" (Ackerman, 1970b), Ackerman reflects on the fact that in previous descriptions of his techniques he had never really related much about his personal style. He had never mentioned his use of first names, his humor, and how he tried to make family encounters interesting and pleasant for himself and for the family, apparently because his long training as a psychoanalyst had inculcated certain taboos against informality and intimacy with patients. He concluded that if teachable principles did underlie his work, they were probably inextricably bound up with his personal performance as a therapist. Thus Ackerman came to see family therapy as a unique and spontaneous expression of the therapist's personality in a therapeutic role.

Ackerman's contributions to the field of family psychotherapy are extensive and important. He was one of the earliest clinicians to envision whole family treatment, and he had the personal inventiveness and energy to initiate it. By the late forties he was pointing out that trying to treat family members through individual therapy without bearing in mind the configuration of the family led to therapeutic problems. He suggested (Ackerman, 1954) that the same therapist might sometimes treat a husband and wife, or mother and child; any such treatment would help the therapist focus on the relationship between the people, and also help the therapist to distinguish the patient's fantasies from the reality of the family situation. Very early Ackerman recommended that family groups be evaluated as wholes, and that these evaluations be followed by therapy of the family group and individual therapy for selected family members. He always concentrated on the fact that people were both individuals and members of the family group.

Ackerman's second important contribuiton was made as a brilliant artist of family therapy technique. He was one of the great geniuses of the movement. Those who studied with him and observed his treatment of families all attest to his clinical wizardry. He was a dynamic catalyst, active, open, and forthright, never rigid or shy. He interacted with families in a highly emotional and effective manner. Nor was he content to remain always in the office, for he recommended frequent home visits (Ackerman, 1966).

Despite his brilliance as a therapist, Ackerman's theoretical ideas do not go much beyond pointing out that individuals are intricately involved in families. Perhaps his major enduring contribution was his consistent stress on individual persons and whole families; he never sacrificed his interest in individuals to an interest in family systems. He believed that the goals of family therapy should be not only to resolve symptoms, but also to enhance family functioning, individual happiness, and inoculate family members against future stress. In sum, he was interested in symptoms, as well as in health and growth, but he never had much to say about the systems of whole families.

Finally there are Ackerman's contributions as a teacher, which may be his most important legacy to those students who were fortunate enough to work directly with him. He taught them a great deal about style and specific techniques; his writing, however, offers very little in the way of a systematic strategy for working with families. His articles are often colorful, but rarely concrete or explicit. First and foremost he consistently recommended that therapists be emotionally involved with families, and work in a highly confrontive manner to transform dormant conflicts into open discussions. If the therapist offers sufficient security by handling families in a calm, firm way, family members will be enabled to catalyze affective interchanges. If they trust the therapist, they will feel safe enough to fight openly. Ackerman's model of the therapist was as a catalyst, active, open, and forthright; he also stressed that therapists be concerned with transference and countertransference distortions, as well as with the reality of family-therapist interactions. In his view, therapists need to provoke controversy to surface latent conflicts from the psychic level to the level of family interaction. Some of his recommendations are vague; for instance, that the therapist must evaluate the outer and inner reality of the family and then stir family members to open up (Ackerman, 1966). This suggestion and others like it to the effect that the therapist should penetrate the family façade may be interesting, but they are not particularly instructive. How does the therapist provoke candid disclosures? Ackerman did it by calling attention to defenses that family members used ("tickling the defenses"); challenging cliches; and interrupting fruitless bickering over unimportant matters. Ackerman's techniques suggest that he was somewhat more concerned with the content of family conflicts than with the process by which family members dealt with them—more interested in secrets and hidden conflicts (particularly those involving sex and aggression) than in emotional distance and proximity among family members or their patterns of communication. Ackerman was one of the innovators and geniuses of the field; but except on the basis of personal contact, it is somewhat difficult to learn how to do family therapy from him.

Carl Whitaker. Even among the company of strong-willed and colorful founders of family therapy, Carl Whitaker stands out as the most dynamic and irreverent. His approach to individual psychotherapy was always radical and provocative, and he brought this same style to his innovative work with families. Whitaker's view of psychologically troubled people is that they are alienated from their emotions and frozen into stereotyped, safe, and predictable routines (Whitaker and Malone, 1953). In response, Whitaker turns up the emotional temperature. His "Psychotherapy of the Absurd" (Whitaker, 1975) is a blend of warm support and unpredictable emotional goading, designed to loosen people up and help them get in touch with their immediate experience.

Given his bold and inventive approach to treatment, it is not surprising that Whitaker was one of the first to break with psychiatric tradition in order to experiment with family treatment. In 1943 he and John Warkentin, working as co-therapists in Oakridge, Tennessee, began including spouses and eventually children in their patients' treatment. Whitaker was among the first to use co-therapy for treatment, and he continues to feel that a supportive co-therapist is essential to enable family therapists to react spontaneously without fear of unchecked countertransference.

In 1946 Whitaker accepted the chair of Psychiatry at Emory University, in Atlanta. He was joined by Warkentin and Thomas Malone. Together they continued to experiment with family treatment. During this period Whitaker initiated a series of conferences that eventually led to the first major meeting of the family therapy movement. Beginning in 1948 Whitaker, Warkentin, and Malone began twice-yearly conferences during which they observed and discussed each other's work with families. They found these sessions to be enormously helpful; mutual observation, using one-way vision screens, has since then been one of the hallmarks of family therapy.

In 1953 Whitaker invited John Rosen, Albert Scheflen, Gregory Bateson, and Don Jackson to participate in the semiannual conference on families, which was held that year in Sea Island, Georgia. Each took turns demonstrating his own approach with the same family, while the others observed and afterwards joined in for a group discussion and analysis. This kind of cross-fertilization of ideas has continued to characterize the family therapy movement; clinicians openly display their work, both for teaching and for mutual enrichment.

Whitaker resigned from Emory's Department of Psychiatry in 1955, and entered private practice with his colleagues. While still in Atlanta, Whitaker continued to practice and write about his unique brand of therapy (Whitaker, 1958). He and his partners at the Atlanta Psychiatric Clinic developed an experiential form of psychotherapy that utilized a number of highly provocative techniques as well as the force of their own personalities.

In 1965 Whitaker left Atlanta for the University of Wisconsin, where he continued to practice and teach, becoming, one of the elder statesmen of the family therapy movement. He travels widely, giving workshops and presentations at conventions, and he has been on the Editorial Board of *Family Process* since its inception.

When the family therapy movement first began Whitaker was less well-known to students than were many of the other first generation family therapists. Perhaps this was due to his atheoretical position. Whereas Jackson and Haley and Bowen developed theoretical concepts that were intriguing and easy to grasp, Whitaker has always eschewed theory in favor of creative spontaneity. His work has therefore been less accessible to students than that of other family therapists. Nevertheless, he has always had the respect of his peers, and people who have had the chance to observe his work can see that there is method to his madness.

To begin with, Whitaker deliberately creates tension by teasing and confronting families, in the belief that stress is necessary for change. In the process, he does not have an obvious strategy, nor does he use structured techniques, preferring, as he says, to let his unconscious run the therapy (Whitaker, 1976). Although his work seems totally spontaneous, even outrageous at times, there is a consistent theme. All of his interventions have the effect of promoting flexibility and change. He views the core problem in families as emotional sterility, and his treatment is to open individuals up to their own feelings, and help them share these feelings within the family.

Ivan Boszormenyi-Nagy. Ivan Boszormenyi-Nagy came to family therapy from psychoanalysis and he has been one of the seminal thinkers in the family therapy movement since its earliest days (see Chapter 4). In 1957 he founded the Eastern Pennsylvania Psychiatric Institute (EPPI), in Philadelphia, as a center for research and training in families and schizophrenia. Because he was a respected scholar/clinician and an able administrator, Nagy was able to attract a number of highly talented colleagues and students. Among these were James Framo, one of the few psychologists in the early family therapy movement; David Rubenstein, a psychiatrist who later conducted a separate family therapy training program; and Geraldine Spark, a social worker who worked with Nagy as a co-therapist, co-director of the unit, and co-author of *Invisible Loyalties* (Boszormenyi-Nagy and Spark, 1973). This group was joined by Gerald Zuk, a psychologist who became interested in families while working with mentally retarded persons. Zuk later developed a "triadic-based" approach to family therapy (1971), in which he conceptualized the therapist as a member of the system in treatment. In triadic-based family therapy, the therapist begins as a mediator, but then takes sides in order to shift power alignments in the family. According to Zuk (1971, p. 73), "By judicious siding, the therapist can tip the balance in favor of more productive relating, or at least disrupt a chronic pattern of pathogenic relating."

In 1960 Albert Scheflen moved from Temple University to EPPI and joined with Ray Birdwhistle to study body language in the process of psychotherapy. Ross Speck, who did his psychiatric residency in the early 1960s, developed, along with Carolyn Attneave, "network therapy," which broadened the context of treatment far beyond the nuclear family. In this approach as many people as possible who are connected to the patient are invited to attend therapy sessions. Frequently as many as fifty people, including the extended family, friends, neighbors, and teachers, are brought together for approximately three 4-hour sessions, and guided by a minimum of three therapists to discuss ways to support and help the patient change (Speck and Attneave, 1973).

Aside from his sponsorship of these students and colleagues, Nagy has himself made major contributions to the study of schizophrenia (Boszormenyi-Nagy, 1962), and family therapy (Boszormenyi-Nagy, 1966, 1972; Boszormenyi-Nagy and Spark, 1973). Nagy described himself as a therapist who went from being an analyst, prizing secrecy and confidentiality, to a family therapist, fighting the forces of pathology on an open battlefield. One of his most important contributions was to introduce the criterion of morality to therapeutic goals and techniques. According to Nagy, neither the pleasure-pain principle, nor transactional expediency is a sufficient guide to human behavior. Instead, he believes that family members have to base their relationships on trust and loyalty, and that they must balance the ledger of entitlement and indebtedness.

Salvador Minuchin. Minuchin was an early entry into the field and his accomplishments rank him as one of the most influential of all family therapists. Salvador Minuchin trained in his native Argentina, and developed a family approach to treating delinquents at the Wiltwyck School for Boys in New York. The use of family therapy with urban slum families was a new development, and publication of his ideas (Minuchin, Montalvo, Guerney, Rosman, and Schumer, 1967) led to his being invited to become the director of the Philadelphia Child Guidance Clinic. Minuchin brought Braulio Montalvo and Bernice Rosman with him and they were joined in 1967 by Jay Haley; together they set about transforming a traditional child guidance clinic into a family therapy center.

Minuchin's first notable achievement at the Philadelphia Child Guidance Clinic was a unique program for training indigenous members of the local black community as paraprofessional family therapists. The reason for this special effort is that cultural differences often make it very difficult for white middle-class therapists to understand and relate successfully to urban blacks and hispanics.

In 1969 Minuchin received a grant to support his training program.

This helped launch an intensive two-year program in which Minuchin, Haley, Montalvo, and Rosman developed a highly successful approach to training as well as one of the most important systems of family therapy. According to Haley, one of the advantages to training people with no previous experience as clinicians to become family therapists is that they have less to unlearn, and are therefore less resistant to thinking in terms of systems. Minuchin and Haley sought to capitalize on this by developing an approach with the least possible number of theoretical concepts. Simplicity continues to be one of the hallmarks of "structural family therapy."

The major features of the training were hands-on experience, on-line supervision, and extensive use of videotapes. Minuchin himself is a practical, technique-oriented clinician, and he believes that therapists are best taught by experience. Once they have seen a few families, therapists, he believes, are ready to appreciate and utilize systems theory. Traditionally, psychotherapy supervision is done after the session, and takes the form of telling students what they should have done. In contrast, Minuchin and Haley supervised by actually observing sessions and interrupting to provide redirection when necessary. They did this by knocking on the door and entering or by calling into the treatment room by telephone or through "bugs in the ear." Instead of learning afterward what they did wrong, therapists learned, on the spot, how to do it right. Later, the group studied videotapes for a more in-depth analysis of what works and what does not.

The structural family therapy that Minuchin and his colleagues developed (Minuchin, 1974) begins with the observation that family transactions, when they are repeated, develop a patterned regularity, or structure. For example, when new parents bring home their first baby from the hospital they must work out a system for parenting. Since they have no previous experience, their initial interactions are unprogrammed and somewhat unpredictable. When the baby cries in the middle of the night, will the mother get up and nurse the child in the nursery, or will the father get up and bring the baby to her? Who will change the baby's diapers when both parents are present? And how early and often will the new parents leave the baby with a babysitter in order to resume their relationship as husband and wife? These questions are soon answered, and the results shape the family's structure.

The nature of the family's structure is determined by emotional *boundaries* which keep family members either close or distant. Either pattern, closeness leading to *enmeshment,* or distance leading to *disengagement,* may be more or less functional for any particular family. This is a point frequently missed by beginning family therapists, who often assume that any family pattern that differs from their own should be changed. Problems begin, according to Minuchin, when a family fails to modify its structure to fit changing circumstances. When this happens, the family needs help.

The techniques of structural family therapy fall into two general strategies. First, the therapist must accommodate to the family in order to join them. To begin by confronting and challenging the family's preferred mode of relating is to insure that they will resist. If instead the therapist begins by trying to understand and accept the family, they will be more likely to accept treatment. Once this initial *joining* is accomplished, the structural family therapist begins to use *restructuring* techniques. These are active and directive maneuvers designed to disrupt dysfunctional structures by strengthening *diffuse boundaries* and softening *rigid* ones (Minuchin and Fishman, 1981).

In the 1970s, under Minuchin's leadership, the Philadelphia Child Guidance Clinic became one of the outstanding centers for family therapy and training. The clinic itself is a large and marvelously equipped building with excellent facilities for videotaping, "live supervision," workshops, and conferences; there are even small apartments for hospitalizing whole families. Minuchin stepped down as director to pursue his special interest in treating psychosomatic families, especially those with anorexia nervosa (Minuchin, Rosman, and Baker, 1978).

Other Early Centers of Family Therapy. In New York, Israel Zwerling, who had been analyzed by Nathan Ackerman, and Marilyn Mendelsohn, who had been analyzed by Don Jackson, organized the Family Studies Section at Albert Einstein College of Medicine and Bronx State Hospital. Andrew Ferber was named Director in 1964, and later Philip Guerin, a protegé of Murray Bowen, joined the section. Nathan Ackerman served as a consultant to the group, and they assembled an impressive array of family therapists with diverse orientations. Included were Chris Beels, Elizabeth Carter, Monica McGoldrick Orfanidis (now Monica McGoldrick), Peggy Papp, and Thomas Fogarty (Guerin, 1976).

Philip Guerin became Director of Training of the Family Studies Section in 1970, and in 1972 established an extramural training program in Westchester. Shortly afterward, in 1973, Guerin founded the Center for Family Learning in New Rochelle, New York, where he developed one of the strongest family therapy training programs in the nation.

In Galveston, Texas, Robert MacGregor and his colleagues developed "multiple impact therapy" (MacGregor, 1967). It was a case of necessity being the mother of invention. The clinic where MacGregor was located served a large population scattered widely over southeastern Texas, and many of his clients had to come from great distances. Because they had to travel so many miles, most of these people were unable to return for weekly therapy sessions. Therefore, in order to make the maximum possible impact in a short time, MacGregor assembled a large team of professionals who worked intensively with the families for two full days. The treatment team consisted of psychologists, social workers, psychiatric residents, and trainees. They met with the family together and in various subgroups in a series of sessions; in between sessions the treatment team discussed their findings and refined their strategies of intervention. Although few family therapists have used such marathon sessions, the team approach to treating families has continued to be one of the hallmarks of the field.

In Boston, the two most significant early contributions to family therapy were both in the existential-experiential wing of the movement. Norman Paul developed an "operational mourning" approach to family therapy designed to uncover and ventilate unresolved grief. According to him, this cathartic approach is useful in almost all families, not only those who have suffered an obvious recent loss.

Also in Boston, Fred and Bunny Duhl set up the Boston Family Institute, where they developed "integrative family therapy" (Chapter 6). The Duhls, along with David Kantor and Sandy Watanabe, combined ideas from several family theories and added a number of expressive techniques, including *family sculpting*.

In Chicago, the Chicago Family Institute and the Institute for Juvenile Research were important parts of the early scene in family therapy (Guerin, 1976). At the Family Institute, Charles and Jan Kramer developed a clinical training program which was later affiliated with the Northwestern University Medical School. The Institute for Juvenile Research also mounted a training program under the leadership of Irv Borstein, with the consultation of Carl Whitaker.

I will conclude this section by mentioning the contributions of Christian Midelfort. Midelfort's pioneering work in family therapy was slow to gain recognition. He began treating families of hospitalized patients in the early 1950s; delivered what was probably the first paper on family therapy at a professional meeting in 1952, at the American Psychiatric Association Convention; and published one of the first complete books on family therapy in 1957. Nevertheless, he remained isolated from the rest of the family therapy movement while he continued to practice as a staff psychiatrist in a clinic in LaCrosse, Wisconsin. Only recently have his pioneering efforts been recognized (Broderick and Schrader, 1981). Midelfort's method of treating families was based on the group therapy model, and it combined psychoanalytic techniques with support and encouragement. At first his concern was to counsel family members on the best ways to help the identified patient, but gradually he evolved a systems viewpoint and conceived of the family as the patient. His technique, which is described in

Chapter 5, was to encourage family members to give each other the love and support that was initially provided by the therapist.

SUMMARY

As we have seen, family therapy has a short history, but a long past. For many years therapists resisted the idea of seeing members of a patient's family in order to safeguard the privacy of the patient-therapist relationship. Freudians excluded the real family in order to uncover the unconscious, introjected family; Rogerians kept the family away in order to provide the unconditional acceptance that they thought necessary to help clients rediscover their own inner promptings; and hospital psychiatrists discouraged family visits which were apt to disrupt the benign milieu of the ersatz hospital family.

Despite the good reasons for keeping family members isolated from an individual's psychotherapy, there were also distinct disadvantages. To begin with, individual psychotherapy is predicated on relative stability in the patient's environment—otherwise, removing the individual from the environment in order to change him or her would not make sense. When families were undergoing crisis and conflict, the patient's improvement sometimes made the family worse. Thus it became clear that change in any one person changes the whole family system. Eventually it also became apparent that changing the family might be the most effective way to change the patient. Once they began to appreciate the reciprocal impact of patients and their families, several therapists decided to try treating the whole family together. In retrospect, what seems remarkable is not that families have a prepotent effect on patients, but that it took so long to put the implications of this into practice.

When they began to experiment with family therapy, clinicians drew on previous work in psychoanalysis, interpersonal psychiatry, group therapy, the child guidance movement, communications theory, social psychology, marriage counseling, and research on schizophrenia.

Psychoanalysis focused attention on the role of the family in personality development, but isolated the family entirely from treatment. Psychoanalytic treatment depends upon the interpretation of resistance and transference, nurtured in a special and private relationship between analyst and analysand. Analysts have always strongly opposed *any* contact with family members in order to protect the transference.

As an observer of personality development, Freud discovered many things that were useful to family therapists. On the other hand, many of his conclusions were not congenial to family therapy, and these created prejudices that later had to be overcome. Freud illuminated the impact of the first few years of family life on personality patterning, but he neglected the crucial periods of adolescence and beyond. He revealed the power of irrational and unconscious forces, but underrated the powers of reason. He discovered distorted images of the family in projections, transference, and fantasy, but lost sight of the reality of current family interaction.

For Freud, the family was an instrument for disciplining the child's biologically determined instinctual urges, and for enforcing repression. Children epitomize animal pleasure; parents personify society's restraints. Since pleasure is antisocial, the family is antipleasure. This conception gives family relationships a puritanical, self-denying, and sacrificial flavor. Missing from this account is the idea of love as a positive force in family relations.

Freud also regarded men as the dominant members of the family group, subordinating women to inferior roles. Arguably this attitude reflected cultural realities in the nineteenth century, but it is an idea whose time has gone.

Those who adapted Freud's ideas to the study and treatment of families had to neutralize his tendency to isolate the individual from the group and to dissociate the inside of the mind from outside behavior and interaction. Nevertheless, most of the pioneers of family therapy were familiar with Freudian theory, and they found its core concepts invaluable for understanding people, if not always for treating them.

Psychoanalysts also turned their attention to neglected aspects of Freud's theory—among them Fromm, Horney, and Sullivan, whose interpersonal theory of psychiatry gave greater emphasis to social forces acting on personalities. Although these interpersonal psychiatrists did not themselves treat families, their ideas inspired those who did.

Obvious parallels between small groups and families led some family therapists to treat families as though they were just another form of group. They were well served in this endeavor by a large volume of literature on group dynamics and group therapy. Some even saw therapy groups as models of family functioning, with the therapist as father, group members as siblings, and the group collectively as the mother (Schindler, 1951). While group therapists experimented with married couples in groups, some family therapists began to conduct group therapy with individual families. Among these, John Bell was the most significant and his family group therapy continues to influence the field today (see Chapter 5).

As therapists gained more experience with families they discovered that the group therapy model was not entirely appropriate for families. Therapy groups are comprised of separate individuals, strangers with no past or future outside the group. Families, on the other hand, consist of intimates who share the same myths, defenses, and points of view. Moreover, family members are not peers who can relate democratically as equals; generational differences create hierarchical structures which cannot be ignored. For these reasons, most family therapists abandoned the group therapy model, replacing it with a variety of systems models.

The child guidance movement contributed the team approach to family therapy. At first, members of interdisciplinary teams were assigned to different family members; but gradually, as they came to appreciate the interlocking behavior patterns of their separate clients, they started integrating and later combining their efforts. The child guidance movement began in this country in 1909 as a creation of the juvenile courts, in order to treat delinquent children who were considered disturbed. Soon these clinics broadened the scope of their population to include a wide range of disorders, and at the same time they broadened the unit of treatment from the child to include the family. At first family therapy was seen as a better means of helping the patient; later it was conceived as a way to serve the needs of the entire family.

Research on family dynamics of schizophrenia is probably the best known chapter in the history of family therapy. The names of Gregory Bateson, Don Jackson, Jay Haley, Murray Bowen, Theodore Lidz, and Lyman Wynne are familiar to most students, as are some of their concepts: *metacommunication, double-bind, differentiation, triangulation, marital schism, marital skew, rubber fence,* and *pseudomutuality.*

Schizophrenic families offer a caricature of family life; their deviant patterns of communication and interaction are plain to see. Those who studied these families relied primarily on natualistic observation, and therefore their conclusions were often more clinically compelling than experimentally rigorous. Double-binds, for example, are not countable; they are not objective entities, but perceived experiences like the "bats" on a Rorschach inkblot. Moveover, since the double-bind is a pattern, not an event, and does not reside in the binder, or the victim, or the message, or the moment, the concept is virtually unresearchable by traditional experimentation.

There are two other common criticisms of the family research on schizophrenia: first, that the interactional mechanisms observed in these families cannot be extended to normal families; second, that the family's role in causing schizophrenia is difficult to reconcile with evidence of genetic determinants. In fact, the observational studies of schizophrenic families may reveal more about precipitating and maintaining schizophrenia than about its etiology. Nevertheless, those who studied the family dynamics of schizophrenia did more than anyone else to launch the family therapy movement.

As a form of treatment, family therapy was preceded by marriage counseling and psychoanalytic treatment of couples. Marital counseling was begun outside the mainstream of clinical psychiatry, and has continued to be an important function of family and social agencies. The history of professional marriage counseling is not as well known as some of the other precedents of family therapy, because its practitioners have not produced an extensive scholarly literature. Nonetheless, marriage counselors contributed a great deal to the techniques of family therapy, and they continue to provide solutions to family problems that are widely sought.

Psychoanalysts have long recognized that married partners are attracted to each other and bound together by unconscious complementary motivations. An unsolved problem of psychoanalytic therapy is the influence exerted by the patient's changed behavior on the spouse. Spouses change in response, and these changes affect the patient in a circular process. To turn these interlocking influences to advantage, some analysts started treating spouses, at first concurrently and later conjointly. The major American figures in this field were Clarence Oberndorf in the 1930s and Bela Mittleman in the 1940s.

In the following decade, Jackson and Haley, Ackerman, and Whitaker reported on their own versions of marital therapy. But since these people were also treating families, the field of marital therapy was absorbed into the whole family therapy movement at this point.

Who was the first to practice family therapy? This turns out to be a difficult and controversial question. As in every field, there were some visionaries who anticipated the recognized development of family therapy. Freud, for example, occasionally saw "Little Hans" together with his father in 1909. However, such experiments were not sufficient to challenge the hegemony of individual therapy until the climate of the times was receptive. In the early 1950s family therapy was begun independently in four different places: John Bell began family group therapy at Clark University (Chapter 5), Murray Bowen started treating families of schizophrenics at the Menninger Clinic and later at NIMH (Chapter 8); Nathan Ackerman began his psychoanalytic family therapy in New York (Chapter 4); and Don Jackson and Jay Haley started communications family therapy in Palo Alto (Chapters 9 and 10).

All these pioneers had distinctly different backgrounds and clinical orientations. Not surprisingly, therefore, the approaches that they developed to family therapy were also quite different. This diversity still characterizes the field today. Had family therapy been started by a single person, as was psychoanalysis, it is unlikely that there would have been so much creative competition so soon.

In addition to those people just mentioned, others who made significant contributions to the beginning of family therapy include Wynne, Lidz, Satir, Whitaker, Nagy, Midelfort, MacGregor, and Minuchin. Even this list leaves out a number of important figures; for what began after a long period of incubation quickly grew and spread. By the 1960s there were literally hundreds of family therapists. Today the field is so large and complex that it will take an entire chapter (Chapter 2) just to provide a descriptive overview.

REFERENCES

Ables, G. The double bind: Paradox in relationships. Doctoral Dissertation, Boston University, 1975.

Ables, G. Researching the unresearchable: Experimentation on the double bind. In C.E. Sluzki & D.C. Ransom (Eds.), *Double bind: The foundation of the communication approach to the family.* New York: Grune & Stratton, 1976.

Ackerman, N.W. The unity of the family. *Archives of Pediatrics,* 1938, *55,* 51–62.

Ackerman, N.W. Interpersonal disturbances in the family: Some unsolved problems in psychotherapy. *Psychiatry,* 1954, *17,* 359–368.

Ackerman, N.W. A dynamic frame for the clinical approach to family conflict. In N.W. Ackerman, F.L. Beatman & S.N. Sherman (Eds.), *Exploring the base for family therapy.* New York: Family Services Association of America, 1961.

Ackerman, N.W. Family psychotherapy—theory and practice. *American Journal of Psychotherapy,* 1966, *20,* 405–414.

Ackerman, N.W. Family interviewing: The study process. In N.W. Ackerman (Ed.), *Family therapy in transition.* Boston: Little Brown, 1970a.

Ackerman, N.W. The art of family therapy. In N.W. Ackerman (Ed.), *Family therapy in transition.* Boston: Little Brown, 1970b.

Ackerman, N.W. & Sobel, R. Family diagnosis: An approach to the preschool child. *American Journal of Orthopsychiatry,* 1950, *20,* 744–753.

Amster, F. Collective psychotherapy of mothers of emotionally disturbed children. *American Journal of Orthopsychiatry,* 1944, *14,* 44–52.

Andres, F.D. An introduction to family systems theory. Georgetown Family Symposium, Washington, D.C., 1971.

Anonymous. Differentiation of self in one's family. In J. Framo (Ed.), *Family interaction.* New York: Springer, 1972.

Bales, R.F. *Interaction process analysis.* Cambridge, Mass.: Addison-Wesley, 1950.

Bateson, G. Information and codification: A philosophical approach. In J. Ruesch &

G. Bateson (Eds.), *Communication: The social matrix of psychiatry.* New York: Norton, 1951.

Bateson, G. Cultural problems posed by a study of schizophrenic processes. In A. Auerbach (Ed.), *Schizophrenia: An integrated approach.* New York: Ronald Press, 1959.

Bateson, G. The birth of a matrix or double-bind and epistemology. In M.M. Berger (Ed.), *Beyond the double bind.* New York: Brunner/Mazel, 1978.

Bateson, G., Jackson, D.D., Haley, J. & Weakland, J. Toward a theory of schizophrenia. *Behavioral Science,* 1956, *1,* 251–264.

Bateson, G., Jackson, D.D. & Weakland, J.H. A note on the double-bind—1962. *Family Process,* 1963, *2,* 154–161.

Beatman, F.L. In V.W. Eisenstein, (Ed.), *Neurotic interaction in marriage.* New York: Basic Books, 1956.

Beavers, W.R., Blumberg, S., Timken, K.R. & Weiner, M.F. Communication patterns of mothers of schizophrenics. *Family Process,* 1965, *4,* 95–104.

Bell, J.E. *Family group therapy.* Public Health Monograph #64. Washington, D.C.: U.S. Government Printing Office, 1961.

Bell, J.E. Recent advances in family group therapy. *Journal of Child Psychology and Psychiatry,* 1962, 1–15.

Benne, K.D. History of the T-group in the laboratory setting. In L.P. Bradford, J.R. Gibb & K.D. Benne (Eds.), *T-group theory and laboratory method.* New York: Wiley, 1964.

Bennis, W.G. Patterns and vicissitudes in T-group development. In L.P. Bradford, J.R. Gibb & K.D. Benne (Eds.), *T-group theory and laboratory methods.* New York: Wiley, 1964.

Berger, A. A test of the double-bind hypothesis of schizophrenia. *Family Process,* 1965, *4,* 198–205.

Bion, W.R. Experience in groups. *Human Relations,* 1948, *1,* 314–329.

Boszormenyi-Nagy, I. The concept of schizophrenia from the point of view of family treatment. *Family Process,* 1962, *1,* 103–113.

Boszormenyi-Nagy, I. From family therapy to a psychology of relationships; fictions of the individual and fictions of the family. *Comprehensive Psychiatry,* 1966, *7,* 408–423.

Boszormenyi-Nagy, I. Loyalty implications of the transference model in psychotherapy. *Archives of General Psychiatry,* 1972, *27,* 374–380.

Boszormenyi-Nagy, I. & Spark, G.L. *Invisible loyalties: Reciprocity in intergenerational family therapy.* New York: Harper & Row, 1973.

Bowen, M. A family concept of schizophrenia. In D.D. Jackson (Ed.), *The etiology of schizophrenia.* New York: Basic Books, 1960.

Bowen, M. Family psychotherapy. *American Journal of Orthopsychiatry,* 1961, *31,* 40–60.

Bowen, M. Family psychotherapy with schizophrenia in the hospital and in private practice. In I. Boszormenyi-Nagy & J.L. Framo (Eds.), *Intensive family therapy.* New York: Harper & Row, 1965.

Bowen, M. Principles and techniques of multiple family therapy. In P.J. Guerin

(Ed.), *Family therapy: Theory and practice*. New York: Gardner Press, 1976.

Bowen, M., Dysinger, R.H. & Basamania, B. The role of the father in families with a schizophrenic patient. *American Journal of Psychiatry*, 1959, *115*, 1017–1020.

Bowlby, J.P. The study and reduction of group tensions in the family. *Human Relations*, 1949, *2*, 123–138.

Brown, G.W. Experiences of discharged chronic schizophrenic patients in various types of living groups. *Milbank Memorial Fund Quarterly*, 1959, *37*, 105–131.

Broderick, C.B. & Schrader, S.S. The history of professional marriage and family therapy. In A.S. Gurman & D.P. Kniskern (Eds.), *Handbook of family therapy*. New York: Brunner/Mazel, 1981.

Burgum, M. The father gets worse: A child guidance problem. *American Journal of Orthopsychiatry*, 1942, *12*, 474–485.

Burkin, H.E., Glatzer, H. & Hirsch, J.S. Therapy of mothers in groups. *American Journal of Orthopsychiatry*, 1944, *14*, 68–75.

Ciotola, P.V. The effect of two contradictory levels of reward and censure on schizophrenics. Doctoral Dissertation, University of Missouri, 1961.

Cooley, C.H. *Human nature and the social order*. New York: Scribners, 1902.

Dicks, H.V. Concepts of marital diagnosis and therapy as developed at the Tavistock Family Psychiatric Clinic, London, England. In E.M. Nash, L. Jessner & D.W. Abse (Eds.), *Marriage counseling in medical practice*. Chapel Hill, N.C.: University of North Carolina Press, 1964.

Fisher, S. & Mendell, D. The spread of psychotherapeutic effects from the patient to his family group. *Psychiatry*, 1958, *21*, 133–140.

Freeman, V.J., Klein, A.F., Riehman, L., Lukoff, I.F. & Heisey, V. Family group counseling as differentiated from other family therapies. *International Journal of Group Psychotherapy*, 1963, *13*, 167–175.

Freud, S. (1911) Psychoanalytic notes upon an autobiographical account of a case of paranoia (dementia paranoides). In Freud, S. *Three case histories*. New York: Collier Books, 1963.

Fromm-Reichmann, F. Notes on the development of treatment of schizophrenics by psychoanalytic psychotherapy. *Psychiatry*, 1948, *11*, 263–274.

Fromm-Reichmann, F. *Principles of intensive psychotherapy*. Chicago: University of Chicago Press, 1950.

Ginsburg, S.W. The mental health movement and its theoretical assumptions. In R. Kotinsky & H. Witmer (Eds.), *Community programs for mental health*. Cambridge: Harvard University Press, 1955.

Greenberg, G.S. The family interactional perspective: A study and examination of the work of Don D. Jackson. *Family Process*, 1977, *16*, 385–412.

Grunwald, H. & Casell, B. Group counseling with parents. *Child Welfare*, 1958, *1*, 1–6.

Guerin, P.J. Family therapy: The first twenty-five years. In P.J. Guerin (Ed.), *Family therapy: Theory and practice*. New York: Gardner Press, 1976.

Guindon, J.E. Paradox, schizophrenia and the double bind hypothesis: An exploratory study. Doctoral Dissertation, University of Washington, 1971.

Haley, J. The family of the schizophrenic. *American Journal of Nervous and Mental Diseases*, 1959, *129*, 357–374.

Haley J. Control in brief psychotherapy. *Archives of General Psychiatry*, 1961, *4*, 139–153.

Haley J. *Strategies of psychotherapy*. New York: Grune & Stratton, 1963.

Haley, J. Development of a theory: A history of a research project. In C.E. Sluzki & D.C. Ransom (Eds.), *Double bind: The foundation of the communication approach to the family*. New York: Grune & Stratton, 1976.

Handlon, J.H. & Parloff, M.B. Treatment of patient and family as a group: Is it group therapy? *International Journal of Group Psychotherapy*, 1962, *12*, 132–141.

Hirsch, S.R. & Leff, J.P. *Abnormalities in parents of schizophrenics: A review of the literature and an investigation of communication defects and deviances*. London: Oxford University Press, 1975.

Hoffman, L. *Foundations of family therapy*. New York: Basic Books, 1981.

Jackson, D.D. Suicide. *Scientific American*, 1954, *191*, 88–96.

Jackson, D.D. Family Therapy in the family of the schizophrenic. In M. Stern (Ed.), *Contemporary psychotherapies*. Glencoe, Ill.: The Free Press, 1961.

Jackson, D.D. Family rules: Marital quid pro quo. *Archives of General Psychiatry*, 1965, *12*, 589–594.

Jackson, D.D. & Weakland, J.H. Schizophrenic symptoms and family interaction. *Archives of General Psychiatry*, 1959, *1*, 618–621.

Jackson, D.D. & Weakland, J.H. Conjoint family therapy: Some considerations on theory, technique, and results. *Psychiatry*, 1961, *24*, 30–45.

Johnson, A.M. & Szurek, S.A. Etiology of anti-social behavior in delinquents and psychopaths. *Journal of the American Medical Association*, 1954, *154*, 814–817.

Kasanin, J., Knight, E. & Sage, P. The parent-child relationships in schizophrenia. *Journal of Nervous and Mental Diseases*, 1934, *79*, 249–263.

Kaslow, F.W. History of family therapy in the United States: A kaleidoscopic overview. *Marriage and Family Review, 1980, 3*, 77–111.

Kingsley, V.C. The effects of the double-bind conflict and sex of the experimenter on the conceptual functioning and visual discrimination of male good and poor premorbid schizphrenics. Doctoral Dissertation, New York University, 1969.

Kirby, K. & Priestman, S. Values of a daughter (schizophrenic) and mother therapy group. *International Journal of Group Psychotherapy*, 1957, *7*, 281–288.

Kluckhohn, F.R. & Spiegel, J.P. Integration and conflict in family behavior. Report No. 27, *Group for the Advancement of Psychiatry*, Topeka, Kansas, 1954.

Knoblochova, J. & Knobloch, F. Family therapy in Czechoslovakia: An aspect of group-centered psychotherapy. In N.W. Ackerman (Ed.), *Family therapy in transition*. Boston: Little, Brown and Company, 1970.

Kubie, L.S. Psychoanalysis and marriage. In V.W. Eisenstein (Ed.), *Neurotic interaction in marriage*. New York: Basic Books, 1956.

Kuhn, T.S. *Structure of scientific revolutions*. Chicago: University of Chicago Press, 1970.

Laing R.D. *The divided self.* London: Tavistock Publications, 1960.

Laing, R.D. Mystification, confusion and conflict. In I. Boszormenyi-Nagy & J.K. Framo (Eds.), *Intensive family therapy.* New York: Harper & Row, 1965.

Levy, D. *Maternal overprotection.* New York: Columbia University Press, 1943.

Lewin, K. *Field theory in social science.* New York: Harper, 1951.

Lidz, R.W. & Lidz, T. The family environment of schizophrenic patients. *American Journal of Psychiatry,* 1949, *106,* 332–345.

Lidz, T., Cornelison, A., Fleck, S. & Terry, D. Intrafamilial environment of the schizophrenic patient. I: The father. *Psychiatry,* 1957a, *20,* 329–342.

Lidz, T., Cornelison, A., Fleck, S. & Terry, D. Intrafamilial environment of schizophrenic patients. II: Marital schism and marital skew. *American Journal of Psychiatry,* 1957b, *20,* 241–248.

Lidz, T. & Fleck, S. Schizophrenia, human integration, and the role of the family. In D.D. Jackson (Ed.), *The etiology of schizophrenia.* New York: Basic Books, 1960.

Lidz T., Parker, B. & Cornelison, A.R. The role of the father in the family environment of the schizophrenic patient. *American Journal of Psychiatry,* 1956, *113,* 126–132.

Low, A.A. *The technique of self-help in psychiatry after-care. Vol. 3 Lectures to relatives of former patients.* Chicago: Recovery, Inc. 1943.

Lowrey, L.G. Group treatment for mothers. *American Journal of Orthopsychiatry,* 1944, *14,* 589–592.

Luft, J. *Group Processes.* Palo Alto, California: National Press Books, 1970.

MacGregor, R. Progress in Multiple Impact Theory. In N.W. Ackerman, F.L. Beatman & S.N. Sherman (Eds.), *Expanding theory and practice in family therapy.* New York: Family Services Association, 1967.

Mahler, M.S. & Rabinovitch, R. The effects of marital conflict on child development. In V.W. Eisenstein (Ed.), *Neurotic interaction in marriage.* New York: Basic Books, 1956.

Marsh, L.C. Group therapy and the psychiatric clinic. *American Journal of Nervous and Mental Diseases,* 1935, *821, 381–393.*

Midelfort, C.F. *The family in psychotherapy.* New York: McGraw-Hill, 1957.

Minuchin, S. *Families and family therapy.* Cambridge: Harvard University Press, 1974.

Minuchin, S. & Fishman, H.C. *Family therapy techniques.* Cambridge: Harvard University Press, 1981.

Minuchin, S., Montalvo, B., Guerney, B.G., Rosman, B.L. & Schumer, F. *Families of the slums.* New York: Basic Books, 1967.

Minuchin, S., Rosman, B.L. & Baker, L. *Psychosomatic families: Anorexia nervosa in context.* Cambridge: Harvard University Press, 1978.

Mittleman, B. Complementary neurotic reactions in intimate relationships. *Psychoanalytic Quarterly,* 1944, *13,* 474–491.

Mittleman, B. The concurrent analysis of married couples. *Psychoanalytic Quarterly,* 1948, *17,* 182–197.

Mittleman, B. Analysis of reciprocal neurotic patterns in family relationships. In V.W. Eisenstein (Ed.), *Neurotic interactions in marriage*. New York: Basic Books, 1956.

Montague, A. Marriage—A cultural perspective. In V.W. Eisenstein (Ed.), *Neurotic interaction in marriage*. New York: Basic Books, 1956.

Moreno, J.L. *Psychodrama*. New York: Beacon House, 1945.

Nichols, M.P. & Zax, M. *Catharsis in psychotherapy*. New York: Gardner Press, 1977.

Nichols, W. Doctoral programs in marital and family therapy. *Journal of Marital and Family Therapy*, 1979, *5*, 23–28.

Oberndorf, C.P. Psychoanalysis of married couples. *Psychoanalytic Review*, 1938, *25*, 453–475.

Parsons, T. & Bales, R.F. *Family socialization and interaction*. Glencoe, Ill.: Free Press, 1955.

Phillips, M. Response to "double-bind" messages in relation to four dimensions of personality and two maternal child rearing attitudes: A study of interpretational and feeling preferences of late adolescents. Doctoral Dissertation, New York University, 1970.

Potash, H.M. Schizophrenic interaction and the concept of the double-bind. Doctoral Dissertation, Michigan State University, 1965.

Ringuette, E.L. & Kennedy, T. An experimental study of the double-bind hypothesis. *Journal of Abnormal Psychology*, 1966, *71*, 136–141.

Ross, W.D. Group psychotherapy with patients' relatives. *American Journal of Psychiatry*, 1948, *104*, 623–626.

Ruesch, J. & Bateson, G. (Eds.), *Communication: The social matrix of psychiatry*. New York: Norton, 1951.

Satir, V. *Peoplemaking*. Palo Alto, California: Science and Behavior Books, 1972.

Schaeffer, R.L. Training schizophenics and neurotics to recognize double binds: A comparison. Doctoral Dissertation, Adelphia University, 1972.

Schindler, W. Counter-transference in family-pattern group psychotherapy. *International Journal of Group Psychotherapy*, 1951, *1*, 100–105.

Schreiber, A.W. An experimental double-bind and communicativeness. Doctoral Dissertation, City University of New York, 1970.

Sherif, M. *An outline of social psychology*. New York: Harper and Brothers, 1948.

Singer, M.T., Wynne, L.C. & Toohey, M.L. Communication disorders and the families of schizophrenics. In L.C. Wynne, R.L. Cromwell & S. Matthysse (Eds.), *The nature of schizophrenia*. New York: Wiley, 1978.

Skynner, R. *Systems of family and marital psychotherapy*. New York: Brunner/Mazel, 1976.

Slavson, S.R. *An introduction to group therapy*. New York: The Commonwealth Fund, 1943.

Sluzki, C.E., Beavin, J., Tarnopololsky, A. & Vernon, E. Transactional disqualification. *Archives of General Psychiatry*, 1967, *16*, 494–504.

Smith, E.K. The effect of double-bind communications upon the state of anxiety of normals. Doctoral Dissertation, University of New Mexico, 1972.

Sojit, C.M. Dyadic interaction in a double-bind situation. *Family Process*, 1969, *8*, 235–259.

Speck, R. & Attneave, C. *Family networks: Rehabilitation and healing*. New York: Pantheon, 1973.

Spiegel, J.P. The resolution of role conflict within the family. *Psychiatry*, 1957, *20*, 146.

Stierlin, H. *Psychoanalysis and family therapy*. New York: Jason Aronson, 1977.

Strodtbeck, F.L. The family as a three-person group. *American Sociological Review*, 1954, *19*, 23–29.

Strodtbeck, F.L. Family interaction, values, and achievement. In D.C. McClelland, A.L. Baldwin, A. Bronfenbrenner & F.L. Strodtbeck (Eds.), *Talent and society*. Princeton, N.J.: Van Nostrand, 1958.

Uzoka, A.F. The myth of the nuclear family. *American Psychologist*, 1979, *34*, 1095–1106.

Watzlawick, P.A., Beavin, J.H. & Jackson, D.D. *Pragmatics of human communication*. New York: Norton, 1967.

Weakland, J.H. The "double-bind" hypothesis of schizophrenia and three-party interaction. In D.D. Jackson (Ed.), *The etiology of schizophrenia*. New York: Basic Books, 1960.

Whitaker, C.A. Psychotherapy with couples. *American Journal of Psychotherapy*, 1958, *12*, 18–23.

Whitaker, C.A. Psychotherapy of the absurd: With a special emphasis on the psychotherapy of aggression. *Family Process*, 1975, *14*, 1–16.

Whitaker, C.A. A family is a four-dimensional relationship. In P.J. Guerin (Ed.), *Family therapy: Theory and practice*. New York: Gardner Press, 1976.

Whitaker, C.A. & Malone, T.P. *The roots of psychotherapy*. New York: Blakiston, 1953.

Whitehead, A.N. & Russell, B. *Principia mathematica*. Cambridge: Cambridge University Press, 1910.

Wynne, L.C. The study of intrafamilial alignments and splits in exploratory family therapy. In N.W. Ackerman, F.L. Beatman & S.N. Sherman (Eds.), *Exploring the base for family therapy*. New York: Family Services Association, 1961.

Wynne, L.C. Knotted relationships, communication deviances, and metabinding. In M.M. Berger (Ed.), *Beyond the double bind*. New York: Brunner/Mazel, 1978.

Wynne, L.C., Ryckoff, I., Day, J. & Hirsch, S.I. Pseudo-mutuality in the family relationships of schizophrenics. *Psychiatry*, 1958, *21*, 205–220.

Yalom, I.D. *The theory and practice of group psychotherapy*. New York: Basic Books, 1970.

Zuk, G.H. *Family therapy: A triadic-based approach*. New York: Behavioral Publications, 1971.

2

The Contemporary Context of Family Therapy

INTRODUCTION

In the preceding chapter we saw how family therapy was developed independently by several different clinicians. Moreover, since these innovators came from diverse backgrounds including psychoanalysis, communications theory, and group therapy, they developed distinct and unique systems of treatment. Today, these separate and competing approaches, which will be the focus of Section II of this book, are the source of family therapy's complexity and vitality. In the present chapter I will give an overview of the contemporary scene in family therapy, describing the major current developments in the field as well as the centers that are most active in teaching and training. Before doing so, however, I will summarize the essential and enduring beliefs that emerged from the history of family therapy and are now the core concepts and methods of family therapy.

ENDURING CONCEPTS OF FAMILY THERAPY

Family therapy is more than a novel therapeutic technique; it is a whole new approach to understanding human behavior. Prior to family therapy, behavior was considered to be a product of individual personalities as influenced by discrete events in the past. This *monadic* view, based on *linear causality*, was replaced by the idea that behavior is a product of *family systems* which operate according to *circular causality*.

The Family as Context. For a long time, individual therapists recognized the importance of family influences in shaping the personality, but assumed that internal representations of childhood events exerted a more dominant influence than ongoing family interactions. Consistent with this viewpoint, psychotherapists isolated patients from their natural environment in order to manipulate aspects of their internally organized behavior. Family therapists, on the contrary, believe that the dominant forces in personality development are located externally in current interactions in the family system. This is the fundamental premise of family therapy as an orientation: that people are products of their social context, and that any attempt to understand them must include an appreciation of their families.

A corollary of the family orientation is that the most effective way to treat people is to alter their family interactions. As a method, family therapy usually, but not always, involves bringing the family together for treatment. But even those therapists—for example, Bowenian and strategic therapists—who do not necessarily meet with whole families design their interventions to affect family interactions.

Emergent Properties of Groups. Family therapy was a product of many converging lines of study, each of which contributed important concepts and techniques to the field as we know it today. Group-dynamics theorists contributed the idea of a transcendent group process. Groups are more than just the sum of their individual members, and they cannot be understood simply by adding up the personalities involved. When people join together in a group, processes emerge which reflect not only the individuals' personalities, but also collective patterns of interaction described as *group dynamics*.

Similarly, field theorists explained behavior as a function not merely of intrapsychic forces and interpsychic processes, but also as a product of larger emotional fields in which people exist. While it is possible to expand the system of forces in the environment to progressively larger foci, family therapists have rarely found it useful to include more than the extended family in their field of observation, although many family practitioners do include the therapist in their analyses. The influence of extended families is demonstrated by the fact that symptoms in nuclear families often surface at a time of major changes in families of origin. A grandparent's death, for example, may lead to a mother's becoming overly restrictive with her children, which in turn may result in one of them becoming symptomatic.

Group therapists discovered that thinking about both group dynamics and individual dynamics enabled them to achieve the best results. Family therapists applied the notion of group dynamics to families and used systems theory to elaborate the nature of these interpersonal forces. Some family therapists stress group forces to the exclusion of individual ones; others integrate concepts from group dynamics and individual dynamics.

Group therapy served as one of the original models for family treatment. Although the limitations of group therapy methods have become apparent to family therapists, most family therapists continue to use the group therapy technique of promoting interactions among group members as one of the major strategies of treatment.

Disorders of Childhood as a Family Problem. The child guidance movement began as a confident attempt to prevent serious adult psychopathology by resolving problems in young children, before the problems became entrenched. As they gained experience, child-guidance clinicians discovered that individual therapy for children was not effective enough to combat powerful forces in the family. Consequently they expanded their conceptual model from a monadic to a dyadic one, and extended treatment to mothers and their children. The child guidance movement also contributed the team approach to treatment, which is so prominent in many schools of family therapy.

Dyadic and Triadic Models of Behavior. Family therapy also passed through a series of conceptual stages, from regarding individuals as the unit of pathology to dyadic and eventually triadic models. Locating pathology in the individual personality did not begin with psychoanalysis; it has always been a natural way to think about psychological problems. If someone has a problem, something inside must be bothering them. This point of view has been maintained in Freudian theory, as well as in most other theories of psychotherapy. The monadic model was later extended by social psychiatrists and object relations theorists to include the dyadic concept of interlocking pathology or object relations. Meanwhile, the intrapsychic apparatus was further subdivided into structures, among which conflicts develop. Family therapists demonstrated that since behavior is interactive, one person's behavior is always in relation to another's. Moreover, the pair's relationship turns out to reflect the influence of third parties. A boy's behavior depends upon his relationship with his mother and that, in turn, depends upon her relationship with her husband.

Psychopathology as Serving a Family Function. Severely disturbed families provide a magnified focus on processes that operate in all families, but are not always so easy to observe. Studies of the etiology of schizophrenia led to the conclusion that deviance was not necessarily negative, but that on the contrary, the deviancies of schizophrenics were manifestations that had meaning in their families, and served a function in those families. R.D. Laing's concept of *mystification* is based on the idea that the denial and blurring of unpleasant reality can drive young people mad, and that their madness can preserve the fragile equilibrium of their families.

Another important finding was that often when the patient got better, someone else in the family got worse. This, and the tenacity with which these families resisted change, led Jackson to coin the term *family homeostasis.* The concept of homeostasis emphasized the negative feedback mechanisms by which families preserve their stability within a closed system. But Jackson also observed what he called a "runaway" in families. This is a deviation-amplifying process which creates stress and change. Other family therapists, including Minuchin and Whitaker, have emphasized the function that crisis and stress play in creating a climate for change.

Jackson's concept of homeostatic processes is more easily remembered than the runaway, but is not necessarily more significant. The runaway describes the kind of discontinuous change that can occur in systems. These sudden leaps, which are often unpredictable and irreversible, are utilized by strategic therapists to change family systems by provoking what Rabkin (1970) calls "saltatory" change.

Circular Causality. Among those studying the etiology of schizophrenia, the Bateson group, Murray Bowen, and Lyman Wynne had the greatest impact on family therapy. Bateson is usually thought of as an innovator, and rightly so, but he was also a student and a synthesizer who introduced theoretical ideas from general systems theory and cybernetics to the family field. Family therapy is based on a new paradigm of thought, fashionably known as the "new epistemology." The central concept of this new way of thinking is the idea of *circularity.*

Before the advent of family therapy, explanations of psychopathology were based on linear models—medical, psychodynamic, and behavioral. In all of these, etiology was conceived in terms of prior events—disease, emotional conflict, or learning history—which caused symptoms in the present. The patient is the locus of malfunction in all of these models. Family therapy was part of a profound shift in the paradigm of scientific thinking, a shift from linear to circular thinking.

Using the concept of circularity, family therapists changed the way we think of psychopathology from something caused by events in the past to something that is a part of ongoing, circular causal loops. The concept of linear causality is based on a Newtonian model, in which the universe is like a billiard table where the balls act unidirectionally on each other. Bateson believed that the world of living things is poorly represented by such a model, because it neglects to account for communication and relationships as well as force.

One way to illustrate the difference between these two viewpoints is the example of the difference between kicking a stone and kicking a dog (Hoffman, 1981). If you kick a stone, the energy transmitted by the kick will move the stone a certain distance, depending upon the force of the kick and the weight of the stone. But if you kick a dog, the outcome is not predictable on the basis of these forces. What happens will depend upon the relationship between you and the dog. The dog may cower, run away, or bite you, depending upon how the relationship is defined and how the dog interprets the kick. Moreover, the dog's response will also send information back to you. If the dog bites you, you may not kick him again.

Circularity changes the way we think about treatment as well. No longer do we see the therapist as an active subject and the client as a passive object. Both are part of a larger field in which they, and many other elements, act and react upon each other, exerting multiple and circular influences. A circular model forces us as therapists to consider ourselves as elements in the fields we wish to change.

Boundaries and Triangles. Murray Bowen's studies of schizophrenia led him to formulate two of the most influential concepts of family theory: *boundaries* and *triangles*. The importance of boundaries was first described in the concept of the *undifferentiated family ego mass*, the emotional "stuck-togetherness" of families with inadequate interpersonal boundaries. This lack of differentiation, which is similar to Wynne's *pseudomutuality* and Minuchin's *enmeshment*, is extremely pronounced in families of schizophrenics, but it is also found to some extent in all families. This quality of fusion is a bridge to psychoanalytic theory of the self, and it also defines the goal of Bowenian family theory: *differentiation of the self.*

Bowen also called attention to the importance of triangles in all human interactions. According to Bowen, two-person emotional systems always form three-person systems when they are stressed. As long as things are calm, a wife and husband, or boss and employee, can keep their relationship between them. But when problems develop, the one who becomes most anxious will relieve tension by triangling in a third person. A wife may complain about her husband to her mother; an employee may spend lunch hours grousing to colleagues about the boss. These triangles cool emotions when things get too hot in the original pair, but they also prevent meaningful resolution of problems. The process of detriangulation is an essential part of many family therapies, including Bowen's.

Family Roles. Lyman Wynne's studies of how thought disorder is communicated in schizophrenic families contributed the concepts of *pseudomutuality* and the *rubber fence* to the emerging field of family therapy. These concepts, along with Lidz's ideas about *marital schism* and *marital skew* drew attention to the importance of role relations in families, and helped create a shift in perspective from the content to the process of family interactions. Once they began to see the process of family interactions, family theorists could begin to treat families as organizations which behave like organisms.

General Systems Theory. Members of Bateson's schizophrenia project analyzed the communication in schizophrenic families and developed many of the concepts and techniques that launched the family therapy movement. By far the most influential conceptual contribution of the Palo Alto group was the application of general systems theory to family dynamics (Watzlawick, Beavin, and Jackson, 1967). According to systems theory, families have a unity or *wholeness* that is greater than the sum of their parts. Therefore, a change in one family member changes the whole system. In addition to wholeness, systems are characterized by: *nonsummativity*, an *emergent quality*, *feedback* (in families, communication), *homeostatic mechanisms*, *rules*, *circularity*, *transactions*, and *process*. Although they usually treated families as *closed systems*, the Palo Alto group described them as *open systems*, in which there is a continuous exchange of input and output between the system and the environment.

Levels of Communication. The *double-bind* is the most famous concept to emerge from the Bateson group's studies of family pathology, but the idea that communication has at least two levels—report and command—was probably more significant to the practice of family therapy. Today, family therapists of all persuasions are attuned to the importance of communication. They are aware that one cannot *not* communicate, and they understand that all messages have metacommunicative properties. Whatever other aspects of family dynamics they focus on, family therapists are necessarily involved with communication, and their efforts are guided by concepts which are the legacy of Bateson and his Palo Alto colleagues.

FUNDAMENTALS OF FAMILY TREATMENT

The first people to actually treat families began with few established principles and techniques; they were exploring new territory and did not have maps to guide them. Nevertheless, within a decade these pioneers had discovered many of the most important features of family problems and had invented ways of dealing with them.

From Intrapsychic to Interpersonal. When family therapy was first beginning, the dominant model in the field was psychoanalysis, and many of the first principles of family therapy were developed in reaction to perceived shortcomings of the psychoanalytic approach. Psychoanalysis is a protracted exploration of the past, designed to foster growth through insight; family therapy is a brief, action-oriented approach designed to resolve symptoms by changing behavior in the present.

Although he continued to use psychodynamic formulations, Ackerman shifted the focus of diagnosis and treatment from the individual to the family. He was still concerned with unexpressed feeling and unconscious motives, but he shifted the field of exploration from the intrapsychic to the interpersonal. Ackerman's work was a transition between psychoanalytic theory of individuals and systems theory of families. His was still a therapy of uncovering; his concern was not just with the clarity of communication, but also with uncovering repressed contents.

From Content to Process. Jackson, Haley, and Satir developed approaches to family therapy that were considerably more systems-oriented. Their focus was on the process of communication, which they interpreted as the medium of feedback in cybernetic family systems.

The shift from content to process is one of the most significant features of family therapy. Content is the language of linear causality; process is the language of circular dynamics. Individual patients and families try to understand their problems by focusing on content. When asked to discuss their difficulties, they give histories: "First we moved to the city, and then we put Kimberly in private school; the next thing we knew she was arrested for shoplifting!" These histories are based on monadic, linear, and historical views of causality that make up most people's view of the world. But the shift from sequential actions of individuals to transactions within systems requires a shift of attention from content to process. The "facts" of a case usually obscure the process of family communication that conveys transactional reality.

Each of these three pioneers of family therapy emphasized a different aspect of communication. Jackson's main interest was cognition; Satir's was feeling; and Haley's was power.

Outwitting Communicational Resistance. Jackson saw families as *rule-governed systems*, and he emphasized their *homeostatic mechanisms*. By focusing on the conservative tendencies of families, Jackson influenced family therapists to expect automatic resistance to change. The positive result of this was the development of numerous strategic tactics for outwitting resistance. A negative consequence has been a tendency to conceive of families as objects of intervention, and as opponents to be outwitted, instead of as partners in a collaborative effort.

Jackson's major strategy for change was the *therapeutic double-bind*, a term used loosely to describe various paradoxical techniques, including *prescribing the symptom*. Patients are usually understood as unfortunates, afflicted with symptoms they cannot control. If they are told to change, they usually plead helplessness. But if they are told not to change—to perform their symptoms—they are caught in a bind; they have to change something, either their symptomatic behavior, or their pretense to helplessness.

Paradoxical directives have become one of the most important technical devices in family therapy. Used judiciously, they force change, treating the family as a system whose rules do not work, but that will not be changed by rational understanding. Paradoxical techniques are the mainstay of strategic family therapy, and are also incorporated by many nonstrategic therapists.

Another of Jackson's influential discoveries was the use of *relabeling,* a technique whereby the therapist restates a situation so that it is seen in a new way. The point is to change the way that reality is perceived so that new behaviors will follow. For example, if an obstreperous six-year-old is labeled "hyperactive," parents will seek professional treatment. But if the child is relabeled as "naughty," then the parents are more likely to discipline and control the child. The new label upsets the homeostatic balance of the system, and forces a change so as to incorporate the new label. Relabeling, or *reframing,* as it is usually called today, is a major tactic in strategic therapy as well as an adjunct in almost every other form of family therapy.

Communicating Feelings. Satir's concern was to improve the way family systems communicate, especially the way individuals express their feelings. Although she worked with families, she has always been primarily interested in individuals. Her lasting contributions include emphasizing respect for individuals and their feelings of self-esteem; establishing a climate of emotional acceptance and expressiveness in families; and popularizing family therapy. Satir's reverence for feelings and many of her specific techniques now form an important part of experiential family therapy.

Communication and Therapeutic Directives. Haley's conception of family relationships is that they take place through communication, and that communication takes place on different levels. At the simplest level is the content of communication, but every message is also seen by Haley as an attempt to define the relationship. Thus, Haley's main concern has been with power; his analysis and treatment focuses on the struggle for control.

His model of therapy is the relationship between the hypnotist and subject. The goal is to get rid of the problems by forcing the subject to behave differently. Therefore, a prerequisite is to gain control of the therapeutic relationship. This can either be done directly by assuming the stance of an expert and demanding compliance, or indirectly by assuming a one-down stance and provoking noncompliance. In practice this translates into using directives, reframing, and warning families of "the dangers of changing too fast."

Whatever the cause of psychiatric problems, the therapeutic issue is what to do about them. Haley relies on directives because he believes that understanding does not solve problems, changing behavior does. He uses directives to get families to behave differently in their lives outside of therapy.

The use of directives has become one of the most widespread techniques of family therapy. Experientialists use directives to promote affective experiences in therapy sessions; behaviorists use directives to teach parents new ways of disciplining their children; structural family therapists use directives in the form of tasks between sessions; Bowenian therapists use directives to advise patients how to improve relations with their parents; and strategic therapists use directives to outwit resistance and provoke change. There is no question that directives are a useful tool in family therapy. However, when directives are the main focus of treatment, therapists become overly central; they direct families in order to manipulate them to relate differently to problems. The therapist who relies primarily on directives takes over the responsibility for solving problems, instead of helping families improve their functioning so that they will learn how to solve their own problems.

Whether or not this appears to be a problem depends upon whether you see the job of family therapy as helping families learn to solve problems or simply as relieving their symptoms.

Making Families Responsible for Solving Their Own Problems. Murray Bowen is at the opposite end of the spectrum from Haley. Haley tries to get stalled families moving by giving them a push or at most a tuneup; Bowen gives them a thorough overhaul. When Bowen took the radical step of hospitalizing whole families, he was putting into practice the ideal that people can best be treated in their natural context. In addition, he was preventing families from shifting responsibility for their disturbed members onto the clinical staff. Whereas Haley does therapy by temporarily taking over, Bowen believes that families should be forced to assume responsibility for their own dilemmas. Today, family therapy schools are divided on this issue; strategic and behavioral therapists assume responsibility for solving problems, while most other orientations strictly avoid taking over this responsibility.

Involving the Extended Family. Bowen was also first in the family movement to draw attention to the wider kinship network. He did so originally by assembling all of the people involved with his schizophrenic patients— family and staff—in large group therapy sessions. These meetings were the prototype for multiple family and couples groups, which Bowen later used, as well as for network therapy, developed by Speck and Attneave. Bowen found these large meetings to be a valuable source of information, but disappointing for achieving therapeutic results. Consequently, he developed a theory based on the extended family system, but in practice he met only with individuals and couples. Bowen's technique of sending patients to work out their relationships in the extended family has not been widely adopted by other schools of family therapy, but his emphasis on the importance of triangles in intergenerational networks has been.

The One-Way Mirror and Videotaping. Conjoint family interviews and observing behind the one-way mirror were two methodological innovations of profound significance. When a patient is interviewed in a consulting room it is natural to conceive of him or her as the locus of the problems; when patients are observed interacting with their families it is impossible to see only one person as the problem. Bringing symptomatic families together for observation was the beginning of family therapy.

Equally important was the use of the one-way mirror, which enhanced observation and therapy alike. From their vantage behind the glass, researchers and clinicians have been able to study the processes of family interaction, and help the therapist in the room organize observations and plan interventions. The mirror somehow seems to filter out the affect from family meetings. This helps explain why after a session the therapist is worn out, but the observers are not: the therapist feels responsible to *do* something, not just observe. It is remarkably easier to understand family interactions when they are observed from behind the screen.

Another hallmark of family therapy, live supervision, is a by-product of the one-way mirror. Instead of waiting until the end of a session to tell therapists what they did wrong, the supervisor who observes a session in progress can call or enter to tell them how to do it right. Observation and live supervision have helped make obsolete the concept of the therapist as a free-standing agent. The ability to work in concert with supervisors and colleagues behind the glass is one of the most powerful weapons in the family therapist's arsenal.

Among the technological accoutrements of family therapy, the television camera has played almost as prominent a role as the one-way mirror. By videotaping and reviewing their work, therapists are able to see the small movements and repetitive patterns of family dynamics; seeing differently enables therapists to think differently. In the process, they become much more skilled observers. Moreover, studying a videotape is one of the few ways to really see oneself in action, which is invaluable for improving therapeutic technique.

Miscellaneous Contributions. None of the other early concepts and methods were as popular as those I have just mentioned, but there were other significant contributions. John E. Bell treated families as groups, helped parents learn to negotiate with their children, and introduced the idea that therapy can be conducted in planned stages. Christian Midelfort worked with families in order to help them mobilize latent forces of love and support. Norman Paul's technique of *operational mourning* was another attempt to stimulate healing emotional experiences in families.

Ivan Boszormenyi-Nagy's work initially drew little attention outside the scholarly wing of family therapy. Recently, however, his combination of psychoanalytic, systems, and ethical principles has become more influential, as increasing numbers of family therapists are becoming interested in integrating psychoanalytic theory and family therapy.

Carl Whitaker is one of the major figures in the field, but his impact has been more personal than conceptual. His contributions include emphasizing the value of cotherapy, and teaching—by example—that family therapy can be a spontaneous and provocative experience.

Finally, Minuchin's concept of family structure is one of the most influential ideas in the field. Today, relatively few family therapists fail to take into account the structure of families, regardless of their technical strategies.

FAMILY THERAPY AND INDIVIDUAL PSYCHOTHERAPY

For many years individual therapy was the only model of treatment for psychological ills. Although the various schools of individual therapy had conceptual disagreements with one another, they shared a number of unquestioned basic assumptions. Rogerians and Freudians, for example, may have disagreed as to whether low self-esteem or repressed drives was the root cause of psychopathology, but they never doubted that the primary forces shaping and maintaining behavior are located within the individual, and therefore that treatment requires only the presence of the patient and a therapist. When family therapy first got started it was seen as another method to treat the same problem. The patient was still the patient. The opposition put forward by individual therapists was based on the belief that the technique of bringing in the family was potentially destructive to the confidentiality and supportiveness of the therapeutic relationship.

It soon became clear that family therapy was more than another way to treat individual patients, it was a new way of defining the problem. The patient was now the family. This shift involved a fundamental redefinition of personality development, abnormal behavior, and treatment. Family therapy became part of a new paradigm of thinking that challenged previous basic assumptions.

Individual therapies recognize the primary importance played by family life in shaping the personality; but they assume that these influences become internalized, and that intrapsychic personality dynamics become the dominant forces that determine behavior. Treatment, therefore, can and should be directed at the person and his or her personal makeup. Family therapy, on the other hand, acknowledges that past experiences are encoded in individuals, but considers these influences to be weaker than current interpersonal interactions. Treatment, from the family perspective, is most powerful and effective when it is applied directly to the organization of the family.

Individual therapies understand personality formation as an internal process; symptoms are seen as the result of conflicts *within* the person. The environment is considered only as a contributory source of stress, activating latent inner conflicts. Because the environment is seen as providing the external challenge that evokes internal conflicts, treatment is carried out in isolation, in a private relationship with the therapist. The goal of individual psychotherapy is to change the way the patient handles his or her own internal experience, to equip him or her to go forth better able to negotiate the environment.

In family therapy, the dominant influences on behavior are thought to be located externally, in the ongoing life of the family. To the extent that personality is shaped by early experiences, these are viewed as real interactions and perceptions rather than distorted fantasies. What happens to the young child is thought to be the result not of internal conflict but of the realities of family living. Symptom formation is also viewed as the result of conflict between the individual and the environment, but with a different emphasis. Individual therapies consider symptomatic individuals to be inadequately equipped to deal with the environment, and they try to change the individual. Family therapy considers dysfunctional families to be inflexible in responding to the natural strivings of the developing child, and tries to change the family.

When family therapy was young, traditional psychotherapists attacked it. In many institutions, senior clinicians and administrators, schooled in the individual paradigm, challenged family therapy's legitimacy and opposed its practice. As family therapy grew and became an accepted force in the field, the hostilities ceased, but there was little exchange between the two competing ideologies.

Once it is understood that family therapy is not a method but an orientation to clinical problems, the conceptual dichotomy between individual therapy and family therapy dissolves. From a family-therapy point of view, all psychological treatment *is* treatment of families, whether one, two, or several people are present, and whether or not the therapist includes the whole family in his or her assessment. Bowenian and strategic therapists, for example, are no less systems-oriented simply because they often do therapy with one person at a time.

Today, the differences between individual and family therapy are often less than those between rival schools of family therapy. What therapists think about problems and how they treat them are more important than how many people are in the treatment room.

PROLIFERATION OF
RIVAL SCHOOLS OF FAMILY THERAPY

In the 1950s family therapy was a radical new experiment, practiced in relative isolation by a small group of clinicians who had little contact with each other. In the sixties family therapy emerged as a growing force in the mental health field; its practitioners drew strength from sharing their ideas, but often had to contend with a psychiatric establishment that was resistant to the whole idea of family treatment. Just as clients are accustomed to thinking of one person as the patient and are reluctant to accept the suggestion that the whole family may be involved, so were many clinicians. In most clinics and training institutions family therapists were attacked as violators of sacred norms, or tolerated as not-quite-respectable mavericks. Gradually, however, the family therapy movement grew and became respectable. What started out as heresy became a new orthodoxy.

When family clinicians were fighting for legitimacy there was a tendency to think of family therapy as a monolithic enterprise. But even from the beginning there were distinct differences between, say, Murray Bowen and Nathan Ackerman, or John Bell and Don Jackson. As family therapy grew these differences became clearer and more pronounced. The major development of the 1970s was the working out of separate systems vying with each other for the allegiance of the growing number of clinicians who wanted to become family therapists. Carlos Sluzki (1983, p. 24) explained this jockeying for pre-eminence in economic terms:

> During its first 10 or 15 years, the situation in the family therapy field was akin to that of the western frontier of the U.S. during the mid-1800s. There was a lot of territory to occupy and explore, an undeclared war with the previous inhabitants (in family therapy's case, psychodynamically-oriented and classical psychiatrists) and a prevailing spirit of adventure and expansionism. Back then, family therapists were, for the most part, not too preoccupied with staking out their personal domains since like-minded neighbors were few and far between and they were more concerned with developing common defenses against the unfriendly elements in the mental health establishment.

Over the last 10 years, however, there has been a population explosion within the field as well as a dramatic increase in the commercial advantages of having control of part of its territory. As a result, people have been known to surreptitiously move fences, erect huge stockages, dispute certain areas and even claim as their own territories that were previously defined as common grounds. During the last 10 years, we have witnessed a Balkanization of the field into sectors based on political rather than scientific boundaries. We have also seen the rise of a "star" system, based on maintaining those artificial boundaries for politico-economic reasons. The consequence of all this has been the development of more and more "brand-name" models and increased bickering about whose technique washes whiter.

At the close of the 1960s the ideas of communications theory were probably the most popular and influential in the field. Watzlawick, Beavin, and Jackson's *Pragmatics of Human Communications* (1967) was widely read and served as both an introduction and a manual of family therapy to a very large audience. In the early 1970s structural family therapy emerged as the most popular approach in the field. The simple and practical nature of structural theory, Minuchin's charismatic style, and the extensive training facilities of the Philadelphia Child Guidance Clinic combined to capture center stage in the movement. In the latter part of that decade, various strategic forms of family therapy gained prominence, and a major polarization developed between strategic and nonstrategic therapists. Today, these competing camps engage in serious, often heated debates, trading charges of manipulation, gimmickry, naivete, and ineffectiveness.

In the 1980s there has been a recognizable trend toward integrating concepts and methods of the different schools of family therapy. There continue to be several distinct approaches, but they differ more in theory than in technique. The result of this blurring of distinctions is a growing mutual appreciation among practitioners from totally different paradigms. Behavioral family therapists, for example, have been using effective techniques of operant conditioning for years. But as long as they were isolated from other approaches by mutual ignorance and mistrust, these ideas had little influence on other schools. Now that this isolation is breaking down, the various sects are borrowing more freely from each other. Behaviorists are incorporating structural theory as an organizing framework, analysts occasionally use paradoxical injunctions, and so on.

The fifties was the decade of discovery, the sixties was a fight for acceptance, and the seventies was a time of proliferation of competing schools; the eighties may see a synthesis of the best that the field has to offer—an ironing out of the wrinkles, what Kuhn (1962) called "working out the puzzles of normal science."

CLASSIFYING THE FIELD
OF FAMILY THERAPY

In the early days of family therapy it was often compared with individual therapy, as though "it" were a single entity. This was a reflection of the fact that family therapists were pioneers, trying to stake a claim to some of the territory occupied by psychodynamic theory. But even then family therapy was a field of diverse approaches. The pioneers were united in challenging the hegemony of psychoanalysis, but they differed in terms of background, professional identity, and working context.

In the 1960s the family therapy movement spread and different approaches proliferated. Today, family therapy has been incorporated into the accepted order of things. No longer do family therapists seek to legitimize their work as an alternative to individual therapy. Instead, the leaders of family therapy have been more concerned with defining unique brands of family treatment than they have been with uniting around common issues. As a result, there are now so many different approaches to family therapy that it is difficult to keep track of them all.

Several authors have attempted to bring order to the field by devising systems of classification for the various models of treatment. One of the first was Jay Haley (1962) who wrote a satirical piece in which he divided the field into several different schools. Three schools were designed for moderately disturbed families: the "Dignified School of Family Therapy" (J.E. Bell) in which the therapist does not take sides in family conflicts; the "Dynamic Psychodynamic School of Family Diagnosis" (N.W. Ackerman) where the therapist sides with different members at different times, gets pulled in different directions, and often wishes to flee the room; and the "Chuck It and Run School" (C. Fulweiler) in which the therapist does just that, retreating behind a mirror and leaving the family to fight it out. Haley described two schools which treat seriously disturbed families. The "Great Mother School" (V. Satir) emanates benevolent concern and attempts to generate a friendly atmosphere; while in the "Stonewall School" (D. Jackson) the therapist bedevils the family into health. Finally, Haley described four "Multiplication Schools" which utilized more than one therapist. The

"Eyebrows School" (R.D. Laing) uses two therapists; the "Brotherly Love School" (A.S. Friedman) uses two therapists who make home visits; the "Total Push in the Tall Country School" (R. MacGregor) uses a different therapist for every family member; and the "Hospitalize the Whole Damn Maelstrom School" (M. Bowen) hospitalizes the entire family. Haley's scheme is amusing, but more descriptive than analytic. He also left out what might have been described as the "Svengali School" (J. Haley) in which the therapist outwits families, whether they like it or not.

Alexander (1963) described three different approaches to family problems that were prevalent in mental health agencies in the early 1960s. The *collaborative treatment* model, common to child guidance clinics, called for different members of the family to be treated by separate therapists. *Concommitant treatment* was an approach to marriage counseling where the spouses were seen separately by the same therapist. *Conjoint treatment*, where the family or one of its subsystems was seen together, was still relatively uncommon. Alexander's description is based merely on who is seen; it considers neither how problems are conceptualized nor how they are treated.

Olson (1970) was the first to consider how psychological problems are conceptualized and to relate this to treatment. He classified the mental health field in terms of five basic theoretical frameworks, and described the treatment unit, therapeutic focus, and goal of each. The *intrapersonal framework*, held by most individual psychotherapists, treats the individual, focuses primarily on intrapsychic change with a secondary focus on interpersonal change, and strives for improvement and growth of the self. Collaborative or concurrent marital or parent-child therapy follows the *interpersonal framework*. Treatment is designed collaboratively for relatives; the focus is primarily interpersonal, secondarily intrapsychic; and the goal of treatment is to improve family relationships. The *quasi-interactional framework* is illustrated by parent-child behavior modification. Here, the treatment unit is the individual, the focus is on developing interactional skills, and the goal is improving modes of interaction. Group therapists and multiple family group therapists adhere to an *interactional framework*. The treatment unit is a stranger group, the focus is mainly on group process, with a secondary focus of the intrapsychic, and the goal is improvement of the self in terms of ability to relate to others. In the *transactional framework*, the treatment unit is a natural group, the focus is on marital and family systems, and the goal is to improve family inter-relationships. This is the model followed in conjoint family therapy and network therapy.

The Committee on the Family of the Group for the Advancement for

Psychiatry (GAP, 1970) surveyed the field of family therapy in 1965–1966 and identified three theoretical positions. *Position A* therapists were psychodynamically-oriented individual therapists who occasionally saw families. These therapists considered the family as a stressor with which the patient must cope. They emphasized diagnosis, history-taking, expression of affect, and insight. *Position Z* therapists share a family-systems orientation. They see family therapy as an orientation to all problems, and all therapeutic interventions are seen as family interventions. The patient is considered only the "identified patient" or "symptom bearer" who exposes the dysfunction of the entire family system. These therapists share an ahistorical focus on present interactions, eschew diagnosis, and concentrate on underlying relationship problems. *Position M* is the middle ground, blending psychodynamic and family systems concepts. After dividing the field from A to Z, the committee report left it to the reader's imagination to apply the scale to specific practitioners in the field.

Zuk (1971) described an intensification of the psychodynamic versus systems theory ideological split in the period from 1964 to 1970, and, using the GAP Committee's classification, he identified the major *A position* therapists as Wynne, Boszormenyi-Nagy, and Framo, and their *Z position* counterparts as Haley, Jackson, and Zuk.

One of the best known classifications of family therapy is Beels and Ferber's (1969) comparison of *conductors* and *reactors*. Beels and Ferber believed that theories were simply rationalizations for clinical behavior, and their emphasis on personal style was consonant with the anti-theory spirit of the sixties. *Conductors* are dominant, active, forceful, and charismatic leaders, among them Ackerman, Satir, Bowen, Minuchin, MacGregor, Paul, and Bell. *Reactors* are quieter, less directive therapists, who respond to the family's lead. Among the reactors there are two types: *reactor-analysts*, such as Wynne, Boszormenyi-Nagy, Framo, and Whitaker; *reactor-systems purists* included Jackson, Haley, and Zuk. Because they focused on personal style, Beels and Ferber's schema is better understood as a classification of family therapists rather than of the field of family therapy. The people who originate an approach translate their ideas into practice through the vehicle of their personalities; what emerges is a distinctly personal product. But for the people who come after, style is less important. Everyone has a personal manner; but in order to master a system of therapy and its techniques, it is necessary to begin by subduing some of the self. The apprentice's style is constrained by the discipline of learning the method; later, when techniques have become almost second nature, the therapist can interact more spontaneously.

Although they were describing therapists, not therapies, Beels and Ferber touched upon what is in fact a major distinction among the current schools of family therapy. Just as some therapists are conductors, some therapies are prescriptive (strategic); and as other therapists are reactors, other therapies are elicitory (psychoanalytic).

Foley (1974) compared five leading family therapists—Ackerman, Bowen, Haley, Jackson, and Satir—in terms of three issues: "What is a family?" "What should the outcome of family therapy be?" and "How does a family change?" He also rated these therapists according to how much emphasis they place on eight specific dimensions of therapy: history, diagnosis, affect, learning, values, conscious versus unconscious, transference, and therapist as a model or teacher. (Table 2-1). Although some of Foley's judgments seem mistaken—he considers Jackson and Haley to have a High interest in learning, Ackerman to have only a Medium interest in the unconscious, and Haley and Jackson to place a High emphasis on the therapist as teacher—his attempt to classify therapists in terms of how they

Table 2-1
Foley's (1974) Classification of Leading Family Therapists

DIMENSION OF THERAPY	EMPHASIS		
	High	Medium	Low
1. History	Bowen, Satir	Ackerman, Jackson	Haley
2. Diagnosis	Ackerman	Bowen, Jackson	Haley, Satir
3. Affect	Ackerman, Satir	Haley	Bowen, Jackson
4. Learning	Ackerman, Bowen, Haley, Jackson, Satir	——	——
5. Values	Ackerman, Bowen, Jackson	Haley, Satir	——
6. Conscious *vs.* Unconscious	——	Ackerman, Bowen, Jackson	Haley, Satir
7. Transference	——	Ackerman	Bowen, Haley Jackson, Satir
8. Therapist as teacher	Ackerman, Bowen, Haley, Jackson, Satir	——	——

relate to the practical dimensions of therapy is commendable.

Foley also developed a scheme for classifying family therapists, based on both the GAP (1970) report and Beels and Ferber's (1969) classification. This two-dimensional model (Figure 2-1) describes therapists according to whether they are active or observant, and whether they are systems oriented or analytic. Foley did not, however, attempt to actually classify specific approaches using his model.

Guerin (1976) wrote an insider's history of family therapy, and then devised a comprehensive theoretical classification of the schools of family therapy. His system was developed in response to what he considered an antitheoretical bias in earlier classifications. According to Guerin, describing therapists as conductors or reactors (Beels and Ferber, 1969) and as active or observant (Foley, 1974) overemphasizes style at the expense of theory.

Guerin took the GAP report as a starting point, dividing therapists into psychodynamic or systems thinkers, and then subdivided each of these groups into a variety of subtypes:

A. *Psychodynamic*
  1. *Individual:* dynamically oriented therapists who occasionally see families.
  2. *Group:* J.E. Bell, Wynne, Beels.
  3. *Experiential:* Whitaker, Ferber.
  4. *Ackerman-type:* Nathan and Norman Ackerman, Israel Zwerling.
B. *Systems*
  1. *Strategic:* Haley, Jackson, Watzlawick, Weakland.
  2. *Structural:* Minuchin.
  3. *Bowenian:* Bowen.

Guerin's classification is a useful advance over previous, purely descriptive ones, because it includes conceptual differences and names the leading practitioners in the various schools. However, basing a classifying scheme on a single dimension (psychodynamic versus systems) oversimplifies the theoretical bases of different family therapies.

In 1977 Steidl and Wexler classified the spectrum of family therapies by merely describing several schools of family therapy. They listed communications, psychodynamic, structural, and Bowenian as the major schools of family therapy. This listing provided an overview of the field, but said nothing about the conceptual or methodological differences involved.

Madanes and Haley's (1977) classification is the most comprehensive description and cogent analysis of the field of family therapy. According to them, the major dimensions on which family therapies differ are: past *vs.* present; interpretation *vs.* action; growth *vs.* presenting problem; general method *vs.* specific plan for each problem; unit of one, two, or three people; equality *vs.* hierarchy; and analogical *vs.* digital thinking.

The *psychodynamic school* focuses on individual personalities, and emphasizes the past, both as cause and cure. Symptoms are seen as the result of repressed past experiences, and treatment is designed to bring past ideas and experiences into awareness. The method is *interpretative*, and the goal is *growth*, not symptom resolution. Psychodynamic therapists follow a *general method* in all cases. The theory conceptualizes people in terms of intrapsychic structures and families as collections of *individuals*. Therefore, *equality* is emphasized more than hierarchy. Treatment is *analogical*—therapists are interested in metaphor and meaning rather than discrete elements of behavior.

The *experiential* school emphasizes the present and fosters emotional experience in the session as the main tool of therapy. Experientialists use interpretations, but these often take the form of confrontations, designed to break down resistances instead of analyzing them. They are concerned with *growth*, not problem-solving, and use a smiliar *method* with all families. Although experientialists use interactions as the stage for emotional

Figure 2-1
Foley's (1974) Two-dimensional Model for
Classifying Family Therapists

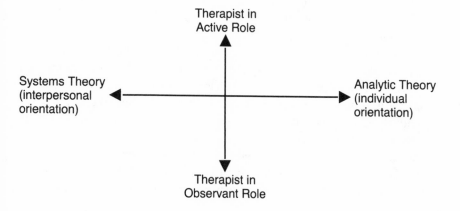

expressiveness, their focus of change is on the *unit of one*. Equality is the experiential model of families, and the approach is *analogical* since it is concerned with the meaning of experience.

Unlike these two schools, *behavioral family therapy* comes out of learning theory rather than Freudian psychology. But like them it is derived from a method of individual psychotherapy. Behaviorists focus on the *present*, but in terms of modifying specific behavior rather than expressing feelings. They work with *action*; instead of making interpretations, they give directions for changing behavior. They concentrate exclusively on the *presenting problem* and design *procedures to fit specific problems*. The conceptual model is a *unit of two persons*, in which one is taught to modify the behavior of the other. Hierarchy is not a relevant issue for this school, and family life is modeled on *equality*. The behaviorists are concerned with *digital* behaviors rather than their analogical meaning.

The *extended family systems school* differs from the preceding ones in not being an offshoot of individual psychology. Madanes and Haley mention two variations of this approach: assembling all of the significant people in a patient's life in one large group, or sending the patient to visit the family of origin. They describe both as focusing on the present, although many people would consider visiting the family of origin as a way of resolving problems from the past. In any case, this school clearly emphasizes *growth* and follows a *general method* in all cases. Extended family therapists emphasize rational understanding of family dynamics, but they use *directives* rather than interpretations to produce change. The focus of this school is on a *unit of three*. In fact, Murray Bowen is the major person in the field to emphasize triangles in human relationships. Intergenerational *hierarchies* are critical to this theory, and therapy is *analogical*.

The two remaining schools in Madanes and Haley's classification both derive from communications theory. (In fact, Haley himself was a link from communications to structural and to strategic family therapies.) *Structural family therapy* concentrates on patterns of interaction in the *present*. Structuralists work with *action* in the session. When they do use interpretations, it is to reinforce interactional changes, not to foster insight. Since this school is concerned with structural problems that underlie symptoms, it tends to be *growth-oriented*. It follows a *specific plan for every problem*, works with *units of three*, and emphasizes *hierarchies*. Parents are expected to fill the role of family executives, not to relate to their children as equals. Madanes and Haley do not mention whether they consider this approach analogical or digital, but it appears to be *digital* in its focus on sequences of interaction, and *analogical* in conceptualizing these exchanges as having meaning in structural terms.

The strategic school focuses on communication in the *present*, and utilizes directives to change behavior through *action*. These directives may be straightforward or paradoxical. Strategists are narrowly concerned with *solving the presenting problem*, and they plan *specific strategies for every problem*. According to Madanes and Haley, problems are seen as involving at least *two* and usually *three people*. Hierarchy is taken into account, and the approach is *digital* in its focus on presenting problems, but *analogical* in conceptualizing how those problems are maintained.

Ritterman (1977) described two approaches to family therapy, communications and structural, in terms of general theoretical models, the *mechanistic* and the *organismic*. Incidentally, much of what Ritterman called the "communications approach" is today represented by the strategic school. The mechanistic world view, derived from Newtonian physics, analyzes phenomena using the model of a machine composed of elementary particles to which forces are applied. The major corollaries of the mechanistic model are *elementarism* (analyzing things by breaking them down into their basic elements) and *antecedent-consequent causality* (in which change is conceived as caused by stimulation from outside the mechanism.)

The organismic world view, derived from biology, assumes that the model for natural as well as social sciences should be based on structured, biological systems, in which energy rather than matter is primary and the system is an active whole, not a passive assemblage of parts. Its basic corollaries are *holism* (the whole is greater than the sum of its parts because of its organization) and *reciprocal causality* (systems and their environments exert mutual influences on each other).

According to Ritterman, communications family therapy exemplifies the mechanistic model, because communications begin by breaking the family system into its smallest elements, bits of communication called messages (elementism). Symptoms are represented as messages which are linked to other messages in additive chains of stimulus and response (antecedent-consequent causality). The analysis of how problems are maintained follows a closed systems model—despite frequent references to open systems by communications theorists—based strictly on the relationship among the parts (communicators) *inside* the system.

The communications model of therapy is designed to resolve problems, not reorganize family systems. This is often described in terms of interrupting problem-maintaining feedback loops. "It is as though the family is conceived of as a...clogged computer that needs to be reprogrammed" (Mitchell, 1967, p. 197).

According to Ritterman, structural family therapy is consistently faithful to an organismic world view. She quotes from Minuchin (1974, p. 89) to illustrate the structural commitment to the whole family (holism).

> In essence, the structural approach to families is based on the concept that a family is more than the individual biopsychodynamics of its members. Family members relate according to certain arrangements, which govern their transactions. These arrangements, though usually not explicitly stated or even recognized, form a whole—the structure of the family. The reality of the structure is of a different order from the reality of the individual members.

Rather than breaking the family system into its elements, bits of communication, Minuchin considers communication as an activity of the whole family that reveals its structure. Moreover, the structural model examines the whole family, both in terms of its subsystems and in relation to larger systems. Problems are treated as representing conflict in the entire system, with all subsystems having an interlocking impact (reciprocal causality).

Treatment consists of joining the family in a position of leadership to form a new—therapeutic—system; evaluating the structure of the family by stimulating interacting; and restructuring the family system. The goal is always a change in the organization of the whole, rather than simply correcting blockages in one particular sequence of behavior.

Ritterman's epistemological analysis calls attention to important philosophical issues. In this respect, her contribution is consistent with Guerin's (1976) call for more theoretical analyses in the field of family therapy. Ritterman's discussion, however, is overly abstract and somewhat unfair. She begins with the assumption that theoretical models from natural science are applicable to the social sciences, and that one, the organismic, is preferable to another because it is more recent. She also exaggerates the differences between the communications and structural theories, overlooking the fact that they have similar roots and that Jay Haley was a bridge from one approach to the other.

In her conclusion, Ritterman suggests that her classification makes it possible to group together philosophically similar family therapy models (communications theory and family behavior theory), as well as family therapies and compatible models in other fields (structural family theory and Piagetian theory). Moreover, as Levant (1980) pointed out, Ritterman's model can be extended to encompass other schools of family therapy. By considering whether they focus on internal subjective states of individual members or on the external behavior of the whole group, as well as the elementaristic-analytic versus holistic dichotomy, it is possible to classify families using the two-dimensional model in Figure 2-2.

Paolino and McCrady's (1978) classification of the field of marital therapy into psychoanalytic, systems, and social learning theory models can be extended to family therapy as well. Although it is quite broad, this division is both accurate and pragmatic. To some extent, however, it does simply describe that there are three different camps of people who treat families, rather than distinguishing between them on the basis of ideological differences. Since Paolino and McCrady's purpose was to survey the literature in the field, their scheme is fine; there are three separate literatures. Unfortunately, it neglects to consider such theoretical divisions of the field as those based on monadic, dyadic, or triadic models; or practical divisions such as growth versus symptom relief.

After reviewing previous classifications, Levant (1980) concluded that it is more useful and appropriate to examine inductively the various schools of family therapy than to impose external categories (such as Ritterman's 1977 world views) on the field deductively. Levant's classification first divides the field into historical and ahistorical approaches; then he subdivides the

Figure 2-2
An Extension of Ritterman's (1977) Paradigmatic
Classification of Family Therapy Theories

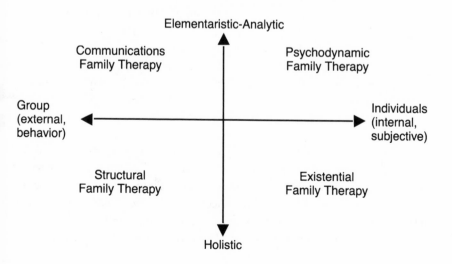

ahistorical approaches according to whether they focus on changing the structure and process of the family, or on providing an intense affective experience. The three therapeutic paradigms are: historical approaches; structure/process approaches; and experiential approaches.

1. *Historical:* Concerned with the person in the system, especially those attachments to the past that affect current functioning and future generations.
   a. *Psychodynamic:* Wynne, Lidz, Ackerman, Framo, Friedman, Zinner, Shapiro, Searles, Paul, Beels, and Epstein.
   b. *Multigenerational:* Bowen
   c. *Intergenerational:* Boszormenyi-Nagy and Spark.
2. *Structure/Process:* Concerned with current patterns of interaction which are believed to maintain the problems that families present with. The aim is to reorder the family system so that it will no longer need or support symptomatic behavior.
   a. *Communications:* Jackson, Haley, Watzlawick, and Weakland.
   b. *Problem-solving:* Haley.
   c. *Brief problem focused:* Watzlawick, Weakland, and Fisch.
   d. *Strategic:* Rabkin.
   e. *Triadic:* Zuk.
   f. *Structural:* Minuchin.
   g. *Behavioral:* Patterson.
   h. *Others:* Satir, Bandler, Grinder, Selvini Palazzoli, Hoffman, and Papp.
3. *Experiential:* Concerned with providing an intense affective experience for family members so that their own self-actualizing tendencies will be liberated.
   a. *Gestalt:* Kempler, Rabin, Hatcher, and the Kaplans.
   b. *Experiential:* Whitaker, Warkentin, Malone, Napier, and Ferber.
   c. *Client-centered:* van der Veen and Levant.

Levant partially succeeded in his aim of classifying the field in a way that is both conceptually meaningful and useful for evaluative comparison. The listing of thirteen separate schools of family therapy gives a comprehensive orientation to the field, and the theoretical distinction between structural approaches and experiential approaches is interesting. On the other hand, the distinction between historical and ahistorical paradigms does not capture a major conceptual dimension. Bowen, for example, is interested in history, but also in structural change. The more important distinction in the field is between individual models and systems models. Even within his own terms, Levant has made a few errors in classification. Behavioral therapists, for example, may be interested in the process of behavioral sequences, but they do not aim to alter the nature of family systems. Moreover, some of the listings of representatives of the various schools are not up to date (omitting most of the major figures in the behavioral school), and others are based on a single publication rather than a knowledge of the field (including Warkentin and Malone as family therapists, and omitting Selvini Palazzoli and Hoffman from the strategic school).

My own attempt to organize the field is the subject of the bulk of this book. In "Section II: Systems of Family Therapy," I describe eight schools of family therapy, chosen to represent the major approaches to conceptualizing and treating families. In some cases the fit between a school and its practitioners is uncomplicated. *Structural family therapy,* for instance, is a coherent, well-recognized approach, and it is readily identified with its leading practitioner, Salvador Minuchin. In the case of the *behavioral* and *strategic* schools, there are several leading figures, but they are acknowledged practitioners of those approaches. It is necessary to subdivide both of these schools, however, into separate branches to reflect the diversity within a basic consistency. *Experiential family therapy* also includes several clinicians who are readily identified with this approach. Here too, though, there is a fair amount of diversity, and at times it is necessary to differentiate the ideas and methods of particular therapists.

The other four schools are less easily defined. Two approaches, *family group therapy* and *communications therapy,* belong more to the past than the present. They are included because they represent coherent systems of family therapy, and because both continue to have an impact on the field. *Extended family therapy* is primarily about Murray Bowen's therapy; network therapy was included because its emphasis on expanding treatment beyond the nuclear family fits well with Bowenian therapy. Multiple family therapy fits less well in this chapter; it was included because its method involves people outside the nuclear family, although it is conceptually limited to the nuclear family. The *psychoanalytic school* includes a variety of different figures who share a belief that combining a depth-psychological understanding of individuals with an interactional family treatment is the optimal way to deal with human problems.

My goal was to classify the field of family therapy in a way that is comprehensive and based on conceptual rather than personal differences. In the process I encountered two major difficulties. First, some of the approaches did not fit neatly together conceptually. Multiple family group therapy, for instance, could have as easily been included with family group therapy as with extended family therapy. Second, some practitioners are not easily classifed. Virginia Satir, for example, has made contributions to communications and experiential therapy; Peggy Papp has changed from an experiential to a strategic model; and some people, like Fred and Bunny Duhl, combine elements from several schools in their work. The final classification is intended merely as a convenient way to organize the field. It is not meant to represent a novel view; rather it is a comprehensive grouping in familiar terms. Chapters 4 through 11 describe the various schools of family therapy; comparison and analysis are deferred until the final chapter.

THE FAMILY THERAPY ESTABLISHMENT

Now that family therapy has become a significant force in the mental health field, its practitioners have developed a power structure with institutions and recognized authorities. These institutions and authorities make up the family therapy establishment, with its own professional organizations, literature, and training centers.

It is never easy to describe the current scene in family therapy because the field is constantly changing. Every year new journals are introduced, significant advances are made in theory and technique, and major personalities move from one center to another. Nevertheless, in this section I will describe the family therapy establishment as it appears in the winter of 1982–83.

Professional Organizations. The American Association for Marriage and Family Therapy (AAMFT) was organized in 1942 by Lester Dearborn and Ernest Graves as a professional organization to set standards for marriage counselors. In 1970 it was expanded to include family therapists, and the United States Department of Health, Education, and Welfare designated the AAMFT to establish standards for certification of training programs in marital and family therapy. To accomplish this task, a ten-member Accreditation Commission was set up, and today this group offers official sanction to training programs throughout the country.

The AAMFT is a large group whose main goal is organizing and credentialing the field. Its membership is dominated by counselors who seek credibility as mental health providers. Nevertheless, the group has a membership of over 9,000 members, including some of the leading authorities in the field such as Carl Whitaker and Jay Haley.

The other professional family therapy organization is a small group of experienced clinicians and teachers. The American Family Therapy Association (AFTA) is an academy of advanced professionals, interested in exchanging ideas; they leave government approval and credentialing to the AAMFT.

The American Family Therapy Association was started in 1977, following a discussion of the editorial board of *Family Process*. Its first officers were: President, Murray Bowen; Vice President, John Spiegel; Executive Vice President, Gerald Berenson; Secretary, James Framo; and Treasurer, Geraldine Spark. This group of approximately 500 family therapy teachers and researchers meets yearly to share ideas and develop common interests. It is a think tank whose annual meeting is made up of interest groups where a variety of clinical, teaching, and research topics are discussed. Requirements for membership include having been a teacher of family therapy for at least five years and having made a thoughtful contribution to the field.

Literature. The first book devoted entirely to diagnosis and treatment of families was Nathan Ackerman's the *Psychodynamics of Family Life*, published in 1958. The first journal in the field, *Family Process*, was founded in 1961 by the Ackerman Institute and the Mental Research Institute. Today there is a steady stream of books on family therapy, and more than a dozen journals devoted primarily to family treatment. In fact, the family-therapy literature proliferates at such a rate, that it's difficult to keep up with it. The *Recommended Readings* section located at the back of this volume is a selective guide to some of the classic books and articles in the field.

In 1961 Don Jackson and Nathan Ackerman founded the first family therapy journal, *Family Process*. Under the editorial leadership of Jay Haley and later Donald Bloch, *Family Process* has continued to publish the best and most influential articles in the field; its editorial board and advisory editors read like a list of who's who in the movement. Carlos Sluzki took over the editorship when Bloch stepped down in 1983, and seems certain to maintain the high standards set by his predecessors.

Today, *Family Process* has at least a dozen rivals. Second in terms of readership, is the *Journal of Marital and Family Therapy*, the official organ of the American Association for Marriage and Family Therapy. It was first published in 1975 as *Journal of Marital and Family Counseling*; it was renamed in 1979. Alan Gurman recently took over from Florence Kaslow as editor. Some of the other journals in the field, like *American Journal of Family Therapy, Marriage and Family Living, International Journal of Family Therapy,* and *International Journal of Family Counseling* are well-established publications with formats similar to that of *Family Process.*Many others are recent entries to the field and have more specialized formats. One, *The Marriage and Family Review,* has been around for a while, but under the editorship of Marvin Sussman it has gone to new format, featuring selected themes of current significance.

The *Family* was started 10 years ago by Philip Guerin when he opened the Center for Family Learning in New Rochelle. This journal is devoted to practical issues of applying Bowenian theory to a variety of clinical problems. Another journal representing a particular viewpoint is the *Journal of Strategic and Systemic Therapies,* which includes articles of theoretical as well as practical significance. A new thematically-organized quarterly, *Family Therapy Collections,* was scheduled to publish its first issue in 1983, as was also *Family Systems Medicine,* edited by Donald Bloch and devoted to the growing area of collaboration between family-medicine practitioners and systems thinkers.

Finally, there are two publications devoted to news and features. The field of family therapy is growing so rapidly that it is difficult to keep up with the latest publications, conferences, workshops, and ideas. The *Family Therapy News* and *The Family Networker* keep readers informed about what is happening. The fact that the *Family Therapy Networker* now has the third largest readership in the field—surpassed only by *Family Process* and the *Journal of Marital and Family Therapy*—attests to the interest in these journalistic calendars.

Training Centers. Family therapy is now practiced and taught at numerous institutions throughout the world. A recent survey by Bloch and Weiss (1981) listed 213 family therapy training programs in the United States, 11 in Canada and 21 in Europe. Since the number is growing at such a rapid pace, this listing must be considered a conservative estimate.

The largest number of training programs is affiliated with universities, but the oldest and most influential centers are free-standing family institutes. I shall list here some of the best-known current centers of family therapy training and briefly describe their programs.

The *Ackerman Institute for Family Therapy* in New York City was founded as the Family Institute by Nathan Ackerman in 1960. Following Ackerman's death in 1971, the center was renamed in his honor and the directorship was assumed by Donald Bloch. Ackerman's psychoanalytic influence is still represented in Bloch's work, although recently the staff of the Ackerman Institute offers diverse models of family therapy. Lynn Hoffman's application of systemic therapy has also made the Ackerman Institute a leading center in the strategic family therapy camp. (Hoffman now offers training at her new center in Amherst, Massachusetts.)

The Ackerman Institute's training program is one of the most complete and intensive in the country. They offer a full range of clinical services as well as varied educational opportunites. Further information may be obtained from: Robert Simon, M.D., 149 East 78th St., New York, New York 10021.

The *Center for Family Learning* in New Rochelle, New York, was founded by Philip Guerin in 1973. Guerin and his long time colleague Thomas Fogarty were trained in family systems therapy by Murray Bowen at Georgetown University and taught together at the Family Studies Section of Albert Einstein College of Medicine prior to founding the Center. The multigenerational model, as interpreted by Guerin and Fogarty, continues to be the source of treatment and training at the Center. There are over a dozen faculty, many of whom are also affiliated with colleges and universities throughout the Middle Atlantic states.

The Center provides clinical service to families throughout the greater New York City area, under the clinical direction of David R. Chabot. The mainstay of the training program is a three to four year sequence, with an optional fifth year. During the first year students learn the basics of family systems theory, and apply the theory to families they treat, to families they observe in treatment by members of the faculty, and to themselves as members of their own families. The second year focus is on CFL's typology of families and the clinical methods developed to deal with these different symptom presentations. The third year is devoted to a shaping and honing of the therapist's clinical artistry and the development of subspecialties. In addition, The Center for Family Learning has a wide variety of seminars, workshops, and extra-mural training programs available to family clinicians throughout the country and publishes a bi-annual journal, *The Family.* The contact person for additional information is: Philip J. Guerin, Jr., M.D., 10 Hanford Avenue, New Rochelle, New York 10805.

The *Family Institute of Westchester,* located in Mount Vernon, New York, is directed by Elizabeth Carter. The staff also includes Fredda Herz, Monica McGoldrick, and Ken Terkelson. All of these people were trained in extended family systems theory, but they teach an integrated model which includes aspects of structural and strategic therapy as well.

The Institute has been in operation since 1977 and is primarily known for its training program. The training offered includes a comprehensive program of supervision, seminars, and small groups which takes three years to complete. There is also a two-year externship which meets weekly. In addition to the training offered on site, members of the teaching staff are among the most popular speakers at workshops and conventions throughout the country. Additional information is available from: Lillian Fine, Administrator, 147 Archer Avenue, Mount Vernon, New York 10605.

The *Philadelphia Child Guidance Clinic* became one of the leading centers of family therapy in the world during the 1970s. It was here that Salvador Minuchin and his colleagues defined and promulgated the concepts of structural family therapy. Among these collaborators were Braulio Montalvo and Bernice Rosman who still work at the Child Guidance Clinic. When Minuchin retired as director he was followed in that position first by Harry Aponte and then by Ronald Liebman. Although retired, Minuchin nevertheless remains an active presence at the Clinic. (Minuchin and his wife, Patricia, now offer their own training program in New York City.)

Unlike most of the other centers of family therapy training which are located in small clinics and old houses, the Philadelphia Child Guidance Clinic is a large, modern, well-equipped facility that is physically part of the Children's Hospital of Philadelphia. It has an inpatient unit for children and families, outpatient clinics, and departments of training, research, and pediatric liaison. The Philadelphia Child Guidance Clinic is formally affiliated with the Departments of Psychiatry and Pediatrics of the University of Pennsylvania School of Medicine. There is an elaborate network of videotaping equipment, and over 300 staff are involved in the Clinic's activities.

Due to the popularity of structural family therapy and to its excellent physical facilites, the Child Guidance Clinic probably has trained more family therapists than any other center in the world. The training programs include an internship, various clinical practica, an extern program, supervisory groups, evening courses, child psychiatry and behavioral pediatrics fellowships, workshops, and conferences. Additional information can be obtained by writing to: H. Charles Fishman, M.D., Director of Training, Philadelphia Child Guidance Clinic, Two Children's Center, 34th Street and Civic Center Boulevard, Philadelphia, Pennsylvania 19104.

The *Georgetown Family Center,* located in Washington, D.C., was organized to teach family systems theory as developed by Murray Bowen. Bowen founded and still directs this center, which is affiliated with Georgetown University Medical School. The Center provides clinical service to people in the Washington, D.C. area, and training to family clinicians from all over the country. The training programs include a weekly, three-year postgraduate program, and a special postgraduate program for out-of-towners that meets for three consecutive days, four times a year, over a three-year period. There is also a full-time fellowship for psychiatrists and part-time internships for graduates of their other training programs. A description of these programs is available from: Michael Kerr, M.D., Director of Training, The Georgetown Family Center, 4380 MacArthur Blvd. N.W., Washington, D.C. 20007.

The *Family Therapy Institute of Washington, D.C.* is where Jay Haley and Cloe Madanes practice and teach their brand of strategic family therapy. Haley came to Washington after several years at the Philadelphia Child Guidance Clinic, and the training model offered at the Family Therapy Institute reflects Haley's unique integration of structural concepts and strategic methods. The Institute offers treatment provided by a multidisciplinary staff to families with a wide range of problems. Haley and Madanes also offer supervision, seminars, and workshops to professionals from all over the country. Inquiries may be made to: Cloe Madanes, Family Therapy Institute of Washington, D.C., 4602 N. Park Avenue, Chevy Chase, Maryland 20815.

The *Center for Family Studies/The Family Institute of Chicago* was founded as the Family Institute of Chicago, in 1968, to carry out education, research, and training in family systems. Charles Kramer, the founder and director, is a graduate of the Chicago Institute of Psychoanalysis, and one of the early figures in the field who integrated psychoanalytic theory with systems concepts. The training model of this center is eclectic, combining concepts and methods from psychoanalytic, structural, Bowenian, and strategic family therapies.

The Family Institute of Chicago is a Division of the Institute of Psychiatry of Northwestern Memorial Hospital, and its staff members hold faculty appointments in the Department of Psychiatry and Behavioral Sciences of Northwestern University Medical School. Eleven professional staff members are supplemented by 47 part-time faculty. The Education Section, headed by Noble Butler, offers teaching, supervision, and consultation to staff, residents, and students in the Institute, and to persons and agencies in the professional community in the Midwest. They offer a full range of clinical services, courses, seminars, workshops, and conferences. Research is an important component of the clinical as well as the educational programs. Brochures may be obtained from Noble Butler, Ph.D., 10 East Huron, Chicago, Illinois 60611.

The *Family Systems Program* is a training unit of the Institute for Juvenile Research, which is funded by the Illinois Department of Mental Health. It was founded in 1974 by Irving Berstein, who initiated many of the program's basic features. He was succeeded by Celia Falicov, who helped the Institute define a rigorous treatment philosophy and Howard Liddle, who expanded the visibility of the program at the national level and developed a highly-structured training program with built-in objectives and evaluations. The current faculty—Director Douglas Breunlin, Richard Schwartz, and Betty Karrer—is developing a treatment and training model which integrates structural and strategic family therapies. The staff offers a wide range of training opportunities, including courses, workshops, and one-year clinical and supervisory externships. One of the hallmarks of the Family Systems Program is the systematic evaluation of training carried out by the staff (Breunlin, Schwartz, Krause, and Selby, 1983). For information write to: Douglas Breunlin, MSSA, Family Systems Program, 907 South Wolcott, Chicago, Illinois 60612.

The *Boston Family Institute,* founded in 1969, is the oldest free-standing family therapy institute in New England. Its codirectors, Fred and Bunny Duhl are leading figures in the experiential school, and are both nationally active in the family therapy movement. The model of treatment practiced and taught at this center is Integrative Family Therapy, an eclectic blend of systems theory and experiential exercises. The training process, which is described in Bunny Duhl's book, *From the Inside Out and Other Metaphors,* combines self-awareness and personal exploration of families with didactic and practical training. The Institute offers a variety of training programs, including a two-year part-time certificate training program, and an intensive one-year program for practicing therapists. For further information, write to: Bunny S. Duhl, Co-Director, The Boston Family Institute, 251 Harvard Street, Brookline, Massachusetts 02146.

The *Family Institute of Cambridge,* in Massachusetts, was founded in 1976 by David Kantor, Barry Dym, and Carter Umbarger. Kantor left in 1980, and two additional directors were then added—Richard Chasin and Sallyann Roth.

In both theory and therapeutic technique, the Family Institute relies primarily on the tenets of general systems theory. There is some secondary interest in psychodramatic techniques. All aspects of theory and therapy are organized around a theme of the reciprocity between individual psychology and family dynamics.

The two major internal training sequences are an intensive program for clinicians with some experience, and a basic program introducing students to family-systems theory and therapy. In addition to these training programs, the Family Institute offers a wide variety of seminars and workshops, group supervision, and conferences. Detailed information about training programs is available from: Marsha Morgan, Administrative Director, The Family Institute of Cambridge, 256 Concord Avenue. Cambridge, Massachusetts 02138.

The Mental Research Institute (MRI) in Palo Alto, California was founded in 1959 by the late Don Jackson. Today, MRI's focus is on research and training from an interactional or systemic point of view. Some of the most well-known staff members of MRI are Paul Watzlawick, John Weakland, Richard Fisch, and Arthur Bodin.

MRI accepts Masters level and above candidates into a wide variety of training programs, including workshops, coninuing seminars, month-long residency programs, clinical externships, and supervisory groups. In addition, many of the staff members are among the stars of the family therapy workshop circuit. For further information about MRI's training programs you may write to: Director of Training, 555 Middlefield Road, Palo Alto, California 94301.

RESEARCH IN FAMILY THERAPY

Family therapy has grown from an experimental innovation to a major movement, because a vast number of people are convinced that it works. Clinical practitioners, students, and patients accept the evidence of their own experience as proof that family therapy concepts and methods are valid. But while the data of personal experience are important and useful, the ultimate test of family therapy's effectiveness is empirical research. Any treatment that claims to resolve human problems is too important to accept or reject uncritically. Families and their therapists invest too much and have too much at stake to put their trust in received opinions. Furthermore, even after the question of family therapy's overall effectiveness is settled, there remain a number of other more specific questions: Which systems of family therapy works best with which clinical problems? Are two therapists better than one? What is the optimal group of family members to work with? There are several excellent reviews of research available which discuss these questions, among them Gurman and Kniskern, 1978; Wells and Dezen, 1978; Jacobson, 1979; Benningfeld, 1978; and Strelnick, 1977.

When family therapy was introduced it immediately raised many questions: Does it work? How do the results of family treatment compare with those of individual therapy? What are the most effective techniques in family therapy? For the most part the answers to these questions came in the form of position papers and statements of belief, rather than from empirical research. Commenting on this state of affairs, Parloff (1961, p. 445) observed that:

> The relevant literature is vast, yet very little of it would be classed by the rigorous investigator as research. Most of the contributors to the area have been clinician-naturalists who, having perhaps a Freud-like vision of themselves, have made salutory advances from observations to conclusions with a maximum of vigor and a minimum of rigor.

Ten years later, Olson (1970) found little change, and suggested that the autonomy and unconnectedness of the several different professions engaged in family therapy was responsible for the lack of co-ordinated efforts to study the field. Gurman—a psychologist—noted (1971) that family therapy grew up in child guidance and social work agencies, where psychologists, who do most of the research in the field, are less actively involved than psychiatrists and social workers.

When Wells and his colleagues (1972) published the first review of outcome studies of family therapy, they could find only 13 relevant reports. But in 1978, when Gurman and Kniskern analyzed the outcome research in marital and family therapy they presented results from over 200 studies. By this time there were enough studies to support the overall effectiveness of family therapy, but not enough to answer many of the more specific questions being asked.

By 1978 there were 77 studies of marital and family therapy which reported gross rates of improvement. These studies included heterogeneous samples of patients, therapists, and forms of treatment. Studies of marital therapy showed positive change in 65 percent of the cases treated, as compared with individual therapy for similar problems which showed only a 48 percent rate of improvement. Furthermore, there were significantly higher rates of patient deterioration as a result of individual therapy.

About half of the studies of family therapy involved children or adolescents as the identified patient (IP) and about half involved adult IPs. Child and adolescent patients improved 71 percent, and adult patients improved 65 percent. These figures are similar to those reported in individual therapy (Bergin, 1971). When these results are broken down by treatment setting,

76 percent improved in outpatient settings, and 59 percent improved in day hospitals. This result is not surprising considering that day hospital patients tend to be chronic, marginally compensated psychotics and severe borderline personality disorders.

Taken together these studies lend substantial empirical support to the overall effectiveness of family therapy. Among the reports of gross improvement rates of family therapy the most impressive results have been reported on the effectiveness of structural family therapy. Minuchin and his colleagues have demonstrated a 90 percent success rate in the treatment of serious, psychosomatic disorders (Minuchin *et al.*, 1975; Rosman *et al.*, 1976) and heroin addicts (Stanton and Todd, 1979). The results of these studies are particularly convincing because the measures of change employed were highly objective indices, including blood sugar level for diabetics, weight gain for anorectics, and urine samples for heroin addicts.

Comparative studies examine not just the gross rates of improvement, but the differential effectiveness of various types of treatment. Studies comparing different formats of marital therapy have found that conjoint marital therapy and conjoint group marital therapy are superior to alternative treatments where spouses are seen separately in 70 percent of all comparisons, and inferior in only 5 percent. These clear-cut findings have helped speed the demise of concurrent and collaborative marital therapies (Gurman, 1973).

Gurman and Kniskern (1978) found 21 studies comparing family therapy to other types of treatment, primarily outpatient individual treatment. Every one of these studies showed family therapy to be equal or superior to the alternatives. The comparative study that attracted the most attention was Langsley's family crisis therapy project (Langsley *et al.*, 1968, 1969), later replicated by Rittenhouse (1970). Three hundred acutely disturbed patients for whom hospitalization was recommended were randomly assigned to either short-term, family-centered crisis therapy or to conventional inpatient treatment. Family treatment was clearly superior to hospitalization in terms of length and frequency of readmissions, and was able to avert instead of simply delaying hospitalization. This study may be criticized for not including a true control group and for confounding the effects of hospitalization versus nonhospitalization with those of family therapy versus other forms of psychotherapy. Nevertheless, avoiding hospitalization for 150 seriously disturbed patients is an impressive demonstration of the effectiveness of family therapy.

In another comparative study, this one extremely well-designed, Wellisch, Vincent, and Ro-trock (1976) compared family therapy to individual therapy in the treatment of adolescent inpatients. Family therapy emerged superior on a variety of self-report and observational measures. At 3-month followup none of the adolescents treated with family therapy had been rehospitalized, while 43 percent of those treated individually had been rehospitalized.

In 1978 Gurman and Kniskern found 31 controlled studies of nonbehavioral marital and family therapy. Eighteen of 31 comparisons showed family therapy to be superior to no-treatment controls; 11 showed a tie; and two studies (both of which were considered to involve inappropriate criteria) showed family treatment to be worse than no treatment. Gurman and Kniskern (1978, p. 845) concluded that in the aggregate these studies offer evidence of the effectiveness of nonbehavioral marital and family therapies:

> Moreover, largely positive results emerge on the basis of a wide variety of criteria, on change measures from a number of evaluative perspectives, for many types of marital and family problems, from therapy conducted by clinicians of all the major therapeutic disciplines, and in therapy carried out in a number of treatment settings.

Reviewing the somewhat more extensive research literature on the outcome of behavioral marital and family therapy, Gurman and Kniskern (1978) found behavioral couples therapy superior to control conditions in 7 to 11 studies (analogue and naturalistic), and superior to alternative forms of treatment in 8 to 16 comparisons. They concluded that these studies provide suggestive evidence of the effectiveness of behavioral marriage therapy, but noted that the large number of nonclinical analogue demonstrations with minimally-distressed couples makes this evidence less persuasive than that for nonbehavioral treatment.

Behavioral family therapy, which is based on educating and training parents as opposed to working with whole family groups, showed positive change in parents' reports about their problem children's behavior in the majority of 34 studies. These good results were specific to the behaviors targeted for change, and did not generalize to other behavior; nor did the results generalize from home to school, or remain at high rates of improvement at follow-up. Because of the lack of evidence for generalization or endurance of these behavior changes, behavioral family therapy cannot be said to have resulted in fundamental changes in the families treated.

Even less empirical information is available on the specific factors that influence family therapy outcome. Although the data are limited, experienced therapists seem to be more effective than inexperienced ones (Freeman *et al.,* 1969; Griffin, 1967; Roberts, 1975; Schrieber, 1966; Shellow *et al.,* 1963).

Cotherapy has been claimed by many family therapists to be superior to single therapist treatment, but the empirical results have shown no difference (Gurman, 1973), although cotherapy does appear to be useful in couples groups (Gurman, 1975). Somewhat more data is available showing the importance of therapist relationship skills. Warmth, empathy, and genuineness appear to be very important in keeping families in treatment beyond the first interview (Shapiro, 1974; Shapiro and Budman, 1973; Waxenberg, 1973). Moreover, the therapist's ability to model meaning clarification (Jones, 1969); the positive perceptions of family members (Graham, 1968); and the therapist's ability to facilitate depth of experiencing (DeChenne, 1973) also seem to be important relationship skills for family therapists. Technical skills may be necessary but are apparently not sufficient without more refined relationship skills.

Off to a slow start, research in family therapy has burgeoned in recent years. Thus far there is sufficient empirical evidence to say that family therapy is an effective form of treatment for a wide variety of clinical problems. Although there is little that can be said yet about the specific ingredients of successful family therapy, the rapid increase in the number and sophistication of studies in the field is fast closing this information gap.

SUMMARY

Family therapy was born in the 1950s of multiple parents. In the sixties this fledgling discipline struggled to gain acceptance as a legitimate member of the family of mental health providers. In the 1970s family therapy, by then a respectable and powerful force, was split into several rival camps, each proclaiming distinctive programs. Reading the details of these methodological prescriptions (Chapters 4–11) and accepting the jargon in which they are expressed leads to an exaggerated idea of fragmentation in the field. More careful study reveals a set of shared beliefs that constitute the core concepts and methods of family therapy.

The fundamental principles of family therapy are simple and elegant. People are products of their natural contexts, the most significant of which is the family; psychological disorders are therefore not individual problems, but family problems. Although these disorders seem to be handicaps they are actually part of the family's attempt to maintain a viable and cohesive structure. Families may be understood as systems, operating not as collections of individuals, but as emergent, whole entities. Understanding how family systems work is greatly enhanced by the concepts of circular causality, levels of communication, boundaries, and triangles.

Family therapy as a treatment method began when clinicians first brought families together for observation. Doing so forced a shift in focus from intrapsychic content to interpersonal process. Instead of trying to understand what is going on inside people, family therapists began to manipulate what goes on between them. Clarifying communication, and issuing tasks and directives were the first methods used to outwit resistance and to help families change. Even in the early days of family therapy, however, different practitioners developed alternate strategies and tactics of change.

Today, these differences are responsible for the development of several competing orientations, whose existence has inspired several attempts to classify the field. My own classification of the field into eight systems of family therapy is based upon concepts and methods rather than personalities. The eight systems—psychoanalytic, group, experiential, behavioral, extended family, communications, strategic, and structural—is a reasonably clear guide to the field, although it is often necessary to point out distinctions within schools as well as between them.

Family therapy is such a fast-developing field that it is difficult to describe the current scene; as soon as you begin, it changes. My picture of the family therapy establishment reflects the way it appears at the beginning of the 1980s. This establishment includes two major professional organizations, the AAMFT and the AFTA, and a number of leading institutions and training centers. Although there are too many high-quality training programs to list them all, I selected a sample of the oldest and best known programs in the country—the Ackerman Institute, Center for Family Learning, Family Institute of Westchester, Philadelphia Child Guidance Clinic, Georgetown Family Center, Family Therapy Institute of Washington, D.C., Family Institute of Chicago, Family Systems Program, Boston Family Institute, Family Institute of Cambridge, and the Mental Research Institute.

Family therapy's growth over the past twenty-five years has been truly remarkable. It gained a foothold when its techniques proved useful; but mass acceptance came not because its critics saw the light, but because the original opponents retired and a new generation of clinicians grew up who took family theory for granted. Now many of the axioms of family therapy are overexposed and underexamined. With an evangelical fervor, family therapists proclaim a new epistemology and tout the latest innovations in technique. The only trouble is, what if it doesn't work? The surest proof, empirical research, is just now becoming available. There are many studies that verify the overall effectiveness of family therapy, but too few that deal with specific questions about which methods work with which patients and in what circumstances.

Family therapy is a uniquely human enterprise, not wholly reducible to scientific measurement. But if it works, we should be able to demonstrate that it does; and if some methods are better than others that, too, should be studied. History is filled with examples of healing rituals whose success owed more to the enthusiasm of their proponents than to the effectiveness of their concepts and methods. Such panaceas, that were later debunked or found to have limited uses, are especially prevalent in mental health where hope and trust exert powerful and often unrecognized influences. Family therapy has now lasted too long to be a fad; but it is still a young discipline in need of continued experimentation and study.

REFERENCES

Alexander, I.E. Family therapy. *Marriage and Family Living*, 1963, *25*, 146–154.

Beels, C.C. & Ferber, A. Family therapy: A view. *Family Process*, 1969, *8*, 280–332.'

Benningfeld, A.B. Multiple family therapy systems. *Journal of Marriage and Family Counseling*, 1978, *4*, 25–34.

Bergin, A.E. The evaluation of therapeutic outcomes. In A.E. Bergin & S.L. Garfield (Eds.), *Handbook of psychotherapy and behavior change*. New York: Wiley, 1971.

Bloch, D.A. & Weiss, H.M. Training facilities in marital and family therapy. *Family Process*, 1981, *20*, 133–146.

Breunlin, D.C., Schwartz, R.C., Krause, M.S. & Selby, L.M. Evaluating family therapy training: The development of an instrument. *Journal of Marital and Family Therapy*, 1983, *9*, 37–47.

DeChenne, T.K. Experiential facilitation in conjoint marriage counseling. *Psychotherapy*, 1973, *10*, 212–214.

Foley, V.D. *An introduction to family therapy*. New York: Grune & Stratton, 1974.

Freeman, S.J.J., Leavene, E.J. & McCullock, D.J. Factors associated with success or failure in marital counseling. *Family Coordinator*, 1969, *18*, 125–128.

Graham, J.A. The effect of the use of counselor positive responses to positive perceptions of mate in marriage counseling. *Dissertation Abstracts International*, 1968, *28*, 3504A.

Griffin, R.W. Change in perception of marital relationship as related to marital counseling. *Dissertation Abstracts International,* 1967, *27,* 3956A.

Group for the Advancement of Psychiatry. *Treatment of families in conflict: The clinical study of family process.* New York: Jason Aronson, 1970.

Guerin, P.J. Family therapy: The first twenty-five years. In P.J. Guerin (Ed.), *Family therapy: Theory and practice.* New York: Gardner Press, 1976.

Gurman, A.S. Group marital therapy: Clinical and empirical implications for outcome research. *International Journal of Group Psychotherapy,* 1971,*21,* 174–189.

Gurman, A.S. Marital therapy: Emerging trends in research and practice. *Family Process,* 1973, *12,* 45–54.

Gurman, A.S. Some therapeutic implications of marital therapy research. In A.S. Gurman & D.G. Rice (Eds.), *Couples in conflict: New directions in marital therapy.* New York: Jason Aronson, 1975.

Gurman, A.S. Contemporary marital therapies: A critique and comparative analysis of psychoanalytic, behavioral and systems theory approaches. In T.J. Paolino & B.J. McCrady (Eds.), *Marriage and marital therapy.* New York: Brunner/ Mazel, 1978.

Gurman, A.S. & Kniskern, D.P. Research on marital and family therapy: Progress, perspective and prospect. In S. Garfield & A. Bergin (Eds.), *Handbook of psychotherapy and behavior change,* Second edition. New York: Wiley, 1978.

Haley, J. Whither family therapy? *Family Process,* 1962, *1,* 69–100.

Haley, J. Toward a theory of pathological systems. In P. Watzlawick & J. Weakland (Eds.), *The interactional view.* New York: Norton, 1977.

Hill, R. & Hansen, D.A. The identification of conceptual frameworks utilized in family study. *Marriage and Family Living,* 1980, *22,* 299–311.

Hoffman, L. *Foundations of family therapy.* New York: Basic Books, 1981.

Jacobson, N.S. Behavioral treatments for marital discord: A critical appraisal. In M. Hersen, R.M. Eisler & P.M. Miller (Eds.), *Progress in behavior modification,* Vol. 7. New York: Academic Press, 1979.

Jones, B.S. Functions of meaning-clarification by therapists in a psychotherapy group. *Dissertation Abstracts International,* 1969, *29,* 3706A.

Kuhn, T. *The structure of scientific revolutions.* Chicago: University of Chicago Press, 1962.

Langsley, D., Flomenhaft, K. & Machotka, P. Follow-up evaluation of family crisis therapy. *American Journal of Orthopsychiatry,* 1969, *39,* 753–759.

Langsley, D., Pittman, F. Machotka, P. & Flomenhaft, K. Family crisis therapy—results and implications. *Family Process,* 1968, *7,* 145–158.

Levant, R.F. A classification of the field of family therapy: A review of prior attempts and a new paradigmatic model. *The American Journal of Family Therapy,* 1980, *8,* 4–16.

Madanes, C. & Haley, J. Dimensions of family therapy. *Journal of Nervous and Mental Disease,* 1977, *165,* 88–98.

Minuchin, S. *Families and family therapy.* Cambridge, Mass.: Harvard University Press, 1964.

Minuchin, S., Baker, L., Rosman, B., Liebman, R., Milman, L. & Todd, T. A conceptual model of psychosomatic illness in children. *Archives of General Psychiatry,* 1975, *32,* 1031–1038.

Mitchell, C. Problems and principles in family therapy. In N.W. Ackerman (Ed.), *Expanding theory and practice in family therapy.* New York: Family Services Association of America, 1967.

Olson, D.H. Marital and family therapy: Integrative review and critique. *Journal of Marriage and the Family,* 1970, *32,* 501–538.

Paolino, T.J. & McCrady, B.J. (Eds.), *Marriage and marital therapy.* New York: Brunner/Mazel, 1978.

Parloff, M.B. The family in psychotherapy. *Archives of General Psychiatry,* 1961. *4,* 445–451.

Rabkin, R. *Inner and outer space.* New York: Norton, 1970.

Rittenhouse, J. Endurance of effect: Family unit treatment compared to identified patient treatment. *Proceedings, 78th Annual Convention of the American Psychological Association,* 1970, 535–536.

Ritterman, M.K. Paradigmatic classification of family therapy theories. *Family Process,* 1977, *16,* 29–148.

Roberts, R.V. The effects on marital satisfaction of brief training in behavioral exchange negotiation mediated by differentially experienced trainers. *Dissertation Abstracts International,* 1975, *36,* 457B.

Rosman, B.L., Minuchin, S., Liebman, R. & Baker, L. Input and outcome of family therapy in anorexia nervosa. In J.L. Claghorn (Ed.), *Successful psychotherapy.* New York: Brunner/Mazel, 1976.

Schrieber, L. Evaluation of family group treatment in a family agency. *Family Process,* 1966, *5,* 21–29.

Shapiro, R. Therapist attitudes and premature termination in family and individual therapy. *Journal of Nervous and Mental Disease,* 1974, *159,* 101–107.

Shapiro, R. & Budman, S. Defection, termination, and continuation in family and individual therapy. *Family Process,* 1973, *12,* 55–67.

Shellow, R., Brown, B. & Osberg, J. Family group therapy in retrospect: Four years and sixty families. *Family Process,* 1963, *2,* 52–67.

Sluzki, C. Interview on the state of the art. *Family Therapy Networker,* 1983, *7,* (1), 24.

Stanton, M.D. & Todd, T.C. Structural family therapy with drug addicts. In E. Kaufman & P. Kaufmann (Eds.), *The family therapy of drug and alcohol abuse.* New York: Gardner Press, 1979.

Steidl, J.H. & Wexler, J.P. What's a clinician to do with so many approaches to family therapy? *The Family,* 1977, *4,* 59–66.

Strelnick, A.H. Multiple family group therapy: A review of the literature. *Family Process,* 1977, *16,* 307–326.

Watzlawick, P., Beavin, J. & Jackson, D.D. *Pragmatics of human communication.* New York: Norton, 1967.

Waxenberg, B.R. Therapists' empathy, regard and genuineness as factors in staying or dropping out of short-term, time-limited family therapy. *Dissertation Abstracts International,* 1973, *34,* 1288B.

Wellisch, D. Vincent, J., & Ro-trock, G. Family therapy versus individual therapy: A study of adolescents and their parents. In D.H. Olson (Ed.), *Treating relationships*. Lake Mills, Iowa: Graphic Press, 1976.

Wells, R.A. & Dezen, A.E. The results of family therapy revisited: The nonbehavioral methods. *Family Process*, 1978, *17*, 251–274.

Wells, R.A., Dilkes, T. & Trivelli, N. The results of family therapy: A critical review of the literature. *Family Process*, 1972, *7*, 189–207.

Zuk, G.H. Family therapy: 1964–1970. *Psychotherapy: Theory, Research and Practice*, 1971, *8*, 90–97.

3

The Theoretical Context of Family Therapy

INTRODUCTION

heories are necessary to explain how unwanted behavior develops, and how it can be changed. In the field of family therapy practice has outrun theory, with the result that underlying theoretical assumptions about behavior and change are often implicit and unstated. The problem with unstated assumptions is that they are not easily examined, questioned, or challenged. Only when theoretical assumptions are explicit can they be discussed, tested, and refined.

Theories are not arid abstractions divorced from practice, or a collection of heuristic but unrelated clinical hypotheses. They have an important— perhaps essential—practical utility. In family therapy, they serve as a basis for conceptual understanding of family systems and how they operate. This use of theory as an organizing framework to explain total family functioning is very practical, for it provides therapists with strategies for treatment. And although some therapists eschew theory altogether, claiming that good therapy is intuitive, and the effective therapist need only "be a real self" (Whitaker, 1976), many others find a well-defined theoretical approach a guide for deliberate and decisive action.

The family therapy movement is based on more than the discovery of a new method and an enlarged social unit of treatment. It is a product of a new epistemology, a new way of thinking about the nature of mind and about the determinants of behavior (Hoffman, 1981).

Most family therapists are clinicians, relatively uninvolved with family theories, which have been largely the province of sociologists. When clinicians have talked theory, they have usually described or rationalized, posthoc, their therapeutic methods. This state of affairs is changing somewhat, but even now anyone interested in studying family theory will have to go to the literature of sociology.

Hill (1966) was among those who documented the inadequacies of family theory in the sixties. He recommended that clinical training programs include systematic training in theory construction and also that students be taught several of the current conceptual frameworks, instead of being indoctrinated in only one model. He also believed that students should be encouraged to build new taxonomies and improve existing ones; be trained in codification to help them reduce theoretical overlap and duplication; and be stimulated to construct theoretical schemas and models from which hypotheses could be derived. Such training would help to assure the relevance of research and clinical observations.

Among the most influential theoretical analyses of family functioning are those of Talcott Parsons and his colleagues. An excellent introduction to some of these ideas can be found in *Family Socialization and Interaction Processes* (Parsons and Bales, 1955). Parsons believed that there is constancy in structure and function in families, although they may evolve somewhat in relation to the rest of society. For example, families are becoming somewhat more specialized as the traditional functions of the extended kinship group are taken over by other social agencies such as schools, churches, businesses and government.

Nonetheless, the nuclear family retains almost exclusive control over certain vital areas, primarily the socialization and stabilization of personality. According to Parsons the latter is dependent upon the former. Personality develops not primarily by modification of instincts, but by differentiation of internalized object systems (compare Freud's superego, and George Herbert Mead's idea of taking the role of the other); personality may thus be considered a kind of mirror image of the social structures the child experiences, many of which are located in the nuclear family.

Parsons and Bales (1955) described the growing specialization and isolation of the nuclear family. Middle class families are likely to own their own homes, be financially independent, and live away from their families of origin. Economic forces are a significant determinant of this shift. Primary incomes are now derived from occupational earnings, rather than from sharing in parents' wealth, business, or farm; as people move to where they can find work, families become progressively more scattered. This of course has some negative consequences. The marital pair, deprived of the support of their kin, must depend ever more on each other. Marriage is thus more important and more burdened. Similarly, as parents, the couple is unsupported by grandparents, aunts, and uncles, and the parenting becomes similarly strained.

In the nuclear family, children are exposed to four main role types. The first two, based on generation, are biologically determined. The second two, sex roles, are more sociological and traditional. The female role is *expressive*, the male *instrumental*. The expressive role involves emotional support, management of tensions, and care and support of the children. The instrumental role involves managerial decisions, solution of group tasks, and discipline of the children. This polarity has been criticized on empirical and logical grounds, and recently on philosophical and moral grounds as well. Although it is a sexist dichotomy, it does accurately describe traditional roles in marriage.

Parsons also delineated four functional requirements of the family as a social system. These are: adaptivity, goal gratification, integration, and pattern maintenance. The nuclear family, according to Parsons' (Parsons and Bales, 1955) analysis, is a small group that shares the characteristics found in all small groups of similar size, but with significant differences. Like other small groups, the family is differentiated along two axes—relative power and the instrumental-expressive axis. The fact that this pattern characterizes families in a wide variety of different cultures suggests that it is not fortuitous, but functional.

One point of Parsons' sociological analysis is particularly important for family clinicians to remember: as a socializing unit, the family is never independent, but is a subsystem imbedded in the larger society. Children are not socialized by their families alone, but by other social institutions as well—not the least of which is television.

At the beginning of the 1960s there were five major theoretical approaches to family study: developmental, structural-functional, symbolic, interactional, and situational (Broderick, 1971). Parsons, for example, integrated interaction theory with structural–functional theory, and added a developmental dimension by integrating Freudian psychosexual development into his model of the family.

By the end of the sixties only three of the five theories remained viable: the interactional, developmental, and structural-functional. To these were added balance theory (Heider; Newcomb); exchange theory (Thibaut and Kelley; Homans); and most importantly, general systems theory (von Bertalanffy).

Those who pioneered the study and treatment of schizophrenic families may have known little sociology, yet they found themselves dealing with the structure and function of groups. They invented a sociology of family interaction without reference to established sociological theories. Their concepts grew out of observing the interactions of whole families in contrast to the sociological method of interviewing single family members.

In the early days of family therapy, clinicians were concerned with defending patients against the influence of their families. Schizophrenic patients were seen as victims of double-binding parents and schizophreno-genic mothers. Further observation led to a profound shift away from this conception of patients versus parents. It soon became clear that all the members of the family were victims, and that the whole family needed to be changed. The family was no longer seen as an aggregate of individuals, but as a system. Here we come to one of the central, but most easily misunderstood ideas in family therapy. Traditional concepts of individual psychology were inadequate; some form of a theory of systems was necessary. This much is known by virtually all students of family therapy, and most of them can give a reasonable definition of a system. However, there is an enormous difference between having an academic understanding of systems and actually reorganizing your thinking so that you *experience* families as systems. It is extremely difficult to transcend the habit of seeing people as independent individuals. Nor will simply studying this section on systems theory reorganize your way of thinking. That requires practice and experience. The discussion that follows will serve as an introduction and a first step to adopting a systems perspective. But thinking in terms of systems requires a profound shift in our approach to human relations, and it will take a great deal of concentrated effort to actually learn to *see* systems.

GENERAL SYSTEMS THEORY
AND CIRCULAR CAUSALITY

During the first half of the twentieth century psychology was dominated by mechanistic reductionist theories of the stimulus-response variety. Behavior was considered to be shaped by outside forces, which for behaviorists, were classical and operant conditionings, and for psychoanalysts, were early childhood experiences.

The advent of family therapy revealed the inadequacies of these models of behavior. Imposing concepts about individuals on families simply did not work. Those who treated families as nothing more than the sum of their individual members soon discovered that they were missing something. Nor was it enough to think in terms of separate individuals influenced by their interactions. The shift from individual to systems thinking is discontinuous, and requires the introduction of new theoretical models.

Family therapists also began to examine basic assumptions about causality. Initially, troubled families were treated as a collection of disturbed individuals. Later, it became clear that families are mutually causative systems, whose complementary behavior reinforces and perpetuates the nature of their interactions. Two major theoretical shifts were instrumental in the new, family oriented approach to behavior: one shift from mechanical to systems theory, and another from linear to circular causality.

The terms *systems* and *systems theory* are often used so vaguely and ambiguously as to dull their usefulness as explanatory concepts. Sometimes *systems theory* is used to refer to a particular school of family therapy (Bowen, 1966); at other times it is used to mean simply thinking about families rather than individuals. But not all thinking about families is guided by systems theory. In fact, many people continue to treat families as collections of individuals.

A system is a complex of interacting elements and the relationships which organize them. Or, as Gregory Bateson (1971) defined it, a system is a unit with a feedback structure and therefore capable of processing information. Families can be described as systems, as can environments and societies;

even individuals can be described as systems (Schafer, 1976).

The two most well-known variants of systems theory are cybernetics and general systems theory. Although the two are often equated, they are not the same. General systems theory is the broader of the two concepts, referring to all self-regulating systems, of which the cybernetic or feedback model is one type.

Cybernetics is a term coined by Norbert Weiner (1948) to describe systems which regulate themselves by means of feedback loops. The basic elements in a cybernetic system are a receptor, a center and effector, and a feedback loop. Stimuli (or information) are received by the receptor and transmitted to the center, which reacts to the message and amplifies its signal. The message is then carried to the effector which reacts by discharging an output. The output is monitored by a feedback loop to the receptor, which enables it to modify subsequent responses.

The concept of self-regulating, cybernetic systems is applicable to thermostatically controlled heaters, guided missiles, and many biological functions which subserve physiological homeostasis, such as the Krebs cycle, the maintenance of blood sugar levels, and physiological thermo-regulation.

Cybernetics is closely associated with communications theory and information theory; cybernetics emphasizes the control mechanisms, while the other two emphasize the messages.

The cybernetic model is important to family theorists, because it introduces the idea of circular causality by way of the feedback loop. In linear causality, event A causes event B. This is the familiar model of independent and dependent variables, and stimulus-response behaviorism. From the perspective of circular causality any delineation of before and after, or cause and effect, is purely arbitrary. Instead, behavior is seen as a series of moves and countermoves in a repeating cycle. A husband may be convinced that his wife's nagging (cause) makes him withdraw (effect). She is equally likely to believe that his withdrawal causes her to nag. A systems theorist would instead see their behavior as part of a circular pattern: the more she nags the more he withdraws, *and* the more he withdraws, the more she nags. Who started the sequence is not considered relevant for resolving it, because once underway these sequences seem to be self-perpetuating.

The participants in such a sequence are trapped in the epistemology of the linear model. Each thinks, "If only I try harder (more nagging, or more withdrawal) I can make the other one change." But change rarely occurs, because instead of changing the dysfunctional pattern, they simply act it out more forcefully. Even when blaming ("Her nagging makes me withdraw") is replaced by confessions of guilt ("Maybe my withdrawal makes her nag") the illusion of linear causality is maintained.

Family therapists tend to think linearly and overemphasize homeostasis, thus positing a dualism between one part of the system and another. Inadvertently, most fall back upon a mechanical model of a closed feedback system. Perhaps pathological families, because they are stuck at points of transition, seem to fit a homeostatic model. Therapy, however, should be based on a more fluid model; it should help them get unstuck and move to a different level of adjustment.

A major difference between cybernetics and general systems theory is that cybernetics is a more mechanistic model. According to Weiner (1954) the basic principles governing self-regulating machines are found in human behavior as well. Goal-seeking machines, like household furnaces or guided missiles, require a means of control and communication to achieve their tasks. The same is true of human beings. As with self-regulating machines, Weiner (1954) believed that the adequacy of a person's adjustment depends upon the adequacy of the information coming to the person.

Von Bertalanffy, who developed general systems theory, argued that the cybernetic model is too mechanistic. People are not like machines, he maintained, but are active and creative, exerting control over their surroundings not only in their motor output, but also in perceptual selection and cognitive structuring of their sensory input. While the cybernetic model is useful, it probably does not explain certain unique activities of living creatures, including play and creativity. Therefore, von Bertalanffy believed that a new systems model was needed for the life sciences, because the functioning of whole systems could not be deduced from an analysis of their separate parts. Systems theory was developed to go beyond mechanistic physics to include the interfunctioning of parts that make up whole systems, and beyond static concepts to take account of the temporal quality of life and the omnipresence of change.

Two concepts were precursors of general systems theory—organismic biology and open systems. Von Bertalanffy believed that living organisms are organized wholes, not just the sum of their separate parts. Organismic biology focused not on the isolated parts of processes, but on the organizing relationships themselves. Notions of organization, absent in conventional physics, were emphasized, including wholeness, growth, and differentiation (Gray and Rizzo, 1969).

Von Bertalanffy (1967) also believed that living organisms were essentially open systems, maintaining themselves with continuous inputs from, and outputs to, the environment. He emphasized living systems as wholes, in contrast to previous analytic and summative approaches; he substituted a dynamic conception of life for previous static and machine analogies; and he attributed primary activity to living organisms, rather than primary reactivity.

A system is closed if there is no influx of energy and therefore no change in the system's components. Organic systems are open—they exchange materials, energies, or information with the environment. An example of a closed system would be a chemical reaction taking place in a sealed container. Although the closed systems model may be applied to families, it is often inadequate. A teenaged boy's depression for instance, may be understood as a function of his family, viewed as a closed system. Perhaps his depression results from an over-involvement with his mother, which in turn is related to the mother's emotional distance from the father. However, if we take into account the family's environment, we may wonder if the son's depression and his over-involvement with his mother could be related to a lack of friends, and no extracurricular activities at school. Likewise, the father's emotional distance from his wife may be related to his preoccupation with his career. No single event in this view is said to *cause* the others; they are all said to be interrelated; and indeed family therapy is less concerned with the way pathological sequences originate than it is with how to change them.

Among the properties of open systems are *wholeness, feedback,* and *equifinality* (Watzlawick, Beavin, and Jackson, 1967). Because systems behave as wholes, change in any one part will cause change in the entire system. Applied to families, this means that a family is not simply a collection of individuals, but a coherent composite that behaves as an irreducible unit. The behavior of every individual in the family is related to and dependent upon the behavior of all the others. Thus it is not surprising that improvement in one family member will cause repercussions—positive and negative— in the others.

Open systems are regulated by feedback. Inputs from family members or from the environment are acted upon and modified by the family system. In addition to the input, the therapist must consider the nature of the system and its feedback mechanisms, if he or she is to understand how to help the family change. Feedback can be either positive or negative. Negative feedback characterizes homeostasis, and plays an important role in maintaining the stability of relationships. Negative feedback means that when information comes into the system, it is counteracted in a way that maintains stability. It is called *negative* because it operates to reduce any tendency toward deviation. A common example of negative feedback is the tendency of many families to label any steps toward maturity and independence as "mad" or "bad" (Watzlawick, *et al.,* 1967).

Positive feedback, on the other hand, leads to change. Information received by the system is used to amplify the output deviation, and this acts as a positive influence on the trend toward change. Negative feedback maintains stability; positive feedback leads to change. All families that stay together must use some degree of negative feedback in order to maintain their equilibrium in the face of developmental and environmental stresses. However, for learning and growth to occur, families must also incorporate positive feedback.

Equifinality means that the same result may be reached from different beginnings (von Bertalanffy, 1968). In open systems, different initial conditions may yield the same final result, and different results may be produced from the same "causes." This principle implies that in order to understand families it is more important to consider the ongoing organization of their interactions than either the genesis or the product of these interactions.

Systems theory helps to generalize principles discovered in one field to applications in other fields. For example, certain kinetic principles may apply to such different entities as chemical systems, human populations, and economic processes (von Bertalanffy, 1967). Von Bertalanffy generalized the biological principles of open, self-regulating systems to explain, by analogy, personality, group relations, and social systems. He pointed out that humanity in the mass does not consist of an aggregation of isolated individuals; it is instead organized in systems of various orders, from small groups, such as families, to the largest group, civilization. This being the case, he argued, psychiatric practice should not be confined to the level of the individual.

Systems theory has revolutionized the way family therapists think about families, and made possible a number of powerful new methods of treatment. At times it has produced an adversarial attitude between advocates of individual therapy and family therapy. This is unfortunate and unnecessary.

Traditional models need not be discarded in favor of systems theory. We can retain psychoanalytic insights into motivation and personality, and learn also to examine systems interactions and the social context. These models are not inherently contradictory. Each is separately useful as far as it goes, but neither is the whole truth or the only way to understand behavior. Even among those family therapists most committed to systems thinking there is still room for appreciation of the anxiety, anguish, and loneliness of individuals. Clinicians need not be limited either to an individual or to a systems viewpoint, but can use both—just as a photographer may use telescopic as well as wide-angle lenses.

INDIVIDUAL DEVELOPMENT AND FAMILY LIFE CYCLE

Psychological problems develop when people are faced with more stress than they can tolerate. Some of us can cope with more stress than others, but everyone is vulnerable at some point. Whether or not someone develops symptoms of disturbance depends upon the strength of his or her personal resources and the degree of stress. The most obvious stressors are external events, such as the breakup of a love affair, the death of a friend, or the loss of a job. Equally important, though not always equally apparent, are stresses which arise at transitions from one phase of development to another. As Minuchin (1974) and Haley (1976) have observed, families are most likely to encounter difficulties in the transition between one developmental stage and another.

Most of what has been written about developmental stages concerns the development of individuals. So deep rooted is the individual orientation to psychology that even when talking about family development, most people think in terms of collections of individuals. Child development continues to be among the most intensely studied aspects of human behavior. Recently, however, development in the adult years has begun to receive increased attention. The fact that Gail Sheehy's *Passages: Predictable Crises of Adult Life* (1976) was a nationwide bestseller attests to the growing interest in the life cycle of adults.

Families as well as individuals have life cycles. Everyone is familiar with the milestones of the nuclear family's life cycle: courtship, marriage, birth, child rearing, old age, and death. But because of the ingrained habit of thinking of families as nothing but collections of individuals, most people imagine family life cycles as simply the concurrent development of a group of individuals. Although families are comprised of individuals, they are also social systems with unique operating principles. Therefore this section will include a section on the family life cycle, as well as summaries of child and adult development.

Child Development. In the half-century since child psychology became an established discipline, psychologists have studied the physical, emotional, social, and cognitive attributes of the growing child. Their work has produced a vast literature, both popular and scholarly, and their findings have been adduced to support varying theories of human behavior, from psychoanalytic to behavioral. At various times students of child development have been particularly concerned with one or another aspect of the child's makeup. Among the best known and influential observations are the developmental sequences of the child's motor behavior described by Gesell, of emotional behavior described by Freud, of social behavior described by Erikson, and of cognitive behavior described by Piaget.

Born relatively tiny and helpless, infants grow and develop rapidly. In six to twelve months they triple their weight (Duvall, 1977), and they begin immediately to use the abilities they were born with, including crying, sucking, burping, and waving their arms and legs. Movements, which at first are crude and haphazard, soon become more refined and goal-directed.

The normative sequences of motor development were identified and described by Arnold Gesell (1929) and his colleagues at Yale. Gross motor development normally proceeds in an orderly sequence which begins with postural control, followed by voluntary locomotion. By six months most children can lift and hold their heads up (Shirley, 1931). Some children are able to sit unsupported by as early as five months; by twelve months 90 percent of infants are able to do so. Crawling comes next (36–40 weeks), followed by standing (40 weeks) and finally walking (12–15 months; Gesell, 1929).

Fine motor movement and learning also develop rapidly. The newborn sucks everything possible, looks around, and craves stimulation during most of the waking hours. By the end of the first year little children have learned to work hard for what they want, to initiate activities, play games, and enjoy socializing. Infants and their parents interact first to satisfy basic needs and later for the pure joy of each other's company. As mother and father express their love by cuddling and fondling; the baby learns to respond by cooing and smiling.

By the second year the child is walking and talking and begins to get into everything. Two-year-olds are already adept at problem-solving, and at remembering and finding things. The baby's first words are eagerly anticipated; later they are regarded as incessant chattering.

During recent years the process of language development has attracted considerable interest from various schools of psychology. Psychologists agree that language acquisition depends upon an interaction between biological and cultural factors. But there is lively debate as to the relative importance of each.

Learning theorists argue that language is learned by gradual imitation and social reinforcement, whereas developmental psychologists maintain that imitation cannot account for the speed and complexity of verbal development. Lenneberg (1967) believes that a child must first abstract the language, after which it becomes aware of the relationship among various types of words. Once equipped with these semantic principles, the child is thought to be able to generate his or her own language.

Among the best known advocates of the developmental approach to psycholinguistics is Noam Chomsky (1957), who maintains that knowledge of language results from the interplay of genetically-determined structures of the mind, maturational processes, and interaction with the environment. According to Chomsky, children learn the rules of language and then are able to express their intended meaning through spoken words.

The child's rapid motor development is easily observed and has been long studied; but the emotional significance of early childhood was underestimated prior to Freud's monumental discoveries. Sigmund Freud (1856–1939), who authored the best known theory of the stages of normal childhood development, did not study either normal development or children. Instead, he derived his conclusions from clinical studies of neurotic adults whom he believed to have suffered developmental conflicts in childhood. His observations led him to speculate about the usual course of child development. Although many of Freud's conclusions are now widely accepted, they were startling and controversial in the late nineteenth and early twentieth century, because he postulated the existence of hidden and irrational motivational forces and so challenged our view of ourselves as a basically rational and logical beings.

Two concepts, *psychic determinism* and the *unconscious*, are the cornerstones of psychoanalytic theory (Brenner, 1955). The first term refers to Freud's belief that all behavior is meaningfully determined; the second to a reservoir of memories and impulses of which people are usually unaware. Not reason or altruism, but basic animal drives are the root cause of human behavior.

People may think—consciously—that they are motivated by lofty principles; but Freud taught us that much of what we do is motivated by hidden, irrational, instinctual forces—primarily sexuality, and secondarily aggression. Because these impulses conflict with social requirements, individuals mask (repress) their basic impulses and seek indirect forms of gratification. Conflict is the basic and inevitable characteristic of psychological life, and all mental phenomena are the result of an interplay between physical drives and the restraining influence of the environment.

Freud expanded and modified his theories over half a century, and even the briefest summary of his theory of personality has to mention several different aspects of psychic functioning. These various ways of explaining the psychology of the person are the *topographic, dynamic, economic, structural,* and *genetic* models of the mind.

The *topographic model* divides the mind into three levels, according to their accessibility to awareness: *conscious, preconscious,* and *unconscious*. *Conscious* refers to the mental contents of which we are presently aware; *preconscious* to that which can easily be recalled; and *unconscious* to those wishes, memories, and impulses which cannot ordinarily be recognized. If we avoid the temptation to reify the unconscious into an actual physical structure, it is a very useful explanatory concept.

The *dynamic model* postulates that all behavior results from the (dynamic) interaction among various agencies of the mind and between instinctual impulses and environmental counterforces. Thus the psyche is always in tension; drives are seeking discharge to attain pleasure, and inhibitory tendencies delay the direct expression of drives in order to avoid pain.

According to Freud's *economic model,* people have a fixed quantity of psychic energy, derived from drives and existing in a closed, intrapsychic system. This energy is divided among various components of the mind. When it is bound up in unconscious conflicts, we feel fatigue and apathy.

Freud's *structural* and *genetic models* are the most familiar, and the most easily related to child development. The structural model divides the mind into an *id, ego,* and *superego*. Like the conscious and unconscious aspects of the mind, these three agencies should be understood not as "things" which actually exist somewhere in the brain, but as metaphors for describing processes of mental functioning. The id contains the congeries of basic drives which seek immediate discharge according to the pleasure principle. The simple act of sneezing exemplifies id functioning: tension is felt and immediately reduced through reflexlike discharge. This type of functioning is not sufficient to serve the needs of the infant, because he or she is not able to satisfy his or her own desires and parents do not always provide immediate or complete surcease from tension. Temporary frustration is inevitable, and in turn stimulates growth in the complexity of psychic functioning.

The frustrating aspects of reality bring about psychological processes, called ego functioning, which devise ways to secure pleasures that are not immediately or automatically available. Thus, delay of gratification is the precursor to thinking and planning. Once developed, the ego co-determines all behavior by mediating the demands of id, environment, and the third psychic structure, the superego.

The superego is the repository of internalized social values, taught by the parents and other authority figures. The infant's long dependence on parents invests their prohibitions with the strong force of imperative. At first children learn to be "good" to avoid being punished. Later, through identifying with their parents, they are "good" because it feels right. Uncritical acceptance of received parental values occurs early in life, and these values are subsequently relatively inaccessible to critical re-evaluation.

The *genetic* aspect of psychoanalytic theory emphasizes the prepotent effects of early experience on later behavior. Freud believed that behavior can only be understood in terms of early environmental influences on innate biological impulses. Primary among these is the sexual drive. Freud contended that the sexual instinct, broadly interpreted, is active in children from birth onward. At first sexual energy, or *libido,* is diffuse and unfocused; only gradually does it become attached to specific aims and objects in a series of psychosexual stages.

The first pleasurable activity of newborns is feeding. Accordingly, during the first stage of psychosexual development, the *oral stage* (0–2 years), the infant is preoccupied with the pleasures of sucking and eating. Noting that infants and even older children happily suck their thumbs or pacifiers even in the absence of nourishment, Freud postulated that sucking is innately pleasurable and that this pleasure is sexual in nature.

Infants are profoundly helpless during this stage of life, and so the *oral stage* is characterized by dependency and acquisitiveness. Too much frustration or gratification during this, or any other stage, may lead to *fixation.* Thus the infant who was not given adequate opportunity to experience the passive pleasures of sucking may be fixated at the oral stage, and later, especially at times of stress, regress to a passive, dependent mode of behavior.

The *anal stage* follows the oral, and lasts from approximately 2 to 3 years of age. During this time the child is faced with the first social obligation, toilet training. The child must regulate his or her own impulses and desires in order to please the parents. Usually the child undertakes this responsibility willingly and derives great pleasure in pleasing the parents by learning to control bowel habits.

Ideally, parents will be patient and understanding, not too strict and demanding. Anxious parents, however, may be too harsh with children who have little accidents. This harshness may lead to fixation at the anal stage, with conflicts over expulsion and retention; a person who is fixated at this point, is characterized by orderliness, parsimony, and obstinancy.

Most children master the task of toilet training by about age 3, and then proceed to the *phallic stage*. As they discover the intensely pleasureable sensation they get from touching their genitals in infantile masturbation, the genitals replace the anal zone as the primary locus of sexual pleasure. This is the beginning of the phallic stage which lasts from about 3 to 5 years of age.

With this growing awareness of his or her own sex, the child now experiences an upsurge of sexual feelings toward the parent of the opposite sex. Freud called the boy's wish to possess his mother and displace his rival father, and the girl's desire for her father and jealousy of her mother, the *oedipus complex*. It soon becomes obvious that these wishes are unrealistic and the child learns to repress them, and replace them with identification with the same sex parent. The child thus tries to become a person who will some day be able to possess someone of the opposite sex.

After the oedipal conflict is resolved the child enters *latency,* a period of relative quiescence of sexual feelings which lasts until puberty. While the sexual feelings are relatively dormant, the latency-age child begins to focus more outside the family, at school, and with friends.

With puberty begins the *genital stage,* during which reawakened sexual feelings are focused on peers instead of parents. In their early teens most children relate primarily to members of their own sex; but by the late teens most have started dating, which lays the groundwork for lasting relation-ships and mature sexuality.

After Freud's epochal discoveries, his followers explored other aspects of psychic life, notably *ego functioning* and *social behavior.* Ego analysts, such as Hartmann and Rapaport, argued that the ego does not derive from the id as a result of conflict with the environment. Instead they believed that the ego was autonomous and relatively conflict-free. Their investigations produced a rich body of knowledge of our rational capabilities, which helped round out Freud's illumination of the irrational.

Other analytic thinkers filled the gaps in understanding of social life left by Freud's emphasis on the biological side of human behavior. Among the most notable of these was Erik Erikson (1950) who developed one of the most complete and influential theories of the stages of social development. Erikson distinguished eight stages in the life cycle, from birth to maturity. Each stage is a product of the interaction between the individual and society. Only the five stages of childhood will be outlined here.

The first stage is a period of total dependency, during which the child who is well cared for develops self-acceptance and *basic trust*. The child who is mistreated emerges from this stage with a feeling that the environment is essentially malevolent.

During the second and third years, a child whose parents encourage independent strivings will develop a sense of *autonomy*. If, on the other hand, the parents suppress the child's independence, he or she will feel shame and doubt, which may lead to withdrawal and apathy.

Given parental affection and support, the child between three and six begins to take *initiative* to develop new roles in the family; he or she delights in experimentation and creativity. If, however, family control is too harsh the child experiences a profound sense of guilt, which inhibits the desire for independence and initiative.

The latency-age child (about age 6) is particularly interested in learning. With some degree of success in school the child acquires a sense of *industry* and competence. But if the child is crippled by anxieties or is too harshly criticized, he or she is deprived of confidence and begins to feel inferior.

The biological and social changes that occur during puberty cause discontinuity and bewilderment among adolescents. Earlier doubts and conflicts re-emerge, and are added to new ones created by rapid changes. Adolescents question everything, including themselves. Outward defiance and rebelliousness are common, but the need for belonging may result in blind adherence to peer-group values. The central problems of this stage are acceptance of self, achievement of successful interpersonal relationships, and preparation for a career. A favorable outcome involves a resolution of the *identity crisis* and a new level of integration and continuity. Failure to resolve the identity crisis leads to diffusion and confusion of social and sexual roles, with maladaptive patterns of behavior including delinquency and promiscuity.

Another extremely significant approach to the child's development is the *cognitive theory* of Jean Piaget and his followers. Using his own three babies as subjects, he studied the logic of their actions and their slow construction of fundamental categories for understanding the world: object, space, time, and activity. With older children he concentrated on their long struggle to comprehend the way objects endure: that objects continue to exist even when out of sight, and that matter retains its mass even when its shape is transformed.

According to Piaget (1954), intelligence is neither a matter of gradual conditioning, as behaviorists maintain, nor the result of innate mechanisms that unfold with age. Rather, intelligence is a product of the child's active adaptation to the external world. It originates in the biological substrate and evolves through successive stages as a product of the interaction between the functional characteristics of the child and the properties of the environment. Children can only utilize experiences which their cognitive capacities are able to handle. They reach out to assimilate new experience within the limits of their capacity, and then accommodate by reorganizing and expanding those capacities. Piaget's three periods of cognitive development are: the *sensorimotor stage* (0–2 years); the *stage of concrete operations* (2–11 years); and the *stage of formal operations* (11–15 years).

In the first stage, sensorimotor activity provides the raw material from which cognition is generated. The infant's actions and their results are internalized, forming mental images which give rise to conceptual thinking. The infant's first tools for dealing with the environment are a set of motor and sensory reflexes. With these the child first experiences then manipulates the environment. Passive hearing and seeing give way to active listening and looking; passive motor reflexes are followed by active manipulation and locomotion. By the end of the sensorimotor stage, the child has learned about the existence and permanence of objects, and makes a distinction between himself or herself and the external world.

Piaget divided the second period of cognitive development into two parts: the *preoperational period* (2–7 years); and the *period of concrete operations* (7–11 years). The major task of the preoperational period is to internalize the sensory and motor impressions that constitute the beginnings of representational experience. The child begins by thinking only in terms of specific actions, but gradually begins to engage in symbolic thinking which includes, but is not limited, to language.

In the first stage, sensorimotor images were the source of all cognitive activity. In the second stage, imitation and play are the vehicles for symbolic thinking. Accommodation and assimilation each govern different aspects of learning (Piaget, 1963). Children demonstrate accommodation by imitating certain sequences of their parents' behavior. Their play is a product of assimilation, for in play they are not bound by the intrinsic properties of objects. Instead, they incorporate objects into their games as their imagination dictates. A broom can be a horse, and two chairs can serve as a train. During this period the child's thinking is egocentric, concrete, and action-oriented.

The subperiod of *concrete operations* occurs from about the seventh to the eleventh year of life. The child begins to coordinate concrete schemata into more complex and abstract concepts. Thinking becomes logical and less tied to immediate perception. Thinking is also no longer predominantly egocentric, which has a pronounced impact on social behavior. No longer limited to his or her own point of view, the child is now capable of genuinely reciprocal relationships. Mutual respect develops where once there was no awareness of the needs of others. Language continues to be an important tool for conceptualization, and children actively communicate to check out and refine their view of reality.

The stage of *formal operations* (from about 11 to 15 years) is when the most advanced types of concepts are developed. At this time hypothetical-deductive reasoning becomes possible. The adolescent's intellectual functioning is no longer determined by objects, actions, and physical relationships, but allows for potential realities, relationships among abstract concepts, and the implications of various assumptions.

The adolescent's more abstract conceptualizing enables him or her to generalize from one set of solutions to another. Therefore, he or she can rise above concrete reality and conceive of possibilities never experienced, and plan for future occupations of which he or she has no firsthand knowledge. So powerful is this formal thinking that adolescents develop a new kind of egocentricism. They come to believe that their own ideas are unique and superior. They challenge received values, and become interested in the purpose and meaning of life.

Child development continues to be an area of intense research interest; among the best known of recent investigators are T. Berry Brazelton and Jerome Kagan.

Brazelton is one of a growing number of pediatricians (including LaBoyer) who advise treating newborns with more comfort and stimulation in order to enhance their subsequent emotional and intellectual development. Brazelton and his colleagues have demonstrated that teaching new parents about the many and complex things their infants can do increases the parents' responsiveness and interaction. Parents who are aware of their infants' abilities play more with them, and this leads to significantly higher scores on measures of psychological and motor development at one year.

Jerome Kagan's studies have led him to conclude that physiological maturation plays a major role in cognitive growth, which usually unfolds in a well-ordered sequence. These ideas are based on his work at Harvard's child development laboratory, and they are supported by observations that in children of all cultures many abilities emerge at about the same age. Kagan's studies have made it clear that behavioral advances depend, at least in part, on correlated changes in the brain.

Adult Development. The majority of family therapists work in clinics for children, and most families present problems focused on children. Therefore, family therapists tend to be more familiar with the stages of child development than with those of adulthood. If a family is having problems, clinicians are liable to think first about developmental stresses of the children, such as the birth of a sibling, entering school, or adolescence. It may be equally useful to think about the developmental stresses of the parents. When children are entering school, their parents may be struggling with problems of self-definition; and as children are entering adolescence, their parents may be experiencing their own midlife crises.

Although students of human development still concentrate on child-hood more than any other period, there has been a recent upsurge of interest in the problems of adulthood. Gail Sheehy's book, *Passages,* was a best seller for many weeks, and Hollywood has recently turned out a spate of movies dealing with middle adulthood: *Kramer vs. Kramer, Middle Age Crazy, Ordinary People.* A more scholarly account of adult development has been published by Daniel Levinson called *The Seasons of a Man's Life.* (Levinson, 1978).

Levinson's book, based on extensive interviews of 40 men, is a description and analysis of typical patterns of adult development with an emphasis on early and middle adulthood. Levinson chose not to include women in his sample, sacrificing breadth for depth. Levinson divided adulthood into early, middle, and late periods and describes the transition points between these stages as the crucial turning points in the life cycle. During these transitions, men modify their previous life structures and develop new ones appropriate to the subsequent stage of maturity. The transition points are sources of renewal—or stagnation—that shape subsequent periods.

Entry into a new period often reactivates unresolved problems and con-flicts of previous periods. Therefore, when a family comes for treatment, therapists should first explore current situational crises. Once these are under-stood, or their absence verified, therapists should explore possible current developmental problems. Finally, therapists should look for continuing problems from earlier developmental stages to see if unresolved tasks are hampering adjustment to the current situation.

Table 3–1 depicts the stages of adult development as described by Levinson. Naturally, stages of maturity are not set chronologically, but vary from person to person (Lidz, 1976). Levinson found individual variations on common themes and patterns; however, he also found consistency among the men he studied, with only a few years difference between those earliest and those latest to reach developmental epochs.

One of the observations that emerged from Levinson's study is that becoming a mature adult is a much longer and more complex process than is generally recognized. The Early Adult Transition lasts from approximately 17 to 22 years of age, and its major task is moving into the adult world. If an adolescent separates too early from his family, he may remain tied to them emotionally, often as a pseudo-adult whose frustrated yearning for parental support interferes with mature growth and true independence. Most of the subjects in Levinson's study gradually loosened the ties to their parents during their twenties. As they approached 30, most had become increasingly indifferent to and alienated from their parents.

These years are described by Erik Erikson as the first of three stages of adulthood, *Intimacy and Distantiation vs. Self-Absorption.* According to Erikson (1959) the achievement of real intimacy with friends or lovers is only possible after a reasonable .sense of identity has been established.

Table 3-1
Developmental Periods of Adulthood
as Described by Daniel Levinson

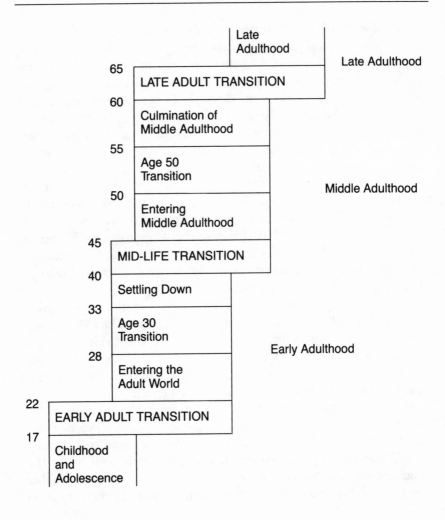

Distantiation, the counterpart of intimacy, is the readiness to combat those forces who are inimical to one's well-being. This ability to engage in competitive encounters is one of the hallmarks of a mature person.

Levinson's findings cast doubt on the usual view that young men conclude most of the uncertainty of adolescence by their early twenties and thereafter move onto a stable, steady life course. In fact the twenties and thirties may be the most stressful decades of the entire life cycle. Most of those in Levinson's sample had a significant personal crisis in their twenties, and did not really achieve a stable life structure until close to age 30.

This instability is increased by a fast changing and highly differentiated society like ours, where the available number and variety of choices of career and life style increase the psychological burden involved in choosing. In more traditional cultures it is usually taken for granted that children will follow the same traditions and careers as their parents. In our society change, not continuity, is the norm, and the great majority of young Americans form a life in early adulthood that is quite different from their parents'.

Between the ages of 22 and 28 most young men are engaged in Entering the Adult World. Men in this season of their lives are engaged first in exploration and then in creating a stable life structure. They explore a variety of possibilities in order to discover and generate options. This is a time when young adults "hang loose," and are wary of permanent commitments. Even what seem to be binding choices, like a career or a marriage, have a provisional quality.

In their late twenties people begin to create a stable life structure. By this time most are working at an occupation and are married with a family. It is a time of great responsibility. Ideally, a balance is struck between exploration and creating a stable structure. But people vary. Those who delay marrying or choosing a career beyond age thirty may find that their options have become restricted; those who make these choices prematurely may find that they are tied to the wrong spouse or the wrong job.

The satisfactory resolution of those choices is relevant to Erikson's second stage of adulthood, *Generativity vs. Stagnation*. Those people who have successfully established an identity and achieved an intimate relationship then develop the wish to help establish and nurture future generations. This drive is usually expressed in child bearing and rearing, but may also be applied to other forms of creativity and altruism. Erikson (1959) observed that those people who do not develop their capacity for generativity often begin to indulge themselves as though they were their own one and only child.

Next in Levinson's scheme is the Age 30 Transition, which lasts from about 28 to 33. This is the time when the provisional, exploratory quality of the twenties ends; life becomes more serious. Decisions and commitments are now felt to be for real. If a man wants to change, he feels that he better do so now. For many men this hardening of the life structure is stressful, and an "age thirty crisis" is common.

By the time he is about 33, according to Levinson, a man will have dealt more or less successfully with four major tasks: 1) forming a dream; 2) forming a mentor relationship; 3) forming an occupation; and 4) forming a marriage and family. Levinson used the word *forming* deliberately to emphasize that these are creative, ongoing tasks, not simply things that are chosen once.

Levinson found that all men have a guiding dream, more or less articulated and conscious. For some the dream takes a dramatic form that is unlikely to be realized. Such men dream of becoming superstars who reach the pinnacle of success and are showered with attention. For others the dream may be more mundane, yet still inspiring and sustaining. Such men dream of being good at their work and devoted husbands and fathers.

Another essential need of young men is for a mentor to support them as they try to realize their dreams. The mentor is part parent, part peer, and may be nearly as important to a young adult as parents are to a young child. A man's personality is enriched by internalizing significant features of the mentor.

Levinson found that men do not simply decide on a career in their early twenties and then stick with it. Instead, forming an occupation is a complex process that extends over much of early adulthood. Unfortunately, people have to make initial and crucial choices often before they have the knowledge and insight to choose wisely; however, those who do make a wrong choice have the option of changing. Even those who make the right initial choice must make further choices as their careers develop and as both they and circumstances change.

Like his occupation, a man's marriage and family are complex projects which evolve over an extended period of time. Many men do not really commit themselves to being husbands—with the attendant accommodation, sacrifices and devotion that this role requires—until years after the wedding ceremony. Likewise, a man does not automatically become a parent in the fullest sense when his first child is born.

The next season in a man's life occupies the period from about 33 to 40 years, and is called Settling Down. The two major tasks of this stage are establishing a niche in society and working toward advancement. During these years a man invests himself in those structures that are most important to him: work, family, friends, leisure activities and community. For the majority of men life seems to revolve around two centers, career and family, and judging from the amount of relative attention devoted to each, career is primary for most men. Indeed, many men turn to their wives and children for love and attention only after they come to realize that they will never get the kind of acclaim they dreamed of in their occupations.

Sadly, Levinson found that very few men maintain any close friendships. Friendship seems to come naturally during the school years; during adulthood it must be planned for and worked at, and most people simply do not give friendship a very high priority in their lives.

As a man begins to come into his own, he may break with his mentor, just as an adolescent separates from his family. Becoming one's own man provides a sense of accomplishment and allows the man in his late thirties to move into constructive authority in the role of father, senior at work, and friend of other adults. The feeling of becoming one's own person and being able to act as mentor to others is an essential part of adult maturity.

Women frequently change the course of their lives some time between the ages of thirty-five and forty. Before those years their lives center around their children; once their children are in school and they have time to look around and see where they are going, many resume their educations or careers; or they may become more involved in social and community activities.

Levinson discusses the Midlife Transition occurring at age 40–45, as a bridge between early and middle adulthood. Middle adulthood is a time of frustration; it is ushered in by a period of stocktaking which may stimulate uneasiness or even a crisis. Women usually go through this transition at a somewhat earlier age (Lidz, 1976).

In this time of assessing his success or failure a man has three tasks: 1) terminating the era of early adulthood; 2) initiating middle adulthood; and 3) resolving a series of polarities.

The initial focus is on the past. As he reappraises his life a man discovers how much of it has been based on illusions. For some this is a devasting realization; life seems nothing but "a tale told by an idiot, full of sound and fury, signifying nothing." Other men perceive giving up past illusions as liberating, and feel free to develop more relaxed life goals.

In middle age adults are at the peak of their powers. After considering the past successes or failures and inner satisfactions, people shift from thinking about the past to the future. Many consider ways to modify the structure of their lives, even though they realize that after forty it becomes increasingly difficult to make radical changes.

The basic polarity to be resolved in the midlife transition is between youth and age. In middle age, a man must give up certain youthful qualities (with some regret and some relief), and find positive pleasure in being older. Beyond survival, men are concerned that their lives have some meaning. They begin to accept their mortality, but want to leave some legacy for the future. They are interested not only in the wellbeing of their children, but also in the future of the companies, universities and towns in which they have invested their energies. Erikson (1959) considers this "generativity" a major accomplishment of middle life; "stagnation" is its negative counterpart.

Individuation seems to proceed in cycles, being especially prominent in adolescence and at the midlife transition. In early adulthood men readjust this balance, but their reappraisal requires turning inward. They examine and readjust their guiding dream. Most keep the dream, but make it less absolute, they learn to enjoy the process of living, and they no longer strive only for success. By forty the dream of great professional success is usually found to be unattained and unattainable. This discovery may rob life of its meaning for a while and precipitate a midlife crisis. Many resolve the crisis by replacing some of their concern for advancement and recognition by devloping an ability to derive intrinsic satisfaction from their work.

Levinson's study leaves off at the period of Entering Middle Adulthood (45–50). Less is known about these middle and late adult years; but the family problems of this period, including coping with adolescent children and subsequently with the empty nest syndrome, have had much attention (Walsh, 1982). After the children leave home, husbands and wives must renew their marriage relationship. Those who have maintained a strong bond find this to be a time of satisfaction and serenity. For others it is a time of frustration and conflict. The changes of these years usually affect mothers more than fathers, especially those women who feel deprived of the meaning of their lives when their children leave. The capacity to shift to other interests is essential to achieving a satisfying middle and old age.

Other losses must also be accepted in the middle years. Parents, relatives and friends die, physical ability begins to decline, and career flexibility begins to diminish. Some of the factors that help in coping with these changes are the security of a good marriage, satisfying leisure interests, and a meaningful vocation.

Erikson (1959) describes the final achievement of mature life as "integrity." A life well-lived gives a sense of inner peace and a conviction of personal significance. A series of unsuccessful adaptations leads to "despair" in old age. Achieving integrity means accepting one's life as it is—without undue regret or recrimination—with the wisdom to realize that the past is over and cannot be altered. Those who cannot accept their lives as they are fall into despair; they feel their lives have been wasted, and they end with self-hatred and bitterness toward others.

Retirement is a major transition for the mature man, as well as for his wife. Just as with other turning points, retirement may be welcomed or feared. For those who choose to retire and are financially secure, it offers a long-awaited opportunity to withdraw from the world of work and enjoy a variety of relaxed leisure interests. For those who are forced to retire, or who are unable to afford a comfortable standard of living, it comes as a cruel blow. In fact, only about a third of retired persons are dissatisfied, and most of these have financial problems, poor health, or have been widowed. Less than 10 percent are unhappy because they miss working (Lidz, 1976).

Adjustment to old age depends upon a variety of factors—economic, social, and personal. Researchers have identified three personalities among men who adjust well to retirement, and two among those who do poorly (Lidz, 1976). The *mature* type realistically accept themselves and their circumstances. They find satisfaction relating to people and in various activities. They think of their lives as rewarding and take old age in their stride. The *rocking chair* type welcome the opportunity to be free from responsibility and to indulge their passivity in old age. The *armored* group overcompensate for their fear of physical decline by keeping active and avoiding thinking about death.

Among the poorly adjusted, the *angry* ones are bitter about failing to achieve their dreams, and blame others for their disappointments. These people are unable to face growing old with equanimity. The other poorly adjusted group are the *self-haters,* who blame themselves for failing in life. They feel that they have always failed, and as they get older they feel progressively more inadequate.

Lidz (1976) believes that although some degree of disengagement may be necessary in adjusting to old age, those elderly persons who remain productively active are the happiest. The realities of physical and economic limitations must be accepted, but old age can still be a period of growth and satisfaction.

As they approach advanced old age, people's hopes for their remaining years tend to be modest. They wish to live out their years with dignity, to continue to be able to care for themselves, and to be useful and appreciated. They hope to find serenity and contentment, and to avoid becoming senile or invalid. Ending life in a nursing home or mental hospital, away from friends and family, is usually dreaded.

Adjustment to old age is determined partly by the personality, physical and mental robustness, and inner resources of the elderly person. In addition, the support and nurturance given by family and society are critical as the elderly person becomes less self-sufficient. The type of life the elderly lead is due to the generosity of others, as well as their own efforts. Even though their lives may be coming to an end, they are still critically important members of their families.

Family Life Cycle. Studies of the family life cycle begin with the formation of the family during courtship and marriage. After they are formed, most families first expand to accommodate growing children and then later contract as the children leave home to become adults. Duvall (1977), who wrote the pioneering work on family development in the 1950s, divided the family life cycle into eight stages and outlined the developmental tasks of each stage (Table 3–2).

Solomon (1973) condensed Duvall's eight stages into five and explained how to use them as a diagnostic schema for treatment planning. In the first stage, *Marriage,* the tasks are separation from families of origin, and investment of primary commitments in the marriage. The newly-married couple begins to learn how to meet each other's needs, in a process that continues for many years. In the second stage, *Birth,* the couple must develop new roles as mother and father, without neglecting their relationship as wife and husband. The third stage, *Individuation,* begins when the first child enters school. The tasks here are to accept the children's growing independence, and encourage their socialization. Parents may err by either prolonging their children's dependency or by pushing them toward premature independence, so that although the children may leave home at an early age, they often return dependent and defeated. In the fourth stage, *Departure of the Children,* adult children must separate from their parents and develop outside relationships as their primary sources of gratification. The parents must learn to let go. If the parents' marital relationship is stable and gratifying, it will be easier for them to relinquish the children. If not, then they may try, consciously or unconsciously, to keep their children dependent upon them. In the fifth stage, *Integration of Loss,* the parents are faced with losses in economic, social, and physical functioning. Solomon (1973) believes that awareness of these developmental stages and the major tasks involved will enable therapists to identify the maturational conflicts that have brought families into treatment.

Noting that family sociologists tend to be more aware of family life cycle stages than are clinicians, Barnhill and Longo (1978) summarized Duvall's stages and described how clinicians can make use of these ideas. Borrowing the psychoanalytic concepts of fixation and regression, Barnhill and Longo pointed out that at times of stress families often revert to earlier modes of functioning. Consequently therapists need to understand something about the developmental stages that families pass through. Even if a developmental transition is not the obvious precipitant, life cycle problems nearly always interact with other problems. Therapists therefore need to recognize, not only the family's current situation, but also points of fixation at earlier levels.

Table 3-2
Duvall's Stages of the Family Life Cycle

Stage	Developmental tasks
1. Married couples without children.	Establishing a mutually satisfying marriage. Adjusting to pregnancy and the promise of parenthood. Fitting into the kin network.
2. Childbearing families (oldest child birth–30 months).	Having, adjusting to, and encouraging the development of infants. Establishing a satisfying home for both parents and infants.
3. Families with preschool children (oldest child 2½–6 years).	Adapting to the critical needs and interests of preschool children in stimulating, growth-promoting ways. Coping with energy depletion and lack of privacy.
4. Families with children (oldest child 6–13 years).	Fitting into the community of school-age families. Encouraging children's educational achievement.
5. Families with teenagers (oldest child 13–20 years).	Balancing freedom with responsibility. Establishing postparental interests and careers.
6. Families launching young adults (first child gone to last child's leaving home).	Releasing young adults with appropriate rituals and assistance. Maintaining a supportive home base.
7. Middle-aged parents (empty nest to retirement).	Rebuilding the marriage relationship. Maintaining kin ties with older and younger generations.
8. Aging family members (retirement to death of both spouses).	Coping with bereavement and living alone. Closing the family home or adapting it to aging. Adjustment to retirement.

Barnhill and Longo suggested that a simple problem-solving approach is sufficient with families who come to treatment with a clear external stressor as a focus. However, because families do tend to get stuck at developmental transitions, they encourage therapists to look for unsuccessfully negotiated transitions, particularly when there is no other clear-cut precipitant. Therapists, they point out, need to focus not so much on developmental stages, as on the transitions from one to another. Accordingly, they highlighted the following transitions between family life cycle stages:

0–1   Commitment
1–2   Developing new parent roles
2–3   Accepting the new personality
3–4   Introducing the children to institutions outside the home
4–5   Accepting adolescence
5–6   Experimenting with independence
6–7   Preparations to launch
7–8   Letting go, facing each other again
8–9   Accepting retirement and old age

Elizabeth Carter and Monica McGoldrick (1980) have described the family life cycle from the multigenerational family systems point of view developed by Murray Bowen. From this perspective the significant forces affecting individuals stem not only from their nuclear families, but also from previous generations of their extended families. Carter and McGoldrick's book describes the following six stages of the family life cycle:

(1)   The Unattached Young Adult
(2)   Joining of Families Through Marriage
(3)   The Family with Young Children
(4)   The Family with Adolescents
(5)   Launching Children and Moving On
(6)   The Family in Later Life

Adolescence is well known to be a tumultuous period in family life (Blos, 1962), but what follows is neither easy nor insignificant. According to Lidz (1976), the major tasks of the young adult are choosing a career and a marital partner. The transition to young adulthood is a difficult period and one in which the degree of mature resolution of relationships with the family of origin plays a powerful determining role on career and marriage choices (Meyer, 1980). The preliminary challenge of the unattached young adult is coming to terms with the family of origin. Optimum resolution of the transition from adolescence to adulthood entails separating from the family, achieving emotional maturity, and developing an independent self-identity. Failure to achieve a mature separation may take the form of prolonged dependency and attachment, or emotional cutoff and reactive flight. The overly dependent person is liable to make career and marital choices based on parental expectations rather than self-defined interests. When emotional entanglement with parents results in reactive flight, life decisions are often made with rebellious defiance that masquerades as independence.

Resolution of family ties does not of course depend solely upon the young adult. Parental overattachment may also hinder mature development and true autonomy of the children. If an unhappy marriage is stabilized by the presence of the children, parents may be particularly threatened by the independence of their adult children. Such parents may act in subtle and not so subtle ways to prolong their children's dependence.

As their children grow up, most parents are also facing a changing relationship with their own parents. The grandparents are likely to be slowing down and becoming less capable, economically and physically less self-sufficient. Although the stresses of old age that affect the grandparents may not directly affect the emerging young adult, the anxiety that affects the parents will be transmitted to the third generation. If one of the grandparents dies or becomes seriously ill, the parents may be even more threatened by the sense that they are losing their growing children. The parents' own level of emotional maturity and independence from their own parents will determine how much anxiety they experience as their parents grow older. The more mature the parents, the more stress they can withstand without undue anxiety. Thus, what appears to be a developmental accomplishment of one person, the young adult, is actually interconnected with family development in earlier generations.

Meyer (1980) suggests that therapists treating young adults should help them change, rather than just feel better. Working to change interpersonal behavior instead of intrapsychic feeling states is a principle of most family therapies. It may be particularly relevant to young adults, who are faced with concrete decisions that affect all succeeding phases of life.

Meyer also cautions therapists not to support the tendency of young adults to blame their difficulties on their parents. Doing so not only reinforces a habit of projecting responsiblity, it also encourages reactive distance from the parents. Instead of blaming their parents, floundering young adults should be helped to understand them. Trying to understand the personal and family forces acting on their parents helps struggling young adults achieve a more objective view of the dynamics of the emotional system of which they are a part.

Therapists, especially young ones, have a tendency to identify with young adult patients. One result of this is that they may join in blaming the parents. Another consequence of this identification is a tendency to, tacitly if not explicitly, advise certain specific decisions. Meyer points out that young adults are particularly sensitive to others who seem to have a stake in their actions, and unfortunately their simultaneous need for approval and need to demonstrate independence may impair their ability to decide what they themselves want to do. Therapists who are objective and rational enough to remain strictly neutral avoid restimulating conflicts with authority. If the therapist does not feel responsible for what a young adult patient does, it is much easier to foster understanding without trying to influence the direction of decision making.

The next stage of the family life cycle is the joining of families through marriage. The decision to marry is unquestionably one of life's most important. Unfortunately, it is not always carefully considered; it is usually motivated more by unconscious needs than by rational judgment (Mittleman, 1948), and it is frequently made on the basis of prevalent myths about marriage (Lederer and Jackson, 1968). Furthermore, although the couple may think that they are marrying only each other, they are actually joining two complex, extended family systems (McGoldrick, 1980).

Marriage requires years of deliberate effort. It is not—contrary to the fantasies of many single people—a dreamland that one simply enters into; it must be developed and improved. Unhappily, many people stack the cards against themselves by failing to pick a suitable partner. In fact, choosing a mate may be the most neurotic major life decision that most people make.

A person's marital choice is powerfully affected by the degree to which relations with the family of origin have been resolved in a mature way (Moss and Gingles, 1959). Even the timing of most marital decisions is influenced by extended family events, although most couples are unaware of this synchrony (Friedman, 1974). The sense of aloneness which accompanies the illness or death of a family member pushes many people to seek refuge in marriage. Similarly, many people suddenly decide to marry their hometown boy friend or girl friend after they move away and are unable to find friends or romance. In their rush to escape loneliness people often blind themselves to problems in the relationship, even though they may already be well aware that problems exist.

Whether the decision to marry is made in haste or not, it is frequently an attempt to compensate for a feeling of emptiness or incompleteness, rather than a way of enriching the life of an already mature person (Fromm, 1968). Ideally, people should work out what they want for themselves, and then join in marriage as two whole people. Unfortunately, most people look to their spouses to make up for deficiencies in their family life or themselves. We have all heard of those who married to get out of their parents' house; they may be only the most obvious examples of a phenomenon that affects most marital decisions. A person may have already left the family and its emotional turmoil, but the decision to marry may be unconsciously motivated by the desire to recreate the emotional fusion of the original family.

According to Friedman (1974), couples who marry younger or older than average (22–25 years) may be fleeing from unresolved tension in their families of orientation, or they may be having trouble separating from the family's emotional enmeshment. Similar inferences may be drawn about couples who decide to marry after having known each other for a very brief or a very long period of time, and those who have an unusually short or long interval between their engagement and wedding.

As they move from courtship to marriage many couples become disillusioned and frustrated. The letdown often begins with the wedding ceremony and honeymoon. Even couples who have lived together before marriage may find their relationship burdened by the feeling of obligation that goes with marriage. As Jay Haley (1963) once observed, they begin to wonder whether they are staying together because they want to or because they must. Myths of marital bliss are displaced onto the wedding ceremony (McGoldrick, 1980), and fantasies of perfect sexual and emotional harmony are anticipated for the honeymoon. Unfortunately, these rites of passage rarely live up to exaggerated expectations.

Most dating couples have a romanticized view of each other and of marriage. Lederer and Jackson (1968) called this the "utopia syndrome." Most believe that they are marrying "for love" (Duvall, 1977), but unconscious needs for sex, nurturance, and approval may predominate. Many people lose their good judgment during courtship and are unprepared to make the effort required for a marriage to succeed.

According to Lederer and Jackson (1968) the attributes of a good marriage are tolerance, respect, honesty, and the desire to stay together, usually between people with similar backgrounds, interests and values.

Whether their backgrounds are similar or dissimilar all couples must learn to accommodate to each other in the early phase of their marriage (Minuchin, 1974). The popular, romanticized view of marriage may mask the difficulties of mutual accommodation. Couples must work out routines for eating, sleeping, conversing, having sex, watching television, and a myriad of other daily functions. They must also decide which traditions to maintain from their original families and which to develop for themselves. They must renegotiate relationships with siblings, friends, and parents.

Among the most difficult aspects of accommodation is working out relationships with the in-laws. This problem is unique to our species, because as Haley (1963) quipped, having in-laws is what distinguishes humankind from the rest of the animal kingdom. All other animals separate from their families when they mate. Many people wish they could do the same.

In-law relationships may be dreaded before marriage and avoided afterward, from a stereotyped fear of intrusion. But the breaking of family ties only places more emotional demands upon the marriage. When the relationship to a spouse is the only significant relationship someone has, that person will be overly sensitive to the spouse's every reaction. Any hint of rejection or sign of differentness will be threatening and may lead to emotional fusion or stormy conflict.

Complicating the task of mutual accommodation is that many spouses look for unilateral changes from their partners (Lederer and Jackson, 1968). When this is not forthcoming—and of course no change will occur as long as each spouse waits for the other to start—one or both spouses often triangle in an outside person or interest in order to stabilize the marriage. A husband who cannot get his wife to stop nagging may begin to withdraw into drinking; the wife who cannot get the attention she wants from her husband may concentrate on her career while neglecting the marriage.

All too frequently, young married people believe that having children will stabilize their relationship. Most couples only have a short period to adjust to marriage before the birth of the first child. Parenthood is an even more permanent commitment than marriage. Today, young couples are thinking more seriously about whether or not to have children (Bradt, 1980). Some of the reasons for this may be narcissism (Lasch, 1978), or the availability of more effective means of birth control. More and more, parenthood is seen as an unwelcome sacrifice by working women who now constitute 50 percent of the workforce.

Though the situation is beginning to change, parenthood still means motherhood. Even when women work, their husbands do not stay home to care for the children; instead families with two working parents are likely to arrange for child care out of the home, which is available as soon as children are toilet trained.

Although many couples no longer take having children for granted, childless couples are still a small minority. At one extreme are couples with no room in their lives for children; at the other, are couples who want children in order to fill the void of sterile and unsatisfactory lives. These parents think of children as vessels for their own unfulfilled dreams and ambitions. Unfortunately, having children to make up for a feeling of emptiness is as likely to result in emotional conflict as is choosing a mate for the same reasons. In such child-focused families (Bradt, 1980) children may be used to provide a substitute for other satisfying adult relationships, fill the void left by an emotionally distant spouse, and make up for a lack of (past as well as present) intimacy with parents.

The presence of children often results in less intimacy for the marital couple. Having them diminishes the couple's privacy, and the demands of child-rearing may leave little time and energy for the couple to spend on themselves. Yet sustaining intimacy in the marriage is essential to the well-being of the children (Bradt, 1980). Too little emotional intensity between husband and wife usually results in too much emotional intensity between parents and children. Even intact nuclear families often become the functional equivalent of single-parent families. The mother and child relationship is often overly intense, like the third leg of a triangle (Bowen, 1966) that draws mother closer and leaves father more distant.

Like marriage, parenthood is celebrated as a joyous time of fulfillment, but like marriage it is also a strenuous responsibility. Women generally begin their commitment to motherhood during pregnancy, since it is impossible for them to ignore the new life growing inside of them. Once the baby is born, caring for it is a round-the-clock job, leaving the parents very little time between feedings, changing diapers, and bathing. Exhaustion and discouragement are common during this stressful time, and many young parents experience the postpartum blues (Duvall, 1977). Eventually the baby becomes stabilized around a regular routine and begins to sleep through the night. This welcome change provides some rest for the parents, and the household settles down to a more peaceful and orderly place. By now the young parents are more adept at caring for the baby. Gradually the baby develops from a tiny creature who alternately sleeps, screams, eats, and wets into a person, and the family moves into the childrearing phase, which lasts for many years.

The new baby develops rapidly, growing and learning at a tremendous rate. Although much of this development seems innately programmed, the way in which the parents relate to the baby has an enormous impact. Not only must the parents learn to meet the needs of the baby competently, but they must do it in a way that reconciles their roles as spouses as well as parents. Furthermore, they must integrate conflicting theories about how to raise the baby.

Because young families today usually live apart from their extended families most of the functions of child rearing fall on the parents, particularly the mother. In addition to caring for the baby, most young mothers do the shopping, wash the clothes, cook, clean house, assume responsiblity for the family's social life, and try to be good wives to their husbands. It is a heavy load of responsibility, which is hard for others to appreciate, and its demands leave most young mothers chronically tired and stressed.

Today's fathers may accept more responsiblity for child care than in the past, but they are are still unlikely to share the burden equally. The young father also probably finds that his wife needs increased understanding and support, and he must also learn to share her attention with a very demanding little rival.

The developmental tasks of the childrearing stage consist of establishing the young family as a stable unit, co-ordinating conflicting developmental tasks of each member, and mutually supporting the needs of mother, father, and baby. The young family that manages to meet the needs of all its members and coordinate their interrelations will emerge from this period well equipped to handle future developmental hurdles. Those who fail to meet the challenges of this stage will be predisposed to have difficulty in all subsequent periods.

Many families keep to themselves for a while after the birth of the child, but they soon expand their sphere to include increased interaction with friends, neighbors, and in-laws. Grandparents come into their own at this time. Sooner or later most parents leave their precious infant with a babysitter, and begin to resume their marital romance as well as their social life. In many communities parents take turns minding each other's children. Having children tends to bring people together.

Families typically decide to have a second child when the first is somewhere between 2 and 5 years of age (Duvall, 1977). Most couples accept the second child with more equanimity than the first. There is less disruption and anxiety the second time around. The additional children form a new family unit, the sibling subsystem. Within this system brothers and sisters learn to compete, to co-operate, and to resolve conflicts. Parents can maximize the chances for children to learn to deal with siblings and friends by not settling all of their arguments and instead letting the children learn to work things out among themselves.

Between childhood and adulthood comes adolescence, often the stormiest period for the entire family. With the advent of sexual maturation, complex cognitive abilities, and new physical capacities, adolescents not only can, but must, begin to break away from childhood dependency to the social world outside the family (Blos, 1979). For the adolescent this means learning to venture out from the family matrix without abruptly severing family ties and the support they provide. For the parents this means gradually relinquishing control, and increasing the flexibility of family boundaries to accommodate their children's growing independence. At the same time their children are entering adolescence, many parents must learn to refocus their attention on their own midlife marital and career issues.

One of the factors which makes adolescence a painful process is that only by rejection, or at least revision, of customary family patterns does the adolescent become a separate person, an adult. Most adolescents begin by challenging their families with change. From their contact with broader and more current cultural influences they bring new styles, language, mannerisms, and values into their families. In this way they serve as conduits for new social trends from the world at large (Ackerman, 1980). They also bring new people, some of whom may be alien, into contact with their families. This age-old situation of generational separateness and polarization is often referred to as the generation gap.

Those late to discover this age-old gap (especially parents) tend to lament its existence and look for ways to "solve" it. But although problematic, the generation gap is not a problem, it is part of the normative development of the adolescent phase of the family life cycle. Without this generational conflict no adolescent psychological differentiation and restructuring would occur.

The conflicts that rage within adolescents have been described extensively, notably by Erik Erikson. According to Erikson (1950), the primary task of adolescence is gaining an ego identity, which in turn is a precursor to establishing the capacity for intimacy. The difficulties of establishing an identity as a separate person lead to what Erikson called "the identity crisis," the resolution of which marks the end of late adolescence. Others within the psychoanalytic tradition, including Peter Blos (1962, 1979), have documented the inner turmoil caused by psychic instability and vulnerabiltiy of the adolescent.

The growing pains of the adolescent are tied to turmoil within each parent, and often cause conflicts between the parents as well as between the parents and their adolescent child. The parents may find their teenager fluctuating between child and adult, a critic bent on exposing hypocrisy, especially in his parents. He is liable one day to condemn his father's materialism and the next day sneer at his father's failure to achieve material success; she criticizes her mother's willingness to be a household drudge, then turns and says she's a sloppy housekeeper. When adolescent children behave as though nothing their parents say or do is acceptable, the parents' personal resources are sorely tested. A stable coalition between the parents will enable them to deal effectively with inevitable conflicts with their offspring, but often other sources of stress also may make it difficult for parents to cope with their adolescents' rebellion.

A sterile marriage, a career disappointment, or trouble with the extended family will all make it harder for parents to deal with a child's adolescent passage. Disappointments in their own lives may make it more difficult for parents to grant their children the increasing independence they need. Other problems may so preoccupy parents that they have little time to provide the stable and nurturant base from which adolescents can venture back and forth. A divorced mother may find her son's dating intolerable, and she may try to keep him close to her to stave off her own inner emptiness. A father engaged in an extramarital affair may ignore his daughter, thereby denying her the mixture of support and protection she still needs from him.

As teenagers become more independent, their parents may feel rejected and disrespected. At the same time, adolescents are likely to feel distrust and deprecation. These negative feelings accelerate the shift in orientation from family to friends. How well teenagers have been prepared to make their own lives outside the family will decide whether or not they can avoid the widely publicized problems of excessive drinking, drug abuse, venereal disease, and pregnancy. Underlying these manifestations of conflict are certain core conflicts between parents and their adolescent children: control versus freedom; parental responsibility versus shared responsibility; social versus academic values; mobility versus stability; open communication, including outspoken criticism, versus respect with peace and quiet; and dedicated lives versus an uncommitted stance (Duvall, 1977). Successful resolution of these conflicts is made more likely by parents who encourage independence, but stand firm against unreasonable testing of limits.

Sooner or later adolescence ends for most people, and they leave their families as unattached young adults. For the rest of the family, this is the period of "launching children and moving on" (Carter and McGoldrick, 1980). The post-childrearing stage has been dubbed the "empty nest" (McIver, 1937), and is often thought to be traumatic, especially for the mother. However, Harkins (1978) studied 318 normal women and found that they did not suffer from an empty nest syndrome. Instead, for most of them relinquishing the primary role of parent was a positive and liberating experience. Parents who are most successful at launching their children into their own independence are those whose emotional lives do not revolve around the continuing dependence of their children (Solomon, 1973). By giving to and caring for their children, parents lay the groundwork for the children to feel that they have continued support. By letting them go, parents help their children to establish autonomy as separate persons.

When the children begin to leave there are physical and emotional changes in the make-up of the family. Parents must rearrange their physical facilities and resources; sometimes meet increased expenses, such as college, a wedding, or a new home; reallocate responsibilities among grown and growing children; and renew their marital relationship.

For some parents this is a time of fruition. As the children leave they are free to take up new interests and new roles. With childrearing behind them many parents look forward to the realization of their full potential. A mother may return to work, a father may go back to school. For others, this can be a time of disruption and deprivation of familiar roles. Without their children, many parents in our child-centered culture feel a sense of loss and disintegration. Some of these parents do not even regard autonomy and independence as worthwhile goals for their children. These parents may cling to their children, preventing them from ever really leaving home, or be devastated when their children finally do break away.

At about the time their children leave home, many people must also cope with disability or death of their own parents. Once again, problems in any one generation will send tremors throughout the family. Once the grandparents die, parents themselves become the oldest generation, and the family moves into later life.

Like the elderly, the family in later life has been generally stereotyped or ignored (Walsh, 1980). Recent political and journalistic attention has generated more understanding and compassion for the problems of aging. As old people must cope with retirement, widowhood, illness and discrimination, their families must readjust, providing support for the older generation without exaggerating their dependency.

Retirement—especially when it entails financial restrictions—is often a profoundly disruptive experience. The retired person suddenly loses a life-long vocation, a feeling of productivity, and the social life inherent in most work settings. Without other interests—and people—to turn to, retirement can be a major trauma.

Retirement also affects the spouse and the marriage. Where once there were separate spheres of activity and a structured boundary, now the married couple is together much of the time. While many couples welcome having more time to be with each other, too much togetherness is liable to strain most relationships.

The death of a spouse is one of life's greatest traumas. Women are four times as likely as men to be widowed (Walsh, 1980), and the prospect of widowhood is a serious concern for women from middle age onward (Neugarten, 1970). Between the ages of 55 and 65, 25 percent of women become widows (Lidz, 1976), and because of the greater longevity of women, relatively few remarry or find a male companion. Life is far from over for a sixty-year-old widow, but it can be very lonely.

The shock of widowhood brings a terrible sense of loss, of disorientation, and of loneliness. For the elderly, this stress comes at a particularly difficult time, and they are acutely prone to sickness or death. Death and suicide rates rise alarmingly in the first year after a spouse dies (Neugarten, 1970). By virtue of experience, women may be better able to manage their households, but their social life is likely to be more restricted. The loneliness of an elderly widow is most likely to be alleviated if there are strong family ties.

As they reach advanced old age most people must face the prospect of illness and dependency. They may hope for serenity and contentment, but must cope with a progressive loss of independence. Most old people hope they will not become a burden to anyone. Successful adjustment, however, demands that they accept their limitations as well as strengths. Although most elderly people do maintain good health (Walsh, 1980), they worry about physical and mental deterioration.

Once again, the family's response is a critical factor in determining how old people will cope with the prospect of failing health. Obviously, the family can be a source of support. On the other hand, if children become too helpful, doing what their parents can do for themselves, the parents will become progressively more dependent.

Contrary to popular belief, most elderly people are not shunted off to nursing homes. In fact only 4 percent of all elderly persons live in institutions, and of those almost half have organic brain syndromes (Streib, 1972); the average age of admission is eighty (Butler, 1975). But when institutional placement is deemed necessary, guilt and anxiety tend to reverberate throughout the family. Suspicion and jealousy among the siblings of the middle generation can lead to painful conflicts over who is to decide where the parents will go, and who is to pay.

Finally, most families will have to deal with terminal illness in their elderly members. Death is profoundly difficult to understand, much less accept, and families may defend themselves from the awful truth, just as individuals do. Family members may respond with denial, anger and guilt (Kubler-Ross, 1969) when told that a grandparent is dying. If they have trouble accepting the truth, they may try to hide it from the dying person. While understandable, this dissimulation is generally considered dysfunctional, because it leads to emotional distance and misunderstanding— precisely when the dying person, and the whole family, are sorely in need of closeness and understanding.

Murray Bowen (1976) has written a poignant account of his own experience of helping a family cope with the death of one of its members. Because individuals are not separate unto themselves, death happens not to one person but to the whole family. According to Bowen, adaptive coping with a death in the family depends as much on direct and open communication within the family system as it does on overt expression of grief by individuals. Perhaps families can best handle the shock of death by combining the open discussion advocated by Bowen with the cathartic release often recommended.

By now it should be clear that family therapists need to be aware of the stresses impinging upon mature and aging adults. Whatever the age and presenting problems of the identified patient, the problems of elderly family members should be considered. However, it is not enough to be familiar with the separate issues of the older generation—retirement, illness, and widowhood. Because problems in one generation do not cause problems in another in linear fashion, adequate conceptualization and treatment require an understanding of how the developmental burdens of one generation interact in circular fashion with those simultaneously occurring in other generations.

Problems most often occur when diverse developmental strivings are incompatible. Consider the following example.

> After twenty years of concentrating most of their energy on childrearing, Shirley and Clint O'Banion were becoming more involved in their marriage and in community affairs. Now that their children were grown, Shirley and Clint were spending more time together, and Shirley was running for a seat on the town council.
>
> Just six months before the election Shirley's father died. The death of the family patriarch shook the entire family to its roots. The whole, very large, clan came together to share their grief, and to support Shirley's mother. But after an intense period of mourning the family members resumed the business of living. All, that is, except Shirley's mother.
>
> This poor woman's life had been so intertwined with that of her husband that she was unable to accept his death and unable to cope with life on her

own. Finally, after a series of unsuccessful attempts to bolster her position as a self-sufficient widow, Shirley and Clint invited her to move in with them.

Problems developed when the non-complementary needs in three generations collided. Shirley's mother needed closeness, Shirley and Clint needed distance, and their children needed a mixture of freedom and support.

At a time when Shirley wanted to resume her political activities, her mother was moody and begged not to be left alone. Reluctantly, Shirley complied, and suspended her campaign for the town council to be with her mother. Unfortunately, she took out her anger and resentment on Clint. Tense and frustrated after a full day with her mother, Shirley picked fights with Clint over the least little slight. He responded by withdrawing, spending more and more time at work.

Furthermore, Shirley's mother, a strict woman easily given to criticism began to argue with her grandchildren about their independent ways. Caught in the middle, Shirley tended to side with her mother. Thus, what had been a smooth transition into independence was accelerated, and the children cut off contact with their parents.

As this story illustrates, family assessment should include not only the stresses affecting one, two, or three generations, but also how these stresses interact. Finally, it is wise to remember that many families who seek treatment are not "sick," but average families suffering the pains of accommodating to developmental transitions.

Our review of family life cycle development has been confined to the typical, intact family. Naturally, there are numerous variations on this theme. Interested readers may wish to review the section on variations in the family cycle in Carter and McGoldrick's *The Family Life Cycle: A Framework for Family Therapy* (1980).

THE FAMILY UNIT

Family clinicians, exposed to the limited range of families who seek psychiatric treatment, are liable to develop a distorted impression of American family life. Seeing only such families does not provide the observer with an adequate perspective on families in general, and does not teach him or her about the nature and extent of problems that all families face. Professionals who daily must deal with the crises of dysfunctional families are liable to have an overly pessimistic impression of modern family life. Nor is the general public immune to negative portrayals of family life. Clinical and journalistic accounts of family violence, incest, illegitimacy, and divorce make news; harmonious family functioning does not. It is easy to conclude that modern family life is in serious decline, but some understanding of the modern history and current social trends of the family teaches us otherwise. In this section, I shall offer a brief summary of current sociological information about the family.

The rising divorce rate, reports of widespread child abuse, accounts of violence between spouses, and the rapidly increasing rate of illegitimate births are symptoms of disturbance in current family life, and their prevalence has led many people to assume there has been a decline in the stability of the American family. Other trends, while not necessarily negative, also point to a possible decline in the importance of the nuclear family. These include the growing number of couples who elect not to have children; the increasing number of people who live together without legally marrying (unwed couples, homosexual couples, communal living groups); mothers who elect to have children but not husbands; and the increasing frequency and acceptance of extramarital sexual relationships. These changes raise a number of ethical and practical concerns, including their effect on child development and on our ideas about what constitutes a "family."

Our view of the traditional nuclear family has been shaken by a variety of alternative life styles which have become increasingly prevalent in the 1960s and 1970s. Family therapists must now accept the fact that families come in different sizes, shapes, and colors (McGoldrick, Pearce, and Giordano, 1982). Unfortunately, however, many consider a normal family to be made up of a wage-earning father, an economically and socially dependent mother, and two or more children. It is difficult for many of us to shake this stereotype, despite the observable fact that there are alternate family structures and a growing pluralism in family forms. Indeed, American family life has experienced a striking shift toward instability since 1960. Rapidly rising rates of divorce, illegitimacy, single-parent families, and alternate family structures all serve witness to the fact that the nuclear family is not a fixed and stable entity.

Several reasons have been put forth to explain this growing instability. For one thing, the post-war baby boom resulted in a bulge in the number of children who reached adolescence in the 1960s. Adolescents tend to be confused, questioning, and rebellious; when parents and school authorities are sure enough of their own values they can provide a mixture of restraint, understanding, and love that will counteract this adolescent instability. However, in the sixties, possibly because there were so many of them, the adolescents seem to have been able to destabilize their parents and society.

Another possible factor increasing the instability of family life is the reevaluation in sexual mores. The sexual revolution has weakened cultural support for the institution of monogamous marriage by making sex outside of the traditional context of marriage more acceptable. Attacks on the nuclear family norm also have come from various intellectual sources. The institution of the family clearly conserves the established order, and in the sixties the new left revived the Marxist critique of the family as being predicated on property relations and male supremacy. Marxists view the family as an apparatus indispensable to the bourgeois order (Donzelot, 1979), an anchorage point of private property, and a pivotal institution for reproducing the ruling hierarchy and ideology. In short, the family is an agent of the established order.

Feminists perceive the family as an institutionalized perpetuation of patriarchal domination. Because many married couples adopt a polarized complementarity, with the man occupying a dominant role at home while also pursuing a career, and the woman subordinated to her husband and forced to take full responsibility for housekeeping and childrearing, some feminists have suggested that the family is inherently sexist. Consequently, some women have chosen to avoid marriage altogether; others have married, but attempted to work out a more egalitarian relationship.

Finally, the family norm has come under fire from populationists (Carlson, 1980). These critics are alarmed by worldwide overpopulation, and advocate zero population growth. This means discouraging families from continuing to have more and more children. The widespread availability of oral contraceptives and legal abortions gives couples the technical resources to choose more freely when and whether to have children.

Thus there has been widespread rejection of traditional family forms and values among young adults, supported by various liberal and intellectual critiques. Consequently, in the sixties alternate family forms and life styles proliferated. Television, a conservative barometer of public opinion, reflected these changes as programs like *Father Knows Best* and *Ozzie and Harriet* gave way to *One Day At a Time* and *Three's Company*.

In place of the nuclear family, therefore, sociologists, family counseling journals, and the press document the existence of alternative models based on mutability, choice, experimentation, self-fulfillment, liberated sexuality, and limited reproduction (Carlson, 1980). Legitimate life styles now include not only the nuclear family, but also group marriage, polygamy, polyandry, communal arrangements, homosexual pairings, open marriages, heterosexual and nonmonogamous cohabitation, and the single life style.

In unmarried-couple families the commitment of the partners is based on emotional rather than legal bonds. People who opt for this alternative to marriage believe that a relationship should endure only as long as it meets the needs of the individuals involved. Traditionalists point out that without a legal contract couples are more readily apt to split up when problems and conflicts arise, and that this freedom to leave is most particularly a problem when children are involved.

Many women who consider themselves liberated have chosen to have children without also having a husband. Many of the women in these single-mother households are professionals, who want a "total female experience," including motherhood as well as a career. Although they decide to have children without immediate plans to marry, most do not foreclose the possibility of marriage at a later date; they usually have someone else to care for their babies while they are at work. Other single mothers may not have planned to have children, but once they have, keep the babies rather than give them up for adoption. It is not uncommon for such a woman to move in with her parents, who then become some combination of parents and grandparents to the child. Clinical data show that even those women who want children but not husbands usually feel lonely, and wish to get married as their children get older.

Although communal living groups are not new, they have become increasingly common. Some are organized around religious movements, while others are simply social group domestic households, many composed of young urban adults who have decided they want a more rustic, presumably more wholesome, lifestyle. These people usually live together on small farms; many sustain themselves by farming, laboring, and doing a variety of crafts. Their lifestyle is deliberately informal and relaxed, and their approach to childrearing is casual and spontaneous. Most of these groups put a premium on sharing, which extends to child care. Like communes throughout history, most of these groups do not last more than a few years. Those organized around a religious creed and those that are economically self-sufficient tend to be the most stable.

The impact on the development of children of these various alternative forms of family has been the subject of much interest, speculation, and argument. There are only a few careful and objective sociological studies, however; one such is Bernice Eiduson's (1979) "Emergent Families of the 1970's: Values, Practices and Impact on Children."

Eiduson headed an interdisciplinary team at U.C.L.A. that conducted a longitudinal study comparing the childrearing practices of 150 alternative life style families with 50 traditional nuclear families. Using an extensive array of interviews, questionnaires, home observations, and psychological as well as medical tests, the group followed the study families from the third trimester of the mother's pregnancy. The data reported thus far go only as far as preschool development, but additional information will be forthcoming as the families develop.

Eiduson found that concern for the child's welfare began with the pregnancy in all families. Among the alternative life style mothers this meant, for example, a marked decrease in drug use. Although many continued to use marijuana occasionally, they virtually all stopped using amphetamines, hallucinogens, and other powerful drugs. Similarly, all the mothers became concerned about appropriate nutrition, and there were no differences in health or nutrition during pregnancy between the alternatives and traditional mothers.

Despite their advance intentions to be more creative and experimental about birth and child care, most of the alternative families studied reverted to the relatively traditional practices, with which they were familiar, for birth and during the baby's first year of life. That is to say, like most of us, alternative families became more cautious and conservative in the face of a stressful new situation. For example, although many had planned to have the birth at home, only 20 percent of the nontraditional parents actually did so. This conservative tendency continued to operate in all phases of child care and socialization, resulting in experiences which brought the alternative life style families much closer to traditional nuclear families once children were born. Eiduson concluded that differences in the home milieu were not reflected in differences with regard to caretaking and socialization of infants. Apparently the biological and emotional needs of babies sensitize parents and are the most salient determinants of behavior during the first year of life, regardless of the parents' environment or philosophy. All who have had children will undoubtedly agree that the babies' needs determine how they are treated, especially during their infancy.

Another finding was that among all families, even the most committedly communal, the mother-child bond is strongly maintained. In cases where the maternal tie was disrupted (for example, when mother and child were separated after the child was six months old, or where the mother was depressed or addicted), the children tended to develop serious problems.

At the moment, alternative lifestyle parents are becoming increasingly reintegrated into the mainstream culture. The young adults of the sixties and seventies are getting older, moving back from the farm, and re-entering school and the workforce. At the same time, mainstream parents are adopting some of the alternative values and practices. Nuclear families are becoming less sexually repressive, more interested in equality of the sexes, and more flexible in structuring family roles (Eiduson, 1979).

Another area of even keener concern and more intense controversy is that of urban black families. Here too there is no shortage of stereotypes.

Until recently, social scientists accepted the idea that black families are adapted to a disorganized and pathological life style. As an example, in *The Negro Family: The Case for National Action,* Daniel Patrick Moynihan (1965) disseminated the view that slavery had destroyed the African culture as well as the stability of black families. Slavery, he said, had made Afro-American families despise their heritage, and by separating men from their wives and children, had created a matriarchal society, a "tangle of pathology," and a "crumbling culture." The flaw in this thesis is that it interprets black family life on the basis of middle-class white standards, which are accepted as normal, instead of studying black families on their own terms and then looking at the consequences for family members.

The thesis that slavery destroyed black family life, and that blacks do not develop strong family ties has been challenged by historical scholars (Genovese, 1974; Gutman, 1976). According to Eugene Genovese (1974), family sentiments during slavery were deeply ingrained, and men and women struggled against great odds, but with considerable success, to keep family units together.

Other studies of black culture have stressed the strengths of black families. Robert Hill (1971), for example, pointed out five resources of black families:

1. Strong kinship bonds. Black families, especially the poor, maintain close extended family ties, and exhibit a willingness to help out when members of the family run into problems.
2. Strong work orientation.
3. Adaptability of family roles. Black families tend toward more egalitarian decision-making between husbands and wives.
4. High achievement orientation. Although not matched by optimism, blacks do have a powerful motive for success.
5. Positive orientation toward religion.

Despite these strengths, the economic plight of blacks in America continues to be severe, and this has an effect on family life. Three-fifths of the black population live in the inner slums of our large cities, and unemployment is double that for whites (McQueen, 1979). McQueen's data also show an increase in unmarried parents and a decrease in husband and wife families from 74 percent in 1960 to 61 percent in 1975. White families show a similar trend, but in 1975, 87 percent were still comprised of a husband and a wife. Illegitimacy rates are also rising. In conclusion, McQueen (1979) postulated three reasons for disruption of stable black families: economic distress due to inflation, unemployment, and racial discrimination; a shortage of black males due to a pronounced discrepancy in life span between black men and women; and changing norms for marriage and family life.

Patterns of family life are probably affected more by social class than by nationality, religion, geographical region, or even race. Substantial differences in how parents of different social classes rear their children result chiefly from values that are determined by economic conditions.

All parents want their children to be honest, happy, considerate, obedient, and dependable (Kohn, 1979). Middle and working class parents also want their children to respect the rights of others. The higher the social class, the greater the emphasis on self-direction and the less on the value of conformity to external authority.

Parent-child relationships are structured along two principal axes: support and restraint. In general, middle-class parents emphasize support, while working-class parents emphasize restraint (Kohn, 1979). In 1950 the tendency had been for mothers to specialize in support and fathers in restraint (Parsons and Bales, 1955); but today both parents tend to share these instrumental and affective roles, especially middle-class parents.

Like these other variants, the single-parent family is not necessarily pathological. Approximately 16 percent of the families in this country are headed by a single parent, usually a woman (Beal, 1980). Most of these women are divorced (44 percent) or widowed (35 percent); few were never married. When parents divorce, the mother usually is awarded custody; because the divorce rate is getting higher, the incidence of single-parent families is also increasing. Currently over 10 million children are being reared in mother-headed, single-parent homes (Hetherington, Cox, and Cox, 1979). Although fathers are somewhat more likely to gain custody today than they were in the past, only about 10 percent of children of divorce live with their fathers.

Single-parent families are not inherently pathological, although the terms used most often in the literature — "father-absent families" and "broken homes" — imply that they are. Couples considering divorce may prolong a bad marriage in order "not to hurt the children." On the other hand, many couples considering divorce feel that the children will be happier if their parents are happier; and indeed, research on the impact of single-parenting does indicate that children reared in single-parent homes are more well-adjusted than those reared in conflict-laden intact families (McCord, McCord, and Thurber, 1962; Nye, 1957). Children in two-parent families where the fathers are emotionally unavailable, because of occupational demands or rejection, show decrements in cognitive achievement (Hetherington, *et al.* 1979); this indicates that having a father who is not involved or who is cold and rejecting may be just as detrimental to a child's development as having a father who is totally absent. Furthermore, the finding that divorce has a more pronounced detrimental effect on the children's cognitive functioning than does the father's death, can be attributed to the fact that divorce is preceded by psychological withdrawal.

The absence of a father, either physical or psychological, does have a detrimental effect on cognitive functioning as measured by intelligence tests and school performance (Biller, 1974; Shinn, 1978). Hetherington offered three possible explanations for this finding. First, fathers are oriented to achieving and problem-solving; in their absence children may be deprived of these influences. Second, there is more anxiety-provoking stress in single-parent families. Finally, children receive less adult attention and academic encouragement in single-parent homes.

Fathers also seem to have more traditional views on sex roles, and the presence of warm, dominant, masculine fathers is associated with a more feminine identification for girls. Boys, but not girls, show some deviations in sex-role typing if the father is absent before the child reaches the age of five. After the preschool years, the presence or absence of the father does not exert much influence on sex-role behavior (Hetherington, *et al.*, 1979).

Girls who lose their fathers seek husbands more like them than do girls from intact families. Apparently, girls who lose their fathers retain idealized images; girls who grow up with their fathers in the home develop a more balanced view, seeing their shortcomings as well as their virtues. On the other hand, daughters of divorced mothers tend to see all men in a negative light, have more problematic heterosexual relations (Hetherington, *et al.*, 1979), and have a higher rate of delinquency (Biller, 1974).

Boys in mother-headed families are more antisocial and impulsive; they are less controlled, less able to delay gratification, and more rebellious against adult authority figures (Hetherington, *et al.*, 1979).

Most writers (Beal, 1980; Hetherington, *et al.*, 1979) conclude that the developmental disruptions cited above are not mainly due to the absence of the father, but to the stress on and lack of support for the mother and her children. Beal (1980) defined the problem of single parents as "task overload." Divorce usually leaves a woman with small children and in economic distress. When a woman has to return to work following divorce, the children not only lose their father's presence in the home, but they also see less of their mother. Furthermore, mother and children are liable to become increasingly isolated. Usually they will be cut off from the father's family, sometimes from the mother's as well if her family disapproves of the divorce. And the mother is liable to spend less time with the old friends she and her husband knew as a couple. Despite all these pressures on the single-parent mother, many women handle the situation remarkably well. Indeed, for many, the liberation from an unhappy marriage can mark the beginning of greater fulfillment as a person and as a parent..

Mental health professionals can help single-parent families by helping the single parent cope with added responsibilities, find relief from stress, and develop increased social and emotional support. With proper guidance the children can take on some of the parental responsibilities and avoid taking sides between their divorcing parents.

What is normal and what is not is in part culturally determined. Family therapists, most of whom are white and middle-class, must be aware that social and cultural values shape the transactions in the families they treat, and that these values may differ from their own. Don't stereotype families; work with, not against, their values. Trying to impose your own cultural values or cognitive system upon families in treatment is destructive if not futile.

SUMMARY

Research and theory are not esoteric, academic exercises; they are practical necessities for sound clinical work. Without a theoretical framework, therapists may proceed haphazardly, relying on intuition and uncoordinated techniques. Family therapy is diffcult enough without the unnecessary burden of conceptual confusion. Theories about how families function help us understand what makes them tick, and why they have the problems they do. Even more important, theories provide the conceptual basis for planning effective healing strategies. Each of the systems described in this book has its own theoretical model, but some significant concepts are shared by all. They have been the subject of this chapter.

Family therapy is not just another method of treatment; it is a whole new way to think about people and their problems. This point of view—thinking about families instead of individuals—required a new conceptual paradigm, not derivable from previous theories. No longer are people considered as separate entities, acting and interacting; instead they are thought of as members of complex systems embedded in still larger systems — family, group, community, and nation. When family therapists limit their focus to the nuclear and extended families they do so for practical reasons, not because they are unaware of larger social contexts.

In order to do family therapy, as opposed to psychotherapy with individuals, it was necessary to develop models of the family as an active whole, not reducible to the sum of its parts. General systems theory represents just such a conceptual leap, which is why it has played a pivotal role in the development of family therapy. Using general systems concepts, clinicians were able to think of families as rule-governed organic wholes, rather than as collections of individuals interacting according to the dictates of their separate personalities.

Similarly, the idea of circular causality expanded our view of sequences of behavior and improved our ability to modify interpersonal interactions. Most people are trapped in the linear presupposition that if event A precedes behavior B, then A causes B. If a friend is rude to you (A), you may decide not to call him (B), and conclude that A caused B. Your friend may believe the converse, that is, that B caused A. A third friend, however, with an expanded perspective, may observe a sequence of ...A-B-A-B-A...and conclude that both behaviors are a series of moves and countermoves in a repeating cycle. The concept of circular causality alerts family therapists to look for similar sequences in family interactions.

A widespread misconception about family therapy is that it focuses only on visible interactions and ignores the personal and private experiences of individual family members.Although systems theories and psychological theories are often set against each other, neither is right or wrong, and neither can replace the other. They are different ways of describing the same thing, and both are useful. Wise family therapists are familiar with individual-based, psychological approaches as well as with relationship-based family approaches; by integrating the two types of theories, family therapists have expanded their knowledge and improved their practice.

Families often seek treatment when some event occurs in the environment which creates stress for the family. More often, however, families come for treatment at a time when they are experiencing a developmental crisis. For this reason, it behooves family therapists to know the major facts and theories of individual development.

The most well-known and comprehensive theory of personality development is psychoanalysis. Freud taught that behavior is motivated by unconscious drives, and that growing up occurs in a series of stages in which different components of drives become prominent and then are tamed.

Freud's followers built upon his theory by adding observations about social development and ego psychology. Among the most influential were Erikson, who developed a theory of the stages of social developement, and Piaget, who descibed the stages of cognitive development.

Most personality theories concentrate on childhood developments, but lately there has been an upsurge of interest in the problems of adulthood. Recent studies have confirmed Freud's belief that the major problems of adulthood are "love and work," and at the same time have disproved the idea that adults work out stable life structures in their early twenties. Separating from the family of origin, exploring various life structures, marrying, and choosing an occupation are complicated and protracted ventures, and most people do not form stable adult life structures until they are in their thirties. Even after that there are normative crises in middle adulthood as people reappraise their lives and begin to realize that many of their dreams won't come true. Finally, adults face problems of retirement and gradual decline of physical and economic resources, all of which have a significant impact on the entire family.

Just as children and adults experience developmental life crises, so do families. Studies of the family life cycle describe typical patterns as families pass through marriage to childrearing, and eventually to retirement, old age, and death. By keeping track of parallel life cycle developments in three generations, family therapists can better appreciate the context of the problems that families bring to treatment. Of course not all family units are alike; and good family therapists do not try to squeeze their client families into the molds of their own cultural forms and values.

REFERENCES

Ackerman, N.J. The family with adolescents. In E.A. Carter & M. McGoldrick (Eds.), *The family life cycle: A framework for family therapy*. New York: Gardner Press, 1980.

Barnhill, L.R., & Longo, D. Fixation and regression in the family life cycle. *Family Process*, 1978, *17*, 469–478.

Bateson, G. A systems approach. *International Journal of Psychiatry*, 1971, *9*, 242–244.

Beal, E.W. Separation, divorce, and single-parent families. In E.A. Carter & M. McGoldrick (Eds.), *The family life cycle: A framework for family therapy*. New York: Gardner Press, 1980.

Beckett, J.A. General systems theory, psychiatry and psychotherapy. *International Journal of Group Psychotherapy*, 1973, *23*, 292–305.

von Bertalanffy, L. General systems theory and psychiatry: An overview. Paper presented at the annual meeting of the American Psychiatric Association, May 1967.

von Bertalanffy, L. General systems theory. New York: George Braziller, 1968.

Biller, H.G. *Parental deprivation: Family, school, sexuality and society.* Lexington, Mass.: Heath, 1974.

Blos, P. *On adolescence: A psychoanalytic interpretation.* New York: Free Press, 1962.

Blos, P. *The adolescent passage.* New York: International Universities Press, 1979.

Bowen, M. The use of family theory in clinical practice. *Comprehensive Psychiatry,* 1966, *1,* 345–374.

Bowen, M. Family reaction to death. In P.J. Guerin (Ed.), *Family therapy: Theory and practice.* New York: Gardner Press, 1976.

Bradt, J.O. The family with young children. In E.A. Carter & M. McGoldrick (Eds.), *The family life cycle: A framework for family therapy.* New York: Gardner Press, 1980.

Brenner, C. *An elementary textbook of psychoanalysis.* New York: International Universities Press, 1955.

Broderick, C.B. Beyond the conceptual frameworks: A decade of development in family theory. *Journal of Marriage and the Family,* 1971, *33,* 139–159.

Butler, R.N. Psychiatry and the elderly: An overview. *American Journal of Psychiatry,* 1975, *132,* 893–900.

Carlson, A.C. Families, sex, and the liberal agenda. *The Public Interest,* 1980, *58,* 62–79.

Carter, E.A., & McGoldrick, M. The family life cycle and family therapy: An overview. In E.A. Carter & M. McGoldrick (Eds.), *The family life cycle: A framework for family therapy.* New York: Gardner Press, 1980.

Chess, S., & Hassibi, M. *Principles and practice of child psychiatry.* New York: Plenum, 1978.

Chomsky, N. *Syntactic structure.* The Hague: Mouton, 1957.

Donzelot, J. *The policing of families.* New York: Pantheon Books, 1979.

Duvall, E.M. *Marriage and family development.* New York: Lippincott, 1977.

Eiduson, B.T. Emergent families of the 1970's: Values, practices, and impact on children. In D. Reiss & H. Hoffman (Eds.), *The American family: Dying or developing.* New York: Plenum Press, 1979.

Erikson, E.H. *Childhood and society.* New York: Norton, 1950.

Erikson, E.H. Growth and crises of the healthy personality. *Psychological Issues,* 1959, *1,* 50–100.

Friedman, E.H. The nature of the marital bond. Paper presented at the 11th Georgetown University Family Therapy Symposium, 1974.

Fromm, E. *The art of loving.* New York: Harper & Row, 1968.

Genovese, E.D. *Roll, Jordon, roll: The world the slaves made.* New York: Random House, 1974.

Gesell, A. *Infancy and human growth.* New York: Macmillan, 1929.

Glick, P.C. & Norton, A.J. Number, timing, and duration of marriages and divorces in the U.S. *Current Population Reports,* Series P. 20, No. 297, Bureau of the Census, Oct. 1976.

Gray, W. & Rizzo, N.D. History and development of general systems theory. In W. Gray, F.J. Duhl, & N.D. Rizzo (Eds.), *General systems theory and psychiatry.* Boston: Little, Brown and Company, 1969.

Gutman, H.C. *The black family in slavery and freedom: 1750 – 1925.* New York: Pantheon, 1976.

Haley, J. *Strategies of psychotherapy.* New York: Grune & Stratton, 1963.

Haley, J. *Problem-solving therapy.* San Francisco: Jossey-Bass, 1976.

Harkins, E. Effects of the empty nest transition: A self report of psychological well-being. *Journal of Marriage and the Family,* 1978, *40,* 549–550.

Hetherington, E.M., Cox, M., & Cox, R. The development of children in mother-headed families. In D. Reiss & H. Hoffman (Eds.), *The American family: Dying or developing.* New York: Plenum Press, 1979.

Hill, R. Contemporary developments in family theory. *Journal of Marriage and the Family,* 1966, *28,* 10 – 26.

Hill, R. *Strengths of black families.* New York: Emerson Hall, 1971.

Hoffman, L. *Foundations of family therapy.* New York: Basic Books, 1981.

Jung, C.G. *Psychological types: The psychology of individuation.* New York: Harcourt Brace, 1961.

Kohn, M.L. The effects of social class on parental values and practices. In D. Reiss & H. Hoffman (Eds.), *The American family: Dying or developing.* New York: Plenum Press, 1979.

Kubler-Ross, E. *On death and dying.* New York: Macmillan, 1969.

Lasch, C. *The culture of narcissism.* New York: Norton, 1978.

Lederer, W.J., & Jackson, D.D. *The mirages of marriage.* New York: Norton, 1968.

Lenneberg, E.H. *The biological foundations of language.* New York: Wiley, 1967.

Levinson, D.J. *The seasons of a man's life.* New York: Ballantine Books, 1978.

Lidz, T. *The person.* New York: Basic Books, 1976.

McCord, J., McCord, W., & Thurber, E. Some effects of parental absence on male children. *Journal of Abnormal and Social Psychology,* 1962, *64,* 361–369.

McCullough, P. Launching children and moving on. In E.A. Carter & M. McGoldrick (Eds.), *The family life cycle: A framework for family therapy.* New York: Gardner Press, 1980.

McGoldrick, M. The joining of families through marriage: The new couple. In E.A. Carter & M. McGoldrick (Eds.), *The family life cycle: A framework for family therapy.* New York: Gardner Press, 1980.

McGoldrick, M., Pearce, J.K., & Giordano, J. (Eds.), *Ethnicity and family therapy.* New York: Guilford, 1982.

McIver, R.M. *Society: A textbook of sociology.* New York: Farrar and Reinhart, 1937.

McQueen, A.J. The adaptation of urban black families; Trends, problems, and issues. In D. Reiss & H. Hoffman (Eds.), *The American family: Dying or developing.* New York: Plenum Press, 1979.

Meyer, P.H. Between families: The unattached young adult. In E.A. Carter & M. McGoldrick (Eds.), *The family life cycle: A framework for family therapy.* New York: Gardner Press, 1980.

Minuchin, S. *Families and family therapy.* Cambridge, Mass.: Harvard University Press, 1974.

Mittleman, B. The concurrent analysis of married couples. *Psycholanalytic Quarterly,* 1948, *17,* 182–197.

Moss, J.J., & Gingles, R. The relationship of personality to the incidence of early marriage. *Marriage and Family Living,* 1959, *21,* 373–377.

Moynihan, D.P. *The Negro family: The case for national action.* U.S. Department of Labor, 1965.

Neugarten, B. Dynamics of transition from middle age to old age: Adaptation and the life cycle. *Journal of Geriatric Psychiatry,* 1970, *4,* 71–87.

Nye, F.I. Child adjustment in broken and unhappy unbroken homes. *Marriage and Family Living,* 1957, *19,* 356–360.

Parsons, T. & Bales, R. F. *Family socialization and interaction processes.* Glencoe, Ill.: Free Press, 1955.

Piaget, J. *The construction of reality in the child.* New York: Basic Books, 1954.

Piaget, J. *The origins of intelligence in children.* New York: Norton, 1963.

Schafer, R. *A new language for psychoanalysis.* New Haven: Yale University Press, 1976.

Sheehy, G. *Passages: Predictable crises of adult life.* New York: E.P. Dutton, 1976.

Shinn, M. Father absence and children's cognitive development. *Psychological Bulletin,* 1978, *85,* 295–324.

Shirley, M.M. *Postural and locomotor development.* Minneapolis: Minnesota University Press, 1931.

Solomon, M.A. A developmental conceptual premise for family therapy. *Family Process,* 1973, *12,* 179–188.

Streib, G. Older families and their troubles: Familial and social responses. *The Family Coordinator,* 1972, *21,* 5–19.

Walsh, F. The family in later life. In E.A. Carter & M. McGoldrick (Eds.), *The family life cycle: A framework for family therapy.* New York: Gardner Press, 1980.

Walsh, F. (Ed.), *Normal family processes.* New York: Guilford, 1982.

Watzlawick, P., Beavin, J.H., & Jackson, D.D. *Pragmatics of human communication.* New York: Norton, 1967.

Weiner, N. *Cybernetics, or control and communication in the animal and the machine.* Cambridge, Mass.: Technology Press, 1948.

Weiner, N. *The human use of human beings: Cybernetics and society.* New York: Doubleday, 1954.

Whitaker, C. The hindrance of theory in clinical work. In P.J. Guerin (Ed.), *Family therapy: Theory and practice.* New York: Gardner Press, 1976.

Part **II**

Systems of
Family
Therapy

4

Psychoanalytic Family Therapy

d espite the antipathy of many family therapists to psychoanalysis, psychoanalytically-trained clinicians have been in the vanguard of the family therapy movement—among them Nathan Ackerman, Ian Alger, Murray Bowen, Lyman Wynne, Theodore Lidz, Israel Zwerling, Ivan Boszormenyi-Nagy, Carl Whitaker, Don Jackson, and Salvador Minuchin. Furthermore, many practitioners exhibit distinctly analytic influences in their work. There seems to be a paradox here; psychoanalysis is essentially an intrapsychic theory and a therapy of individuals, and family therapy is a social systems theory and a therapy of family group relationships. How, then, can there be a psychoanalytic family therapy?

The pioneer family therapists with psychoanalytic backgrounds abandoned the depth psychology of individuals and built constructs of relationships. Instead of focusing on the unconscious vicissitudes of instinctual

179

drives, the early family therapists studied the realities of family and social interactions. Some of the well-known concepts that illustrate this social emphasis are Lidz's (Lidz, Cornelison, Fleck, and Terry, 1957) "marital schism" and "marital skew," Wynne's (Wynne, Ryckoff, Day, and Hirsch, 1958) "pseudomutuality," and Bowen's (1966) "emotional fusion."

During the 1950s and 60s, much of the theoretical development within the mainstream of psychoanalysis was in object relations theory and self psychology (Erikson, 1963; Kernberg, 1966; Klein, 1946; Kohut, 1971). In this chapter I will attempt to integrate some of these newer developments in psychoanalytic theory with psychoanalytic family therapy.

SKETCHES OF LEADING FIGURES

Psychoanalysis is a conservative discipline, modifying and refining its basic concepts, rather than replacing them with new ones. Therefore, it is appropriate to begin by acknowledging Freud's contribution to the psychoanalytic study of family life. Freud's psychology was a study of instinctual drives, from their untamed beginnings to their eventual domestication by the demands of social living. Much of this process takes place within the family; consequently, Freud viewed the family as the context within which the child learns to control and channel impulses in socially acceptable ways. Since most of this learning occurs very early in life, and since sexual frustration is highly charged with anxiety, many of these crucial interactions are repressed and unconscious. Therefore, Freud emphasized the projection of irrational fantasy in the transference relationship to the therapist, rather than the real interactions within the family. Presented with a symptomatic child like Little Hans, Freud (1909) was more interested in analyzing the child's unconscious oedipus complex than in treating the family. Thus, although Freud studied the developmental psychology of children, he was concerned with the influence of the family on individual personality development, rather than with family dynamics.

Flugel (1921) also presented a psychoanalytic view of the family in the early 1920s. But, like Freud's, his work was also limited to a focus on intrapsychic processes, and a therapy limited to patient-therapist dyads.

Major advances were achieved in the psychoanalytic understanding of family dynamics by child analysts who began to analyze mothers and children concurrently (Burlingham, 1951). An example of the fruits of these studies is Adelaide Johnson's (Johnson and Szurek, 1952) explanation of the transmission of superego lacunae, gaps in standards of personal morality which are passed on by parents who tell their children such things as: "Don't tell Daddy, but you can play with his tennis racquet"; or, "I know the traffic light is red, but I don't see any policemen."

Subsequently, the concurrent analysis of married couples revealed the family as a group of interlocking intrapsychic systems (Oberndorf, 1933; Mittelmann, 1948; Martin and Bird, 1953). This idea remains an important feature of the psychoanalytic view of families. Most contemporary family therapists view the family as functioning in terms of a single organic unity, but psychoanalytic therapists are concerned with complex interactions among individual family members.

From the 1930s to the 50s, more and more psychoanalytic researchers became interested in the family. Erik Erikson explored the sociological dimensions of ego psychology. Erich Fromm's observations about cultural forces and the struggle for individuality foreshadowed later work by Bowen and others on the process of differentiation within the family. Harry Stack Sullivan's interpersonal theory emphasized the mother's role in transmitting anxiety and insecurity to her children. Moreover, although he did not treat families, Sullivan transformed the treatment milieu at Sheppard and Enoch Pratt Hospital into a kind of surrogate family for his young schizophrenic patients.

Theodore Lidz at Yale, and Murray Bowen and Lyman Wynne at NIMH applied interpersonal psychiatry in direct observational studies of families of schizophrenics. Bowen and Wynne both made important contributions later to the practice of family therapy, but the initial impact of their work was primarily limited to research on the transmission of schizophrenia. Their psychoanalytically-informed studies showed that pathological communication, roles, and thinking linked parental psychopathology and schizophrenia in the offspring.

In the 1940s Henry Dicks (1963) established a Family Psychiatric Unit at the prestigious Tavistock Clinic in England, where teams of psychiatric social workers attempted to reconcile couples who had been referred by the divorce courts. By the 1960s, Dicks (1967) was applying object relations theory to the understanding and treatment of marital conflict. Also at the Tavistock, John Bowlby (1949) described conjoint family interviews as an adjunct to individual psychotherapy; he saw the parents of one of his adolescent patients in an effort to resolve a treatment impasse. His report of this case is, like many others, an isolated example of a clinician experimenting with family sessions, but without much notice or lasting influence.

While serving as the chief psychiatrist at Menninger's Child Guidance Clinic, Nathan Ackerman began by following the traditional orthopsychiatric approach—that is, he treated the child and a social worker saw the mother. By the 1940s, however, he began to experiment with having one therapist interview both mother and child, and even the entire family. Unlike others before him, Ackerman did not stop with experimental dabbling with family sessions; instead he recognized the leverage derived from seeing whole families, and came to view the family as the most appropriate unit for diagnosis and treatment.

In 1957 Ackerman opened the Family Mental Health Clinic at New York City's Jewish Family Service. In 1960 he founded what was then called the Family Institute, and now is known as the Ackerman Institute. His book, The *Psychodynamics of Family Life*, published in 1958, was the first one devoted to diagnosis and treatment of families. In 1961 he and Don Jackson co-founded *Family Process*, the most influential journal in the field.

Classical Freudians assumed that the individuals they treated lived in stable environments. Dreams and fantasies were the royal roads to the unconscious, and consequently they did not think it was necessary to know anything about the real family environment. But Ackerman realized that family environments are rarely stable, dependable, or predictable; rather than ignore or reject them, however, he believed that they could be changed for the better by treating people in the context of their families (Ackerman, 1966). Moreover, he wrote (Ackerman, 1958) that accurate understanding of the unconscious requires an understanding of its dynamics in the context of conscious experience and the reality of family and social interactions. Since people do not live in isolation, Ackerman believed they should not be treated in isolation.

Although most of the treatment now conducted at the Ackerman Institute is far removed from Ackerman's own psychoanalytic background and ideas, his influence is still present, especially in the work of Donald Bloch.

Ivan Boszormenyi-Nagy, also a psychoanalyst, developed another important center of family therapy at the Eastern Pennsylvania Psychiatric Institute (EPPI) in 1957. Among his colleagues and students at EPPI were David Rubenstein, James Framo, Geraldine Spark, and Ross Speck. Nagy's writings (Boszormenyi-Nagy and Framo, 1965; Boszormenyi-Nagy and Spark, 1973) merit careful study by serious students of family therapy.

Among others who have incorporated psychoanalytic theory and family therapy are: Helm Stierlin (1977), Robin Skynner (1976), William Meissner (1978), Nathan Epstein, Henry Grunebaum, and Clifford Sager.

THEORETICAL FORMULATIONS

Psychoanalysis is primarily the study of individuals and their instinctual drives, and family therapy is the study of social relationships; the bridge between the two is psychoanalytic *object relations theory*. Psychoanalysis conceptualizes all family interactions in terms of object relations, which are the internalized residues of early parent-child interactions. The capacity to function as a friend, lover, spouse, and parent is largely a consequence of one's childhood relationships with parents. The unconscious remnants of these internalized objects form the core of the self.

Object relations theory may be defined as the psychoanalytic study of the origin and nature of interpersonal relationships, and of the intrapsychic structures which grew out of past relationships and remain to influence present interpersonal relations. The emphasis is on those mental structures that preserve early interpersonal experiences in the form of *self*-and *object-images*. The roots of object relations theory lie in Freud's discovery of the oedipus complex and how it influences treatment through transference and resistance.

Although Freud acknowledged the importance of early family relationships, his emphasis was on how the family context affected the evolution of instinctual expression. What interested him was never so much the real family as his patients' distorted, unconscious perceptions of it. The family was perceived not as a realistic arena for the development of group relations, but as a medium within which individuals developed their own personalities. Freud's emphasis on instincts as opposed to interpersonal relations, however, does not mean he devalued social life. He simply believed that the psychobiology of instincts needed to be understood first, and in his later writings he turned his attention to ego psychology (Freud, 1923) and interpersonal relations (Freud, 1921).

Freud's original focus was on bodily appetites, particularly sex. While these appetites obviously involve other people, they are primarily biological needs and the relationships they involve are secondary matters. Sex cannot be divorced from object relations, but on the other hand sexual relations can be more physical than personal. This is less true of aggression, to which Freud turned his interest in later years, because aggression is not an organic appetite; it is a dynamic behavior pattern originating in anger towards other people. As Guntrip (1971) put it, aggression is a personal reaction to "bad" object relations. Therefore, as Freud's interest shifted from sex to aggression, the interpersonal, object-relational side of his thinking came to the fore. Eventually he ceased to regard anxiety as damned-up sexual tension, and considered it to be the ego's reaction to danger from other people.

Subsequently, Melanie Klein's observations of the role of aggression in infancy also led her to think about object relations. She combined Freud's psychobiological terms and concepts with her own brilliant insights into the mental life of little children to develop psychodynamic object-relational thinking.

Klein's theory (Segal, 1964) stemmed from her observations of the infant's developing relationship with the first significant object, namely the mother. According to Klein, the infant does not form impressions of the mother based solely upon real experiences of her, but instead filters these experiences through an already developed inner fantasy life. The infant's innate makeup contains forces of love and hate, which are experienced before the real objects themselves; as physical perception of real objects develops, it is filtered through the distortions of an already formed inner world. The infant does not develop impressions of a "bad" mother from actual experience; he projects his own aggressive fantasies onto her. The child then re-introjects—that is, internalizes—these objects that cause pain, which leads to a cruel superego and severe anxiety. Unlike orthodox Freudians, Klein believed that superego formation and oedipal conflicts begin in the first two years of life. The infant thus never experiences real objects objectively, because what he experiences depends more upon his own innate makeup than on any real behavior of real objects. The environment confirms, but does not originate the baby's primary anxieties and inner conflicts (Segal, 1964).

The infant's first internalized objects are fragmented; that is, they are experienced as *part objects,* and as either "good" or "bad." In place of Freud's instinctual maturational phases—oral, anal, phallic, and genital—Klein postulated two developmental positions which depend on the role of object relations. Introjection of bad objects, such as a dry breast or the angry face of mother, generates anxiety and fear, which leads the baby into what Klein (1946) called the *paranoid position.* If the child also has sufficient positive experiences, the introjection of these good objects helps to alleviate introjected anxieties and fears.

At about the time of weaning, the infant begins to experience the mother as one person, with both good and bad qualities. In addition, the infant discovers that he has the capacity to hurt the ones he loves. In consequence, the baby is depressed at becoming ambivalent toward mother and feels guilty about the capacity to inflict pain upon her. This leads to the *depressive position,* which in turn is instumental in the development of the oedipal conflict beginning in the second year of life.

Klein has been criticized for her failure to follow her own observations to their logical conclusion—namely, that object relations are more relevant than instinctual developments to personality development. Ronald Fairbairn went much further than Klein in the direction of object relations and away from drive psychology. His radical version of object-relations theory stressed the ego as object-seeking and down played the role of instincts—making love more important than sex.

Because internal object relations are developed from the earliest and most primitive forms of interpersonal interaction, it is not surprising that the major advances in this field have been made by people like Klein and Fairbairn who treated and studied very young children and disturbed adults. In the late 1930s and 1940s, based on his work with schizoid patients (1952), Fairbairn elaborated the concept of *splitting.* Freud had originally mentioned splitting as a defense mechanism of the ego; he defined it as a lifelong coexistence of two contradictory dispositions which do not influence each other. Fairbairn's view of splitting is that the ego is divided into structures which contain (a) part of the ego; (b) part of the object; and (c) the affect associated with the relationship. To the degree that splitting is not resolved, object relations retain a kind of "all good" or "all bad" quality.

The primitive ego uses splitting to keep positive and negative images separate, at first because positive and negative experiences happen separately, and later on as a way to avoid anxiety. Splitting, which prevents the anxiety associated with negative (aggressive) images from being generalized through-out the ego, usually disappears in the second year of life as positive and negative images are synthesized. If it is excessive, however, splitting inter-feres with integration of these images and precludes a realistic development of the representational world.

Internalization of object relations starts on a relatively primitive level and, as the child grows, becomes more sophisticated. *Introjection* is the earliest and most primitive form of the internalization process. The child reproduces and fixates its interactions with the environment by organizing memory traces which include images of the object, the self interacting with the object, and the associated affect. Included are good and bad internal objects, each with images of the object and the self. Thus, if mother yells, images of a bad mother and an unworthy self are stored. Introjection is a crude and global form of taking in, as if those fragments of self-other interaction were swallowed whole.

Identification, a higher level of internalization, involves the internalization of a role. In the earliest introjections, object- and self-images are not clearly differentiated; in identification they are. The result of identification is that the child takes on certain roles and behaves in the same way the parents do. A child of two can be seen to imitate the parents in a variety of ways.

Ego identity (Erikson, 1956) represents the most sophisticated level of the internalization process. It is the over-all organization of synthesized identifications and introjections. Ego identity involves a consolidation of inner structures, which provides a sense of coherence and continuity of the self. Ego identity includes a consolidated self-concept and a consolidated world of object representations. At the highest level of development, according to Kernberg (1976, p. 73),

> A harmonious world of internalized object-representations, including not only significant others from the family and immediate friends but also a social group and a cultural identity, constitute an ever growing internal world providing love, reconfirmation, support, and guidance within the object relations system of the ego. Such an internal world, in turn, gives depth to the present interaction with others. In periods of crisis, such as loss, abandonment, separation, failure, and loneliness, the individual can temporarily fall back on his internal world; in this way, the intrapsychic and the interpersonal worlds relate to and reinforce each other.

In their observations of infants and young children, Spitz and Bowlby emphasized the child's profound need for physical attachment to a single and constant object. If this primitive need is denied, the result will be *anaclitic depression* (Spitz and Wolf, 1946), a turning away from the world and withdrawal into apathy. According to Bowlby (1969), attachment is not simply a secondary phenomenon, resulting from being fed, but a basic need in all, including human, animals. We must have a secure and loving human attachment in infancy if we are to become secure adults. Those who do not have this experience are excessively vulnerable to even the slightest lack of support, and become chronically overdependent. In psychoanalytic terms, this is the explanation for the genesis of *enmeshed* families. The quality of the first object relationship affects all later relationships, including marriage.

Margaret Mahler observed infants and young children and described the essential role of a process of separation-individuation. For the first month of life, which Mahler described as the *autistic phase,* infants are concerned primarily with their own bodily needs and sensations. The second, or *symbiotic phase,* lasts from approximately 2 to 6 months, during which the good mother relieves the baby's tension by feeding, changing, holding, and smiling. The more adequate the care given during this phase, the higher the child's self-esteem will be. After this the child begins a gradual process of separation from the mother, progressively renouncing symbiotic fusion with her. The result of successful separation and individuation is a well-differentiated and internally-integrated organization of the self (Mahler, Pine and Bergman, 1975). Failure to achieve separation and individuation undermines the development of a cohesive sense of self and a differentiated sense of identity, resulting in an overly intense emotional attachment to the family. Dependence and attachment to parents handicaps a person's ability to negotiate the extrafamilial world. Depending upon the severity of the failure to separate, crises are liable to develop when the child reaches school age, enters adolescence, or prepares to leave home as an adult.

The shift in emphasis from biology to object relations can also be seen in the work of Americans such as Horney, Fromm, and Sullivan, whose level of analysis was more social and cultural than depth analytic. In his theory of interpersonal psychiatry, Harry Stack Sullivan (1953) emphasized the ways that individuals function in interpersonal situations; he thought that was more important than how an individual expresses instinctual impulses. In every interpersonal situation the participants interact with each other on the basis of past relations with others. Sullivan pointed out the crucial impor-tance of the early mother-child interaction on the *self-system,* or *self-dynamism.* The nature of these interactions leads to three types of *personifications* which determine the nature of the self-system. When the mother is warm and nurturing the child feels good; when the mother rebuffs the child's need for tenderness or frustrates its needs, the child feels bad; and when the child is exposed to extreme pain or frustration, it dissociates to escape anxiety which would otherwise be intolerable. These experiences create the self-dynamisms: *good me, bad me,* and *not me,* which then become part of the person's response to future interpersonal situations.

Sullivan has been enormously influential in this country, although he has been criticized for neglecting Freud's insights into the instinctual deter-minants of behavior (Kernberg, 1976), and for neglecting intrapsychic, unconscious conflicts related to internalized object relations, while stressing actual present and past interpersonal relations (Guntrip, 1961). In Sullivanian theory, the child is at the mercy of the environment. The child searches for *security* and *satisfaction,* and develops a self-system derived from interpersonal relations with the parents by repudiating those actions which cause the parents anxiety. Thus, the extent of the parents' anxiety sets the limits on the child's healthy growth and development.

More recently, Erik Erikson (1956, 1963) has theorized that introjections and identifications, along with social roles, form the basis of *ego identity*. In his formulations on the process of socialization, Erikson has never abandoned the instinctual basis of Freudian theory. He recognizes the influence of sexual and aggressive drives, and accepts the importance of the oral stage of development; however he stresses the importance of *basic trust,* in the relationship between mother and child. In order for basic trust to develop, the infant needs physical comfort and protection from undue anxiety, frustration, and rejection. Armed with basic trust the growing person can face new situations with confidence and equanimity; without it new experiences bring fear and apprehension. The child who successfully negotiates the stages of Eriksonean development emerges with basic trust and a clear sense of ego identity.

To understand object-relations theory it is essential to bear in mind that it is not objects that are in the psyche, but fantasies of objects. As Edith Jacobson (1964) pointed out, the object is never perceived exactly as it is; what is perceived is a representation that reflects the subjective experience of the object. Thus, object relations are determined, not only by how the object behaves toward the subject, but also by how the subject perceives and then integrates that behavior. In *The Brothers Karamazov,* Dostoevsky, speaking through the monk Zossima, makes exactly this point.

> From the house of my parents I have brought nothing but pleasant memories, for there are no memories more precious than those of one's early childhood in one's own home, and that is almost always so, if there is any love and harmony in the family at all. Indeed, precious memories may be retained even from a bad home so long as your heart is capable of finding anything precious.

The internal world of object relations never exactly corresponds to the actual world of real people. It is an approximation, strongly influenced by the earliest object images, introjections, and identifications. This inner world gradually matures and develops, becoming progressively synthesized and closer to reality. The individual's internal capacity for dealing with conflict and failure is intimately related to the maturity and depth of the internal world of object relations. Trust in one's self and one's goodness is based on the confirmation of love from internalized good objects.

NORMAL FAMILY DEVELOPMENT

The distinction between normal and abnormal family development is less clearly drawn by psychoanalytic writers than by family therapists in other schools. Since most family therapists are primarily interested in treating clinical problems, their conceptualizations tend to focus on how these problems develop. Although they are mainly interested in psychopathology, psychoanalysts are also concerned with the facts of normal personality development. Following Freud, they take clinical phenomena and psychopathological developments as starting points from which to retrace the development of personality, normal and abnormal. Bear in mind, therefore, that many of the events described in this section as normal family development have the potential to produce behavior disorders, and that most of the events described as behavior disorders also have normal counterparts.

The psychoanalytic model of normal development contains concepts drawn from object-relations theory, attachment theory, and theories of the self—all of which are modifications and additions to Freud's psychology of drives. The first stage of object relations is an objectless stage. Freud called this *primary narcissism;* Mahler calls it *autistic.* The newborn's responses are limited to conditioned reflexes. Gradually, sensation, perception, and memory develop, shaping the infant's experience and encoding the influence of other people. Thereafter, the entire process of growth depends upon the ego's relations with objects, at first as actual interactions with real objects, and later as unconscious residues of these first interactions. According to Freudian models, psychological well-being depends upon: (a) gratification of instincts; (b) realistic control of primitive drives; and (c) co-ordination of independent psychic structures. According to object-relations theory, achieving and preserving psychic wholeness through good object relations is the key to psychological adjustment.

The child's innate potential does not mature in sublime indifference to the interpersonal world. The infant needs a facilitating environment in order to thrive. This environment does not have to be an unattainable ideal; an "average expectable environment" featuring "good-enough mothering" (Winnicott, 1965a) is sufficient. This continuously helping, fostering, nursing environment at first accepts the infant's immature dependence; as time goes on, it supports the growing child's tentative ventures into independence, and eventually ratifies the child's finding a life of his own through personal relations with others.

The parents' capacity to provide good-enough mothering and sufficient security for the baby's developing ego depends upon whether they themselves feel secure. To begin with, the mother must be secure and selfless enough to channel most of her energy into supporting and caring for her infant. She drains interest from herself and her marriage and focuses it on the baby. As the baby comes to need less from the mother, she gradually recovers her self-interest, which allows her to permit the child to become independent (Winnicott, 1965b). At the same time she also redevelops an interest in the marital relationship.

If the early relationship with mother is secure and loving, the infant will gradually be able to give her up, meanwhile retaining her loving support in the form of a good internal object. In the process most little children adopt a *transitional object* (Winnicott, 1965b) to ease the loss—a soft toy or blanket that the child begins to cling to during the period when he or she starts to realize that mother is a separate object and can go out of sight. The toy that Mommy gives reassures her anxious baby; it is a reminder that stands for her and keeps alive the mental image of her until she comes back in person. When Mommy says, "Goodnight," the child hugs the teddy bear until morning when Mommy returns.

The outcome of good object relations in infancy is the emergence of a secure and successfully differentiated identity. The little child who has been cared for by consistently loving and reliably supportive parents develops a sense of "libidinal object constancy" (Kernberg, 1966). The child *knows* that he or she is loved and worthwhile. This sense of worth endows the child with a capacity to delay gratification, tolerate frustration, and achieve competent ego functioning; he or she has a coherent and cohesive sense of self, and is able either to be with others or to be independent. The child with a backlog of good object relations matures with the ability to tolerate closeness as well as separateness.

The child's identity is continually enriched and revised, especially at nodal points of development such as the oedipal period, puberty, and adolescence. But the search for identity does not end with adolescence (Erikson, 1959); the sense of identity continues to be shaped by experiences in adulthood, especially social relations, career development, and family life (Levinson, 1978). Although popular culture treats the search for identity as a narcissistic quest (Lasch, 1978), for Erikson it means finding one's identity in relation to social groups, including the family.

The early attachment between mother and child has been shown to be a critical aspect of healthy development (Bowlby, 1969). Close physical proximity and attachment to a single maternal object are necessary preconditions for healthy object relations in childhood and adulthood.

The infant needs a state of total merging and identification with the mother as a foundation for future growth of a strongly formed personal self.

After passing through the normal autistic and symbiotic phases, the child enters a long *separation-individuation period* at approximately 6 months (Mahler, Pine, and Bergman, 1975). First efforts at separation are tentative and brief, as symbolized playfully in the game of peekaboo. At about 8 months the child begins to experience *stranger anxiety* (Spitz, 1965). Exaggerated stranger anxiety is a sign that the child is not secure in separating from mother; absence of stranger anxiety indicates that the child has not established a firm bond to mother as a primary object.

Soon the little child begins to creep and then to crawl, first away from and then back to mother. What enables the child to practice separating is the awareness that mother is constantly there for assurance, like a safe harbor. At a similar stage Harlow's infant monkeys alternately venture out to explore and then return to cling to their mothers. Those without mothers remain huddled in the corner of their cages.

Learning to walk enables the toddler to become very much more independent and separate from mother. The one-year-old child plays a variety of games that are used to practice separation and reunion. Toys and objects are hidden and then found, with shrieks of delight. If all goes well the child achieves a sense of self, separate from mother, by about age three. He or she will have developed a sense of confidence and self-esteem that goes along with realistic recognition of interpersonal boundaries.

The necessary and sufficient condition for successful completion of separation-individuation is the reliable and loving support of a good mother. "Predictable emotional involvement on the part of the mother seems to facilitate the rich unfolding of the toddler's thought processes, reality testing and coping behavior..." (Mahler, *et al.,* 1975, p. 79). The *good-enough mother* is physically and emotionally present; her support of separation-individuation results in the child's achieving a firm sense of identity and a lifelong capacity for developing nonsymbiotic object relations.

Recently, Otto Kernberg and Heinz Kohut have brought theories of the self to center stage in psychoanalytic circles. Although both Kernberg and

Kohut began with observations of severe character disorders, their work illuminates the organization of the normal inner psychic world and the integration of the self.

According to Kernberg (1966), pleasure and pain organize good and bad internalized object relations; they are the major motivational system which organizes intrapsychic experience. The earliest introjections occur in the process of separating from the mother. If separation is successful and securely negotiated, the child establishes him- or herself as an independent being. When the introjective process is positive and constructive, the child absorbs part of the mother's personality, in modified form, for constructive use. Ideally, part of what the child internalizes is conflict-free and independent of drive pressures and defensive needs.

The mother must have a capacity to tolerate separation and withdrawal in order to accept the child's growing independence. If the child is excessively dependent and clings in fear of separation, or if the mother is made anxious by the loss of the symbiotic relationship, or is excessively rejecting, the process is subverted. In the normal outcome, loving parents are the objects of selective and partial identifications, in which only those features that are in harmony with the image of the self are internalized. As Kernberg (1966, p. 243) says,

> Actually, the enrichment of one's personal life by the internal presence of such selective, partial identifications representing people who are loved and admired in a realistic way without indiscriminate internalization, constitutes a major source of emotional depth and well-being.

Normal development of the self includes the integration of positive and negative internalized images. Normally the child's ego development reaches a stage where positive and negative introjections are synthesized to provide a realistic and balanced view both of others and of the self in relation to others.

In Kohut's (1971) theory of the self, the separation-individuation phase is crucial in the formation of a sense of self that is strong, good, and cohesive. Healthy negotiation of this developmental epoch depends upon the availability of parental *self-objects* who respond with approval to the child's grandiose fantasies, thereby relieving feelings of helplessness. The child who is thus able to overcome feelings of helplessness is able to recognize that he or she and mother are separate persons, each with their own needs. In this way the child is able to tolerate separation from the mother and to develop a sense of goodness and strength. Moreover, if mother remains warm and loving during the process of separation, the little child retains a sense of loveableness while achieving individuality and strength. The child who sees approval and acceptance in the mirror of parental eyes develops a strong self, capable of tolerating victory and defeat as well as acceptance or rejection throughout adult life.

From the psychoanalytic perspective, the fate of family development is largely determined by the early development of the individual personalities that make up the family. If the spouses are mature and healthy adults, then the family will be healthy and harmonious. According to Skynner (1976), the characteristics of optimally well-developed families are as follows: affiliative, open, reaching out to others; respect for separateness and individuality; open, clear communication; firm parental coalitions, sharing of power; flexible control by negotiation; spontaneous interactions, with humor and wit; initiative; and the encouragement of uniqueness, and lively, strong character development.

DEVELOPMENT OF BEHAVIOR DISORDERS

Nonpsychoanalytic family therapists tend to identify pathology in the nature of interactions *between* people; psychoanalytic therapists identify pathological trends *within* the interacting people. According to classical psychoanalytic conflict theory, symptoms are attempts to cope with unconscious conflicts and the anxiety which signals the emergence of repressed impulses. Structurally, these conflicts are between the id and the ego: an instinctual drive seeks expression in a struggle against an opposing restraint (Fenichel, 1945). While agreeing that this basic formulation remains valid, object-relations theorists have added the notion that not only behavior, but also psychic structure, evolves out of early experiences with others. Therefore, psychopathology is seen as reflecting the consequences of untoward early object relations.

As psychoanalytic thinkers shifted their emphasis from instincts to object relations, infantile dependence and incomplete ego development became the core problems in development, in place of the oedipal complex and repressed instincts. Fear-dictated flight from object relations, which begins early in childhood, is now considered to be the deepest root of mental illness.

Psychoanalysts trace the roots of behavior disorder to the earliest months of life when parents first begin interacting with their infant. One of the important reasons for psychopathology is considered to be that the child develops distorted perceptions by attributing qualities belonging to one person to someone else. Freud (1905) discovered this phenomenon and called it "transference" when his patient, Dora displaced feelings for her father and a family friend onto him, and terminated treatment abruptly just as it was about to succeed. Others have observed similar phenomena and called them by other names—"scapegoating" (Vogel and Bell, 1960); "trading of dissociations" (Wynne, 1965); "merging" (Boszormenyi-Nagy, 1967); "irrational role assignments" (Framo, 1970); "symbiosis" (Mahler, 1952); "family projective process" (Bowen, 1965). Regardless of name, all are variants of Melanie Klein's (1946) concept, *projective identification*.

Projective identification is a process whereby the subject perceives an object as if the object contained elements of the subject's personality, *and* evokes behavior and feelings from the object that conform to these projected perceptions. Unlike projection, projective identification is a truly interactional process. Not only do parents project anxiety-provoking aspects of themselves onto their children, the children collude and behave in a way that fulfills their parents' fears. By doing so they may be stigmatized or scapegoated, but they also gratify aggressive impulses, as, for instance, in delinquent behavior (Jacobson, 1964); they realize their own omnipotent fantasies; they receive subtle reinforcement from their families; and they avoid the terrible fear of rejection for not conforming (Zinner and Shapiro, 1972). Meanwhile the parents are able to avoid the anxiety associated with having certain impulses; experience vicarious gratification of the projected impulses through their children; and still punish the children for expressing them. In this way an intrapsychic, structural conflict becomes externalized, with the parent acting as the superego punishing the child for acting on the dictates of the id.

> The J. family sought help controlling 15-year-old Paul's delinquent behavior. Arrested several times for vandalism, Paul seemed neither ashamed of nor able to understand his compulsion to strike out against authority. As therapy progressed, it became clear that Paul's father harbored a deep but unexpressed resentment of the social conditions which made him work long hours for low wages in a factory, while the "fat cats didn't do shit, but still drove around in Cadillacs." Once the therapists became aware of Mr. J.'s strong but suppressed hatred of authority, they also began to notice that he smiled slightly when Mrs. J. described Paul's latest exploits.

The descriptions of disturbed family relations made by psychoanalytically-trained observers during the 1950s and 60s focused on identifying features of the family environment conducive to the development of schizophrenia. For the most part these theorists dealt with dyadic concepts— "emotional divorce" (Bowen, Dysinger, and Basamania, 1959), "marital schism" and "marital skew" (Lidz, Cornelison, Fleck, and Terry, 1957); and they emphasized adult roles and communication—"role reciprocity" (Mittlemann, 1948); "pseudomutuality" (Wynne, Ryckroff, Day, and Hirsch, 1958).

In exploring the unique and emergent characteristics of family relationships and dynamics, these early investigators saw that family patterns are built upon the personality dynamics of the individual family members. Subsequently most family therapists ignored the individuals in the system. It may now be time to reemphasize the underlying personality dynamics within individual family members.

More recent descriptions of family pathology by psychoanalytic clinicians either suggest or are explicitly based on arrested ego development and pathological early object-relations. Skynner (1981) lists the following major features of disturbed families: diffuse interpersonal boundaries, unclear identities, satisfaction from fantasy as opposed to reality, difficulty coping with separation and loss, attempts to preserve past states of relationship— often fantasied—and attempts to manipulate others into rigidly held views of them. Many of these concepts are clearly related to the developmental tasks described above.

From an object-relations point of view, inadequate separation and individuation, as well as introjection of pathological objects are critical determinants of poor adult adjustment. Whether premature or delayed, difficulty in separating creates lasting problems. Guntrip (1969, p. 128) described how separation anxiety weakens the ego, as follows:

> However caused, the danger of separation, whether by desertion or withdrawal, is that the infant, starting life with a primitive and quite undeveloped psyche, just cannot stand the loss of his object. He cannot retain his primitive wholeness for more than a short period in the absence of mother and cannot go on to develop a strong sense of identity and selfhood without an object-relation. Separation-anxiety then is a pointer to the last and worst fear, fear of the loss of the ego itself, of depersonalization and the sense of unreality.

Failure to develop a cohesive sense of self and a differentiated sense of identity causes a prolonged and intensely emotional attachment to the family. This dependence on and attachment to parents handicaps a person's ability to develop a social and family life of his or her own. This, in object-relations terms, explains the enmeshment that characterizes so many clinic families (Minuchin, 1974).

The parents' own failure to accept the fact that their children are separate beings can take extreme forms, leading to the most severe types of psychopathology. Several investigators have remarked that anorexia nervosa is a problem that results from inadequate separation and individuation (Bruch, 1978; Masterson, 1977). Often the parents' own serious personality disorders prevent them from understanding and accepting their children's need for independence. Such parents cannot tolerate separation or deviation from their rules, and respond to independent ventures with extreme overcontrol. The result is that the children do not develop a separate sense of self; they do not differentiate their own needs from those of their parents; and they become overly compliant, "perfect" children. Lidz (Lidz, Cornelison, and Fleck, 1965) described a mother of identical twins who, when she was constipated, would give her two sons an enema or laxative.

The compliant facade of "false self" (Winnicott, 1965b) of these children is adaptive only as long as they remain at home with their parents. That is why poorly differentiated children usually face a crisis in adolescence, a time when developmental pressures for independence conflict with infantile family attachments. The outcome may be continued dependence or a violent adolescent rebellion. But the teenager who rebels as a reaction against strong unresolved dependency needs is ill-equipped for mature social relations—not to mention marriage. Behind a facade of proud self-reliance, such individuals harbor deep longings for dependence and tend to be extremely emotionally reactive. When they marry they may seek constant approval; they may automatically reject control and influence; they may exhibit both responses.

> In their first couples therapy session, Mr. and Mrs. B.'s complaints were mirror images. He claimed that she was "bossy and demanding," while she said that he "had to have everything his own way and wouldn't listen to anybody." An exploration of Mr. B.'s family history revealed that he was the youngest child in a closely-knit family of five. He described his mother as warm and loving, but said she tried to smother him, and that she discouraged all of his efforts to be independent. Subjected to these same pressures, his two older sisters conformed and still remain unmarried, living with their parents. Mr. B., however, rebelled against his mother's domination and left home to join the Marines at age 17. As he related his experience in the Marine Corps and subsequent successful business ventures, it was clear that he was fiercely proud of his independence.
>
> Once the story of Mr. B.'s success in breaking away from his overcontrolling

mother was brought out into the open, both Mr. and Mrs. B. had a clearer understanding of his tendency to overreact to anything he perceived as controlling. Deeper analysis subsequently revealed that while Mr. B. staunchly rejected what he called "bossiness," he nevertheless was terribly concerned with securing praise and approval. Apparently, he had learned to fear his deep-seated dependency needs, and he protected himself with a facade of "not needing anything from anybody." Nevertheless, the needs were still there, and had in fact been a powerful determinant of his choice of a wife.

Much of the current psychoanalytic thinking about the effects of pathological object relations have come from Otto Kernberg's and Heinz Kohut's studies of borderline character disorders and narcissistic personalities. While the majority of persons seeking family therapy are not so severely disturbed, a great many people suffer from these disorders to a lesser extent.

In treating borderline personality disorders, Kernberg (1966) was struck by the fact that his patients alternately expressed complementary sides of a conflict, one minute expressing libidinal or aggressive impulses, the next minute behaving defensively in just the opposite manner. He deduced that their behavior was the result of marked compartmentalization of ego states due to a *splitting of the ego*. In borderline personalities, early conflict-ridden object relations are easily triggered, resulting in expression of contradictory ego states that are split off from one another. Good and bad partial objects are swallowed whole and remain as potential expressions without being integrated or modified.

The essence of Kernberg's position is that borderline pathology is an object relations disorder. Excessive rage is its cause, and splitting is the defense against it. Borderline patients are liable to sudden outbursts of anger, then equally suddenly will change to warm, friendly, and dependent behavior. When provoked to rage, their image of the hated person corresponds to an early image of mother; their self-image as a rejected or attacked little child corresponds to an image internalized from early interactions.

The cause of pathological introjection is maternal overprotection or rejection, or both. The child who is exposed to inadequate parenting takes in narcissistic grandiosity, or devaluation and narcissistic rage. Moreover, failure to develop positive forms of identification impairs the child's ability to establish a cohesive self, adequately differentiated from others. Instead, the emerging self is organized around pathological introjects; this results in a sense of inadequacy and an inability to tolerate frustration or criticism without feeling rejected to the point of threatened destruction.

The development of a *grandiose self* has been described by Kohut (1971). According to Kohut, the narcissistic personality is also an object-relations disorder, stemming from pathological defense against dependency. The grandiose self develops from merging the real self, the idealized self and the idealized object. Outwardly, narcissistic personalities may show either grandiosity, or worthlessness and shame. They seek involvements and attachments to complete their inner narcissistic deficits in order to stabilize a fragile equilibrium. They may be able to form relationships, but not as one whole person to another.

To the extent that pathogenic introjects form the core of the self, there is a propensity for projection. Meissner (1978) describes this as the *paranoid process;* split-off and repressed parts of the self are externally displaced, distorting object relations. Pathological introjects not only create a poor self-image, they contaminate relations with others as well. This process causes transference reactions, and it seriously affects marital choices, and ultimately the dynamics of family life.

When it comes to marital choice, psychoanalysts assure us, love is blind. Freud (1921) wrote that the overvaluation of the loved object when we fall in love leads us to make false judgments based on *idealization.* The loving attachment to the object reflects an overflow of narcissistic libido, so that the object of our love becomes a substitute for our own unattained ego ideal. What is loved in the object is that which we seek in ourselves but have failed to attain. The more the object satisfies a narcissistic need, and the more the person surrenders to the beloved, the more the person's own ego is impoverished.

Psychoanalysts point out that marital choice is based partially on the desire to find an object who will complement and reinforce unconscious fantasies (Dicks, 1963). Depending upon the nature of these fantasies, some people expect their partners always to gratify them, and others expect their partners never to gratify them. Moreover, people tend to seek mates with complementary needs (Meissner, 1978); this point is illustrated in those marriages where one partner is dominant and the other submissive. Such relationships may be both stable and functional; beginning therapists are therefore well advised not to impose their own values and preferences, or to try to "save" women from doll's-house marriages, or rescue men from being dominated by their wives.

Further complicating marital choice is the fact that we learn very early to hide some of our real needs and feelings in order to win approval. Children who are insecure tend to develop an outward appearance of being good, and to deny and repress impulses and feelings that they fear may lead to rejection. Winnicott (1965a) dubbed this phenomenon the *false self*—children behave "as if" they were perfect angels, pretending to be what they are not. But because they are only acting, their emotional responses lack depth and genuineness. Such children do not trust other people to accept their real selves, and they use their false selves to protect their fragile self-esteem and inner vulnerability.

In its most extreme form, the development of a false self leads to schizoid behavior (Guntrip, 1969); even in less severe manifestations it affects the choice of a marital partner. During courtship, both partners are eager to please and therefore present themselves in the best possible light. Powerful dependency needs, narcissism, or homosexual impulses may be submerged before marriage; but once married, the spouses reveal themselves without camouflage—warts and all.

Marital choice is heavily influenced by the mutual fit of the two partners' projective systems. Typically, each wants the other to be an idealized parent. But since this need was frustrated in childhood, it is defended against and is neither directly felt nor revealed. The honeymoon may therefore turn out to be no honeymoon at all, as a woman realizes that the tower of strength she thought she married is in fact not her father, but a very young man with dependency needs of his own. Likewise, a new husband may discover that he is now the target of those angry hysterics that he had previously seen directed only against his wife's mother.

In addition to feeling freer to be themselves after marriage, many spouses actually regress to an earlier stage of development. Normally, fragmented introjections are gradually synthesized in childhood, so that they eventually come closer to external reality. But these early introjects are retained in "non-metabolized form," as Kernberg (1966) put it, under the influence of pathologically fixated, severely disturbed early relationships, and unmodified splitting. Early nonintegrated object-images remain ready to surface when restimulated in adult life. This is especially true of intensely negative experiences at an early age, which have an overwhelming influence on all subsequent object relations.

While they are teenagers living with their parents, most people react to stress and frustration in immature ways, such as pouting or attacking angrily. Such behavior is not likely to be accepted by peers, so that people tend to suppress it outside their families and while they are living on their own. However, after they marry, so that they are once again in a family situation, many people begin again to act like adolescents. Consequently the first few months of marriage can be very trying.

Families as well as individuals seem to have *general developmental levels* and experience fixation and regression. According to Skynner (1981), families pass on a general level of development from one generation to the next.

Developmental failures are part of every family's inheritance; for example, a woman who did not get good-enough mothering will probably fail in this role herself. Often the signs of developmental failure may be manifest in sexual or aggressive acting out; such symptoms often obscure the object-relations root of the problem. But Guntrip (1971, p. 40) has cautioned,

> I have never yet met any patient whose overintense sexuality and/or aggression could not be understood in object-relational terms, as resulting from too great and too early deprivations of mothering and general frustration of healthy development in childhood.

Most families function adequately until they are stressed, at which time they become "stuck" in rigid and dysfunctional patterns (Barnhill and Longo, 1978). When faced with stress, families tend to decompensate to earlier levels of development. The amount of stress a family can tolerate depends upon its level of development and the type of fixations its members may have.

Like individuals, families may pass through one developmental stage and on to the next without having totally resolved the issues of the transition. Thus there may be partial fixations at one or more stages of the family life cycle. When stressed, the family not only re-experiences old conflicts, but also falls back on old patterns of coping. Consequently, family therapists need to identify fixation points and regressive patterns of coping, as well as current difficulties.

Psychiatrists, and especially psychoanalysts, have been criticized (Szasz, 1961) for absolving people of responsibility for their actions. . To say that someone has "acted-out" "repressed" sexual urges through an extramarital affair is to suggest that he or she is not to be held accountable for infidelity. One psychoanalyst, however, Ivan Boszormenyi-Nagy, stresses the idea of ethical accountability within families. Good family relationships include behaving ethically with other family members, and considering each member's welfare and interests. Nagy believes that family members owe one another *loyalty*, and that they acquire *merit* by supporting each other. To the degree that parents are fair and responsible, they engender loyalty in their children; however, parents create loyalty conflicts when they ask their children to be loyal to one parent at the expense of disloyalty to the other (Boszormenyi-Nagy and Ulrich, 1981).

Pathological reactions may develop from *invisible loyalties*. These are unconscious commitments that children take on to help their families to the detriment of their own well-being. For example, a child may get sick to unite parents in concern. Invisible loyalties are problematic because they are not subject to rational awareness and scrutiny. The similarity between invisible loyalties and object-relations concepts is not surprising; many of Nagy's concepts redescribe traditional psychoanalytic concepts in the language of relational ethics. Another example is his (1967, 1972) concept of *interlocking need templates,* essentially the same thing as projective identification.

Nagy believes that symptoms develop when the trustworthiness of relationships breaks down because caring and accountability are absent. But while emphasizing such ethical and transactional considerations, Nagy does not neglect the subjective experience and unconscious dynamics of individual family members (Boszormenyi-Nagy and Ulrich, 1981, p. 160):

> There is no theoretical parsimony in trying to invalidate the significance of drives, psychic development, and inner experience. On the contrary, it appears that the intensive, in-depth relational implications of psychoanalytic theory need to be explored, expanded, and integrated with the other contextual dimensions.

The other contextual dimensions referred to are *facts, power alignments,* and *relational ethics.*

While most psychoanalytic thinkers would agree that it is appropriate and necessary to consider individual rights and responsibilities within the family, some have pointed out that individual boundaries are blurred by unconscious connections with other family members. Kernberg (1975), for example, writes that blurring of boundaries between the self and others is a result of projective identification, since part of the projected impulse is still recognized within the ego.

Marriage on the surface appears to be a contract between two responsible people; at a deeper level, however, marriage is a transaction between hidden internalized objects. Contracts in marital relations are usually described using the terms of behavioral or communications theories; but Sager's (1981) treatment of marital contracts also considers the unconscious and intrapsychic factors that are based on earlier introjected childhood influences. Each contract has three levels of awareness: 1) verbalized, though not always heard(!); 2) conscious but not verbalized, usually because of fear of anger or disapproval; and 3) unconscious. Each partner acts as though the other ought to be aware of the tems of the contract, and is hurt and angry if the spouse does not live up to these terms. Spouses who behave like this do not accept each other's real personality and identity; each wants the other to conform to an internalized role model, and punishes the other when these unrealistic expectations are disappointed (Dicks, 1963). Even when such behavior is overtly resisted, it may at the same time be unconsciously colluded with. It is valid and useful to emphasize individual rights and responsibilities in real relationships (Boszormenyi-Nagy, 1972), but it is also true that at an unconscious level a marital pair may represent a single personality, with each spouse playing the role of half self and half the other's projective identifications. This is why people tend to marry those with needs complementary to their own (Meissner, 1978).

A similar dynamic operates between parents and children. Even before they are born, children exist as part of their parents' fantasies. The anticipated child may represent, among other things, a more devoted love object than the spouse, someone to succeed where the parent failed, or a peace offering to re-establish loving relations with grandparents.

Zinner and Shapiro (1972) coined the term *delineations* for parental acts and statements that communicate the parents' images to their children. Pathogenic delineations are based more on the parents' defensive needs than on realistic perception of the children; moreover, parents are strongly motivated to maintain defensive delineations despite anything the children actually do. Thus it is not uncommon to see parents who insist upon seeing their children as bad, helpless, and sick, or brilliant, normal, and fearless, regardless of the truth.

Any and all of the children in a family may suffer from such distortions, but usually only one is identified as "the patient" or the "sick one." He or she is chosen usually because of some trait that makes him or her a suitable target for the parents' projected emotions. These children should not, however, be thought of as helpless victims. In fact, they collude in the projected identification in order to cement attachments, assuage unconscious guilt, or preserve their parents' shaky marriages. Often, the presenting symptom is symbolic of the denied parental emotion. A misbehaving child may be acting out her father's repressed anger at his wife; an overly dependent child may be expressing his mother's fear of leading an independent life outside the home; and a bully may be counterphobically compensating for his father's projected insecurity.

Intrapsychic personality dynamics are obscured by psychological defenses, which mask the true nature of an individual's feelings, both from himself and from others. *Family myths* (Ferreira, 1963) serve the same function in families, simplifying and distorting reality. Stierlin (1977) elaborated on Ferreira's view of family myths and developed the implications for family assessment and therapy. Myths protect family members from facing certain painful truths, and also serve to keep outsiders from learning embarassing facts. A typical myth is that of family harmony, familiar to family therapists, especially those who have worked with conflict-avoiding families. In the extreme, this myth takes the form of "pseudomutuality" (Wynne, *et al.,* 1958) found in schizophrenic families. Often the myth of family harmony is maintained by the use of projective identification; one family member is delegated to be the bad one, and all the others insist they are happy and well-adjusted. This bad seed, may be the identified patient or sometimes a deceased relative.

Families often view outsiders, especially family therapists, as intruders who want to stir up painful and embarassing memories. The more they fear such inquiries, the more they cling to family myths. Therapists must neither be fooled by these myths, nor make the mistake of attacking them prematurely.

GOALS OF THERAPY

The goal of psychoanalytic family therapy is to change the personalities of the family members so that they will be able to interact with one another as whole, healthy persons on the basis of current realities rather than unconscious images of the past. Plainly this is an ambitious task and often therapists will accept less. Families in acute crisis are treated with understanding and support to help them through their crisis. Once the crisis is resolved, the psychoanalytic family therapist hopes to engage the family in long-term reconstructive psychotherapy. Some families accept, but many do not. When the family is motivated only for symptom relief, the therapist must support its decision to terminate, lest the family members drop out *and* feel that they have failed. Some psychoanalytic family therapists deliberately plan short-term treatment. In these cases, just as in individual short-term dynamic psychotherapy (e.g., Sifneos, 1972), it is considered essential to narrow the field of exploration by selecting a specific focus for treatment. A notable exponent of short-term psychoanalytic family therapy is Christopher Dare, at the Maudsley Hospital in London. Although it is not common, some psychoanalytic family therapists also engage in explicitly crisis-oriented family therapy (Umana, Gross, and McConville, 1980).

To the extent that psychoanalytic family therapists opt for crisis resolution with symptom-reduction as the only goal, they tend to function much like other family therapists. Hence, they focus more on supporting defenses and clarifying communication than on analyzing defenses and uncovering repressed needs and impulses. When the goal is personal growth and structural change, more technical psychoanalytic methods are employed and therapy is extended for a year or more.

It is easy to say that the goal is personality change; it is rather more difficult to specify precisely what is meant by "change." The kind of change most commonly sought after is described as *separation-individuation* (Katz, 1981) or *differentiation* (Skynner, 1981); both terms emphasize the growth and independence of individuals from their families of origin, and thus reflect the prominent influence of object relations-theory. (Perhaps an additional reason for emphasizing separation-individuation is the fact that enmeshed families are more likely to seek and to remain in treatment than are isolated or disengaged families). Individual therapists often think of individuation in terms of physical separation. Thus, adolescents and young adults may be treated in isolation from their families in order to help them become more independent. Family therapists, on the other hand, believe that emotional growth and autonomy are best achieved by working through the emotional bonds within the family. Rather than remove individuals from their families, psychoanalytic family therapists convene families to help them learn how to let go of one another in a way that allows each individual to be independent as well as related. Individuation neither requires, nor is achieved by, severing relationship bonds. The following extended example illustrates how the goals of psychoanalytic family therapy were implemented within a particular family.

Three months after he went away to college, Barry J. had his first psychotic break. A brief hospital stay made it clear that Barry was unable to withstand separation from his family without severely decompensating; therefore, the hospital staff recommended that upon discharge he should live apart from his parents with only minimal contact, in order to help him become an independent adult. Accordingly, he was discharged to a supportive group home for young adults and seen twice weekly in individual psychotherapy. Unfortunately, he suffered a second breakdown, and within two months was once again hospitalized.

As the time for discharge from this second hospitalization approached, the ward psychiatrist decided to convene a meeting of the entire family in order to discuss plans for Barry's post-hospital adjustment. During this meeting it became painfully obvious that powerful forces within the family were binding Barry and impeding any chance for genuine separation. Barry's parents were both pleasant and effective people who separately were most engaging and helpful. Towards each other, however, they displayed an icy hatred. During those few moments in the interview when they spoke to each other, rather than of Barry, their hostility was evident. Only their concern for and involvement with Barry, their youngest, prevented their relationship from becoming a battleground—a battleground upon which Barry feared one or both of them might be destroyed.

At the staff conference following this interview two plans for disposition were advanced. One group, recognizing the powerful pathological influence of the family, recommended that Barry be removed as far as possible from the family and treated in individual psychotherapy. Only by isolating Barry from his parents, they argued, was there hope that he could mature into an independent person. Others on the staff disagreed, arguing that only by treating the family conjointly could the collusive bond between Barry and his parents be resolved. After lengthy discussion the group reached a consensus to try the latter approach.

Most of the early family meetings were dominated by the parents' anxious concern about Barry: about the apartment complex where he lived, about his job, about his friends, about how he was spending his leisure time, about his clothes, about his grooming—in short, about every little detail of his life. Gradually, with the therapists' support, Barry was able to limit how much of his life was open to his parents' scrutiny. As he did so, and as they were less able to preoccupy themselves with him, they began more and more to focus on their own relationship. As Barry became more successful at handling his own affairs, his parents became openly combative with each other.

Following a session during which the parents' marital relationship was the primary focus, the therapist recommended that the parents come for a few separate sessions in addition to the regular family meetings. In these separate sessions, unable to divert their attention to Barry, the J.s fought viciously, leaving no doubt that theirs was a seriously destructive relationship. Rather than getting better in treatment, their relationship got worse.

After two months of internecine warfare—during which time Barry continued to improve—Mr. and Mrs. J. sought a legal separation. Once they were separated, both parents seemed to become happier, more involved with their friends and careers, and less worried about Barry. As they further released their stranglehold on their son, both parents began to develop a warmer and more genuine relationship with him. Even after the parents divorced they continued to attend family sessions with Barry. In place of the original tensely symbiotic bond, a more balanced relationship between Barry and his parents gradually emerged. Resolution of hidden conflicts, and working through of unconscious loyalties, led to genuine autonomy of separate persons—enjoying but no longer needing each other—an outcome far better than isolation.

CONDITIONS FOR BEHAVIOR CHANGE

As any student knows, psychoanalytic therapy achieves personality change and growth through insight; but the idea that insight cures is a misleading oversimplification. Insight is necessary, but not sufficient for successful psychoanalytic treatment. In psychoanalytic family therapy, family members expand their insight by learning that their psychological lives are larger than their conscious experience, and by coming to understand and accept repressed parts of their personalities. Just as in individual therapy, interpretations, to be effective, should be limited to preconscious material—that which the patient is almost aware of; interpretations of unconscious material arouse anxiety, which means they will be rejected. Whatever insights are achieved, however, must subsequently be *worked through* (Greenson, 1967)—that is, translated into new and more productive ways of behaving and interacting.

Some (Kohut, 1977) have even suggested that psychoanalytic treatment works not so much by insight as by reducing defenses, so that patients simply experience and express repressed parts of themselves. From this point of view, it may be more important for family members to express and gratify their unconscious needs and repressed sexuality and aggression than to learn to understand them better. Regardless of which position is taken, most therapists work to do both—that is, both foster insight and encourage expression of repressed impulses (Ackerman, 1958).

Analytic therapists foster insight by penetrating beneath surface phenomena to the hidden meanings below. In individual therapy, dreams and free associations are considered to be *manifest content,* not to be taken at face value. Likewise, manifest family interactions are thought to be disguised versions of the latent feelings hidden behind them. Nonanalytic family therapists accept the meaning of the family's manifest interactions; analytic family therapists attempt to uncover other material, especially that which is hidden, unconscious, and from the past. According to Framo (1970, p. 158), "The family cannot undergo deep or meaningful change if the therapists deal only with current, immediate interactions among the members."

Naturally, families defend against exposing their innermost feelings. After all, it is a great deal to ask of anyone to expose old wounds and embarassing emotions. Psychoanalysts deal with this problem by creating a climate of trust and by proceeding very slowly. But the risk of exposure is far greater in family therapy. Not only do family members have to acknowledge painful feelings, they are asked to do so in front of the very people they most want to hide them from. A therapist might offer as an interpretation the idea that a man hates his wife because he blames her for depriving him of the freedom of his lost youth. In individual treatment, the patient may acknowledge this fairly readily, wonder why he has suppressed his feelings, and begin to explore the roots of his reactions. But imagine how much more difficult it is to admit its truth and acknowledge his feelings in front of his wife.

Since patients in family therapy are likely to be concerned about public exposure as well as self-protection, therapists must offer them a great deal of security. Such security is necessary both for uncovering material for analysis, and also for working through this material in family interaction. Once an atmosphere of security is established, the analytic family therapist can begin to identify projective mechanisms and bring them back into the marital relationship. Then the spouses can reinternalize parts of themselves that they had projected onto their mates. Once they no longer need to rely on projective identification, they can acknowledge and accept previously split-off, guilt-ridden libidinal and aggressive parts of their own egos. The therapist helps the spouses to work through the introjects of their parents so that they can see how their present difficulties have emerged from unconscious attempts to perpetuate old conflicts arising from their families of origin. This work is painful and cannot proceed without the continual security offered by a competent and supportive therapist.

Any form of family therapy derived from psychoanalytic principles must establish a climate of sufficient safety to expose and analyze object-relational images, internalized at an early age. Moreover, in order to work through these insights, secure social interactions must be nurtured in family treatment sessions so that unfinished developmental tasks can be uncovered and surmounted. Speaking to this point, Guntrip (1971) wrote that analysts who emphasize instinct theory can blame treatment failures on the great strength of their patients' sexuality and aggression. But from an object-relations perspective, such failures are more likely to be seen as the therapist's failure to make the treatment relationships secure. For the therapist, this means listening, without becoming overly intrusive; for family members, this means learning to hear each other's complaints as statements of feeling and requests for change, rather than as attacks that threaten their ego integrity.

Transference, the *sine qua non* of individual psychoanalysis, is also considered essential for psychoanalytic family therapy. Individual patients reveal their unconscious assumptions about people by acting them out in the therapeutic relationship. Family members reveal repressed images of past family relationships in their current interactions with family members, as well as with the therapist.

To some, the idea of transference seems relevant only to individual therapy, where in the absence of a real relationship most of the patient's feelings toward the therapist must be inspired by fantasy. What need is there to think of transference in family therapy, when the "real" relationships are actually present? In fact, transference is ubiquitous in all emotionally significant relationships. By re-experiencing and acting out repetitious past patterns—toward the therapist, or other family members, or both—a person can begin to view these interactions objectively and, with the therapist's help, begin to break up repetitious pathological cycles. According to Nagy (1972, p. 378) family therapy offers an even more fertile field for utilizing transference than does individual therapy.

> Beginning family therapists are soon struck with a different climate for therapeutic transference as they begin to see families rather than isolated individuals. The chief reason for this is the fact that family relationships themselves are embedded in a transference context and the family therapist can enter the ongoing transference relationship system rather than having to recreate it as a new relationship in the privacy of an exclusive therapist-patient work relationship.

Elsewhere, Nadelson (1978, p. 123), wrote,

> Since marital conflict may be viewed as a result of the mutual projection, by each partner, of early internalized objects, and thus may become the battleground for past conflict, the therapist must be aware of each spouse's transference projection onto the partner as well as onto the therapist.

When two or more generations of family members are present in treatment it often becomes painfully obvious how certain distortions in one relationship are rooted in repetitions of previous experiences. Here psychoanalytic family therapists have great information, and the leverage to rework developmental experiences in such a way as to modify pathological introjects. In describing the interrelations among family members' pathology, Ackerman (1966) coined the felicitous phrase, "a cluster of interpenetrating illnesses."

By gathering whole families for treatment, the psychoanalytic therapist broadens the number of transference reactions, but mutes their intensity. Transference to the therapist exists, but because the family is present, it is less intense than in private therapy. As Nagy (1972) has observed, "parentification" of the therapist is antithetical to existing family ties. Both the real and transferential reactions to other family members divert a good deal of the emotional energy that otherwise might be focused on the therapist. Furthermore, the aloofness and ambiguity of the therapist is less marked in family than in individual therapy.

For most psychoanalytic family therapists, transference is the operative model for understanding family emotional systems. "It is as if the family members evolve a more or less stable transference-countertransference configuration among themselves" (Meissner, 1978, p. 81).

The field of observation is enlarged for the psychoanalytic therapist who can see not only the real relationships among the generations that are assembled, but also the vestiges of previous generations and past interactions encoded as object images and manifest as transference. As in individual therapy, the family therapist ignores transference at his peril. But although awareness of transference, as well as resistance and projection, must guide the therapist's interventions, these reactions need not always, or only, be interpreted. Some therapists within the psychoanalytic framework prefer to offset interactions based on transference rather than to interpret them (Boszormenyi-Nagy and Ulrich, 1981).

Two of the major considerations in family therapy are who should be included in treatment, and on whom should the help be focused. Some approaches, as, for instance, strategic and behavioral, focus on helping the identified patient, even though the family may be seen conjointly. Most psychoanalytic family therapists (Boszormenyi-Nagy, 1972; Ackerman, 1958) seem to agree that the commitment should be to *all* family members; however, they are more likely to mean helping individuals to grow and mature, than helping the family as an organic whole. "To help an individual or couple in marital conflict one must help each partner move toward a higher level of personality development" (Blanck, 1967, p. 160).

The nature of this "higher level of personality development" has been defined in both structural and object-relations terms. For example, Nadelson (1978, p. 146) emphasized the structural aim of bringing instinctual drives under the dominion of the ego, when she wrote,

> The ultimate aim of interpretation and working through in psychoanalytically oriented marital therapy is the neutralization and integration of aggressive and libidinal needs so that behavior is motivated more in the service of the ego and less by impulse and intrapsychic conflict.

When aggressive and libidinal impulses are interpreted and experienced, they become conscious. Once they become aware of such impulses, family members are better able to integrate them into their lives and thus overcome their pathological, controlling power.

The personal growth aimed for in psychoanalytic treatment can also be sought in terms of improved object relations. For family members to overcome pathological attachments to each other, they must be helped to become whole individuals. As Guntrip put it, "Psychotherapy is the reintegration of the split-ego, the restoration of lost wholeness" (1971, p. 94). The split ego, which developed from bad object relations early in life, is resolved by good object relations, first in psychotherapy and subsequently in interactions within the family.

TECHNIQUES

In classical psychoanalysis, therapeutic change is achieved by *analysis:* confrontation, clarification, interpretation, and working through (Greenson, 1967). Even when modifications are made, as in psychodynamic psycho-therapy where cathartic techniques, suggestion, and manipulation are employed (Bibring, 1954), interpretation remains the decisive technique. This holds true for psychoanalytic family therapy as well. However, psychoanalytic clinicians doing family therapy are more inclined to include other, not strictly analytic, techniques because in family treatment the patients can begin to use awareness and start to behave differently in their families without having to leave the treatment room.

Before the therapist can attempt to change families, he or she must formulate an understanding of them. Here, psychoanalytic therapists are particularly well equipped, because they have available a comprehensive theory of personality and behavior. Moreover, as some authors (Dare, 1979) have pointed out, psychoanalytic understanding is useful for developing a comprehensive picture of family dynamics even when treatment techniques are drawn from other approaches. Thus, the early psychoanalytic family therapists used psychoanalytic concepts for understanding families, but resorted to other methods, especially facilitating communication, for treatment.

What distinguishes psychoanalytic from most other diagnostic formula-tions of families is that, as we discussed above, they understand the individ-ual family members' intrapsychic dynamics; in fact, the majority of psychoanalytic concepts are about individuals or dyads. But since psycho-analytic family therapists must also deal with larger relationship systems, they also must consider the family's interpersonal dynamics as well as the intrapsychic lives of its members.

The following is an abbreviated sketch of an initial psychoanalytic evaluation of a family.

After two sessions with the family of Sally G., who was suffering from school phobia, the therapist made a preliminary formulation of the family's dynamics. In addition to the usual descriptions of the family members, the presenting problem, and their history, the formulation included assessments of the parents' object relations and the collusive, unconscious interaction of their marital relationship.

Mr. G. had been initially attracted to his wife as a libidinal object who would fulfill his sexual fantasies, including his voyeuristic propensities. Counterbalancing his sexual feelings was a tendency to idealize his wife, the dynamic reaction to his libidinal impulses. Thus he was deeply conflicted and intensely ambivalent in his sexual relations with her.

At another level, Mr. G. had unconscious expectations that she would be the same long-suffering, self-sacrificing kind of person that his mother was. Thus, he longed for motherly consolation from her. However, these dependent longings were threatening to his sense of masculinity, so he behaved outwardly as though he were tough, self-sufficient, and needed no one. That he had a dependent inner object inside himself was shown by his own tender solicitude toward his wife and children when they were ill. But they had to be in a position of weakness and vulnerability to enable him to overcome his defenses enough for him to gratify his own infantile dependency needs vicariously.

Mrs. G. expected marriage to provide her with an ideal father, someone who would be loving, nurturing, and supportive. Given this unconscious expectation, the very sexuality that attracted men to her was also a threat to her wish to be treated like a little girl. Like her husband, she too was highly conflicted about sexual relations. Raised as an only child, she always expected to come first. She was even jealous of her husband's warmth toward Sally, and attempted to maintain distance between father and daughter by her own intense attachment to Sally.

At the level of her early self-object images, she was a jealous, greedy, demanding little girl. Her introjection of her mother provided her with a model of how to treat a father figure. Unfortunately, what worked for her mother with her father did not work for her with her husband.

Thus, at an object-relations level, both spouses felt themselves to be deprived little children, each seeking automatic gratification of wishes, each wanting to be taken care of without having to ask. When these magical wishes were not granted, both of them seethed with angry resentment. Eventually they reacted to trivial provocations with the underlying rage, and horrible quarrels erupted.

When Sally witnessed her parents' violent altercations, she became terrified that her own hostile and murderous fantasies might come true. Although her parents hated their own internalized bad parent figures, they seemed to act them out with each other. Further enmeshing Sally in their conflict was the fact that the ego boundaries between herself and her mother were blurred. It was almost as though mother and daughter shared one joint personality.

Dynamically, Sally's staying home from school could be seen as a desperate attempt to protect her mother-herself from her father's attack, and to defend both her parents against her own, projected, murderous fantasies.

Nonanalytic clinicians tend to focus their evaluations on overt communications and interactions, as well as conscious hopes and expectations. But from a psychoanalytic perspective such descriptions only scratch the surface. Unconscious forces constitute the core of family life. However, this does not mean that psychoanalytic clinicians deal only with the psychology of individual personality defects. Psychoanalysts who work in family therapy recognize that family dynamics are more than the additive sum of individual dynamics. Thus, Henry Dicks (1967, pp.8–9) wrote, "But such [personality] defects have mainly become organized around the marriage without necessarily invading or disturbing other facets of personality functioning, *e.g.,* the work sphere or the area of social relations." Individuals may bring impaired object relations to family life, but it is the unconscious fit between family members that essentially determines adjustment.

Applying object-relations theory to family evaluation, Dicks (1967) has proposed three levels upon which to assess the marital relationship: (1) social and cultural backgrounds, and commonality of interests; (2) conscious expectations of roles for self and spouse; and (3) the fit between unconscious self-images and object-images. If a couple is in harmony on any two of these levels, Dicks believes they will stay together, even in the face of constant conflict. However, if they are incompatible on two of three levels, the marriage will probably end in divorce.

Dicks' analysis helps to explain why many couples seem to remain together despite constant fighting, and why other couples who seem content enough suddenly split up. Presumably the battling couples who cleave together fit each other's unconscious needs, and their object-images dovetail. In discussing one such couple, Dicks (1967, p.119) wrote,

> At the level of social value judgements, I would have no hesitation in rating the marriage of Case Ten as more living, deeper and "truer" than the conventional whited sepulchres in which no sleeping dog is permitted to raise his head, let alone bark.

Ackerman who himself described (1961) the primary diagnostic task of the family therapist as uncovering conflict within and between family members recommended (1958) home visits as a useful part of the standard family evaluation. During these informal visits he suggested that the therapist focus on interactional patterns, roles, and the emotional climate of the home. Such visits no doubt do provide excellent data; but may have been more useful to early family therapists who were interested in interpersonal interactions than they are for an object-relations analysis of individual personalities and their mutual fit.

Analysts do not postpone treatment until they have made an exhaustive study of their cases; on the contrary, psychoanalytic therapists do not complete their evaluations, do not even arrive at a final diagnosis, until the end of treatment. Ordering and classifying the dynamics of a case is not considered to be complete until the dynamics have been observed to change over time during the course of treatment. Psychoanalytic family therapists do emphasize assessment, but even so consider it merely begun at the outset of the treatment; its completion comes in the course of therapy itself.

After the preliminary psychodynamic assessment the therapist must decide who to include in treatment. Ackerman (1961) recommended that all the people living under the same roof be present in all initial family interviews; he suggested that subsequently, any and all subsets of family members, including separate individuals, might be met with. Psychoanalytic family therapists today work with every possible combination of family members. Perhaps most common, however, is treatment of marital couples; most psychoanalytic clinicians will prefer to emphasize the adult nucleus of the family because it is consistent with their own verbal and intellectual level.

From an object-relations point of view (Dicks, 1963), marriage is a transaction between hidden, internalized objects. These internal objects, which reflect the parenting and marital relationships in the spouses' original families, are brought into awareness by interpretations of the unconscious bases of the couple's interactions. Frequently, couples are found to have dominant *shared internal objects* (Dicks, 1967), based on unconscious assimilation of parent figures. Such couples do not relate to each other as real persons, but as angry or loving parents, to be tormented or idealized.

Some aspects of internalized objects are conscious, readily expressed, and easily examined. These accessible aspects are based upon direct identification with consciously perceived parental models, or overcompensation against negative images. A bullying husband may be overcompensating for feeling weak, like his father. His behavior seems to say, "I won't be pushed around the way Dad was." Such consciously-held object images will emerge regardless of therapeutic technique; however, in order to get unconscious images to emerge, psychoanalytic clinicians rely upon a nondirective exploratory style.

Psychoanalytic patients are taught to *free associate*—that is, to follow their thoughts as they occur spontaneously, without planning or censorship. This technique is the best way to bring unconscious material to the surface.

While the patient free-associates, the analyst occasionally asks clarifying questions, but mostly listens with silent interest. Eventually, the analyst begins to interpret significant material, particularly resistance and transference.

Psychoanalytic family therapists generally follow this basic approach. To begin with, family members are invited to speak freely about their concerns with very little interruption or guidance from the therapist. This may not sound different from what other family therapists do, but psychoanalytic family therapists are far more nondirective than practitioners of other schools. This nondirectiveness comes out in both obvious and subtle ways. Strategic therapists ask pointed questions about behavioral sequences surrounding symptoms; structuralists direct family members to engage in extended dialogues; psychoanalytic therapists tend to just listen. This is not to say that they do not ask questions or that their interest is not selective. The point is, they are convinced that the spontaneous flow of their patients' thoughts and feelings provides important clues to their underlying concerns; their free associations also reveal patterns of family interactions. Psychoanalytic therapists intervene very little, much less often than others. Once a new family starts discussing its problems, most psychoanalytic therapists scrupulously refrain from comments or questions until the spontaneous flow of the family's dialogue subsides (Dicks, 1967).

Not only do they generally avoid explicitly directing what their patients say, psychoanalytic therapists are also careful not to be drawn into offering advice; nor do they try to manipulate their patients' lives. Most other family therapists also deny or minimize the amount of advice they give; but some do so frequently, however inadvertently—as in the following case.

> Summarizing her fourth session with the Z. family, a psychology intern reported that they had responded quite well to an important interpretation. She then proceeded to review the detailed process notes of the session with her supervisor.
>
> Midway through the session, Mr. Z. described an argument with his wife that took place during the week. He had come home late from work, and his wife began to nag and scold him. Previously when this happened Mr. Z. would feel terribly hurt, and go off sulking and thinking how cruel and unfair his wife was to him. This time, however, her nagging provoked him to fight back, and they had a terrific row. At this point in the narrative, the therapist intervened, saying, "So, this time you stood up for yourself. And no doubt afterwards, you felt better, didn't you?" Mr. Z. said that yes, he did feel better afterwards, and then fell silent.
>
> Listening to this material, the supervisor realized that although Mr. Z.'s fighting back was a step in the right direction, the therapist's intervention was

not an interpretation, but a thinly veiled manipulation; futhermore, it closed off exploration of the couple's dynamic interaction. Certainly, Mr. Z. was aware that his pouty withdrawal in the face of criticism from his wife was not an adaptive response. What he did not yet understand were the unconscious reasons for his doing so—what awful consequences he anticipated in his fantasy, who it was his wife reminded him of, and what her conscious and unconscious feelings were about arguing with a man. By simply giving Mr. Z. a verbal pat on the back at this juncture the therapist helped to seal off this crucial data.

The following are examples of advice-giving and persuasion passing as interpretations. Notice that the interventions are statements of widely held beliefs and personal opinions, rather than uncovering comments based specifically on material revealed by the patients.

A husband reported that after feeling anxious and depressed at the office all day, he had stopped on the way home and bought a bouquet of flowers for his wife. She, pleased with the gift, was especially warm and friendly that evening, and the husband felt reassured. The therapist commented, "That's good; you have to give to get."

After several sessions in which he was silent and depressed, a teenaged boy finally began to argue with his mother, angrily accusing her of not understanding him and playing favorites with his brother and sister. Just as the mother was about to respond, the therapist intervened, saying, "That's good. It's good to let your feelings out. If you'd express your anger more you wouldn't get so depressed."

In the first example, the therapist, by delivering a hackneyed bit of advice, missed an opportunity to explore the husband's anxiety and the reasons why he was reluctant to simply tell his wife that he was unhappy. In the second, the therapist's "interpretation" precluded an exploration of what the youngster imagined would happen if he asked for more attention from his mother. Moreover, it also obscured the mother's response, and took it out of the session. If she responds to her son's complaints in an angry or rejecting fashion after the session, even if it is reported, the interaction will not be directly available in the session for therapeutic intervention. Thus, the advantage of being able to work through and integrate the boy's new behavior was lost.

Psychoanalytic family therapy is certainly more active than classical psychoanalysis; nevertheless, it remains a nondirective uncovering technique. The discipline involved in learning to interfere minimally and to scrutinize one's responses to eliminate unessential or leading interventions is a critical part of psychoanalytic technique, with individuals or with families. Interpretations should neither reassure nor direct people; they should facilitate the emergence of new material, forgotten or repressed, and mobilize feelings previously avoided (Dicks, 1967).

In addition to limiting interpretations to specific material revealed by their patients, psychoanalytic therapists also limit the number of interpretations they make. Two or three per session is typical. Most of the rest of the analytic therapist's activity is devoted to eliciting material without becoming overly directive. Sessions typically begin with the therapist inviting family members to discuss current experiences, thoughts, and feelings. In the initial session, a typical opening might be, "Could the two of you begin by discussing the difficulties you've been having?" In subsequent meetings, the therapist might begin either by saying nothing or perhaps, "Where would you like to begin today?" The therapist then leans back and lets the family talk, with minimal direction or interference with the spontaneous flow of their communication. Questions are limited to requests for amplification and clarification. "Could you tell me more about that?" "Have the two of you discussed how you felt about moving to Chicago?"

When the initial associations and spontaneous interactions dry up, the psychoanalytic therapist probes gently, eliciting history, people's thoughts and feelings, and their ideas about other family members' perspectives. "What does your father think about your problems? How would he explain them?" This technique underscores the analytic therapist's interest in assumptions and projections.

Although I have repeatedly emphasized the nondirective nature of psychoanalytic technique, it is far from a passive approach. While family members are speaking about whatever is on *their* minds, the therapist is actively analyzing what is being said for derivatives of drives, defenses, ego states, and manifestations of transference. Psychoanalytic therapists, more than most others, order the raw data of family dialogues by fitting them to their theory. The bare facts are always ambiguous; psychoanalytic theory organizes them and makes them meaningful.

In addition to fitting the raw data to theory, the psychoanalytic therapist also directs it by pursuing the past. Particular interest is paid to childhood memories of and associations to interactions with parents. The following vignette shows how transitions are made from the present to the past.

> Among their major disappointments in each other Mr. and Mrs. S. both complained bitterly that the other one "doesn't take care of me when I'm sick, or listen to my complaints at the end of the day." Not only did they share the

perception of the other one's lack of "mothering," they both steadfastly maintained that they were very supportive and understanding. Mrs. S.'s complaint was typical: "Yesterday was an absolute nightmare for me. The baby was sick and fussy, and I had a miserable cold. Everything was twice as hard for me and I had twice as much to do. All day long I was looking forward to John's coming home. But when he finally did, he didn't seem to care about how awful I felt. In fact he only listened to me for a minute before he started telling some dumb story about his office." Mr. S. responded by telling a similar story, but with the roles reversed.

At this point the therapist intervened to ask both spouses to describe their relationships with their mothers. What emerged were two very different but very revealing histories.

Mr. S.'s mother was a child of the depression, for whom self-reliance, personal sacrifice, and unremitting struggle were paramount virtues. Though she loved her children, she withheld warmth, affection, and nurturance lest they become "spoiled and soft." Nevertheless, Mr. S. craved his mother's succorance and constantly sought it. Naturally, he was often rebuffed. A particularly painful memory for him was of a time he had come home in tears after getting beaten by a bully in the school yard. But instead of the loving comfort he hoped for, his mother scolded him for "acting like a baby," and told him he had to learn to fight his own battles. Over the years he learned to protect himself from these rebuffs by developing a rigid facade of independence and strength.

With the second significant woman in his life, his wife, Mr. S. maintained his rigid defensiveness. He never talked about his problems, but since he continued to yearn for compassionate understanding, he resented his wife bitterly for not drawing him out. His own failure to risk rejection by asking for support served as a self-fulfilling prophecy, confirming his expectation, "She doesn't care about me."

Mrs. S.'s background was quite different from her husband's. Her parents were indulgent and demonstrative. They doted on their only child, communicating their love by expressing constant, anxious concern for her well-being. When she was a little girl, the slightest bump or bruise was the occasion for lavish expressions of solicitous concern. She came to marriage used to talking about herself and her problems. At first Mr. S. was enchanted. "Here is someone who cares about feelings," he thought. But when he discovered that she didn't ask him to talk about his own concerns, he became resentful and progressively less sympathetic. This convinced her, "He doesn't care about me."

After the historical roots of current family conflicts have been uncovered, interpretations are made about how family members continue to re-enact past, and often distorted, images from childhood. The data for such interpretations come from transference reactions to the therapist or to other family members, as well as from actual descriptions of childhood memories.

Even more so than in individual therapy, psychoanalytic therapists who work with families deal less with recollections of the past than with re-enactments of its influence, manifest as transference. For this reason it is considered essential to create and maintain a milieu in which patients feel safe enough to relive some of their crucial unresolved conflicts, and to reactivate their early relationship images.

The following case demonstrates how the therapist's permissive acceptance enables family members to gradually shed their outer defenses and to reveal their basic conflicts and object images, which provide the material for mutative interpretations.

> The H.'s were a wealthy, highly educated family, who were concerned with their oldest child's listlessness, irritability, and poor performance in school. Despite the fact that the boy showed all the signs of a mild depressive episode, the therapist insisted upon seeing the whole family.
>
> In the first few sessions, the family was very polite and dignified, with each one playing a recognizable role. Alex, the identified patient, described his discouragement and lack of interest in school, while his parents expressed their concern, alternately supportively and critically. Alex's younger sister Susan, a lively and robust child, showed little concern for her brother, and generally spoke much more about her life outside the family than her brother did.
>
> At first the family was so composed and collected that the therapist began to experience reality as they did: namely, that nothing was wrong in the family, except for Alex. After a time, the parents had a few disagreements about how to respond to Alex, but they quickly submerged them. Gradually, however, as they felt safer in therapy—safer than they did alone together at home—Mr. and Mrs. H. began to argue more and more openly. During this process the therapist made no interpretations, but concentrated her efforts on accepting the couple's arguing, while gently blocking any efforts to detour their conflict. Because they felt protected by the therapist, the spouses allowed the full fury of their feelings to be expressed, and their arguments became increasingly vituperative.
>
> By uncovering the hidden conflict in the marriage, and blocking the scapegoating of the identified patient, the therapist was following the same course that most nonanalytic therapists would pursue. At this point, she did not simply stay with the couple's conflict, but instead began to explore their separate childhood histories. In short, having uncovered their conflict, she sought to trace its genetic source.
>
> What emerged from Mr. H.'s portrait of his childhood was a picture of a boy who had learned to appease his hypercritical mother by not openly challenging her. Moreover, since he did not expect much positive reaction from her, he generally avoided her company as much as possible.

For her part, Mrs. H. described her close relationship with a dominant mother and a lifelong disdain for her father, a man who was very successful professionally, but played only a marginal role in her upbringing.

Only after extensive exploration of these early object relations did the therapist begin to interpret the couple's current conflictual behavior. Mr. H., she pointed out, believed that he had to mollify his wife (like his mother), but didn't expect any understanding or support from her, so he withdrew from her and lavished his affection on his children. In their early married years, Mrs. H. struck back in self-defense; she demanded that he spend more time with her, talk more, and be more attentive. Eventually, however, she accepted his withdrawal (as she had seen her mother do with her father), and redirected her angry disappointment to her son. In short, these two apparently sophisticated adults were behaving, unconsciously, like children; he like a frightened child hiding from a harsh, critical mother, and she like a domineering woman hopelessly enraged at the lack of a relationship with her husband.

In this case, the therapist analyzed and interpreted the unconscious images that played a large part in the family's conflict. In addition, her permissive acceptance of the couple's loud arguments provided them with a permissive superego figure to be incorporated through the transference relationship. Psychoanalytic family therapists are aware that their influence is not confined to rational analysis, but also includes a kind of re-parenting. Thus, therapists may act in a more controlling or permissive fashion depending upon their assessment of the particular needs of the family.

One psychoanalytic family therapist who was acutely aware of his personal influence on families was Nathan Ackerman. His recommendations on technique (Ackerman, 1966) were designed to penetrate family defenses in order to surface hidden conflicts over sex and aggression. To begin with, he advocated a deep personal commitment and involvement with families. His own style was intimate and provocative. Unlike the traditionally reserved and aloof analyst, Ackerman related to families in a very open and personal manner. In this regard he wrote (1961, p. 242):

> It is very important at the outset to establish a meaningful emotional contact with all members of the family, to create a climate in which one really touches them and they feel they touch back.

After making contact, Ackerman encouraged open and honest expression of feeling by being open and honest himself. His spontaneous self-disclosure of his own thoughts and feelings made it hard for family members to resist doing likewise.

Ackerman certainly made full use of his warm and charismatic personality, but he did more than simply "be himself" and "let it all hang out" in family sessions. He also made conscious and deliberate use of confrontive techniques to tease family secrets and conflicts out from behind their defensive overlays. His own memorable phrase to describe this was "tickling the defenses." Always aware of people's tendency to avoid what is painful or embarassing, he teased, cajoled, and provoked family members to open up and say what was really on their minds.

Naturally, psychoanalytic family therapists emphasize that much of what is hidden in family dialogues is not consciously withheld, but rather repressed into unconsciousness. The approach to this material is guarded by resistance, and when it is manifest it is often in the form of transference. In fact, it is fair to say that the goal of any form of psychoanalytic psychotherapy is to overcome resistance and to work through the past in the transference of the present.

Resistance is any conscious or unconscious behavior that blocks or impedes therapy. In families, resistance is collusive and more often manifest in overt behavior than it is in private therapy. Frank discussions of problems with other families are often painful, and most people go to great lengths to avoid them. Some of the common forms of resistance include seeking individual therapy or separate sessions to avoid facing family problems; persistently talking to the therapist instead of talking to other family members, despite the therapist's urging; avoiding conflictual topics; scapegoating; becoming depressed to avoid the danger of angry confrontations; and steadfastly refusing to consider one's own role in problematic interactions.

Most psychoanalytic family therapists deal with resistance by interpreting it early in its appearance. The family technique for interpreting resistance is different from that used in individual therapy. In individual therapy the aim is primarily to foster insight into the nature and meaning of resistance; therefore, resistances are generally not interpreted until they become obvious to the patient. Moreover, the most effective interpretations are elicited from the patient, rather than given by the therapist. For example, in individual psychotherapy a psychoanalytic therapist would wait for three or four recurrences before discusing a patient's lateness. Confronting lateness on its first occurence is merely liable to make the patient defensive, and thus impede understanding of the reason he or she is tardy. After the lateness (or other form of resistance) has become a recognizable pattern, the therapist will ask the patient to consider its meaning.

By contrast, family therapists interpret resistance more directly and sooner. The reason for this is that resistance in family therapy is more likely to take the form of acting-out, so that family therapists have to meet resistance with confrontation very early on. The following vignette illustrates the interpretation of resistance.

Mr. and Mrs. Z. had endured ten years of an unrewarding marriage, with an unhappy sexual relationship, in order to preserve the fragile security that being married offered them. Mrs. Z.'s totally unexpected and uncharacteristic affair forced the couple to acknowledge the problems in their marriage, and so they consulted a family therapist.

Although they could no longer deny the existence of problems, both spouses exhibited major resistance to confronting their problems openly. Their resistance represented personal reluctance to acknowledge certain of their feelings, and a joint collusion to avoid frank discussions of their relational problems.

In the first session, both partners said that married life had been "more or less okay"; that Mrs. Z. had some kind of "midlife crisis"; and that it was she who needed therapy. This request for individual therapy was seen as a resistance to avoid the painful examination of the marriage, and the therapist said so. "It seems, Mr. Z., that you'd rather blame your wife for the problems than consider how the two of you may both be contributing to the difficulties. And you, Mrs. Z., seem to prefer accepting all the guilt in order to avoid confronting your husband with your dissatisfaction and anger."

Accepting the therapist's interpretation and agreeing to examine their marriage together deprived the couple of one form of resistance, as though an escape hatch had been closed to two reluctant combatants. In the next few sessions both spouses attacked each other vituperatively, but they talked about her affair and his reactions rather than about problems in their relationship. These arguments were not productive because whenever Mr. Z. felt anxious he attacked his wife angrily, and whenever she felt angry she became depressed and guilty.

Sensing that their fighting was unproductive, the therapist said, "It's clear that you've put each other through a lot of unhappiness and you're both quite bitter. But unless you get down to talking about specific problems in your marriage, there is little chance that you'll get anywhere."

Thus focused, Mrs. Z. timidly ventured that she'd never enjoyed sex with her husband, and wished that he would take more time with foreplay. He snapped back, "Okay, so sex wasn't so great, is that any reason to throw away ten years of marriage and start whoring around!" At this point, Mrs. Z. buried her face in her hands and sobbed uncontrollably for several minutes. After she regained her composure, the therapist intervened, again confronting the couple with their resistance: "It seems, Mr. Z., that when you feel anxious, you get angry. Now what is it that makes you so anxious about discussing sex?" Following this the couple was able to talk about their feelings about sex in their marriage until near the end of the session. At that point, Mr. Z. again lashed out at his wife, calling her a whore and a bitch.

Mrs. Z. began the following session by saying that she had been extremely depressed and upset, crying off and on all week. "I feel so guilty," she sobbed. "You *should* feel guilty!" retorted her husband. Once again, the therapist intervened. "You use your wife's affair as a club to bludgeon her with. Are you still afraid to discuss specific problems in the marriage? And you, Mrs. Z., cover your anger with depression. What is it that you're angry about? What was missing in the marriage? What did you want?"

This pattern continued for several more sessions. The spouses who had avoided discussing or even thinking about their problems for ten years used a variety of resistances to veer away from them in therapy. The therapist persisted in pointing out their resistance, and urged them to talk about specific complaints.

Psychoanalytic family therapists endeavor to foster insight and understanding; they also urge families to consider what they are going to do about the problems they discuss. This effort—part of the process of working through — is more prominent in family therapy than in individual therapy. Nagy, for example, considers that family members must not only be made aware of their motivations, but also held accountable for their behavior. In "Contextual Family Therapy" (Boszormenyi-Nagy and Ulrich, 1981), he points out that the therapist must help people face the intrinsically destructive expectations involved in invisible loyalties, and then help them find more positive ways of making loyalty payments in the family ledger. What this boils down to is developing a balance of fairness among various family members.

Ackerman too stressed an active working through of insights by encouraging families to constructively express the aggressive and libidinal impulses uncovered in therapy. In order to alleviate symptoms impulses must become conscious; but an emotional experience must be associated with increased intellectual self-awareness in order for lives to change. To modify thinking and feeling is the essential task of psychoanalytic therapy, but family therapists are also concerned with supervising and analyzing changes in behavior.

EVALUATING THERAPY
THEORY AND RESULTS

Psychoanalytic therapists have generally been opposed to attempts to evaluate their work, using empirical standards. Since symptom reduction is not the goal, it cannot serve as the measure of success. And since the presence or absence of unconscious conflict is not apparent to family members or outside observers, whether or not an analysis can be considered successful has to depend on the subjective clinical judgment of the therapist. Psychoanalytic clinicians of course consider that the therapist's observations are entirely valid as a means of evaluating theory and treatment. The following quotation from the Blanks (1972, p. 675) illustrates this point. Speaking of Margaret Mahler's ideas, they wrote,

> Clinicians who employ her theories technically question neither the methodology nor the findings, for they can confirm them clinically, a form of validation that meets as closely as possible the experimentalist's insistence upon replication as criterion of the scientific method.

Another example of this point of view can be found in the writing of Robert Langs. "The ultimate test of a therapist's formulation," says Langs (1982, p. 186), "lies in the use of the therapist's impressions as a basis for intervention." What then determines the validity and effectiveness of these interventions? Langs does not hesitate; the patient's reactions, conscious and unconscious, constitute the ultimate litmus test. "True validation involves responses from the patient in both the cognitive and interpersonal spheres."

Is the ultimate test of therapy then the patient's reactions? Yes, and no. First, the patient's reactions themselves are open to various interpretations — especially since validation is sought not only in direct manifest responses but also in unconsciously encoded derivatives. Moreover, this point of view does not take into account the changes in patients' lives that occur outside the office or consulting room. Occasionally therapists report on the outcome of psychoanalytic family therapy, but mostly as an uncontrolled case study. One such unsubstantiated report is Dicks's (1967) survey of the outcome of psychoanalytic couples therapy at the Tavistock Clinic, in which he rated as having been successfully treated 72.8 percent of a random sample of cases.

SUMMARY

Psychoanalytically-trained clinicians were among the first to practice family therapy. However, when they began treating families most of them traded in their ideas about depth psychology for those of systems theory. The result was most often an eclectic mix of psychoanalytic and systems concepts, rather than a true integration.

In recent years the mainstream of psychoanalytic thinking has become increasingly dominated by object-relations theory and self psychology. In this chapter, I have sketched the main points of these theories, and shown how they are relevant to a psychoanalytic family therapy which integrates depth psychology and systems theory. A few practitioners have combined elements of both; none has achieved a true synthesis. Psychoanalytically-trained therapists have yet to utilize object-relations theory to develop a genuinely psychoanalytic approach to treating troubled families.

REFERENCES

Ackerman, N.W. *The psychodynamics of family life*. New York: Basic Books, 1958.

Ackerman, N.W. The emergence of family psychotherapy on the present scene. In M.I. Stein (Ed.), *Contemporary psychotherapies*. Glencoe, Illinois: The Free Press, 1961.

Ackerman, N.W. *Treating the troubled family*. New York, Basic Books, 1966.

Barnhill, L.R. & Longo, D. Fixation and regression in the family life cycle. *Family Process*, 1978, *17*, 469–478.

Bibring, E. Psychoanalysis and the dynamic psychotherapies. *Journal of the American Psychoanalytic Association*, 1954, *2*, 745–770.

Blanck, G. & Blanck, R. Toward a psychoanalytic developmental psychology. *Journal of the American Psychoanalytic Association*, 1972, *20*, 668–710.

Blanck, R. Marriage as a phase of personality development. *Social Casework*, 1967, *48*, 154–160.

Boszormenyi-Nagy I. Relational modes and meaning. In G.H. Zuk & I. Boszormenyi-Nagy, (Eds.), *Family therapy and disturbed families*. Palo Alto: Science and Behavior Books, 1967.

Boszormenyi-Nagy, I. Loyalty implications of the transference model in psychotherapy. *Archives of General Psychiatry*, 1972, *27*, 374–380.

Boszormenyi-Nagy, I. & Framo, J. (Eds.), *Intensive family therapy: Theoretical and practical aspects*. New York: Harper and Row, 1965.

Boszormenyi-Nagy, I. & Spark, G. *Invisible loyalties: Reciprocity in intergenerational family therapy*. New York: Harper and Row, 1973.

Boszormenyi-Nagy, I. & Ulrich, D.N. Contextual family therapy. In A.S. Gurman & D. Kniskern (Eds.), *Handbook of family therapy*. New York: Brunner/Mazel, 1981.

Bowen, M. Dysinger, R.H. & Basamania, B. The role of the father in families with a schizophrenic patient. *American Journal of Psychiatry*, 1959, *115*, 1017–1020.

Bowen, M. Family psychotherapy with schizophrenia in the hospital and in private practice. In I. Boszormenyi-Nagy & J.L. Framo (Eds.), *Intensive family therapy*. New York: Hoeber, 1965.

Bowen, M. The use of family theory in clinical practice. *Comprehensive Psychiatry,* 1966, *7,* 345–374.

Bowlby, J. The study and reduction of group tension in the family. *Human Relations,* 1949, *2,* 123–128.

Bowlby, J. *Attachment and loss, Vol. 1: Attachment.* New York: Basic Books, 1969.

Broderick, C.B. & Schrader, S.S. The history of professional marriage and family therapy. In A.S. Gurman & D. Kniskern, (Eds.), *Handbook of family therapy.* New York: Brunner/Mazel, 1981.

Bruch, H. *The golden cage.* Cambridge, Mass.: Harvard University Press, 1978.

Burlingham, D.T. Present trends in handling the mother-child relationship during the therapeutic process. *Psychoanalytic Study of the Child.* New York: International Universities Press, 1951.

Dare, C. Psychoanalysis and systems in family therapy. *Journal of Family Therapy,* 1979, *1,* 137–151.

Dicks, H.V. Object relations theory and marital studies. *British Journal of Medical Psychology.* 1963, *36,* 125–129.

Dicks, H.V. Marital tensions. New York: Basic Books, 1967.

Dostoyevsky, F. *The brothers Karamazov.* New York: Penguin Books, 1958.

Erikson, E.H. The problem of ego identity. *Journal of the American Psychoanalytic Association,* 1956, *4,* 56–121.

Erikson, E.H. Identity and the life cycle. *Psychological Issues,* 1959, *1,* 1–171.

Erikson, E.H. *Childhood and society.* New York: Norton, 1963.

Fairbairn, W.D. *An object-relations theory of the personality.* New York: Basic Books, 1952.

Fenichel, O. *The psychoanalytic theory of neurosis.* New York: Norton, 1945.

Ferreira, A. Family myths and homeostasis. *Archives of General Psychiatry,* 1963, *9,* 457–463.

Flugel, J. *The psychoanalytic study of the family.* London: Hogarth Press, 1921.

Framo, J.L. Symptoms from a family transactional viewpoint. In N.W. Ackerman (Ed.), *Family therapy in transition.* Boston: Little, Brown, 1970.

Freud, S. (1905) Fragment of an analysis of a case of hysteria. *Collected papers.* New York: Basic Books, 1959.

Freud, S. (1909) Analysis of a phobia in a five-year old boy. *Collected papers, Vol. III.* New York: Basic Books, 1959.

Freud, S. (1921) Group psychology and the analysis of the ego. *Standard Edition, 17,* 1–22. London: Hogarth Press, 1955.

Freud, S. (1923) The ego and the id. *Standard Edition, 19,* 13–66. London: Hogarth Press, 1961.

Greenson, R.R. *The theory and technique of psychoanalysis.* New York: International Universities Press, 1967.

Guntrip, H. *Personality structure and human interaction.* London: Hogarth Press, 1961.

Guntrip, H. *Schizoid phenomena, object relations theory and the self.* New York: International Universities Press, 1969.

Guntrip, H. *Psychoanalytic theory, therapy, and the self.* New York: Basic Books, 1971.

Jacobson, E. *The self and the object world*. New York: International Universities Press, 1964.

Johnson, A. & Szurek, S. The genesis of antisocial acting out in children and adults. *Psychoanalytic Quarterly*, 1952, *21*, 323–343.

Katz, B. Separation-individuation and marital therapy. *Psychotherapy: Theory, Research and Practice*, 1981, *18*, 195–203.

Kernberg, O.F. Structural derivatives of object relationships. *International Journal of Psychoanalysis*, 1966, *47*, 236–253.

Kernberg, O.F. Countertransference. In *Borderline conditions and pathological narcissism*. New York: Jason Aronson, 1975.

Kernberg, O.F. Object-relations theory and clinical psychoanalysis. New York: Jason Aronson, 1976.

Klein, M. Notes on some schizoid mechanisms. *International Journal of Psycho-Analysis*, 1946, *27*, 99–110.

Kohut, H. *The analysis of the self*. New York: International Universities Press, 1971.

Kohut, H. *The restoration of the self*. New York: International Universities Press, 1977.

Langs, R. *Psychotherapy: A basic text*. New York:, Jason Aronson, 1982.

Lasch, C. *The culture of narcissism*. New York: Norton, 1978.

Levinson, D.J. *The seasons of a man's life*. New York: Ballantine Books, 1978.

Lidz, T. Cornelison, A., & Fleck, S. *Schizophrenia and the family*. New York: International Universities Press, 1965.

Lidz, T. Cornelison, A., Fleck, S. & Terry, D. The intrafamilial environment of schizophrenic patients; II: Marital schism and marital skew. *American Journal of Psychiatry*, 1957, *114*, 241–248.

Mahler, M.S. On child psychosis and schizophrenia: Autistic and symbiotic infantile psychoses. *Psychoanalytic Study of the Child, Volume 7*, 1952.

Mahler, M., Pine, F. & Bergman, A. *The psychological birth of the human infant*. New York: Basic Books, 1975.

Martin, P.A. & Bird, H.W. An approach to the psychotherapy of marriage partners. *Psychiatry*, 1953, *16*, 123–127.

Masterson, J.F. Primary anorexia nervosa in the borderline adolescent—an object-relations view. In P. Hartocollis (Ed.), *Borderline personality disorders: The concept, the syndrome, the patient*. New York: International Universities Press, 1977.

Meissner, W.W. The conceptualization of marriage and family dynamics from a psychoanalytic perspective. In T.J. Paolino, & B.S. McCrady (Eds.), *Marriage and marital therapy*. New York: Brunner/Mazel, 1978.

Minuchin, S. *Families and family therapy*. Cambridge: Harvard University Press, 1974.

Mittlemann, B. The concurrent analysis of married couples. *Psychoanalytic Quarterly*, 1948, *17*, 182–197.

Modell, A.H. *Object love and reality*. New York: International Universities Press, 1968.

Nadelson, C.C. Marital therapy from a psychoanalytic perspective. In T.J. Paolino & B.S. McCrady (Eds.), *Marriage and marital therapy*. New York: Brunner/Mazel, 1978.

Oberndorf, C.P. Psychoanalysis of married couples. *Psychoanalytic Review*, 1938, *25*, 453–475.

Sager, C.J. Couples therapy and marriage contracts. In A.S. Gurman & D.P. Kniskern (Eds.), *Handbook of family therapy*. New York: Brunner/Mazel, 1981.

Segal, H. *Introduction to the work of Melanie Klein*. New York: Basic Books, 1964.

Sifneos, P.E. *Short-term psychotherapy and emotional crisis*. Cambridge: Harvard University Press, 1972.

Skynner, A.C.R. *Systems of family and marital psychotherapy*. New York: Brunner/Mazel, 1976.

Skynner, A.C.R. An open-systems, group analytic approach to family therapy. In A.S. Gurman & D. Kniskern (Eds.), *Handbook of family therapy*. New York: Brunner/Mazel, 1981.

Spitz, R.E. *The first year of life*. New York: International Universities Press, 1965.

Spitz, R. & Wolf, K. Anaclitic depression: An inquiry into the genesis of psychiatric conditions early in childhood. *Psychoanalytic Study of the Child*, 1946, *2*, 313–342.

Stierlin, H. *Psychoanalysis and family therapy*. New York: Jason Aronson, 1977.

Sullivan, H.S. *The interpersonal theory of psychiatry*. New York: Norton, 1953.

Szasz, T.S. *The myth of mental illness*. New York: Hoeber-Harper, 1961.

Umana, R.F., Gross, S.J. & McConville, M.T. *Crisis in the family: Three Approaches*. New York: Gardner Press, 1980.

Vogel, E.F. & Bell, N.W. The emotionally disturbed as the family scapegoat. In N.W. Bell & E.F. Vogel (Eds.), *The family*. Glencoe, Ill.: Free Press, 1960.

Winnicott, D.W. *The maturational process and the facilitating environment: Studies in the theory of emotional development*. New York, International Universities Press, 1965a.

Winnicott, D.W. *The maturational process and the facilitating environment: Studies in the theory of emotional development*. New York, International Universities Press, 1965a.

Wynne, L.C. Some indications and contraindications for exploratory family therapy. In I. Boszormenyi-Nagy & J.L. Framo (Eds.), *Intensive family therapy*. New York: Hoeber, 1965.

Wynne, L.C. Some guidelines for exploratory family therapy. In J. Haley (Ed.), *Changing families*. New York: Grune & Stratton, 1971.

Wynne, L., Ryckoff, I., Day, J. & Hirsch, S. Pseudomutuality in the family relations of schizophrenics. *Psychiatry*, 1958, *21*, 205–220.

Zinner, J. & Shapiro, R. Projective identification as a mode of perception and behavior in families of adolescents. *International Journal of Psychoanalysis*, 1972, *53*, 523–530.

5

Group
Family
Therapy

INTRODUCTION

most of the pioneers of family therapy were trained in psychoanalytic psychodynamics. When they began treating families, they shifted from individual to systems dynamics for explanatory principles. Some extrapolated from their understanding of intrapsychic dynamics, while others turned to the new literature on general systems theory to explain families. Outside the United States, group dynamics theory probably had a more significant influence on family therapy than either psychoanalysis or general systems theory. The theory of group dynamics and group psychotherapy was readily applicable to families, and thus group methods were the source of inspiration for a school of family therapists, most notable among whom was John Elderkin Bell. Families are groups with some unique properties and some properties shared with all groups. To the extent that families are like other groups they are a dynamic field of interacting social forces to which the principles of group dynamics are applicable.

Another congenial notion that family group therapists found in the group therapy literature is the idea that the essence of the individual is social. People develop in and are defined by their social contexts. Therefore, since psychological disturbances must have their origin in disturbed social relationships, the resolution of these disturbances may best be achieved in a social network.

Group therapists had found that an individual's symptoms were reactivated in therapy groups, which made the group an ideal place to observe and treat problems. Group therapists had also discovered that serving the group as a whole was the most effective way to serve its members. Family therapists reasoned that this would also hold true in the person's primary group, the family, and they were right. They further assumed that they could transfer the techniques of group therapy directly to families, and here they met with mixed success. It was certainly convenient to have a ready-made set of techniques to rely on, and the early results of family group therapy were positive. Gradually, however, as the field of family therapy matured, the unique systems properties of families have become more appreciated and the techniques of group therapy are less and less relied on in contemporary family therapy.

SKETCHES OF LEADING FIGURES

Group therapy influenced the beginnings of family therapy in two ways. First, many of the early family therapists turned to the group therapy model and the group dynamics literature to guide their efforts to treat families. Second, many of the pioneers of family therapy were themselves products of group therapy training and experience. These clinicians emphasized the similarities between the two approaches; for instance Midelfort (1957) stated that family therapy is an example of group therapy.

Developments in theory and research on small groups were applied first to group psychotherapy and later to family group therapy. One of the first to describe the process of group development was Bales (1950), who observed that groups have an *equilibrium problem*—namely, that they must balance the *group task*, productivity, with individual *social-emotional needs*. Another important group theorist was Bion (1961), who identified three emotional undercurrents in group development: *dependency, pairing,* and *fight-flight*. Subsequently, Bennis and Shepard (1956) identified 6 stages of group development that arise as members deal with problems of dependence and affiliation: *dependence-submission, counterdependence, resolution, enchantment, disenchantment,* and *consensual validation.* Schutz (1958) saw 3 stages: *inclusion, control,* and *affection.* Perhaps the most influential contributions to the group dynamics literature were made by Kurt Lewin (1951); Lewin's field theory led directly to applications in group therapy and encounter groups.

Of those who applied the group therapy model to family therapy, John Elderkin Bell is by far the most significant and the best known. So true is this, that this chapter is largely an exposition of his ideas. But there are also others who deserve to be mentioned in the history of family group therapy, including Rudolph Dreikurs, Christian Midelfort, S.H. Foulkes, and Robin Skynner.

Rudolph Dreikurs was a student of Alfred Adler, who put Adler's ideas into practice in child guidance clinics in Chicago. Adler (1931) believed that neurosis stems from childhood experiences of overprotection or neglect, and that the most effective time to intervene is in childhood when the person is still malleable. Accordingly, Adler organized child guidance clinics in Vienna in the early part of this century where he helped children develop positive self-images and strengthen their social feelings. Dreikurs followed Adler's techniques in many ways, including children's groups, community groups, parents' groups, and family therapy groups. As far back as 1951, Dreikurs wrote an article, "Family Group Therapy in the Chicago Community Child Guidance Centers," in which he spelled out his belief that problems in children are best dealt with by meeting with all members of the family (Dreikurs, 1951, p. 292).

> Discussion and therapy deal with the dynamics that operate within the family. Since the problems of the child express his *inter*personal conflicts within the family, rather than any *intra*personal conflict, the counselor deals with all members of the family who unwittingly take part in the conflict.

Dreikurs's technique with families combined emotional support and encouragement with interpretations and suggestions about modifying unhappy interactions. He encouraged families to discuss their mutual problems in an open, democratic spirit, and he urged them to institute a regular "family council," in order to carry the model of family group therapy into the family's daily life.

Despite the fact that his approach anticipated many later developments in family therapy, Dreikurs's work did not gain wide attention, nor did it have much direct influence on the field. Insofar as the field of family therapy is concerned, he is one of those people who possess foresight and imagination, but whose ideas do not take hold because they are not developed in a receptive professional context.

Christian Midelfort is another early figure in family therapy whose influence was largely restricted to his own place and time. Midelfort trained at the Henry Phipps and Payne-Whitney psychiatric clinics under Adolph Meyer, Oskar Diethelm, and Thomas Rennie; he practiced at the Lutheran Hospital in LaCrosse, Wisconsin. Charged with responsibility for treating fairly seriously disturbed patients, Midelfort decided that the only way to achieve lasting results was to include the patients' families in treatment. Although he still considered the patient as the focus of treatment, Midelfort developed an array of family therapy techniques that anticipated many later developments in psychoanalytic and family group therapies. One example of his inventiveness was that he hospitalized other members of the family in order to avoid totally removing a psychiatric patient from his or her social context. His own background in psychoanalysis determined his basic attitudes about psychopathology, but the exigencies of treating severely disturbed patients gradually changed his treatment approach so that it became more supportive. He came to believe that love is the most important element in treating emotional disorders. People need love to flourish; psychiatric patients are people in whom this need has been frustrated. Midelfort, therefore, saw his task as stimulating families to give and receive love. He considered family therapy a form of group therapy, and believed that the therapist should take two roles—an involved group member and its leader.

S.H. Foulkes was an English psychoanalyst and one of the organizers of the group therapy movement in Great Britain. Although he began conducting conjoint family therapy interviews early in the 1940s, his work is little known to family therapists, because his major interest and his publications are in group analytic therapy. As an analyst, Foulkes was aware of the complex interacting forces on individual personalities. Emotional disturbance, he realized, can not be regarded as in a vacuum, limited to an individual patient. Instead, Foulkes perceived the disturbance of the individual as embedded in a disturbed field of social forces. His term for the social forces in the group analytic situation was the *group matrix* (Foulkes, 1965); his analogous term for the patient's natural group was the *network*. The network covers not only the nuclear but also the extended family group and friends. Since psychological problems are due in part to pathological processes in interpersonal interactions, the network of communication became Foulkes's object of treatment in groups and families. He believed that it is impossible to change the patient without changing the network.

In families, psychodynamic bonds count more than kinship ties; therefore networks may include some people who are not official members of the family. The implication of this idea is that therapists should not decide *a priori* who to convene for treatment, but should start with the referred patient and then work with whoever is discovered to have strong psychodynamic ties to that person. Foulkes argued that psychiatric disturbance is a social process, and treatment should be conducted with all of the people who have an essential connection with the patient's basic conflicts, symptoms, and problems.

Foulkes's influence on British psychiatry was enormous. Among his followers is Robin Skynner, whose work overlaps the psychoanalytic (see Chapter 4) and group approaches to families. More of a synthesizer than an innovator, Skynner has not had wide influence in this country, but he has written a useful guide to analytic and group-oriented family therapy (Skynner, 1976).

Skynner's training in child and adult psychiatry led naturally to an interest in the family as a whole; and his group analytic apprenticeship with Foulkes helped shape his method of working with families. He began treating families in 1962 and has been an active force in the British family therapy movement. His orientation to families is revealed in the following remark: "The family, like the small group of strangers, is seen as possessing inherent potentials for constructive understanding and for facilitating growth and positive change, as well as for creating confusion and blocking development" (Skynner, 1976, p. 192).

The most influential person in family group therapy was and is John Elderkin Bell. One of the originators of family therapy, Bell began seeing families in 1951, although he did not report his work until later (Bell, 1961). Bell's professional training was in education and he began to practice therapy as a teacher. His early work was highly structured and directive, and he approached families as though they were students in a class on family life. Over time, however, he became less of an educator and more of a therapist, the difference being a progressively refined awareness of family dynamics and resistance to change.

Bell (1975) credits his start as a family therapist to a fortunate misunderstanding. When he was in London in 1951, Bell was under the mistaken impression that Dr. Bowlby of the Tavistock Clinic was experimenting with group therapy for families, which stimulated him to try this approach as a means of dealing with behavior problems of children. It turned out that Bowlby was only interviewing family members as an adjunct to treating children, but Bell did not learn this till later. Bell thought that if so eminent an authority as Bowlby was using family therapy, it must be a good idea.

When Bell started treating families he was encouraged by the success of his newly devised method, although he continued to revise his approach. As he began to report on his work, he gained wide influence in the 1960s; he is now recognized as one of the fathers of family therapy and remains one of its most thoughtful spokesmen.

THEORETICAL FORMULATIONS

Family group theory derives from the application of small group theory, which in turn stems from social psychology and sociology, to the natural family group.

Cartwright and Zander (1968) listed eight theoretical orientations to the analysis of groups:

1. *Psychoanalytic theory* derives from Freudian psychology and concerns motivational and defensive processes in individuals in relation to group life.

2. *Field theory* holds that behavior is the result of a field of interdependent forces. Just as in physics, events (social behaviors) are seen as determined by their relations to other events in the same system.

3. *Interaction theory* views the group as a system of interacting individuals.

4. *Systems theory* analyzes groups in terms of the structure and function of interlocking elements.

5. The *sociometric* orientation emphasizes interpersonal attraction among group members.

6. The *general psychology* orientation extends theoretical analyses of individual behavior to group behavior. By limiting attention to individual motivation, perception, and learning, this orientation excludes the transcendent properties of groups.

7. The *empirical-statistical* model holds that basic laws of group behavior can be discovered through factor analysis of data about individuals.

8. The *formal-models* orientation attempts to construct internally consistent formal models of group behavior, using mathematical analyses.

Information about how small groups develop and function was developed in social-psychological and sociological theory and research. These discoveries led to the development of group psychotherapy. Most theories of group dynamics begin with the data of interaction between group members. This interactional focus characterizes virtually all students of group behavior. But there are also forces within individual group members that operate in the formation of groups, some of which were first elucidated by Freud.

Although he is best known for his work on the psychology of individuals, Freud was also interested in interpersonal relationships. Many would consider his *Group Psychology and the Analysis of the Ego* (Freud, 1921) the first major text on the dynamic psychology of the group. According to Freud, the major requirement for transforming a collection of individuals into a group is the development of *leadership*. In addition to manifest tasks of organization and direction, the leader also serves as a parent figure on whom the members become more or less dependent. Given the presence of a leader, the psychological cement responsible for strong group ties is a mixture of imitation, identification, empathy, relatedness, sympathy, common purpose, mutual interest, and a shared recognition of having something in common. *Identification* is a basic mechanism in group formation, because the members identify with the leader who serves as a parent surrogate, and they also identify with one another as siblings. *Empathy,* a second major mechanism in group dynamics, enables members to experience their group life through one another. These two mechanisms promote positive feeling within the group and help to limit aggressiveness. Even *narcissism* is important in group development, because members project some of their own narcissism onto the group, which makes the group itself become an important entity.

Transference occurs in groups when members repeat in their relationships with the therapist and other group members unconscious attitudes and feelings that were derived from interactions with childhood figures. It may be obvious that such transference reactions are inappropriate in a group of strangers, but it is equally inappropriate for members of a family group to react to each other on the basis of past realities. An adult man who expects his mother to be completely understanding and supportive may be making a transference distortion just as much as if he were to expect similar reactions from women in a therapy group.

Freud's concept of *resistance* in dyadic therapy also applies to groups in general and to family group therapy in particular. Resistance occurs when group members, seeking to ward off anxiety, oppose the progress of treatment. Resistance to treatment may be manifested by individual family members as silence, hostility, refusing to attend sessions, or avoiding painful topics. The family as a whole group may also resist treatment, which can be seen in scapegoating, superficial chatting, prolonged dependency on the therapist, or outright refusal to follow therapeutic suggestions.

Like Freud, Bion (1961) also attempted to develop a group psychology of the unconscious, and he described groups as functioning on a *manifest level* and a *latent level*. At the manifest level, groups come together to work on a task that is conscious and rational. On this level, they need a leader to guide and direct them. Below this level, group members join together to fulfill powerful, but unconscious, basic needs. These needs are always present, but tend to recede when the group is busy with the conscious task; they rise to the surface when the group has little to do.

At the latent level, groups seek a leader who will meet their *dependency needs*, permit them to gratify their sexual needs, and lead them in *fight or flight* when danger threatens. These needs give rise to three *basic assumptions*, which characterize groups at one time or another. The basic assumptions are that the real purpose of the group is *dependency, pairing*, or *fight-flight*.

Freudian concepts, extrapolated from the individual to the group, remain part of the theoretical structure of group psychology; but most of the concepts in the study of groups focus less on individuals than on the interactions among them. Although many therapists continue to apply psychoanalytic concepts to the understanding of families and other small groups, considerably more attention is now paid to the action between, not within, group members.

Whole groups, including families, are usually defined by structure; subgroups are defined by function. In fact, total groups rarely appear in one place at the same time. Most of the time groups, including families, operate as subgroups. It isn't the family that cleans the house, it's Mom and the kids; it isn't the family that plans a move, it's Mom and Dad.

The processes of group formation in families are action processes leading to accommodation of complementary and conflicting demands of family members (Bell, 1975). The action processes can be specified in terms of *purposes* (motivation); *media* (verbal and nonverbal channels of communication); *mechanisms* (decision, evaluation, revision); and *form* (structure of relationships).

Hearn's (1957) analysis of the formation of small groups is equally useful for understanding families. Initially, group (or family) interactions are situation-specific and purposive. Later, relationships and patterns of interaction become automatic and are treated as ends in themselves. In order to simplify their operations, groups undergo a progressive reduction of the number of ways group members interact. But sometimes, especially when problems arise, a group must increase the complexity of its structure and interactions. Hence, groups are subject to periodic expansion and contraction. Subgroups are formed and dissolved as other action steps are needed.

A work group may spin off an ad hoc committee to deal with a particular problem. In a family, Dad and the kids may team up to take care of the housework while Mom is sick.

According to Kurt Lewin's (1951) field theory, conflict is an inevitable feature of group life, as members vie with one another for adequate *life space*. Just as animals need their own territory, people seem to need their own "space," and for this reason there is an inherent tension between the needs of the individual and those of the group. The amount of conflict generated by this tension depends upon the amount of restriction imposed by the group, compared with the amount of mutual support it gives in exchange. How groups deal with this conflict depends partly on their structure and partly on their leadership. A poorly-organized and poorly-led group distributes tension unevenly; consequently, tension tends to disrupt the functioning of part of the group. This is one explanation for the concept of scapegoating in family therapy. On the other hand, a well-organized and well-led group distributes tension evenly, maximizing the group's capacity to handle problems.

What distinguishes Lewin's model of group tensions from earlier theories is that it is *ahistorical*. Instead of resorting to the personal histories of group members for explanations, Lewin based his analysis totally on the current nature of the group itself. This ahistorical model is the reason why most group-oriented therapies focus on the *here-and-now*. It is also the basis for believing that *process*, rather than *content*, holds the key to understanding and modifying group function. Although he was not a clinician himself, Lewin's theories had a major impact on psychotherapists, shifting their focus from the individual to the group, from the intrapsychic to the interpersonal, and from the retrospective to the experiential.

Role theory, which has influenced so many branches of psychology, occupies a prominent place in theories of group functioning. Every position in a group structure has an associated role, which consists of expected and prescribed behavior for the occupant of that position. In family groups some roles are biologically determined, while others depend upon the specific dynamics of the group. Sex roles, kinship roles of mother, father, son, and daughter, and age roles of infant, child, teenager, and adult are obvious, but not necessarily more significant than such assigned roles as "the strong one," "the scapegoat," or "the baby." According to Cooley (1902), multiple roles are the key to understanding individual motives.

The number and character of role conflicts provide a basis upon which to evaluate the functioning of social systems (Brown, 1965). In families, role conflicts can occur within or between roles; some are chronic, while others develop in the face of changing circumstances. *Intra-role* conflict exists when a single role calls for contradictory performances, such as when a child is expected to be both independent and obedient. *Inter-role* conflict exists when two or more roles are not complementary, as for example when a woman is expected to be strong as a mother, but helpless as a wife. Notice that the notion of role conflict makes no reference to personalities. The problem is not in the person, but in the design of the system.

There can also be problems in how well roles and personalities fit each other. A private and isolated man may have trouble filling the role of a warm and loving father. Thus personality and role are not exclusive or independent of each other; they are mutually determinative. Parsons (1950), speaking as an analytically-oriented sociologist, emphasized the internalization of family roles as a determining influence on the development of personality. Over time, roles tend to become stereotyped, and thus limit flexibility in individuals and in the group (Bales, 1970). Clinicians like Speigel (1971) and Bell (1975) developed the clinical implications of role theory and applied them to the diagnosis and treatment of families. Speigel made conflict and complementarity central to his conception of role theory; Bell emphasized the impact of role rigidity on family dysfunction.

As this brief summary demonstrates, family group theory is an amalgam, combining sociological concepts derived from group dynamics with clinical concepts derived from group therapy. Some of these concepts play an academic, supporting role; others are directly applied to solving the practical problems of treating family groups.

NORMAL FAMILY DEVELOPMENT

The growth process, from birth onward, takes place in a group setting. From the start, the child is a member of an interacting group. Since the family shares a number of properties in common with other groups, some family therapists have discovered that concepts in the literature of group dynamics are useful for explaining the processes of normal development.

One of the first to describe the process of group development was Bales (1950) who introduced the notion of an *equilibrium problem* in group development. To be successful, groups must achieve a balance between the productivity necessary to carry out the *group task* and the harmony needed to meet the *social-emotional* needs of the individual members. Although Bales's conclusions were based on observations of laboratory groups, they are equally applicable to normal family development. The same is true of Bion's (1961) three emotional modalities—*dependency, pairing, fight-flight*—which underlie the development of families as well as other groups. Bennis and Shepard (1956) identified *dependence* and *independence* as the two major developmental problems of groups. Within the period of dependency, they found three distinct phases—dependence-submission, counterdependence, and resolution. Within the period of independence they found subphases of enchantment, disenchantment, and consensual validation. And, William Schutz (1958) considered the most important stages of group development to be *inclusion, control,* and *affection.*

A number of studies in group dynamics indicate that *cohesiveness* is a major criterion of well-functioning groups. Cohesiveness here refers to the group's attractiveness, morale, and co-ordination. The greater the group's cohesiveness, the greater is its social influence and the more likely are its members to conform to group standards (Shaw, 1981). *Need compatibility* is another factor that determines whether or not a group functions well (Shaw, 1981). When the members of the group have needs which are compatible with each other, the group will function smoothly. If not, there is conflict. Extrapolating this finding to families, we may assume that compatibility of needs would make good marriages. This assumption has been supported by studies demonstrating that need compatibility predicts marital choice (Winch, 1955) and marital adjustment (Meyer and Pepper, 1977). Elsewhere Bell (1975) lists "complementarity of aims" as one of the major criteria of normal family development. Speaking of the healthy and efficient family, he wrote (Bell, 1975, p. 180):

> It shows, by the mutual satisfaction of its members and by action in concert, that complementary aims exist and are supporting the functions and structure of the group as a group.
> It has available multiple methods for accommodating the mutually incompatible demands of its individual members. It demonstrates from day to day a variety of patterns by which it faces and handles the conflicts between individuals and factions within it.
> It has a means of repeatedly evaluating the consequences of its achievements of accommodation.
> It chooses to operate flexibly, so that new methods of accommodation may be discovered and taken up when radical shifts are required.

According to Midelfort (1957), love is the ingredient most necessary for normal family development. The normal family provides love through approval, understanding, and affection. This gives children a base of security from which they grow into competent individuals and members of groups. Having received enough love to make them secure, they are capable of functioning autonomously and, as social beings, able to give love to others.

Beyond those already mentioned, many of the concepts about normal group development in the group dynamics literature are restricted to the process of group therapy. Therapy groups are made up of peers and strangers who are selected by the therapist; families are not. Moreover, since the group leader is both more prestigious and more of an unknown quantity to group members than are parents to their children, studies of how group members define themselves in terms of the leader (Yalom, 1970) are less applicable to family development. Another aspect of the group dynamics literature that limits concern with the history of normal development is the ahistorical approach introduced in Lewin's (1951) field theory. Accordingly, family group therapists have been more interested in the quality of here-and-now interactions than in how they developed.

DEVELOPMENT OF BEHAVIOR DISORDERS

The ahistorical orientation of group dynamics also affects the family group therapist's view of behavior disorders. There is less interest in the development than in the description of disorder, and a greater tendency to describe disorder as embedded in the dynamics of family interactions. Symptoms are considered as disturbed and disturbing group processes. But the group does not *cause* disturbance in its members; rather, the behavior of the members is part of the disturbance of the group. This is another way of saying that family group therapists rejected linear causality in favor of circular causality, which they described in terms of "group dynamics."

As soon as he began seeing whole families, Bell was aware of the circular causality of problems, which he contrasted with the linear, psychoanalytic view that parents cause problems in their children. In his words (Bell, 1961, p. 48):

> Because psychoanalysis has emphasized the importance of early childhood and its genetic processes in personality formation, there has grown up a tendency to ask about the nature of the parent in relation to the child, to single out the more significant influences of the parent on the child that occur at particular stages of child development, and to evaluate the parents in terms of certain value systems that have been implicit in or the product of such conceptions as the oral and anal phases of development or the Oedipus

complex. Thus the evaluation is made from the standpoint of the child, as though the interpreter were looking at the parents through the child's eyes.

In family group therapy it is not possible to empathize with a child to the extent of evaluating the parents only from his perspective. To do so would lead to thinking of the parent primarily in terms of his contribution to the child's pathology. It is not hard to see how parents would be offended at being reminded that the sins of the fathers are visited upon the children. In family therapy we have to think, also, that the sins of the children are visited upon the parents.

Family group therapists are less concerned with the origins of psychopathology than with the conditions that support and maintain it. The perpetuation of pathology is viewed as meaningful, and necessary if the group is to continue to operate as it has been organized. This is why, when an individual is treated in isolation, the group will confront and oppose his changed behavior. Moreover, if symptoms are resolved in one member of a natural group, they will break out in another. In the family, if "the patient" improves, someone else will have to take on the role of the sick one as a means of maintaining the family's pattern of functioning. What may look like progress is resisted in order to preserve what has become the status quo.

The specific aspects of group dynamics that are associated with the development of behavior disorder include stereotyped roles, breakdowns in communication, and blocked channels for giving and receiving love.

Rigidity of roles forces group interactions to occur in a narrow, stereotyped range. The number of roles is reduced and individuals are not allowed to escape from roles that perpetuate the status quo. One manifestation of this is constricted communication. If a father is trapped in the role of a depressed patient, then he will not be able to communicate as an assertive or angry husband. As Bell says, (1975, p. 185):

> Acting in a disturbed way is a role, just as being a "model child," "the baby," "the black sheep," and so on, are roles. Such roles are imposed on a particular individual because the family has discovered that this structuring seems to be the best way to handle the complex interrelations that exist within the family.

Acute symptoms may be regarded as signs of a family member's needs and wants. The symptom is an attempt to communicate these needs and to prevent the group from ignoring them. In normal families, needs which arise at changes in the life cycle may be communicated directly. Then the group can understand and restructure itself to meet these needs. In the face of changing circumstances, the group must develop alternative avenues of interaction. If they are stuck with inflexible roles and an unvarying structure, the group malfunctions. Because it is threatening, communication about disturbance and frustrated needs is blocked, misunderstood, or rejected. The result is often a symptomatic disturbance in the person whose needs are unmet.

If the needs which generate acute symptoms continue to go unmet, the symptoms, themselves, may be perpetuated as a role. Chronic symptoms and the "sick role" then are maintained by the pattern of family interactions. The symptomatic one takes on the function of preserving what has become the status quo. The following brief clinical narrative illustrates this process.

> Jonathan was an only child who seemed to flourish on his parents' attention. He was especially close to his mother, and the two of them never seemed to mind his father's frequent business trips as long as they had each other for company. But when he turned five and started school, something happened to Jonathan. He was at first very enthusiastic about kindergarten and eagerly looked forward to "playing with all the other kids." His mother was pleased with how well her "little man" was adjusting to school, but she did not like the idea of his staying after school to play with the other boys in the school playground.
>
> At first Jonathan protested his mother's restrictions, but he soon gave up and grew moody instead. The moodier he got the more solicitous and protective his mother became. Moreover, as mother continued to hover over Jonathan, father became even more distant.
>
> Jonathan's entry into school was a life cycle transition that called for an expansion of roles in the family. Instead of only being "Mommy's little man," it was time for Jonathan to also take on the roles of schoolboy and playmate. Unfortunately, this family was structured too rigidly to tolerate such a transition. Jonathan's role of "Mommy's little man" was critical in stabilizing the parents' comfortably distant relationship.
>
> Had the family entered treatment shortly after this transition, when Jonathan's symptoms were acute, it is likely that the problems could have easily been resolved. Unhappily, they did not. Jonathan's moodiness soon took on a life of its own. No longer, "Mommy's little man," he became "poor Jonathan," a quiet but sad little boy, who would rather help his mother around the house than play with other children.

Since verbal communication is the primary vehicle in group therapy, it is not surprising that family group therapists consider poor communication to be one of the major features of family pathology. This attitude is not unique to them. Communication difficulties are so often cited as a problem in unhappy families that the concept has become a cliché, so universally applied that it often loses meaning.

Even the general public is preoccupied with problems in communicating. In fact, when people who come for marital therapy are asked what their trouble is, the most common answer is, "communication." But even if nearly everyone does have trouble communicating, this fact does not explain what caused their problems. Is trouble in communicating the cause or the effect of family problems? The answer depends partly on one's theory of pathology, but even more on the nature of treatment. Family group therapy was developed at a time when there was little sophisticated theory about systems dynamics. It was a pragmatic approach, based more on technique than theory; and the essence of the technique was to analyze the process of group communication. Naturally then, poor communication had to be considered an essential feature of family pathology. But still, this should be understood more as a descriptive than an explanatory statement. Family group therapists talk about poor communication in the families they treat, but they do little to explain how this problem developed. Nevertheless, "poor communication" may be as good an "explanation" as "headache" is when the only medicine available is aspirin.

Another aspect of family pathology, lack of love, is also more a descriptive than an explanatory idea. According to Midelfort (1957), psychiatric problems develop when families are unable to provide sufficient love and understanding. Midelfort's "explanation," however, may be a consequence of his method of treatment, which is primarily supportive and nurturing. If providing love is the cure, than lack of love must be the disease.

In the families that he studied, Midelfort found obedience to be more prized than affection, and reward and punishment to be of more concern than giving and receiving love. He noted that it is particularly common in depressed families to express love only when there is strict conformity to the family pattern.

GOALS OF THERAPY

The goal of treating family groups is the same as treating stranger groups: promoting individuation of group members and improving their relationships and interactions. The group and its members are seen as inextricably intertwined; growth in one means growth in the other. By today's standards, this notion is hardly revolutionary, but family group therapy was a groundbreaking approach; today most of its tenets are familiar, but in the 1950s many of these ideas were radically new.

Individual growth is promoted when unmet needs are verbalized and understood, and when overly confining roles are explored and expanded. When family members are released from their inhibitions they are able to develop new forms of expression to channel interpersonal communication. But, just as individual growth does not mean isolation, the goal of family group therapy also includes greater family cohesiveness. Family cohesiveness is thought to be both a wish and a duty of family members. Bell (1961) and Midelfort (1957) believe that people have a deep longing for a closer family bond; they both endeavor to help the families they work with achieve this goal. Moreover, family group therapists also consider it everyone's duty to support the needs of their families.

The family group therapist puts a boundary around the family by meeting with them as a group. This enables them to learn to act together as a group. But the family group therapist allows the family to determine its own objectives. The therapist supports the family in setting their own goals and priorities, but does not impose his or her own (Bell, 1976). All therapists make this claim, but few live up to it. My observations of Bell's work suggest that he does not impose his values or set specific goals for families, although he does have general goals always in mind.

In describing the signs that a family is ready for termination, (Bell, 1975) implicitly revealed his general goals for treatment. Treatment is complete when the family has resolved or learned to cope with the presenting symptoms; when they show increased co-operation, independence, and humor; when their interactions are freer and more open; when all family members experience greater security; and when there is greater flexibility in family roles.

If a dysfunctional group is seen as one where roles have become rigid and inflexible, then therapy should be aimed at exploring and expanding roles. Furthermore, if communication has been impoverished by role rigidity, then improved communication becomes the means to meet the goal of improved group functioning. Enhanced communication, which is often considered an end in itself, can better be understood as a means to an end. The family with clear and open communication can voice unmet needs, reduce distorted perceptions of each other, share feelings, solve problems, and alternate flexibly among a variety of roles. When nonverbal signs and symptoms of distress are put into words, the family can change and restructure itself. Often these changes take the form of increasing the range and flexibility open to family members.

Although it can be described in many ways and explained as serving other ends, the primary aim of family group therapy is simply this: to improve verbal communication among family members. A theoretical analysis of group dynamics could be used to elaborate more complex goals of a functional group, but this would distort, rather than enrich, the understanding of family group therapy. The goal of this approach reflects the fairly simple view of families and their problems that was prevalent among the average clinical practitioners of the 1950s. While Gregory Bateson was laboring with his complex systems analyses, most clinicians thought that the way to help troubled families was simply to have them sit down and talk to one another. Moreover, as soon as these families did begin to converse, they had enough communicational problems to keep therapists busy for a long time correcting these errors, without having to spend time on issues of systems dynamics.

CONDITIONS FOR BEHAVIOR CHANGE

Action and insight are the primary vehicles of change in family group therapy. As in group therapy, members of the group meet regularly to discuss their problems, while the therapist encourages them to talk openly and critiques the process of their interaction. Opinions as to which of these two mechanisms, action or insight, takes precedence have changed, both in family therapy in general, as well as in family group therapy. Bell's (1961) early view was that insight is the prerequisite that enables family members to change their behavior. Therefore, he first interpreted their behavior to them, and then helped them change. As he gained more experience with families, he came to see that the effect works better the other way around. Now (Bell, 1975) he believes that the first step is to help families change their patterns of behavior through direct influence. Only after they have begun to interact more productively does he add interpretations, so that insight can solidify the behavioral changes.

Families, stuck in rigid patterns of behavior and perception, operate as *quasi-stationary equilibria* (Lewin, 1951) that resist change. The therapist joins the group as an outsider, which enables family members to relate to him or her in new ways. Once the therapist joins the group, it becomes a new group, with new possibilities for perception and interaction. For example, children who are accustomed to not being listened to by grownups, tend to make themselves "heard" by disruptive behavior. But if the therapist demonstrates a willingness to listen, the children may learn to express their feelings verbally rather than in action. The same is true of parents, who may suddenly "grow up" when they begin to interact with a family therapist. This introduces new perspectives for the entire family, as demonstrated by the following vignette.

> Mrs. Smith complained of her husband's sullen manner and of his incompetence around the home. The children shared their mother's image. When their daddy came home from work, he always seemed to be tired and he rarely played with them. When the family came to treatment, the therapist was immediately struck by Mr. Smith's withdrawn posture and seeming disinterest. However, unlike Mrs. Smith and the children, the therapist did not assume that this stereotyped behavior was characterological or immutable. After all, since he was a successful attorney, the therapist assumed that Mr. Smith must be both reasonably sociable and competent at work.
>
> Instead of accepting his posture of withdrawn disinterest, the therapist began to draw him out, at first about his work, and later about his views of the children. In this context, Mr. Smith dropped the role he played at home and took up the one he played at work. As he spoke with energy and enthusiasm to the therapist, the rest of the family began to see him in a new light.

Once they revise their stereotypes, family members may begin to re-evaluate and respond to each other in new and more productive ways. This enables them to test out new behavior, maintaining changes that prove useful, and rejecting those that do not. The therapist's role in this process may be described as promoting social interaction through communication, permitting the family to experience, appraise, and reorder its relational processes. The therapist disrupts unsatisfactory patterns of relationship, encourages the family to clarify and examine its goals, and helps them to modify goals to make them more productive for the whole group and its members. The therapist demonstrates, by the way he or she relates to individuals and subgroups, the possibility of more fluid communication and more flexibility in roles and functions.

As I have said, the general model of cure is to disrupt stereotyped patterns of interaction and promote flexible alternatives. Within this general framework, there are specific mechanisms thought to produce change in family group therapy. To begin with, the therapist declares and demonstrates a leadership role (Foulkes, 1965). This means taking active charge of the conduct of therapy sessions; it does not mean directing and advising the family. The therapist does not impose his or her model of behavior on the family, nor does the therapist tell them how to solve their problems. While many therapists are tempted to impose their own preferred styles of relating onto families, by doing so they seriously interfere with the families' autonomous functioning. Directiveness and advice-giving were not a part of analytic group therapy and they do not play a role in family group therapy.

The primary medium of exchange in group therapy is verbal communication, and therefore it is not surprising that family group therapists consider improved communication to be the major vehicle through which behavior change is accomplished. "Improving communication" as a goal of psychotherapy has become such a cliché that clinicians seldom question how improving communication leads to change. In family group therapy, improved communication leads to exploring relationships, restructuring roles, enhancing flexibility of the whole group as a system, and to bolstering the family's problem-solving abilities.

In another context, Yalom (1970) listed ten curative factors in group psychotherapy. These are: imparting of information, instillation of hope, universality, altruism, the corrective recapitulation of the primary family group, imitative behavior, interpersonal learning, group cohesiveness, and catharsis. Most of these factors rely on verbal communication, and their applicability to family therapy is readily apparent. Even the factor that Yalom calls the corrective recapitulation of the family group can be seen as relevant once it is realized that (a) families don't generally meet to discuss their relationships, outside of family therapy; and (b) family therapy may reactivate earlier experiences of family life, which, though no longer operative, still have a powerful unconscious influence.

Group-oriented therapists promote communication by concentrating their interventions on *process* rather than *content* (Bion, 1961; Yalom, 1970). The same is true of family group therapists. This is an important point, and one that is easy to overlook. Most approaches to psychotherapy are analytic — in the sense that they analyze a whole into its constituent parts. Psychoanalysts treat individuals as systems of interacting structures (id, ego, superego) in conflict, and most family therapists analyze families in subsystems of dyads or triads. The group model, on the other hand, treats the group as an organic whole, and attempts to deal with the process of interaction in the whole group. When the group model is applied to families, the total group interaction is the focus of observation and intervention.

Because they focus on the whole, and the field of observation is large and complex, family group therapists work with what is observable, with minimal inference. They generally do not meet with less than the whole group and, while they may occasionally work with the process of interaction in a subgroup, they prefer to focus on the social interaction of the entire family.

Families, like other groups, are thought to evolve through a series of stages in the process of therapy. Bell (1976) lists seven stages in the process of family group therapy. In the *initiation*, family and therapist get to know each other, exploring their expectations and working out the rules of their relationship. *Testing* is Bell's term for the next period, during which rules are probed as participants test out which will be adhered to and which deviated from. Next comes a *struggle for power* as individuals and subgroup coalitions maneuver to establish who will have power and under what circumstances. In the phase of *settling on a common task* the group and its individual members work out the tasks to which they will devote their energies. Once the tasks are established, members of the group work on both shared and individual problems in their *struggles toward completion of the common task*. *Achieving completion* comes when inclusive conciliation is reached among the group members. The final phase is *separation* during which the family leaves the therapist behind and resumes their independence. These stages are thought to develop spontaneously; they are not programmed by the therapist, but knowledge of them enables the therapist to lead the family group in solving their problems as these evolutionary developments proceed.

The primary technique for changing the process of the family group's interactions is simple interpretation. Not interpretation in the psychoanalytic sense of elucidating unconscious meanings, but in the descriptive sense of pointing out patterns of behavior that the family is not aware of. This reliance on interpretation is typical of the model of cure in group therapy, and it was typical of early family therapy. Today many family therapists consider this somewhat naive because it neglects, or at least grossly underestimates, the role of resistance.

In therapy groups the participants are strangers, and although each one of them is more or less resistant to personal awareness and change, the group does not have a long history of preferred patterns of interaction. In this context, there may be less resistance to changing the process of group interactions; therefore, simply pointing out what is going on may be an effective technique. The same is not, however, true of families. Families have a history during which they have worked out patterns of communication and interaction. These patterns are maintained because they are familiar and because they work—at least in keeping anxiety to a minimum. Moreover, participants are selected for therapy groups with an eye to including different personalities and defensive styles. Group members with an obsessive personality style are more likely to be affected by interacting with more expressive peers, and vice versa. Families, on the other hand, are like badly selected groups in that defenses and pathological attitudes are shared by all. Therefore, families have strong vested interests in the processes of their interactions, and a therapy that tries to change this by merely describing these patterns is likely to fail.

In Midelfort's (1957) view the family therapist is more of a midwife than an interpreter. According to him, members of unhappy families are severely frustrated from lack of love. The therapist's job is to help clear away obstacles and bring forth the love that is inside of them. This supportive and nurturant view of the process of change probably reflects the fact that Midelfort worked with sicker families than did Bell. As evidence of his parental stance with families, Midelfort (1957) wrote that family therapy may have to be continued throughout the life of severely disturbed families.

As a result of improving the process of their interactions, families become more efficient systems for handling problems. In family group therapy, the therapist doesn't direct problem-solving, but helps the family to become more effective at solving their own problems. One example of how this is done is Bell's early work with families. In his classic paper, "Family Group Therapy" Bell (1961) advised family therapists to help families solve one small problem very early in treatment. This, he suggested, would boost their faith in themselves and in the process of therapy. He cautions, however, that the family, not the therapist, must solve the problem. The therapist should neither select the problem nor tell the family what to do to solve it. The goal is not simply to get the problems solved, but to get the family to become a more effective and confident problem-solving group. In Bell's words, "The family will stay independent of the therapist so that they do not attribute success in problem-solving to the therapist, nor assume that to solve problems the family must seek a therapist's help" (Bell, 1976, p. 140).

In Kurt Lewin's (1951) field theory, *unfreezing* small groups is considered to be the first step in changing them. Similarly, Bell (1961) described the status of the family unit as a balance of forces. Change, he believed, results from a redistribution of forces within the group. He also thought that when family members begin to talk about problems, they are likely to mobilize a dormant impetus to solve them. One way this occurs is through the catharsis of blocked feelings, especially anger. "To move into the position to act constructively in changing their perceptions of one another, and the ways in which they wish to relate, the family must first rid the group of the accumulation of hostility from the past" (Bell, 1975, p. 137). Catharsis of unhappy feelings is thought to make room for dormant positive feelings. Midlefort's (1957) conception of therapy, as clearing away obstacles to giving and receiving love, is similar. The point is that the constructive forces are in the family; the therapist doesn't put them there, he or she only brings them out. Psychoanalytically-oriented family group therapists think in terms of bringing out unconscious positive and constructive impulses through the use of empathy. According to some, the therapist gives love, but responds to the family's reciprocated love by connecting it within the family, not between the family and the therapist. The therapist's affection and understanding mobilize similar positive responses among family members, which strengthens the bonds in the group.

Another way that talking about problems promotes latent forces to solve them is through the mobilization of guilt. According to Bell, "It would appear that family welfare is for many a stronger motivation than personal gain; at least the effort expended is less complicated by guilt. Thus family group therapy exploits a most forceful motivation" (1961, p. 50). Another more positive way of describing the cohesive, problem-solving force in families is to say that removing obstacles, intrapsychic and interpsychic, enables families to give and receive love and respect. From this perspective, the therapist's job is seen to be catalyzing expressions of love and trust within the family.

As families begin to discuss solutions to their problems, the therapist does not give advice; he or she creates the opportunity for the family to work on the problems, but then stays out of it. The therapist controls the process of what goes on in the sessions, but scrupulously refrains from advising or directing what goes on outside.

One of the ways the therapist influences the process of the family dialogue is to model listening. As the family members talk, the therapist listens intently, demonstrating to the speaker what it feels like to be heard and understood. Other therapeutic interventions are designed to block interference, argument, and blaming.

After expression comes analysis. Once members of the family have had a chance to express their feelings—and be listened to—the therapist begins to explore why those feelings were present, and why they were held back. As always, the family group therapist believes that what families can understand, they can change.

Interpretations are designed to revise some of the family's dysfunctional conceptions about the nature and causes of their problems. The therapist's remarks have the effect of reducing blame and guilt. Beginning therapists tend to focus on blame more easily than guilt. Even though parents commonly attack and criticize their children, they often privately blame themselves and feel guilty. Intervention around the surface content, the manifest attack, may reinforce a significant residual problem, the guilt. A parent whose guilt is masked by criticizing his children may be relieved by being chastised by a therapist, because the chastisement bolsters that parent's defenses without altering the fact that responsibility for change is projected. But when both blame and guilt are assuaged, responsibility for change need no longer be evaded. In family group therapy, change is viewed as a mutual responsibility of parents and children.

TECHNIQUES

The techniques of family group therapy are similar to those of analytic and supportive group therapy. The role of the therapist is that of a *process leader.* The model of the family is a democratic group; the therapist relates to the family democratically, just as the members relate to each other. As process leaders, therapists do not impose their goals on families, but rather help them set their own. As Bell (1976) noted, families may comply with a therapist's objectives, but unless these objectives correspond to their own, the changes will not last. "Thus I have knowingly adopted the process of intermediary leadership, and restrained my impulses to improve, educate, direct, and dominate families" (Bell, 1976, p. 136).

Family members are treated equally. The therapist sees all of them as people with something to say, and often in need of help saying it; the therapist encourages everyone in the family to open up and express their points of view. There is little concern with structure; few attempts are made to reinforce the parents' hierarchical position. If anything, there is a tendency to give extra support to the children, and to encourage their communication and interaction. Therefore, group-oriented family therapists often begin treatment by asking the children for their points of view, and make an effort to support the children as they try to express their thoughts and feelings.

Bell, whose work exemplifies this supportive stance toward the children, even begins treatment with a specially planned *child-centered phase.* In fact, his original approach (Bell, 1961) was carefully orchestrated into a series of such stages. He began treatment by meeting separately with the parents, with the stated purpose of hearing their story and explaining the method of family group therapy to them. In so doing it seems he was also asking their permission and co-operation.

In this initial meeting, Bell coached the parents to listen attentively to their children so as to insure that the children would open up. Moreover, he warned the parents that the children were likely to make some demands for changes in the family rules, and he encouraged the parents to accede to some of these. He also prepared the parents for the likelihood that their children would express a good deal of hostility when they began to open up. His purpose was to support the children's expression of feelings and to gain their trust and co-operation in the process of negotiating to solve family problems.

Family group therapists generally begin the first meeting with the whole family by explaining the purpose for bringing them together and by establishing ground rules for the meetings. In addition, family group therapists make explicit attempts to convert their clients to the point of view that problems are a product of families, not individuals. Bell describes the rationale he offers to families (Bell, 1975, p. 7) in the first session.

> At this first session I tell the children that I have talked with their mother and father and that we are getting together because they feel the family is not as happy as it should be. I aim to structure the situation by including the following in my comments during the first session. I recognize, first, that grownups are big, strong, sometimes bossy, and often fail to understand children. As a result they sometimes so run the family that the children are afraid to talk about their real feelings and real wishes. Second, that this therapy is a unique situation in that I am a grownup who is here to make sure that each child gets a chance to talk about the things that seem to him to make the family unhappy. Third, that I am on the children's side, as indeed the parents really are, but that the parents sometimes don't know how to take the children's side best, and that we can help them here to understand what the children feel and want. Fourth, that their mother and father really want to change things so that the children will be happier and be able to have more say in how the family is to be run. Fifth, that I am to see that everyone gets a chance to talk about important things and to work out together the plans for the family, but that I am only an umpire or a referee. I will not make decisions for the family.

This elaborate opening statement, from Bell's early days, implies that family members can rather easily be motivated to examine and change their behavior. Today's family therapists might consider that Bell underestimated the family's resistance to change. Such a long introduction also implies that the therapist is a powerful outside figure to whom the family defers, a model probably more appropriate for group therapy with strangers than family therapy, since the family resists outside influences and also tend to induct therapists into the family group.

During the *child-centered phase* of family group therapy, children are encouraged to air their grievances, while their parents refrain from making demands of their own. Bell reassures the children that they will not be punished if they speak up, and he backs up this promise by blocking parental retaliation. He also asks the children to take the lead in proposing solutions to the problems they voice. Many children respond by asking for unilateral concessions from their parents: "I want Mommy and Daddy to let me watch cartoons on Saturday." Other children are more prepared to seek solutions through compromise: "If I clean up my whole room on Saturday, then I should be allowed to come downstairs and watch cartoons."

Once the children have spoken up, and have been rewarded with some changes, then it is the parents' turn to open up. This begins the *parent-centered stage* of treatment. Parents usually begin by complaining about their children's behavior. Moreover, because they were purposefully restrained while their children complained, parents are likely to be angry during this stage. Again, it is important to shield the children from parental onslaughts and to help them continue to express their own feelings. This is a period of catharsis of dysphoric feelings, which can lead to increased tolerance in the home. In Bell's (1975, p. 10) words:

> Often when the hostility gets most intense we have the bonds between the members of the family strengthened as for instance when Mickey, an 11-year-old who had threatened to run away from home three weeks earlier, said during a particularly intense conference: "But I don't want to run away any more. I love you too much." But it is not only the children who provide these positive feelings. Parents at this stage often say to the child, "Now I realize how wrong I have been," or "I guess the real problem is not with you but with us."

Even when he switches to the concerns of the adults, Bell's treatment remains focused on the entire family. The same is not true of many other family group therapists, who tend to shift to couples' (as opposed to parents') problems as soon as possible. Although many parents *do* have marital problems that interfere with their parenting, such an eager switch to a couples focus often reflects the therapist's training and the fact of feeling more comfortable with adults.

Finally, there is a *family-centered stage* during which the therapist equalizes support for various family members while they continue to improve their communication and solve their problems. During this process the therapist determines which family members need to be supported and what kind of support will be effective. Support for someone who is blocked in communication may take the form of simple encouragement, or of interpreting blocks and resistances. The following vignette (Bell, 1975, p. 136) exemplifies Bell's directive style of intervening.

> After remaining silent for several sessions, one father came in with a great tirade against his son, daughter and wife. I noticed how each individual in his own way, within a few minutes, was withdrawing from the conference. Then I said, "Now I think we should hear what Jim has to say about this, and Nancy should have her say, and perhaps we should also hear what your wife feels about it." This restored total family participation without closing out the father.

A second approach to this situation would be to describe the group process, rather than to direct it. That is, to say something like, "You seem very angry, but I noticed that while you were talking your children turned away and your wife started to fidget in her chair." This approach draws the family's attention to the process of their interaction, and is typical of nondirective group and family group therapy.

During all of the discussions, the family group therapist stimulates conversation and interprets reasons for silence and negative feelings. Anything that interferes with balanced self-expression is considered resistance and is dealt with accordingly. Often this entails confronting someone by describing his or her nonverbal behavior. "Mr. Brown, I notice that you've been silent, but I think you've been telling us something with your hands." Attempts to talk privately with the therapist are also seen as resistance, and these too are derailed. "Well, I wonder whether we really should talk privately. After all we are here to talk these things out in the family, and I wonder why you feel you can't talk in front of them."

Bell originally interpreted freely the motivations and defenses of individual family members. However, his experience with this technique taught him that interpretations based on intrapsychic inferences were singularly unproductive in family treatment, and so he began to concentrate more and more on reporting to families his observations of the sequence of their interactions. He gives (Bell, 1975, p. 205) an example from his practice.

> "I noticed when you were saying this, Mr. Jones, that Mrs. Jones was opening and shutting her lips, and Jimmy was flicking his finger at a spot on the table."

Such direct attention to nonverbals is most effective when there is a block or interruption in meaningful communication.

Most of the interpretations in family group therapy focus on the process of interaction. Bell (1961) has described these interpretations as occurring in one of four varieties—reflective, connective, reconstructive, and normative. *Reflective interpretations* describe what the therapist sees going on at the moment. Also called *mirroring*, these interventions are designed to confront the family with unproductive aspects of its functioning. The following remark is what Bell would call a reflective interpretation. "I notice that whenever your wife says something critical you just hang your head, and that you never answer her back." In psychoanalytic terminology this is called a "confrontation," because its aim is not merely to foster insight, but to criticize and suggest a change.

Connective interpretations point out unrecognized links between different actions among family members. Such an interpretation might take the form of describing reciprocal behavior between two family members, or of reminding people that they seem to have had similar experiences. *Reconstructive interpretations* explain how events in the family's history provide the context for some current experience. *Normative interpretations* are remarks designed to support or correct a family member by comparing that person's behavior to what most people do. For example:

> Kevin, aged 12, lived in a family of women. His parents divorced when he was 6, after which he and his mother and two sisters moved in with an unmarried aunt. The family sought treatment for Kevin's "aggressive behavior," but it soon became apparent that the problem was that he was ostracized for anything that reminded his mother of his father. Thus, he was criticized for wanting to play football, being muddy, and watching television.
>
> At one point, Kevin's mother reproached him for "spending a whole hour watching television cartoons on Saturday morning." Here, the therapist intervened with a normative interpretation, saying "One hour, is that all? Most kids his age watch TV for three or four hours on Saturday morning."

> When Mrs. Banion became moody and disconsolate shortly after her first child was born, both she and her husband thought it was a case of postpartum depression. They were, therefore, surprised when the therapist they called asked to see all three of them for an evaluation. In that meeting, Mrs. Banion began by describing how unhappy she was, and how guilty that made her feel, "Because I love my baby, and this should be the happiest time of my life." So saying, she burst into tears, and sobbed, "It's just too much! I can't cope with it all." Despite the fact that Mrs. Banion was terribly upset and crying hard, the therapist noticed that her husband made no move to take the baby from her arms or to comfort her. He just sat there. His facial expression showed that he

was clearly upset and sympathetic, but still he just sat there. The therapist then asked the couple to describe how they divided the child's rearing chores. "Oh, that's my job," said Mrs. Banion. "Gary's too busy with his work." As it turned out, Mrs. Banion had assumed total responsibility for the new baby; her husband did not so much as change a diaper. In response to this information the therapist made a rather lengthy normative interpretation, explaining that "A new baby is a tremendous responsibility and requires an enormous amount of work. There's feeding, and changing, and bathing; and, I don't imagine either of you two have been getting much sleep these days?" The couple nodded vigorously, looking relieved that the therapist understood and was sympathetic. "And Gary, I understand you have your job, and that the two of you feel that the baby is Susan's job; but it is too big a job for one person. Susan, you're depressed because you are simply overwhelmed, you need some help from Gary. It's not a question of your failing in any way, it's just that taking care of a baby requires both parents. In my day, families stayed closer to home, and there was always an aunt or a grandmother to help out. Husbands— fathers—didn't have to. That's where this idea that taking care of a baby is a woman's job comes from. But these days, most young fathers help out quite a bit, changing diapers, playing with the baby, or sometimes taking the baby for a ride or a walk, so Mom can get some rest."

As this example suggests, family group therapists do not limit themselves to analyzing the process of communication and interaction. In fact, some of them use many of the techniques of supportive therapy, including reflection of feelings, encouragement, and suggestion. The degree to which such active, manipulative techniques are employed depends upon the predilections of the therapist and the nature of the patient population. Midelfort, who worked primarily with families of hospitalized patients, made extensive use of supportive techniques. He considered that many schizophrenic families were unable to manage without lifelong contact with a family therapist. In depressed families he found (Midelfort, 1957) that many of the patient's family members were also depressed and helpless, and needed the organizational and supervisory talents of a therapist to hold things together and to keep them going. With psychopathic families, Midelfort believed that it is the therapist's job to supply those missing social and cultural values which, when integrated into family life, inhibit impulsiveness.

Most family group therapists are less supportive and directive than Midelfort, and confine their manipulations to managing the group process within sessions. To this end they may silence a dominant member in order to create an opening for others to speak, or they may help someone put feelings into words by rephrasing what he or she had said.

In its early days, family group therapy was often the method chosen by beginners. It was an approach that required little familiarity with systems dynamics, and even at a time when few clinicians had much experience with families, most had received some training and experience with groups. Relatively inexperienced family therapists often used this method with families in crisis, and treated "better"—that is, more stable and highly motivated—cases with individual therapy. For these reasons family group therapy tended at the beginning to be relatively brief and crisis-oriented. As therapists became more skillful and practiced, however, families who came in crisis were often converted to a systems view and remained in treatment for a longer time. Bell, for example, generally saw families from about two months to about a year-and-a-half.

EVALUATING THERAPY THEORY AND RESULTS

Family group therapy is a pragmatic, clinical approach. Its practitioners have been concerned, not with theory building or research, but with clinical effectiveness. Therefore, its value has been measured by its usefulness to family group therapists and by the few reports of successful outcome.

Most of the early cases treated by John Bell (1961) were referred because of behavioral problems in one of the children. With this population, he reports a successful outcome in a great majority of cases. Midelfort (1957), who used family group therapy with a more seriously disturbed population, provided slightly more specific data on its outcome. Using family group therapy with 9 cases of hospitalized schizophrenics, 3 were improved but suffered at least one recurrent episode; 3 were improved with no recurrence; and 3 were not improved and had to be committed to state hospitals. According to Midelfort the major reason for success was not anything specific in the therapeutic method; it was that loving relatives took part in the treatment. Where relatives were not present or not supportive, treatment generally failed.

Midelfort (1957) also cited clinical data on the treatment of 90 families, all of whom had one member diagnosed as a psychopathic personality. Of these, 50 benefitted substantially, to the extent that the identified patient was able to control his impulses and to socialize more effectively.

One reason why it is difficult to assess family group therapy is that its methods have been appropriated by so many people that it hardly exists any longer as a separate approach. I said earlier that this was one of the original approaches to treating families, and that, as they gained experience, most family therapists modified this approach to incorporate ideas from systems theory and techniques to handle resistance to change. On the other hand, the major concepts and methods of family therapy are so basic that they have been incorporated into almost all forms of family therapy. Thus, family group therapy has met the fate of many innovations; it has been a victim of its own success, and absorbed by everyone in the field.

SUMMARY

Family group therapy was started by clinicians who had a background in group therapy, and by others who applied ideas of group dynamics to families. It was an approach widely used in the 1960s; but more recently some of its methods have been absorbed into newer approaches, and others have been discarded as more appropriate to group therapy than family therapy.

The leading practitioner of family group therapy is John Elderkin Bell who, along with Ackerman, Jackson, and Bowen, should be considered one of the originators of family therapy. Bell first considered family group therapy to be a battle between parents and their children, so that his basic strategy was to allow first one and then the other side to express themselves. Except for giving a little extra protection to the children, Bell remained pretty much in the background, confident that open communication would make it possible for families to resolve their own problems.

Interventions in family group therapy focus on the process of interaction, and are designed to confront families with their dysfunctional patterns of communication. These process interventions are designed to engage families and to move them through the stages of group development.

Family group therapists are directive to the extent of encouraging people to speak when they appear to have something to say. Otherwise, they are relatively passive and confine themselves to describing the processes they see in families. In therapy groups made up of strangers with contrasting defenses and personality styles, this approach is effective; moreover, therapists in these groups can act as catalysts who stir members to confront and challenge each other. Families, however, share defenses and pathological attitudes, and so therapists cannot rely on other group members to challenge family norms. That is why the therapist who treats families more actively confronts family patterns of interaction and looks for ways to circumvent the defenses that are more powerful in families than in groups of strangers.

REFERENCES

Adler, A. *Guiding the child.* New York: Greenberg, 1931.

Bales, R.F. *Interaction process analysis: A method for the study of small groups.* Cambridge, Mass.: Addison-Wesley, 1950.

Bales, R.F. *Personality and interpersonal behavior.* New York: Holt, Rinehart & Winston, 1970.

Bell, J.E. *Family group therapy.* Public Health Monograph No. 64, Washington: U.S. Government Printing Office, 1961.

Bell, J.E. *Family therapy.* New York: Jason Aronson, 1975.

Bell, J.A. A theoretical framework for family group therapy. In P.J. Guerin (Ed.), *Family therapy: Theory and practice.* New York: Gardner Press, 1976.

Bennis, W.G. & Shepard, H.A. A theory of group development. *Human Relations,* 1956, *9,* 415–437.

Bion, W.R. *Experiences in groups.* London: Tavistock Publications, 1961.

Brown, R. *Social psychology.* New York: The Free Press, 1965.

Cartwright, D. & Zander, A. (Eds.), *Group dynamics: Research and theory.* New York: Harper & Row, 1968.

Cooley, C.H. *Human nature and the social order.* New York: Scribner, 1902.

Dreikurs, R. Family group therapy in the Chicago community child-guidance centers. *Mental Hygiene,* 1951, *35,* 291–301.

Foulkes, S.H. *Therapeutic group analysis.* New York: International Universities Press, 1965.

Foulkes, S.H. *Group analytic psychotherapy: Method and principles.* London: Gordon & Breach, 1975.

Freud, S. (1921) Group psychology and the analysis of the ego. *Standard Edition Vol. 18.* London: Hogarth Press, 1955.

Gleitman, H. *Psychology.* New York: Norton, 1981.

Hearn, G. The process of group development. *Autonomous Groups Bulletin,* 1957, *13,* 1–7.

Lewin, K. *Field theory in social science.* New York: McGraw-Hill, 1951.

Meyer, J.P. & Pepper, S. Need compatibility and marital adjustment in young married couples. *Journal of Personality and Social Psychology,* 1977, *35,* 331–342.

Midelfort, C.F. *The family in psychotherapy.* New York: McGraw-Hill, 1957.

Parsons, T. Psychoanalysis and the social structure. *Psychoanalytic Quarterly,* 1950, *19,* 371–380.

Schutz, W.C. *FIRO: A three-dimensional theory of interpersonal behavior.* New York: Holt, Rinehart and Winston, 1958.

Shaw, M.E. *Group dynamics: The psychology of small group behavior.* New York: McGraw-Hill, 1981.

Skynner, A.R.C. *Systems of family and marital psychotherapy.* New York: Brunner/Mazel, 1976.

Spiegel, J. *Transactions.* New York: Science House, 1971.

Winch, R.F. The theory of complementary needs in mate selection: A test of one kind of complementariness. *American Sociological Review,* 1955, *20,* 52–56.

Yalom, I.D. *The theory and practice of group psychotherapy.* New York: Basic Books, 1970.

6

Experiential Family Therapy

INTRODUCTION

a n experiential branch of family therapy emerged from the humanistic psychology of the 1960s that like the individual humanistic therapies emphasized immediate, *here-and-now* experience. The quality of ongoing experience was both the criterion of psychological health, and the focus of therapeutic interventions. Experiential family therapists today still emphasize the emotional component of personalities, since they consider feeling-expression to be the medium of shared experience and the means to personal and family fulfillment.

Experiential therapy was most popular when family therapy was young, when therapists talked about systems change, but borrowed their techniques from individual and group therapies. Experiential family therapists drew heavily from Gestalt therapy and encounter groups. Other expressive techniques, such as *sculpting* and *family drawing*, bore the influence of the arts and of psychodrama. Because experiential treatment emphasizes sensitivity and feeling-expression, it was not as well suited to family therapy as were other approaches that deal with systems and action; consequently, the experiential approach has lately been used less and some of its early exponents, such as Peggy Papp, have adopted systems concepts and methods. The approach remains vital in the hands of such people as Carl Whitaker, Virginia Satir, and Walter Kempler, and they and other experiential family therapists have introduced a number of expressive techniques that any family therapist may find useful.

SKETCHES OF LEADING FIGURES

The dean of experiential family therapists is Carl Whitaker. He was among the first in the field to treat families, and he has remained one of the leading exponents of a free-wheeling approach, aimed at loosening the rigid patterns that keep families from being sensitive and responsive. Iconoclastic, even outrageous at times, Whitaker nevertheless retains the respect and admiration of the family therapy establishment.

After Dr. Whitaker completed his psychiatric residency at Syracuse University, he worked at the University of Louisville College of Medicine and at the Oakridge Hospital; then he went to Emory University. In 1955 Whitaker formed the Atlanta Psychiatric Clinic with eight other therapists, including Thomas Malone, John Warkentin and Richard Felder. Experiential psychotherapy was born in this group, which published a number of highly provocative and challenging papers. Since 1965, Whitaker has been at the University of Wisconsin Medical School, and in private practice in Madison.

A second major figure among experiential family therapists is Virginia Satir, who was one of the members of the early Palo Alto group. She emphasizes communication as well as emotional experiencing, so that her work must be considered in both the communications and experiential traditions. Satir is more important as a clinician and teacher than an innovative thinker. Beginners will find some useful suggestions in her book, *Conjoint Family Therapy* (Satir, 1967), but her real impact has been on the families she has worked with and on those professionals lucky enough to observe her in action.

Another Californian who has written a great deal about experiential family therapy is Walter Kempler. Kempler brings many of the ideas and techniques of Gestalt and other emotive therapies to his work with families. He writes about procedures commonly found in encounter groups and existential-humanistic individual therapies, which demonstrate the roots of experiential family therapy.

Fred and Bunny Duhl, co-directors of the Boston Family Institute, have introduced a number of expressive techniques into experiential family therapy. They use nonverbal means of communication, such as *spatialization* and *sculpting* (Duhl, Kantor, and Duhl, 1973), as well as *roleplaying* and *puppets* (Duhl and Duhl, 1981). Their approach which they call "integrative family therapy," is an amalgam of elements from numerous sources, including psychodrama, experiential psychotherapy, cognitive psychology, structural family therapy, and behavioral psychotherapy. The Duhls are included in this Experiential Family Therapy chapter because of their technical contributions, rather than because their work fits neatly into this, or any other, conceptual scheme.

Experiential family therapy derives from existential and humanistic psychology, so that experientialists share a commitment to freedom, individuality, and personal fulfillment. Otherwise, they are relatively atheoretical. The hallmark of this approach is the use of techniques designed to open individuals to their inner experience and to unfreeze family interactions. Experiential approaches reached their greatest popularity in the 1960s (Nichols and Zax, 1977), and have since then largely been displaced by developments in more systems-oriented therapies. Once feeling-expression occupied center stage in psychological therapies; today, that place is held by behavior and cognition. Psychotherapists have discovered that people think and act; but that does not mean we can ignore the immediate emotional experience that is the main concern of experiential family therapy.

THEORETICAL FORMULATIONS

Carl Whitaker may have best expressed the experientialists' position on theory in his "The Hindrance of Theory in Clinical Work" (Whitaker, 1976a). In this article Whitaker describes what he considers to be the chilling effect of theory on intuition and creativity in psychotherapy. Theory may be useful for beginners, Whitaker says, but his advice is to give up theory as soon as possible in favor of just being yourself. He quotes Paul Tillich's existential aphorism, "Being is becoming," to support his own contention that psychotherapy requires openness and spontaneity more than theory and technique; and he cites the fact that technical approaches usually do not work for second-generation therapists. For instance, Carl Rogers and Joseph Wolpe were themselves quite successful using theoretically-inspired technical procedures; their students, however, were less successful, and Whitaker suggests that the reason for their failures was that they could not be creative themselves when they were copying the theoretical structure of their mentors. Although Whitaker doesn't mention this point, it also may be due to the fact that theories of clinical innovators are only secondary elaborations—that is, afterthoughts and rationalizations—of methods that suit their personal styles, and that do not work for other people.

Whitaker says that therapists who base their work on theory are likely to substitute dispassionate observation for caring, and goes on to imply that theory is a refuge from the anxiety-provoking experience of sharing a family's life stress. Instead of having the courage just to "be" with the family and help them grapple with their problems, theoretically-inclined clinicians use theory to create distance in the name of objectivity. This sentiment is echoed by Kempler (1981, p. 45), who wrote, "Theorizing, if not theory, is treacherous." The danger he alludes to is that theories may bias and contaminate experience.

Most people consider psychotherapy to be a mixture of art and science; for experiential therapists art is 90 percent, science 10. The search for theory, according to this viewpoint, then arises from an attempt to escape the tension and anxiety of being fully with unhappy families. However, Whitaker suggests therapists do not need theories to handle stress and anxiety; what they do need are supportive co-therapists and wise, helpful supervisors. In short, it is not technique but personal support which enables therapists to do their best. By avoiding theory, Whitaker believes that he forces families to establish their own theoretical way of living. This is a form of active parenting which carries a deep respect for the individual and for the unique identity of each family he works with.

No theory is, of course, itself a theory. To say that therapy should not be constrained by theory is to say that it should be loose, creative, open, and spontaneous. Therapists should offer their own feelings, fantasies, and personal stories, if that's what they feel like doing, and if that's what they think it takes to help families become more aware and sensitive.

Despite Whitaker's disdain for theory, however, experiential family therapy is very much a child of the existential, humanistic, and phenomenological tradition: all experiential family therapists, including Whitaker, owe some of their inspiration to thinkers in this tradition.

Philosophers like Edmund Husserl and Martin Heidegger (1963) were the first to work out the implications for clinical practice contained in existential thought. Their ideas were assimilated and developed by Ludwig Binswanger (1967), who formulated a new theory of the psychotherapeutic process, but remained tied to the psychoanalytic method. The same may be said of Medard Boss (1963), the developer of "Daseinsanalysis," which also differs from psychoanalysis more in theory than in practice. Much of the theorizing done by these existential psychologists stemmed from their reaction to perceived shortcomings of psychoanalysis and behaviorism. In place of *determinism*, the existentialists emphasized *freedom* and the necessity to discover the essence of one's *individuality* in the immediacy of experience. Instead of being pushed by the past, they saw people as pulled toward the future, impelled by their *values* and personal *goals*. Psychoanalysis posited a structuralized model of the mind; existentialists treated persons as wholes. Finally, existentialists substituted a positive model of humanity for what they believed was an unduly pessimistic psychoanalytic model. They believed that people should aim at personal fulfillment rather than settle for partial resolution of their neuroses.

These new ideas were translated into new practices of psychotherapy by Victor Frankl, Charlotte Buhler, Fritz Perls, Rollo May, Carl Rogers, Eugene Gendlin, Sidney Jourard, R.D. Laing, Carl Whitaker, and others. The most influential of these new approaches were Frankl's (1963) *Logotherapy;* Perls' (1969) *Gestalt Therapy;* Rogers' (1951) *Client-Centered Therapy;* and Gendlin's (1962) *Experiencing.* Incidentally, it was probably Whitaker and Malone (1953) who first used the term, "experiential psychotherapy."

The theoretical statements of experiential psychotherapists generally consist of a series of loosely connected constructs and statements of position. Most of them are melioristic, and often the language is more colorful and stagy than clear and precise. Take, for instance, the following sample from Whitaker and Keith (1981, p. 190).

> Metacommunication is considered to be an experimental process, an offer of participation that implies the clear freedom to return to an established role security rather than be caught in the "as if" tongue-in-cheek micro-theater.

That trap is the context that pushes son into stealing cars or daughter into incest with father while mother plays the madame. The whimsy and creativity of the family can even be exaggerated to where family subgroups or individuals are free to be nonrational or crazy.

According to Virginia Satir (1972, p. 21), "So many of the words professional people use to talk about human beings sound sterile and lack life-and-breath images," that she prefers folksy and concrete images. Consequently, much of the writing done by experientialists is more evocative than elucidative.

Despite the paucity of elegant theoretical statements, there are a number of basic theoretical premises that define the experiential position on families and their treatment—a basic commitment to individual awareness, expression, and self-fulfillment. Whitaker emphasizes that self-fulfillment depends upon family cohesiveness, and Satir stresses the importance of good communication with other family members; but the basic commitment is to individual growth. Moreover, while there is some talk about family systems (Satir, 1972), the experiential model of families is more like a democratic group than a system with structure and a hierarchy. Hence there is great emphasis on flexibility and freedom with respect to family roles and the distribution of power. Roles are thought to be reciprocal. If one spouse is a quiet, private person, the other is apt to be sociable and outgoing. Treatment is generally designed to help individual family members find fulfilling roles for themselves, without much concern for the needs of the family as a whole. This is not to say that the needs of the family system are denigrated, but they are thought to follow automatically on the heels of individual growth. At times, the family may even be portrayed as the enemy of individual freedom and authenticity (Laing and Esterson, 1970).

Theories about families as systems are translated into techniques that facilitate communication and interaction. The emphasis on stimulating interpersonal interaction implies an acceptance of whatever level of individual experience and understanding is already present. This is where experiential theory differs (as does psychoanalytic theory) from most systems approaches, for the emphasis is on expanding immediate personal experience. The assumption is that such expansion on an individual level will break new ground for the family group, and the consequent new material and increased awareness will, almost automatically, stimulate increased communication and sharing of feelings among family members. Families will talk more when their members have more to say.

Underlying much of the work of experiential family therapy is the premise, seldom mentioned, that the best way to promote individual and family growth is to liberate affects and impulses. Efforts to reduce defensiveness and unlock deeper levels of experiencing rest on this basic assumption.

NORMAL FAMILY DEVELOPMENT

Existential family therapists subscribe to the humanistic faith in the natural goodness and wisdom of unacculturated human feelings and drives. Left alone, people tend to flourish, according to this point of view. Problems arise because this innate tendency toward *self-actualization* (Rogers, 1951) runs afoul of social (Marcuse, 1955) and familial (Laing and Esterson, 1970) counterpressures. Society enforces repression in order to tame people's instincts sufficiently to make them fit for harmonious group living. Unhappily, socially required self-control is achieved at the cost of "surplus repression" (Marcuse, 1955) and emotional devitalization. Families add their own additional controls to achieve peace and quiet, perpetuating outmoded *family myths* (Gehrke and Kirschenbaum, 1967) and using *mystification* (Laing, 1967) to alienate children from their experience.

In the ideal situation, these controls are not excessive, and children grow up in an atmosphere that supports their feelings and their creative impulses. Parents listen to their children, accept their feelings, and validate their experience, which helps the children to develop healthy channels for expressing their emotions and drives. Affect is valued and nutured; children are encouraged to experience things passionately and to express the full range of human emotions (Pierce, Nichols, and DuBrin, 1983).

Mental health is viewed as a continuous process of growth and change, not a static or homeostatic state. "The healthy family is one that continues to grow in spite of whatever troubles come its way" (Whitaker and Keith, 1981, p. 190). Furthermore, the healthy family deals with stress by pooling its resources, and by sharing problems, not dumping them all on one family member.

Experiential therapists describe the normal family as one which supports individual growth and experience. In so doing, clinicians may unwittingly foster a dichotomy between the individual and the family: "bad" families repress people, "good" ones leave them alone. Neither Carl Whitaker nor Virginia Satir falls into this trap, although Whitaker seems ambivalent about accepting the necessity for an organized family structure. At times he speaks of the need for hierarchy and generational boundaries, while at other times he emphasizes creative flexibility. The following quotation (Whitaker and Keith, 1981, p. 190) shows his vacillation on this point:

The healthy family maintains a separation of the generations. Mother and father are not children and the children are not parents. The two generations function in these two separate role categories. Members of the same generation have equal rank. However, there is a massive freedom of choice in periodic role selection and each role is available to any member. Father can be a five-year-old, mother can be a three-year-old, the three-year-old can be a father, the father can be a mother, depending upon the situation, with each family member protected by an implicit "as if" clause.

In any case, Whitaker sees the family as an integrated whole, not a confederation of separate individuals. Other experientialists often seem to think of the whole as less than the sum of its parts. Kempler (1981), for example, emphasizes *personal responsibility*, which he defines as each person maximizing his or her own potential. Some call this narcissim (Lasch, 1978), but experientialists assume that enhanced personal commitment automatically leads to greater commitment to others.

Satir (1972) describes the normal family as one that nurtures its members. Individual family members listen to and are considerate of each other, enabling them all to feel valued and loved. Affection is freely given and received. Moreover, family members are open and candid with each other. "*Anything* can be talked about—the disappointments, fears, hurts, angers, criticisms as well as the joys and achievements" (Satir, 1972, p. 14).

Satir also considers flexibility and constructive problem-solving to be characteristic of a functional, healthy family. Nurturing parents, she says, realize that change is inevitable; they accept it and try to use it creatively. Her description of the "nurturing family" brings to mind the world portrayed by Norman Rockwell on the covers of *The Saturday Evening Post:* warm and pleasant, but not quite true to life. Perhaps Satir's (1972) idealized version of family life should be taken as a prescription for, rather than a description of, healthy family living.

In general, experiential family therapists describe the family as a place for sharing experience with others. The functional family supports and encourages a wide range of experiencing; the dysfunctional family resists awareness and blunts responsiveness. The vitality of each person's individual experience is the ultimate measure of sanity. Kempler (1981) elaborates on this point, listing three criteria of psychological health. First is the ability for people to state who they are and what they want. Such a person walks in, introduces him- or herself, and says "I need some help. In recent months I've been unable to cope with . . . ." This quality is often spoken of as making "*I*" *statements*, "*I* want," "*I* feel," and so on. The second criterion is the capacity to be a separate person and to accept the differences of others. Third is the willingness and ability to remain in the *here-and-now.* Healthy people accept the truth and richness of their experience in each moment. This enables them to say who they are and what they want—and to accept the same from others. Functional families are secure enough to be passionate; dysfunctional families are frightened and bloodless. Neither problem-solving skills nor particular family structures is nearly as important as expanding open, natural, and spontaneous experiencing. The healthy family offers its members the freedom to be themselves, and supports privacy as well as togetherness.

DEVELOPMENT OF BEHAVIOR DISORDERS

From the experiential perspective, denial of impulses and suppression of feelings are seen as the root causes of family problems. Dysfunctional families are rigidly locked into self-protection and avoidance (Kaplan and Kaplan, 1978). In Sullivan's (1953) terms, they seek *security,* not *satisfaction.* They are too busy trying not to lose to ever dare to win.

Such families function automatically and mechanically, rather than through awareness and choice. Their presenting complaints are many, but the basic problem is that they smother emotion and desire. Laing (1967) describes this as the *mystification* of experience, and he holds the parents responsible. Parents are not, of course, the villains. The process is circular. Kempler (1981) also speaks of family pressure for loyalty and cohesion as interfering with individuals' loyalties to themselves. The untested premise in these unhappy families is that assertiveness or confrontation would lead to emotional chaos. The sad result is that feelings are never openly acknowledged.

According to Whitaker (Whitaker and Keith, 1981), there is no such thing as a marriage, only two scapegoats sent out by their families to perpetuate themselves. Each is programmed to recapitulate the family of origin; together they must work out the inherent conflict in this situation. Feeling helpless and frustrated, they cling even more to what is familiar, thus intensifying, rather than alleviating, their problems. Each strenuously resists the other's accustomed ways of doing things. When couples present in this stage of accommodation, one may appear sicker than the other. But, according to Whitaker (1958), the degree of disturbance in spouses almost always turns out to be similar, even if at first they appear manifestly different.

Couples who remain together eventually reach some kind of accommodation. Whether it is based on compromise or unilateral concession, it lessens the previous conflict. Dysfunctional families, terrified of conflict, cling rigidly to the structures and routines that they work out together. Having experienced being different—and not liking it—they now cling to togetherness. Once again, alternatives are dismissed or blocked from awareness.

What distinguishes dysfunctional families is that the flow of their behavior is clogged with unexpressed action, robbing them of flexibility and vitality. They appear to be fixed and rigid. Clinicians readily discern fixed triangles and subgroups; anyone can see their rigidity.

Avoidance of feelings is described as the cause and effect of family dysfunction. Kempler (1981) lists a number of devices commonly used to avoid feelings: asking questions, instead of stating opinions; using the editorial we ("We are worried about Johnny"); and changing subjects. The attention that the experientialists pay to these protective conversational devices used to avoid intimacy reflects their concern with relatively minor forms of psychic difficulty.

Experiential family therapists believe that a climate of emotional deadness leads to symptoms in one or more family members. However, because they are as concerned with positive health as with clinical pathology, experientialists point to the "normal" casualties that others might overlook. Whitaker (Whitaker and Keith, 1981) speaks of "the lonely father syndrome," "the battle fatigue mother syndrome," "the infidelity syndrome," and "the parentified child syndrome." These "normal" problems concern experiential family therapists just as much as do the symptoms of recognized psychopathology. Experiential family therapists also look for culturally invisible pathologies, such as obesity, heavy smoking, and overwork. These symptoms of family trouble are "invisible," because they are regarded as normal.

Systems-oriented family therapists (see Chapters 8, 9, 10, 11) generally look no deeper than interactions between family members to explain psychopathology. But experientialists, like psychoanalysts, are concerned as much with individuals as with systems, and consider intrapsychic problems when explaining psychopathology. For example, Kaplan and Kaplan (1978) speak of projection and introjection as intrapsychic defenses which lead to interpersonal problems in the family. Members of such families disown parts of themselves, and fit together by adopting complementary, although rigidly limiting, roles. One person's "strength" is maintained by the other's "weakness." The ongoing, patterned interactions in such families are described as "confluent," meaning ritualized playing-out of roles. The majority of clinical examples from the experiential family therapy literature are about families with a depressed or critical wife and a reasonable, but ineffectual husband. Moreover, unlike other family therapists, experientialists describe patterns of family dysfunction using the individual or a dyad as the unit of analysis. Kempler (1981), who is a typical member of the Gestalt-and-encounter wing of experiential therapists, describes dyadic patterns of avoiding intimacy with clever names—"pouter-shouter"; "crier-shrieker"; "shrew and mouse."

Dysfunctional families are made up of people incapable of autonomy or of real intimacy. They don't know themselves and they don't know one another. The root cause is *alienation* from experience—what Kempler (1981) calls "astigmatic awareness." Their communication is restricted because their awareness is restricted. They don't say much to each other because they don't feel much. They don't really experience their own experience, much less share it with other family members.

Many of the experientialists' descriptions of disordered behavior are based on concepts borrowed from other orientations. Perls' notion of *unfinished business* is frequently referred to (Kempler, 1965). Whitaker, who has worked with almost all of the major figures in family therapy, uses Minuchin's concepts of *enmeshment* and *disengagement* (Whitaker and Keith, 1981), as well as many of Bowen's notions about *triangles* and *emotional cutoff* from the extended family (Napier and Whitaker, 1978). He also uses the concept of *projective identification,* although he does not call it by that name (Whitaker and Keith, 1981, p. 196).

> If a mother is guilty about her early sex life, she may pressure the oldest son to be a priest or the oldest daughter to be a nun. If mother was frustrated in her effort to go to medical school, she may pressure son to become a family doctor.

Whitaker also speaks of family pathology as arising from an impasse in a transition in the family life-cycle, or not adapting to changing circumstances. While this is anything but novel, it is certainly consistent with the experientialists' emphasis on the need for change and flexibility. They consider not changing in the face of changing circumstances as more pathogenic than doing something positively destructive. In this model, sins of omission outweigh sins of commission.

In her portrayal of troubled families, Satir (1972) emphasizes the atmosphere of emotional deadness. Such families are cold; they live in a climate of forced politeness; they are bored, sullen, and sad. There is little evidence of warmth or friendship; the family seems to stay together merely out of habit and duty. The adults don't enjoy their children and the children learn not to value themselves or care about their parents. In consequence of the lack of action in the family, these people avoid each other, and preoccupy themselves with work and other activities outside the family.

It is important to notice that the "dysfunction" Satir describes is not the same as the clinical pathology in diagnostic manuals. Satir, like others in the experiential camp, is just as concerned with "normal" people who lead lives of quiet desperation as with the more blatantly disturbed people who usually present themselves to clinics. As Satir (1972, p. 12) puts it,

> It is a sad experience for me to be with these families. I see the hopelessness, the helplessness, the loneliness. I see the bravery of people trying to cover up—a bravery that can still bellow or nag or whine at each other. Others no longer care. These people go on year after year, enduring misery themselves or in their desperation, inflicting it on others.

GOALS OF THERAPY

Growth, not stability, is the goal of experiential family therapy. Symptom relief, social adjustment, and work are considered important, but secondary to increased personal integrity (congruence between inner experience and outer behavior); greater freedom of choice; less dependence; and expanded experiencing (Malone, Whitaker, Warkentin, and Felder, 1961). The painful symptoms that families present with are regarded as tickets of admission (Whitaker and Keith, 1981); the real problem is emotional sterility. The aim is for individual family members to become sensitive to their needs and feelings, and to share these within the family. In this way, family unity is based on lively and genuine interaction, rather than on repression and self-abnegation.

Experiential therapists have a tendency to focus on individuals and their experience. In Kempler's (1981, p. 27) case the commitment to the individual is acknowledged: "I consider my primary responsibility to people—to each individual within the family—and only secondarily to the organization called family." In common with others in the existential-humanistic tradition, experiential therapists believe that the way to emotional health is to uncover deeper levels of experiencing—the potential for personal fulfillment locked inside of all of us. It's what's inside that counts. Virginia Satir (1972, p. 120) stated the goals of family therapy in this way:

We attempt to make three changes in the family system. First, each member of the family should be able to report congruently, completely, and obviously on what he sees and hears, feels and thinks, about himself and others, in the presence of others. Second, each person should be addressed and related to in terms of his uniqueness, so that decisions are made in terms of exploration and negotiation rather than in terms of power. Third, differentness must be openly acknowledged and used for growth.

When experiential methods are applied to treating family systems (rather than to individuals who happen to be assembled in family groups), the goal of individual growth is merged with the goal of achieving a strengthened family unit. Carl Whitaker's work nicely embodies this dual goal. According to him, personal growth requires family integration, and vice versa. A sense of belongingness and the freedom to individuate go hand in hand. In fact, it is often necessary to bring parents emotionally closer together to enable their children to leave home, since many children cannot leave unless they sense that their parents will be happy without them.

In addition to the general goal of increasing the creativity of the family and its members, experiential therapists also try to help every family work out its own particular problems. But this work is done with a minimal amount of systematic conceptualization or advanced planning. In fact, many of the goals may be unconscious during therapy and can only be acknowledged in retrospect (Napier, 1977). Experiential therapy includes rational and nonrational elements. Rational goals are designed to promote conscious awareness and understanding, nonrational to increase spontaneity and sincerity. A conscious experience of inner potentials (affects, fantasies, impulses) will deprive them of their pathogenic influence, and liberate their life force. The result of increased awareness is a *reintegration* of repressed or disowned parts of the self. Most experientialists emphasize the feeling side of human nature: creativity, spontaneity, and the ability to play.

Whitaker advocates "craziness," nonrational, creative experiencing and functioning as a proper goal of therapy. If they let themselves become a little crazy, he believes, families will reap the rewards of zest, emotionality, and spontaneity.

When writing about their treatment goals, experiential clinicians emphasize the value of experience for its own sake. Whitaker (1967), for example, sees all therapy as a process of expanding experience, which he believes leads toward growth. In Gestalt-therapy terms this is known as finishing *unfinished business*. Inactive responses stultify experience. Experiential therapists bring these to the fore and help translate them into action (Kempler, 1965). By promoting more intensive experiencing, experiential family treatment brings about greater self-awareness, clarity of experience, range of functioning potential, and self-direction (Kaplan and Kaplan, 1978).

New experience for family members is thought to break down confluence, disrupt rigid expectancies, and unblock awareness—all of which promotes individuation (Kaplan and Kaplan, (1978). Bunny and Fred Duhl (1981) say their goal is a heightened sense of competence, well-being, and self-esteem. Expanded awareness of self and others is thought to promote flexible behavior, in place of automatic, stereotyped habits. Because the Duhls emphasize behavior change as a consequence of enhanced experiencing, they define explicit behavioral goals in collaboration with their patients.

Most family therapists consider that an increased sensitivity and growth in individuals serves the broad aim of enhanced family functioning. Some experiential family therapists keep the family-systems goal implicit, and devote relatively few of their interventions to promote it; others perceive individual growth as explicitly linked to family growth, and so devote more of their attention to promoting family interactions. The Duhls (1981) espouse "new and renewed integration" within and between family members as mutually reinforcing goals of treatment. Whitaker (1976a) presumes that families come to treatment because they are unable to be close, and therefore unable to individuate. By helping family members to recover their own potential for experiencing, he believes he is also helping them recover their ability to care for one another.

CONDITIONS FOR BEHAVIOR CHANGE

Among the misconceptions of those who are new to family therapy is that families are fragile and therapists must be cautious to keep from breaking them. A little experience teaches that the opposite is true. Most families are so rigidly structured that it takes therapeutic dynamite to change them. Effective family therapy requires powerful interventions—indeed, it is the basic maneuvers for producing change, that distinguish therapeutic systems. Experiential family therapists consider emotional experiencing the pivotal method for bringing about therapeutic change.

Experiential clinicians use evocative techniques and the force of their own personalities to create personal encounters, therapeutic regression, and intimate disclosure. The vitality of the therapist as a person is one major force in therapy; the vitality of the *encounter* is another. This powerfully personal experience is thought to help establish caring, person-to-person relationships among all family members. August Napier (Napier and Whitaker, 1978) wrote, in *The Family Crucible,* a nice description of what experiential family therapists think causes change. Breakthroughs occur when family members risk being "more separate, divergent, even angrier," as well as "when they risk being closer and more intimate." Outbursts of anger are often followed by greater intimacy and warmth, because the unexpressed anger that keeps people apart also keeps them from loving one another.

Because feeling-expression and intimate experience within sessions are believed to be crucial, anxiety is stimulated and prized. (The opposite more cerebral approach is used by such therapists as Murray Bowen.) Experiential family therapists are alternately provocative and warmly supportive. In this way they help families dare to take risks that may make them more anxious, at least temporarily. This permits them to drop protective, defensive patterns and really open up with each other.

Existential encounter is believed to be the essential force in the psycho-therapeutic process (Kempler, 1973; Whitaker, 1976a). These encounters must be reciprocal; instead of hiding behind a professional role or using devices to maintain distance from families, the therapist must be a genuine person who catalyzes change using his or her personal impact on families. As Kempler (1968, p. 97) said:

> In this approach the therapist becomes a family member during the interviews, participating as fully as he is able, hopefully available for appreciation and criticism as well as he is able to dispense it. He laughs, cries and rages. He feels and shares his embarrassments, confusions and helplessness. He shares his fears of revealing himself when these feelings are a part of his current total person. He sometimes cannot share himself and hopefully he is able to say at least that much.

Therapists are advised to attend to their own responses to families. Are they anxious, angry, or bored? Once noted, these reactions are to be shared with the family. Whitaker and his colleagues at the Atlanta Psychiatric Clinic (Whitaker, Warkentin, and Malone, 1959) pioneered the technique of spontaneously communicating their feelings *fully* to patients. These therapists often seemed highly impulsive, even falling asleep and reporting their dreams. According to Kempler (1965, p. 61), "By being, as nearly as possible, a total person, rather than playing the role of therapist, the atmosphere encourages all members to participate more fully as total personalities." He translates this into action by being extremely self-disclosing, even in his opening statements to families. At times this seems more self-indulgent than provocative. For example, he says, (Kempler, 1973, p. 37) "If the therapist is hungry he should say so: 'I'm getting hungry. I hope I can make it until lunchtime.'"

By being a "real person," open, honest, and spontaneous, the therapist believes he or she can teach family members to be the same. As Whitaker (1975) said, if the therapist sometimes gets angry, then patients can learn to deal with anger in others and in themselves. While this is a compelling point of view, its validity rests on the assumption that the therapist is a worthwhile model—not only a healthy, mature person, but also one whose instincts are trustworthy and useful to families. Experiential therapists have great faith in themselves as valid standards against which family members can measure themselves.

This is an attractive idea, and one that seems to work in the hands of experienced practitioners like Carl Whitaker. However, younger and less experienced therapists should not overestimate the salutary effects of their personal disclosures, nor should they underestimate the potential for countertransference in their emotional reactions to families.

Experiential family therapists share the humanistic faith that people are naturally healthy, and if left to their own devices will be creative, zestful, loving, and productive (Rogers, 1951; Janov, 1970; Perls, Hefferline and Goodman, 1951). The main task of therapy is therefore seen as overcoming defenses which are an accretion of interpersonal and cultural inhibitions. Indeed, the primary curative mechanism in experiential family therapy is unblocking resistances to experiencing, within and between family members. This unfreezing process is accomplished by mobilizing stress and fostering regression. In the ensuing emotionally-charged atmosphere family members achieve a heightened awareness of their immediate personal experience; feelings are expressed, and unsatisfied needs emerge.

Some of the experiential family clinicians pay more attention to resistance to feeling within family members than to the resistance of the family system to change. For example, Kempler's conception of interlocking family patterns is that they are easily resolved by the therapist's pointing them out. "Often in families, merely calling attention to the pattern is sufficient for one or more members to stop their part in it, thereby eliminating the possibility of continuing that interlocking behavior" (Kempler, 1981, p. 113). Kempler believes the objective of experiential therapy is to complete interpersonal encounters. He often seems to achieve this objective by pushing family members through impasses. But, just as is true with encounter groups (Lieberman, Yalom, and Miles, 1973), these changes will probably not be sustained without being repeated and worked through in a climate of understanding.

Dysfunctional families have strong conservative or homeostatic predilections; they opt for safety rather than satisfaction. Since needs and passions are messy, unhappy families are content to submerge them; experiential therapists are not. Clinicians like Whitaker believe that it is important to be effective, not safe. Therefore he deliberately aims to generate enough stress to destabilize the families he works with.

Just as stress opens family dialogues and makes change possible, therapeutic regression enables individual family members to discover and reveal hidden aspects of themselves. Once these personal needs and feelings emerge, then they become the substance of progressively more intimate interpersonal encounters within the family.

What sets experiential family therapy apart from most other family treatments is the belief that promoting family interaction is not sufficient for change. Most other approaches begin with an interpersonal focus; their aim is to help family members open up and tell each other what is on their minds. Presumably, however, this means that they will be sharing only what is already conscious. As a result, family members may have fewer secrets from each other, but they will continue to have secrets from themselves, in the form of unconscious needs and feelings. Experiential family therapists, on the other hand, believe that increasing the experience levels of individual family members will also produce more honest and intimate family interactions. In the process of experiential therapy, family members will say more to each other, because they have more to say. The following example demonstrates this "inside out" process of change.

> After an initial, information-gathering session, the L. family was discussing ten-year-old Tommy's misbehavior. For several minutes Mrs. L. and Tommy's younger sister took turns cataloging all the "terrible things" Tommy did around the house. As the discussion continued, the therapist noticed how uninvolved Mr. L. seemed to be. Although he dutifully nodded agreement to his wife's complaints, he seemed more depressed than concerned. When asked what was on his mind, he said very little, and the therapist got the impression that, in fact, very little *was* on his mind—at least consciously. The therapist didn't know the reason for his lack of involvement, but she did know that it annoyed her, and she decided to say so.
>
> *Therapist (to Mr. L.):* You know what, you piss me off.
>
> *Mr. L.:* What? (He was shocked; people he knew didn't speak that way.)
>
> *Therapist:* I said, you piss me off. Here your wife is concerned and upset about Tommy, and you just sit there like a lump on a log. You're about as much a part of this family as that lamp in the corner.
>
> *Mr. L.:* You have no right to talk to me that way (getting angrier by the minute). I work very hard for this family. Who do you think puts bread on the table? I get up six days a week and drive a delivery truck all over town. All day

long, I have to listen to customers bitching about this, and that. Then I come home and what do I get? More bitching. "Tommy did this. Tommy did that." I'm sick of it.

Therapist: Say that again, louder.

Mr. L.: I'm sick of it! I'm sick of it!!

This interchange dramatically transformed the atmosphere in the session. Suddenly, the reason for Mr. L.'s disinterest became clear. He was furious at his wife for nagging and complaining about Tommy. She, in turn, was displacing much of her feeling for her husband onto Tommy, as a result of Mr. L.'s emotional unavailability. In subsequent sessions, as Mr. and Mrs. L. spent more time talking about their relationship, less and less was heard about Tommy's misbehavior.

Following her own emotional impulse, the therapist in the example above increased the affective intensity in the session by attacking a member of the family. The anxiety generated as she did so was sufficient to expose a hidden problem. Once the problem was uncovered, it did not take much cajoling to get the family members to fight it out.

Although the reader may be uncomfortable with the idea of a therapist attacking a family member, it is not at all unusual in experiential therapy. What makes this move less risky than it may seem is the presence of other family members. When the whole family is there, it seems to make it safe for therapists to be quite provocative with much less risk of hurting or driving patients away than is true in individual treatment. And as Carl Whitaker (1975) points out, families will accept a great deal from a therapist once they are convinced that he or she genuinely cares about them.

While experiential family therapists emphasize expanded experiencing for individuals as the vehicle for therapeutic change, they are also now beginning to advocate inclusion of as many family members as possible in treatment. As experientialists, they believe in immediate personal experiencing; as family therapists, they believe in the interconnectedness of the family. To be truly strong, individuals must achieve a sense of family relatedness. The family may be likened to a team in which none of the players can perform adequately without the unity and wholeness of the group. Accordingly, the problems of individuals are extended to include the involvement of others, and family members are asked to consider their own part in maintaining behavior that they complain of in others. If a husband complains of his wife's sexual unavailability, he will be asked to deal with his contribution to the problem.

Carl Whitaker (1976b) now believes that it is important to work with three generations. He pushes for at least a couple of meetings with the larger family network, including parents, children, grandparents, and divorced spouses. Inviting these extended family members is an effective way to help them support treatment, instead of opposing and undermining it. It also provides additional information and helps correct distortions.

Whitaker believes that children should always be included, even when they are not the focus of concern. He finds it difficult to work without children, who, he believes, are invaluable for teaching parents to be spontaneous and honest. In order to overcome possible reluctance to attend, Whitaker invites extended family members as consultants, "to help the therapist," not as patients. In these interviews, grandparents are asked for their help, for their perceptions of the family (past or present), and sometimes to talk about the problems in their own marriage (Napier and Whitaker, 1978). Parents may begin to see that the grandparents are different from the images of them they introjected twenty years before. The grandparents, in turn, may begin to see that their children are now adults.

In addition to the increased therapeutic opportunities available when the larger family is present, it seems likely that small changes in the large family group have more powerful repercussions than large changes in one subsystem. Since family therapy is based on the premise that changing the system is the most effective way to change individuals, it follows that a cross-generational group holds the greatest potential for change. In fact it may be that the real reason why many family therapists do not include the extended family is that they lack the nerve or the leverage to bring them in.

TECHNIQUES

According to Walter Kempler (1968), experiential psychotherapy has no techniques, only people. This epigram neatly summarizes the experientialists' emphasis on the curative power of the therapist's personality. As Kempler's remark suggests, most experiential clinicians believe that it isn't so much what therapists do that matters, but who they are. If the therapist is rigid and uptight, then the treatment is likely to be too cool and professional to generate the intense emotional climate deemed necessary for experiential growth. If, on the other hand, the therapist is an alive, aware, and fully-feeling person, then he or she will be able to awaken these potentials in families.

Carl Whitaker endorses this position, and is himself the paradigmatic example of the spontaneous and creative therapist. The point is: therapists who want to foster openness and authenticity in their patients must themselves be open and genuine. However, this point is at least partly rhetorical. Whoever they *are*, therapists must also *do* something. Even if what they do is not highly structured and carefully planned, it can nevertheless be described. Moreover, experiential therapists tend to do a lot; they are highly active and some (including Kempler) use quite a number of structured techniques.

In fact, experiential therapists can be divided into two groups with regard to therapeutic techniques. On the one hand, some employ highly structured devices such as *family sculpting* and *choreography* to stimulate affective intensity in therapy sessions; on the other, therapists like Carl Whitaker rely on the spontaneity and creativity of just being themselves with patients. Whitaker hardly plans more than a few seconds in advance; he certainly does not use structured exercises and tactics. However, underlying both these strategies is a shared conviction that therapy should be an intense, moving experience in the here-and-now. Whether they use gimmicks or just their own impulses, all experiential therapists aim at creating a genuine personal encounter with the families they treat.

Just as experiential therapists are theoretically eclectic, many of their techniques are also borrowed from a variety of sources. For example, the theatrical and psychodramatic origins of *family sculpting* and *choreography* are quite evident. Similarly, Whitaker's work with the extended family seems to derive from Murray Bowen's work. Experiential family therapists have also drawn on encounter groups (Kempler, 1968) and Gestalt-therapy techniques (Kaplan and Kaplan, 1978).

The techniques of experiential family therapy are designed to disrupt defensiveness and foster emotional spontaneity and genuineness. Observing or reading descriptions of their sessions reveals a rich variety of techniques —from individual humanistic psychotherapies, psychodrama, and encounter groups. Although all the therapists discussed in this chapter employ many evocative techniques, they differ sharply with regard to how self-consciously they do so. Some plan and structure sessions around one or more well-practiced techniques, while others are deliberately unstructured and nonstrategic; they emphasize *being with* the family rather than *doing something*, and say that techniques should not be planned, but allowed to flow from the therapist's personal style and spontaneous impulses. Principal speaker for the latter view is Carl Whitaker. Techniques, Whitaker believes (Keith and Whitaker, 1977), are a product of the therapist's personality and of the co-therapy relationship. His own numerous published case studies reveal a playful, nonstructured approach. When children are present, Whitaker is a model parent, alternately playing with the kids in an involved, loving manner, and disciplining them with a firmness and strength. Patients learn from being with Carl Whitaker to become more spontaneous and open, and to feel more worthwhile.

Since he favors a personal and intimate encounter over a theory-guided or technique-bound approach, it is not surprising that Whitaker's style is the same with individuals, couples, or groups (Whitaker, 1958). He assiduously avoids directing real-life decisions, preferring instead to stimulate his own affective involvement with patients. He works to create intimate discussions in sessions rather than to encourage real life behavioral changes.

A comparison between Whitaker's early work (Whitaker, Warkentin and Malone, 1959; Whitaker, 1967) and his later reports (Napier and Whitaker, 1978) shows that he has changed. He started out as deliberately provocative and outlandish. He might fall asleep in sessions, and then report his dreams; he wrestled with patients; he talked about his own sexual fantasies. Today he is much less provocative. Indeed, reading some of his early reports makes one wonder of this behavior how much was genuinely spontaneous and how much a studied pose; how much was for the relationship, how much for himself, and how much for the titillation of observers.

Because Whitaker's treatment is intense and personal, he believes it essential that two therapists work together. Having a cotherapist to share the emotional burden and to interact with keeps the therapist from being totally absorbed in the emotional field of the family. The deep emotional involvement characteristic of experiential family therapy activates powerful countertransference reactions in the therapist. A detached, analytic stance minimizes such feelings; an intense involvement maximizes them. All family therapy tends to activate the therapist's own feelings toward types of family members; experiential family therapy maximizes such feelings. The trouble with countertransference is that it tends to be unconscious. Therapists are more likely to become aware of such feelings after sessions are over. Easier still is to observe countertransference in others, which is one of the values of cotherapists.

Whitaker and his Atlanta Psychiatric Clinic colleagues wrote an excellent treatise on countertransference in family therapy (Whitaker, Felder and Warkentin, 1965), suggesting that experiential family therapists should be emotionally involved—"in" the family, but not "of" the family. The therapist who is emotionally involved in the family should be able to identify with each of the family members. Thinking about experiences you have had that are similar to the family member's, or asking yourself, "What would I like or need if I were that person?" facilitates the process of identification.

In order to minimize potential destructive acting out of countertransference feelings, Whitaker recommends sharing feelings openly with the family, and always working with a cotherapist. Feelings expressed to the family are more useful and less likely to be lived out than if they remain hidden. At times, however, even the therapist may be unaware of such feelings. This is where having a cotherapist is important, because very often the cotherapist is able to recognize such feelings in a colleague, and so can either discuss them after a session, or counteract them during the session.

Young therapists are especially likely to be critical of parents and sympathetic-toward the kids; the best prevention for such countertransference reactions is personal maturity. A mature person has the freedom to enter intense relationships, personal and professional, without becoming enmeshed or reacting as though to his or her own parents. Adequate training, experience, and supervision also immunize therapists against taking sides. In addition, having a strong and rewarding family life will minimize the likelihood of the therapist's seeking ersatz gratification of personal needs with patients.

To resolve countertransference problems, Whitaker recommends that the therapist maintain an overview of the family as a whole, so that he or she will be less likely to get entangled with individuals or subgroups. But the most important method of controlling countertransference is the cotherapy relationship. A strong investment in the cotherapy relationship (or treatment team) keeps therapists from becoming part of the family. Therapists who see families without a cotherapist may bring in a consultant to help achieve the emotional distancing necessary to maintain an objective view.

Because of their interest in current thoughts and feelings, most experientialists eschew history taking (Kempler, 1965) and formal assessment (Kaplan and Kaplan, 1978). Kempler (1973, p. 11) once stated his disdain for diagnosis: "Diagnoses are the tombstones of the therapist's frustration, and accusations such as defensive, resistant, and secondary gain are the flowers placed on the grave of his buried dissatisfaction." His point seems to be that the objective distance necessary for formal assessment removes the therapist from a close emotional interaction with families; moreover, since diagnostic terms tend to be pejorative, they may serve to discharge hostility while masquerading as scientific objectivity.

For most experientialists, assessment is implicit, and occurs automatically as the therapist gets to know the family. In the process of getting acquainted and developing an empathic relationship, the therapist learns what kind of people he or she is dealing with. Whitaker begins by asking each family member to describe the family and how it works. "Talk about the family as a whole." "What is the family like, how is it structured?" In this way, he gets a composite picture of individual family members and their perceptions of the family group. Notice also that by directing family members toward the structure of the family as a whole, he shifts attention away from the identified patient and his or her symptoms.

Kempler, who conducts family therapy much like an encounter group, often begins by sitting down and saying nothing. This device generates anxiety and helps create an atmosphere of emotional intensity. There is, however, something paradoxical about opening like this; it seems nondirective and it seems to be a way of decentralizing the therapist, but it is neither. In fact, by refraining from saying anything, the therapist calls attention to himself, and is in a very controlling position. Any idea that his opening device signals a nondirective approach is dispelled by the transcripts of encounter group style family therapists (Kempler, 1981). Whether they open with silence or by inquiring into specific content areas, they soon become extremely active and directive — they ask questions, direct conversations, and actively confront evasive or defensive family members.

Whitaker's first sessions (Napier and Whitaker, 1978) are quite structured, and include taking a family history. For him, the first contacts with families are opening salvos in "the battle for structure" (Whitaker and Keith, 1981). He labors hard to gain enough control to be able to exert maximum therapeutic leverage. He wants the family to know that the therapists are in charge, and he wants them to accept the idea of family therapy. This begins with the first telephone call. Whitaker (1976b) insists that the largest possible number of family members attend; he believes that three generations are necessary so that he can be sure the grandparents will support, not oppose, therapy; furthermore, their presence helps correct distortions. If significant family members will not attend, Whitaker may refuse to see the family. Why begin with the cards stacked against you?

Most of what experiential family therapists do is aimed at stimulating emotional experience and interaction. To achieve these ends, they use a combination of their own provocativeness and a number of structured, expressive techniques. Experiential therapists begin to push and confront families from the outset (Kempler, 1973). Their interventions tend to be creative and spontaneous, and are described as letting the unconscious operate the therapy (Whitaker, 1967). Many seem to develop genuine and personal attachments to patients, and do not hesitate to side with first one family member, then another.

Among experiential, if not all family therapists, Carl Whitaker is the most outspoken proponent of the idea that therapists should use their own personalities to effect change. Whitaker considers the therapist's personal adequacy, ability to be caring, firmness, and ability to be unpredictable far more effective tools than any therapeutic techniques. He believes that a therapist's wisdom, experience, and creativeness will guide his or her interventions better than any preconceived plan or structure. This approach, of course, works better for therapists who are wise, experienced, and creative than for those who are not.

Experiential family therapists help families to become more real, direct, and alive by modeling this behavior for them. They don't just point the way, they lead the way. Most are very provocative. Whitaker (Napier and Whitaker, 1978), for example, in one session asked a teenage daughter if she thought her parents had a good sex life. Kempler (1968) describes the therapist as a catalyst and as an active participant in family interactions. As a catalyst, he makes suggestions and gives directives. Typical directives include telling family members to look at each other, speak louder, repeat certain statements, or rephrase a remark to make it more emotional. He (Kempler, 1968) cites an example of telling a husband that he whimpered at his wife and whimpered at the therapist. Moreover, this was said in a sarcastic tone, deliberately designed to arouse the man's anger, "Tell her to get the hell off your back—and mean it!" The decision to become an active participant in family encounters depends largely on the therapist's own level of emotional arousal. If he gets upset or angry, he's liable to say so. "I can't stand your wishy-washy answers!" The avowed purpose of such bluntness is to teach —by example—the use of "I" statements. As Kempler (1981, p. 156) remarks, "The expressed experiential 'I' ness of the therapist is the epitome of experiential intervention." He frequently challenges and even argues with family members, while freely acknowledging that his behavior has largely to do with his own frustration.

Although they can be blunt, these therapists also put definite limits on how far they push people. Kempler (1968) says that therapists should be spontaneous, but not impulsive; and most experientialists agree that only a very warm and supportive therapist can afford to risk being pushy and provocative. Napier and Whitaker (1978) also espouse setting limits on the "let it all hang out" credo that sometimes is used to justify permitting family members to engage in destructive fights.

Whether they are provocative or supportive, experiential family therapists are usually quite active and directive. Instead of being left to work out their own styles of interaction, family members are frequently told, "Tell him (or her) what you feel!" or asked, "What are you feeling now?" Just as the best way to get a school-teacher's attention is to misbehave, the best way to get an experiential therapist's attention is to show signs of feeling, without actually expressing it.

Therapists observe nonverbal signs of feeling; they notice how interactions take place; they notice whether people are mobile or rigid; and they try to identify suppressed emotional reactions. Then they try to focus awareness (Kaplan and Kaplan, 1978). By directing attention to what a person is experiencing at the moment, the therapist may induce a breakthrough of affect or a revelation of previously withheld material. When family members appear to be blocked or disrupted, the therapist focuses on the ones who seem most energized.

> *Therapist:* I see you looking over at Dad whenever you ask Mom a question, what's that about?
> *Johnny:* Oh, nothing—I guess.
> *Therapist:* It must mean something. Come on, what were you feeling?
> *Johnny:* Nothing!
> *Therapist:* You must have been feeling something. What was it?
> *Johnny:* Well, sometimes when Mommy lets me do something, Dad gets real mad. But instead of yelling at her, he yells at me (crying softly).
> *Therapist:* Tell him.
> *Johnny:* (Angrily, to the therapist,) Leave me alone!
> *Therapist:* No, it's important. Try to tell your Dad how you feel.
> *Johnny:* (Sobbing hard) You're always picking on me! You never let me do anything!

Experiential therapists use a great number of expressive techniques in their work. With some, this amounts to a kind of eclectic grab bag, as the following remark from Bunny and Fred Duhl (1981, p. 511) suggests.

> For us, we feel free to choose a particular technique or methodology as one chooses a tool from a tool box—that is, the appropriate one for the specific job—in order to achieve the goal of a changed system interaction in a manner that fits all participants, goals, and processes.

Among the techniques available in the experiential family therapy tool box are *family sculpture* (Duhl, Kantor, and Duhl, 1973); *family puppet interviews* (Irwin and Malloy, 1975); *family art therapy* (Geddes and Medway, 1977); *conjoint family drawings* (Bing, 1970); and *Gestalt therapy* techniques (Kempler, 1973). Included among the accoutrements of experiential therapists' offices are toys, doll houses, clay, teddy bears, drawing pens and paper, and batacca bats. Although these props are commonly used in play therapy, experiential therapists do not limit their use to children.

In *family sculpture,* originated by David Kantor and Fred Duhl, the therapist asks each member of the family to arrange the others in a meaningful tableau. This is a graphic means of portraying each person's perceptions of the family, in terms of space, posture, and attitude. Peggy Papp calls her version of this technique "family choreography" to emphasize that it is a fluid form of realigning relationships (Papp, 1976).

The following example of sculpting occurred when a therapist asked Mr. N. to arrange the other members of the family into a scene typical of the time when he comes home from work.

> *Mr. N.:* When I come home from work, eh? Okay. (To his wife,) Honey, you'd be by the stove, wouldn't you?
> *Therapist:* No, don't talk. Just move people where you want them to be.
> *Mr. N.:* Okay.

He guided his wife to stand at a spot where the kitchen stove might be, and placed his children on the kitchen floor, drawing and playing.

> *Therapist:* Fine. Now, still without any dialogue, put them into action.

Mr. N. instructed his wife to pretend to cook, but to turn frequently to see what the kids were up to. He told the children to pretend to play for a while, but then to start fighting, and complaining to Mommy.

> *Therapist:* And what happens when you come into the house?
> *Mr. N.:* Nothing. I try to talk to my wife, but the kids keep pestering her, and she gets mad and says to leave her alone.
> *Therapist:* Okay, act it out.

As the family mimed the scene that Mr. N. had described, each of them had a powerful awareness of how he felt. Mrs. N. acted out trying to cook, and referee the children's fights. The children, who thought this a great game, pretended to fight, and tried to outdo each other getting Mommy's attention. When Mr. N. "came home," he reached out for his wife, but the children came between them, until Mrs. N. finally pushed them all away.

Afterwards, Mrs. N. said that she hadn't realized her husband felt pushed away. She just thought of him as coming home, saying hello, and then withdrawing into the den with his newspaper and bottle of beer.

Family sculpture, choreography, or *spatializing* (Jefferson, 1978) is also used to illuminate scenes from the past. A typical instruction is, "Remember standing in front of your childhood home. Walk in and describe what typically happened." With this technique, the idea is to make a sculpture using people and props to portray one's perceptions of family life. It is a useful device to sharpen sensitivity, and it provides valuable information to the therapist. It is probably most useful if it suggests changes, which are then acted upon. "Do you like it that way? If not, change it to be the way you want it to be. And if you really care, then do something about it between sessions."

Another structured expressive exercise is *family art therapy.* Kwiatkowska (1967) instructs families to produce a series of sequentially ordered drawings, including a "joint family scribble," in which each person makes a quick scribble and then the whole family incorporates the scribble into a unified picture. Bing (1970) has families draw a picture of themselves as family. Rubin and Magnussen (1974) ask for joint murals, as well as two- or three-dimensional family portraits.

Elizabeth Bing (1970) describes the *conjoint family drawing* as a way to warm families up and free them to express themselves. In family drawings the basic instruction is, "Draw a picture as you see yourselves as a family." The resulting picture may disclose perceptions that have not previously been discussed, or may stimulate the person drawing the picture to realize something that he or she had never thought of before.

> A father once drew a picture of the family that showed him off to one side, while his wife and children stood holding hands. Although he was portraying a fact well known to his wife and himself, they had not spoken openly of it. Once he produced his drawing and showed it to the therapist, there was no avoiding discussion. In another case, when the therapist asked each of the family members to draw the family, the teenaged daughter was quite uncertain what to do. She had never thought much about the family, or her role in it. When she started to work, her drawing just seemed to emerge. After she finished, she was somewhat surprised to discover that she had drawn herself closer to her father and sisters than to her mother. This provoked a lively discussion between her and her mother about their relationship. Although the two of them spent time together, the daughter didn't feel close, because she thought her mother treated her like a kid, never talking about her own concerns, and showing only a superficial interest in the daughter's life. For her part, the mother was surprised, and not all displeased, that her daughter felt ready to establish a relationship on a more equal, sharing basis.

Another projective technique designed to increase expressiveness is the *symbolic drawing of family life space* (Geddes and Medway, 1977). First the therapist draws a large circle. Then he or she instructs the family that everything inside the circle is to represent what is inside the family. Persons and institutions thought not to be part of the family are to be placed outside in the environment. Each person in the family is to draw a small circle, representing himself or herself, and place it inside the family circle, in a position meaningfully related to the others. As the family complies with these instructions, the therapist reflects their apparent perceptions. "Oh, you feel you are on the outside, away from everyone else?" "It looks like you think your sister is closer to your parents than you are?"

In *family puppet interviews*, Irwin and Malloy (1975) ask one of the family members to make up a story using puppets. This technique, originally used in play therapy with small children, is supposed to be a vehicle for expression and for highlighting conflicts and alliances. In fact, its usefulness is probably limited to working with small children. Most adults resist expressing anything really personal through such a childlike medium. Even a frightened eight-year-old knows what's up when a therapist says, "Tell me a story."

Roleplaying is another favorite device of experiential therapists. Its use is based upon the premise that experience, to be real, must be felt and exposed in the present. Recollection of past events and consideration of hoped-for or feared future events can be made to have more impact by roleplaying them in the immediacy of the session. Kempler (1968) encourages parents to fantasize and roleplay scenes from childhood. A mother might be asked to roleplay what it was like when she was a little girl, or a father might be asked to imagine himself being a boy caught in the same dilemma as his son is.

Most of the experiential family therapists frequently break off the family dialogues to work with individuals. At times this may be to explore emotional blocks, investigate memories, or even analyze dreams. "The individual intrapsychic work may require a few minutes or it may take an entire session. In some instances it has taken the better part of several sessions" (Kempler, 1981, p. 203). The reason for the individual work is the belief that an individual's unfinished business prevents him or her from encountering others in the family.

When someone is mentioned who is not present in the session therapists may introduce Gestalt *there-and-then* techniques (Kempler, 1973). If a child speaks about her grandfather, she may be asked to speak to a chair, which is supposed to personify him. These techniques have proved very useful in individual therapy (Nichols and Zax, 1977), intensifying emotional experiencing by bringing memories into focus and by acting out suppressed reactions. Whether or not such devices are necessary or useful in family therapy is open to question. In individual treatment patients are isolated from the significant figures in their lives, and roleplaying may be useful to approximate being with those people. But since family therapy is conducted with at least some of the most significant people present, it seems doubtful that roleplaying or other means of fantasy are necessary. If emotional action is wanted, plenty of it is to be had simply by opening the dialogue between family members.

Whitaker (1975) uses a technique similar to roleplaying, which he calls "psychotherapy of the absurd." This consists of augmenting the unreasonable quality of a patient's response to the point of absurdity. It often amounts to calling a person's bluff, as the following example illustrates.

Patient: I can't stand my husband!
Therapist: Why don't you get rid of him, or take up with a boyfriend?

At other times, sarcastic teasing is used, like mock fussing in response to a fussy child. The hope is that patients will get objective distance by participating in the therapist's distancing; the danger is that patients will feel hurt at being made fun of.

EVALUATING THERAPY THEORY AND RESULTS

Experiential family therapists are not much interested in verifying their theories or their results. Their writings reflect a concern with providing potent affective experiences in therapy. The idea that emotional expression and interaction produces change is more or less taken for granted. Even Alvin Mahrer (1982), one of the most productive researchers and scholars among experiential psychotherapists, believes that outcome studies of psychotherapy are essentially useless. His position is that such studies may be of interest to administrators or insurance companies, but they have little impact on practitioners. Instead, he recommends studying "in-therapy outcomes": what therapeutic interventions lead to desired consequences on patients' behavior?

Although Mahrer (1982) and others (Pierce, Nichols, and DuBrin, 1983) have begun to examine such "in-therapy outcomes" in individual treatment, there are as yet no empirical studies of experiential family therapy. What is offered instead as verification are anecdotal reports of successful outcome (Napier and Whitaker, 1978; Duhl and Duhl, 1981), and descriptions of techniques that are seen to be effective in catalyzing emotional expression within sessions (Kempler, 1981).

Experiential family therapists aim to provide a useful experience for the families they treat, but they do not seem to believe that every family member must change overtly to validate their efforts. Moreover, these therapists believe that change frequently comes in small ways which may be difficult to measure. If, as a result of experiential therapy, a family is able to make more direct contact with a schizophrenic son, this would be considered a success.

Whitaker (Whitaker and Keith, 1981) offers little empirical evidence of the success of his approach; instead he cites the goodwill of the community, referrals from previous patients, and the satisfaction of families after treatment as evidences of success. He also mentions his own satisfaction as a therapist, stating that when therapy is unsuccessful therapists become burned-out and bitter.

SUMMARY

Experiential family therapy is designed to change families by changing family members, reversing the direction of effect usually envisioned by family therapists. Experientialists conceive of and treat families as groups of individuals rather than as systems. Enhanced sensitivity and expanded awareness are the essential aims of treatment.

In addition to focusing on *intra*personal change, experiential family therapy is also distinguished by a throughgoing commitment to growth as opposed to problem-solving. Personal growth and self-fulfillment are seen as innate human tendencies that naturally emerge once interferences and defensiveness are reduced. Treatment is therefore aimed at reducing defenses within and between family members. Experientialists challenge and question that which is familiar and automatic. They interrupt automatic behavior and make the familiar strange, believing that once automatic behavior is interrupted, the potential exists for alternative behavior to be more functional and satisfying.

In order to introduce novelty and enhance immediate experiencing, therapists use their own lively personalities as well as numerous structured, expressive techniques. Like encounter group leaders, experiential family therapists act as *agents provocateur* for intense emotional awareness and expression. Therapy is viewed as an existential encounter, conducted by therapists who participate fully and spontaneously. Interventions are said to arise out of the therapist's aliveness and creativity. At various times these interventions take the form of self-disclosure, teasing, sarcasm, humor, personal confrontation, paradoxical intention, and modeling.

These free-wheeling responses may seem intimidating, but the risk is minimized when there are other family members—and frequently cotherapists—present. Nevertheless, any therapy that features personal disclosure from the therapist has the potential to make the therapist—his or her experience, needs, values and opinions— more important than the patients. The following statement, for instance, was made by a prominent experiential family therapist: "I'm almost ready for you people. I'm still thinking about the previous session which was quite moving" (Kempler, 1977, p. 91). Such a remark is fraught with problematic implications and makes the therapist seem oblivious to the needs of the family. One excuse for saying it would be that it enables the therapist to focus completely on the present; but it is also fair to say that such a remark tends to divert interest from what the family members feel to what the therapist feels.

Experiential family therapy derives from existential, humanistic, and phenomenological thought, from which it gets the idea that individual freedom and self-expression can undo the devitalizing effects of culture. Beyond this, however, experiential family therapy tends to be relatively atheoretical. Consequently, this approach has no way to systematically conceptualize family dynamics, and instead simply borrows concepts and techniques from other approaches.

Its essential vitality lies in its techniques for promoting and expanding intense experience. Most people learn to blunt the full range of their experiencing as they grow up; indeed, defensive avoidance of anxiety may be the most prominent motivating force. Experiential therapy takes families who have become refractory to emotional experience and puts some of the oomph back in their lives.

At its best, experiential therapy helps people uncover their own potential aliveness. Experience is real, it is a fact. Therapy conducted on the basis of putting people in touch with their own genuine experience has an undeniable validity. Moreover, when this personal discovery is conducted within the family, there is a good chance that family relations can be revitalized by authentic interaction among people who are really being themselves.

In order to reduce defensiveness and heighten emotional experience, experiential family therapists are highly active. Unfortunately, it is difficult to be active without also becoming interpretative and directive. Even the best of those who practice in this tradition (Napier and Whitaker, 1978) find it hard to resist telling people what they should be, rather than simply helping them find out who they are. Moreover, provocative directions such as, "Tell her to get the hell off your back and mean it!" (Kempler, 1968), often seem to produce compliant shows of feeling, rather than genuine emotional responses. When emotional resistance is truly reduced, feelings will emerge without the direction of a therapist.

In experiential therapy the emphasis is on experience, not understanding, and experiential practitioners seem to have ambivalent attitudes about the utility of insight and understanding. Most, like Whitaker (Whitaker, *et al.,* 1961), emphasize the nonrational forces in treatment, so that the intellectual side of human nature is subordinated to the feeling side. Whitaker's (Whitaker and Keith, 1981) statement that insight doesn't work—recognition is not change—is typical. Elsewhere, his treatment is described (Napier, 1977) as providing a complex emotional experience, not "intellectual nagging." However, case studies of experiential family therapy are filled with examples of advice giving and interpretation. Psychotherapists—of all persuasions—are as prone as the rest of humankind to offer advice and render judgment, and experiential family therapists indulge in this behavior no less often than do members of other schools. The Duhls (Duhl and Duhl, 1981) for example, recognize the need for insight to support emotional change, and have criticized what they call "intervention without education."

Once, the idea that families are systems was both novel and controversial; today it is the new orthodoxy. Now that the pendulum has swung so far in the direction of systems thinking, individuals and their private joys and pains are rarely mentioned. Surely one of the major contributions of experiential family therapy is to remind us not to lose sight of the person in the system.

REFERENCES

Bartlett, F.H. Illusion and reality in R.D. Laing. *Family Process,* 1976, *15,* 51–64.

Bing, E. The conjoint family drawing. *Family Process,* 1970, *9,* 173–194.

Binswanger, L. *Being-in-the-world: Selected papers of Ludwig Binswanger.* In J. Needleman (Ed.), New York: Harper Torchbooks, 1967.

Boss, M. *Psychoanalysis and Daseinanalysis.* New York: Basic Books, 1963.

Duhl, B.S. & Duhl, F.J. Integrative family therapy. In A.S. Gurman & D.P. Kniskern (Eds.), *Handbook of family therapy.* New York: Brunner/Mazel, 1981.

Duhl, F.J., Kantor, D. & Duhl, B.S. Learning, space and action in family therapy: A primer of sculpture. In D.A. Bloch (Ed.), *Techniques of family psychotherapy.* New York: Grune & Stratton, 1973.

Frankl, V.E. *Man's search for meaning.* New York: Washington Square Press, 1963.

Geddes, M. & Medway, J. The symbolic drawing of family life space. *Family Process,* 1977, *16,* 219–228.

Gehrke, S. & Kirschenbaum, M. Survival patterns in conjoint family therapy. *Family Process,* 1967, *6,* 67–80.

Gendlin, E.T. *Experiencing and the creation of meaning.* New York: Macmillan, 1962.

Heidegger, M. *Being and time.* New York: Harper and Row, 1963.

Irwin, E. & Malloy, E. Family puppet interview. *Family Process,* 1975, *14,* 179–191.

Janov, A. *The primal scream.* New York: Dell, 1970.

Jefferson, C. Some notes on the use of family sculpture in therapy. *Family Process,* 1978, *17,* 69–76.

Kaplan, M.L. & Kaplan, N.R. Individual and family growth: A Gestalt approach. *Family Process,* 1978, *17,* 195–205.

Keith, D.V. & Whitaker, C.A. The divorce labyrinth. In P. Papp (Ed.), *Family therapy: Full length case studies.* New York: Gardner Press, 1977.

Kempler, W. Experiential family therapy. *The International Journal of Group Psychotherapy.* 1965, *15,* 57–71.

Kempler, W. Experiential psychotherapy with families. *Family Process,* 1968, *7,* 88–99.

Kempler, W. *Principles of Gestalt family therapy.* Oslo, Norway: Nordahls, 1973.

Kempler, W. *Experiential psychotherapy within families.* New York: Brunner/Mazel, 1981.

Kwiatkowska, H.Y. Family art therapy. *Family Process,* 1967, *6,* 37–55.

Laing, R.D. *The politics of experience.* New York: Ballantine, 1967.

Laing, R.D. & Esterson, A. *Sanity, madness and the family.* Baltimore: Penguin Books, 1970.

Lasch, C. *The culture of narcissism: American life in an age of diminishing expectations.* New York: Norton, 1978.

Lieberman, M.A., Yalom, I.D. & Miles, M.B. *Encounter groups: First facts.* New York: Basic Books, 1973.

Mahrer, A.R. *Experiential psychotherapy: Basic practices.* New York: Brunner/Mazel, 1982.

Malone, T.P., Whitaker, C.A., Warkentin, J. & Felder, R.E. Rational and nonrational psychotherapy. *American Journal of Psychotherapy,* 1961, *15,* 212–220.

Marcuse, H. *Eros and civilization.* New York: Beacon Press, 1955.

Napier, A.Y. Follow-up to divorce labyrinth. In P. Papp (Ed.), *Family therapy: Full length case studies.* New York: Gardner Press, 1977.

Napier, A.Y. & Whitaker, C.A. *The family crucible.* New York: Harper & Row, 1978.

Nichols, M.P. & Zax, M. *Catharsis in psychotherapy.* New York: Gardner Press, 1977.

Papp, P. Family choreography. In P.J. Guerin (Ed.), *Family therapy: Theory and practice.* New York: Gardner Press, 1976.

Perls, F.S., Hefferline, R.E. & Goodman, P. *Gestalt therapy.* New York: Delta, 1951.

Perls, F.S. *Gestalt therapy verbatim.* Lafayette, Calif.: Real People Press, 1961.

Pierce, R., Nichols, M.P. & DuBrin, J. *Feeling expression in psychotherapy.* New York: Gardner Press, 1983.

Rogers, C.R. *Client-centered therapy.* Boston: Houghton Mifflin, 1951.

Rubin, J. & Magnussen, M. A family art evaluation. *Family Process,* 1974, *13,* 185–200.

Satir, V.M. *Conjoint family therapy.* Palo Alto, Calif.: Science and Behavior Books, 1967.

Satir, V.M. The family as a treatment unit. In J. Haley (Ed.), *Changing families.* New York: Grune & Stratton, 1971.

Satir, V. *Peoplemaking.* Palo Alto, Calif.: Science and Behavior Books, 1972.

Simon, R.M. Sculpting the family. *Family Process,* 1972, *11,* 49–51.

Sullivan, H.S. *The interpersonal theory of psychiatry.* New York: Norton, 1953.

Whitaker, C.A. Psychotherapy with couples. *American Journal of Psychotherapy*, 1958, *12*, 18–23.

Whitaker, C.A. The growing edge. In J. Haley & L. Hoffman (Eds.), *Techniques of family therapy*. New York: Basic Books, 1967.

Whitaker, C.A. Psychotherapy of the absurd: With a special emphasis on the psychotherapy of aggression. *Family Process*, 1975, *14*, 1–16.

Whitaker, C.A. The hindrance of theory in clinical work. In P.J. Guerin (Ed.), *Family therapy: Theory and practice*. New York: Gardner Press, 1976a.

Whitaker, C.A. A family is a four-dimensional relationship. In P.J. Guerin (Ed.), *Family therapy: Theory and practice*. New York: Gardner Press, 1976b.

Whitaker, C.A. , Felder, R.E. & Warkentin, J. Countertransference in the family treatment of schizophrenia. In I. Boszormenyi-Nagy, & J.L. Framo (Eds.), *Intensive family therapy*. Hagerstown, Maryland: Harper & Row, 1965.

Whitaker, C.A. & Keith, D.V. Symbolic-experiential family therapy. In A.S. Gurman & D.P. Kniskern (Eds.), *Handbook of family therapy*. New York: Brunner/Mazel, 1981.

Whitaker, C.A. & Malone, T.P. *The roots of psychotherapy*. New York: Blakiston, 1953.

Whitaker, C.A., Warkentin, J., & Malone, T.P. The involvement of the professional therapist. In A. Burton (Ed.), *Case studies in counseling and psychotherapy*. Englewood Cliffs, N.J.: Prentice-Hall, 1959.

7

Behavioral
Family
Therapy

INTRODUCTION

behavioral family therapists use learning theory techniques devised for treating individuals and apply them to problems encountered by families. Still tied to methods for shaping the behavior of individuals, behavioral family therapy has yet to treat families as systems, either conceptually or clinically. Behavior therapists have developed powerful, pragmatic techniques that they administer to a variety of family problems, but most of the emphasis in this kind of family therapy is on behavioral parent training, behavioral marriage therapy, and treatment of sexual dysfunctions.

The distinctive methods of behavioral family therapy mostly involve the application of classical and operant conditioning treatments for individuals. Target behavior is precisely specified in operational terms; operant conditioning, classical conditioning, social learning theory, and cognitive mediational principles are then used to produce change. As more and more behavior therapists have begun to treat family problems, they have come to incorporate a number of nonbehavioral techniques—fostering empathy and support, for instance, and improving communication. However, even when applying such time-honored techniques, behaviorists continue to use a methodical and directive approach. More than any other therapeutic technique, behavior therapy is characterized by careful assessment and evaluation. Analysis of behavioral sequences prior to treatment, assessment of therapy in progress, and evaluation of its final results are the hallmarks of all forms of behavioral therapy. In fact, careful observation and assessment of changes probably are more essential to behavioral therapy than any other factors. When behavioral therapists apply their techniques to families, they are explicit and direct; and they measure their results. This is consistent with the credo of behavior therapy, namely that behavior is determined more by its consequences than its antecedents.

The theories and techniques of behavioral family therapy are, for the most part, applications of those applied to individuals. Therefore, I will begin by describing the development of behavior therapy in general, and then consider its application to family problems.

SKETCHES OF LEADING FIGURES

Behavior therapy is a direct descendant of the laboratory investigations of Ivan Pavlov, the Russian physiologist whose work on conditioned reflexes led to the development of *classical conditioning*. In classical conditioning an *unconditioned stimulus* (US), such as food, which leads to an *unconditioned response* (UCR), like salivation, is paired with a *conditioned stimulus* (CS), such as a bell. The result is that the conditioned stimulus begins to evoke the same response. Pavlov published the results of his laboratory work with animals, and also reported on the application of his techniques to abnormal behavior in humans (Pavlov, 1932, 1934). Subsequently, Watson applied classical conditioning principles to experimentally induce a phobia in Little Albert (Watson and Raynor, 1920); and Mary Cover Jones successfully resolved a similar phobia in the case of Peter (Jones, 1924).

In the 1930s and 1940s, extensions and elaborations of Pavlov's conditioning theory were applied to numerous clinical problems. Nevertheless, classical conditioning was still viewed as having limited practical utility. Then, in 1948, Joseph Wolpe introduced *systematic desensitization*, with which he achieved great success in the treatment of phobics; his work generated enormous interest in behavioral treatment. According to Wolpe

(1948), anxiety is a persistant response of the autonomic nervous system acquired through classical conditioning. Systematic desensitization deconditions the anxiety through *reciprocal inhibition*, by pairing responses that are incompatible with anxiety to the previously anxiety-arousing stimuli. For example, if someone was frightened of snakes, Wolpe would first teach the person how to relax deeply, and then have the person imagine approaching a snake in a graded hierarchy of stages. Each time the person became anxious, he or she would be told to relax. In this way the anxiety evoked by imagining snakes would be systematically extinguished by reciprocal inhibition.

The application of classical conditioning methods to family problems has been primarily in the treatment of anxiety-based disorders, including agoraphobia and sexual dysfunctions, pioneered by Wolpe (1958) and later elaborated by Masters and Johnson (1970) at Washington University.

By far the greatest influence on behavioral family therapy was B.F. Skinner's idea of *operant conditioning*. The term *operant* refers to responses voluntarily emitted by the organism, as opposed to involuntary or reflex behavior. The frequency of operant responses is determined by their consequences. Those responses which are *positively reinforced* will occur more frequently; those that are *punished* or ignored will be *extinguished*. In 1953 Skinner published an enormously influential book, *Science and Human Behavior*, in which he presented a behavioristic approach to all human activity.

The operant conditioner carefully observes behavior, and then quantifies it according to its frequency and rate. Then, to complete a *functional analysis* of the behavior, he or she notes the consequences of the behavior to determine the *contingencies of reinforcement*. Finally, to change the frequency of the behavior, the operant conditioner alters the contingencies of reinforcement. For example, someone interested in a child's temper tantrums would begin by observing when they occurred and what their consequences were. A typical finding might be that the child throws a tantrum whenever his parents denied his requests, and that the parents frequently give in if the tantrums were prolonged. Thus, the parents would be discovered to have been reinforcing the very behavior that they least wanted to. To eliminate the tantrums, they would be taught to ignore or punish them. Moreover, they would be told that giving in, even occasionally, would maintain the tantrums, because behavior that is partially or intermittently reinforced is the most difficult to extinguish. If the child were aware of the contingencies, he might think, "They're not giving me what I want now, but if I keep fussing they will eventually give in; if not this time, then the next."

Skinner, who first used the term "behavior therapy," argued convincingly that behavior problems are important in their own right, not simply as symptoms of underlying psychic conflict. The first professional journal in this field, *Behavior Research and Therapy,* in 1963, elicited a flood of outcome and process studies demonstrating dramatic and impressive behavior change. One question that arose in these early days was, how permanent were the behavior changes? Yes, it was clear that behavior therapists could shape new sequences of behavior; but would these changes last? In learning theory terms, this is a problem of *generalization,* a problem which remains crucial to any form of psychotherapy. It is better to consider this question a problem to be solved, rather than as something to be debated. Behavior therapists have been able to generalize their results by using naturalistic reinforcers, using family members as therapists, and by *fading* (gradually decreasing) external contingencies. Generalization is now programmed, rather than expected or lamented.

Operant conditioning was first applied to children and later to treating marital dyads. Operant conditioning is particularly effective with children, because parents have considerable control over their reinforcers and punishments. Gerald Patterson has probably been the most influential figure in the field of behavioral parent training. Among others prominent in this field are Anthony Graziano, Rex Forehand, and Daniel and Susan O'Leary.

One of the first applications of operant conditioning to family therapy was reported by Stuart (1969). Stuart, who might be considered the grandfather of behavioral couples therapy, initially transferred operant principles, used to modify children's behavior, to couples in distress. He applied a reciprocal reinforcement paradigm in which couples learned to (a) list the behavior they desired from each other; (b) record the frequency with which the spouse displayed the desired behavior; and (c) specify exchanges for the desired behavior. In this early work, tokens were used for reinforcers; subsequent workers have used more social reinforcers.

Katkin (1978) reported success with *charting* in the treatment of a paranoid jealous wife. In charting, the patient is asked to keep an accurate record of the problem behavior. Katkin's ploy was to ask the wife to record the frequency of her irrational accusations. This approach illustrates the early attempts to approach family problems through the treatment of individuals. It also illustrates the adaptation of nonbehavioral techniques—in this case, paradoxical intention.

Other early applications of behavior therapy to conjoint couples treatment included teaching spouses how to shape positive behaviors in one another (Liberman, 1970) and having them analyze the consequences of their behavior and learn to interrupt negative interaction chains (Friedman,

1972). Mutual efforts to change behavior were given even more structure by introducing behavioral contracts—written agreements to exchange desired behavior (Rappaport and Harrell, 1972). At present the leading figures in behavioral marital therapy include Robert Weiss, Neil Jacobson, Richard Stuart, and Gayola Margolin.

Two additional developments have further increased the popularity and influence of behavior therapy. First, many nonbehavioral family therapists selectively include behavioral interventions in their work. A good example is Minuchin's (Minuchin, Rosman, and Baker, 1978) use of operant conditioning in his work with anorexia nervosa. Second, a rapprochement has been achieved between stimulus-response conditioning models and cognitive theories (Mischel, 1973). Many behavioral therapists are now beginning to consider the role of various "internal" processes, such as attitudes, thoughts, and feelings. In addition, family systems theory is influencing behavioral family therapists, which further reduces the differences between systems. Gerald Patterson, for instance, once a pure operant behaviorist, has become interested in systems theory, and an article in *Family Process* by Spinks and Birchler (1982) dealt with resistance in behavioral family therapy.

THEORETICAL FORMULATIONS

Theory follows practice in most family therapies. Successful techniques are developed first, and only later are theories adduced to explain the results. But this is less true of behavioral approaches. The claim that behavior therapy is strictly based upon research and laboratory technology (Barton and Alexander, 1975) has been challenged (Gurman and Knudson, 1978), but it is nevertheless true that behavioral family therapy was developed after the major theories supporting it had already been well established.

The basic tenets of behavior therapy were not developed specifically in relation to family problems, but are assumed to be directly applicable to them. Behavioral strategies relate more to how behavior is changed than to how families function; therefore the theoretical foundations of behavioral family therapy are those of behavior therapy in general.

Those approaching behavior therapy for the first time are often confused by references to *learning theory, behavior modification, behavior therapy,* and *social learning theory.* Are these terms synonymous or do they mean different things? Although sometimes used interchangeably, each of these expressions has its own meaning. *Learning theory* refers to the general body of principles discovered in laboratory experiments on learning and conditioning. These laws are the scientific foundation upon which behavioral treatment rests. *Behavior modification* and *behavior therapy* have been used interchangeably, although some distinctions have been made between them. Lazarus (1971) suggested that *behavior modification* refers to strict operant procedures, while *behavior therapy* is associated with counterconditioning methods for treating anxiety. *Behavior modification* has lately been less often used and seems to conjure up an image of being mindlessly controlled among the public, who sometimes confuse the ends of behavior control with the efficiency of methods used to achieve it. Because the term *behavior therapy* is now commonly used to refer to all operant and nonoperant behavioral treatments, I will follow this usage. *Social learning theory* is a broad approach to human behavior, integrating principles from social, developmental, and cognitive psychology along with those principles of learning derived from experimental psychology. In social learning theory, environmental influences are still the primary concern, but private thoughts and feelings are also used to understand behavior. This framework takes into account the pervasive effects of social influences on behavior.

The central premise of behavior therapy is that *behavior is maintained by its consequences*. It follows from this that behavior will resist change unless more rewarding consequences result from different behavior (Patterson, 1971b). Elaborating the consequences of behavior as well as the cues that elicit it requires an understanding of *stimuli* and *reinforcements*.

Four different stimulus functions are described by learning theorists: eliciting stimuli, discriminative stimuli, neutral stimuli, and reinforcing stimuli. *Eliciting stimuli* are aspects of a situation that reliably produce a response. These are particularly relevant to classical conditioning, where certain eliciting stimuli are known to produce reflex-like responses. *Discriminative stimuli* signal the occasions when a particular response will be followed by a certain consequence. Because they have been associated with these consequences in the past, discriminative stimuli have acquired a cuing function that makes particular responses more probable. Children, for example, quickly learn to detect certain discriminative stimuli which indicate that their parents "really mean it" when they say something. *Neutral stimuli* have no direct relationship to behavior, but conditioning can establish a link between a previously neutral stimulus and a response. Thus Pavlov's dogs responded to a bell only after it had been paired with feeding. *Reinforcing stimuli* are consequences of behavior which affect the probability of future responses. They are cues that reinforcement will follow.

Responses are usually defined as *respondent* or *operant*. Respondents are those that are under the control of eliciting stimuli, and their consequences do not usually affect their frequency of occurrence. Operants are behaviors that are not automatically elicited by some stimulus, but whose occurrence is affected by their consequences. From a systems point of view, the distinction between respondents and operants is problematic. Operants are causes, while respondents are effects. From a linear viewpoint this is a useful distinction, but when we think in terms of circular causal chains the usefulness of this distinction breaks down. With a nagging wife and a withdrawing husband, what is cause and what is effect? Is the nagging an operant or a respondent behavior?

Some responses may not be recognized as operants—something done to get something—just because people are not aware of the reinforcing payoffs. For example, crying is usually reinforced by attention, although the people providing the reinforcement may not realize it. In fact, a variety of unpleasant behaviors, including nagging and temper tantrums, are reinforced by attention. Even though the attention may be unpleasant—yelling—it may be the most social interaction that the nagging spouse or tantruming child receives. Thus, responses are often maintained under conditions that are counterintuitive.

Reinforcements are consequences that effect the rate of behavior, either accelerating or decelerating it. Consequences which accelerate behavior are called *reinforcers*, while those that decelerate behavior are known as *punishers*. Within the class of reinforcers there are: (a) *positive reinforcers*, positive or rewarding consequences; and (b) *negative reinforcers*, aversive consequences which are terminated after a response is made. Thus, parents can positively reinforce their child's cleaning her room by rewarding her after she does it, or negatively reinforce her by nagging until she does it.

Punishment can take the form of (a) *aversive stimuli*, such as yelling or spanking, or (b) *withdrawal of positive stimuli*, such as having to sit in the corner or being "grounded" for a week. Punishment and negative reinforcement are often confused, but do have distinctly different meanings.

Reinforcement and punishment may be either primary or secondary. *Primary reinforcers* are natural or biological outcomes, including sex and food; *primary punishments* might be physical pain or loud noises. *Secondary reinforcers* are ones that have acquired a positive meaning through social learning, like praise or eye contact, while *secondary punishers* include criticism or withdrawal of attention. Because attention has such a powerful influence on behavior, focusing attention on undesirable behavior often provides unintended social reinforcement.

Extinction occurs when no reinforcement follows a response. Inattention, as many people know, is often the best response to behavior that you do not like. The reason why many people fail to credit this is because withholding of a response rarely leads to immediate cessation of unwanted behavior. This is because most behavior has been partially or intermittently reinforced, and therefore takes a long time to extinguish.

The relationship between a response and its consequence defines the *contingencies* governing that response. *Reinforcement schedules* describe the relationship between responding and the occurrence of consequences. When reinforcement occurs at irregular intervals, the response becomes more resistant to extinction. Perhaps you can think of a reinforcement schedule with such regular contingencies of reinforcement that even a few occurrences of nonreinforcement would be sufficient to convince you that no further reinforcement is forthcoming.

While it is easy to see how simple responses can be reinforced, it may be less clear how more complicated responses, including responses not yet in someone's repertoire, can be learned. One way for this learning to occur is by successive approximation, or *shaping*. For example, parents can shape a child's learning to play soccer by paying attention to and praising the child's gradual development of the component skills of the game. Negative behavior can also be shaped, as in those families where children only get attention for progressively more angry and destructive behavior.

In addition to shaping, *modeling* is also used to teach complex or new behavior (Bandura, 1969). People often learn by emulating others, particularly if the models are perceived as successful or prestigious, and if their behavior is seen to lead to reinforcing consequences (Bandura and Walters, 1963). Modeling can be used by a therapist or a family member who exhibits a desired behavior which is then imitated by another member of the family. The amount of learning that takes place during modeling depends upon the degree to which the target family member pays attention, has the capacity to understand and rehearse the new behavior, and can reproduce the behavior. Modeling has been found to be an effective way to shortcut the long and tedious process of trial-and-error learning.

To many people, behavior therapy seems mindless and mechanistic. With all their talk about schedules of reinforcement and controlling behavior, behavior therapists seem to ignore thoughts and feelings. While this may have been true of early behaviorists, it is less true today. Recently there has been a rapprochement between pure stimulus-response behaviorism (Skinner, 1953) and cognitive theories (Mahoney, 1977). Inner events such as cognitions, verbalizations, and feelings are now recognized as events which function as stimuli in controlling overt behavior. This is a point made over and over again by various writers on behavioral family therapy (Weiss, 1978; Jacobson, 1981), but in the opinion of this author cognitive events play a more important role in the theory than in the practice of behavior therapy.

As behavior therapists shifted their attention from individuals in isolation to family relationships, they came to rely on Thibaut and Kelley's (1959) *theory of social exchange*. According to this theory, people strive to maximize "rewards" and minimize "costs" in relationships. When applied to marriages this behavioral economics provides the basis for understanding the reciprocity which develops between spouses. In a successful marriage both partners work to maximize mutual rewards, while minimizing costs. By contrast, in unsuccessful marriages the partners concentrate on minimizing costs, with little expectation of reward. Unhappily married people are too busy trying to protect themselves from being hurt to ever hope for mutual satisfaction. Each person can trim the costs of relating by giving less value (for example, by withdrawing) or by shifting to negative reinforcement and punishment. According to Thibaut and Kelley, behavior exchanges follow a norm of reciprocity over time, so that parity or equilibrium is established for the exchange. Aversive or positive stimulation from one person tends to produce reciprocal behavior from another. Thus, pleasantness begets pleasantness, and hatefulness begets hatefulness.

In its early days behavior therapy tended to focus on individuals rather than relationships. This focus is reflected in the early reports of behavioral marital therapy in which therapists treated spouses separately in individual sessions (Goldiamond, 1965) or treated only one spouse. For example, in two of three marital therapy cases reported by Lazarus (1968) only the wife was treated, offered desensitization and assertive training to help her establish a more balanced and effective relationship with her husband. Other therapists have taught wives the principles of reinforcement and extinction so that they could modify their husbands' behavior (Goldstein, 1971; Goldstein and Francis, 1969).

Asked to treat children, behaviorists initially began seeing them individually. Later, like systems theorists, they began to consider the other people in the children's environments as part of the problem. But unlike systems theorists, behaviorists continue to operate with a linear point of view. The parents' behavior is seen as *causing* the children's behavior. Moreover, despite disclaimers to the contrary (Gordon and Davidson, 1981; Liberman, 1970), the unit of behavioral analysis is *dyadic* rather than *triadic*. The focus is on changing interactions between a parent (usually the mother) and a child, or between one spouse and another. Little or no attention is paid to how these relationships are affected by others in the family. Gordon and Davidson (1981, p. 522) acknowledge that deviant child behavior may be related to other problems in the family, but suggest that this is much exaggerated by systems theorists.

> Clinical experience indicates that deviant child behavior occurs in families with *and* without marital discord. The simple presence of marital discord in these families may or may not be causally related to the child's problems.

From a systems point of view such a statement seems naive; the authors apparently fail to recognize that *overt* discord may be absent precisely *because* the spouses have triangulated their conflict onto a child. Social learning theory is relatively simple, but family dynamics are not.

NORMAL FAMILY DEVELOPMENT

Behaviorists de-emphasize historical data in favor of analyses of current sequences of behavior. As a result behavioral family therapists have little to say about the development of normal or abnormal behavior. Instead they focus their attention on descriptions of the current state of affairs. Moreover, most of their descriptions of healthy family relationships are extrapolated from descriptions of distressed families.

According to the behavior exchange model (Thibaut and Kelley, 1959), a good relationship is one in which giving and getting are balanced. Another way to say this is that a good relationship has a high ratio of benefits relative to costs. This kind of general statement adds little to everyday commonsense notions of family satisfaction. But behaviorists have begun to spell out, in empirical studies, some of the details of what makes a relationship satisfactory. For example, Weiss and Isaac (1978) found that affection, communication, and child care are the most important behaviors leading to marital satisfaction. Earlier, Wills, Weiss, and Patterson (1974), in a pioneering behavioral analysis of satisfaction in marriage, found that affectional and instrumental *dis*pleasures were more important than pleasures in determining marital satisfaction. They found that the exchange of displeasurable responses reduced marital satisfaction significantly more than pleasurable responses increased it. A good relationship, then, is one in which there is an exchange of pleasant behavior, and, even more important, a minimal amount of unpleasant behavior. In other words, good relationships are under positive reinforcing control.

Because behaviorists focus on overt behavior, they have tended to look at the benefits of family life in terms of manifest and tangible events. Thus they tend to overlook the fact that unconscious benefits are among the most important sources of satisfaction and stability in family life. Moreover, the behavior exchange model posits a *comparison level* or evaluation of cost/benefit reward ratio offered by the partner as compared with possible relationships outside the family. Here the behavioral bias may underestimate the importance of one's own self-evaluation of worth. Some people may be satisfied with a low benefit to cost ratio, because they feel that they "don't deserve any better." Furthermore, your own evaluation of the benefits of family life is also influenced by previous models (especially parents), and by images of an ideal partner. Clinical experience demonstrates that some people are dissatisfied despite being married to partners who behave in a very rewarding fashion. Perhaps for these people, internal images of what married life "should be" are more important than the overt behavior of their spouses. Put in terms of social learning theory, there is a need to consider not only the stimuli provided by other family members, but also the way these stimuli are perceived. An increasing attention to cognitive variables will allow behavior therapists to take such ideas into account.

Effective communication is also considered by behaviorists as an important feature of good relationships (Gottman, Markman, and Notarius, 1977). Good communication increases the rewards and pleasures of relating by leading to effective stimulus control over behavior. Clear communication enables family members to discriminate among and between behavioral events, and enhances their ability to be understanding and to give support. It is considered important that family members be good listeners, with understanding, although not necessarily agreement.

Families in treatment often express their desire to be free from problems, and many look to therapists to solve their problems for them. Unfortunately, problems are part of life. Therefore, healthy families are not problem-free, but do have the ability to cope with problems when they arise. Recognizing this, behavioral family therapists stress that both problem-solving skills and the ability to resolve conflicts are criteria for successful marriages (Jacobson and Margolin, 1979). In a good relationship each person is able to speak openly and directly about conflicts. Each is able to keep issues in perspective and discuss specific behaviors that are of concern. Moreover, each is willing and able to understand the other's viewpoint.

When problems arise or when circumstances change, families need the skill to change behavior. Some behaviorists consider communication skills to be the most powerful determinant of marital success (Markman, 1979), while others emphasize sexual gratification (Master and Johnson, 1970).

Many people assume that good family relationships will occur naturally if people are well matched and if they love each other. Behaviorists, on the other hand, consistently emphasize the need to develop relationship skills. Good marriages, they believe, are not made in heaven, but are a product of learning effective coping behavior. Jacobson (1981, p. 561) describes a good relationship as one in which the partners maintain a high rate of rewards.

> Successful couples adapt effectively to the requirements of day-to-day intimacy. In particular, they expend their reinforcement power by frequently acquiring new domains for positive exchange. Spouses who depend on a limited quantity and variety of reinforcers are bound to suffer the ill effects of satiation. As a result, over time their interaction becomes depleted of its prior reinforcement value. Successful couples cope with this inevitable reinforcement erosion by varying their shared activities, developing new common interests, expanding their sexual repertoires, and developing their communication to the point where they continue to interest one another.

Like others, behaviorists emphasize the capacity for adaptability, flexibility, and change; they stress that these are not personality traits but skills that can be learned, most easily in relationships that are under the stimulus control of rules and where there is a consensus about what the rules are (Weiss, 1978). Moreover, the rules should be comprehensive and flexible rather than narrow or rigid (Jacobson and Margolin, 1979). In these happy relationships rewards exceed costs; social reinforcement is dispensed equitably and at a high rate. Moreover, these relationships are built upon positive control, rather than upon negative reinforcement, punishment, and coercion (Stuart, 1975).

DEVELOPMENT OF BEHAVIOR DISORDERS

Behaviorists view symptoms as learned responses, involuntarily acquired and reinforced. Unlike their nonbehavioral colleagues, behavioral family therapists do not seek underlying meaning in symptoms, nor do they posit conflict in or between spouses as leading to problems in the children. Instead, they concentrate their attention on the symptoms themselves and look for environmental responses that reinforce the problem behavior.

At first glance it would seem unlikely that family members reinforce undesirable behavior. Why, for example, would parents reinforce temper tantrums in their children? Or why would a wife reinforce her husband's withdrawal, when it appears to cause her so much pain? The answer is not to be found in some kind of convoluted motive for suffering, but in the simple fact that people often inadvertently reinforce precisely those responses that cause them the most distress.

Naturally it is easy to see how other people cause their own problems. How many times have you seen parents threaten their children with punishment that they do not carry out? And most of us still remember how our own parents failed to reward us for certain skills and achievements. The local shopping center, American family life's public stage, is a good place to observe how often harried parents both fail to punish misbehavior and to reward good behavior in their children. And while it is considerably more difficult, it is also possible to observe how often you yourself use reinforcement to shape the behavior of people around you.

It is also possible to observe that "punishments" may have an effect opposite to what is intended. Consider the following scenario.

> Five-year-old Sandy is playing quietly with tinker toys while her father reads the newspaper. After a few minutes, she knocks the tinker toys off the table and onto the floor. Her father puts down the paper and tells her to be quiet. A little later she starts singing; again her father tells her to quiet down. Finally, she begins making so much noise that her father slams down the paper, storms into the room where she's playing, and gives her a long lecture on the virtues of playing quietly and not disturbing her parents.

What is Sandy apt to learn from this episode? That if she makes enough noise she'll get her father's attention.

Parents usually respond to problem behavior in their children by yelling at them or spanking them. These reactions may seem to be punishment, but they may in fact be reinforcing, because attention—even from an angry parent—is an extremely powerful *social reinforcer* (Skinner, 1953). The truth of this fact underlies the sound advice to, "Ignore it and it will go away." The problem is that most parents have trouble ignoring undesirable behavior in their children. Notice, for example, how quickly children learn that certain words get a big reaction from their parents. Moreover, even when parents do resolve to ignore certain misbehavior, they usually do not do so consistently. This can make things even worse, because *intermittent reinforcement* is the most resistant to extinction (Ferster, 1963).

In addition to the countless behavior problems that are unwittingly maintained by parental attention, other problems persist because many parents don't know how to make effective use of punishment. Parents make threats that they cannot or do not follow through on; they punish so long after the fact that the child does not associate the punishment with the bad behavior; they use punishments so mild that they have no effect; or they use punishments so severe as to cause fear and anxiety instead of discriminative learning.

Systems thinkers of course would protest that these statements are based on a linear view of causality: children continue to misbehave *because* their parents use ineffective contingencies of reinforcement. And it is true that most behavioral family therapists do operate with a linear model; some, however, offer more complex models. For example, Liberman (1972) describes the family as a system of interlocking reciprocal behaviors; Gerald Patterson describes patterns of *reciprocal reinforcement* in families. Consider the behavior of a mother and daughter in the supermarket.

> The little girl asks her mother for a candy bar; the mother says, "No." The child begins crying and complaining, and the mother says, "If you think I'm going to buy you candy when you make such a fuss you have another thing coming, young lady!" But the child escalates her tantrum, getting louder and louder. Finally, the exasperated and embarassed mother gives in, saying, "All right, if you'll quiet down first I'll buy you some cookies."

Obviously, the child has been more reinforced for throwing the temper tantrum than for being quiet. Not so obviously, but also true, the mother has been reinforced for giving in to temper tantrums by her child's ceasing the aversive behavior following the agreement to buy cookies. Thus a spiral of undesirable behavior is maintained by reciprocal reinforcement.

Behavioral family therapists have described a number of defective patterns of reinforcement in cases of marital discord. Azrin, Naster, and Jones (1973) listed the following causes of marital discord:

1. Receiving too little reinforcement from the marriage.
2. Too few needs given marital reinforcement.
3. Marital reinforcement no longer provides satisfaction.
4. New behaviors are not reinforced.
5. One spouse gives more reinforcement than he or she receives.
6. Marriage interferes with extramarital sources of satisfaction.
7. Communication about potential sources of satisfaction is not adequate.
8. Aversive control predominates over positive reinforcement.

The use of *aversive control* is often cited as a major determinant of marital unhappiness. In dysfunctional marriages spouses react to problems with attempts at aversive control—nagging, crying, withdrawing, or threatening. Rarely do these couples think to shape positive alternatives, so that the spouses feel more and more negatively about each other. If someone yells at you to stop doing something, you will probably feel upset and anxious; you may understand what the person wants you to do, but you certainly won't feel like going out of your way to please that person.

In distressed marriages there are fewer rewarding exchanges and more punishing exchanges, verbal and instrumental (Stuart, 1975). Spouses typically reciprocate their partners' use of punishment, and a vicious circle develops (Patterson and Reid, 1970). Partners enter marriage expecting that the rewards of being married will exceed the rewards of remaining single. Marriage provides countless opportunities for rewarding exchanges, and well-functioning couples exchange many benefits. However, when there is a failure to exchange benefits, the reward system shifts from positive to aversive control. The wife whose generosity toward her husband is neither acknowledged nor reciprocated begins to demand her share of exchanged rewards. Unfortunately, as Weiss (1978, p. 189) observed, "Forced rewards, like solicited compliments, lose their value."

People in distressed family relationships also have poor problem-solving skills (Vincent, Weiss, and Birchler, 1975; Weiss, Hops, and Patterson, 1973). When they discuss a problem, they frequently change the subject; they phrase wishes and complaints in vague and critical ways; and they respond to complaints with countercomplaints. The following exchange demonstrates sidetracking, cross-complaining, and name-calling, all typical of distressed marriages.

> "I'd like to talk about all the sweets you've been giving the kids lately."
> "What sweets? Talk about me, you're always stuffing your face. And what do you ever do for the kids? You just come home and complain. Why don't you stay at the office? The kids and I get along better without you."

According to Patterson and Reid (1970), reciprocity also exists between parents and children; parents who behave aversively toward their children get the same in return. This also holds true for the use of negative reinforcement. Children as well as parents develop patterns of reinforcement which exert a powerful controlling effect. Some manipulative children are consciously aware of these contingencies, but often they are as oblivious to the consequences of their responses as are their parents.

Most behavioral analyses point out the lack of reinforcement for adaptive strivings in distressed families. The old adage, "The squeaky wheel gets the grease," seems to apply in such families. Depressions, headaches, and temper tantrums tend to elicit concern and therefore more attention than prosocial behavior. Because this process is unwitting, family members are often mystified about what they do to maintain maladaptive behavior.

Behavior therapists believe that since abnormal behavior is learned and maintained by the same processes as normal behavior, it can therefore be treated directly, without reference to underlying causes.

GOALS OF THERAPY

The goals of behavioral family therapy are quite specific and limited: modifying specific behavior patterns to alleviate the presenting symptoms. There is little concern with systems change or with growth and development. Symptom change is not thought to lead to symptom-substitution, but to inaugurate a positive spiral of behavior, and is dealt with by techniques designed to substitute desirable alternative behaviors (Allyon and Michael, 1959).

The behavioral family therapist tailors treatment to fit each family; the goal is to eliminate undesirable behavior or increase positive behavior as defined by the family (Azrin, Naster, and Jones, 1973). Sometimes it may be necessary to redefine a family's goal of decreasing negative behavior in terms of increasing positive and incompatible behavior (Umana, Gross, and McConville, 1980) or to one that is interpersonal rather than centered in one individual. But these changes are essentially strategies to solve the presenting problem and not related to developing broader goals.

Couples often state goals of reducing aversive behavior, but this pain-avoidance strategy merely reduces dissatisfaction without increasing positive feelings (Weiss, 1978). Therefore, behavioral couples therapists also help spouses increase their satisfaction by accelerating positive behavior. "The goal of behavioral marital counseling is to provide couples with behavior change operations based upon positive control procedures" (Weiss, 1978, p. 206).

The general goals of behavioral therapy are to increase the rate of rewarding interactions by fostering positive behavior change; to decrease the rate of coercion and aversive control; and to teach more effective communication and problem-solving skills (Gurman and Knudson, 1978).

Some of the goals of behavioral family therapy may be shaped by the clientele and setting in which it is practiced. Behavior marital therapy, for example, is most frequently practiced in university teaching clinics. The therapists are often graduate students, and much of the treatment is conducted on an experimental basis. Clients in these settings tend to be relatively young and advantaged; and clients and therapists are often close to each other in age, outlook, and values. Not surprisingly, therapy in such a context often becomes a collaborative effort between people who feel each other to be peers, and a fair amount of teaching goes on. In case studies of behavioral family therapy, many of the interventions take the form of interpretations designed to foster conscious insight. For example, Liberman (1972) reported on his treatment of a couple in which the woman got her husband's attention only when she had headaches. Liberman explained the dynamics of this to the couple; thereafter the husband started paying attention to appropriate wifely and motherly behavior, while ignoring the headaches.

What this demonstrates is that behavioral family therapists aim not only to alleviate symptoms, but also to teach skills and foster understanding so that families will be able to solve their own problems in the future. This point is also supported by Robert Weiss (1978), who suggests that many forms of behavioral family therapy are more concerned with prevention than with cure.

CONDITIONS FOR BEHAVIOR CHANGE

The basic premise of behavior therapy is that behavior will change when the contingencies of reinforcement are altered. To begin with, a *functional analysis of behavior* is required to identify the antecedents and consequences of the target behavior. Once this is complete, a specific approach is usually designed for specific problems. Each family is treated as a unique case, whose therapy program is conceived of as a single-subject experiment. However, there are a number of principles that define the effective conditions for changing behavior.

Careful observation is considered a prerequisite to attempts to control behavior. Great emphasis is placed on measurement and scientific methodology. The first task of the therapist is to observe and record the frequency and duration of problem behavior, as well as the stimulus conditions that precede it and the reinforcement that follows it. This enables the therapist to design an individually adjusted treatment program.

The primary approach in behavioral family therapy is operant rather than classical conditioning (with the exception of treating sexual dysfunctions), and the focus is on changing dyadic interactions (parent-child or spouse-spouse). This dyadic focus differs from the triadic approach of systems oriented family therapists. Although some behavioral family therapists (Liberman, 1970) have disputed this distinction, I believe that this is a major difference between behavioral and nonbehavioral family therapists.

In general, behaviorists de-emphasize the "art" of therapy, treating it instead as a technical procedure dependent largely upon the application of learning theory. Some behavioral writers have argued that change will occur if correct behavioral principles are applied regardless of the individual personality or style of the therapist (Stuart, 1969; Hawkins, Peterson, Schweid, and Bijou, 1966). A few behavioral therapists emphasize that complex skills and great tact are required to conduct family therapy; but many of the articles in this field imply that one merely needs to read the literature to be equipped to conduct psychotherapy. Moreover, behavioral approaches are usually taught in graduate psychology programs by faculty who have more theoretical knowledge than practical experience.

Behavioral family therapy consists of a number of highly structured procedures which focus on technique more than on patients or therapists. Little attention is paid to patients' histories, unconscious motivations, or complex intrafamilial interactions. There appears to be minimal concern with overcoming resistance—a phenomenon that most other therapies emphasize as a major challenge in treating psychological disorders. Systems theorists have discovered that any ongoing social system resists change, either from within or without. Despite this, behaviorists believe that people seeking psychotherapy are capable of rational, collaborative effort to change. As Spinks and Birchler (1982, p. 172) put it:

> Most behaviorists view so-called resistance phenomena as the results of ineffective case management. That is, resistance is a sign that the treatment model or the therapist have been unsuccessful, not that the clients inherently resist change or will not change.

As their experience with families increases, behavioral family therapists do tend to incorporate principles and techniques from systems theory into what they do. Gerald Patterson, for example, cites Minuchin's structural family therapy; Gary Birchler integrates systems theory and behavioral marital therapy (Birchler and Spinks, 1980; Spinks and Birchler, 1982). According to Birchler, straight behavioral family therapy is overly structured and fails to deal with underlying relationship dynamics. In addition, the elaborate assessment procedure, which may take up three or four sessions, is burdensome to many patients.

Behavioral therapists invariably refer to the people they work with as "clients," not patients. Although they are not the only ones to use this word, it underlines their skills-oriented approach. Behavioral parent trainers (Gordon and Davidson, 1981) and marital therapists (Stuart, 1969) believe that the goals of treatment can usually be reached without attending to the parents' or spouses' individual difficulties. Only when such problems noticeably interfere with treatment are they addressed (Spinks and Birchler, 1982).

A major tenet of behavioral family treatment is that behavior change is better achieved by accelerating positive behavior than by decelerating negative behavior. Moreover, there is a concerted effort to minimize coercion by aversive control or extinction, because it is believed that most distressed families already use these approaches to excess. Therefore, only positive reinforcement is consistently and widely used in behavioral family therapy.

Behavioral family therapists directly manipulate contingencies of reinforcement in the families they treat, and may provide reinforcement themselves when the family members comply with their instructions. Once new behaviors are established, therapists counsel family members to use intermittent positive reinforcement and then to fade out material reinforcements in favor of social ones. Following this direct control, therapists teach family members how to observe and modify their own contingencies of reinforcement so that they may maintain their initial gains using self-control procedures.

Applying learning theory to families is quite different from observing white rats in laboratory mazes. In behavioral family therapy it is important not to make simplistic assumptions about what may be rewarding and what may be punishing. Instead, it is critical to examine the interpersonal consequences of behavior. The therapist must find out what is reinforcing for each person and each family, rather than assume that certain things are universally rewarding. Moreover, a variety of different behaviors may be aimed at the same payoff. For example, a child might throw tantrums, whine, or drop things at various times, but all of these may be reinforced by parental attention. Therefore, in order to understand how to help families change, the therapist must shift attention from the behavior (R) to the consequences (KC).

In recent years, behavior therapists have begun to consider cognitive mediating variables as important determinants of behavior (Mahoney, 1977), and these ideas have been incorporated in new forms of cognitive-behavioral therapy (Meichenbaum, 1977). As yet, however, they have had little influence on the practice of behavioral family therapy. Specific applications of cognitive learning approaches have not been tested in treating families, but, as O'Leary and Turkewitz (1978) have pointed out, much of what occurs in any good marital therapy is a discussion of the assumptions that each spouse holds. Such informal discussions of attitudes and assumptions have yet to affect the prevailing approach to treating families, which continues to focus on operant reinforcement of overt behavior.

TECHNIQUES

Since behavioral family therapy is usually practiced as either parent training, marital therapy, or treatment of sexual dysfunction, I shall describe each of these approaches separately.

Behavioral Parent Training. The process of psychotherapy begins with the therapist redefining the client's conception of the nature of the problem and of the appropriate solution. Most family therapists assume that the family, not the individual, is the problem, so that the whole family should be convened to solve it. Behavioral therapists, on the other hand, accept the parents' view that the child is the problem, and generally meet with only one parent and the child. Child training is usually done with mothers, although some behaviorists (Gordon and Davidson, 1981) recommend that both parents and even older siblings be included.

Clients also expect therapy to be a kind of education, and behavior therapists tend to operate as educators (Liberman, 1972). Thus, from the outset, behavioral family therapists employ a model which accords with the typical parents' view of the nature of their problems and the sort of solutions that would be helpful.

Behaviorists say that what distinguishes them is not so much a set of techniques, but the fact that they apply principles from experimental and social psychology to clinical problems, and that they carefully verify the results of their procedures. Liberman (1972) thus refers to therapeutic tactics as "behavioral change experiments," and the literature is replete with a variety of behavioral techniques, together with empirical demonstrations of their utility. In fact behavioral parent training has been successfully applied to almost every type of behavioral problem in children (Graziano, 1977; O'Dell, 1974). Graziano (1977) categorized children's behavioral problems as: (1) somatic symptoms—seizures, eating problems, toilet training; (2) complex syndromes—brain damage, retardation, psychosis; (3) negativistic and aggressive behavior—hyperactivity, fighting, physical and verbal abuse; (4) fears and phobias—school phobia, fear of loud noises; (5) language and speech disorders—elective mutism; and (6) common behavior problems in the home such as bedroom cleaning, persistent whining, getting dressed.

The many techniques developed to address these various problems can be grouped in three major categories: operant conditioning, respondent conditioning, and cognitive/affective techniques. By far the most commonly used approach is operant conditioning, where the reinforcers employed may be tangible or social. In fact, smiling, praise, and attention have found to be as effective as money or candy (Mischel, 1968; Bandura, 1969). Operant techniques may be further divided into *shaping, token economies, contingency contracting, contingency management,* and *time out. Shaping* (Schwitzgebel and Kolb, 1964) consists of reinforcing change in small steps that gradually approximate the desired goals. *Token economies* (Baer and Sherman, 1969) use a system of points or stars to reward children for successful behavior. In this very popular approach, children collect some kind of reward once they have accumulated a sufficient number of tokens. *Contingency contracting* (Stuart, 1971) involves agreements by the parents to make certain changes following changes made by their children. *Contingency management* (Schwitzgebel, 1967) consists of giving and taking away rewards and punishments based upon the children's behavior. *Time out* (Rimm and Masters, 1974) is a punishment involving making children sit in the corner or sending them to their rooms.

Respondent conditioning techniques involve the modification of physiological responses. The most common of these are systematic desensitization (Wolpe, 1969), assertiveness training (Lazarus, 1971), aversion therapies (Risley, 1968), and sex therapies (Masters and Johnson, 1970). Most of these approaches (particularly the last one) are primarily used with adults, but have also been applied to training parents to use with their children. Some of the commonly used cognitive/affective techniques include thought-stopping (McGuire and Vallance, 1964), rational emotive therapy (Ellis, 1962), modeling (Bandura, 1969), reattribution (Kanfer and Phillips, 1970), and self-monitering (Rimm and Masters, 1974). Although behaviorists proudly point to the incorporation of cognitive therapy into their procedures, little is actually used in behavioral family therapy. Parents have been trained individually and in groups, through lectures, assigned readings, programmed materials, discussions, modeling, and direct coaching. Practitioners begin by deciding what responses to modify and which techniques to employ. The research literature provides some guidelines, but here as elsewhere clinicians tend to favor the approach they are most familiar with.

In common with other forms of behavioral family therapy, parent training begins with an extensive assessment procedure. The exact procedure varies from clinic to clinic, but most assessments are based upon Kanfer and Phillips's (1970) *SORKC* model of behavior: *S* for stimulus, *O* for the state of the organism, *R* for the target response, and *KC* for the nature and contingency of the consequences. The following example illustrates how this assessment model is applied.

In the case of parents who complain that their son pesters them for cookies between meals and throws tantrums if they do not give him any, the tantrums would be considered the target behavior, *R*. *O,* the state of the organism, might turn out to be mild hunger, or, even more likely, boredom. The stimulus, *S,* might be the sight of cookies in the cookie jar; and the nature and contingency of the consequences, *KC,* might be that the parents give in by feeding the boy cookies occasionally, and especially if he makes enough of a fuss.

Like any useful diagnostic scheme, the *SORKC* model begins to suggest solutions as soon as it is applied.

In simple cases, such as the one above, applying the *SORKC* model is straightforward, but it quickly becomes more complex with families, where there are long chains of interrelated behavior and therapists must examine the mutual impact of behavior on each family member. Consider the following.

Mr. & Mrs. J. complain that their two small children whine and fuss at the dinner table. A home observation reveals than when Mr. J. yells at the children for misbehaving they start to whine and stand by their mother's chair.

Given this sequence it is not difficult to apply the *SORKC* model. Imagine, however, that the above sequence is only part of a more complex picture.

In the morning, Mr. J. makes a sexual overture to his wife, but she, tired out from taking care of the children, rolls over and goes back to sleep. Mr. J. is hurt and leaves for work after making some hurtful remarks to his wife. She, feeling rejected by her husband, spends the entire day playing with the children for solace. By the time she has to cook dinner, Mrs. J. is exhausted and exasperated with the children. Mr. J. comes home after a difficult day at the office and tries to make up with his wife by hugging her. She responds but only perfunctorily because she is busily trying to cook. While she's at the stove, the children and Mr. J. vie for her attention, each one wanting to tell her something. Finally, she blows up—at her husband—"Can't you see I'm busy!" He goes into the den and sulks until dinner is ready. Just as his wife finds it difficult to express her anger at the children and takes it out on him, Mr. J. has trouble directing anger at his wife and so tends to divert it onto the children. At the dinner table he yells at them for the slightest infraction, at which they whine and turn to their mother. She lets one sit on her lap while she strokes the other's hair.

In this longer, but not atypical sequence, what is stimulus and what response? Obviously these definitions become circular, and their application depends upon the perspective of the observer.

Assessment in behavioral parent training entails defining, observing, and recording the frequency of the behavior that is to be changed, as well as the events that precede it and those that follow it. Early reports in this field involved simple, discrete behavior such as temper tantrums and enuresis. But since the late sixties, parent training has been used with more severe and complex problems, making a clear definition of the behavior to be assessed an essential first step.

Assessment methods fall into one of three categories: interview, observation, and baseline data collection. Interviews, usually with the mother, are designed to provide basic information, such as a definition of the problem, and a list of potential reinforcers. Observations may be conducted behind a one-way mirror or during a home visit. Baseline data, collected prior to the initiation of therapy, may be recorded by therapists or by one or more family members. Typically parents are trained to pinpoint problem behavior, to observe and record its occurrence, and to note the occurrence and frequency of various events which might serve as stimuli and reinforcers.

Keefe, Kopel, and Gordon (1978) outline a five-stage model of behavioral assessment: (1) problem identification; (2) measurement and functional analysis; (3) matching treatment to client; (4) assessment of ongoing therapy; and (5) evaluation of therapy outcome. As this outline illustrates, assessment is an integral part of behavioral treatment from beginning to end. The problem-identification stage begins with an interview of one or both parents. Gordon and Davidson (1981) recommend that the child not be included, in order to minimize distractions and to maximize the parents' candor. These authors suggest that a child who is present and hears all the parents' complaints will be unwilling to participate in therapy. However, it seems that excluding the child supports the parents' view that the child is *the* problem, and that the parents, not the child, will profit from treatment.

Parents generally find it difficult to pinpoint specific problem behavior; instead their complaints are phrased in terms of personality traits. "The problem with Johnny is that he is lazy—shy, hostile, hyperactive, or disrespectful." Therapists respond by probing for descriptions that have concrete behavioral referants, and by developing a picture of the interactions between the parents and child. The question, "What does Johnny *do* that makes you think he's lazy?" helps pinpoint the problem. When this is followed by an inquiry such as, "And what do you do when he does that?", a picture of the interaction emerges. Asking for detailed descriptions elicits information about the frequency, intensity, duration, and social consequences of the problem behavior. Behaviorally-oriented checklists and questionnaires are also administered. These provide information that may have been omitted or overlooked in interviews. The final product of this stage of the assessment is the selection of target behaviors for modification.

The measurement and functional analysis stage consists of actually observing and recording the target behavior, as well as its antecedents and consequences. This may be done by the parents at home or by the therapists in the clinic.

In the next stage the therapist designs a specific treatment package to match the particular needs of the family. Among the factors considered are the degree to which environmental control is possible; whether or not serious interpersonal problems between the parents may preclude their working together collaboratively; possible psychological problems in either parent which might interfere with parent training; and whether or not other forms of treatment might be more effective or economical.

The second consideration, possible conflict between the parents, is usually assumed to be of critical importance by nonbehavioral therapists. But behavioral therapists vary considerably in the degree to which they consider parental conflict to be a problem. Most minimize the role of conflict between the parents, as the following quotation (Gordon and Davidson, 1981, p. 526) illustrates.

> On several occasions we have observed parents whose marriage is characterized by extreme dislike for each other who have, nevertheless, been able to put aside their differences in order that they may work together in a constructive fashion to help their child.

Once the assessment is complete the therapist decides which behaviors should be increased and which decreased. To accelerate behavior, the *Premack principle* (Premack, 1965) is applied; that is, high probability behavior (particularly pleasant activities) is chosen to serve as a reinforcer for behavior with a low probability of occurrence. At one time it was thought that reinforcers must satisfy some basic drive, such as hunger or thirst; but it is now known that behaviors chosen more frequently (given a wide variety of choices) can serve as reinforcers for those chosen less frequently. The following example shows how the Premack principle can be applied in parent training.

Mrs. G. stated that she couldn't get her five-year-old son Adam to clean up his room in the morning. She went on to say that she had already tried rewarding him with candy, money, and toys, but "Nothing works!" A functional analysis of Adam's behavior revealed that, given his choice of things to do, the most probable behaviors were watching television, riding his bicycle, and playing in the mud behind his house. Once these activities were made contingent upon tidying his room, he quickly learned to do it.

A variety of material and social reinforcers have been employed to accelerate desired behaviors, but as the Premack principle demonstrates, to be effective reinforcers must be very popular with the particular child in question. Money or candy may seem like powerful rewards but for some children they may not be as effective as a chance to play in the mud.

Once effective rewards are chosen, parents are taught to shape the desired behavior by reinforcing successive approximation to the therapeutic goals. They are also taught to raise the criteria for reinforcement gradually, and to present reinforcement immediately, contingent upon the desired behavior. Once the child is regularly performing the desired response, reinforcement becomes intermittent in order to increase the durability of the new behavior.

Although parents are taught to apply operant conditioning principles to their children, behavioral therapists generally do not apply these same principles to the parents whom they are training. Instead they rely on the assumption that the process of training is inherently reinforcing. There are exceptions to this, however, as the following (Rinn, 1978, p. 378) illustrates.

It is advisable that the clinician be as reinforcing as possible (*e.g.,* praise, smiles, excited voice) whenever the family carries out homework assignments and procedures. Therapists who are not particularly enthusiastic about the importance of data collection have a tendency to reinforce low rates of data presentation from families.

Deceleration techniques apply contingent punishment and extinction. The most common technique for decelerating behavior is *time out* from positive reinforcement. Basically this means ignoring or isolating the child after he or she misbehaves. This procedure has been shown to be effective with a wide variety of child problems (Forehand and MacDonough, 1975). Studies have shown that a duration of about five minutes is the most effective (Pendergrass, 1971). Children are first warned, to give them a chance to control their own behavior, before they are put into time out. Other techniques used to decelerate behavior include verbal reprimand, ignoring, and isolation. Simply repeating commands to children has been shown to be a most ineffective way to change their behavior (Forehand, Roberts, Doleys, Hobbs, and Resnick, 1976). Response contingent aversive stimulation (LeBow, 1972) is little used with families, although it has been used effectively by therapists working directly with children (Jacobson and Martin, 1976).

Because of the inconvenience of reinforcing behavior immediately after it occurs, *token systems* have been very popular with parent trainers. Points are earned for desirable behavior and lost for undesirable behavior (Christophersen, Arnold, Hill, and Quilitch, 1972). The principles of behavioral parent training are clearly delineated in the following case study.

> Mrs. F. is a twenty-five-year-old housewife and mother of two small children; she came to the clinic complaining of headaches and crying spells. The intake interviewer found her to be mildly depressed, and although she had symptoms of a passive dependent personality disorder, concluded that the depression was primarily a situational reaction to her difficulty in coping with her children. Suzie, age 5, was a shy child who rarely played with other children and had frequent temper tantrums. Robert, who was 8, was more outgoing and sociable, but did very poorly in school. Between them the children were a handful, and Mrs. F. felt helpless and resentful in her dealings with them.
>
> A functional analysis of behavior revealed that Suzie's shyness resulted in her getting a great deal of extra attention from her anxious mother. Whenever Suzie declined an invitation to play with other children, her mother spent a great deal of time talking with her and doing special things to make her feel better. The therapists selected social behavior (not shyness) as the first target response, and instructed Mrs. F. to reinforce all efforts at socializing, and to ignore Suzie when she avoided social contact. Thereafter, whenever Suzie made any attempt to socialize with other children, Mrs. F. would immediately reinforce her with attention and praise. When Suzie chose to stay home rather than play with other children, her mother ignored her, busying herself instead with her own activities. In three weeks Mrs. F. reported that Suzie had made remarkable changes and "seemed to have gotten over her shyness."
>
> Following this initial successful experience the therapist felt it was time to help Mrs. F. tackle the more difficult problem of Suzie's temper tantrums. Since the temper tantrums were unlikely to occur while the family was at the clinic or during a home visit, the therapist instructed Mrs. F. to make observational notes for a week. These notes revealed that Suzie generally had her tantrums when either of her parents denied her requests for a treat or some special indulgence, such as staying up an extra half an hour to watch television. Moreover, tantrums were especially likely to occur at the end of the day when Suzie and her parents were tired. Mrs. F. reported that "We've tried everything. Sometimes we try to ignore her, but that's impossible, she just screams and

shrieks until we can't stand it anymore. Then we sometimes spank her, or sometimes give her what she wants—just to shut her up. Sometimes after we spank her she cries so much that we let her stay up and watch television until she calms down. That usually works to quiet her down."

After listening to this description, the therapist explained as gently and carefully as she could how Mr. and Mrs. F. had inadvertently been reinforcing the tantrums, and told them what they would have to do to stop them. For the next week, the F's were instructed to ignore temper tantrums whenever they occurred. If they occurred at bedtime, Suzie was to be put in her bed; if she continued to cry and scream, she was to be left alone until she stopped. Only when she stopped were her parents to talk with her about what was on her mind. The following week Mrs. F. reported that the temper tantrums had indeed decreased, except for one night when they took on a new and more troubling form. When Suzie was told that she would not be able to stay up late to watch television, she began to yell and cry as usual. Instead of relenting, Mrs. F. put Suzie in her room and told her to get ready for bed. Once she realized that her parents were going to ignore her, as they had earlier in the week, Suzie began to scream and smash things in her room. "It was awful, she was completely out of control. She kicked and struck out at everything in sight, even smashing the little dog-shaped lamp I bought her. We didn't know what to do, so just that once we let her stay up." Again the therapist described the consequences of such behavior, and explained to Mrs. F. how, should Suzie again become destructive, both parents should hold her until the tantrum subsided.

At the next session, Mrs. F. described how Suzie did "get out of control again." This time, instead of giving in, the parents held her as they had been told. Mrs. F. was amazed at the fury and duration of the resulting tantrum. "But we remembered what you said—there was no way we were going to give in!" It took twenty minutes, but Suzie finally calmed down. This, it turned out, was the last time Suzie ever became so violent during a temper tantrum. Nevertheless she did continue to have an occasional tantrum during the next few weeks of therapy. According to Mrs. F., the few tantrums that did occur seemed to take place in different settings or under different conditions than the usual episodes at home, which Suzie had now learned would not be reinforced. For example, one episode took place in a supermarket, when Suzie was told she could not have a candy bar. By this time, however, Mrs. F. was thoroughly convinced of the necessity of not reinforcing the tantrums, and so she did not. Because she was embarrassed at all the noise her daughter was making in public, she did find it necessary to take her out of the store. But she made Suzie sit in the car and took pains not to let it be a pleasant experience for her. Very few tantrums followed this one.

Next the therapist turned her attention to the problem of Robert's poor performance at school. A careful assessment revealed that Robert rarely brought assignments home from school, and when asked usually denied that he had any homework. After checking with Robert's teacher the therapist discovered that the children generally did have homework, and that they were expected to work between thirty minutes and an hour a night. Mrs. F. selected a high probability behavior—watching television—and made it contingent upon Robert's having first completed his homework assignment. For the first two weeks of this regimen, Mrs. F. found it necessary to call the teacher every night to verify the assignments. But soon this was no longer necessary. Doing homework fairly quickly became a habit for Robert and his grades increased from Ds and Cs to Bs and As by the end of the school year. At this point, everyone was happier, and Mrs. F. felt the family no longer needed help.

A follow-up session in the fall found things continuing to go well. Suzie was now much more sociable and had not had any temper tantrums in months. Robert was doing well in school, although he had begun to neglect some of his more difficult assignments. To address this, the therapist explained to Mrs. F. how to institute a token system, and she was able to use it with excellent results in a short space of time.

In this case the therapist met with the mother and instructed her in the use of operant conditioning principles. Another format is to observe parent and child interacting behind a one-way mirror in the clinic. In this way, the therapist gets a first-hand look at what actually happens. With this approach, parents can be taught how to play with their children, as well as how to discipline them, and how to negotiate with them. Sometimes the observing therapist may communicate to the parents through a remote microphone, called a "bug in the ear."

The techniques that have been described are particularly effective with small children and preadolescents. With teenagers the use of contingency contracting (Alexander and Parsons, 1973; Rinn, 1978) is a more widely used procedure. Contracting is introduced by the therapist as a way for everybody in the family to get something by compromising. Both parent and teenager are asked to specify what behavior they would like the other to change. These requests form the nucleus of the initial contract. In order to help family members arrive at contracts, the therapist models, prompts, and reinforces: (a) clear communication of content and feelings; (b) clear presentation of demands; leading to (c) negotiation with each person receiving something in exchange for some concession.

Alexander and Parsons (1973) recommend starting with easy issues while the family is learning the principles of contingency contracting. Success in dealing with minor issues will increase the family's willingness to deal with more difficult problems. Some parents are reluctant to negotiate with their children to "do things that they *should* do anyway, without being bribed." In fact, these parents have a legitimate point, and they should be helped to understand the difference between rules, which are nonnegotiable, and privileges, which can be negotiated.

Behavioral parent training is also conducted in general child-training programs, which are designed for preventive education. The content of these programs varies from general principles of operant behavior to specific techniques for dealing with specific problems. They usually begin with an introduction to social learning theory. Following this, parents are instructed in pinpointing behaviors and selecting one or two for modification. After being taught to analyze the antecedents and consequences of the target behavior, parents learn to monitor the frequency and duration of the responses. Many of these programs include instruction in charting, or graphing, the target behavior. Parents are also taught how to state and enforce rules, and the necessity for being consistent. Usually, techniques for accelerating desired behavior are used concommittantly. Training in the use of positive reinforcement includes helping the parents to increase the frequency and range of reinforcers that they apply. In addition to increasing behavior that their children are already engaging in, the parents are taught to develop new behaviors through shaping, modeling, instructing, and prompting.

Behavioral Marriage Therapy. Most forms of psychotherapy begin as art and move toward science; behavioral marriage therapy did the reverse, beginning as science and moving toward art. Early reports in the literature (Goldiamond, 1965; Lazarus, 1968) consisted of relatively straightforward application of learning theory principles to problems of married couples. A strictly operant conditioning approach was common (Goldstein, 1971), and therapists were relatively naive about the interpersonal dynamics of families. Since that time behavioral marriage therapy has become increasingly popular and increasingly sophisticated. Therapists have become aware, not only of the dynamics of the marital relationship, but also of the dynamics of the therapeutic relationship. Robert Liberman writes (1972, p. 332) about the importance of creating and maintaining a positive therapeutic alliance.

> Without the positive therapeutic alliance between the therapist and those he is helping, there can be little or no successful intervention. The working alliance is the lever which stimulates change. In learning terms, the positive relationship between therapist and patient(s) permits the therapist to serve as a social reinforcer and model; in other words, to build up adaptive behaviors and allow maladaptive behaviors to extinguish. The therapist is an effective reinforcer and model for the patients to the extent that the patients value him and hold him in high regard and warm esteem.

As in other forms of behavioral therapy, marriage therapy begins with an elaborate, structured assessment process. This process usually includes clinical interviews, ratings of specific target behaviors, and standard marital assessment questionnaires. Most widely used of the latter is the Locke-Wallace Marital Adjustment Scale (Locke and Wallace, 1959), which is a 23-item questionnaire covering various aspects of marital satisfaction, including communication, sex, affection, and social activities and values. Rating scales are used to describe and quantify couples' most troublesome problems. Weiss and his colleagues at the Oregon Marital Studies Program ask couples to record their spouse's "pleasing" and "displeasing" behavior during the week.

Assessments are designed to reveal the strengths and weaknesses of the marital relationship, and the manner in which rewards and punishments are exchanged. Several relationship skills are evaluated, including the ability to discuss relationship problems, current reinforcement value for one another, skill in pinpointing relevant reinforcers in the relationship, competencies in sex, child-rearing, financial management, distribution of roles, and decision-making.

Interviews are used to specify and to elaborate target behaviors, first revealed on the structured assessment devices. Some attempt is also made during interviews to understand the etiology of the problems that couples describe as well as to discover problems other than those noted by the spouses themselves. In general, however, behavioral marital therapists de-emphasize interviews (Jacobson and Margolin, 1979) in favor of written questionnaires and direct observation of couples' interactions. Jacobson (1981) offers an outline for pretreatment assessment which is reproduced in Table 7-1.

After completing the assessment, the behavioral clinician presents the couple with an analysis of their relationship described in social learning theory terms. In doing so, therapists take pains to accentuate the positive, striving to maintain positive expectancies and a collaborative set (Jacobson, 1981). Married partners tend to state their goals negatively, in terms of decelerating aversive behavior: "I want less arguing from him"; or, "She nags too much." Most have difficulty describing behavior that they want their spouses to accelerate. To help them do so, some therapists (Azrin *et al.*, 1973) assign a homework task asking the spouses to make a list of pleasing things their partners do during the week. Reviewing these lists in the following session provides the opportunity to emphasize the importance of giving positive feedback.

Since disturbed marital interaction is viewed as resulting from low rates

Table 7-1
Jacobson's Pre-treatment Assessment for Marital Therapy

A. Strengths and skills of the relationship

What are the major strengths of this relationship?
Specifically, what resources do these spouses have to explain their current level of commitment to the relationship?
What is each spouse's current capacity to reinforce the other?
What behaviors on the part of each spouse are highly valued by the other?
What shared activities does the couple currently engage in?
What common interests do they share?
What are the couple's competencies and skills in meeting the essential tasks of a relationship: problem-solving, provision of support and understanding, ability to provide social reinforcement effectively, sexual capabilities, child-rearing and parenting skills, ability to manage finances, household responsibilities, interpersonal skills regarding interaction with people outside the relationship?

B. Presenting Problems

What are the major complaints, and how do these complaints translate into explicit behavioral terms?
What behaviors occur too frequently or at inappropriate times from the standpoint of each spouse?
Under what conditions do these behaviors occur?
What are the reinforcers that are maintaining these behaviors?
What behaviors occur at less than the desired frequency or fail to occur at appropriate times from the standpoint of each spouse?
Under what conditions would each spouse like to see these behaviors occur?
What are the consequences of these behaviors currently, when they occur?
How did the current problems develop over time?
How are current lines of decision-making authority drawn?
Is there a consensus on who makes important decisions in regard to various areas of the relationship?
What kinds of decisions are made collectively as opposed to unilaterally?

C. Sex and affection

Are the spouses physically attracted to one another?
Is either currently dissatisfied with rate, quality, or diversity of sex life together?
If sex is currently a problem, was there a time when it was mutually satisfying?
What are the sexual behaviors that seem to be associated with current dissatisfaction?
Are either or both partners dissatisfied with the amount or quality of nonsexual physical affection?
Are either or both partners currently engaged in an extramarital sexual relationship?

If so, is the uninvolved partner aware of the affair?
What is the couple's history regarding extramarital affairs?

D. Future prospects

Are the partners seeking therapy to improve their relationship, to separate,
   or to decide whether the relationship is worth working on?
What are each spouse's reasons for continuing the relationship despite current
   problems?
What steps has each spouse taken in the direction of divorce?

E. Assessment of social environment

What are each person's alternatives to the present relationship?
How attractive are these alternatives to each person?
Is the environment (parents, relatives, friends, work associates, children)
   supportive of either continuance or dissolution of present relationship?
Are any of the children suffering from psychological problems of their own?
What would the probable consequences of relationship dissolution be for
   the children?

F. Individual functioning of each spouse

Does either spouse exhibit any severe emotional or behavioral problems?
Does either spouse present a psychiatric history of his/her own? Specify.
Have they been in therapy before, either alone or together? What kind of
   therapy? Outcome?
What is each spouse's past experience with intimate relationships?
How is the present relationship different?

—From Jacobson (1981).

of positive reinforcement exchanged by couples (Stuart, 1969; Patterson
and Hops, 1972), a major treatment strategy is to increase positive control
while decreasing the rate of aversive control. This strategy is promoted both
while the couple is interacting at the clinic, and by assigning them homework to alter their pattern of interaction at home. A second major strategy is
to improve communication, which in turn facilitates couples' abilities to
solve problems. Stuart (1975) lists five intervention strategies which summarize the behavioral approach to treating troubled marriages. First, couples are taught to express themselves in clear behavioral descriptions, rather
than in vague and critical complaints. Second, couples are taught new
behavior exchange procedures, emphasizing positive in place of aversive
control. Third, couples are helped to improve their communication. Fourth,
couples are encouraged to establish clear and effective means of sharing
power and making decisions. Fifth, couples are taught strategies for solving

future problems, as a means of maintaining and extending gains initiated in therapy.

Behavior-exchange procedures are taught to help couples increase the frequency of desired behaviors. Couples are advised to express their wishes and annoyances specifically and behaviorally. A typical device is to ask each spouse to list three things that he or she would like the other to do more often. These can provide the basis for a trade, or *quid pro quo*. While explicity exchanging "strokes" in this way, spouses are implicitly learning ways of influencing each other through positive reinforcement. An alternative tactic is to ask each partner to think of things the other might want; do them, and see what happens. Weiss and his associates direct couples to have "love days," where one spouse doubles his or her pleasing behaviors toward the other (Weiss and Birchler, 1978). Stuart (1976) has couples alternate "caring days," where one spouse demonstrates caring in as many ways as possible.

The major intent of these procedures is to help couples establish *reinforcement reciprocity,* based on rewarding behavior, in place of coercion. Positive control is doubtless more pleasant and effective than aversive control. However, the concept of reinforcement reciprocity imples a symmetrical relationship, and although this pattern may characterize the majority of clients seen in university clinics, it surely does not apply to all; and it certainly does not apply to the majority of clients seen in other settings. Like it or not, many marriages are more complementary than symmetrical, and such couples may not be well served by therapeutic techniques based upon reciprocity of (overtly) exchanged behavior.

Behavioral marriage therapists try to help spouses learn to ask for what they want, rather than to expect the other to intuit it. In fact, the whole field has moved from stressing patterns of reinforcement to working on communication and problem-solving (Weiss, 1978). Unlike some other marital therapists, however, behavior therapists emphasize communication that is change-oriented rather than expression-oriented. The stress is always more on resolving conflicts than on expressing feelings. Because of this, some critics (Gurman and Kniskern, 1978) have suggested that behavioral marriage therapists try to eliminate arguing and expressions of anger in the pursuit of dispassionate problem-solving. "Do not complain, criticize, interrupt, disagree harshly, show disinterest, etc. 'Be docile, be quiet, be still,' to borrow a phrase" (Gurman and Kniskern, 1978, p. 133). I too agree that behavior marital therapy often seems mechanical and dispassionate. For example, Jacobson (1981) recommends that couples not try to solve a problem while they are fighting about it, but postpone the discussion to a prearranged problem-solving session. "Couples report that if they postpone the discussion to the next scheduled problem-solving session, by the time the session occurs the problem seems trivial" (Jacobson, 1981, p. 579). Perhaps, but it also seems likely that the interval of postponement allows for the reconstitution of defensiveness, and, further, that the feelings involved are suppressed, not resolved. Jacobson (1981, p. 580) says that angry exchanges occur in all relationships, "but they do not lead to behavior change." On the other hand, many relationships based on chronic suppression and avoidance of angry feelings result in disengagement and a facade of intimacy. Angry feelings are part of being alive; to suppress them is to deaden oneself. Moreover, angry outbursts may often be the prelude to opening up and then solving problems. Couples therapists often need to rekindle smoldering conflicts before either open expression *or* problem-solving can occur.

Training in communications skills may be done in a group format (Ely, Guerney, and Stover, 1973; Hickman and Baldwin, 1971; Pierce, 1973) or with individual couples. The training includes instruction, modeling, roleplaying, structured exercises, behavior rehearsal, and feedback (Jacobson, 1977; Patterson, Hops, and Weiss, 1973; Stuart, 1976). Couples are taught to be specific, to phrase requests in positive terms to avoid attacking, to respond directly to criticism instead of cross-complaining, to talk about the present and future rather than the past, to listen without interruption, to minimize punitive statements, and to eliminate questions that sound like declarations (O'Leary and Turkewitz, 1978).

After explaining these principles, therapists invite the couples to incorporate them in their discussions, during which the therapists provide feedback. Many therapists recommend that couples replay previous arguments, and ask the spouses to paraphrase each other's remarks before replying to them.

Once a couple has been taught to communicate in ways that are conducive to effective problem-solving, they are introduced to the principles of *contingency contracting*, which means changing something contingent on the partner's making changes. There are two forms of contract negotiation used in behavioral family therapy. The first of these is the *quid pro quo* contract (Knox, 1971; Lederer and Jackson, 1968), where one spouse agrees to make a change after a prior change by the other. Contracting is highly structured and the agreements are usually written down. Each spouse specifies desired behavior changes, and with the therapist's help the couple constructs agreements. At the end of the session a written list is made and each spouse signs it. According to Rappaport and Harrell (1972), written agreements act as references, obviating the need to rely on memory; they can be easily modified; they act as cues (discriminative stimuli), reminding spouses of their agreements; and they symbolize the couple's commitment to change. Such a contract might take the following form.

Date _____

This week I agree to:

(1) Come home from work by 6 P.M.
(2) Play with the children for half an hour after supper.

_____
Husband's signature

Contingent upon the above changes, I agree to:

(1) Go bowling once a week with my husband.
(2) Not serve leftovers for supper on week nights.

_____
Wife's signature

This kind of contracting substitutes positive for aversive control, and ensures that changes in one spouse are immediately reinforced by the other (Eisler and Hersen, 1973). Therapists should guide the couple's choices of reinforcement so that the rewards desired by one spouse are not aversive to the other, and also make sure that contracts for sexual behavior are avoided (O'Leary and Turkewitz, 1978).

Jacobson and Martin (1976) have argued that *quid pro quo* contracts are more efficient and less time-consuming than other forms. However, the *quid pro quo* arrangement requires one spouse to be the first to change. In an atmosphere of mistrust and animosity, neither may be willing to do so. An alternative form of contracting is the *good faith* contract, in which both spouses agree to make changes that are not contingent upon what the other does (Weiss, Hops, and Patterson, 1973). Each spouse's independent changes are independently reinforced. In the example cited above, the husband who comes home each night by 6 P.M. and plays with the children after supper might reward himself by buying a new shirt at the end of the week, or be rewarded by his wife with a back rub. Knox (1973) has suggested a combined form of contracting, using good faith contracts until appropriate changes are initiated and then switching to *quid pro quo* contracts once an atmosphere of trust and confidence is established.

Problem-solving training is initiated to deal with problems that are too conflictual or complicated for simple exchange agreements. The key to successful problem-solving is to develop a collaborative set between the spouses. Negotiations are preceded by a careful and specific definition of problems. Only when the spouses agree on the definition of a problem can they effectively begin to discuss a solution. Discussions are limited to only one problem at a time. Each spouse begins by paraphrasing what the other has said, and they are taught to avoid making inferences about the other's motivation—especially inferences of malevolent intent. They are also encouraged to avoid verbal abuse and other aversive responses. When defining a problem it is most effective to begin with a positive statement; instead of saying, "You never...", spouses are taught to say, "I appreciate the way you... And, in addition, I want..."

Behavior therapists are very active in these discussions, teaching structured procedures for problem-solving and giving feedback. The discussions are frequently punctuated by such therapist comments as, "You just interrupted him." "As soon as she makes a request, you change the subject." "When you blamed her for the problem the two of you started arguing instead of planning. Whenever you accuse each other of being unfair you get sidetracked from solving the problem at hand."

The drawback to the activity and directiveness of behavioral marriage therapists is that couples may learn what they are doing wrong, without having sufficient independent practice to correct it. There is a real danger that such a directive approach will tie couples into a prolonged relationship in which they are dependent upon the therapist to referee their fights and tell them how to solve their disagreements. To avoid fostering such dependent relationships most nonbehavioral family therapists remain sufficiently decentralized to promote independent self-sufficiency on the part of their clients (Minuchin, 1974; Ables and Brandsma, 1977). It seems to me that behavioral therapists do create highly dependent relationships with their clients. Indeed, their literature emphasizes the need to resolve dependency by gradually tapering off treatment. O'Leary and Turkewitz (1978) describe four stages in the therapeutic relationship: courtship, engagement, marriage, and disengagement. During the disengagement stage, the therapist gradually withdraws direction and control. The skills learned in therapy must be generalized so that couples can use them independently of the therapist. For this reason, most behaviorists recommend that termination be gradual, so that the therapist's influence can be faded out.

Treatment of Sexual Dysfunction. Some people do not consider sex therapy to be a form of family therapy. Even Masters and Johnson (1970), progenitors of this treatment, do not regard themselves as behavior therapists. However, complaints about sexual problems are so frequently encountered by family therapists, that I will summarize the techniques of sex therapy here to give students a basic familiarity with this approach.

It is often difficult to decide whether to focus directly on sexual problems or to treat them as a symptom of underlying problems in the relationship. At times it may be possible to resolve sexual problems indirectly by working on the interpersonal relationship (Gill and Temperley, 1974). On the other hand, sometimes what appear to be intractable interpersonal problems can be resolved with improvements in a couple's sexual relationship (Kaplan, 1974). In all cases, the decision as to whether or not to treat sexual dysfunction directly should be based upon informed clinical judgment, not ignorance of the techniques available.

Prior to the publication of Masters and Johnson's *Human Sexual Inadequacy* in 1970, the prevailing treatment for sexual dysfunction was a combination of analytic discussion and commonsense suggestions. Men suffering from premature ejaculation were often advised to think distracting, nonsexual thoughts during intercourse. For women who failed to reach orgasm the most common advice was to fake it.

Wolpe's (1958) introduction of *systematic desensitization* led to major advances in the treatment of sexual dysfunction. According to Wolpe, most sexual problems are the result of conditioned anxiety reactions. His therapy consists of instructing couples to engage in a graded series of progressively more intimate encounters, avoiding thoughts about erection or orgasm. A second behavioral approach that frequently proved effective was *assertive training* (Lazarus, 1965; Wolpe, 1958). In assertive training, socially and sexually inhibited persons are encouraged to accept and express their needs and feelings.

While these behavioral remedies were often effective, the real breakthrough came with the publication of Masters and Johnson's (1970) approach. This was followed by a number of others who applied and extended Masters and Johnson's basic approach (Lobitz and LoPiccolo, 1972; Kaplan, 1974).

Although the specific details vary, the same general approach to treatment is followed by most sex therapists. The first step is a careful and thorough assessment. Included in the assessment is a complete medical examination to rule out organic problems, and extensive interviews to determine the nature of the dysfunction as well as to establish goals for treatment. In the absence of organic problems, cases involving lack of information, poor technique, and poor communication in the sexual area are most amenable to sexual therapy. Moreover, those people suffering from premature ejaculation, vaginismus, or orgasmic dysfunction generally respond well to brief treatment (5–20 sessions); cases of ejaculatory incompetence, erectile failure, and lack of sexual desire are generally more difficult to resolve (Heiman, LoPiccolo, and LoPiccolo, 1981).

Following the assessment, clients are presented with an explanation of the role of conditioned anxiety in problems with sex, and they are told how anxiety developed and is being maintained in their sexual relationship. Insight and attitude change are thus a fundamental part of this "behavioral" therapy. Not only may a couple's ignorance be creating problems, but they may also harbor attitudes about sex that are incompatible with the aims of treatment. John Bancroft, who uses a behavioral approach to treat sexual problems, noted (1975, p. 149) that, "Changing attitudes is an essential part of treatment which has been sadly neglected by behaviour therapists." Kaplan (1974) makes extensive use of psychoanalytic theory and technique to deal with attitudinal resistance. Attitudes may be changed by confronting clients with discrepancies between their attitudes and reality; by subtly fostering behavior change, so that attitude change follows to keep pace; and by facilitating the cathartic expression of feelings.

Treatment begins with the *sensate focus*. In this phase of treatment, couples are given homework assignments to explore each other's bodies in order to discover areas which are pleasurable to touch, and to find the most pleasurable ways of touching them. Intercourse and genital contact are forbidden during this period to remove undue anxiety and fear of failure.

The sensate focus assignments are a means of *in vivo desensitization*. Couples who are highly anxious and fearful of "having sex" learn to overcome their fears through a gradual and progressive experience of caressing and massaging each other. As their anxiety declines and desire mounts, they are gradually given permission to engage in progressively more intimate exchanges. While they are engaged in sensate focus assignments the couples are also taught to communicate more effectively about sex. In the process of giving each other feedback, verbally and nonverbally, they are taught the importance of providing positive as well as negative feedback (Heiman *et al.*, 1981). Sex therapists also emphasize the need to become comfortable initiating and refusing sexual contact. The couples are taught how to initiate sex without the ambiguity or poor timing stemming from their history of tension, anxiety, and dread. Each spouse also learns to say "No" gently but firmly, and not let guilt lead them into activities that they find distasteful. In this way, a structure of healthy communication about sex is developed and incorporated by the couple.

Once the sensate focus exercises have gone smoothly, the therapists initiate specific techniques to deal with specific problems. Although the techniques are numerous (Masters and Johnson, 1970; Kaplan, 1974; Heiman, *et al.*, 1981), most rely on some form of desensitization to reduce anxiety, while techniques for sexual enhancement are applied. For the man's impotence or the woman's unresponsiveness an elaboration and extension of the sensate focus is employed. The couple is encouraged to divert their attention away from genital responses to other, less anxiety-provoking pleasures. Gradually this "pleasuring" approximates intercourse.

For *premature ejaculation*, the treatment of choice is the *squeeze technique* (Semans, 1956), in which the woman stimulates the man's penis until he begins to feel the urge to ejaculate. At that point, she squeezes the frenulum firmly between her thumb and first two fingers until the urge to ejaculate subsides. Stimulation begins again until another squeeze is necessary.

Techniques to deal with *erectile failure* are designed to reduce performance anxiety and increase sexual arousal. These include desensitization of the man's anxiety; discussions in which the partners describe their expectations; increasing the variety and duration of foreplay; the *teasing technique* (Masters and Johnson, 1970), in which the woman alternately starts and stops stimulating the man; and beginning intercourse with the woman guiding the man's flaccid penis into her vagina.

Many sex therapy programs have a stated time limit, so that termination is anticipated from the start. Otherwise sex therapy is usually terminated by joint agreement of therapist and clients. Successful termination generally occurs with many, though not necessarily all, of the sexual problems resolved. In my experience, satisfactory resolution usually seems to involve both an increase in pleasure and some re-evaluation of the self and the relationship. Many couples are content to have improved their sexual relationship even if it does not quite live up to their fantasies. As in any form of directive treatment, it is important for sex therapists to gradually fade out their involvement and control. Therapeutic gains are consolidated and extended by reviewing the changes that have occurred; by anticipating future trouble spots; and by planning to deal with problems according to principles learned in treatment.

EVALUATING THERAPY THEORY AND RESULTS

Behavior therapy was born and bred in a tradition of research, and so it is not surprising that behavioral family therapy is the most carefully studied form of family treatment. Almost all reports of behavioral family therapy are accompanied by some assessment of outcome, and there are hundreds of reports of successful parent training, couples' treatment, and sex therapy. However, the majority of these are single case studies, both anecdotal and experimental in nature. They do help substantiate the efficacy of the behavioral approach to treating problems in family living, but such case reports are probably better considered demonstrations than investigations. In addition, there are also a host of controlled experimental studies of behavioral family therapy. Gordon and Davidson (1981) summarized studies of the effectiveness of behavioral parent training, and found that the majority of measures yielded positive results in the majority of cases. They report hundreds of documented successes with a wide variety of problem children. The outcome criteria in studies of parent training are usually based on parents' and observers' frequency counts of prosocial and deviant behavior. Researchers have found that more advantaged families show distinctly better results from behavioral parent training (O'Dell, 1974). This is not surprising, considering the heavy emphasis on didactic presentation in this approach.

A typical finding is that targeted behavior improves; only marginal changes, however, can be seen for nontargeted problem behavior. Apparently the specific focus on presenting symptoms in this approach lends leverage to resolving focal complaints, but only minimally improves general family functioning. Moreover, improvements do not generalize from home to other settings, such as school (Gurman and Kniskern, 1978). Finally, there is a tendency for therapeutic gains to decrease sharply between termination and follow-up.

The behavioral literature also contains a large number of empirical studies of marital therapy. These studies are usually done on brief treatment (approximately nine sessions) and the most common criteria of success are observers' ratings and couples' self-reports. Noticeably absent from such studies are therapists' evaluations. In 1978, Gurman and Kniskern (1978) reported on 8 controlled analogue studies; 2 showed behavioral couples therapy to be significantly better than no treatment; in 5 controlled, comparative analogue studies behavioral couples therapy was found to be more effective than alternative forms of treatment in only one case. In the same survey, Gurman and Kniskern found that 6 of 7 naturalistic comparative studies favored behavioral couples therapy. These findings provide support for the efficacy of this approach; however, as the authors noted, behavioral therapy is still relatively untested on couples with severe marital problems. When they updated their survey in 1981, Gurman and Kniskern (1981) found similar results, and concluded that behavioral marriage therapy appears to be about as effective for mild to moderate marital problems as are nonbehavioral approaches.

Several studies have shown that the most effective ingredient in any form of marital therapy is increasing couples' communications skills (Jacobson, 1978, 1979). Jacobson's studies strongly support his approach, based on observational measures of communication and self-reported marital satisfaction. Liberman and his colleagues (Liberman *et al.,* 1976) found that on objective measures of marital communication behavioral marriage therapy in a group setting was more effective than insight-oriented couples groups. However, the two approaches did not differ in effecting increased marital satisfaction. O'Leary and Turkewitz (1978) have shown that behavior exchanges procedures are effective, especially with young couples; older couples tend to respond more favorably to communications training.

Despite the tremendous growth of public and professional interest in sex therapy, there are still few well-controlled studies of its effectiveness. In a careful review, Hogan (1978) found that most of the literature consists of uncontrolled, clinical case studies. These reports are little more than box scores of successes and failures. Absent are pre- and post-measures, detailed specification of techniques, points of reference other than therapists', and follow-up data. Moreover, since most of these reports come from a handful of therapists, it is impossible to discern what is being evaluated—the techniques of sex therapy, or the skill of these particular therapists. Consequently, only a few tentative conclusions are possible.

The greatest success rates with sexual therapy have been found in treating vaginismus, orgasmic dysfunction, and premature ejaculation. Vaginismus, the spastic contractions of vaginal muscles, has been successfully treated in 90–95 percent of cases (Fuchs, *et al.,* 1973). Eighty-five to 95 percent of the women who had never previously achieved orgasm, did so after treatment. Success rates are lower, 30–50 percent, when limited to those who had previously reached orgasm during coitus (Heiman, *et al.,* 1981). The reported success rates for treatment of premature ejaculation using the squeeze technique (Masters and Johnson, 1970) are uniformly high, 90–95 percent.

For men who had never had erectile functioning, the success rates are between 40 and 60 percent. For those who once had adequate erectile functioning, and then developed difficulty, success rates average 60–80 percent (Heiman, *et al.,* 1981). Retarded ejaculation or failure to ejaculate is relatively uncommon; consequently there are fewer reported treatment cases. Among this small sample, reported success rates range from 50–82 percent (Heiman, *et al.,* 1981). Treatment of individuals with very low levels of interest in sex is relatively new (Kaplan, 1979) and there are as yet few statistics. According to Heiman and the LoPiccolos (Heiman, *et al.,* 1981), such cases respond well to sex therapy.

The fact that there are relatively few published studies should not obscure the fact that sex therapy appears to be an effective procedure for some very vexing problems. Most observers (Gurman and Kniskern, 1981) agree that it should be considered the treatment of choice, especially where there are minimal nonsexual problems.

SUMMARY

Although behavior therapists have begun to apply their techniques to family problems, they have done so, for the most part, within a linear frame of reference. Behavioral problems are regarded as *caused* by dysfunctional patterns of reinforcement between parents and children, or between spouses. Therefore, behavioral family therapy is used to teach parents how to apply learning theory to control their children; to help couples substitute positive for aversive control; and to decondition anxiety in partners with sexual problems. Behavioral family therapists give very little consideration to complex and circular family interactions.

Family symptoms are treated as learned responses, involuntarily acquired and reinforced. Treatment is generally time-limited, and symptom-focused. The behavioral approach to families is based on social learning theory, which is a complex and sophisticated model, according to which behavior is learned and maintained by its consequences, and can be modified by altering those consequences.

The behaviorists' systematic analysis of behavior and their insistence on technically sound interventions make it clear that a therapist's personality is not all that is needed to help people change. Behaviorists do not believe that therapists have to *be* something—warm, self-disclosing, empathic—rather than *do* something. Instead, they believe that personal skills are required, rather than styles, and that to treat behavior problems you need a conceptual framework with technical skills.

An essential adjunct to social learning theory is Thibaut and Kelley's exchange theory, according to which people strive to maximize interpersonal "rewards" while minimizing "costs." Social behavior in a relationship is maintained by a high ratio of rewards to costs, and by the perception that alternative relationships offer fewer rewards and more costs (comparison level of alternatives). In this view, marital and family conflicts occur when optimal behavior-maintaining contingencies do not exist, or when dysfunctional behavior change methods are applied. In unhappy families, coercion replaces reciprocity.

The general goals of behavioral family therapy are to increase the rate of rewarding exchanges; to decrease aversive exchanges; and to teach communication and problem-solving skills. Remediation of problem behavior is the primary goal; prevention of future problems is secondary. Specific techniques are applied to target behaviors; in the process, families are also taught general principles of behavior management.

The behaviorists' focus on modifying the consequences of problem behavior accounts for some of the strengths and weaknesses of behavioral family therapy. By narrowly concentrating their attention on presenting problems, behaviorists have been able to develop an impressive array of effective techniques. Even such relatively intractable problems as delinquent behavior in children and severe sexual dysfunctions have yielded to behavioral technology. On the other hand, behavior is only part of the person, and the problem person is only part of the family. Any form of therapy must deal with the whole person, who not only acts, but also thinks and feels. Different therapies may concentrate on only one of these three human functions—psychoanalysts concentrate on thinking, just as behaviorists concentrate on action—but to be successful a therapy must address all three.

Unhappiness may center around a behavioral complaint, but resolution of the behavior may not resolve the unhappiness. Treatment may resolve the symptom and fail the family. Attitudes and feelings may change along with changes in behavior, but not necessarily. Mere behavior change may not be enough for family members whose ultimate goal is to feel better. "Yes, he's doing his chores now," a parent may agree. "But I don't think he *feels* like helping out. He still isn't really part of our family." Behavior is not what family members in distress are only concerned about, and to be responsive to all their needs, behavioral family therapists need to deal with cognitive and affective material as well as behavioral.

Although behavioral family clinicians recognize the need to modify interpersonal interactions, they generally limit their attention to interactions between units of two, and they tend to accept the family's definition of one person (or couple) as *the* problem. Virtually no consideration is given to the role of marital problems in behavioral treatment of children, and behavioral couples therapists rarely discuss the role that children play in marital distress.

Behaviorists hardly ever treat whole families. Instead they bring in only those subsystems that they consider central to the targeted behaviors. Unfortunately, failure to include—or even consider—whole families in treatment may be disastrous. A therapeutic program to reduce a son's aggressiveness toward his mother can hardly succeed if the father wants an aggressive son, or if the father's anger toward his wife is not more directly addressed. Moreover, if the whole family is not involved in change, new behavior will not be reinforced and maintained.

Despite these shortcomings, behavioral family therapy offers impressive techniques for treating problems with children and troubled marriages. Furthermore, its weaknesses can be corrected by broadening the focus of conceptualization and the scope of treatment to include whole families as systems.

REFERENCES

Ables, B.S. & Brandsma, J.M. *Therapy for couples*. San Francisco: Jossey-Bass, 1977.

Alexander, J.F. & Barton, C. Behavioral systems therapy with families. In D.H. Olson (Ed.), *Treating relationships*. Lake Mills, Iowa: Graphic Publishing, 1976.

Alexander, J.F. & Parsons, B.V. Short-term behavioral intervention with delinquent families: Impact on family process and recidivism. *Journal of Abnormal Psychology*, 1973, *51*, 219–225.

Azrin, N.H., Naster, B.J. & Jones, R. Reciprocity counseling: A rapid learning-based procedure for marital counseling. *Behavior Research and Therapy*, 1973, *11*, 365–383.

Baer, D.M. & Sherman, J.A. Reinforcement control of generalized imitation in young children. *Journal of Experimental Child Psychology*, 1964, *1*, 37–49.

Bancroft, J. The behavioral approach to marital problems. *British Journal of Medical Psychology*, 1975, *48*, 147–152.

Bandura, A. *Principles of behavior modification*. New York: Holt, Rinehart & Winston, 1969.

Bandura, A. & Walters, R. *Social learning and personality development*. New York: Holt, Rinehart & Winston, 1963.

Barton, C. & Alexander, J.F. Therapist skills in systems-behavioral family intervention: How the hell do you get them to do it? Paper presented at the Annual Meeting of the Orthopsychiatric Association, Atlanta, 1975.

Birchler, G.R. & Spinks, S.H. Behavioral-systems-marital therapy: Integration and clinical application. *American Journal of Family Therapy*, 1980, *8*, 6–29.

Christophersen, E.R., Arnold, C.M., Hill, D.W. & Quilitch, H.R. The home point system: Token reinforcement procedures for application by parents of children with behavior problems. *Journal of Applied Behavior Analysis*, 1972, *5*, 485–497.

Eisler, R.M. & Hersen, M. Behavior techniques in family-oriented crisis intervention. *Archives of General Psychiatry,* 1973, *28,* 111–116.

Ellis, A. *Reason and emotion in psychotherapy.* New York: Lyle Stuart, 1962.

Ely, A.L., Guerney, B.G. & Stover, L. Efficacy of the training phase of conjugal therapy. *Psychotherapy: Theory, Research and Practice,* 1973, *10,* 201–207.

Ferster, C. Essentials of a science of behavior. In J.I. Nurnberger, C.B. Ferster & J.P. Brady (Eds.), *An introduction to the science of human behavior.* New York: Appleton-Century-Crofts, 1963.

Forehand, R. & MacDonough, T.S. Response contingent time out: An examination of outcome data. *European Journal of Behavioural Analysis and Modification,* 1975, *1,* 109–115.

Forehand, R., Roberts, M.W., Doleys, D.M., Hobbs, S.A. & Resnick, P.A. An examination of disciplinary procedures with children. *Journal of Experimental Child Psychology,* 1976, *21,* 109–120.

Friedman, P.H. Personalistic family and marital therapy. In A.A. Lazarus (Ed.), *Clinical behavior therapy.* New York: Brunner/Mazel, 1972.

Fuchs, K., Hoch, Z., Paldi, E., Ambramovici, H., Brandes, J.M., Timor-Tritsch, I. & Kleinhaus, M. Hypnodesensitization therapy of vaginismus: Part I. "In Vitro" method. Part II, "In Vivo" method. *International Journal of Clinical and Experimental Hypnosis,* 1973, *21,* 144–156.

Gill, H. & Temperly, J. Time-limited marital treatment in a foursome. *British Journal of Medical Psychology,* 1974, *47,* 153–161.

Goldiamond, I. Self-control procedures in personal behavior problems. *Psychological Reports,* 1965, *17,* 851–868.

Goldstein, M.K. Behavior rate change in marriages: Training wives to modify husbands' behavior. *Dissertation Abstracts International,* 1971, *32 (1-B),* 559.

Goldstein, M.K. & Francis, B. Behavior modification of husbands by wives. Paper presented at the National Council on Family Relations, Washington, D.C., 1969.

Gordon, S.B. & Davidson, N. Behavioral parent training. In A.S. Gurman & D.P. Kniskern (Eds.), *Handbook of family therapy.* New York: Brunner/Mazel, 1981.

Gottman, J., Markman, H. & Notarius, C. The topography of marital conflict: A sequential analysis of verbal and nonverbal behavior. *Journal of Marriage and the Family,* 1977, *39,* 461–477.

Graziano, A.M. Parents as behavior therapists. In M. Hersen, R.M. Eisler & P.M. Miller (Eds.), *Progress in behavior modification.* New York: Academic Press, 1977.

Gurman, A.S. & Kniskern, D.P. Research on marital and family therapy: Progress, perspective and prospect. In S.L. Garfield & A.E. Bergin (Eds.), *Handbook of psychotherapy and behavior change: An empirical analysis.* New York: Wiley, 1978.

Gurman, A.S. & Kniskern, D.P. Family therapy outcome research: Knowns and unknowns. In A.S. Gurman & D.P. Kniskern (Eds.), *Handbook of family therapy.* New York: Brunner/Mazel, 1981.

Gurman, A.S. & Knudson, R.M. Behavioral marriage therapy: A psychodynamic-systems analysis and critique. *Family Process,* 1978, *17,* 121–138.

Hawkins, R.P., Peterson, R.F., Schweid, E. & Bijou, S.W. Behavior therapy in the home: Amelioration of problem parent-child relations with a parent in the therapeutic role. *Journal of Experimental Child Psychology,* 1966, *4,* 99–107.

Heiman, J.R., LoPiccolo, L. & LoPiccolo, J. The treatment of sexual dysfunction. In A.S. Gurman & D.P. Kniskern (Eds.), *Handbook of family therapy.* New York: Brunner/Mazel, 1981.

Hickman, M.E. & Baldwin, B.A. Use of programmed instruction to improve communication in marriage. *The Family Coordinator,* 1971, *20,* 121–125.

Hogan, D.R. The effectiveness of sex therapy: A review of the literature. In J. LoPiccolo & L. LoPiccolo (Eds.), *Handbook of sex therapy.* New York: Plenum Press, 1978.

Jacobson, N.S. Problem solving and contingency contracting in the treatment of marital discord. *Journal of Consulting and Clinical Psychology,* 1977, *45,* 92–100.

Jacobson, N.S. Specific and nonspecific factors in the effectiveness of a behavioral approach to the treatment of marital discord. *Journal of Consulting and Clinical Psychology,* 1978, *46,* 442–452.

Jacobson, N.S. Behavioral marital therapy. In A.S. Gurman & D.P. Kniskern (Eds.), *Handbook of family therapy.* New York: Brunner/Mazel, 1981.

Jacobson, N.S. & Margolin, G. *Marital therapy: Strategies based on social learning and behavior exchange principles.* New York: Brunner/Mazel, 1979.

Jacobson, N.S. & Martin, B. Behavioral marriage therapy: Current status. *Psychological Bulletin,* 1976, *83,* 540–556.

Jones, M.C. A laboratory study of fear: The case of Peter. *Journal of Genetic Psychology,* 1924, *31,* 308–315.

Kanfer. F.H. & Phillips, J.S. *Learning foundations of behavior therapy.* New York: Wiley, 1970.

Kaplan, H.S. *The new sex therapy: Active treatment of sexual dysfunctions.* New York: Brunner/Mazel, 1974.

Kaplan, H.S. *Disorders of sexual desire and other new concepts and techniques in sex therapy.* New York: Brunner/Mazel, 1979.

Katkin, S. Charting as a multipurpose treatment intervention in family therapy. *Family Process,* 1978, *17,* 465–468.

Keefe, F.J., Kopel, S.A. & Gordon, S.B. *A practical guide to behavior assessment.* New York: Springer, 1978.

Kimmel, C. & Van der Veen, F. Factors of marital adjustment in Locke's Marital Adjustment Test. *Journal of Marriage and the Family,* 1974, *36,* 57–63.

Knox, D. *Marriage happiness: A behavioral approach to counseling.* Champaign, Ill.: Research Press, 1971.

Knox, D. Behavior contracts in marriage counseling. *Journal of Family Counseling,* 1973, *1,* 22–28.

Lazarus, A.A. The treatment of a sexually inadequate male. In L.P. Ullmann & L. Krasner (Eds.), *Case studies in behavior modification.* New York: Holt, Rinehart & Winston, 1965.

Lazarus, A.A. Behavior therapy and group marriage counseling. *Journal of the American Society of Psychosomatic Medicine and Dentistry,* 1968, *15,* 49–56.

Lazarus, A.A. *Behavior therapy and beyond.* New York: McGraw-Hill, 1971.

LeBow, M.D. Behavior modification for the family. In G.D. Erickson & T.P. Hogan (Eds.), *Family therapy: An introduction to theory and technique.* Monterey, Calif.: Brooks/Cole, 1972.

Lederer, W.J. & Jackson, D.D. *The mirages of marriage.* New York: Norton, 1968.

Liberman, R.P. Behavioral approaches to family and couple therapy. *American Journal of Orthopsychiatry,* 1970, *40,* 106–118.

Liberman, R.P. Behavioral approaches to family and couple therapy. In C.J. Sager & H.S. Kaplan (Eds.), *Progress in group and family therapy.* New York: Brunner/Mazel, 1972.

Liberman, R.P., Levine, J., Wheeler, E., Sanders, N. & Wallace, C. Experimental evaluation of marital group therapy: Behavioral vs. interaction-insight formats. *Acta Psychiatrica Scandinavia,* 1976, Supplement.

Lobitz, N.C. & LoPiccolo, J. New methods in the behavioral treatment of sexual dysfunction. *Journal of Behavior Therapy and Experimental Psychiatry,* 1972, *3,* 265–271.

Locke, H.J. & Wallace, K.M. Short-term marital adjustment and prediction tests: Their reliability and validity. *Journal of Marriage and Family Living,* 1959, *21,* 251–255.

McGuire, R.J. & Vallance, M. Aversion therapy by electric shock: A simple technique. *British Medical Journal,* 1964, *1,* 151–153.

Mahoney, M.J. Reflections on the cognitive learning trend in psychotherapy. *American Psychologist,* 1977, *32,* 5–13.

Markman, H.J. Application of a behavioral model of marriage in predicting relationship satisfaction of couples planning marriage. *Journal of Consulting and Clinical Psychology,* 1979, *47,* 743–749.

Masters, W. H. & Johnson, V. E. *Human sexual inadequacy.* Boston: Little Brown, 1970.

Meichenbaum, D. *Cognitive behavior modification.* New York: Plenum, 1977.

Minuchin, S. *Families and family therapy.* Cambridge: Harvard University Press, 1974.

Minuchin, S., Rosman, B.L. & Baker, L. *Psychosomatic families.* Cambridge, Mass.: Harvard University Press, 1978.

Mischel, W. On the empirical dilemmas of psychodynamic approaches: Issues and alternatives. *Journal of Abnormal Psychology,* 1973, *82,* 335–344.

O'Dell, S. Training parents in behavior modification: A review. *Psychological Bulletin,* 1974, *81,* 418–433.

O'Leary, K.D., O'Leary, S. & Becher, W.C. Modification of a deviant sibling interaction pattern in the home. *Behavior Research and Therapy,* 1967, *5,* 113–120.

O'Leary, K.D. & Turkewitz, H. Marital therapy from a behavioral perspective. In T.J. Paolino & B.S. McCrady (Eds.), *Marriage and marital therapy.* New York: Brunner/Mazel, 1978.

O'Leary, K.D. & Wilson, G.T. *Behavior therapy: Application and outcome.* Englewood

Cliffs, N.J.: Prentice-Hall, 1975.

Patterson, G.R. Behavioral intervention procedures in the classroom and in the home. In A.E. Bergin & S.L. Garfield (Eds.), *Handbook of psychotherapy and behavior change: An empirical analysis.* New York: Wiley, 1971a.

Patterson, G.R. *Families: Application of social learning theory to family life.* Champaign, Illinois: Research Press, 1971b.

Patterson, G.R., Hops, H. & Weiss, R.L. A social learning approach to reducing rates of marital conflict. In R. Stuart, R. Liberman & S. Wilder (Eds.), *Advances in behavior therapy.* New York: Academic Press, 1973.

Patterson, G.R. & Reid, J. Reciprocity and coercion: Two facets of social systems. In C. Neuringer & J. Michael (Eds.), *Behavior modification in clinical psychology.* New York: Appleton-Century-Crofts, 1970.

Patterson, G.R., Weiss, R.L. & Hops, H. Training in marital skills: Some problems and concepts. In H. Leitenberg (Ed.), *Handbook of behavior modification and behavior therapy.* Englewood Cliffs, New Jersey: Prentice-Hall, 1976.

Pavlov, I.P. Neuroses in man and animals. *Journal of the American Medical Association,* 1932, *99,* 1012–1013.

Pavolov, I.P. An attempt at a physiological interpretation of obsessional neurosis and paranoia. *Journal of Mental Science,* 1934, *80,* 187–197.

Pendergrass, V. E. Effects of length of timeout from positive reinforcement and schedule of application in suppression of aggressive behavior. *Psychological Record,* 1971, *21,* 75–80.

Pierce, R.M. Training in interpersonal communication skills with the partners of deteriorated marriages. *The Family Coordinator,* 1973, *22,* 223–227.

Premack, D. Reinforcement theory. In D. Levine (Ed.), *Nebraska symposium on motivation.* Lincoln, Neb.: University of Nebraska Press, 1965.

Rappaport, A.F. & Harrell, J. A behavioral-exchange model for marital counseling. *Family Coordinator,* 1972, *21,* 203–213.

Rimm, D.C. & Masters, J.C. *Behavior therapy: Techniques and empirical findings.* New York: Wiley, 1974.

Rinn, R.C. Children with behavior disorders. In M. Hersen & A.S. Bellack (Eds.), *Behavior therapy in the psychiatric setting.* Baltimore: Williams & Wilkins, 1978.

Risley, T.R. The effects and side effects of punishing the autistic behaviors of a deviant child. *Journal of Applied Behavior Analysis,* 1968, *1,* 21–34.

Romanczyk, R.G. & Kistner, J.J. The current state of the arts in behavior modification. *The Psychotherapy Bulletin,* 1977, *11,* 16–30.

Schwitzgebel, R. Short-term operant conditioning of adolescent offenders on socially relevant variables. *Journal of Abnormal Psychology,* 1967, *72,* 134–142.

Schwitzgebel, R. & Kolb, D.A. Inducing behavior change in adolescent delinquents. *Behavior Research and Therapy,* 1964, *9,* 233–238.

Semans, J.H. Premature ejaculation: A new approach. *Southern Medical Journal,* 1956, *49,* 353–357.

Skinner, B.F. *Science and human behavior.* New York: Macmillan, 1953.

Spinks, S.H. & Birchler, G.R. Behavioral systems marital therapy: Dealing with resistance. *Family Process,* 1982, *21,* 169–186.

Stuart, R.B. An operant-interpersonal treatment for marital discord. *Journal of Consulting and Clinical Psychology,* 1969, *33,* 675–682.

Stuart, R.B. Behavioral contracting within the families of delinquents. *Journal of Behavior Therapy and Experimental Psychiatry,* 1971, *2,* 1–11.

Stuart, R.B. Behavioral remedies for marital ills: A guide to the use of operant-interpersonal techniques. In T. Thompson & W. Docken (Eds.), *International symposium on behavior modification.* New York: Appleton, 1975.

Stuart, R.B. An operant interpersonal program for couples. In D.H.L. Olson (Ed.), *Treating relationships.* Lake Mills, Iowa: Graphic Publishing Company, 1976.

Thibaut, J. & Kelley, H.H. *The social psychology of groups.* New York: Wiley, 1959.

Umana, R.F., Gross, S.J. & McConville, N.T. *Crisis in the family: Three approaches.* New York: Gardner Press, 1980.

Vincent, J.P., Weiss, R.L. & Birchler, G.R. A behavioral analysis of problem solving in distressed and nondistressed married and stranger dyads. *Behavior Therapy,* 1975, *6,* 475–487.

Watson, J.B. & Raynor, R. Conditioned emotional reactions. *Journal of Experimental Psychology,* 1920, *3,* 1–14.

Weiss, R.L. The conceptualization of marriage from a behavioral perspective. In T.J. Paolino & B.S. McCrady (Eds.), *Marriage and marital therapy.* New York: Brunner/Mazel, 1978.

Weiss, R.L. & Birchler, G.R. Adults with marital dysfunction. In M. Hersen & A.S. Bellack (Eds.), *Behavior therapy in the psychiatric setting.* Baltimore: Williams & Wilkins, 1978.

Weiss, R.L., Hops, H. & Patterson, G.R. A framework for conceptualizing marital conflict, a technology for altering it, some data for evaluating it. In L.A. Hamerlynch, L.C. Handy & E.J. Mash (Eds.) *Behavior change: Methodology, concepts and practice.* Champaign, Illinois: Research Press, 1973.

Weiss, R.L. & Isaac, J. Behavior vs. cognitive measures as predictors of marital satisfaction. Paper presented at the Western Psychological Association meeting, Los Angeles, April 1978.

Wills, T.A., Weiss, R.L. & Patterson, G.R. A behavioral analysis of the determinants of marital satisfaction. *Journal of Consulting and Clinical Psychology,* 1974, *42,* 802–811.

Wolpe, J. An approach to the problem of neurosis based on the conditioned response. Unpublished M.D. thesis. University of Witwatersrand, Johannesberg, South Africa, 1948.

Wolpe, J. *Psychotherapy by reciprocal inhibition.* Stanford, California: Stanford University Press, 1958.

Wolpe, J. *The practice of behavior therapy.* Elmsford, New York: Pergamon Press, 1969.

8

Extended Family Systems Therapy

INTRODUCTION

t he pioneers of family therapy recognized that people are products of
their context, but usually limited treatment to the nuclear family. The
approaches considered in this chapter have extended the focus of therapy to
wider circles of family and friends. Bowen, Laqueur, and Speck developed
distinctly different methods of treatment, but they are linked together by a
common concern with extended social networks.

The methods of therapy described in this chapter are among the most
purely systems-oriented approaches to human problems. The emphasis in
understanding and treatment is on intergenerational processes, and wider
kinship and social structures. Child-centered families who present with
concerns about pathology are redirected to adult relationships, both
multigenerational and in social support systems. The therapist's role is seen

as first defining sources of stress, and then coaching family members to establish closer ties with their larger families and communities.

SKETCHES OF LEADING FIGURES

This book has been organized conceptually to avoid as much as possible the cult of personality that pervades the family therapy field, and to put the contributions of various individuals in the broader context of family theories and strategies. This chapter, however, is largely devoted to the work of one person, Murray Bowen.

Bowen's thinking has been a dominant force in the family therapy movement since the early 1950s; his influence has continued to grow and his stature as a commanding figure in the field is now firmly established. His pre-eminent position is due not only to the fact that he has been one of the parent figures in the field, but also to the innovative and comprehensive nature of his system of family theory and technique. He has trained most extended family systems therapists, except Laqueur, Speck, and Attneave.

Bowen was the oldest child in a large, cohesive family living in rural Pennsylvania. By his own account (Bowen, 1972) he was attracted to the study of medicine more by a fascination with complex problems than by the sentiment to help people. In medical school his interests shifted from neurology to neurosurgery, and then to differential diagnosis. During his internship he constructed an artificial heart, and was subsequently awarded a fellowship in surgery. He then served for five years in the military. There he saw widespread psychopathology, matched by equally widespread ignorance about how to deal with it, which inspired him to seek a career in psychiatry. Here, Bowen felt, he could chart a course through largely unknown territory.

Once in psychiatry Bowen turned his attention to the enigma of schizophrenia. Bowen had been thoroughly trained in psychoanalysis, including undergoing a personal analysis. Not surprisingly, therefore, he sought to apply psychoanalytic concepts to schizophrenia. Later he became assistant director at the Menninger Clinic and there he first became interested in the role of the family in schizophrenia. This interest produced the famous live-in research study of schizophrenic families, conducted at the National Institute of Mental Health from 1954 to 1959.

In 1959, Bowen moved to Georgetown University. During his years at Georgetown, Bowen has developed his comprehensive theory of family therapy, inspired an entire generation of students, and become an internationally renowned leader of the family therapy movement.

Two well-known students of Bowen's are Philip Guerin and Thomas Fogarty, both of whom worked closely with him although both now are independent and separate. Many of Bowen's later students, however, have continued to work with him, among them Michael Kerr, Edward Beal, Joseph Lorio, and Charles Paddock. Each is an important representative of the extended family systems tradition, and all have helped transmit Bowen's ideas in their teaching and through papers presented at the annual Georgetown Family Symposia.

Philip Guerin began his psychiatric residency at Georgetown, where he had also gone to medical school. Although he was exposed to competing influences from the psychoanalytic faculty, he eventually resolved his ambivalence in favor of family therapy. However, his early exposure to psychoanalytic theory served him well, and unlike many recently trained family therapists, Guerin remains well-grounded in individual as well as systems theory.

After his second year of residency at Georgetown, Guerin transferred to Einstein where he served as chief resident. He remained in contact with Bowen, however, and also with Thomas Fogarty and Andrew Ferber. Guerin (1972) also cites his personal study of his own family as a major influence on his career as a family therapist.

Guerin is the founder and director of the Center for Family Learning in New Rochelle, New York, where he is influential as a clinician, teacher, and administrator. In addition, Guerin's knack of bringing ideas and people together led him to edit one of the most valuable books in the family therapy literature (Guerin, *Family Therapy: Theory and Practice*), and to organize many workshops and convention programs.

Thomas Fogarty, now a senior faculty member at the Center for Family Learning and an Assistant Clinical Professor of Psychiatry at Einstein, came to psychiatry by a circuitous route. After high school he spent some time in the Army, where he decided to become a physician. After medical school, he did a residency in internal medicine, and began his career in private practice. But he found this boring, and so retooled by completing a residency in psychiatry. He studied with Bowen, whose influence he continues to reflect. Fogarty first directed a community mental health clinic, but he has since chosen to devote himself more to clinical practice and teaching. He has had a major impact on a large number of trainees.

Peter Laqueur began multiple family therapy in 1950 at Creedmore State Hospital in New York, where he was in charge of a one-hundred-bed ward of young schizophrenic patients. He held large joint meetings weekly with patients and their families, and although he found these sessions sufficiently productive to continue them for several years, he eventually decided that the sheer number of people involved (typically about seventeen families) made them too chaotic to be maximally effective. He therefore limited multiple family groups to four to six families. Laqueur was Director of Family Therapy at Vermont State Hospital and a member of the psychiatric faculty at the University of Vermont, until his untimely death.

Ross Speck and Carolyn Attneave expanded therapy not only beyond the individual, but also beyond the family to include "social networks" of forty or fifty friends and relatives. They don't just work with extended families, they create them.

Ross Speck grew up in a small town in Ontario, Canada, where tent revival meetings and annual family reunions impressed him with the helping potential of social networks. In medical school, he specialized in psychiatry, and after four years of residency training served in both the Canadian and American armies. Later—like so many innovators of family therapy—he underwent psychoanalytic training and graduated from a psychoanalytic institute.

Working with schizophrenic families, Speck was impressed with the importance of influences from outside the nuclear family. True, his schizo-phrenic patients seemed acutely sensitive to their immediate families. But they seemed equally responsive to the extended families and friends. By 1964 he had begun including various combinations of friends and neigh-bors as well as relatives in therapy sessions (Speck and Attneave, 1973). In 1966 he organized his first family network of forty people to help resocialize a schizophrenic family. The success of this experiment convinced him that social networks are as important to families as families are to individuals.

Dr. Speck served as the Clinical Director of the Eastern Pennsylvania Psychiatric Institute in Philadelphia, and Head of the Section of Social Psychiatry at Hahnemann Medical College. In 1970, while teaching net-work therapy to the staff on the Philadelphia Child Guidance Clinic, he met Carolyn Attneave. Recognizing each other as kindred spirits with like interests, they began a collaboration which resulted in the publication of *Family Networks* (Speck and Attneave, 1973), on the theory and technique of network therapy.

Carolyn Attneave had been an artist, theater technician, teacher, and journalist (Attneave, 1972) before she began studying for a doctorate in psychology. Her mother's family were Delaware Indians, and she attributes much of her interest in kinship networks to the heritage of Indian culture, where family bonds extend to whole tribes.

Attneave developed her own approach to social network intervention in the 1960s, while working as a consulting psychologist at a community clinic and as co-ordinator of the health department's community guidance services in rural Oklahoma. With not enough clinicians to deal with heavy demands for service, she enrolled various community agencies as well as relatives, colleagues, and friends to help the troubled people who came to the clinic. She activated the network of community resources to help her patients as an Indian would activate the resources of the tribe to solve the problems of its individual members.

Attneave has held a number of university appointments; currently she is a professor at the University of Washington in Seattle.

THEORETICAL FORMULATIONS

Murray Bowen, among the most cerebral of all family therapists, has always been more committed to family as an orientation rather than a method, and more interested in theory than in technique. From his point of view most mental health professionals are too caught up in narrow questions of technique to ever fully grasp what systems theory is all about. Bowen's own theory is among the most carefully worked out and influential of family systems. Although the theory has evolved and expanded, it has always centered around two sets of opposing forces: those that bind personalities in family togetherness, and those that fight to break free toward individuality. The concepts he has used to express this central tension of the human condition have evolved from *mother-child symbiosis*, to *undifferentiated family ego mass*, to *fusion/differentiation*. However phrased, the central premise is that unresolved emotional attachment to one's family must be resolved, rather than passively accepted or reactively rejected, before one can differentiate a mature, healthy personality. Bowen (*e.g.* 1976) frequently cites six interlocking concepts which make up his theory. These are: 1) Emotional triangles; 2) Differentiation of self; 3) Nuclear family emotional system; 4) Family projection process; 5) Multigenerational projection system; and 6) Influence of sibling position.

1) *Emotional Triangles*. Triangles are the molecules of interpersonal systems. Three people are the smallest stable relationship in families, at work, or in social groups. Significant relationships made up of two persons are unstable; when tension arises, a third person or thing is triangulated into the relationship. Two lovers may have a stable relationship as long as anxiety

is low; however, should anxiety and tension arise, one of the lovers will feel so uncomfortable that he or she will tend to triangulate in a third person or thing, by drinking, let us say, or consulting a psychotherapist, or confiding in a friend. In each of these cases the triangulation relieves tension, but impedes resolution of the problem between the pair. The classic instance of triangulation occurs when tension between a husband and wife is defused, though not resolved, by focusing on the children. Instead of fighting with each other, the parents devote their energy and attention to the kids. Unhappily, the greater the unresolved tension the more likely this triangulation will lead to an overly intense attachment between one of the parents and the children; and this tends to produce symptoms in the child.

Emotional triangles are not limited to three separate persons, but may involve any three-sided system. Thus a common family triangle consists of father at point A, relatively distant from mother at point B, who in turn is relatively close to several children, all clustered at point C. Similarly, in work settings there is often a conflicted relationship between the two most powerful authority figures, who remain relatively distant from each other at points A and B. The rest of the work group will tend to form overlapping triangles, with most of them more closely allied with one of the major figures. Usually there is a good deal of talk and gossip about the "others," which tends to prevent genuine contact or resolution of problems between the major figures.

2) *Differentiation of Self.* Differentiation of self, the cornerstone of Bowen's theory, is both an intrapsychic and an interpersonal concept. Intrapsychic differentiation is the ability to separate feeling from thinking. Undifferentiated people hardly distinguish thoughts from feelings; their intellects are so flooded with feeling that they are almost incapable of objective thinking. Their lives are governed by an accretion of feelings from those around them, either blindly adhered to or angrily rejected. The differentiated person, on the other hand, is not a cold fish who only thinks and never feels. Instead, he or she is able to balance thinking and feeling: capable of strong emotion and spontaneity, but also capable of restraint and acting contrary to emotional impulses.

Lack of differentiation between thinking and feeling occurs in context with lack of differentiation between oneself and others. Because they are less able to think clearly, undifferentiated people react emotionally—positively or negatively—to the dictates of family members, science, culture, and religion. These people have little autonomous identity. Instead they tend to be fused with others. They find it difficult to separate themselves from others, particularly on important issues. Asked what they think, they say what they feel; asked what they believe, they repeat what they have heard. They either conform or assume pseudo-independence through counter-conformity. In contrast, differentiated people are able to take definite stands on issues because they are able to think things through, decide what they believe, and then act on those beliefs. This enables them to be in intimate contact with others without being reflexly shaped by them.

3) *Nuclear Family Emotional System.* This concept deals with the emotional forces in families that operate over the years in recurrent patterns. Bowen originally used the term "undifferentiated family ego mass" to describe emotional oneness or fusion in families. Lack of differentiation in the family of origin leads to an emotional cutoff from parents, which in turn leads to fusion in marriage. The less the differentiation of self prior to marriage, the greater the fusion between spouses. Since this new fusion is unstable it tends to produce one of the following: 1) reactive emotional distance between the spouses; 2) physical or emotional dysfunction in one spouse; 3) overt marital conflict; or 4) projection of the problem onto one or more children. The intensity of these problems is related to the degree of undifferentiation, extent of emotional cutoff from families of origin, and level of stress in the system.

4) *Family Projection Process.* This is the process by which parents transmit their immaturity and lack of differentiation to their children. Emotional fusion between spouses creates tension which leads either to marital conflict or emotional distance. A common case is one in which the husband, who is cut off from his family of origin, relates only in a very cool and distant way to his wife. This predisposes her to a relatively intense focus on the kids. Kept at arm's length by her husband, she devotes her emotional energy to the children, usually with the greatest intensity toward one particular child. This child may be the oldest son or daughter, the youngest son or daughter, or perhaps one who looks like one of the parents.

The child who is the object of the projection process becomes the one most attached to the parents (positively or negatively), and the one with the least differentiation of self. Since it relieves his own anxiety, the husband supports the wife's over-involvement with the children. He may do so directly, or indirectly by virtue of his own lack of involvement.

The emotional fusion between mother and child may take the form of a warm, dependent bond, or an angry, conflictual struggle. As the mother focuses her anxiety on the child, the child's functioning is stunted. This underdevelopment enables the mother to overcontrol the child, distracting her from her own anxieties but crippling the child emotionally. Thus infantilized, the child eventually develops symptoms of psychological impairment, necessitating further parental concern and solidifying the family pattern.

5) *Multigenerational Transmission Process.* This concept describes the transmission of the family emotional process through multiple generations. In every generation the child most involved in the family's fusion moves toward a lower level of differentiation of self, while the least involved child moves toward a higher level of differentiation. Bowen's multigenerational transmission concept takes emotional illness not only beyond the individual to the family, but also beyond the nuclear family to several generations. The problem in the identified patient is a product of the relationship of that person's parents, which is a product of the relationship of their parents, continuing back for several generations. The problem does not reside in the child and is not the child's fault; nor are the parents to blame. Instead the problem is the result of a multigenerational sequence in which all family members are actors and reactors.

6) *Sibling Position.* This concept is similar to Toman's (1969) ten personality profiles of children who grow up in different sibling positions. Bowen concurs that children develop certain fixed personality characteristics based on the sibling position in their families. So many variables are involved that prediction is complex, but knowledge of general characteristics plus specific knowledge of a particular family is helpful in predicting what part a child will play in the family emotional process, and in predicting family patterns in the next generation.

Fogarty (1976a) has described individuals as having four dimensions, and relating to others in three channels. The four dimensions of self are: depth, movement toward objects, movement toward persons, and time. The depth dimension includes much that we generally think of as intrapsychic, including thoughts, feelings, dreams, and aspirations. In addition to these attributes of personality, people vary according to the nature and degree of their proclivity for involvement with things, such as possessions, work, or games, as opposed to other people. Finally, Fogarty says, people vary in being fast or slow to think, act, and feel, and in being committed to the status quo or to change. This is the time dimension.

Fogarty's four-dimensional people are linked to one another by three systems: the thinking system, the emotional system, and the operating system. The thinking system of facts, judgments, and opinions functions in proportion to knowledge and information; it dysfunctions in proportion to which fact is confused with feeling. The emotional system provides color and vitality to relationships. Neither good nor bad, right nor wrong, the emotional system either works effectively or it does not. The third system by which people are connected is the operating system. This defines the ways in which people communicate their thoughts and feelings. Silence, withdrawal, talking, or yelling may all be used to convey essentially the same thought or feeling.

Laqueur (1976) applies general systems theory to families and multiple family groups. Families are seen as systems made up of subsystems — individuals — and belonging to larger systems — communities and societies. Likewise, multiple family groups are systems comprising subsystems of families and therapists. These, like all systems, have input, a central processing mechanism, output, and a feedback loop. The feedback loop enables the central processing mechanism to evaluate the quality of output and subsequently control and correct it.

The inputs to family systems include information and energy from subsystems within (individual members) and suprasystems without (community and environment). The family system processes this information and energy, and converts it into output that ensures the survival and growth of the system and the family members that comprise it. In families, the central processing mechanism, the decision-making unit, may be one or both parents, or even all family members.

According to this model, malfunction occurs if inputs are too weak, useless, or overwhelming; if the central processing unit lacks data or organization; if output channels are limited or blocked; if feedback is incomplete, misleading, or redundant; or if too much or too little information, cognitive or emotional, passes from one part of the system to another. Correcting the system — psychotherapy — requires analyzing the focus of disturbance and modifying it. The multiple family group operates as a systems corrector with input from several families, centrally processed by the therapists in collaboration with family members, to produce outputs of better functioning families and individuals. The therapists use general systems theory to guide their work as systems analysts.

Laqueur also uses Lewin's field theory to conceptualize the process of treatment (Laqueur, 1976). The multiple family therapist tries to keep the whole field in mind, while observing interactions in the group. Once individuals are seen as responding to the totality of forces in their context, the participants can be made aware of their influence on and reactance to the surrounding field.

Network therapy is supported not so much by a theory of behavior change, as by a simple faith in people's ability to help one another solve problems. Individuals, particularly those living in cities, are described as cut off from kin and others in the community. This is a sociological and political version of what Bowen describes in dynamic, psychological terms as the cutoff from extended family. Speck and Attneave describe isolation not so much as a function of family conflict, as simply a fact of contemporary culture.

Like Rousseau and most humanistic psychologists, Speck and Attneave have a simple faith in the natural capacities of people to help themselves. Kinship groups and social groups are inherently able to enhance the quality of the lives of their members. Industrialized societies tend to isolate individuals from family and friends; network therapy is designed to reverse this isolation, to reconnect people with the social matrix.

The social network is assumed to have within it the resources necessary for creative solutions to the problems of its members. The network intervenors endeavor to reconnect people in crisis with their social networks, and to stimulate the people in the network to pitch in and help those in trouble. Psychological problems—many of them—are thought to derive from alienation from the resources of family and social relationships; their solution depends on reactivating those relationships (Speck and Attneave, 1973).

NORMAL FAMILY DEVELOPMENT

In Bowen's system there is no discontinuity between normal and abnormal family development. When he began studying normal families in the late 1950s, he discovered many of the same mechanisms he had previously observed in schizophrenic families. This convinced him that there are no discrete categories of families (schizophrenic, neurotic, or normal), but that all families vary along a continuum from emotional fusion to differentiation. The fact that most of Bowen's clinical contact in recent years has been with families of professionals probably reinforces his belief that families are more alike than different.

Optimal family development is thought to take place when family members are relatively differentiated, when anxiety is low, and when the parents are in good emotional contact with their own families of origin. Normally, but not optimally, people reduce contact with their parents and siblings to avoid the anxiety and conflict of dealing with them. Once out of contact with their families, people forget and deny the discord. However, they carry old difficulties in the form of vulnerability to recapitulate them in intense relationships wherever they go. Having learned to ignore their own role in family conflicts, they are unable to prevent recurrences in new relationships. Therefore, people with greater differentiation who remain in contact with previous generations are more stable than people from enmeshed or splintered families. Although problems may not surface immediately in cut-off families, they will eventually occur in future generations.

Another heritage from the past is that the emotional attachment between spouses is identical to the one each had in the family of origin. People who were relatively undifferentiated in their original families will continue to be undifferentiated when they form a new family. Those who handled family conflicts by distance and withdrawal will do the same in their marriages. Therefore, Bowen is convinced that differentiation of autonomous personalities accomplished primarily in the family of origin is both a description of normal development and a prescription for therapeutic improvement. This inescapable link to the past, stressed more strongly in Bowen's approach than any other, is the prevailing feature of normal family development.

In "Systems Concepts and the Dimensions of Self," Fogarty (1976a) elaborates the characteristics of well-adjusted families: 1) They are balanced and can adapt to change; 2) Emotional problems are seen as existing in the whole group, with components in each person; 3) They are connected across generations to all family members; 4) They use a minimum of fusion and a minimum of distance to solve problems; 5) Each dyad can deal with problems between them; 6) Differences are tolerated, even encouraged; 7) Each person can deal on thinking and emotional levels with the others; 8) They are aware of what each person gets from within and from others; 9) Each person is allowed his or her own emptiness; 10) Preservation of a positive emotional climate takes precedence over doing what is "right" or what is popular; 11) Each member thinks it's a pretty good family to live in; and 12) Members of the family use each other as sources of feedback and learning, not as emotional crutches.

In Bowen's system the hallmark of the well-adjusted person is rational objectivity and individuality. A differentiated person is able to separate thinking from feeling, and remain independent of, though not out of contact with, the nuclear and extended family. The degree of differentiation of self depends largely on the course of one's family history, which is a relatively deterministic position. However, as we shall see, it is possible to achieve higher levels of differentiation through the process of family treatment.

Laqueur's model of normal families stresses free and open communication, cognitive and emotional. While he did not describe how such families develop, he views them as functioning much like an effective group. No one in the family is isolated from the others, and no one dominates or controls.

Although he doesn't say so, he implies that he favors a democratic rather than hierarchical structure in families (*e.g.*, Laqueur, 1976).

Speck and Attneave also have little to say about normal family development, but their position can be deduced from reports of their own experience (Speck and Attneave, 1973) and descriptions of the general nature of networks (Speck and Attneave, 1972). The essence of normal development is the existence of close and mutually supportive bonds in families, extended families, and tribes, as well as among friends, neighbors, and work associates. People are not isolated within themselves or within their families; they are members of communities. Communal efforts are necessary to face crises, such as natural disasters or personal illness, and neighborly interaction is necessary for shared celebrations of life, including births, weddings, and holidays.

In order to describe what is normal, one must look beyond the individual to the family and community. The normal family and the normal community are composed of people actively engaged in sharing everyday concern about whatever threatens the community's well-being. The normal community is characterized by acknowledged interdependence; people are connected and involved, not isolated and detached. People *can* help one another, and normally they *do*.

An individual's network is the sum of all the people who have significance and involvement in his or her life. Normally, this network offers a wealth and variety of relationships to give support and enrichment to individuals. Because they are larger and more complex, than primary groups, networks allow greater freedom and flexibility. Normally, people have access to this wider circle of relationships. If they don't, they may have a false sense of autonomy, but are actually impoverished and alienated.

DEVELOPMENT OF BEHAVIOR DISORDERS

According to Bowen, behavior disorders, mild or severe, result from emotional fusion transmitted from one generation to the next. Emotions flood the intellect, impairing rational functioning and competence. The greater the degree of fusion, the more life is programmed by primitive emotional forces, despite rationalizations to the contrary (Bowen, 1975). Furthermore, the greater the fusion between emotions and intellect, the more one is fused to the emotional reactions of other people. Emotional fusion consists of tense interconnection and dependent attachment, overtly expressed or reactively rejected. Both the clinging, dependent person and the aloof, isolated one are equally caught up in emotional fusion; they merely manifest it in different ways. As long as they are emotionally stuck in the positions they occupied in their families of origin, their personal growth is stunted.

Emotional fusion is a reciprocal of differentiation. The fused person has few firmly held convictions and beliefs; he or she seeks acceptance and approval above any other goal, and makes decisions based primarily on feelings rather than rational thought. The undifferentiated person may have few or many opinions, but in either case the opinions are received, not thought out. Creating a good impression is all important, and the undifferentiated person is likely to be either dogmatic or compliant, but rarely able to calmly state his or her own beliefs without trying to inflate self or attack others. The symptom patterns that develop from emotional fusion are unhappy marriages, either combative or emotionally distant; dysfunction in one of the spouses; or projection of problems onto one or more children. The following clinical vignette illustrates how emotional fusion in the family of origin is transmitted.

> After his father died, Mr. Klein and his older sister were reared by their mother. This woman was a relatively mature and thoughtful person, but following the death of her husband she increasingly devoted all her attention to her children. They were her chief preoccupation, and shaping their lives became the major project of her life. Throughout their childhood she insisted that they conform to her standards: she was persistent in correcting their manners, energetic in demanding high performance in school, and highly critical of anything they sought to do outside the home. She discouraged contact with neighbors and school friends, who were engaged in such "frivolous" pastimes as playing ball or going to school dances.
>
> In late adolescence Mr. Klein began to realize the powerful control his mother exerted over him and his sister. The sister was never able to break free from her mother's influence, and remained single, living with her mother for the rest of her life. Mr. Klein, however, was determined to leave home and become independent. Since he had always been told what to think, where to go, and how to behave, it was difficult to move out and be on his own. However, he was strongwilled and energetic; finally, in his mid-twenties, he left home and turned his back on his mother. He moved to a distant city, started working, and eventually married.
>
> The woman he married, Liza, came from a large, closely knit, and affectionate family. She and her four sisters were very much attached to each other and remained best friends throughout their lives. Their relationship with their parents was warm and close; none of the sisters ever questioned this model of family structure.

After she graduated from high school, Liza announced to the family that she wanted to go to college. This was contrary to the family norm that daughters remain at home and prepare themselves to be wives and mothers. Hence a major battle ensued between Liza and her parents; they were struggling to hold on, and she was struggling to break free. Finally she left for college, but she was ever after estranged from her parents. They had forgiven, but not forgotten, her violation of the family tradition.

When Liza and Mr. Klein met they were immediately drawn to one another. Both were lonely and cut off from their families. After a brief, passionate courtship, they married. The honeymoon didn't last long. Never having really differentiated himself from his domineering mother, Mr. Klein was exquisitely sensitive to any effort to direct him. He became furious at his wife's slightest attempt to change his habits or get him to accommodate to her way of thinking and behaving. After years of grating against his dictatorial mother, his patience for control had long since worn thin. Mrs. Klein, on the other hand, sought to re-establish in her new marriage the closeness she had in her family. But in order to be close, she and her husband had to do things together and share similar interests and routines. When she moved toward him, suggesting that they do something, he was angry and resentful, feeling his individuality impinged upon. After several months of conflict and argument, the two settled into a period of relative equilibrium. Mr. Klein put most of his energy into his work, where he felt free and autonomous, leaving his wife to adjust to the distance between them. A year later their first child, David, was born.

Both parents were delighted to have a baby, but what was for Mr. Klein a pleasant addition to the family was for Mrs. Klein the means to fulfill her desperate need to be close to someone. The baby meant everything to her. While he was an infant she was the perfect mother, loving him tenderly and caring for his every need. When he was hungry she fed him; when he was wet she changed him; and when he cried —whenever he cried— she held him. When Mr. Klein tried to get involved with his infant son, his wife hovered about making sure he didn't do anything "wrong" with her precious baby. Naturally this infuriated Mr. Klein, and after a few bitter arguments he gradually left David more and more in his wife's care.

As he learned to walk and talk, David got into mischief, as all little children do. He grabbed things that he wasn't supposed to, refused to stay in the playpen, and fussed whenever he didn't get his way. His crying was unbearable to his mother. She found herself unable to set limits or establish controls on this precious baby whose love she needed so badly. When she put him in his crib for a nap, he cried. Although she desperately needed some time by herself, and little David also needed his nap, she was so unable to stand the crying that after five minutes she went and brought him downstairs. This was the beginning of a lifelong pattern.

David grew up with a distant father and a doting mother, thinking he was the center of the universe. Whatever he wanted, he expected to get; whenever he was frustrated, he threw a tantrum until he got what he wanted. Bad as things were at home, at least the family existed in a kind of equilibrium. Dad was cut off from his wife and son, but he had his work. Mother was cut off from her husband, but she had her baby. Although he was willful and disobedient, he gave her the affection she craved. David's difficulties began when he went off to school. Used to getting his own way, he found it impossible to share with other children, or to abide by the rules. His disobedience and tantrums did nothing to endear him to his schoolmates or teachers. The other children avoided him, and he grew up having few friends. With teachers he acted out his father's battle against any efforts to control him. When Mrs. Klein heard complaints about David's failure to conform to the school's demands, she sided with her son and saw these complaints as resulting from a failure to accommodate to David's specialness and creativity. So she moved him from school to school. But everywhere the conflicts were the same.

David grew up with a terrible pattern of adjustment to school and friends, but retained his extremely close relationship with his mother. The crisis came with adolescence. Like his father before him, David tried to develop independent interests outside the home. However, he was far less capable of separating than his father had been, and his mother was equally incapable of letting him go. The result was the beginning of chronic conflicts between David and his mother. Even as they argued and fought they remained centered on each other. David spent more time battling his mother than doing anything outside the family.

Although he eventually left home at twenty-five, David remained a severely limited person. He hadn't learned the knack of looking after himself, and so had to settle for a series of unrewarding and uninteresting jobs. Never having learned to compromise or adjust to other children, he found it extremely difficult to make friends. He spent the rest of his life as a lonely, isolated, and marginally adjusted person. Worst of all he didn't even have the consolation of the warm relationship with his mother.

David's history illustrates the components of Bowen's theory of behavior disorder. Both of his parents grew up relatively undifferentiated in emotionally fused families. As dictated by their own emotional needs, Mr. and Mrs. Klein's parents held their children too close, too long. This fusion sharply limits independent thinking and acting. Smothered by parents, it's hard to do other than reflexly accept or oppose them.

Except in unusual cases, even emotionally fused children reach a point where they try to break away. But breaking away in such instances tends to be accomplished by emotional cutoff rather than by mature resolution of family ties. In childhood we relate to our parents as children. We depend on them to take care of us, uncritically accept many of their attitudes and beliefs, and behave in ways that are generally effective in getting our way with them. This usually means some combination of being quiet and good, patiently waiting to be rewarded, and being upset and demanding. A good deal of this childish behavior just does not work well in the adult world. However, most of us leave home before ever changing to an adult-to-adult pattern with our parents. We—and they—only begin to change before it's time to leave.

A meek, patient child may become a bit more assertive and demanding in adolescence. Predictably, parents react with disappointment and anger. But instead of weathering the storm and patiently persisting with an adult stance, most people get hurt and withdraw. This is the emotional cutoff. Instead of persisting long enough to transform the relationship to an adult level, people decide that the only way to deal with their parents is to move away. Unhappily, this only gives the illusion of solving the problems.

The girl who didn't get past meek patience with her parents will probably adopt a similar stance outside the home. When it doesn't work, she may react with temper—which also won't work. Those who cut themselves off from their parents to minimize tension carry over their childish repertoire of behavior, unmodified.

According to Bowen, people tend to choose mates with equivalent levels of undifferentiation. This may be manifest in quite different ways—perhaps extreme dependence in one, with extreme independence in the other—but, underneath, the level of immaturity is the same. Observations of sharp increases in problems after nuclear families cut off from extended families (Kerr, 1971) tend to corroborate Bowen's view. When inevitable conflict develops, each spouse will be aware of the contribution of emotional immaturity—in the other one. Each will be prepared for change—in the other one. He will discover that her treating him like a father entails not only clinging dependence, but also emotional tirades and temper tantrums. She will discover that he withdraws the closeness she found so attractive in courtship as soon as she makes any demands. He fled from his parents because he needs closeness, but cannot handle it. Faced with conflict, he again withdraws. Sadly, what turned them on to each other carries the switch that turns them off.

What follows is marital conflict, dysfunction in one of the spouses, debilitating overconcern with one of the children, or various combinations of all three. When families come for help, they may present with any one of these problems. Whatever the presenting problem, the dynamics are similar: undifferentiation in families of origin is transferred to marital problems, which are in turn projected onto a symptomatic spouse or child. Thus the problems of the past are visited on the future.

Laqueur (1976) describes seven varieties of disturbed families. The most severely distrubed are those in which family members are thoroughly isolated from each other. The second type are those families so split by generation that there is little significant interaction between parents and children. The third type of family is split by gender. Fathers and sons form one unit, mothers and daughters another, with little communication across the boundary. The fourth group are families with a symbiotic pair. Two members are intensely fused together, while the rest are cut off, from the pair and from each other. The fifth type of family is dominated by one person, usually the mother. She is clearly and dramatically in charge; all communication and all interaction must go through her. In the sixth variation, one member is scapegoated and distinctly outside the rest of the group. The seventh kind of family is based on a rigid and inflexible hierarchy. Although no one may overtly appear domineering, one person holds all the power and calls all the shots. Often this person will refuse to attend therapy sessions.

Because their writing tends to be sociological and prescriptive, rather than psychological and explanatory, Speck and Attneave say little about the development of disorder. They are more concerned with solving problems than explaining how they develop. What they do say is that there are many reasons for problems in living. The pathology they address directly is that in the system. Dysfunction in individuals is associated with social bonds that are either too loose or too tight (Speck and Attneave, 1973).

Depersonalization and alienation are produced and supported by isolation from family and community. This notion is similar to Bowen's, though nowhere does Speck explain the process as clearly as Bowen does. Alternatively, the structure of the social network can be so rigid that symbiotic ties enfeeble and constrict individuals. Experience is constrained and latent interests wither. In rigid networks, systems change is difficult, and optimal personal growth impossible.

Speck's descriptions of disordered family relationships are not especially novel; for example, he frequently speaks of symbiotic ties between schizophrenics and their mothers. But he does have a wider frame of reference that expands his view and permits him to see potential resources beyond the confines of the family. Individual therapists attempt to resolve a symbiotic attachment by interposing distance and substituting a therapeutic attachment. Family therapists bring the symbiotic pair together to help each of them let go. Network therapists assemble members of the wider family and community to provide multiple sources of leverage, some pushing on the pair to let go, others pulling on each of them to reinvest their energy in other, more productive relationships. In the network therapy framework, pathology is neither in the schizophrenic patient nor in the relationship with the mother. Instead, the problem of concern is the network of fixed or dormant relationships which has shut out the symbiotic pair and left them fused together.

GOALS OF THERAPY

The goal of Bowen's therapy is increased differentiation of self. Nothing else lasts. Genuine change in the family system requires reopening of closed family ties and detriangulation, which creates the conditions for individual autonomy and growth. Symptoms are de-emphasized in a treatment that resembles "in vivo" psychoanalysis. Problems are presumed to inhere in the system, not the person; and change is sought at the level of the system. In order to change the system, and enable family members to achieve higher levels of differentiation, modification must take place in the most important triangle in the family—the one that involves the marital couple. To accomplish this the therapist creates a new triangle, with him or herself and the two primary members of the family. If the therapist stays in contact with the spouses, while remaining emotionally neutral, then the spouses can begin the process of detriangulation and differentiation which will profoundly and permanently change the family system.

The goal of Laqueur's multiple family therapy is to help disturbed families improve their relationship within the family and with the friends and associates outside the family. Laqueur (1972) de-emphasizes individual psychopathology and makes improved relationships and intergroup interfaces the objectives of his treatment. He sees multiple family therapy as an intermediary between poorly functioning families and the surrounding society.

Implicit in any system that emphasizes family change over individual change is that if the family improves, the symptomatic individuals will also improve. No matter how much Laqueur espouses change in the family and group, his work rests on the premise that these systems changes will profit those identified as patients. There are two consequences of de-emphasizing symptomatic improvement in favor of enhanced family functioning. The first is positive. Emphasizing systems goals helps therapists and families to focus on achieving them. This increases the leverage of family therapy. There is, however, a danger of neglecting symptomatic improvement in the presenting patient. Changing the family is a means to help the identified patient, but it is directed at the broader goal of helping everyone in the family. But the original goal of the family is to help the patient. Family therapists must not lose sight of this. While systems change is a legitimate means to that end, and an additional goal, families still have a right to expect help for the problems they come in with.

What makes this more than an abstract issue is that there is a tendency among those who de-emphasize symptomatic improvement to neglect to achieve it. Changing systems and restructuring families should help alleviate the problems the family sought help for. The fact that Laqueur does not discuss symptomatic improvement doesn't mean that he fails to achieve it. Nevertheless, students of family therapy should not let an expanded focus on systems functioning lead them to overlook the importance of alleviating symptmatic behavior in troubled patients. Whatever else they deliver, if family therapists don't deliver that, then "let the buyer beware."

The goal of network therapy is to stimulate the network of family and friends to help solve one another's problems (Speck and Attneave, 1972). In a "culture of narcissism" (Lasch, 1978), people are cut off from the life-enhancing enrichment of the social matrix. Nuclear families are cut off from extended families, friends, and neighbors. Individuals isolated in preoccupation with themselves are depleted by lack of involvement with the larger family and community networks. Network therapy aims to redress this imbalance by stimulating the dormant potential of social networks to help and enrich its component members.

Like Bowen, Speck sees a kinship group larger than the nuclear family as the significant social context. These wider circles—extended family and social network—are significant because they accurately describe what constitutes the social context, and also prescribe what is available for the support and nurturance of people with problems. The usual descriptions of the family are sociological, and stress the decline of the extended family and the ascendancy of the nuclear family as the significant social unit in modern western culture. Likewise, clinicians—if they think of the family at all —tend to think of the nuclear family as *the* family. Bowen's work broadens this base to include ties to the extended family, past and present. Speck limits his goals to the present context, but expands his emphasis to include, not only the family of relatives, but also the "family" of neighbors and friends.

Defining specific goals for therapy seems to become progressively more vague as the unit of treatment gets larger. Changes sought in individuals need to be spelled out in rather specific detail (c.f. Ford and Urban, 1963); goals for nuclear families are somewhat less specific. When Bowen describes goals for the extended family (as opposed to the individual goal of differentiation) it seems enough for him to speak of developing one-to-one relationships and avoiding triangles. The point is not that the goals of extended family work are naive or less well thought-out than those for individuals, but that they are relatively self-evident. Once the point is conceded that people are embedded in a larger social context, it seems obvious what needs to be done: open the system.

Speck says that activating the helping potential of the social network includes strengthening bonds; resolving conflict; changing perceptions; ventilating feelings; and solving problems (Speck and Attneave, 1972). These suggestions help to clarify what is meant by the general goal of stimulating the network to help its members. However, once the general goal is grasped, it seems that a clinician could rely on commonsense and general knowledge of groups as a guide for working with the network. Once the larger frame of reference is accepted, an inventive leader can work out the details.

CONDITIONS FOR BEHAVIOR CHANGE

Bowen believes that change occurs when anxiety is low, and that understanding, not behavior, is the critical vehicle for change. Most family therapists subscribe to the notion that emotional tension leads to processes that are reflected in the structure of family relationships, and that tension is maintained or resolved by the nature of those relationships. But there are clear differences between Bowen and other systems theorists as far as conceptions of what conditions are necessary for change. Strategic and structural therapists believe that behavior change, not understanding, is critical, and that such change is most likely to occur when anxiety is high and conflicts are allowed to surface. Bowen, on the other hand, believes that anxiety breeds emotional fusion, and that change requires understanding and differentiation in a calm, unheated atmosphere. Guerin suggests that if a family comes in during a crisis they should be encouraged to discuss it until their agitation is relieved. Guerin calls this "cooling down the affective overload" (Guerin and Pendagast, 1976). Beginners often make the mistake of trying too quickly to divert new families from their initial concerns to those with more theoretical interest to the therapist. If they do this with hostility or abruptly, they may cause families to drop out prematurely.

Bowen also differs from most systems therapists in believing that meaningful change does not require the presence of the entire family. Instead he believes that change is initiated by individuals or couples who are capable of affecting the rest of the family. His program of treatment can be described as proceeding from inside to out. Differentiation of self, which begins as a personal and individual process, is the vehicle for transforming relationships and the entire family system. For most family therapists treating individuals doesn't make much sense; after all, their fundamental premise is that individuals are products of their social context. Although he also believes this, Bowen's work is predicated on the idea that well-motivated individuals are more capable of change than are larger family groups. The therapeutic process is a cycle in which the individual differentiates a self, which transforms the family system, which leads to further differentiation in the individual.

Part of the process of differentiating a self is to contact as many members of the family as possible and develop a relationship with each of them. How this helps may seem mysterious at first—particularly for people who do not think of their strength or well-being as dependent on family ties. A little reflection reveals that increasing the number of important relationships will enable an individual to spread out his or her emotional energy. Instead of concentrating all emotional energy in one or two family relationships, it is defused into several. Freud had a similar notion on an intrapsychic level. In "The Project for a Scientific Psychology," Freud described his neurological model of the mind. The immature mind has few outlets ("cathexes") for channeling psychic energy, and hence little flexibility or capacity to delay responding. The mature mind, on the other hand, has many channels of response, which permits greater flexibility. Bowen's notion of increasing the emotional family network is like Freud's model, writ large.

Since we learn how to relate to the family during childhood, we learn to relate as children. Because most of us leave our families before we have established adult personalities, we continue to react childishly to our parents, brothers, and sisters. Furthermore, we react similarly in new relationships which re-stimulate the old patterns. Returning to the family—as adults—enables us to understand and modify the old habits. This in turn frees us from acting out childish reactions in future relationships.

Bowen maintains that his treatment approach follows from his theory rather than from his personal style (Anonymous, 1972). Yes and no. Undoubtedly his essentially highly rational and self-disciplined approach has its roots in the core of Bowen's personality. But be that as it may, his techniques of treatment do seem to follow from his theory more than other approaches in the field. The theory postulates fusion in grandparents transmitted to parents and projected onto children; the therapy prescribes differentiation, reversing this process in overlapping stages. Opening closed relationships and resolving triangles in the extended family results in greater differentiation, which then leads to a reduction in problems in the nuclear family. This emphasis on the extended family is one of the unique and defining features of Bowen's system.

Unresolved tensions in families are described as leading to a series of overlapping triangles (Andres, 1971). Conflict between two people is detoured to a third person who is triangled in. With additional tension, a fourth person may be brought in, leaving out the third. In a family with a great deal of tension and an equivalent tendency toward emotional cutoff, the available triangles will eventually be exhausted and the family will triangle in an outsider. The outsider may be a friend, minister, colleague, or psychotherapist. If a stranger comes into contact with two parts of the triangle (for instance, a mother and father), the stranger will either become triangulated or withdraw (Bowen, 1976). If the stranger is a family therapist, he or she can remain in contact with the twosome but avoid getting emotionally triangulated.

Therapy with couples is based on the premise that tension in the dyad will dissipate if they remain in contact with a third person (in a stable triangle)—*if* that person remains neutral and objective rather than emotionally entangled. This therapeutic triangle can reverse the insidious process of problem-maintaining triangulation. Furthermore, change in any one triangle will change the entire family system.

Family therapy with individuals is based on the premise that if one person in the family achieves a higher level of differentiation of self this will enable (or cause) other members of the family to do the same. Bowen teaches individuals about triangles, and then coaches them to return to their families of origin where they work to detriangle themselves, develop greater objectivity, and thus achieve a permanent reduction in their emotional reactiveness. This in turn has a therapeutic impact on all systems of which these individuals are a part.

Laqueur's multiple family therapy is an eclectic form of group therapy, and therefore the conditions for behavior change are similar to those described in the group therapy literature. Yalom's (1970) list of the curative factors in group therapy also applies to family therapy in groups: 1) Imparting information; 2) Instilling hope; 3) Universality; 4) Altruism; 5) Corrective recapitulation of the primary family group; 6) Developing social skills; 7) Imitation; 8) Interpersonal learning; 9) Group cohesiveness; and 10) Catharsis. In fact, Laqueur mentions many of these mechanisms in his own writing.

Among family therapists there are some who rely on insight to change behavior, and others who believe that behavior change can precede—even be independent of—insight. Bowen and Haley are representative examples of these different viewpoints. Laqueur relies both on insight and direct behavior change.

Insight into oneself and one's family is achieved in multiple family therapy primarily through improved communication. In addition, Laqueur mentions learning by analogy, modeling, indirect interpretation, and identification as mechanisms by which families improve their understanding (Laqueur, 1976). Furthermore, families learn not only from the interpretations of the co-therapists, but also from those of other families. Indeed, other families are often more confrontative than the therapists—they know the score and they aren't under any obligation to be supportive. Their messages can also be reinforced by being part of a group consensus. It's harder to deny unanimous opinions of peers than interpretations from a therapist.

Multiple family groups also provide the setting for direct behavior change. The permissive atmosphere, support of the therapists, and presence of a variety of other people all make it possible to experiment with new ways of behaving. This can occur spontaneously, by suggestion, or through roleplaying or other structured techniques. Futhermore, the group may foster a sense of competition—to do what's expected and to get better—which speeds the process of behavior change.

In network therapy, change in the social matrix is thought to be the necessary and sufficient condition for improving the lot of the index patient. Since much of mental disorder is believed to result from alienation from the resources of network relationships (Speck and Attneave, 1973), enhanced family and social ties are thought to be a powerful mechanism for producing behavior change. Here, as in multiple family therapy, the *helper therapy principle* (Caplan, 1964) applies. In network therapy, the helpers may profit just as much as those they help.

Although the basic mechanism of change is simply to open closed or dormant networks, there is a complication. Why were the networks closed in the first place? Naive therapists often think that if people will only begin to communicate, things will get better. What they overlook is the fact that people stop communicating because they had problems when they talked. Opening channels of communication is only part of the solution. People must also be helped to change the problematic aspects of their interaction once they begin to communicate in therapy.

Maybe some problems can be solved simply by getting the network involved; however, in the majority of cases it's likely that once the network is assembled latent conflicts will rise to the surface. These conflicts were responsible for originally closing the network; now they must be resolved or attenuated if the network is to remain intact long enough to be helpful. Once the network is convened, and conflicts that have surfaced are resolved, then members of the network can help in a variety of ways. They can provide the full gamut of psychological support, confrontation, and education. Less dramatically but equally important they can provide various kinds of genuine help: babysitting, social invitations, help in finding jobs, financial support, and so on.

TECHNIQUES

Bowen advocates a variety of methods all aimed at the same goals. Whether treatment involves nuclear families, couples, individuals, or multiple family groups, the effort is directed at modifying the family system. Family is the conceptual unit, though not necessarily the group to be included in treatment sessions. Guerin (Guerin and Pendagast, 1976) recommends accommodating to the family's view of deciding who to include in treatment. If they see the problem as a marital one, the husband and wife may wish to come in without the children. Where one of the children is described as the problem, parents and children should be included. A single family member can be seen individually, but the treatment will still affect the entire family.

Family Therapy with Couples. Whenever possible, Bowen prefers to work with both parents or spouses. When the therapist joins the couple, a therapeutic triangle is formed. If the therapist avoids being emotionally triangulated, the couple will be forced to deal with each other. The emotional tone of sessions should be lively enough to be meaningful, but cool enough to be objective. This is accomplished by asking more, and less, provocative questions, and by regulating the amount of interaction between the spouses. When things are calm, conflicting feelings can be dealt with more objectively, and the spouses can talk rationally with each other. But when feeling outruns thinking, it's best to ask questions which get the spouses to think more and feel less, and to talk to the therapist rather than to each other. Fogarty (1976b) stresses the need for the therapist to maintain control when there is open conflict; otherwise the couple's interaction will be destructive. If they simply fight in therapy the way they do at home—or worse—they will become convinced that change is impossible. One way to minimize conflict with a battling couple is to change the subject. If they attack each other, switch to a discussion about the kids or the extended family. If they still cannot talk calmly, control the fighting by having each talk directly to the therapist. Couples who have argued for years about the same subject are often amazed to discover that the first time they ever really hear the other's position is when they listen as the other talks to the therapist. It is so much easier to hear when you are not planning your own response. If all else fails to cool things down, Fogarty (1976b) recommends seeing the spouses in separate sessions.

Contrary to popular belief, couples do not solve problems just by talking about them. Left to their own devices they tend to argue unproductively, project all responsibility onto the other one, and attack instead of negotiate. Change requires talk *and* willingness to listen, so that each can begin to change personally rather than endlessly demand change of the other. Because of the universal tendency to see only others' contributions to problems, special techniques are required to help family members see the process, not just the content, of interactions; to see their part in the process, instead of just blaming others; and finally to change.

Guerin (1971) recommends the "displacement story" as a device for helping family members achieve sufficient distance to see their own roles in the family system. The displacement story is about other families with similar problems. For example, a couple too busy attacking to listen to each other might be told: "It must be terribly frustrating not getting through to each other. Last year I saw a couple who just couldn't seem to stop arguing long enough to listen to each other. Only after I split them up and they blew off steam for several sessions individually with me did they seem to have any capacity to listen to what the other one was saying."

Guerin also uses films as displacement materials. If the proper esthetic distance is maintained, people can become emotionally involved with a movie so that it has an impact but at the same time remain sufficiently removed to be objective. Underdistancing, in therapy sessions or in some highly provocative movies, results in an emotional experience devoid of reflection. Overdistancing, such as may occur in a lecture or uninteresting film, may lead to a lack of involvement and impact. Guerin selects films like *I Never Sang for My Father, Scenes from a Marriage,* and *Breaking Away* to use as displacement materials for teaching family dynamics to trainees and to families in therapy.

Therapists must always avoid being emotionally triangulated by couples. A major axiom of Bowen's theory is that emotional tension between two people results in their trying to trap a third person in the emotional issues between them (Bowen, 1975). Successful therapy requires that the therapist relate meaningfully to the couple without becoming entangled in the family system. Armed with a knowledge of triangles, the therapist endeavors to remain neutral and objective. This requires an optimal level of emotional distance, which Bowen says (1975) is the point where the therapist can see both the tragic and the comic aspects of the couple's interactions. Keeping detriangled requires a calm tone of voice and talking about facts more than feelings.

As the spouses talk, the therapist concentrates on the process of their interaction, not on the details under discussion. Becoming overly concerned about the content of the discussion is a sign that the therapist is emotionally entangled in the couple's problems. It may be hard to avoid being drawn in by issues as controversial as money, sex, or discipline of children, but the therapist's job is not to settle disputes, it is to help the couple do so. The aim is to get husband and wife to express ideas, thoughts, and opinions to the therapist in the presence of the other spouse. Should one break down in tears, the therapist remains calm and inquires about the thoughts that touched off the tears. If the couple begins arguing, the therapist becomes more active, calmly questioning one, then the other, and focusing the issue on their individual thoughts.

Descriptive labels are helpful devices for seeing the process underlying the content of family interactions. For example, Fogarty (1976b) has described the "distancer/pursuer" dynamic among couples. The more one pursues, and asks for more communication, time, and togetherness, the more the other distances—watches TV, works late, or goes off with the kids. Frequently, spouses alternate pursuing and distancing in different areas. Husbands commonly distance themselves emotionally, but pursue sexually. The trick, according to Fogarty, is, "Never pursue a distancer." Instead, help the pursuer explore his or her own inner emptiness. "What's in your life other than the other person?" It is also important that the therapist not pursue the distancer. When no one is chasing, the distancer will be able to move toward the family.

Bowen betrays a certain indecisiveness about the relative merits of thinking versus feeling, as well as togetherness versus individuality. Sometimes he states that thinking and feeling are equally valid (Bowen, 1976); but he also says that intellectual functioning is uniquely human and represents the apogee of human accomplishment (Bowen, 1975). A similar ambivalence is evident in his discussions of togetherness and individuality. He writes in one place (Bowen, 1975) that relationship systems maintain their equilibrium from two forces, togetherness and individuality, which implies that both are equally valid and worthwhile. On the other hand, he also extols the virtues of individuality and denigrates togetherness. Although he does overemphasize thinking and individuality, his therapy does not suffer from it. Just as emotive therapy is a useful antidote to the intellectual-ized ramblings that often characterize individual therapy (Nichols and Zax, 1977), so Bowen's rational approach offers an effective counter to the emotional haranguing so common in couples therapy. It may be that, just as emotive treatment fosters greater rationality, Bowen's emphasis on reason and separateness creates the conditions necessary for couples to become more loving and affectionate at home.

To underscore the need for objectivity and emotional neutrality, Bowen speaks of the therapist as a "coach" or "consultant." He does not mean to imply coldness or indifference on the therapist's part, but rather to empha-size the calm rationality required to avoid triangulation. In traditional terms this is known as "managing transference and countertransference reactions." And just as analysts are analyzed themselves so they can recognize their own countertransference, so Bowen considers differentiating a self in one's own family necessary to avoid being emotionally triangled by couples. Further-more, Guerin suggests that the best way to develop a genuine understanding of family concepts is to try them out in your own family (Guerin and Fogarty, 1972).

In order to help each spouse define a position as a differentiated self, it's useful for the therapist to establish an "I position" (Guerin, 1971). The more the therapist defines an autonomous position in relation to the family, the easier it is for family members to define themselves to each other. Gradually family members learn to calmly state their own beliefs and convictions, and to act on them without attacking others in the family, or becoming overly upset by their responses. When one partner begins differentiating, the other is discomfited and presses for a return to the status quo (Carter and Orfanidis, 1976). If this emotional counterreaction is weathered calmly, with neither one giving in to opposition or becoming hostile, then both partners move toward a higher level of differentiation. The process takes place in small steps, with spouses alternating between separateness and togetherness. Eventually, when each has a sufficiently well-articulated self, they can come together in mutual caring and respect, rather than in clinging dependency.

After sufficient harmony has been purchased with progress toward self-differentiation, Bowen teaches the couple how emotional systems oper-ate, and encourages them to explore their own families of origin (Bowen,

1971). He prepares them for this by first making occasional references to their families of origin. Once they begin to recognize the relevance of their prior family experience to their current problems, transition to the focus on their families of origin will be smooth. Kerr (1971) suggests that when relationship problems in the nuclear family are being discussed, therapists should occasionally ask questions about similar patterns in the family of origin. If they can see that they are repeating earlier patterns, family members are more likely to recognize their own emotional reactivity. Recently I saw a couple who were unable to decide what to do with their severely disturbed teenaged daughter. Although the daughter was virtually uncontrollable, her mother found it very difficult to consider hospitalization. I asked her what her own mother would have done, and without hesitating, she replied that her long-suffering mother would have been too guilt-ridden ever to consider placement, no matter how much she and the rest of the family might suffer. Little more needed to be said.

More didactic teaching occurs in the transition from brief to long-term therapy. Knowledge of family systems theory enables family members to analyze their own problems, and gives them a framework in which they can continue to change. Such information is useful when tensions have abated, but is risky during periods of conflict and anxiety. At such times, battling family members are liable to distort any statements about how families function as support for one or the other opposing position. So primed are warring spouses to make the other "wrong" in order for them to be "right," that they "hear" much of what the therapist says as being for them or against them. But when they are calm, they abandon the idea that if one is right the other must be wrong, and they can profit from didactic sessions. As they learn about systems theory, both spouses are sent home for visits, to continue the process of differentiation in their extended families. During this phase of treatment—coaching—Bowen believes that infrequent sessions are not only possible, but desirable (1976). Meeting with the therapist only once a month or so forces families to become more responsible and resourceful. It also dissolves a great deal of dependency on the therapist.

Family Therapy with One Person. Bowen's personal success at differentiating himself from his family convinced him that a single highly motivated person can be the fulcrum for changing an entire family system (Anonymous, 1972). Subsequently he made family therapy with one person a major part of his practice. He uses this method with one spouse when the other refuses to participate, or with single adults who live far from their parents or whose parents won't come for treatment. Aside from these cases, in which Bowen has made a virtue out of necessity, he uses this approach extensively with trainees and other mental health professionals. Extended family work with spouses is also the focus of couples treatment after the presenting anxiety and symptoms subside.

The goal of working with individuals is the same as working with larger units: differentiation. With individuals the focus is upon resolving neurotic emotional relationships in the extended family. This means developing person-to-person relationships, seeing family members as people rather than emotionally charged images, learning to observe one's self in triangles, and finally, detriangling one's self (Bowen, 1974).

The extent of unresolved emotional attachment to parents defines the level of undifferentiation. More intense levels of undifferentiation go hand in hand with more extreme efforts to achieve emotional distance, either through internal mechanisms or physical distance. A person may handle mild anxiety with parents by remaining silent or avoiding personal discussions; but when anxiety arises he or she might find it necessary to walk out of the room or even leave town. However, the person who runs away is as emotionally attached as the one who stays home and uses psychological defenses to control the attachment. The one who runs away needs closeness but can't handle it. In marriage and other intense relationships, when tension mounts the person will again withdraw.

Two sure signs of this emotional cutoff (Bowen, 1974) are denial of the importance of the family, and an exaggerated facade of independence. Cut off people boast of their emancipation and infrequent communication with their parents. The opposite of emotional cutoff is an open relationship system, in which family members have genuine, but not confining emotional contact. Bowen's therapy is designed to increase the frequency and intimacy of emotional contact with the extended family. In fact, Bowen finds the results of extended family work superior to working directly on the nuclear family (Bowen, 1974). He believes that it is easier to observe emotional forces in the context of one's parental family, where one's needs are no longer as intimately imbedded (Anonymous, 1972). Perhaps the essentially cognitive and directive nature of his procedure lends itself better to coaching individuals than to working directly with nuclear family groups. Families have a culture and life of their own and it's more effective to enter into the family and influence them from within than to remain outside and attempt to direct them. Bowen's success with individuals, and he really focuses on individuals whether he sees them alone or with their spouses, is at least in part a function of his intellectual approach.

Prerequisites to differentiating a self in the extended family are: 1) some knowledge of how family systems function; and 2) strong motivation to change. It is difficult to sustain the energy to work on the family in the absence of current distress, and many people often work only in spurts from one crisis to the next (Carter and Orfanidis, 1976). When things are calm they relax, and only when problems arise again do they continue their efforts to change.

The actual process of change is begun by learning about one's larger family—who comprises the family, where they lived, what they did, and what they were like. Most people are surprisingly ignorant of their family's history. A basic working knowledge of family, as far back as grandparents, is an adequate beginning. A useful device for organizing this material is the *genogram*.

Genograms are schematic diagrams of families, listing family members and their relationships to one another. Included are ages, dates of marriage, deaths, and geographical locations. Men are represented by squares and women by circles, with their ages inside the figures. Horizontal lines indicate marriages with dates written on the line, and vertical lines connect parents and children. Let us say, in constructing a typical genogram, that I am thirty-four, my wife is thirty-six, and we were married in 1968 (Figure 1).

Figure 8-1

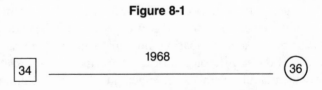

The next diagram shows that we have two children, a daughter aged four and a son aged two, and that we live in Albany, New York (Figure 2).

Figure 8-2

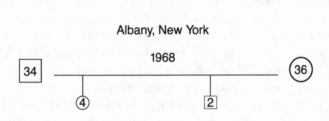

Next the genogram is expanded to include the extended family, beginning with my family of origin (see Figure 3). My father, aged 65, and my
mother, aged 62, live in Washington, D.C.; my brother and his wife live in
Albequerque, New Mexico, with their three children.

Figure 8-3

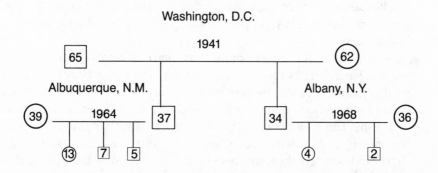

My wife's family of origin, shown by Figure 4, consists of her parents,
who live in Chicago, and her brother who lives in New Jersey. The slash in
the line joining her brother and his wife indicates that they split up in 1978.

Figure 8-4

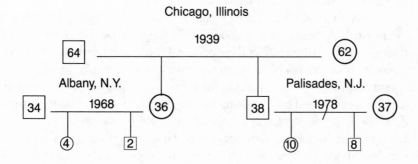

Dates of important events such as deaths, marriages, and divorces,
deserve careful study. These events send emotional shock waves throughout

the family, which may open lines of communication and foster personal contact, or may close off channels; in the latter case issues may get buried and family members progressively more cut off. A divorce may bring the family together or divide it. In some cases, news of the divorce reminds the family that the people divorcing are separate individuals with emotional needs, rather than a self-sufficient unit. Furthermore, family members may discover that it's easier to be with the divorcing spouses one at a time, when they are freed from the chronic tension of being together. In other cases, families take sides after a divorce. One side is "right," the other is "wrong"; the divorce between two people becomes a divorce between two segments of the family.

Another significant piece of information on the genogram is the geographical location of various groups in the family system. Clusters of family groups in one location suggest strong family bonds. In more explosive families, the emotional cutoff is graphically illustrated by extreme distances separating family subunits. Of course it's possible to live in the same community and be separated by emotional distance. Also, many people choose to live where there are career opportunities, a reason that has little to do with family feeling. Nevertheless, the geographical spread of the family is a good clue of underlying emotional patterns.

Filling out the genogram is not an end in itself, nor is it a simple matter. The genogram is only a skeleton which must be fleshed out with important information about the family. In order to put meat on the skeleton's bones, it is necessary to know what to look for. Dates, relationships, and localities are the framework for exploring emotional boundaries, fusion, cutoffs, critical conflicts, amount of openness, and the number of current and potential relationships in the family.

Family members may know some of these things, but not all. For, as recent work by Nisbett and Wilson (1977) suggests, people's reports about their experience often reflect their personal theories of attribution (what is *supposed* to be) rather than accurate observation (what *is*). Sometimes a "good relationship" with parents turns out to be one in which fusion and tension are managed by distancing tactics, such as infrequent contact, superficial conversation, or gossiping about other family members. Therefore it is important to ask for descriptions of family relationships, rather than conclusions about them. Not, "Do you have a good relationship with your parents?" but, "Where do your parents live? How often do you see them, write, or call? What do you and your mother talk about when you're alone together? Do you ever go out to lunch, just you and your dad?" This more detailed kind of inquiry reveals the nature of personal relationships and the existing triangles in the system.

Other kinds of information that help to explain the family include cultural, ethnic, and religious affiliations; educational and economic levels; relationships with the community and social networks; and the nature of the work that family members do. Just as an individual cut off from his extended family is liable to be fused in his nuclear family, a family cut off from social and community ties is liable to be enmeshed in its own emotions, with limited outside resources for dissipating anxiety and distress.

The person who embarks on a quest of learning more about his or her family usually knows where to look. Most families have one or two members who know a great deal about the family—perhaps a maiden aunt, a patriarch, or a cousin who is very family-centered. Phone calls, letters, or, better yet, visits to these family archivists, will yield much information, some of which will produce startling surprises.

Gathering information about the family is also an excellent vehicle for the second step in the differentiation project, which is establishing person-to-person relationships with as many family members as possible. This means getting in touch with people and speaking personally with them, not trying to talk to Mom and Dad together, and not letting Uncle George talk about other people or impersonal topics. If this sounds easy, try it. Few of us can spend more than a few minutes talking personally with family members without getting a bit anxious. When this happens, we're tempted to withdraw physically or emotionally, or triangle in another person. Gradually extending the time of real personal conversation will improve the relationship and help differentiate a self.

There are profound benefits to be derived from developing person-to-person relationships with members of the extended family, but they have to be experienced to be understood. In the process of opening and deepening personal relationships, you will learn about the emotional forces in the family. Some of the family triangles will immediately become apparent; others will emerge only after more careful examination. Usually we notice only the most obvious triangles because we are too emotionally engaged to be rational and astute observers. Few people can be objective about their parents. They are either comfortably fused or uncomfortably reactive. Making frequent short visits will help control emotional reactiveness so that you can become a better observer.

Many of our habitual emotional responses to the family impede our ability to understand and accept others; worse, they make it impossible for us to understand and control ourselves or the situation. It is prefectly natural to get angry and blame people when things go wrong. The differentiated person, however, is capable of stepping back, controlling emotional responsiveness, and reflecting on the best strategies for improving things.

Bowen (1974) calls this "getting beyond blaming and anger," and says that, once learned in the family, this ability is useful for handling emotional snarls throughout life.

Ultimately, differentiating a self requires that you identify interpersonal triangles you participate in, and detriangulate from them. The goal is to relate to the other people without gossiping or taking sides, and without counterattacking or defending yourself. Bowen suggests that the best time to do this is during a family crisis, but it can be begun at any time.

A common triangle is between one parent and a child. Suppose that every time you visit your folks, your mother takes you aside and starts complaining about your father. Maybe it feels good to be confided in; if you're a mental health professional, maybe you'll have fantasies about rescuing your parents — or at least your mother. In fact the triangling is destructive to all three relationships: you and Dad, Dad and Mom, and, yes, you and Mom. In triangles, two poles will be close and two will be distant (Figure 5). Sympathizing with Mom alienates Dad. It also makes it less likely that she will do anything about working out her complaints with him.

Finally, although this triangle may give you the illusion of being close to your mother, it is at best an ersatz intimacy. Nor is defending your father a solution. That only moves you away from Mom toward Dad, and widens the gulf between them. As long as the triangulation continues, personal and open one-to-one relationships cannot develop.

Once the triangle is recognized for what it is, you can make a plan of action so you stop participating in it. The basic idea is to do something, anything, to get the other two people to work out their own relationship. The simplest and most direct approach is to suggest that they do so. In the example just given, you can suggest that your mother discuss her concerns with your father, *and* you can refuse to listen to more of her complaints. Less direct but more powerful is to tell Dad that his wife has been complaining about him, and you don't know why she doesn't tell him about it. She'll be annoyed, but not forever. A more devious ploy is to overagree with Mom's

Figure 8-5

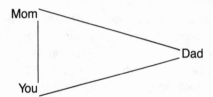

complaints. When she says he's messy, you say he's a complete slob; when she says he's not very thoughtful, you say he's a monster. Pretty soon she'll begin to defend him. Maybe she will decide to work out her complaints with him; or maybe she won't. But either way you will have removed yourself from the triangle.

Once you become aware of them, you'll find that triangles are ubiquitous. Some common examples include griping with colleagues about the boss; telling someone that your spouse doesn't understand you; undercutting your spouse with the kids; and watching television to avoid talking to your family. Breaking free of triangles may not be easy, but the rewards are great. Bowen believes that differentiating an autonomous self requires opening relationships in the extended family, and then ceasing to participate in triangles. The payoff comes not only from enriching these relationships, but also from enhancing your ability to relate to anyone—friends, fellow workers, patients, and your spouse and kids. Furthermore, if you can remain in emotional contact, but change the part you play in the family and maintain the change in spite of family pressure to change back, the family will have to change to accommodate to your change.

Some useful guidelines to resisting the family's attempts to get you to change back to unproductive, but familiar, patterns of the past have been enumerated by Carter and Orfanidis (1976), and by Guerin and Fogarty (1972). Although differentiation in the family can be accomplished on your own, it is best to work with a coach who has successfully guided others through the process. A coach, trained in Bowen's theory, recognizes that the main work of differentiation must be accomplished outside therapy sessions in relationships with the family, rather than during sessions in relationship to the therapist. Therefore, the therapist recognizes the diminished importance of his or her relationship to the client and strives to minimize and discourage transference.

If you do attempt this work, an important rule of thumb is to keep your own counsel. A professional coach can give neutral and objective advice; family members and friends cannot. Keep in mind that the changes you make are for yourself. Arm yourself with a plan to handle the family's counterreactions. As you move in and out of the family system, distinguish between planned and reactive distance. Distance is useful when you want to think, but interpersonal problems are never resolved at a distance.

When a problem arises in the family, examine your own behavior. Problem behavior is an expression of a family process, and you have responsibility for part of that process. The only change anyone can really make is change of self. If you're confused about what you're doing to maintain the status quo, try simply reversing what you were doing. Instead of nagging someone to change, tell them to keep doing what they have been. Instead of pleading with your mother to visit you, start ignoring her. Instead of yelling at the kids, back off and let your spouse do it. Such reversals often have an immediate and dramatic impact on the system.

Re-entry into your family of origin is necessary to open the closed system. Sometimes all that is required is visiting. Other times, buried issues must be raised, activating dormant triangles by stirring up emotions in the system. If you can't move directly toward your father without his withdrawing, move toward other people to whom he is close, thus activating a triangle. If your father is tense about being alone with you, spend some time alone with your mother. This is likely to make him want to have equal time.

In re-entry, it is advisable to begin by opening closed relationships before trying to change conflictual ones. Don't start by trying to resolve the warfare between yourself and your mother. Begin by looking up a sibling or cousin with whom you've long been out of touch. In all contacts deal with personal issues, but avoid stalemated conflicts. If your contacts with some sections of the family are routine and regular, make them more irregular and unpredictable.

Those who continue working on their family relationships beyond the resolution of a crisis, or beyond the first flush of enthusiasm for a new academic interest, can achieve profound changes in themselves, in their family systems, and in their own clinical work. Extended family systems therapy is never finished. Coaching sessions may be spaced at more infrequent intervals, but even when these sessions are discontinued, it is usually with the understanding that the client will continue applying the principles in family, social, and work relations. If the client feels stuck or faces a new crisis, the process can always be renewed. Clients may request refresher appointments after a couple of years, and extended family systems therapists often consult each other if they have difficulty at home or at work.

After treating 1500 families over the course of thirty years, Laqueur came to believe that multiple family therapy is rarely contraindicated. Groups are composed of four to six families, mixed with respect to socioeconomic status and background to ensure heterogeneity. If families are too similar, their conversations may be limited to superficial discussion of common interests. Sessions are held weekly and last for ninety minutes. Groups are open-ended, so that as old families drop out or graduate, new ones can join in. Treatment is generally long-term, lasting for about a year or a year-and-a-half. Recently, however, as hospital stays have become progressively shorter, Laqueur experimented with methods of lessening the duration of treatment (Laqueur, 1976).

Laqueur and his co-therapists conduct multiple family groups like traditional therapy groups with the addition of encounter group and psychodrama techniques. The therapists sit with the twenty or thirty members of the group in an ellipse, and open by explaining the ground rules of treatment. In his opening remarks, Laqueur states plainly that an individual's problems are family problems, and therefore the goal of treatment is to improve family functioning (Laqueur, 1976).

Structured exercises are used to increase the level of interaction and intensity of feeling. Laqueur begins by asking the mothers in the group to come forward and say what they think of themselves, as people and as wives and mothers. Next, the fathers are asked to do the same. Not forgotten are the children, since Laqueur includes all family members in his groups. After their parents have spoken, the kids are asked to divide themselves into two groups, "good" kids and "bad" kids, and to discuss the problems they have in the family. Another encounter exercise used is "yes-no," where two people in conflict face each other and shout "Yes!" or "No!" while pushing against each other. Family sculpting is also used, as are a number of psychodrama techniques (Laqueur, 1976). Laqueur also makes extensive use of television videotape, reviewing sessions for teaching and training, and even replaying segments for group members to illustrate particular aspects of their interactions.

Multiple family therapy goes through three stages, according to Laqueur. In the "initial interest" phase, family members experience a sense of relief at entering treatment and beginning to deal with their problems. They see improvement in other families, which raises their own hopes. These positive expectations usually result in some immediate symptomatic improvement.

Next is the "resistance" stage. No longer permitted to attribute all problems to the identified patients, family members begin to understand that each of them is part of the problem and each must change. The doubt and fear stirred up by this awareness lead to a variety of subtle and not so subtle attempts to avoid responsibility for change. Some may become quiet and angry, some may be "unable" to attend occasional sessions, and others may drop out altogether. However, if families stay for at least five sessions they tend not to drop out, even if they do become discouraged and resistant.

Once they get beyond the greatest period of resistance, families enter the "working through" phase. They become more open and willing to discuss problems. As they begin to accept their shortcomings and capitalize on their strengths, families become more flexible and better able to resolve their problems. They also begin to help other families solve problems, which according to the helper-therapy principle further enhances their competence and self-esteem.

Successful treatment, defined as enhanced family functioning (Laqueur, 1976), is evident when family members like and respect each other, enjoy daily living, understand and support one another, have better insight and improved judgment, are more open to new information, and generally experience satisfaction in relations within the family as well as with people outside the family. With good progress, after a year or so Laqueur recommends to families that they terminate. "Now you're ready to try things on your own," he says. "If things don't work out, come back" (Laqueur, 1972).

Like multiple family therapy, network therapy is conducted with a variety of group techniques. Once assembled, the network is a large collection of individuals and subgroups, without a unifying structure or culture. The first task of the network intervenors is to provide structure and direction—to make the group into a system. According to Speck and Attneave (1973) each network assembly unfolds in six distinct phases:

1) *Retribalization*, which involves reacquaintance and awareness of the presenting problems. It begins with the first telephone call the family makes inviting people to assemble, and lasts throughout the meetings.

2) *Polarization*, in which conflicting positions, primarily generational conflicts, are activated.

3) *Mobilization*, during which tasks are assigned and active efforts to help are inaugurated by concerned group members.

4) *Depression*, which regularly seems to follow initial enthusiasm.

5) *Breakthrough*, when the efforts begun during mobilization start to pay off.

6) *Exhaustion and elation*, which occurs following each meeting as members experience hope and relief. It also occurs following a successful series of network meetings.

Network therapy is usually recommended when there is a family crisis which yields neither to the family's efforts to solve it, nor to more conventional therapeutic solutions. When the network approach is proposed to a family, they are told to invite about forty family members and friends to their house. It's the family's responsibility to assemble the network, to tell them what the problem is, and to explain why they are being called upon to help (Rueveni, 1975).

Because of the large number of participants, a team of three to six therapists, or "network intervenors," is used. The team consists of people who know each other fairly well and can divide responsibility for various tasks. One acts as the speaker for the team; he or she should be skillful with large groups, have good sense of timing, and have a charismatic presence. This person functions like a discussion leader and theatrical director. The other team members try to blend in with the network rather than assume roles as professionals. Team members are more effectively able to catalyze discussions if those present assume they are members of the network.

The leader begins by introducing him or herself, outlining the problem, and explaining the network method. Participants are told that the process may be strenuous; meetings last for two to four hours, and the group may need to meet three to six times. Retribalization is furthered by the introduction of encounter group techniques to alleviate defensiveness and foster a climate of warm involvement. Team members scattered throughout the group encourage those who hang back to join in. After five or ten minutes of shaking hands, jumping up and down, shouting, huddling together, and swaying back and forth, the group experiences a release of tension and a sense of cohesiveness.

The polarization phase begins when the leader identifies and activates conflicting points of view in the network. Participants are divided into two or three subgroups which are arranged in concentric circles. The inner circle might be composed of the nuclear family, the identified patient, his or her friends, or everyone under twenty years of age. This group is then asked to discuss the patient, themselves, and what they know about the main problem. Because the network has been divided according to some important dimension, those in the outer circles are likely to have strong opinions that conflict with what's being said in the inner circle.

In a typical arrangement, the inner circle might consist of the patient and his or her peers; the outer circle might consist of their parents; and a middle circle might be made up of intermediaries (Speck and Attneave, 1973). After the kids have expressed their views, the parents are invited to comment and criticize. They usually do. Finally, the middle group is asked to respond. Their observations tend to produce compromises and a synthesis.

During the mobilization phase, tasks are presented. Subgroups of highly involved and active members of the network are identified and asked to develop plans for solving concrete problems. If the identified patient needs a job, a committee might be formed to help; or if the parents never go anywhere together, a group might be asked to get them started. Throughout this process, the stance of the team members is crucial. If they adopt an authoritarian, doctor-patient position, the network will rely upon them for direction. Network members won't mobilize their own creative resources, they'll just do what they're told until the meetings are over. However, if their faith in people is greater than their need for personal power and control, the network team will be able to delegate responsibility in such a way that the network can become a self-sustaining unit. However strong the temptation, network intervenors must resist taking over and doing "therapy" with various individuals and families.

A period of depression generally follows the mobilization stage. Confrontation and change are both threatening and exhausting; after the initial enthusiasm has worn off, the network tends to lapse into resistance and despair. The members begin to realize just how entrenched are the problems they're wrestling with, and how much effort will be required to solve them. When problems have been confronted squarely, and still there is no resolution in sight, group members may feel somewhat desperate and anxious. The degree of anxiety is a function of the salience of the problems, and the apparent limit to the alternatives for dealing with them.

Depression gives way to determined persistence if the leader is able to mobilize the group affectively and instrumentally. In a case study of network intervention, Uri Rueveni (1975) describes a period of depression in which the problem family felt acutely isolated and abandoned by the rest of the group. Rueveni broke through this impasse by prescribing a cathartic encounter group exercise, "the death ceremony." Family members were asked to close their eyes and imagine themselves dead. The rest of the network members were asked to share their own feelings about the members of the family: their strengths, their weaknesses, and what each of them meant to their family and friends. This dramatic device produced an outflow of feeling and support which carried the network out of depression.

Speck and Attneave (1973) have described breaking the network into problem-solving subgroups, using action instead of affect to get beyond the period of despair. They report assigning a group of friends to the task of getting the adolescent patient to stop abusing drugs and to move out of his parents' house.

Breakthrough is achieved when the network's energies are unleashed and members begin to accomplish the assigned tasks. This may occur after a couple of meetings, or during the latter part of the initial meeting. When it does occur the network team may go home early, leaving the rest of the network to discuss things further and perhaps work out some of the details of their plans.

Sessions generally end with feelings of exhaustion and elation, from which therapists and participants recover between meetings. In general, each phase of this cycle is repeated during every session. If the intervention is successful, members of the network will be mobilized to continue their involvement and assistance after each meeting is concluded. Network intervention may not solve all of the initial problems, but it provides the impetus for family and friends to become involved in mutually supportive ways that will enable them to function as a competent support group through future crises. Once the network has been activated, there's always someone to call when the need arises.

EVALUATING AND VERIFYING THERAPY THEORY AND RESULTS

The status of extended family systems therapy and theory rests not upon empirical research but upon the elegance of Murray Bowen's theory; clinical reports of successful treatment; and the personal profit experienced by those who have worked at differentiating a self in their families of origin.

Bowen's original research with schizophrenic families was more clinical observation than controlled experimentation. In fact, Bowen is decidedly cool to empirical research (Bowen, 1976), preferring instead to refine and integrate theory and practice. The little empirical work that has been done in the field is reported at the annual Georgetown Family Symposia. There, evaluations of various programs and occasional research reports have been presented. One of these, a study by Winer, was of sufficient interest to be published in *Family Process* (Winer, 1971). Winer reported on observations of four families in multiple family therapy, led by Murray Bowen. Over the course of treatment, the experimenter tracked the ratio of self references to other references, and the number of differentiated-self references. Statements considered as differentiated-self references included: speaking for self without blaming; dealing with change or desired change in self rather than in others; distinguishing thoughts from feelings; and showing awareness and goal-directedness. There were two significant findings, both of which supported Bowen's position. First, in early sessions there were fewer self statements; the greatest number referred to "we"and "us," indicating that the spouses did not differentiate separate positions. Second, there was an evolution toward more differentiated "I" statements over the course of treatment. Initially these occurred less than half the time, but after a few sessions differentiated statements predominated.

Although it does support the effectiveness of Bowen's therapy in increasing differentiation, the Winer study did not test the premise that differentiation of self is synonymous with positive therapeutic outcome. In fact, that is an article of faith with Bowen, and it points to a certain circularity in his theory: symptoms indicate emotional fusion, and fusion is demonstrated by the presence of symptoms (Bowen, 1966). These contentions may both be correct and useful, but they are circular.

Bowen repeatedly stresses the importance of theory in clinical practice (Bowen, 1976), and so invites judgment on the basis of his theory. Therefore, it should be noted that although his theory is thorough, consistent, and useful, it is largely a series of constructs based on clinical observation. The basic tenets are not supported by empirical research, and in fact are probably not amenable to confirmation or disconfirmation in controlled experimentation. Bowen's theory, like psychoanalysis, is probably best judged not as true or false, but as useful or not useful. On balance, it seems eminently useful.

The theory is a blueprint for therapy, and the therapy is consistent with the theory. This is not as banal as it sounds, for Bowen's theory is more complex than most and his treatment is faithful to his theory, more so than the techniques of other family therapists to their theories.

Evidence for the effectiveness of extended family systems therapy rests largely on personal experience and clinical reports. Bowen, Laqueur, Speck, and Attneave apparently do at least as well as the standard figures; these are one-third of the patients get worse or no better; one-third of the patients get somewhat better; and one-third get significantly better.

People who develop systems of therapy are influenced by their personal and emotional experiences, and Bowen is more aware and candid than most about this (Anonymous, 1972). His family was middle-class, symptom-free, and relatively enmeshed; and his techniques seem most relevant for this sort of family.

Bowen concentrates on the individuals, who are the subsystems that make up nuclear families; Laqueur, Speck, and Attneave concentrate on the social contexts, suprasystems in which nuclear families are embedded. In all three varieties of extended systems therapy, there is less emphasis on nuclear families and less emphasis on symptom resolution than in most forms of family therapy. Consequently each school tends to measure success by improvement in what they think is most important—individuals for Bowen, groups for Laqueur, and the social network for Speck and Attneave. While changes at these levels are admirable, they should be seen as mediate or additional goals, not substitutes for solving the problems that families ask for help with.

Network therapy is probably the most sensational of the methods reviewed in this chapter. It also differs enough from the mainstream of family therapy for me to point out that it is more crisis intervention than psychotherapy. Although the boundaries are not distinct, crisis intervention tends to be a brief effort to ameliorate an acute situation, with minimal impact on structure—personality structure or family structure. Psychotherapy tends to be lengthier and aims more at structural change.

Network therapy is a powerful affective experience. Members are obviously moved by their participation, and it satisfies a hunger for closeness. Participants describe feeling "high" and consider it a euphoric experience. But does this effect last?

Maybe it lasts longer than the good feelings that follow encounter groups, but it lasts less than the effects of family therapy that modifies the structure of nuclear families. Network therapy may have a profound impact on individuals and families, but the impact is limited to what can be achieved by altering external circumstances and social support systems.

All these therapists are fine clinicians; and they and their students have the advantage of working with theories that are sufficiently specific to provide clear strategies for treatment. Particularly now when family therapy is so fashionable, most people who see families use an eclectic hodgepodge of unrelated concepts and techniques; they are apt not to have a clear theory or a consistent strategy. The unhappy result is that most family therapists are drawn into the families' emotional processes and absorbed in content issues. The treatment that results tends to be haphazard and ineffectual.

Second-generation family therapists, like Guerin and Fogarty, are well-grounded enough in a theoretical system (for them, Bowen's), that they are able to diverge from it and add to it without losing focus. However, third-generation family therapists (students of students) are often left with no clear theoretical underpinning, and their work suffers for it. Interestingly, students of the pioneer family therapists have not been particularly innovative. None of them has surpassed their teachers. These observations underscore the plight of graduate students who are exposed to a variety of approaches, all of which are presented with more criticism than sympathetic understanding. Consequently they are left with no one coherent approach. Probably the best way to become an effective clinician is to begin as a disciple of one particular school. Apprentice yourself to an expert—the best you can find—and immerse yourself in one system. After you have mastered that approach and practiced it for a few years, then you can begin to modify it, without altogether losing focus and direction.

SUMMARY

The diverse methods of Bowenian therapy, multiple family groups, and network therapy were included together in one chapter because they share a common emphasis on extended social and kinship groups. All of these approaches go beyond the nuclear family to explain and alleviate human problems. When it comes to specifics, however, each of them employs unique methods of treatment.

Bowen's conceptual focus is wider than most family therapists', but his actual unit of treatment is smaller. His concern is always with the multi-generational family system, even though he usually meets with individuals or couples. Since he first introduced the "three generational hypothesis" of schizophrenia, he has been aware of how interlocking triangles connect one generation to the next—like threads interwoven in a total family fabric. Although Bowenian therapists are unique in sending patients home to repair their relationships with parents, the idea of intergenerational connections has been very influential in the field.

According to Bowen's theory-based, analytic analysis, the major problem in families is emotional fusion, the major goal is differentiation. Emotional fusion grows out of an instinctual need for others, but is an unhealthy exaggeration of this need. Some people manifest fusion directly as a need for togetherness, while others mask it with a pseudo-independent façade. The person with a differentiated self need not be isolated, but can stay in contact with others and maintain his or her own integrity. Similarly, the healthy family is one that remains in viable emotional contact from one generation to another.

In Bowenian theory the triangle is the universal unit of analysis—in principle and in practice. Like Freud, Bowen stresses the pivotal importance of early family relations. The relationship between the self and parents is described as a triangle and considered the most important in life. Bowen's understanding of triangles is one of his most important contributions and one of the central ideas in family therapy.

For Bowen, therapy is a logical extension of theory. Before you can make any significant inroads into family problems, you must have a thorough understanding of how family systems operate. The cure is to go backwards, to visit your parents, grandparents, aunts, and uncles, and learn to get along with them.

Bowen's theory espouses a balance between togetherness and independence, but the practice has a distinctly intellectual and emotionally distanced character. As a family therapist, Bowen seems more scientific than humanistic, more theoretical than practical. He sees anxiety as a threat to psychic equilibrium, consequently his approach to treatment often seems dispassionate. Bowen moves away from the heat of family confrontations in order to contemplate the history of family relationships. Like moving from the playing field into the stands, patterns become more visible, but it may be more difficult to have an immediate impact.

Bowen's model defocuses on symptoms in favor of systems dynamics. The treatment discourages therapists from trying to "fix" relationships, and instead encourages clients to begin a lifelong effort at self-discovery. This is not, however, merely a matter of introspection, but of actually making contact with the family. Clients are equipped for these journeys of self-discovery with cognitive tools for understanding their own patterns of emotional attachment and disengagement.

Multiple family therapy and network therapy both utilize the resources of people outside the family to broaden the base of emotional support. Neither adds much to existing theories, but both are useful antidotes to the isolation of many families today. Of the two approaches, network therapy seems more useful because it works with the patient's real environment. The whole network may actually be convened only a few times, but its resources continue to be available. Multiple family therapy, on the other hand, uses an artificial group which is unlikely to continue beyond treatment.

The idea of treating a number of families or couples simultaneously does not appear to be well founded. Family therapy is therapy in context, but multiple family therapy is based on an artificial context. Putting an individual patient into a therapy group is an expedient way to mimic real social relations in the treatment setting. Moreover, other group members lend additional validity to therapists' observations about patients' behavior. What works in group therapy may not work for families. Families have within them the real relationships that groups imitate, and families have plenty of leverage for changing their members. Moreover, by adding more than one family or couple to the treatment setting the potential gain of additional perspectives is more than offset by the distraction of skipping from one set of problems to another.

REFERENCES

Andres, F. D. An introduction to family systems theory. Georgetown Family Symposium, Washington, D.C., 1971.

Anonymous. Differentiation of self in one's family. In J. Framo (Ed.), *Family interaction*. New York: Springer, 1972.

Attneave, C. We became family therapists. In A. Ferber, M. Mendelsohn & A. Napier (Eds.), *The book of family therapy*. New York: Science House, 1972.

Bowen, M. The use of family theory in clinical practice. *Comprehensive Psychiatry*, 1966, *7*, 345–374.

Bowen, M. Family therapy and family group therapy. In H. Kaplan & B. Sadock (Eds.), *Comprehensive group psychotherapy.* Baltimore: Williams and Wilkins, 1971.

Bowen, M. Being and becoming a family therapist. In A. Ferber, M. Mendelsohn & A. Napier (Eds.), *The book of family therapy.* New York: Science House, 1972.

Bowen, M. Toward the differentiation of self in one's family of origin. In F. Andres & J. Lorio (Eds.), *Georgetown family symposia, Vol. 1.* Washington, D.C.: Department of Psychiatry, Georgetown University Medical Center, 1974.

Bowen, M. Family therapy after twenty years. In S. Arieti (Ed.), *American handbook of psychiatry, Vol. 5.* New York: Basic Books, 1975.

Bowen, M. Theory in the practice of psychotherapy. In P. J. Guerin (Ed.), *Family therapy: Theory and practice.* New York: Gardner Press, 1976.

Caplan, G. *Principles of preventive psychiatry.* New York: Basic Books, 1964.

Carter, E. & Orfanidis, M.M. Family therapy with one person and the family therapist's own family. In P. J. Guerin (Ed.), *Family therapy: Theory and practice.* New York: Gardner Press, 1976.

Fogarty, T. F. Systems concepts and the dimensions of self. In P. J. Guerin (Ed.), *Family therapy: Theory and practice.* New York: Gardner Press, 1976a.

Fogarty, T. F. Marital crisis. In P.J. Guerin (Ed.), *Family therapy: Theory and practice.* New York: Gardner Press, 1976b.

Ford, D.H. & Urban, H.B. *Systems of psychotherapy.* New York: Wiley, 1963.

Guerin, P. J. A family affair. Georgetown Family Symposium, Washington, D.C., 1971.

Guerin, P. J. We became family therapists. In A. Ferber, M. Mendelsohn & A. Napier (Eds.), *The book of family therapy.* New York: Science House, 1972.

Guerin, P. J. (Ed.), *Family therapy: Theory and practice.* New York: Gardner Press, 1976.

Guerin, P. J. & Fogarty, T. F. Study your own family. In A. Ferber, M. Mendelsohn & A. Napier (Eds.), *The book of family therapy.* New York: Science House, 1972.

Guerin, P. J. & Pendagast, E.G. Evaluation of family system and genogram. In P.J. Guerin (Ed.), *Family therapy: Theory and practice.* New York: Gardner Press, 1976.

Kerr, M. The importance of the extended family. Georgetown Family Symposium, Washington, D.C., 1971.

Laqueur, H.P. Mechanisms of change in multiple family therapy. In C.J. Sager & H.S. Kaplan (Eds.), *Progress in group and family therapy.* New York: Brunner/Mazel, 1972.

Laqueur, H.P. Mulitple family therapy. In P. J. Guerin (Ed.), *Family therapy: Theory and practice.* New York: Gardner Press, 1976.

Lasch, C. *The culture of narcissism.* New York: Norton, 1978.

Nichols, M.P. & Zax, M. *Catharsis in psychotherapy.* New York: Gardner Press, 1977.

Nisbett, R.E. & Wilson, T.D. The halo effect: Evidence for unconscious alteration of judgments. *Journal of Personality and Social Psychology,* 1977, *35,* 250–256.

Ruevini, U. Network intervention with a family in crisis. *Family Process,* 1975, *14,* 193–203.

Speck, R. & Attneave, C. Social network intervention. In C.J. Sager & H.S. Kaplan (Eds.), *Progress in group and family therapy.* New York: Brunner/Mazel, 1972.

Speck, R. & Attneave, C. *Family networks: Rehabilitation and healing.* New York: Pantheon, 1973.

Toman, W. *Family constellation.* New York: Springer Publishing Company, 1969.

Winer, L.R. The qualified pronoun count as a measure of change in family psychotherapy. *Family Process,* 1971, *10,* 243–247.

Yalom, I.D. *The theory and practice of group psychotherapy.* New York: Basic Books, 1970.

9

Communications Family Therapy

The communications model that emerged from Palo Alto has had an enormous impact on the entire field of family therapy. Communications family therapy was no mere application of individual psychotherapy to families; it was a radically new conceptualization that altered the very nature of imagination. The focus on communication was not new. Kraepelin and Bleuler described thought and communications deficits in schizophrenia, and Freud discovered hidden meaning in neurotic communication. What was new was the focus on the process, the form of communication, rather than its content. The communicationists developed techniques of treatment, but their lasting contribution was a whole new way of thinking about families.

Communications theory is an intellectual tradition with roots outside psychiatry. It is closely tied to and derived from general systems theory, cybernetics, and information theory. Many of the originators of communications family therapy were not mental health professionals, and their work reflects their training in anthropology, communications, ethology, ethnology, information theory, cybernetics, social psychology, and hypnosis.

Gregory Bateson, who was the leading figure in communications theory, was an anthropologist; the fact that his work led to family therapy was largely an artifact of the context in which he worked. His research was funded by psychiatry, and he chose schizophrenia as his field of study at a time when schizophrenic symptoms were thought to be crazy and senseless, just as neurotic symptoms had been before Freud. Freud used psychoanalysis to unravel the meaning of neurotic symptoms; the Bateson group used communications analysis to interpret schizophrenic behavior. Moreover, the fact that schizophrenia was generally neglected by the mainstream of psychiatry as a hopeless condition meant that there were fewer vested interests to oppose innovations, such as seeing whole families together.

Bateson's observations led him to conclude that the interchange of messages between people defined their relationships, and that these relationships were stabilized by homeostatic processes in families. His interest was scientific, not therapeutic, and his goal was to develop a general model of human behavior. When Jay Haley and Don Jackson began interviewing families, they were more interested in studying them than in treating them; only gradually did they begin to intervene to help. At first they used interpretations, because they still believed that awareness would bring about change. But, finding that this did not work, they developed new techniques to fit their new ways of thinking. Directives replaced interpretations as the major technique to modify family systems by changing the way that family members communicate with one another.

The paradigms of communications theory were so well received that they were adopted by other schools of family therapy. Virtually every approach now treats communication as synonymous with behavior, and concepts like the *double-bind* and *family homeostasis* have been absorbed in the literature. In fact, it might be said that communications family therapy died of success. Not only have many of its precepts been universally adopted, but in addition, its proponents have branched off to form new schools, especially the strategic, structural, and experiential approaches to family therapy.

SKETCHES OF LEADING FIGURES

Communications therapy was one of the earliest approaches to family therapy, and the history of this orientation is inextricably intertwined with the history of the first decade of the family therapy movement (see Chapter 1). The leading characters in this history were the members of Bateson's schizophrenia project and the Mental Research Institute (MRI) in Palo Alto. Although many of the same individuals were in both groups, Bateson's group was devoted primarily to research, while Jackson's group at MRI concentrated on treatment.

For over twenty years a multidisciplinary group at MRI has been developing and refining theoretical concepts about family functioning based on communications theory. Don Jackson and Jay Haley were the leaders who created and popularized the communications approach to treating families. Nothing in Jackson's traditional psychiatric background portends his radical departure from conventional psychotherapy; he was trained at Stanford where the major influences were Freudian and Sullivanian, Chestnut Lodge, the Washington-Baltimore Psychoanalytic Institute, and the San Francisco Psychoanalytic Institute. In 1951, he became a consultant to the Palo Alto Veterans Administration Hospital, which led to his association with the Bateson project.

Jackson established the Mental Research Institute in November, 1958, and received his first grant in March, 1959. The original staff consisted of Jackson, Jules Riskin, and Virginia Satir. They were joined later by Jay Haley, John Weakland, and Paul Watzlawick. Gregory Bateson served as a research associate and teacher.

Jay Haley has always been somewhat of an outsider. He entered the field without clinical credentials, and first established his reputation as a commentator and critic. His initial impact came from his writing, in which he infused irony and sarcasm with incisive analysis of psychotherapy. In "The Art of Psychoanalysis" (reproduced in Haley, 1963), Haley redefined psychoanalysis, not as a search for insight, but as a game of "oneupsmanship," in which patient and analyst struggle to force the other one into a one-down position (Haley, 1963, p. 193).

> By placing the patient on a couch, the analyst gives the patient the feeling of having his feet up in the air and the knowledge that the analyst has both feet on the ground. Not only is the patient disconcerted by having to lie down while talking, but he finds himself literally below the analyst and so his one-down position is geographically emphasized. In addition, the analyst seats himself behind the couch where he can watch the patient but the patient cannot watch him. This gives the patient the kind of disconcerted feeling a person has when sparring with an opponent while blindfolded. Unable to see what response his ploys provoke, he is unsure when he is one-up and when one-down. Some patients try to solve this problem by saying something like,

"I slept with my sister last night," and then whirling around to see how the analyst is responding. These "shocker" ploys usually fail in their effect. The analyst may twitch, but he has time to recover before the patient can whirl fully around and see him. Most analysts have developed ways of handling the whirling patient. As the patient turns, they are gazing off into space, or doodling with a pencil, or braiding belts, or staring at tropical fish. It is essential that the rare patient who gets an opportunity to observe the analyst see only an impassive demeanor.

In this same paper (1963, p. 198), Haley also tossed a few barbs at other popular forms of psychotherapy.

There is, for example, the Rogerian system of ploys where the therapist merely repeats back what the patient says. This is an inevitably winning system. When the patient accuses the therapist of being no use to him, the therapist replies, "You feel I'm no use to you." The patient says, "That's right, you're not worth a damn." The therapist says, "You feel I'm not worth a damn." This ploy, even more than the orthodox silence ploy, eliminates any triumphant feeling in the patient and makes him feel a little silly after awhile (a one-down feeling). Most orthodox analysts look upon the Rogerian ploys as not only weak but not quite respectable. They do not give the patient a fair chance.

Haley saw patients and families during the years he worked on the Bateson project, but retired from clinical practice in 1962. Since then he has concentrated on studying families, and teaching and supervising family therapy. His writing continues to be witty and critical, and his relationship to the rest of the field continues to be adversarial and iconoclastic.

Haley was studying at Stanford University when he met Gregory Bateson, who hired him to work on the communications project. Haley began to interview schizophrenic patients in order to analyze the strange style of their communication. From these analyses, Haley along with Bateson, Jackson, and Weakland, came up with the famous idea of the double-bind, and only then began to see families in order to confirm their speculations.

As a therapist, Haley was greatly influenced by Milton Erickson, with whom he began studying hypnosis in 1953. Then, after the Bateson project broke up in 1962, Haley worked in research at MRI, until 1967 when he joined Minuchin at the Philadelphia Child Guidance Clinic. It was here that Haley became especially interested in training and supervision, areas in which he may have made his greatest contributions to the field of family therapy.

Bateson himself had a superbly analytic mind, nurtured from an early age in a variety of scientific disciplines, and his scientific background shaped the character of the group's approach to families. Under Bateson's influence, the orientation of the project was anthropological. Members of the group relied on naturalistic observation, rather than experimentation, to form their ideas. Their forte was generating hypotheses, not testing them. Even the double-bind concept was arrived at by deductive conjecture. Given the incongruous nature of schizophrenic communication, Bateson reasoned (Bateson, Jackson, Haley, and Weakland, 1963), it *must* have been learned in the family. Only later was this conclusion supported by observation.

They did not set out to develop a clinical approach; their goal was to observe, not to change families. In fact, they stumbled onto family therapy more or less by accident. When Bateson developed the double-bind hypothesis in 1954 he had never seen a family. He published the idea in 1956, and started seeing families in 1956 or 1957. At first, the group merely wanted to observe patterns of communication, only later were they moved to try to help the unhappy people they had been studying.

THEORETICAL FORMULATIONS

Communications therapists adopted the *black box* concept from telecommunications and applied it to individuals within the family. This model disregards the internal structure of individuals in order to concentrate on their input and output—that is, communication. It isn't that these clinicians deny the phenomena of mind—thinking and feeling—they just find it useful to ignore them. By limiting their focus to what goes on between, rather than within, family members, communications theorists qualify as "systems purists" (Beels and Ferber, 1969).

Communications theorists also disregard the past, leaving speculation about the genesis of behavior to the psychoanalysts, while they search for patterns with which to understand behavior in the present. They consider it unimportant to figure out what is cause and what is effect, preferring to use a model of circular causality in which chains of behavior are seen as effect-effect-effect.

Families are treated as error-controlled, goal-directed systems, and their interactions are analyzed using cybernetic theory, epistemology, general systems theory, and games theory. For example, interactions can be described using a games analogy. Someone who doesn't know how to play chess could discover the rules by watching the game being played and noting the pattern of moves, and this is precisely the strategy used by communications theorists in their analyses of family communications. Beginning with schizophrenic families and branching out to a wide variety of families, these workers observed the patterns of communication to discover regularities, which acted as "rules" of family interactions.

Human communication can be analyzed according to *syntax, semantics,* and *pragmatics* (Carnap, 1942; Morris, 1938). *Syntax* refers to the way words are put together to form phrases and sentences; it is the style in which information is transmitted. Errors of *syntax* are particularly likely in the speech of persons who are learning a new language. This is the domain of the information theorist, who is concerned with encoding information; channels of communication; the capacity, variability, redundancy, and noise inherent in the communication; and the patterning of speech over time. In families this would relate to who speaks to whom, the percentage of speaking time for each member, the parsimony of speech, and the ratio of information to noise. Scheflen (1966) elaborated on channels of communication by including nonlanguage modalities: kinesic and postural, tactile, olfactory, territorial, and artifactual (dress, make-up, props). Thus, *syntax* is concerned with the statistical properties of language, not with its meaning. Meaning is the realm of *semantics*. In families, *semantics* refers to the clarity of language, the existence of private or shared communicational systems, and concordance versus confusion of communication. Finally, there is the *pragmatics*, or behavioral effect, of communication. In order to evaluate the effects of communication, it is necessary to take into account nonverbal behavior and the context of communication, as well as the words used. The pragmatics of communication (Watzlawick, Beavin, and Jackson, 1967) is the primary concern of communications therapists, and is their basis for understanding behavior in any family system.

In *The Pragmatics of Human Communication,* Watzlawick, Beavin, and Jackson (1967) sought to develop a "calculus" of human communication, which they stated in a series of axioms about the interpersonal implications of communication. These axioms are an aspect of *metacommunication,* which means communicating about communication. The first of these axioms is that people are always communicating. Since all behavior is communicative, and one cannot *not* behave, then it follows that one cannot *not* communicate. Consider the following example.

> Mrs. Snead began the first family therapy session by saying, "I just don't know what to do with Roger anymore. He's not doing well in school, he doesn't help out around the house; all he wants to do is hang around with those awful friends of his. But the worst thing is that he refuses to communicate with us."

At this point, the therapist turned to Roger and said, "Well, what do you have to say about all this?" But Roger said nothing. Instead he continued to sit slouched in a chair at the far corner of the room, with an angry sullen look on his face.

The problem is not that Roger is not communicating. In fact, he is communicating that he is angry, mistrustful, and that he refuses to negotiate. Communication may also take place when it is not intentional, conscious, or successful, that is, in the absence of mutual understanding.

A second major proposition is that all messages have a "report" and a "command" function (Ruesch and Bateson, 1951). The report or content of a message conveys information; the command is a statement about the definition of the relationship. Every time people speak, they are not only sending messages, but also defining their relationships. The speaker's message conveys some content and also how the speaker views him or herself and how he or she views the hearer. For example, the message, "Mommy, Sandy hit me," conveys information but also suggests a command, "Do something about it." Notice, however, that the implicit command is slightly ambiguous. The reason for this is that the printed word omits nonverbal and contextual clues. The statement shrieked by a child in tears, has a different command value than if it were spoken by a giggling child. The command aspect of the communication would also be quite different if it were spoken by a small child about a babysitter, or if it were said by an older sibling playing in the backyard.

Not only is language structured in a hierarchy of levels, but Birdwhistell (1952) and Scheflen (1966) have shown that bodily movements are also so organized. Wynne (1970) believes that there are three levels to every communication. In addition to the content and relationship levels, he believes there is also the level of the *task* in which the communicating persons are engaged. Moreover, to be comprehensive, a communications analysis should include not only the communications, but also social relations and cultural regulations. The Palo Alto group focused on the family and their communications; in Philadelphia, Scheflen and Birdwhistell, who had a cultural viewpoint, emphasized the program and the behavioral pattern. The Palo Alto group elaborated on types of interaction in normal and pathological communication; the Philadelphia group pointed out that these patterns of interaction have to be integrated in social patterns in ways that conform to the conventions and values of the culture.

The relationship between speakers is another factor which significantly affects how the command aspects of communication are responded to. For example, a therapist whose aim is to help patients express their feelings would be likely to respond to a husband who is crying by listening sympathetically and encouraging him to continue to express his thoughts and feelings. The man's wife, on the other hand, might well be threatened and upset by his display of "weakness," and try to "cheer him up" by telling him that the problem doesn't really exist or by suggesting ways for him to solve it. In this instance, the therapist can listen to the man's feelings without hearing (or responding to) a command to "do something about them." The wife feels threatened and obligated by the inferred command, and so cannot simply listen.

The command aspect of communications functions to define relationships. "Mommy, Sandy hit me" suggests that the speaker accepts a one-down relationship with Sandy, but insists that mother will intercede to settle any problems. This defining is often obscured because it is usually not deliberate or done with full awareness, and, as we have seen, it depends upon how it is received. In healthy relationships this last aspect recedes into the background. Conversely, problematic relationships are characterized by frequent struggles about the nature of the relationship.

In families, command messages are patterned as *rules* (Jackson, 1965). The regular patterning of interactions stabilizes relationships. These patterns, or rules, can be deduced from observed redundancies in interaction. Jackson used the term *family rules* as a description of regularity, not as a causal or determining concept. Nobody "lays down the rules." In fact, families are generally unaware of them.

The rules, or regularities, of family interaction operate to preserve *family homeostasis* (Jackson, 1967, 1965), an acceptable behavioral balance within the family. Homeostatic mechanisms bring families back to a previous balance in the face of any disruption, and thus serve to resist change. Jackson's notion of family homeostasis describes the conservative aspect of family systems, and is similar to the general systems theory concept of *negative feedback*. Thus, according to a communications analysis, families operate as goal-directed, rule-governed systems.

Communications theorists found in *general systems theory* (von Bertalanffy, 1950) a number of ideas useful to explain how families work. Some of these ideas have been described in Chapters 1 and 3; their application will be further considered in following sections of this chapter. At this point, I would only like to point out that while the communications theorists (Watzlawick, *et al.*, 1967) described families as *open systems* in their theoretical statements, they tended to treat them as *closed systems* in their clinical work. Thus, they concentrated their therapeutic efforts on the nuclear family, with little or no consideration of inputs from the community or extended family.

Relationships between communicants are also described as being either *complementary* or *symmetrical*. Complementary relationships are ones in which one person is one-up, superior, or primary, while the other is one-down, inferior, or secondary. A common complementary pattern is where one person is assertive and the other submissive, with each mutually reinforcing and sustaining the other's position. It is important to understand that one-up and one-down are descriptive terms, not evaluative. Moreover, it is a mistake to assume that one person's position *causes* the other's, or that the one-down position is any weaker than the one-up. As Sartre (1964) pointed out, it is the masochist as well as the sadist who creates the possibility of a sado-masochistic relationship.

Symmetrical relationships are based on equality; the behavior of one person mirrors that of the other. Symmetrical relationships between husbands and wives, where both are free to pursue careers and both share housekeeping and childrearing responsibilities, are often thought of as ideal by today's standards. However, from a communications viewpoint, there is no reason to assume that such a relationship would be any more stable or functional—for the system—than a traditional, complementary one.

Another aspect of communication is that it can be *punctuated* in various ways (Bateson and Jackson, 1964). An outside observer may hear a dialogue as an uninterrupted flow of communication, but each of the participants may believe that what he or she says is caused by what the other says. Thus, punctuation organizes behavioral events and reflects the bias of the observer. Couples therapists are familiar with the impasse created by each spouse saying, "I only do X, because he (or she) does Y." A common example is the wife who says she only nags because her husband withdraws, while he says he only withdraws because she nags. Another example is the wife who says that she would be more in the mood for sex if her husband was more affectionate, to which he counters that he would be in the mood to be more affectionate if she would have sex more often.

As long as couples punctuate their interactions in this fashion, there is little likelihood of change. Each insists that the other causes the impasse and each waits for the other to change first. The impasse is created by the universal tendency for people to punctuate a sequence of interactions so that it appears that the other one has initiative, dominance, or dependency—in other words, power. Children illustrate this when they have a fight and run to a parent, both crying, "He started it!" Their mutual illusion is based on the mistaken notion that such sequences have a discrete beginning, and that one person's behavior is caused by another's in linear fashion.

Communications theory does not posit linear causality or look for an underlying cause of behavior; instead this model assumes circular causality and analyzes specific behaviors occurring at the present time. Considerations of underlying causality are treated as conceptual noise, with no practical therapeutic value. The behaviors that the communications theorist observes are patterns of communications linked together in additive chains of stimulus *and* response. This model of sequential causality enables therapists to treat behavioral chains as *feedback loops*. When the response to one family member's problematic behavior exacerbates the problem, that chain is seen to be a positive feedback loop. The advantage of this formulation is that it focuses on interactions that perpetuate problems, which can be changed, instead of inferring underlying causes, which are not observable and often not subject to change.

NORMAL FAMILY DEVELOPMENT

As "systems purists," the communications family therapists treat behavior as ahistorical. Whether they are describing or treating family interactions, their attention is on the here-and-now, with very little interest paid to development. Normal families are described as functional systems, which like all living systems depend upon two important processes (Maruyama, 1968). First, they must maintain constant integrity in the face of environmental vagaries. This is accomplished through *negative feedback*, which is often illustrated by the example of the thermostat on a home heating unit. When the heat drops below a set point, the thermostat activates the furnace, until the heat returns to the desired temperature.

No living system can survive without a regular pattern or structure. On the other hand, too rigid a structure leaves the system ill-equipped to adapt to changing circumstances. This is why normal families must also have mechanisms for *positive feedback*. Negative feedback minimizes change to maintain a steady state; positive feedback alters the system to accommodate to novel inputs. As children grow older, they change the nature of their input to the family system. The most obvious instance is at adolescence when they seek more involvement with peers and demand more freedom and independence. A family system limited to negative feedback can only resist such changes in order to maintain its inflexible structure. Normal families, on the other hand, also have positive feedback mechanisms and can respond to new information by modifying the structure of the system.

Normal families become periodically unbalanced (Hoffman, 1971); they do so to permit relationships to shift during transition points in the family life cycle. No family passes through these changes in a totally harmonious fashion; all experience stress, resist change, and develop vicious cycles. But normal families are not trapped into perpetuating any destructive patterns that develop; they are able to engage positive feedback mechanisms to modify themselves. Symptomatic families remain stuck, using a symptomatic member to avoid change; normal families are able to change and so do not require any such sacrifice.

Concepts from general systems theory, such as positive feedback, have the virtues of wide applicability and theoretical elegance, but they often seem esoteric and abstract. When we recognize that the channel for positive feedback is communication, it is possible to describe what happens more plainly. Normal families are able to change because they communicate clearly. When their children say that they want to grow up, parents listen.

Most of the research on family communication has been done with disturbed families, and only recently have researchers begun to pay attention to healthy family communication and interaction. One attempt to correct this comes from an unlikely source. Researchers studying children at "high risk" for psychiatric disorders have begun to examine elements of family interaction and communication that provide high risk children with resources that promote healthy functioning.

These researchers have concluded that clear and logical communication on the part of the parents is most important in promoting healthy adjustment in children by providing them with a model for developing cognitive capacities of attending, focusing, remaining task-oriented, and communicating ideas and feelings clearly and directly (Wynne, Jones, and Al-Khayyal, 1982). Wynne and his colleagues have found that mothers' healthy communication predicted successful school adjustment. The same was true for fathers' communication, but the effect was less powerful. When parents communicate clearly in a focused, well-structured, flexible manner, their children are regarded as competent academically and socially by their teachers and peers.

DEVELOPMENT OF BEHAVIOR DISORDERS

Communications theorists developed their conception of behavior disorder by observing patterns of communication in schizophrenic families. In earlier monadic views the peculiarities of schizophrenic speech were believed to be the result of the patient's thought disorder, not the family's pathological communication (Bleuler, 1950). Later, this viewpoint was modified by interpersonal theories of psychopathology, which emphasized the effect of disordered relationships on disordered speech. Sullivan (1944), for example, wrote, "The schizophrenic's speech shows characteristic peculiarities because of recurrent severe disturbances in his relationships with other people and the result is a confusion of the critical faculties concerning the structure of spoken and written language." In Sullivan's *interpersonal theory* of psychiatry, schizophrenic disturbance was no longer considered to be the product of one person's pathology, but was viewed as the result of pathological relationships. Nevertheless, the disturbance was still located in the individual. The relationships may be disturbing, but it is the patient who is disturbed.

The Bateson group carried this line of reasoning a step further. According to them, schizophrenic disturbance is a disturbance of the entire family. The symptoms may be observable in only one member, but they are a function of the whole family system. Moreover, symptoms are seen as communicated messages. At one level, they are statements made by the person with the symptoms; at another level, they are statements made by the system.

According to family communications theorists, the essential function of symptoms is to maintain the homeostatic equilibrium of family systems. Pathological families are considered to be enmeshed in dysfunctional, but very strong, homeostatic patterns of communication (Jackson and Weakland, 1961). Their interactions may seem odd, and they may be unsatisfying, yet they are powerfully self-reinforcing. These families cling to their rigid and inflexible structures, and respond to signs of change as negative feedback. That is, change is treated, not as an opportunity for growth, but as a threat and a signal to change back. Changes that threaten their stability are labeled as "sick," as the following example illustrates.

> Tommy was a quiet, solitary boy, the only child of eastern European immigrant parents. The parents left their small farming community and came to the United States, where they both found factory work in a large city in the northeast. Although they were now safe from religious persecution and their standard of living improved, the couple felt alien and out of sympathy with their new neighbors. They kept to themselves and took pleasure in raising Tommy.
>
> Tommy was a frail child with a number of peculiar mannerisms, but to his parents he was perfect. Then he started school. He began to make friends with other children, and, eager to be accepted, he picked up a number of American

habits. He chewed bubble gum, watched television cartoons, and rode his bicycle whenever he had the chance. His parents were annoyed by the gum chewing and by Tommy's fondness for television, but they were genuinely distressed by his eagerness to play with his friends. They began to feel that he was rejecting their values, and that "something must be wrong with him." By the time they called the child guidance clinic, they were convinced that Tommy was disturbed, and they asked for help to "make Tommy normal again."

In their theoretical papers, communications theorists maintained the position that pathology inheres in the system as a whole (Hoffman, 1971; Jackson, 1967; Watzlawick, Beavin, and Jackson, 1967). The *identified patient* is considered a role with complementary counterroles, all of which contribute to the maintenance of the system. The identified patient may be the victim, but in this framework "victim" and "victimizer" are seen as mutually determined roles—neither is good or bad, and neither causes the other. However, although this circular causality is a consistent feature of their theorizing, communications therapists often lapse into linear causality in their research on psychopathology.

The foundations for a family theory of the etiology of schizophrenia focusing on disturbed patterns of communication were laid down by Gregory Bateson (Bateson, Jackson, Haley, and Weakland, 1956), Theodore Lidz (Lidz, Cornelison, Terry, and Fleck, 1958), and Lyman Wynne (Wynne, Ryckoff, Day, and Hirsch, 1958). All of these researchers believe in circular causality, but their observations emphasized the pathological effect of parental irrationality on the offspring, and they suggest that the disordered thinking observed in the schizophrenic offspring is a result of the parents' thought and communications disorder.

Lyman Wynne's concept of *communication deviance* reflects cognitive and attentional deficits as well as affective and relational deficits. He found that the severity of parental psychopathology was correlated with communication deviance and with the severity of psychiatric disorder in their late adolescent and young adult offspring (Wynne, Singer, Bartko, and Toohey, 1977). Communication in such families isn't focused, and also includes frequent nihilistic, derogatory, disparaging, and critical remarks.

Despite the enthusiasm for the idea that schizophrenia may be caused by disordered communication in the family, the fact is, it is not. Communication deviance is not found in all schizophrenic families, nor is it limited to families so diagnosed. Wynne's view (1968, 1970) is that communications patterns can be regarded as building upon attention-response dispositions which probably have an innate, genetically-determined component.

It is difficult to judge a single communication as normal or pathological. Instead the judgment must be made on a series or sequence of communications. It is possible to study the syntax and semantics, that is the content of speech, for signs of clarity or confusion. For instance, Lyman Wynne found that schizophrenics' speech could be differentiated from that of normals or delinquents (Wynne and Singer, 1963). But when the members of the Palo Alto groups studied the pragmatics of communication, they reported on the metacommunication or command aspects of language.

Symptoms are seen as messages which are responses to persistent communicational quandries. The nonverbal message of a symptomatic family member is: "It is not I who does not (or does) want to do this, it is something outside my control—my nerves, my illness, my anxiety, my bad eyes, alcohol, my upbringing, the Communists, or my wife" (Watzlawick, *et al.*, 1967, p. 80). The symptoms are not considered to be pathological effects *caused by* communication problems in the family; they are seen as embedded in a pathological context, within which they may be the only possible reaction. Among the forms of pathological communication identified by the Palo Alto group are: denying that one is communicating; disqualifying the other person's message; confusing levels of communication; discrepant punctuation of communication sequences; symmetrical escalation to competitiveness; rigid complementarity; and paradoxical communication.

The most pervasive feature of pathological family communications is the use of *paradox*. A paradox is a contradiction that follows correct deduction from logical premises. In family communications, paradoxes usually take the form of *paradoxical injunctions*. A paradoxical injunction, for example, is to demand some behavior which by its very nature can only be spontaneous —"Be spontaneous!" "Be more dominant." "You should have more self-confidence." "Tell me you love me." A person who is exposed to such paradoxical injunctions is caught in an untenable position, to comply—to be dominant or spontaneous—means to be submissive or premeditated. The only way to escape the dilemma is to step outside the context and comment on it, but such metacommunication rarely occurs within families. For one thing, it is difficult to communicate about communication; for another, the first speaker may assert his or her authority and refuse to accept the metacommunication.

Paradoxical communications are a frequent feature of every day life. They are relatively harmless in small doses, but when they take the form of double-binds the consequences are malignant. In the double-bind the two contradictory messages are on different levels of abstraction and there is an implicit injunction against commenting on the discrepancy. A common example of a double-bind is the wife who denounces her husband for not showing feelings, but then attacks him when he tries.

Continual exposure to paradoxical communication is like the dilemma of a dreamer caught in a nightmare. Nothing the dreamer tries to do in the dream works. The only solution is to step outside the context by waking up. Unfortunately, for people who live in a nightmare, it isn't possible to wake up.

GOALS OF THERAPY

The goal of communications family therapy is to take "deliberate action to alter poorly functioning patterns of interaction" (Watzlawick, *et al.*, 1967, p. 145). Because "patterns of interaction" are synonymous with communication, this means changing patterns of communication. In the early days of communications family therapy, especially in Virginia Satir's work, this led to a general goal of improving communication in the family. Later the goal was narrowed to altering those specific patterns of communication that maintained the symptom. By 1974, Weakland wrote that the goal of therapy is resolving symptoms, not reorganizing families: "We see the resolution of problems as primarily requiring a substitution of behavior patterns so as to interrupt the vicious, positive feedback circles" (Weakland, Fisch, Watzlawick, and Bodin, 1974, p. 149).

In this model, the therapist identifies the symptom to be changed as a communicative message, and then looks for behavior that is maintaining the problem. Once this antecedent behavior is discovered, the goal of intervention is to substitute behaviors that are not destructive—that is, that do not perpetuate the symptom. In communications theory terms, this amounts to interrupting positive feedback loops.

The goal of the communications therapist is, like that of the behavior therapist, to interdict behaviors that stimulate or reinforce symptoms. These two models also share the assumption that once pathological behavior is blocked, it will be replaced by constructive alternatives, instead of by other symptoms. The limitation of the behavioral model is that it treats the symptomatic person as the problem, and conceives of the symptom as only a response, rather than as both a response and a stimulus in a chain of interaction. The limitation of the communication model is that it isolates the sequence of behavior that maintains the symptoms, and focuses on two-person interactions without considering third persons. In other words, the communications model underestimates the effect that the communication between A and B has on the relationship and on the communications between B and C. If, for example, a child C is fearful because her mother B yells at her, and her mother yells at her because her husband A is not available, changing only the mother's behavior may result in a different symptomatic behavior in the child; the relationship with the husband must also be addressed.

CONDITIONS FOR BEHAVIOR CHANGE

If behavior is communication, then the way to change behavior is to change communication. According to the communications theorists, all events and actions have communicative properties. Even symptoms can be considered as covert messages, commenting upon relationships (Jackson, 1961). Even a headache that develops from prolonged tension in the occipital muscles is a message, since it is a report on how the person feels and also a command to be responded to. If a symptom is seen as a covert message, then by implication making the message overt eliminates the need for the symptom. Therefore, one of the important ways to change behavior is to bring hidden messages out into the open.

In addition to being multi-channeled, communication is also multi-leveled. Every message is qualified by another message or by the context, which may be congruent or incongruent; lack of congruence creates pathogenic contradictions, paradoxes, and double-binds. As I pointed out above, an essential ingredient of the double-bind is that it is impossible to escape or look at the binding situation from the outside. But no change can be generated from within, it can only come from outside the pattern. So, according to communications theorists (Watzlawick, Beavin, and Jackson, 1967), the paradigm for psychotherapy is an intervention from the outside to resolve relational dilemmas. The therapist is an outsider who supplies what the relationship cannot, a change in the rules.

From the outside position the therapist can point out problematic sequences, or manipulate them in order to effect therapeutic change. The first strategy relies on the power of insight and depends upon cooperation and willingness to change, but the second does not; it is an attempt to beat families at their own games, with or without their cooperation. Included in the second strategy are many of the most clever and interesting tactics of communications therapy, and much more has been written about these than about simple interpretation. Nevertheless, in the early days of family therapy, therapists relied more on pointing out communicational problems than on any other technique.

It is important to realize that communications therapists have used two very different strategies of change. The first, simply pointing out communicational problems, is represented in Virginia Satir's work, and was widely practiced by those who were new to family therapy. The second, less direct, approach was always more characteristic of Haley and Jackson, and eventually it became the predominant strategy. By the time they wrote *Pragmatics of Human Communication,* Watzlawick, Beavin, and Jackson (1967, p. 236) believed that,

> Therapeutic communication, then, must necessarily transcend such counsel as is customarily but ineffectually given by the protagonists themselves, as well as their friends and relatives, [because] bona fide patients—by which we simply mean persons who are not deliberately simulating—usually have tried and failed in all kinds of self-discipline and exercises in will power long before they revealed their distress to others and were told to "pull themselves together." It is in the essence of a symptom that it is something unwilled and therefore autonomous.

Therefore, they recommended interventions to make people behave in ways that would produce change. These manipulative strategies formed the basis of a new system, strategic family therapy (Chapter 10), which is an offshoot of communications theory.

Jackson and Haley's early work with families was influenced by the hypnotherapy that they learned from Milton Erickson. The hypnotherapist works by giving explicit instructions, whose purpose is often obscure. However, before patients will follow direction the therapist must gain control of the relationship. Haley was especially concerned with power and control in relationships. According to him (1963), everyday relationships are dominated by a struggle to achieve control. The same is true in therapeutic relationships.

The first task is to force the patient to concede that he or she is relating to the therapist. But this isn't always easy. Patients insist that their symptoms are not things they do, but things that happen to them. They say, "I have a handwashing compulsion," not "I compulsively wash my hands." Although symptoms affect relationships, they usually do so outside of awareness—otherwise the symptoms wouldn't "work," but would be recognized as manipulative ploys and thereby lose their power. A wife's handwashing compulsion may be a rebellion against a tyrannical husband, but it only works as long as it is seen as involuntary.

Jackson sometimes began by giving patients advice about their symptoms. He did so to point up the problem area, just as an interpretation would do; but at the same time his comments forced an intellectual understanding into action and made the patient focus on the relationship with the therapist —regardless of whether the patient accepted or rejected his advice. Haley (1961) recommended asking certain kinds of patients to do something in order to provoke a rebellious response, which served to make them concede that they were relating to the therapist. He mentions, as an example, directing a schizophrenic patient to hear voices. If the patient hears voices, then he is complying with the therapist's request. If he does not hear voices, then he can no longer claim to be crazy.

Once they have established a measure of control over the therapeutic relationship, communications theorists use paradox to break the "games without end" that their patients are caught up in. Haley argued that therapeutic paradoxes—used wittingly or unwittingly—underlie most successful psychotherapy. In "The Art of Psychoanalysis" Haley (1963) took the position that psychoanalysis worked not by discovering profound truths locked in the unconscious, but by ingeniously creating therapeutic paradoxes from which patients could escape only by giving up their symptoms.

Haley's (1961) direction to hear voices, illustrates the technique of *prescribing the symptom*. By instructing the patient to enact a symptomatic behavior the therapist is demanding that something "involuntary" be done voluntarily. This is a paradoxical injunction, which forces one of two changes. Either the patient performs the symptom, and thus admits that it isn't voluntary; or the patient gives up the symptom. Prescribing the symptom is a form of what the communications theorists called *therapeutic double-binds* (Jackson, 1961). According to Watzlawick, Beavin, and Jackson (1967), the same technique that drives people crazy is used to drive them sane.

Actually, "therapeutic double-bind" is somewhat loose usage, because it does not necessarily involve two orders of message one of which denies the other. To illustrate what he meant by a therapeutic double-bind, Jackson (1961) cited the following case report.

> The patient was a young wife with a martyr complex, who felt that despite her best efforts to please her husband he just would not be satisfied. Jackson sensed that she was probably just "acting nice" in order to cover her intense, but unacceptable, rage at her husband. But the patient bridled when he even suggested that she might be "dissatisfied." In the face of this resistance, Jackson suggested that since her marriage was so important and since her husband's mood had such a profound effect on her, that she should learn to be really pleasing.

By accepting the therapist's suggestion, the patient was admitting that she wasn't really pleasing. Moreover, she was forced to change.

In the above example, the patient is directed to change by doing more of the same. The object is to force the patient to step outside the frame set by her dilemma, with or without her awareness. In order to succeed, therapeutic double-binds, or paradoxical injunctions, must be so cleverly designed as to leave no loophole through which a patient can escape.

The tactics of change employed by the communication therapists focus on altering discrete sequences of interaction that perpetuate symptomatic behavior. Despite their claims to include triadic sequences in their analyses (Sluzki, 1978), most of their interventions are limited to dyadic interactions. Timing is considered to be an important factor in how the family will respond to attempts to change them. At a period of steady-state equilibrium families will resist change; at times of crisis they are more likely to accept change.

According to Jackson's notion of family homeostasis, family systems regulate themselves using symptoms as negative feedback to maintain their equilibrium. In this way, symptomatic families become caught in an increasingly inflexible set of patterns. The task of therapy is to loosen them up by introducing positive feedback to break up stability and equilibrium. The goal is to change the family system so that deviance is no longer necessary to preserve homeostasis.

TECHNIQUES

Technique follows theory in communications family therapy more so than in almost any other treatment approach. Most of these therapists wrote a great deal about the theory of human communications before they began applying their ideas to treatment; and even after they began to describe their work with families, most of the publications had a distinctly theoretical flavor. As a result, communications family therapists appear to have had an intellectual stance and more emotional distance from the families they worked with than other early family therapists. Communications therapy seems to have been done *to* families, more than *with* them.

Formal assessment is typically not used by communications therapists, although Watzlawick (1966) did introduce a *structured family interview.* In this procedure, families are given five tasks to complete, including:

1. Deciding their main problem.
2. Planning a family outing.
3. The parents discussing how they met.
4. Discussing the meaning of a proverb.
5. Identifying faults and placing the blame on the correct person.

While the family worked on these tasks, the therapist, watching behind a one-way mirror, observed the family's patterns of communication, methods of decision making, and scapegoating. Although it is useful for research, the structured family interview has never gained wide acceptance as a clinical tool.

Most of the actual techniques of communications family therapy consist of teaching rules of clear communication, analyzing and interpreting communicational patterns, and manipulating interactions through a variety of strategic maneuvers. The progression of these three strategies from more straightforward to more subtle reflects the growing awareness of how families resist change.

In their early work (Jackson and Weakland, 1961), communications therapists opened by stating their belief that the whole family is involved in the presenting problem. Then they explained that all families develop habitual patterns of communication, including some that are problematical. This attempt to convert families from seeing the identified patient as the problem to accepting mutual responsibility underestimated the family's resistance to change. Later, these therapists were more likely to begin by asking for and accepting a family's own definition of their problems (Haley, 1976).

After the therapists made their opening remarks they asked the family members, usually one at a time, to discuss their problems. While they did so the therapists listened, but concentrated on the process of communication, rather than the topics and content. When someone in the family spoke in a confused or confusing way, the therapist would point this out, and insist that the family members follow certain rules of clear communication. Satir (1967) was the most straightforward teacher, and she advocated teaching and modeling clear communication. When someone said something that was unclear, she would question and clarify the message, and as she did so she impressed on the family some basic guidelines for clear speaking.

One rule is that people should always speak in the first person singular when saying what they think or feel. For example:

Husband: We always liked Donna's boyfriends.

Therapist: I'd like you to speak for yourself; later your wife can say what she thinks.

Husband: Yes, but we've always agreed on these things.

Therapist: Perhaps, but you are the expert on how *you* think and feel. Speak for yourself and let her speak for herself.

A similar rule is that everyone should make personal statements ("I statements") about personal matters. Opinions and value judgments must be understood as that, not passed off as facts or general principles. Owning that opinions are only that is a necessary step to discussing them in a way that permits legitimate differences and the possibility of changing opinions.

Wife: People shouldn't want to do things without their children.

Therapist: So you like to bring the kids along when you and your husband go out.

Wife: Well, yes, doesn't everybody?

Husband: I don't. I'd like to go out, just the two of us, once in a while.

Another rule is that people should speak directly to, not about, each other. This avoids ignoring or disqualifying family members and prevents the establishment of destructive coalitions. For example:

Teenager: (To therapist) My mother always ignores me. Isn't that right, Dad?

Therapist: Would you say that to her?

Teenager: I have told her, but she doesn't listen.

Therapist: Tell her again.

Teenager: (To therapist) Oh, okay. (To mother) Sometimes I get the feeling ... (Shifts back to therapist) Oh, what's the use!

Therapist: I can see how hard it is, and I guess you've kind of decided that it's no use trying to talk to your mom if she isn't going to listen, but in here, I hope we can all learn to speak more directly to each other, so that no one will be ignored.

As this exchange illustrates, it is often quite difficult to teach people to communicate clearly just by telling them how to. It seems like a good idea, but it doesn't work very well. The reason that an active approach to family therapy persists at all is that, with enough insisting, most people will follow the directions, at least for the moment. However, in the face of habits that have been long maintained and that are resistant to change, the new behavior often only lasts for as long as the therapist is there to insist and remind. For this reason, less direct, but more effective, means of influencing family patterns of communication were developed.

In the early days of communications family therapy, Virginia Satir was probably the most transparent and direct therapist, and Jay Haley was the least; Don Jackson occupied a position somewhere in between. In contrast to traditional psychotherapy, where the focus is on individuals, on unconscious unobservable fantasies and misperceptions, past experience, and intrapsychic states, Jackson concerned himself with influence, interaction, and behavior immediately observable in the present.

When he began treating families of schizophrenics, Jackson thought that he needed to protect patients from their families (Jackson and Weakland, 1961), but came to realize that parents and children were all bound together in mutually destructive ways. Even now those who are new to family therapy, especially if they themselves have not yet become parents, tend to identify with the children and see the parents as the bad guys. Not only is this wrong, as Jackson himself later realized, but it leads to alienation of the parents. Parents are the architects of the family, and as the most powerful figures, usually decide whether or not the family will remain in treatment. Young therapists often begin "knowing" the parents are responsible for all the problems. Only later, when these therapists become parents themselves, do they achieve a more balanced perspective—and learn that it's all the children's fault.

Jackson emphasized the need for structure and management in family therapy sessions. He began first sessions by saying, "We are here to work together on better understanding one another so that you all can get more out of your family life" (Jackson and Weakland, 1961, p. 37). Not only does this remark structure the meeting, it also conveys the idea that all members of the family are to become the focus of discussion. Furthermore, it reveals the therapist's goal, and may therefore precipitate a struggle with parents who have generally come only to help the patient, and who are extremely resistant to the idea that they are part of the problem. Jackson thus set the rules right at the outset, and explained fairly openly what he was doing in order to fight resistance, scapegoating, and obfuscation. His style was to anticipate and disarm resistance openly. Today, most family therapists find it more effective to be somewhat subtler, meeting the family's resistance not with psychological karate but with jujitsu—using their own momentum for leverage, instead of opposing them head-on.

Jackson may have found it so difficult to deal with schizophrenic families that he became thus active and intrusive and less worried about being carried along with the families' interactions. In any case, there is a suggestion of combativeness in his writings, as though he saw himself battling against families. He spoke of beating families at their own game (Jackson and Weakland, 1961) by using dual or multiple messages, and provoking them to do something in defiance of therapeutic directives whose real purpose may be concealed (therapeutic double-binds). This is a model of a therapist who conspires to outwit families in a distanced sort of way.

Jackson may have been subtlely combative with families, but Jay Haley was clear and explicit in defining therapy as a battle for control between therapist and patients.[1] For Haley, the important distinction is not between internal processes and the way people relate to others, but between insight and manipulation. Even those of his predecessors who believed that interaction was the key to understanding patients still continued to believe that self-awareness was necessary (and sufficient) to cause change. Haley did not. Instead he believed that therapists need to maneuver so as to achieve a position of power over their patients, in order to manipulate the patients into changing. Although the notion of manipulation may have unpleasant connotations, moral criticism should be reserved for those who use patients covertly for their own ends, rather than used against those who seek the most effective means of helping patients achieve their goals.

Haley's most significant early publication of his ideas was in *Strategies of Psychotherapy* (Haley, 1963). In it he claims that therapeutic paradoxes underlie what therapists of all different persuasions do, and then he ingeniously reanalyzes a number of different therapeutic modalities. His critiques are always lucid and clever. It is, however, a little harder to discern his own strategies and techniques. In *Strategies of Psychotherapy*, Haley reveals his own procedures most directly when he discusses techniques of directive therapy, marriage therapy, and therapeutic paradoxes. He devotes less than two pages in *Strategies* to therapeutic intervention with families, and refers the reader back to his section on marriage therapy.

Haley described the marital relationship in terms of conflicting levels of communication. Conflicts occur not only over what rules the couple will follow in dealing with each other, but also over who is to set the rules. Complexity is introduced because couples may be complementary in some spheres and symmetrical in others. But the complexity goes still further;

---

[1]*Note:* Haley has continued to develop and revise his thinking over the past twenty years; the material in this section is based on the communications model that he followed in the 1960s. Haley's more recent ideas are described in the following chapter, "Strategic Family Therapy."

although it may appear that a wife dominates a dependent husband, the husband may, in fact, provoke the wife to be dominating, thus himself dominating the type of relationship that they have. It takes a coward to make a bully.

Although Haley's analysis of human relations is highly intellectual and rational, he observes that family members have great difficulty being rational about their problems. In fact he tends to exaggerate peoples' inability to understand their own behavior. His therapy therefore tends to be done *to* patients, rather than done *with* them. Although Haley criticizes to the point of ridicule the idea that insight is curative, he does put a lot of faith in simple openness of communication as a way of dealing with problems in couples and marriages. He cites numerous examples of the problems created in families who do not speak openly of certain matters, but deal with them only indirectly. He suggests that if couples will simply bring into the open and discuss underlying resentments and frustrated wishes, these can be resolved through rational communication. Certainly open discussion may be helpful, but usually it's only a beginning. Once submerged material is finally brought to the surface, it means that whatever problems responsible for submerging it in the first place must be dealt with. This is quite a tricky matter. Haley states that symptoms in a spouse serve the same function as symptoms in disturbed children—that is, to avoid defining the relationship and dealing with marital stress. He also says that when the symptoms improve the couple will begin to fight more openly.

According to Haley, the mere presence of the third person, the therapist, helps couples solve their problems. By dealing fairly with each spouse and not taking sides, the therapist disarms the usual blaming maneuvers; in other words, the therapist serves as a referee. Not only does the therapist actively intervene when either spouse fights dirty, but the therapist's mere presence encourages the couple to speak more openly and not hit each other below the belt.

In addition to being referee, the therapist should relabel or redefine the activity of family members with each other. At first the therapist should be permissive and encourage family members to express themselves freely. This is the time for making explicit accusations and protests, so that they can be responded to. Once family members begin to express themselves, the therapist's comments can be directed toward helping participants communicate in problem-solving, rather than in destructive ways. One strategy is to redefine what family members say, stressing the positive aspects of their relationship. "For example," Haley says, "if a husband is protesting his wife's constant nagging, the therapist might comment that the wife seems trying to reach her husband and achieve more closeness with him. If the wife protests that her husband constantly withdraws from her, the husband might be defined as one who wants to avoid discord and seeks an amiable relationship" (Haley, 1963, p. 139).

One of Haley's major strategies is to make explicit the implicit or covert rules which govern family relationships. Dysfunctional rules made explicit become more difficult to follow. For example, some wives berate their husbands for not expressing themselves, but the wives talk so much and criticize so loudly that the husbands hardly have a chance. Once the therapist points this out, it becomes more difficult to follow the implicit rule that the husband should not talk. Haley believed that disagreements about which rules to follow are relatively easily solved through discussion and compromise. Conflicts about who is to set rules are stickier, and require that the therapist be less straightforward. Because the issue of control is too explosive to be dealt with openly, Haley recommends comments which are really subtle directives.

Haley's directives are of two sorts: suggestions to behave differently, and suggestions to continue to behave the same. Straightforward advice, he says, rarely works. When it does, it's likely that the conflict was minor, or that the couple was moving in that direction anyway. Some of Haley's directives are for changes that seem so small that the full ramifications are not immediately apparent. In a couple, for example, where the wife seems to have her own way most of the time, the husband is asked to say "no" on some minor issue once during the week. This seems trivial, but it accomplishes two things. It makes the husband practice speaking up for himself, and it makes the wife aware that she has been domineering. This small beginning gives both spouses a chance to work on changing their part of the interaction. The fact that they are doing so under therapeutic direction often (though not always) makes them more likely to follow the advice.

Haley's suggestion that family members continue to behave in the same way is in fact a therapeutic paradox. If people do something under the therapist's direction, then the therapist gains control over that behavior. It is the therapist, then, who is laying down the rules for the relationship. Moreover, when they are told to continue their dysfunctional behavior, family members may spontaneously change. When a teenager who is rebelling against parents is instructed to continue to rebel, he or she is caught in a paradoxical position. Continuing to rebel means following the direction of an authority figure, and the teenager can maintain the illusion of freedom only by giving up this behavior. Meanwhile the problematic behavior ceases. Sometimes it is more effective to have one spouse suggest that the other continue symptomatic behavior. While this may seem trivial, it produces a major shift, because it alters who defines the nature of the relationship.

EVALUATING THERAPY THEORY AND RESULTS

Communications family therapy is an intellectual and scholarly approach, but one not founded upon empiricism. Bateson and his colleagues in Palo Alto used the natural history method of observation to generate their ideas. Their major theories, including family homeostasis and the double-bind, were based on deductive reasoning—given the nature of their communication, schizophrenics *must* have been exposed to double-binds. Only later did they attempt to verify these conclusions by studying family interactions.

The first concern of the communicationists was theory, not therapy. Strategies for change came later, and were very much a product of the theory. This reverses the usual case, where clinicians develop theories to describe what they have found to be true in therapy. Theories of therapy are thus usually ways of organizing the data of clinical experience. In communications family therapy, theory preceded clinical experience and is often given more prominence.

The first major publication of communications theory was the double-bind paper (Bateson, Jackson, Haley, and Weakland, 1956). Initially it was met with great enthusiasm and wide acceptance. This was followed by a period of intense analysis and research (see Chapter 1), which culminated in serious challenge and criticism. It turns out that many of the concepts of communications theory, like the double-bind, are not subject to empirical confirmation. Instead, these concepts are useful metaphors, much like many of the propositions of psychoanalysis.

Haley actually did quite a bit of careful research on family interactions. Most of it was done not to evaluate therapy, or even a theory of therapy, but to test for differences in communication between schizophrenic and normal families. At one time, the finding that verbal communication in families of schizophrenics can be differentiated from communication in other families (Singer and Wynne, 1963) was taken as support for a family etiology theory of schizophrenia. The problem with this conclusion is that most of the studies in which communications disorders were observed were made after the offspring had already been diagnosed schizophrenic. It is therefore just as likely that the observed disorders of communication are a response to schizophrenia rather than a cause of it.

Two studies by Haley (1968) and Waxler (1974) cast serious doubt on the etiological interpretation. Haley found that normal children were just as able to perform a cognitive task when they were instructed by schizophrenic parents as when instructed by normal parents. Schizophrenic children, on the other hand, were less able than normal children to perform the task when both groups were instructed by their own parents. Waxler (1974) found that schizophrenic parents had only a minor and indirect influence on the performance of normal children.

Joan Liem (1974) compared the etiological and responsive hypothesis in an experimental design similar to those used by Haley (1968) and Waxler (1974). The subjects of this study were members of eleven families with schizophrenic young adult sons and eleven families with normal young adult sons. Their task was to describe common objects and simple human concepts for other family members to identify. The results supported the responsive hypothesis over the etiological one. The observed communications disorders of schizophrenic sons had an immediate negative effect on all parents, normal as well as schizophrenic, who attempted to respond to them. On the other hand, communications disorders were not observed in parents of the schizophrenic sons, nor were their communications found to have a disruptive effect on any of the sons who responded to them.

As these three studies illustrate, the idea that communications disorders cause schizophrenia has not been supported. Moreover, family therapy has proven not very effective with schizophrenic families. However, although communications therapy began as a result of studies of schizophrenia, its validity does not rest on its effectiveness with this disorder. Communications concepts have been so widely adopted by family therapists of all theoretical persuasions that it would be difficult to measure their effectiveness by comparing one approach to others.

The communications therapists themselves have shown little inclination to conduct outcome studies. Whether or not the techniques of communications therapy are effective is a matter for empirical study, not argument. Thus far, however, there is no evidence for the effectiveness of this approach. The only existing outcome study (Weakland, Fisch, Watzlawick, and Bodin, 1974) was too poorly controlled to provide valid conclusions. The absence of controlled outcome studies does not, of course, distinguish communications family therapy from most of the other approaches to family treatment. For the time being, family therapy remains a field where the power of written descriptions is the only source of conviction other than personal experience.

SUMMARY

Communications family therapy was one of the first and possibly the most influential forms of family treatment. Its theoretical development was closely tied to general systems theory and the therapy that emerged was a systems approach *par excellence*. Therapy was a by-product of Gregory Bateson's schizophrenia project. The main product was a set of ideas about human communication and family systems. The fact that their studies had a profound impact on the entire field of psychotherapy is largely an artifact of the psychiatric context that was the source of their funding. Many of these ideas—homeostasis, double-bind, feedback—were absorbed by the entire field of family therapy, so that there is no longer a separate school of communications family therapy.

Bateson assembled a unique group with diverse talents, and he gave them free rein to develop their interests. Among the many subjects that interested them, communication was the common denominator. Communication is the detectable input and output they used to analyze the black box of interpersonal systems. Communication was described as feedback, as a tactic in interpersonal power struggles, and as symptom. In fact, all behavior was considered communication. The trouble is the concept loses precision when it is used so broadly. If all events and actions are treated as communication, then communications analysis may be taken to mean everything, and therefore nothing. Human relations are not all a matter of communication; communication may be the matrix in which interactions are embedded, but human interactions have other attributes as well.

The Bateson group may be best remembered for the concept of the double-bind, but their enduring contribution is that they applied communications analysis to a wide range of behavior, including family dynamics. In fact, the idea of metacommunication is a much more useful concept than that of the double-bind, and it has been absorbed not only by family therapists but also by the general public. Whether or not they are familiar with the term *metacommunication,* most people understand that all messages have both report and command functions.

Another of the most significant ideas of communications theory is that families are rule-governed systems, maintained by homeostatic, negative feedback mechanisms. This accounts for the stability of normal families and explains why dysfunctional families get stuck in outmoded ways of behaving. Because such families do not have adequate positive feedback mechanisms, they are unable to adjust to changing circumstances.

Communications theorists borrowed the open systems model from general systems theory, but their clinical analyses and interventions were based on the closed systems paradigm of cybernetics. This is another example of how this approach was more useful theoretically than pragmatically. In their clinical descriptions, relationships are portrayed as struggles for power and control. Haley emphasized the power struggle between the spouses, and Watzlawick said that the major problem of control in families is cognitive. The therapy that they developed from these ideas was conceived as a power struggle, in which the therapist takes control to outwit the forces of symptom-maintenance.

When communication takes place in a closed system—the fantasies of an individual, or the conversations within a family—there is little opportunity for adjusting the system. Only when someone external to the system provides communicational input can correction occur. This is the premise on which communications family theory is based. The rules of family functioning are largely unknown to the family, and the best way to examine and correct them is to consult an expert in communications.

While there were major differences among the intervention strategies of Haley, Jackson, Satir, and Watzlawick, they were all committed to altering self-reinforcing and mutually destructive patterns of communication. They pursued this goal by direct and indirect means. The direct approach, favored by Satir, sought change by making family rules explicit and by teaching principles of clear communication. This approach could be described as establishing ground rules, or metacommunicational principles, and included such tactics as telling people to speak for themselves and pointing out nonverbal and multi-leveled channels of communication.

The trouble is, as Haley noted, "One of the difficulties involved in telling patients to do something is the fact that psychiatric patients are noted for their hesitation about doing what they are told." For this reason, communications therapists began to rely on more indirect strategies, designed to provoke change, not to foster awareness. Telling family members to speak for themselves, for instance, may challenge a family rule and therefore meet with strong resistance.

Resistances and symptoms were treated with a variety of paradoxical directives, known loosely as therapeutic double-binds. Milton Erickson's technique of prescribing resistances was used as a lever to gain control, as, for example, when a therapist tells family members not to reveal everything in the first session. The same ploy is used to prescribe symptoms, an action that makes unrecognized rules explicit, implies that such behavior is voluntary, and places the therapist in control.

Eventually, communications therapy became a symptom-focused, brief, directive therapy. The focus on symptoms is consistent with the general systems concept of *equifinality*, which means that no matter where systems change begins the final result is the same. Moreover, even when they convened whole families, the communication therapists focused on the marital pair, and they have always been more adept with dyadic than triadic thinking.

Today, the theories of communications therapy have been absorbed into the mainstream of family therapy, and its symptom-focused interventions are the basis of the strategic school of family therapy.

REFERENCES

Bateson, G. & Jackson, D.D. Some varieties of pathogenic organization. *Disorders of Communication,* 1964, *42,* 270–283.

Bateson, G., Jackson, D.D., Haley, J. & Weakland, J. Toward a theory of schizophrenia. *Behavioral Science,* 1956, *1,* 251–264.

Bateson, G., Jackson, D.D., Haley, J. & Weakland, J.H. A note on the double-bind —1962. *Family Process,* 1963, *2,* 154–161.

Beels, C.C. & Ferber, A. Family Therapy: A view. *Family Process,* 1969, *8,* 280–318.

von Bertalanffy, L. An outline of General System Theory. *British Journal of the Philosophy of Science,* 1950, *1,* 134–165.

Birdwhistell, R.L. *Introduction to kinesics.* Louisville, Kentucky: University of Louisville Press, 1952.

Bleuler, E. *Dementia praecox or the group of schizophrenias.* New York: International Universities Press, 1950.

Carnap, R. *Introduction to semantics.* Cambridge: Harvard University Press, 1942.

Haley, J. Control in psychotherapy with schizophrenics. *Archives of General Psychiatry,* 1961, *5,* 340–353.

Haley, J. *Strategies of psychotherapy,* New York: Grune & Stratton, 1963.

Haley, J. Testing parental instructions to schizophrenic and normal children: A pilot study. *Journal of Abnormal Psychology,* 1968, *73,* 559–565.

Haley, J. *Problem-solving therapy.* San Francisco: Jossey-Bass, 1976.

Hoffman, L. Deviation-amplifying processes in natural groups. In J. Haley (Ed.), *Changing families.* New York: Grune & Stratton, 1971.

Jackson, D.D. Interactional psychotherapy. In M.T. Stein (Ed.), *Contemporary psychotherapies*. New York: Free Press of Glencoe, 1961.

Jackson, D.D. Family rules: The marital quid pro quo. *Archives of General Psychiatry*, 1965, *12*, 589–594.

Jackson, D.D. Aspects of conjoint family therapy. In G.H. Zuk & I. Boszormenyi-Nagy (Eds.), *Family therapy and disturbed families*. Palo Alto: Science and Behavior, 1967.

Jackson, D.D. & Weakland, J.H. Conjoint family therapy: Some consideration on theory, technique, and results. *Psychiatry*, 1961, *24*, 30–45.

Lederer, W. & Jackson, D.D. *Mirages of marriage*. New York: Norton, 1968.

Lidz, T., Cornelison, A., Terry, D. & Fleck, S. Intra-familial environment of the schizophrenic patient: IV. The transmission of irrationality. *Archives of Neurology and Psychiatry*, 1958, *79*, 305–316.

Liem, J.H. Effects of verbal communications of parents and children: A comparison of normal and schizophrenic families. *Journal of Consulting and Clinical Psychology*, 1974, *42*, 438–450.

Maruyama, M. The second cybernetics: Deviation-amplifying mutual causal processes. In W. Buckley (Ed.), *Modern systems research for the behavioral scientist*. Chicago: Aldine, 1968.

Morris, C.W. Foundations of the theory of signs. In O. Neurath, R. Carnap & C.O. Morris (Eds.), *International encyclopedia of united science. Volume 1*. Chicago: University of Chicago Press, 1938.

Ruesch, J. & Bateson, G. *Communication: The social matrix of psychiatry*. New York: Norton, 1951.

Sartre, J.P. *Being and nothingness*. New York: Citadel Press, 1964.

Satir, V. *Conjoint family therapy*. Palo Alto: Science and Behavior, 1967.

Satir, V. The family as a treatment unit. In J. Haley (Ed.), *Changing families*. New York: Grune & Stratton, 1971.

Scheflen, A.E. Natural history method in psychotherapy: Communicational research. In L.A. Gottschalk & A.H. Auerbach (Eds.), *Methods of research in psychotherapy*. New York: Appleton-Century-Crofts, 1966.

Scheflen, A.E. Human communication: Behavioral programs and their integration in interaction. *Behavioral Science*, 1968, *13*, 86–102.

Sluzki, C.E. Marital therapy from a systems theory perspective. In T.J. Paolino & B.S. McCrady (Eds.), *Marriage and marital therapy*. New York: Brunner/Mazel, 1978.

Sullivan, H.S. The language of schizophrenia. In J.S. Kasanin (Ed.), *Language and thought in schizophrenia*. New York: Norton, 1944.

Watzlawick, P.A. A structured family interview. *Family Process*, 1966, *5*, 256–271.

Watzlawick, P., Beavin, J.H. & Jackson, D.D. *Pragmatics of human communication*. New York: Norton, 1967.

Waxler, N.E. Parent and child effects on cognitive performance: An experimental approach to the etiological and responsive theories of schizophrenia. *Family Process*, 1974, *13*, 1–22.

Weakland, J., Fisch, R., Watzlawick, P. & Bodin, A.M. Brief therapy: Focused problem resolution. *Family Process,* 1974, *13,* 141–168.

Wynne, L.C. Methodologic and conceptual issues in the study of schizophrenics and their families. *Journal of Psychiatric Research,* 1968, *6,* 185–199.

Wynne, L.C. Communication disorders and the quest for relatedness in families of schizophrenics. *American Journal of Psychoanalysis,* 1970, *30,* 100–114.

Wynne, L.C., Jones, J.E. & Al-Khayyal, M. Healthy family communication patterns: Observations in families "at risk" for psychopathology. In F. Walsh (Ed.), *Normal family processes.* New York: Guilford, 1982.

Wynne, L.C., Ryckoff, I.M., Day, J. & Hirsch, S. Pseudomutuality in the family relations of schizophrenics. *Psychiatry,* 1958, *21,* 205–220.

Wynne, L.C. & Singer, M.T. Thought disorder and family relationships of schizophrenics: I. Research strategy. *Archives of General Psychiatry,* 1963, *9,* 191–198.

Wynne, L.C., Singer, M.T., Bartko, J.J. & Toohey, M.L. Schizophrenics and their families: Recent research on parental communication. In J.M. Tanner (Ed.), *Developments in psychiatric research.* London: Hodden & Stoughton, 1977.

10

Strategic
Family
Therapy

INTRODUCTION

d escended from communications therapy and heir to the best
work in that tradition, strategic therapy is among the most exciting and vital
of the recent developments in family therapy. Taking as their starting point
the communications model of family systems, strategic therapists focus their
attention on repeated sequences of behavior and patterns of communication. Strategic therapy, or problem-solving therapy, or brief therapy, or
systemic therapy, as it is variously called, is method-oriented and problem-
focused. Although they are highly intellectual in their analyses of problem-
maintaining behavior, strategic therapists manipulate behavior with little or
no attempt to instill insight. Several other approaches to family therapy are
offshoots of individual theories of therapy, but strategic therapy derives
from a purely family therapy tradition based on general systems theory and
cybernetics.

Strategic therapists take a *systemic* (circular) view of problem-maintenance and a *strategic* (planned) orientation to change. The analysis is based on systems theory, but the interventions are strictly pragmatic. Jay Haley (1973) coined the term "strategic therapy" when describing Milton Erickson's work, which inspired the intervention strategies of this school. Following Erickson, strategic therapists take responsibility for planning strategies to solve their clients' problems. They set clear goals, which always include resolving the presenting symptoms. It is thus an approach with extreme emphasis on the details of symptoms and less intrinsic interest in families and their over-all growth and welfare.

In the late 1970s strategic therapy became so influential that the field of family therapy was polarized into strategic and nonstrategic camps. The followers of the two approaches regularly engage in serious, often emotional, debates. Nonstrategic therapists accuse strategists of being cold, manipulative, and overemphasizing power and technique. Strategic therapists respond by saying that nonstrategic therapists are nonsystemic, linear thinkers, who fail to grasp the importance of circularity.

SKETCHES OF LEADING FIGURES

There is not one, but several approaches to strategic therapy. The common theoretical background is systems and communication theory; the common therapeutic strategy is interrupting repetitive patterns of interaction in which problems are embedded. The leading strategic therapists are: the late Milton Erickson; Jay Haley and Cloe Madanes; a group at the Institute for Family Studies in Milan, comprised of Mara Selvini Palazzoli, Luigi Boscolo, Gianfranco Cecchin, and Guiliana Prata; Lynn Hoffman and her team at the Ackerman Institute; Richard Rabkin; and members of the Brief Therapy Center of the Mental Research Institute (MRI) in Palo Alto, including Richard Fisch, John Weakland, Paul Watzlawick, and Arthur Bodin.

Although he occasionally treated couples and families, Milton Erickson's practice was devoted primarily to working with individuals. Since he was not primarily a family therapist, his work will not be emphasized in this chapter. However, his brilliant and inventive strategies for solving psychological problems have had such an impact on the development of strategic therapy that this chapter would be incomplete without some discussion of his ideas.

After working as a psychiatrist in a variety of hospital and academic settings, Erickson established a private practice in Phoenix, Arizona, in 1948. Since then his professional life was devoted to maintaining a busy private practice and teaching his skills to others, through consultation, supervision, seminars, and lectures throughout the United States and in several foreign countries. In addition to his membership in a number of psychiatric and medical hypnosis societies, he was the founding president of the American Society for Clinical Hypnosis.

His influence on strategic therapy has been transmitted through his case reports and descriptions of his clinical methods by his students, among them John Weakland and Jay Haley (Haley, 1967, 1973).

Erickson was a genuine original: a legendary figure whose work has aptly been called "uncommon therapy" (Haley, 1973). Although Erickson himself talked about his work from the perspective of hypnosis, of conditioning, or of psychoanalysis, these traditional frameworks do not adequately account for his results. By studying and writing about what Erickson actually did, however, Haley has been able to pinpoint Erickson's contributions to psychological treatment.

Rather than following any standard procedure dictated by a particular theory, Erickson designed a specific approach to fit whatever the problem at hand. Always pragmatic and flexible, he developed an enormous variety of therapeutic strategies. He believed that people's problems are unique and infinitely variable, and he was equally convinced that they can change in a variety of ways. Patients tend to view their situations as traps with only one possible exit, but Erickson assumed that they have a wide range of alternatives. He intervened forcefully to block symptoms and to provoke patients to behave in new, more adaptive ways.

Unlike traditional therapists who emphasize the patient's own responsibility to change, Erickson assumed full accountability for what happens in treatment. He was powerful and directive, but rarely direct. He eschewed understanding in favor of manipulation as a vehicle for change. Two characteristics of Erickson's approach have been particularly influential on other strategic therapists: his use of indirect means of influence, and his acceptance of whatever clients offer.

Erickson began with each new patient by accepting what the patient brings, including hostility or fear. By so doing, he cemented an intense relationship and maneuvered himself into a position where he had leverage to change the patient's behavior. This relationship is crucial, for Erickson's idea was that symptomatic behavior has a social function, and that the way to resolve psychiatric problems is to change the patient's relationships with others, including the therapist.

Many of Erickson's ideas, including his emphasis on the present function and social context of symptoms, helped to stimulate the development of strategic family therapy. Erickson's style of therapy as well as many of his specific strategies are implicit in the work of these therapists, especially in Jay Haley's work. A selection of Erickson's papers appears in *Advanced Techniques of Hypnosis and Therapy* (Haley, 1967), and a comprehensive description of his approach in Jay Haley's *Uncommon Therapy* (Haley, 1973).

Among the most prominent of strategic family therapists is Jay Haley, whose mentors include, besides Erickson, Bateson and Minuchin. Haley's work with Bateson's communications project in Palo Alto and subsequently with Don Jackson at the Mental Research Institute has been described in Chapter 1. His important and influential book, *Strategies of Psychotherapy* (Haley, 1963), summarizes his thinking at that time.

In 1967 Haley left MRI to join Minuchin and Braulio Montalvo at the Philadelphia Child Guidance Clinic. For approximately ten years he was director of family therapy research at the Child Guidance Clinic, as well as a clinical member of the University of Pennsylvania's Department of Psychiatry. His association with Minuchin was productive for both men. Minuchin credits Haley for helping him articulate many of the principles elaborated in *Families and Family Therapy* (Minuchin, 1974), and Haley gives Minuchin credit for helping him understand the structure of families. In Haley's later work (Haley, 1976, 1980), he uses the structural view of family organization as the context within which to apply his strategic techniques. Haley's example may serve to help bridge the gap between competing approaches in the field.

In 1976 Haley left Philadelphia for Washington, D.C. to join the faculty of the University of Maryland Medical School, and to establish his own family therapy clinic with his wife, Cloe Madanes. Madanes, one of the most respected and influential members of the family therapy field, started at the Philadelphia Child Guidance Clinic, where she worked with Haley, Minuchin, and Montalvo. In 1976, Madanes and Haley teamed up to start their own institute in Washington, D.C., the Family Therapy Institute, now one of the major family therapy training centers in the United States.

Mara Selvini Palazzoli is an Italian psychiatrist who practices in Milan. Her interest in families developed from earlier work with anorexia nervosa, where she used psychoanalytic techniques to investigate these dramatic cases of self-starvation. At that time she was particularly interested in the relationships between mothers and daughters, and this interest expanded to encompass the total family context. Eventually she began treating whole families.

In 1967 Selvini Palazzoli established the Institute for Family Studies, which now also includes Luigi Boscolo, Gianfranco Cecchin, and Guiliana Prata. This gifted team has developed a remarkably successful treatment approach that relies heavily on the use of therapeutic paradoxes. The group has been effective after very few sessions even with the most difficult families, including those with children and young adults diagnosed as acute schizophrenics.

Selvini Palazzoli and her colleagues, or the Milan Associates as they now call themselves, first visited the United States in 1977. Their visit was sponsored by the Ackerman Institute, where their ideas have been taken up by Lynn Hoffman. Hoffman began doing family research at the Mental Research Institute in Palo Alto in 1963. Since that time, hers has been one of the most intelligent and articulate voices in the family therapy movement. Now she is a leading American exponent of the systemic model of treatment, based on the work of the Milan Associates.

Hoffman is a faculty member of the Ackerman Institute and head of its Family Treatment Group. Among her collaborators are Olga Silverstein, Gillian Walker, Peggy Penn, John Patten, Joel Bergman, and Jeffrey Ross. The Family Treatment Group uses a team of clinicians to work with "impossible" cases, referred after other methods have failed. Two members of the group act as cotherapists while the others observe behind the one-way mirror. Using a level of systems thinking that is difficult to grasp, they meet with their client families once a month for 8 to about 18 sessions. While the methods used are more synthetic than original, they have nevertheless been remarkably successful. Recently, Hoffman opened her own training center in Amherst, Massachusetts.

Richard Rabkin is a literate and eclectic social psychiatrist. He practices psychotherapy in New York City and teaches at the New York University School of Medicine. His writing and practice reflect a number of diverse influences. He worked for a time at the Wiltwyck School for Boys, where he learned about family therapy and systems theory from Salvador Minuchin and Edgar Auerswald. He was also greatly influenced by the writings of Jay Haley and those of the Brief Therapy group at Palo Alto. And his use of hypnosis is derived from Milton Erickson and Herbert Spiegel.

The Mental Research Institute (MRI) led the way in research and training in family therapy's first decade. Its founding director, Don Jackson, assembled an energetic and creative staff interested in communication, families, and schizophrenia. Among them were Jules Riskin, Virginia Satir, Jay Haley, John Weakland, Paul Watzlawick, and Janet Beavin. This group was responsible for the first formal training program in family therapy (funded in 1962 by NIMH), a library of videotapes of family sessions, and many important contributions to the literature of family interaction research and therapy. Haley's (1963) *Strategies of Psychotherapy*, Satir's (1964) *Conjoint Family Therapy*, and Watzlawick, Beavin, and Jackson's (1967) *Pragmatics of Human Communication* were probably the most popular and influential family therapy books of the 1960s.

In 1967 the Brief Therapy Center of MRI was opened under the directorship of Richard Fisch. The staff included John Weakland, Paul Watzlawick, and Arthur Bodin. Their mission was to develop the briefest possible treatment for psychiatric disorders. What emerged was a very active approach, focused on the presenting symptoms, and limited to ten sessions. This approach was found to be successful both in resolving the presenting problem and in initiating a positive spiral of change in the rest of the family as well.

After Don Jackson's death in 1968, the center of the family therapy movement shifted from Palo Alto to Philadelphia and New York. Jackson was succeeded as director by John Bell in 1968, Jules Riskin in 1973, Nicholas Cummings in 1979, and Carlos Sluzki in 1980.

In recent years, MRI has reemerged as one of the leading centers of family therapy, and the Brief Therapy Center is acknowledged to be among the most creative and influential sources of strategic therapy. Watzlawick, Weakland, and Fisch's (1974) book, *Change: Principles of Problem Formation and Problem Resolution* was one of the first published accounts of strategic family therapy. Together with a follow-up volume, *The Tactics of Change: Doing Therapy Briefly* (Fisch, Weakland, and Segal, 1982), it describes one of the leading methods in this school.

THEORETICAL FORMULATIONS

Strategic therapists are interested more in change than in understanding; consequently they write mostly about technique rather than theory. The hallmark of their approach is designing novel strategies for solving problems. Like most clinicians, their theories are simpler and more pragmatic than those of scholars and academicians. Their work is generally concerned with observing and changing particular sequences of behavior rather than with developing new theories of family functioning.

The theoretical underpinnings of strategic therapy come from general systems theory and cybernetics, via the communications school of family therapy. Among the ideas adopted from the earlier work of Bateson, Jackson, and Haley are: viewing symptoms in context; family homeostasis; double-bind; therapeutic paradox; circularity of family systems; and the need for systems change to resolve the problems of individuals.

Individual problems are regarded as manifestations of family disturbance, and symptoms are seen as communicative. Disturbed behavior is viewed as a social phenomenon, reflecting dysfunction in the family system and best treated by modifying that system (Weakland, Fisch, Watzlawick, and Bodin, 1974). However, unlike communications family therapists, strategic therapists do not assume that the identified patient's symptoms are necessarily a crucial aspect of the family system; therefore, they do not believe that fundamental overhaul of the system is always required. This approach enables them to intervene briefly, attacking only those aspects of the system that appear to be directly involved in maintaining the symptoms. Instead of trying to remake families from the ground up, strategic therapists focus their attention on problem-maintaining sequences of behavior, with the aim of predicting and eventually modifying them. The MRI group in particular believe that minor changes in family systems are often sufficient to resolve problems and initiate progressive development.

Strategic therapists view the family as an interpersonal system analogous to other cybernetic systems. It is circular, rather than linear, with complex interlocking feedback mechanisms and patterns of behavior that are repeated in regular sequences which involve three or more persons. The ideas of circular causality and three (or more) person systems are emphasized particularly by Haley and Selvini Palazzoli. Haley (1976) stresses that a symptom is not a discrete (digital) "bit" of behavior, but is part of an ongoing (analogic) sequence; it has multiple referents, including relationships to the therapist as well as to other family members.

In a linear view of causality an event, B, must be caused by an antecedent event, A. If the last cookie disappears from the cookie jar, it's a safe bet that someone ate it. This linear model explains most physical and chemical actions, but it is less useful for explaining social behavior. Strategic therapists use a circular model for explaining interpersonal events, and focus their attention on repeating sequences of behavior. From this perspective, symptoms are not caused (linearly) by any specific event, but are maintained as part of a vicious circle of interaction. Strategic therapists therefore attempt to resolve symptoms by interdicting these circular patterns, and by creating new behavior patterns in place of the old vicious circles.

If Mrs. Smith's drinking bouts seem to follow her husband's beating her, strategic therapists do not infer that the beating *causes* the drinking—or vice versa. Instead, beating and drinking are seen as reciprocal moves in a destructive family game. This leaves strategic therapists free to interrupt the sequence at the point most amenable to change. In this case the therapist might tell the couple that the beatings are a natural way for a husband to keep his wife in line. This ridiculous statement might enrage the wife enough so that she fights back instead of withdrawing into alcoholism.

Strategic therapists are also less concerned with the etiology of problems than with what maintains them. Regardless of how they get started, most psychological problems persist only if they are maintained by the current behavior of patients and by their interactions with others. Strategic therapists attempt to discover and alter this problem-maintaining behavior. If the problem-maintaining behavior is changed, the problem will be resolved.

Problem-maintaining behavior can be described from monadic, dyadic, or triadic vantage points, depending upon how many people are seen as participating in the sequence. Although Rabkin and the MRI group frequently think in terms of monadic or dyadic cycles, most strategic therapists now focus on triadic problem-maintaining sequences. In fact, Lynn Hoffman (1981) considers the discovery of pathological triads to be one of the foundations of family therapy.

It was Murray Bowen (1966) who first described the triangle as the basic building block of family systems. As soon as tension develops between two members of a triangle, one of them moves toward the third. Triangling in the third person stabilizes the relationship, but often prevents resolution of conflict in the dyad.

Gerald Zuk (1971) also emphasized triadic relationships as critical for understanding and treating families. Minuchin likewise considers triangles, especially those involving a coalition between a parent and child, as a central fact of family structure, and uses the triad as the basis for strategies of intervention (Minuchin, 1974). Minuchin found that triangles involving a split between parents are particularly common among enmeshed families. Treatment in these cases is designed to break up the cross-generational coalitions and solidify the barrier between generations. Haley exemplifies the transition from a dyadic point of view (Haley, 1963) to a triadic one (Haley, 1976). When he wrote *Strategies of Psychotherapy*, he broadened the description of problems from one person to include their function in the interaction between two people. By the time he wrote *Problem-Solving Therapy* (Haley, 1976), he had incorporated ideas from Bowen and Minuchin, and emphasized that behavior could best be understood as a product of interactions involving three or more people.

The trick, says Haley, is to recognize that sequences of behavior may be more complex than they first appear. For example, a child's misbehavior may readily be recognized as having something to do with the child's interaction with his mother. But this dyadic point of view is incomplete, because the mother's behavior is in turn influenced by her husband's as well as her child's actions.

Haley described (1976) the following sequence as typical:

1. Father becomes unhappy and withdraws.
2. Child misbehaves.
3. Mother doesn't deal effectively with the child.
4. Father gets involved, with mother and child.
5. Child behaves.
6. Mother becomes more effective; expects more from father and from child.
7. Father becomes unhappy and withdraws.

The repetitive cycle involves not just the intrapsychic problems of a child, nor even the interaction between the child and his mother. Instead, as Haley emphasizes, from a systems point of view behavior needs to be understood as a function of at least three persons.

Even couples' problems should be understood as triangular rather than dyadic, according to Haley. A married couple doesn't form a totally independent relationship. Instead, the marital dyad is stabilized by a third person. This third leg of the triangle may be a parent, child, friend, or even therapist. A husband and wife who don't get along well may maintain the stability of their relationship by shifting their focus of concern to a child. If the couple enters treatment, the therapist may replace the child in stabilizing the relationship. This frees the child from a destructive triangle, but the solution is temporary unless the therapist helps the couple modify the pattern.

Like Haley, Selvini Palazzoli and her colleagues think in terms of triadic sequences. Their theoretical base is general systems theory and cybernetics. Rather than trying to discover "causes" of problem behavior, they think of families as involved in a game which serves to maintain the homeostasis of the system. They observe the pragmatic effect of various moves and countermoves, all of which are seen as working in the service of the game and its perpetuation.

Steve de Shazer (1975) describes triads consisting of two allies and an isolate, or "odd man out," as typical of families disturbed enough to seek treatment. Since these alliances are usually covert, treatment strategies are generally direct, in order to bring them out into the open, relabel, or unbalance them. Most strategic therapists do not believe that describing covert patterns to the family is enough to initiate change. Instead, they attempt to create novel situations in which the family spontaneously behaves differently.

According to general systems theory, living systems are characterized by a dynamic tension between homeostasis and change. That is, they operate to maintain a pattern of stability, but also are able to grow and adapt. Pathological families are systems in which homeostasis begins to take precedence over change and transformation.

Relentlessly playing out an habitual game to maintain a fixed homeostasis is exactly what gets families into trouble. Families who develop problems are those who don't modify their behavior to fit changing circumstances. Instead of adapting themselves to change, they continue to follow rigid sequences which are no longer functional. Since these outmoded patterns of behavior were once functional, however, families do cling tenaciously to them and resist change. Pathological families sustain their rigid homeostasis through an elaborate set of paradoxes. Families are thus self-regulating systems caught up in destructive games; the family members are the players who cannot change the rules. Furthermore, they tend to resist any outside efforts to get them to modify the rules of a system that they are dependent upon for survival. The more disturbed the family, the more energy they spend maintaining the status quo.

Watzlawick, Weakland, and Fisch (1974) cite mathematical group theory and the theory of logical types to explain two kinds of change: change which occurs within a system that itself remains unchanged; and change which alters the system itself. The former, internal reshuffling, they call *first-order change;* and the second, systemic alteration, they call *second-order change.* In an earlier work (Watzlawick, Beavin, and Jackson, 1967) they called a system limited to internal change without any alteration of the system's structure a "game without end."

The difference between first- and second-order change can be illustrated by a nightmare. As long as the dreamer remains asleep, he or she may attempt to escape danger by dreaming of running away or fighting. These are first-order changes. But if the dreamer surmounts the context of the nightmare by waking up, second-order change is achieved. Families tend to limit themselves to first-order changes when they are trying to resolve their difficulties. Parents of a clinging, dependent child, for instance, may switch from telling the child to stay home to telling the child to go out and play as a way to foster independence; however, this first-order change doesn't alter the basic functioning of a system in which directive parents dictate to a dependent child.

In the face of extreme resistance to change and paradoxical transactions, strategic therapists try to induce change by using therapeutic counter-paradoxes. According to Rohrbaugh and his colleagues (Rohrbaugh, *et al.*, 1977), these strategies take one of three forms: *prescribing, restraining,* and *repositioning.*

In *prescribing strategies,* the therapist instructs the patient to engage in the behavior that is to be eliminated. Examples include practicing an obsessional thought, trying to bring on a headache, and encouraging a rebellious adolescent to rebel. *Restraining strategies* discourage or even deny the possibility of change. For example, the therapist might tell a patient to go slow, or warn the patient of the dangers of giving up his or her symptoms. *Positioning strategies* accept and exaggerate a patient's negativistic stance. If the patient says that things don't look so good, the therapist responds that they look hopeless.

NORMAL FAMILY DEVELOPMENT

John Weakland (1976) quotes a therapist as telling a patient, "Neither you nor I need to explain what is normal." The point of this remark is that pragmatic clinicians are always more concerned with pathology and change than with normality and theory. In Don Jackson's (1967, p. 28) "The Myth of Normality," he expressed skepticism about the existence of the normal family: "As a student of the family for many years, I think it is safe to say that there is no such thing as a normal family any more than there is a normal individual." His point was that there is no one model of health or normality, and therefore he suggested that we replace the concept of normality with the word, conventional.

Strategic therapists do not write much about normal family development, but they do discuss how normal families are able to avoid developing symptoms. Normal families are able to adjust their functioning to meet the demands of changing circumstances. They are able to modify their interactions to accommodate to everyday difficulties and to transitional points of development (Weakland, *et al.*, 1974).

Successful families are also able to avoid creating serious problems out of everyday difficulties. They take action when necessary, but avoid the kind of utopian thinking that makes people try to change things that don't need changing—such as the "generation gap."

Normal families are thought to be organized hierarchically, according to generations. Haley in particular (Haley, 1976) adopts this structuralist point of view; he maintains that normal families respect generational boundaries and avoid covert, cross-generational coalitions. Other strategic therapists stress the need for open acknowledgement of family alliances (Selvini Palazzoli, *et al.*, 1978), but do not emphasize family hierarchy and structure as Haley does.

Relationships in normal families can be complementary or symmetrical; they are understood and accepted as such. This is in contrast to the tendency of pathological families not to accept either alternative. The crux of the difference between normal and pathological families is that normal families tolerate and admit differences, alliances, and even power struggles; pathological families, on the contrary, conceal and mystify any circumstance that runs counter to prevailing family myths. This is thought to be particularly true in schizophrenic families, where relationships are always either pseudocomplementary or pseudosymmetrical (Selvini Palazolli, *et al.*, 1978).

In an attempt to shed more light on the elusive concept of normality, in the 1970s Jules Riskin began studying what he calls "non-labeled" families. One of his findings is that non-labeled families seem to display no scapegoating and do not believe that when something goes wrong someone must be blamed (Riskin and McCorkle, 1979). He also found that these families tend to change over time in the direction of increased affect, increased freedom to interrupt, greater spontaneity, and more sharing of information without being asked. There is, however, the possibility that these changes may be partly an artifact of the frequent interviews conducted by the researchers.

Riskin's data tend to confirm one of the central tenets of communications theory, namely that *rules* and *meta-rules* need to be clear in order to assure both stability and flexibility. In clinic families, therapists assume the task of setting and clarifying rules for homeostatic functioning and rules for change; in healthy families, the parents do this job. Such families acknowledge their problems, discuss the rules for solving them, and modify those rules when necessary in such a way as to prevent ordinary problems from paralyzing the family.

Strategic therapists have too healthy a respect for human diversity to say they can identify clearly the patterns of a normal family life. Normality is not simply the converse of abnormality; how to manage a family and rear children properly remains a mystery. Jay Haley, who has observed hundreds of families, says that family patterns are simply too varied for anyone to be able to adequately describe normal family functioning (Haley, 1976).

DEVELOPMENT OF BEHAVIOR DISORDERS

Strategic therapists address the development of behavior disorders from two perspectives, molar and molecular. The molar point of view applies to the general qualities of dysfunctional families; the molecular point of view explains how specific difficulties become problems through being mis-handled, and how these problems are maintained by attempts to solve them.

Families are described as systems; pathological families maintain an increasingly rigid adherence to homeostatic functioning. These families continue to operate in ways that worked in the past, but are no longer functional in changed circumstances. A young couple may have a successful open marriage built around a great deal of independence and freedom for both of them. They may be comfortable with separate careers, separate vacations, and even separate extramarital relationships. However, such extreme independence is not likely to remain functional for them once children are born and the couple becomes a family. If both parents continue to spend most of their time away from home, the children will not get the nurturance they need. If one spouse takes care of the children without increased support and commitment from the other, that caretaking parent will become emotionally overburdened.

Virtually all observed behavior is structured and maintained primarily by current communicative interaction within an ongoing system of social relationships (Weakland, 1976). Abnormal families are caught in rigid repetitive sequences that permit only a narrow range of behavior. Their inflexibility limits the diversity of their responses. Symptomatic families develop problems because they are not able to adapt to altered circum-stances. They are particularly likely to get stuck at transitional points in the life cycle. Haley (1980), for example, points out the enormous difficulty parents in schizophrenic families have in letting their children leave home.

Symptoms are understood in terms of the context in which they occur and the functions they serve. In disturbed families, symptoms function as homeostatic mechanisms that regulate family life. For example, a couple with little mutual feeling left other than animosity may unite and remain together out of concern for a disturbed child. In this case, the child's disturbance is necessary to preserve the stability of the family.

Another general characteristic of pathological families is inadequate hierarchical organization. According to Haley (1976), functional families are organized hierarchically by generations. If status in the hierarchy is unclear, there will be a struggle to define roles. A child's temper tantrums are symptomatic of an unclear hierarchy. If a child gets what he or she wants by screaming and yelling, then the family is one in which the parents don't insist on executive decision making.

Some families appear to be organized hierarchically, but covert coalitions between children and one of the parents undermine the unity of the parental team (Selvini Palazzoli, *et al.*, 1978). These cross-generational coalitions are liable to cause problems, especially if they are unrecognized. The more covert the coalition, the more serious the symptoms (Hoffman, 1976).

When one of the children in a family has a problem, one parent is usually more concerned and involved. Haley emphasizes the destructive nature of such cross-generational coalitions, and describes various ways of breaking up these unhealthy alignments. The therapist can disrupt the intense parent-child dyad by encouraging even more overinvolvement in the hope that the parent will retreat (Haley, 1963). Alternately, the therapist can focus on the parental dyad, tease out their differences, and help them to resolve their latent conflict (Haley, 1976). In this way, the therapist replaces the child in the triangle. A third alternative is for the therapist to enter by focusing on the peripheral parent's relation to the child, giving that parent a pleasant task to do with the child or putting that parent in charge of disciplining the child.

A chronic problem of abnormal families is that they are rigidly organized, although many do not have a clear hierarchical arrangement. Acute problems develop when they fail to modify their functioning in response to feedback. Families are systems with regular patterns of interaction and corrective feedback. Like all systems, families have rules for how they function. If there is a break in the rules, feedback will be initiated to re-establish the status quo. Every behavior is a communication which stimulates feedback in the form of another communication.

It follows that if a family member behaves symptomatically, this behavior is supported by responses from the other family members that maintain the pathology in order to maintain the rules which preserve homeostasis. Without a change in the rules, the symptoms persist. From this point of view, asking, "What is wrong with this patient?" is unproductive. A more relevant question is, "What is going on in this sysem of interaction that maintains the problem?" (Weakland, 1976).

Mental health professionals are as likely to be part of the problem as part of the solution (Stanton and Schwartz, 1954). By assuming a hierarchical position of leadership and unwittingly taking over for the parents, clinicians put the parents down and confirm their sense of incompetence. They exacerbate existing problems by labeling them pejoratively. Identifying problems is necessary, but giving them diagnostic labels often makes things worse. "Depression" is more difficult to resolve than "laziness," and "schizophrenia" is more difficult to change than "difficulty in holding a job" (Madanes, 1981).

Misguided attempts to solve existing problems are the immediate cause of symptomatic behavior, according to Watzlawick, Weakland, and Fisch (1974). Unfortunately, the symptoms only make things worse: usually families respond to symptoms by redoubling the efforts that produced them in the first place. This results in fighting fire with fuel. Parents who are "sympathetic and understanding" enough to let a sixteen-year-old drop out of school are likely to be even more sympathetic and understanding if he begins to sleep late and mope around the house all day. Thus the symptom is maintained by attempts to solve it—the "solution" *is* the problem.

Rigidly-organized families, especially those with unclear hierarchies, have difficulty responding to changing life circumstances. Even normal families are stressed by transitional events like marriage, birth, adolescence, and death, but they are able to weather these storms without undue strain because they are able to adapt to change. Pathological families respond to problems with solutions that only make things worse. This is the general framework that strategic therapists use to explain behavior disorders.

Since strategists are somewhat less prone than others to generalize, they treat each case as unique. Therefore, to obtain a more detailed understanding of the strategic conception of development of symptoms it's helpful to read case study analyses. The following example is taken from Lynn Hoffman (1981, p. 326).

I treated one family with a boy who had always had trouble in school. He was a likable, spirited seventeen-year-old, but since his early years his mother had engaged in endless battles with him over his school work. He was not doing well during his senior year at a demanding prep school, and had been caught cheating in writing a paper. The boy's anxieties were centered mainly on academic achievement, and psychological tests revealed that he was very nervous about doing anything without exact instructions. The parents were in the process of finding a less demanding and more relaxed school, but the school psychologist had recommended family therapy because the boy's problems were "emotional."

A look at the family showed many strengths. Boy and parents were quite capable of coping with the problem of finding another school. It was hard to understand why, in this family where nonconforming brightness and originality were prized as well as conventional abilities, the son was having such a problem. He seemed like a person who did not have an academic bent but would undoubtedly find his own level of achievement if not pressured. The one who seemed to feel that pressure was necessary was, of course, the mother. There was some hint that the boy, who seemed to be repeating his artistic father's own early school difficulties, reflected the mother's disappointment with her husband, especially his choice of an artistic career, with all the financial problems that implied. But the couple's fondness for each other seemed much too genuine to require such a serious problem to keep their relationship going.

When we went back to the past, the mother disclosed that her own mother was a hard driving perfectionist who had always made this eldest daughter the living proof of her own success. As a little girl, the mother had had to be more brilliant, more responsible, more handsome, more successful, than any other mother's little girl. She ended up with many resentful feelings about her mother, but did not outwardly rebel except in one respect: she chose for a husband a man who was an artist, not the banker or businessman her mother would have preferred. She continued to hold a high standard for herself and for everybody else in the family, especially her son.

It seemed that the only possible move would be to try to break the hold this perfectionistic grandmother still had over her striving daughter, which had made her try so hard to produce the perfect son. Of course the harder she tried, the more the boy resisted (possibly also out of an identification with his father), even though consciously he was doing what he could to live up to her expectations and feeling miserable when he failed.

The therapist told the mother that, in a curious way, she was still showing her mother how hard she was trying, and would always try, to be the best in every way: the best career woman, the best wife, and the best mother. This was the greatest sign of devotion she could possibly pay her mother: that she was still trying to please her at any cost. And this was why she had to continue to pressure her son to succeed: out of loyalty for this mother whose opinion she had long since thought she did not care about.

At the same time the boy was told that by presenting himself as an academic failure, which had been his father's problem, he was not only being loyal to his father but was in some way representing his mother's resistance to her own mother's perfectionism. In this family where there was a rule that failure must never be allowed, he was a kind of pioneer.

The aim of this intervention was to activate a recoil from the structures the mother did not realize she was laboring under; and to redefine the son's apparent disgrace as a way of helping the family, especially his father. The statement to the son would not have been sufficient if it had not been coupled with the mother-grandmother issue, making it hard for the mother to continue her effort to "perfect" her family without feeling that she was playing into the hands of her own deeply resented mother.

A number of changes followed this session. The father announced that he was quitting a poorly paid but stable job he had held for some years and going back into freelance work. His wife, although it obviously cost her something, backed him and said she was proud that he had the courage to leave a job that was unworthy of him. The boy was placed in a school that emphasized athletics, which he was good at, rather than scholarship.

This, then, is an example of a three-generation systemic intervention. We can see how forces coiled within the past can be used as a source of momentum for change in the present. History, used in this way, is no longer dead but alive, carrying within it the means for the destruction of the very patterns it predicted and sustained. This is the systemic use of the past, very different from the older view that to understand or "work through" emotions or attitudes or patterns that are no longer appropriate to the present will eliminate them. They would not be still in use if they were not, in some way, still appropriate.

GOALS OF THERAPY

One goal of all therapies is to solve the presenting problem; strategic family therapists focus singlemindedly on doing just that. Some strategists speak of the need for systems change in order to solve the presenting problem, but Haley is alone among them in suggesting that changing the structure of the family system is in itself an important goal (Haley, 1976). The other strategic therapists focus almost exclusively on symptom resolution, and some (Fisch, 1978) have even criticized Haley for stressing the need to change the family's underlying structure. The clinician's aim is to solve the presenting problem, not rearrange or improve the family. Nevertheless, they quietly hope that change will have a domino effect, improving the family's functioning.

In order to accomplish the primary goal of solving problems, strategic therapists work for mediate goals which include changing repetitive sequences supporting the problems (Selvini Palazzoli, *et al.*, 1978; Watzlawick, *et al.*, 1974); and changing the communicative behavior of family members so as to block symptomatic metaphors and permit more adaptive ones to emerge (Haley, 1976).

The emphasis on solving problems instead of changing families is based on a belief that families are more likely to be stuck than sick. Treatment is therefore designed to help people past a crisis and on to the next stage of development. The time when a young person is leaving home is a particularly vulnerable period (Haley, 1980). Strategic therapists focus on these transitional impasses in order to prevent the repetition of problematic sequences of interaction, and to introduce more complexity as well as new alternatives.

Strategic therapists stress the need to discover and modify the well-intentioned but counterproductive solutions that symptomatic families apply to their own difficulties. Once these mediating behaviors are changed, the primary goal, solving the presenting problem, can be accomplished.

CONDITIONS FOR BEHAVIOR CHANGE

Strategic therapy is pragmatic and symptom-focused. Its adherents are behaviorally-oriented practitioners who regard insight and understanding as neither necessary nor even relevant for solving problems. "Why" explanations may lead to lovely discussions of problems, but rarely to their solution. Asking why a problem has developed is not useful; asking what is being done to perpetuate the problem is. Haley (1976), for example, says that telling people what they're doing wrong doesn't help them change, it only mobilizes resistance. The same is true, Haley believes, of cathartic expression of feeling. He believes changes in behavior alter feelings and perceptions, rather than the other way around.

Strategic therapists focus on present, recurrent sequences of behavior, most explicitly on presenting problems. Although they may be interested in modifying family interactions that are responsible for maintaining symptoms, strategists believe that these problematic interactions are best observed while family members discuss the problems of the symptom bearer.

Tactical maneuvering is a major technique in strategic treatment; equally significant is the fact that these therapies emphasize social settings. Instead of segregating individuals, or viewing them in isolation as early behaviorists did, strategic therapists support individuals in their usual setting. Even with severely disturbed clients, social ties are reinforced instead of severed; the problem-solving approach is applied to persons in context of their primary social groups. Treatment strategies are designed to take the client's social network into account. If someone is hospitalized, the strategic therapist works with the hospital staff as well as the symptomatic person and his or her family (Haley, 1976).

Like all forms of treatment, strategic therapy is based on its way of conceptualizing problems. Problems, in this view, are considered to be maintained by repetitive sequences of interaction; consequently, change is sought by observing and then altering these sequences. Most strategic therapists (Watzlawick, *et al.*, 1974) don't believe that fundamental restructuring of families is necessary to solve their problems. Rather, they aim for a more modest goal of altering problematic sequences. These small but significant changes are thought to produce ripple effects which have a positive impact on family systems (Hoffman, 1976).

Strategic therapists believe that the way to change problem-maintaining sequences of behavior is by influencing the ways family members respond to one another because of the ways they must respond to the therapist. This is often accomplished using implicit or indirect means of influence. Selvini Palazzoli (Selvini Palazzoli, *et al.*, 1974), makes a point of accepting whatever patients have to offer and turning it to good use. Haley (1976) suggests that changes are best achieved in stages, rather than in one fell swoop. Therapists must first spot the sequence of interaction that maintains the problem. Often these sequences turn out to be longer and more complicated than is first apparent. Usually, they involve at least three persons.

Other strategic therapists emphasize the sudden shifts that sometimes produce dramatic changes in systems in one decisive movement. Rabkin (1977) calls this "saltology," or sudden change that may result when a fundamental rule of a system is changed. After the problematic sequence is observed, individualized strategies for change are designed so that they suit particular families.

Strategic therapists, like other action-oriented therapists, take direct responsibility for influencing their patients. They view therapy as a technical matter, requiring rational therapeutic expertise to solve problems. If things don't go well, strategic therapists don't blame the patients, they blame themselves (Selvini Palazzoli, *et al.*, 1978). Here they clearly follow a medical model: the patient brings a problem to the practitioner whose responsibility it is to solve the problem. The strategic therapists thus seek to maximize their power and influence in order to bring about desired changes.

In another way, however, strategists are far from the medical model. Physicians study and describe symptoms in order to define syndromes and discover their etiology. Discovering the cause of a disease is considered essential to finding its cure. In contrast, strategic therapists are not concerned with discovering origins; they wish to identify the factors involved in the organization and persistence of the problems. There is no starting point in an ongoing stream of interaction (Weakland, 1976), and so the linear model of cause and effect is inappropriate, and resolution is primarily a matter of interrupting vicious cycles of feedback.

In researching various examples of significant, but naturally occurring, change Watzlawick, Weakland, and Fisch (1974) found that decisive action was applied to the attempted solution, not to the difficulty itself. First-order change appears to be based on common sense ("more of the same") strategies, and second-order change often appears to be illogical. Therapeutic strategies generally don't follow common sense, because common sense solutions have usually been tried and have failed before people come to therapy (Rabkin, 1977). Therefore, the target of change in their treatment is the attempted solution to problems.

Haley (1976) lists three steps for altering problem-maintaining sequences. First, it is necessary to spot the sequence that maintains the problem. Second, a goal must be selected and agreed upon. Third, a solution, often involving a shift in labeling, is applied. "Reframing," as it is called (Watzlawick, Weakland, and Fisch, 1974), consists of changing the conceptual or emotional viewpoint in order to change the meaning without changing the facts. The situation doesn't change, but the interpretation does. For example, if parents are permitting a child to engage in anti-social behavior because the child is "crazy," a therapist who recognizes their behavior is maintaining the problem, may redefine the child's behavior as "bad."

According to Rabkin, isolating specific problems and setting clear goals is the *sine qua non* of strategic therapy. He believes that therapists should always formulate a diagnosis as a first step. Such diagnoses, he recommends, don't come from the A.P.A.'s statistical manual, but are based on an analysis of the problem and what is preventing its solution. He also suggests that therapists offer a formulation to their patients that names the problem and briefly explains it (Rabkin, 1977). Even though other strategic therapists may prefer to remain more mysterious and keep their ideas to themselves, they will all agree that a clear definition of problems is important, and so is keeping the focus of treatment on the presenting problem. Keeping the focus on symptoms keeps clients motivated.

Adequate motivation, a concern to all clinicians, is considered to be complex as well as critical by the strategic therapists. Because they are concerned with the social context of problem behavior, they must deal with motivation on several levels—within and between individuals, overt and covert, and on the level of compliance. Rabkin (1977) offers a number of practical suggestions to maximize patients' motivations for treatment. Patients who come in demoralized from their many failures, for instance, are given hope that the therapist will be able to help them, which makes them willing to try hard to follow his instructions.

Rabkin also deals with the problem of compliance, which concerns all strategic therapists. The problem with good advice is that people don't usually follow it. Strategic therapists therefore maneuver themselves into a position where patients will follow their suggestions. Rabkin (1977) suggests using "ordeals" and "prestige work" as ways to indirectly increase compliance. "If a patient works, travels, or suffers before getting to see the therapist or during the course of therapy, he will have a greater expectation of benefit than if things are made easy and accessible for him. The role of a pilgrimage in the search for a cure had long been recognized, especially in a religious context, as in the case of Lourdes. I understand that no permanent resident of the city of Lourdes has ever been helped there" (Rabkin, 1977, p. 170). Rabkin's point is that when patients have to make difficult sacrifices to be treated, their hopes are mobilized by the effort. The Milan group takes full advantage of this principle by scheduling sessions at long intervals and at great distances for their clients. Essentially this technique may be summed up as, "You really appreciate those things you have to work for."

"Prestige work" refers to convincing patients that therapists are effective. Ancient shamans used to bedeck themselves in fantastic ritual garments and perform feats of magic to demonstrate their powers. Modern psychotherapists dress casually or formally, depending on their clientele, but they cover their walls with diplomas that certify their competence. Some even resort to more elaborate gimmicks. There is an old joke about a lonely teenager who gets a phone call asking for a date. "Let me think," she says. Then she puts down the phone receiver and dances for joy. Returning to the phone, she assumes her most blasé tone of voice and says, "Well, yes, I guess I'm free." Psychotherapists employ a similar strategy when they look at an open appointment book and say, "Maybe I can squeeze you in next week."

The decisive technique is to give directives. Directives or tasks are designed for both inside and outside therapy sessions, and may be straightforward or paradoxical. In general, strategic therapists are less active in treatment sessions and much of the work is assigned for homework between sessions. Tasks are assigned on the basis of a belief that change is born of action, not understanding. Tasks are carefully designed to fit the case; they are assigned to be done between sessions to insure that what is begun in therapy sessions is generalized to the family's environment. Since problems are considered to be maintained by family interactions, most tasks are designed to involve the whole family. Since change requires action, often action that appears illogical, tasks are generally assigned without explanation or comment. Tasks are tools used to change family systems so that they will be able to manage their own problems.

Carlos Sluzki (1978, p. 378), provides an example. Sluzki was treating a couple who were locked in a relationship in which the wife's nagging, complaining negativism was complemented by the husband's appeasing optimism. Both of them agreed that she was the victimizer and he was the victim. Sluzki praised her for taking on the burden of being the villain, but added that making her husband good while she remained the "mean one" must have given her some satisfaction. But he said, there are no kicks like being the "good guy," and he selfishly monopolizes this role.

Then Sluzki assigned them the following task: He told the husband to respond to any of his wife's statements by being as pessimistic as possible, regardless of his true feelings. Sluzki then directed the wife to remain as pessimistic as always, "in order not to make the task more difficult for her husband."

The task served the following purposes: (1) the prescription acknowledged that he could be genuinely pessimistic; (2) her habitual behavior was being relabeled as a gesture of good will; (3) if they followed instructions, they would quite quickly reach a deadlock that would force her to extricate the positive side of the matter; (4) nobody—but the therapist perhaps —would be blamed for any escalation into pessimism between them, totally eliminating any label of victim and victimizer; and (5) they were being granted a humorous way out of confrontations, which they continued to use thereafter on occasions. In fact, both expressed a remarkable reduction of the conflicts and a general improvement in the relationship from then on, while Sluzki, correspondingly, expressed concern about their unexplainable and too dramatic change.

TECHNIQUES

Although strategic therapists do share both general strategies and specific techniques of treatment, various centers have evolved distinctive procedures. Strategic therapists usually see whole families, but not always. The MRI group will see individuals or couples, and may see only the parents of problem children if the parents prefer. Rabkin sees mostly individuals, as did the late Milton Erickson.

One principle that unites strategic therapists is the belief that common-sense solutions to problems rarely work. People caught up in the dysfunctional process of a system are unable to get far enough outside their context to see what is perpetuating the problem. Consequently their efforts to change are limited to doing more of the same. Strategic therapists are therefore convinced that insight and awareness are not useful for changing behavior. That is why they so frequently rely on therapeutic paradox. They assume resistance, see understanding as invariably useless, and expect clients to do whatever they are told *not* to do. For example, Watzlawick, Weakland, and Fisch (1974) describe a young couple who were bothered by their parents' tendency to treat them like children by doing everything for them. Despite the husband's adequate salary, the parents continued to send money and to lavish gifts on them, refuse to let them pay even part of a restaurant check, and so on. Watzlawick and his colleagues helped the couple solve their difficulty with their doting parents by having them use reverse psychology. Instead of trying to act more competent, the couple was told to act helpless and dependent, so much so, that the parents got disgusted and finally backed off. This approach was clever and successful; but the therapists seem to assume beforehand that having the couple explain to their parents that they wanted more independence wouldn't work, and so they went directly to a paradoxical maneuver.

The strategic therapist asks about the problem, finds out what solution is being tried, and then reverses it. After initial greetings and explanations, the therapist inquires directly about the problem that has made the family come for help. Families are asked to describe the problem in concrete and detailed terms. After everyone present has had a chance to talk, goals are set and clarified. The therapist accepts what the family offers and maintains focus on the presenting complaint. By avoiding confrontations or explanations, strategic therapists hope to minimize resistance. The major techniques for solving problems are assigning tasks and giving directives, many of which are paradoxical and most of which are carried out between sessions.

Most strategic therapists work with a team of observers. Both during and after sessions, therapists and observers meet to analyze the family's behavior and to carefully plan strategies of intervention.

Paradoxical instructions (Erickson, in Haley, 1967, 1973; Frankl, 1960; Haley, 1973, 1976; Hare-Mustin, 1975; Watzlawick, Weakland, and Fisch,

1974) generally appear absurd, often taking the form of prescribing the symptom. What follows is a contest for control between the therapist and the family. Either the symptom does occur, but under the therapist's direction, or it doesn't occur. To win, the family must change.

Within this general framework, various strategic therapists practice their own unique methods of therapy. In the following section, I will describe the approaches of the Brief Therapy Center group at MRI, Jay Haley, and Mara Selvini Palazzoli.

The MRI group. Members of MRI's Brief Therapy Center follow a six step treatment procedure:

1. Introduction to the treatment set-up.
2. Inquiry and definition of the problem.
3. Estimation of the behavior maintaining the problem.
4. Setting goals for treatment.
5. Selecting and making behavioral interventions.
6. Termination.

Patients are accepted for treatment with no prior screening. If there is an opening when a prospective client calls, the secretary schedules an appointment. If there isn't an immediate opening, the person is referred elsewhere. Upon arrival patients fill out a form covering basic demographic data. Next, therapists explain that sessions are recorded and observed, and point out the advantages of having several professionals involved in the case. Therapists also explain that treatment is conducted within a maximum of ten sessions, thereby setting up a powerful expectation of change.

Once the preliminaries are concluded, therapists ask for a clear and specific definition of the major problem. The MRI group share the general opinion (Sifneos, 1979) that patients must be able to define a single major problem in order for brief psychotherapy to succeed. Those patients who cite more than one problem are asked to choose the most important one. If more than one person is involved, each is asked for an opinion.

When a problem is stated in vague terms, such as "We just don't seem to get along," or in terms of presumptive causes, "Dad's job is making him depressed," the therapist helps translate it into a clear and concrete goal.

Because they believe that problems persist only when reinforced in social interaction, the brief therapists pay particular attention to what people do to perpetuate their problems. They start by asking what the patient or family has done to try to correct what is wrong. Often this reveals precisely what has made things worse. For example, the husband who nags at his wife to spend more time with him may succeed only in driving her further away; the parents who sit down and have long talks with their son who fights with his little sister may be reinforcing the fighting with their attention; or the husband who does everything his wife asks to reassure her of his love may feel so resentful that he begins to hate her.

In general, the solutions that tend to perpetuate or exacerbate problems fall into one of three categories:

1. The solution is simply to deny that a problem exists; action is necessary, but is not taken. A fearful child, for instance, avoids going to school, and the parents do nothing, believing that it's "just a phase."

2. The solution is an effort to solve something which isn't really a problem; action is taken when it shouldn't be. For example, parents severely punish a child for masturbating.

3. The solution is an effort to solve a problem within a framework that makes a solution impossible; action is taken, but at the wrong level. Parents try hard, for instance, to motivate a child to do something that the child doesn't yet know how to do (Watzlawick, Weakland, and Fisch, 1974).

When problem-maintaining behavior involves subtle, nonverbal acts, or complicated sequences that include several people, the inquiry is more protracted and detailed. The relevant clues may be disclosed not so much by what people say, as by how they say it, or by who says what to whom. For example, a man's depression may be aggravated by a complicated sequence involving his wife and son. Wishing for more affection from his wife, the man acts gloomy, hoping this will make her more sympathetic. Instead, she criticizes him for moping around, which causes the son to reprove her for not being more understanding. This makes her angry and she withdraws further from the husband, who mopes around even more—and so on. Both his wife and son are trying to help, she by cheering him up, he by telling her to be more sympathetic, but their "help" only makes matters worse. In this case, the therapist provoked the son to criticize the father ("for his own good"), which brought the wife to her husband's defense, and the couple's increased closeness resolved the depression.

Weakland and his colleagues believe that by negotiating very specific and concrete goals, they will motivate clients to change, and they will also give the client a way to evaluate success. Since treatment is brief, they ask the client to state the minimum changes he or she would regard as indicating progress. Vague or overly ambitious goals are redefined to more realistic levels in order to maximize the chances of success.

Once a goal is agreed upon, and the therapists perceive what is maintaining the problem, they design a specific strategy of intervention to block the symptom-maintaining behavior. They often begin by making what appear to be interpretations; actually these statements are devices for "reframing" problems (Watzlawick, *et al.*, 1974) rather than attempts to convey insight. The reframing statements may or may not be "true;" they are not meant to educate but to alter the way family members interact, by changing the meaning attributed to a set of facts. The situation doesn't change, but its interpretation does. If a teenager is refusing to do his chores, reframing this behavior as "striving for independence" rather than rebellion may lead his parents to nag less.

Every attempt is made to fit interventions to the family's specific characteristics in order to make them more palatable. If patients are rebellious or argumentative, directives may be given with the hope that the patients *won't* follow them, but will do something else instead. (Resistance is not—should not be—assumed, but is gauged by reactions to initial interventions.) Directives are also phrased in language that suits the family—behavior to be discouraged may be described to a middle class family as "uncouth," to a working class family as "gross."

The brief therapists give their instructions in a low-keyed, offhanded way. By minimizing the significance of their injunctions they hope to catch patients off guard and to circumvent their usual habit of resisting advice. They suggest change rather than ordering it. And if patients still seem reluctant they back off even further, and suggest that the request may be premature: maybe the patient "isn't ready yet."

Directives are designed to encourage small steps toward desired changes, so that they are more likely to be carried out. Usually the directives are presented as homework to be carried out between sessions.

Paradoxical instructions are a decisive part of the treatment package at the Brief Therapy Center. Typically, they take the form of prescribing symptoms. For example, in one family, the mother forgave her son's frequent misbehavior by explaining that "it's all the result of psychological problems." Accordingly, he was told to misbehave more during the coming week, and his mother was to forgive him "with even more understanding." When such a therapeutic double-bind is given, patients can comply and thus accept the therapists's control, or rebel, in which case the problem improves.

Since most patients have already been exhorted to change many times, they tend to be expert at defeating or ignoring common sense suggestions. Therefore, instead of trying to counter resistance to change, the brief therapists accept it and turn it to good advantage. Instead of saying, "Why don't you change," they are liable to say. "How could you possibly change?" When such paradoxical statements produce progress, they continue the strategy by warning patients to "Go slow," and when there is improvement, they worry out loud that "Things may be moving too fast." These paradoxical cautions are designed to promote rapid change by provoking patients to disprove the therapist's pessimism. In a similar manner, relapses are often prescribed following successful improvement.

The brief therapists make use of observers to fortify their assaults on resistant clients. If a patient consistently disagrees with the therapist, one of the observers may enter and criticize the therapist's lack of understanding, in order to form an alliance with the patient. This puts the observer in a powerful position to offer directives that the patient will accept. Sometimes patients who are skeptical about the therapist's opinion are convinced if they hear that all of the observers concur with the therapist.

Termination is varied to suit the style of the patient, and generally involves a continuation of the stance taken in treatment. With defiant clients, the team may minimize any gains and express skepticism about any future progress. Compliant patients are congratulated for the changes they achieved, and told that they will probably continue to improve. Sometimes patients who have made progress are still insecure, and dread the thought of termination. This situation is handled by "terminating without termination." The therapist says that he thinks treatment was successful but can't be sure; since "only time will tell," he or she proposes they halt treatment, but offers to resume the remainder of the ten sessions if the patient runs into problems.

Jay Haley. Since his classic work, *Strategies of Psychotherapy* (Haley, 1963), much of Haley's writings have been analyses of other people's theories and methods of therapy. Recently, however, he has delineated his own approach to treatment, evolved over two decades (Haley, 1976, 1980). These recent works show the influence of a variety of sources, especially Bateson, Erickson, and Minuchin. What he has evolved is a strategic technical approach, built on an appreciation for family structure and hierarchy.

As far as family dynamics are concerned, Haley takes a structural point of view; he thinks families are organized hierarchically, with the marital couple as the most significant subsystem and triads as the smallest conceptual unit. When it comes to technique, he develops imaginative strategic solutions. His procedure is extremely flexible; he will vary even the duration of sessions, the place of the meetings, and his fees. However, within this variability, there are consistent themes that characterize his general approach.

Haley strongly recommends that therapists work alone, rather than with cotherapists. Working alone, he says (Haley, 1976), enables therapists to move more decisively. A single therapist is able to develop ideas and implement them immediately, without having to wait for agreement with a colleague. He does, however, advocate the use of observers behind one-way mirrors who can consult with the therapist if necessary.

Haley believes that if therapy is to end well, it must begin properly. Therefore he devotes a good deal of time and attention to the opening moves of treatment. Regardless of who is presented as the official patient, Haley begins by interviewing the entire family. His approach to this initial interview is pragmatic and regularly follows four stages: a social stage, a problem stage, an interaction stage, and finally a goal-setting stage.

Families tend to be more ill-at-ease and uncertain than individual patients. Most families don't think there is anything wrong with them, and they may be unwilling or unprepared to accept a therapist's authority and direction. Therefore, Haley makes an effort to help families relax, easing them into what might be an awkward first session. He makes a point of greeting every single member of the family and trying to make each one comfortable. He acts as though he were a host, making sure that all his guests feel welcome. While he is making small talk, Haley observes how each family member behaves and how they all interact.

After this brief social stage, Haley gets right down to business in the problem stage. Before asking for the family's position, he clarifies his own; he introduces himself, repeats what he knows about the family, and explains why he has asked the entire family to come—that is, because he wants to get everyone's ideas and opinions.

One of Haley's abiding concerns is interpersonal power, and he begins jockeying for position right away. As the family enters, he studies their interactions to learn how power is distributed in the system. He notes who is dominant and who is submissive, who is aggressive and who is defensive. He also pays careful attention to how family members relate to him. Usually someone tries to engage the therapist on his or her side, but Haley cautions against being drawn into lasting coalitions with any single family member.

Haley's clear and practical suggestions even address such specific questions as whom to speak to first. Since mothers are usually more central and fathers less involved, the therapist should speak first to the father in order to increase his concern and involvement. This suggestion nicely illustrates Haley's strategic maneuvering, which begins with the first contact and characterizes the course of all subsequent meetings.

Haley speaks directly about the problem and what is to be done about it. He listens carefully to the way that the family defines the problem, making certain to give each person a chance to speak. Until he has heard from all present, he discourages interruptions or discussions. At this point he is more interested in what each person thinks about the problem than in the way they interact.

During this phase of the interview he observes how the family reacts, but does not comment, preferring to file away his observations to guide later interventions. After speaking to each family member, he notices disagreements and conflicts, and redefines what is described as one person's problem to be the problem of several others. For example, the mother may state that the problem is her son, who won't behave; however, as Haley listens to all of the family members, he may see that mother and father don't agree on how to set and enforce rules for their son, and that the other siblings exclude him from their activities. In this way, he reconceptualizes the problem as a systems problem, not merely a problem inside the son.

Once everyone has had a chance to talk, Haley encourages them to discuss their various points of view among themselves. In this, the interaction stage, Haley remains in charge, but in a way that is less obvious, so that the family can relate freely enough to reveal their typical interactional patterns.

As the members of the family talk with each other, Haley observes how the family is organized. Who sides with whom? Who has the most power, and who has the least? Do the parents function as a unit, or does one undercut the other? Haley stresses that most of these questions can best be answered by observing what happens while they are talking with each other, not to him. Little of a family's organization will be revealed if the therapist permits family members to direct all of their comments to him or her.

Haley believes that conducting interviews in this manner not only provides a good deal of information, but also begins the process of change. By focusing on problems and desired changes, a therapist conveys the impression that treatment will be designed to solve problems, not just promote "understanding" or "communication."

Sometimes Haley ends the first session by directing the family to carry out a task. In subsequent sessions directives play a central role in problem-solving therapy. Haley argues that all therapists use directives, wittingly or unwittingly. Just the simple act of reflecting feelings conveys the idea that the therapist is interested in feelings and would like the patient to talk more about them. Even by pointing out that a patient is trying to get the therapist to tell him or her what to do is implicitly directing the patient how to behave. Haley's argument is like Wolpe's (1958) who as a behaviorist points out that all therapy is behavioral, whether the therapist realizes it or not.

Haley says the question is not whether to use directives, but how to use them effectively.

Effective directives are not in the form of simple advice. Advice is rarely helpful, unless patients happen to be ignorant of some piece of information, or unless their problems are minor. As Haley says, advice generally doesn't help because people don't have rational control over what they do.

To design an effective directive, the therapist has to learn what solutions have already been tried and failed. Asking families what they've tried that hasn't worked not only gains information, but also underscores the fact that they haven't been successful and so need the therapist's help. To persuade family members to do a task, they must be convinced that each one will gain something by complying. If the task seems to be one where some win and some lose, it probably won't be carried out. For example, if a husband and wife argue about his not helping out around the house, a good task might be to have him begin doing the dishes. Explaining that by doing the task she'll get some help, and he'll be able to escape the constant arguing will motivate them both to comply.

The following two tasks taken from Haley's *Problem-Solving Therapy* illustrate how he uses them. A couple who were out of the habit of being affectionate with each other were told to behave affectionately in order to "teach their child" how to show affection. In another case, a mother who was unable to control her twelve-year-old son had decided to send him away to military school. Haley suggested that since the boy had no idea how tough his life would be at military school, it would be a good idea for the mother to help prepare him. They both agreed. Haley directed her to teach him how to stand at attention, be polite, and wake up early every morning to make his bed. The two of them followed these instructions as if playing a game, with mother as sergeant and son as private. But after two weeks the son was behaving so well that his mother no longer felt it necessary to send him away.

These were tasks that Haley hoped the family would comply with. He also gives paradoxical directives that are designed to help families change by rebelling against instructions. When they are in a crisis families are so unstable and upset that they are more liable to follow directives that require change than when they are not in crisis. Hence Haley finds paradoxical directives most useful with families who are relatively stable, and thus will not follow instructions.

Many paradoxical directives take the form of telling family members that it might be better if they did not change. This reverse psychology is slightly insulting and challenges people to prove that they *can* change. Parents embroiled in discipline problems with a small child might be told that setting and enforcing rules will create problems for them, because if the child behaved the two of them wouldn't have anything else to talk about. Many couples respond by getting tough with the child and learning to enjoy each other's company in order to prove the therapist wrong.

If families do improve in spite of these restraining tactics, Haley may tell them that the change is only temporary and they'll soon revert to their old ways. This tends to ensure that they will continue to improve, to prove him wrong—and themselves capable.

Paradoxical interventions are designed to overpower resistance by forcing family members to rebel against the therapist's directives and thereby refuse to act out their symptoms. But many therapists are uncomfortable with this approach because they do not like its confrontational nature—to succeed the therapists must provoke defiance. Madanes (1981) uses *pretend techniques* which have a similar purpose, but a gentler style. Instead of creating tension and provoking rebellion, they bypass resistance by using a spirit of playfulness.

One strategy is to ask a symptomatic child to pretend to have the symptom, and encourage the parents to pretend to help. The child can now give up the actual symptom; pretending to have it is quite enough. A person cannot pretend to have a phobia or throw a tantrum, and have a real phobia or a real tantrum at the same time. Moreover, since the parents' concern is also a pretense, the whole situation is transformed from a deadly serious struggle to a playful, make-believe game. The following two case studies summarized from Madanes (1981) illustrate the pretend technique.

In the first case, a mother sought therapy because her 10-year-old son had night terrors. There were also two older daughters and a baby brother. Madanes suspected that the boy was concerned about his mother, who was poor, spoke little English, and had lost two husbands.

Since the boy had night terrors the therapist asked all the members of the family to describe their dreams. Only the mother and the son had nightmares. The mother's nightmare was that someone would break into the house, and the boy's was that he was being attacked by a witch. When Madanes asked what the mother did when the boy had nightmares, she said that she took him into her bed and told him to pray to God. She explained that she thought his nightmares were the work of the devil.

The treatment team's conjecture was that the boy's night terrors were both a metaphorical expression of the mother's fears, and an attempt to help her. As long as the boy was afraid, his mother had to be strong in order to help him; thus she could not be afraid herself. Unfortunately, while she tried to protect him, she frightened him further by talking about God and the devil. Both mother and child were helping each other in unproductive ways.

The family members were told to pretend that they were at home and mother was afraid that someone might break in. The son was asked to protect his mother. In this way the mother had to pretend to need the child's help instead of really needing it. At first the family had difficulty playing the scene because the mother would attack the make-believe thief before the son could help. Thus she communicated that she was capable of taking care of herself; she did not need the son's protection. After the scene was performed correctly, with the son attacking the thief, they all discussed the performance. The mother explained that it was difficult for her to play her part because she was a competent person who could defend herself. Madanes sent the family home with the task of repeating this dramatization every evening for a week. If the son started screaming during his sleep, his mother was to wake him up and play the scene again. They were told that this was important to do no matter how late it was or how tired they were. The son's night terrors completely disappeared.

In the second case, a mother sought psychiatric treatment for her 5-year-old son because he had uncontrollable temper tantrums. After talking with the family for a few minutes Madanes asked the son to pretend to have a tantrum to show her what it was like. The boy said, "Okay, I'm the Incredible Hulk!" He puffed out his chest, flexed his muscles, made a monstrous face, and started screaming and kicking the furniture. Madanes then asked the mother to do what she usually did in such circumstances. The mother responded by telling her son, in a weak and ineffective way, to calm down. She tried to pretend to send him to another room as she tried to do at home with little success. Next, Madanes asked the mother if the boy was doing a good job of pretending. She said that he was.

Madanes asked the boy to repeat the scene. This time he was Frankenstein and his trantrum was performed with a more rigid body posture and a face more appropriate to Frankenstein's monster. Then Madanes talked with the boy about the Incredible Hulk and Frankenstein and congratulated the mother for rearing such an imaginative child.

Following this discussion, mother and son were told to pretend that he was having a tantrum while she was walking him to his room. The boy was told to act like the Incredible Hulk and to make lots of noise. Then they were told to pretend to close the door and hug and kiss. Next Madanes instructed the mother to pretend that she was having a tantrum, and the boy was to hug and kiss her. Madanes instructed mother and son to perform both scenes every morning before school, and every afternoon when the boy came home. After every performance the mother was to give the boy milk and cookies if he did a good job. Thus the mother was moved from a helpless position to one of superiority in which she was in charge of rewarding his make-believe performance. The next week the mother called to say that they did not need to come for therapy because the boy was behaving very well and that his tantrums had ceased.

Haley's concern with family structure and hierarchy is reflected in the fact that he assigns tasks that affect, not only the presenting problem, but also the family's structure. An example from a case treated by Braulio Montalvo illustrates this point. The presenting problem in this case was a small child who lit a fire in the family's apartment while playing with matches. The structural problem in this family was that the mother was isolated from the child who was left to an older brother's supervision. In order to bring about a structural change while focusing on the problem Montalvo instructed the mother to spend a few minutes each day teaching the child the correct way to light matches. This made the child more competent with matches *and* brought her closer to her mother.

Haley describes problem behavior as occurring in the context of sequences of interaction among family members. Although clinicians—not to mention family members—may have a limited awareness of complex sequences, Haley stresses the importance of viewing problem behavior as part of a recurring chain of events. One of the most common sequences is where one parent sides with a child against the other parent. This pattern also illustrates a coalition across generational lines, which is characteristic of malfunctioning families.

1. One parent, usually the mother, has an intense relationship with the child. She attempts to deal with problems by alternately using affection and anger.
2. The child's symptoms worsen.
3. The mother calls upon the father for help.
4. Father steps in to deal with the child.
5. Mother—threatened by loss of her intense closeness with her child —criticizes father's handling of the situation.
6. Father withdraws—from his wife as well as the child.
7. Mother and child are once again enmeshed in the intense relationship that is the context for the child's symptoms.

Changing such a sequence, according to Haley, is best achieved by joining the system and altering it by participating in it. The therapist changes the way family members respond to each other because of the way they must respond to the therapist. He can, for instance, join different coalitions long enough to unbalance them and thus force the family members to regroup.

Haley recommends that dysfunctional family patterns be changed in stages. It is a mistake, he says, to think that families can go directly from an abnormal state to a normal one. The first step is to transform the system into a radically different format. From this antithesis, a synthesis can be developed. If a mother and child are intensely enmeshed, the first stage of change might be to put the father totally in charge. After that happens, it will be easier to guide the family to a more normal pattern where both parents share the responsibility of childrearing. When an overinvolved mother is separated from her child, she will need a new outlet for emotional gratification, and usually she will turn to her husband. This in turn frees the child to become more involved with peers.

Once change is initiated, Haley meets with the family a few more times to ensure that it is stabilized and that family structure is modified in a way that supports the change. After that is done he moves to terminate, making sure that the changes are supported by improved family functioning, so that there is no further need for the therapist.

Mara Selvini Palazzoli. Mara Selvini Palazzoli and her associates, Luigi Boscolo, Gianfranco Cecchin, and Guiliana Prata practice an imaginative form of strategic family therapy at the Institute for Family Study in Milan, Italy. Although they design unique solutions for every case, the team has developed a meticulous treatment strategy within which they practice their innovative tactics.

They always work with male-female cotherapy teams, observed by the other members of the group. (Recently, they have begun using solo therapists.) Sessions are held, on the average, once a month, and are generally limited to 10 for each case. Initially the monthly sessions were necessitated by the fact that many families traveled long distances to the center in Milan, and it was just too difficult for them to come more frequently; however, the long interval between sessions proved to be beneficial. The therapists found that paradoxical prescriptions seem to have a greater impact when they are followed over a long period of time, since when the rules by which a system functions are changed, it takes time for the system to adjust. When one family member begins to behave differently, the others must react, and then the changed person must react to their reactions. Weekly intervals between sessions may be too short for all these adjustments to occur; consequently after each session the team decides how long they will wait till the next one.

The average interval is a month, but it may vary from between two weeks to several months.

Treatment follows a fairly standard format. For all first sessions and most succeeding ones the unit of treatment is all family members living under the same roof. The cotherapists and observers meet before each session to read the chart and discuss the previous meeting. Sessions start with the family discussing their problems. These discussions elicit information and allow the therapists to observe the family's transactional style. At some point during every meeting, the therapists leave the treatment room to discuss the progress of the session with the observers. After this strategy conference, the therapists rejoin the family to make a brief comment and assign a task, which is usually a paradoxical prescription. The next visit is scheduled, and the family leaves; therapists and observers then meet again for a postsession discussion.

Selvini Palazzoli's approach to treatment is not just brief, but sudden. Instead of condensing a gradual approach into a brief time span, she aims to change families in sudden and decisive moves. These decisive blows are like surgery as opposed to medication.

Pathological interactions that maintain problem behavior are governed by fundamental rules. Once these rules are discovered and changed, problem behavior quickly disappears. Families are therefore like groups playing a game, and traditional therapy is like trying to change the players. Selvini Palazzoli believes that none of the players are able to change; what has to be changed are the rules of the game (Selvini Palazzoli, Boscolo, Cecchin, and Prata, 1978). That is what she designs therapy to do.

Like other strategic therapists (Rabkin, 1977; Watzlawick, *et al.*, 1974), Selvini Palazzoli begins maneuvering for leverage in the first telephone contact with new patients. She considers it essential to avoid compromising on certain basic preconditions for treatment, despite heroic efforts on the part of families to get her to do so. Thus, she resists making "emergency" appointments, or meeting with less than the whole family.

In order to understand Selvini Palazzoli's interventions it is first necessary to understand her view of families as engaged in destructive, but self-perpetuating games. To do so requires a radical shift from assuming linear causality to seeing circularity—a shift that is difficult to explain, and even more difficult to accomplish in practice.

Most of us, when we see someone behaving in a certain way or showing signs of emotion, assume this behavior manifests something about the person, or characterizes him or her. If Mr. Jones hangs his head and looks dejected, we assume that he is sad, and perhaps we try to find out why.

Selvini Palazzoli takes the position that it is more useful to understand all behavior as part of a sequence. She perceives Mr. Jones's appearance of sadness not as characterizing something within him, but as something he shows at this moment. Instead of commenting on his sadness or trying to understand why he is sad, she wants to know how his appearance of sadness affects others in the family. The emotion is seen not as a state in Mr. Jones, but as one move in a game in the family system.

Or, take a couple, where one spouse seems to be ready to leave, while the other appears dependent and clings to the marriage. It is a mistake to assume that these attitudes are psychic qualities inherent in the individuals. The two are accomplices in the same game. Each position defines the other, and their behaviors are reciprocal responses. Change, according to Selvini Palazzoli, must occur in their game, not in the two players.

Four fundamental principles operate in Selvini Palazzoli's approach to interviewing families: *hypothesizing, circularity, neutrality,* and *positive connotation* (Selvini Palazzoli, *et al.,* 1978). The first of these principles, *hypothesizing,* means actively thinking about the family before the first session begins. When therapists enter first sessions without seriously considering what they may discover, they tend to be passive information-gatherers. With individuals this is a handicap; with families it is deadly. Families have a set way of doing things and an entrenched view of the nature and cause of their problems. Unless some hypotheses are formulated in advance, therapists will tend to be indoctrinated into the family's official version of their situation.

To prevent this from happening, Selvini Palazzoli and her colleagues have presession planning conferences in which they develop hypotheses about what may be responsible for maintaining the family's problems. These hypotheses are formulated from the group's knowledge of families in general, as well as whatever specific information they have about that particular family. If a youngster has suddenly developed symptoms at home, the group may speculate that the symptoms are a way of preserving the family cohesion, which is threatened by the loss of one of its members.

Once the group develops a hypothesis, the therapist has a point of view, and can actively look for information to confirm or disprove it. If the hypothesis proves correct, therapy proceeds from a clear understanding of the systemic factors underlying the problem. If the hypothesis proves incorrect, another is formulated and investigated, until the group is satisfied that they understand what is supporting the designated patient's symptoms.

Circularity means thinking in terms of relationships and interactions, not in terms of separate individuals. To help them develop a circular viewpoint, the therapists ask about relationships and interactions rather than about individuals and feelings. They will, for instance, routinely ask one person to describe and comment upon the relationship between two other family members; this third person can give a more objective description of the dyad than its members, and such descriptions also reveal the dynamics of the triad. If a child is asked to describe her parents' relationship, she is liable to disclose how she fits in. By saying, "Mommy and Daddy argue a lot, because he always comes home late," the child says something about the marriage and something about an intergenerational coalition.

Another device for revealing circular patterns is to ask family members to describe how they *react* to symptoms, rather than describe the symptoms themselves. Descriptions of symptoms are generally biased toward intrapsychic conceptions based on linear causality. Descriptions of reactions to the symptoms, on the other hand, reveal the circular dances performed by the members of the family.

Neutrality is also considered essential. Neutrality is not a vague moral precept; it refers to behavior, not disposition. Regardless of how they feel, the team members act to balance their support among all family members. By successively aligning with every segment of the family, the therapists end by seeming to be allied with everyone.

The fourth hallmark of the Milan group's approach is the use of *positive connotation*. Symptoms are considered adaptive, and so they are described as favorably as possible. Peculiar communications and strange behavior, as well as frankly symptomatic behavior, are positively attributed to the desire to preserve the cohesion of the family group; therapists describe all behavior this way, never taking sides, always stressing the positive in order to avoid resistance.

Selvini Palazzoli points out that if the team criticizes symptoms, they will then contradict themselves when they later paradoxically prescribe them. How can they prescribe behaviors they had already criticized? If they "accept" a symptom, they tend to express or imply cirticism of the behavior of other family members, tacitly blaming them for causing it, and thus defining the same family members as "good" and the others as "bad." They avoid this by describing all the family's behavior in a positive light.

Describing symptomatic, bizarre behavior positively is, of course, paradoxical; it leads the family to wonder why the cohesion of the group requires the presence of a disturbed member. Furthermore, when the therapists describe both the patient's symptoms and the associated behavior of other family members positively, they are explicitly linking all that goes on in the family system. By underlining and confirming the homeostatic function of the symptom and the others' behavior, the therapists stress the importance of the stability and cohesion of the group. Also, by approving instead of reproaching the system, its members, and its cohesion, the therapists avoid being rejected as threatening outsiders.

Paradoxical prescriptions are a regular feature of the group's technique. The prescriptions are designed with much attention to detail, always include every member of the family, and usually are given in the first session. This underscores the problem-solving nature of treatment, and permits an evaluation of the family's compliance.

Some of the prescriptions take the form of rituals. They engage the whole family in a series of actions which run counter to rigid family rules and myths, but without any overt comment or criticism by the therapists. For example, one family of four was thoroughly enmeshed with a large extended family; they were told to hold family discussions every other night after dinner. They were to lock the door, and each of the four family members had to speak for fifteen minutes about the family. Meanwhile, they were to redouble their allegiance and courtesy to the other members of the clan. Without explicitly challenging this family's exaggerated loyalty to the extended family, and its rule against differentiating from or criticizing them, this ritual helped to break the rigid adherence to that rule. By locking the door and sitting down together the family was forced to clear the field of grandparents, aunts, uncles, and cousins. Furthermore, the therapists had obliged them to talk about the family, which undercut the rule against discussing favorable and unfavorable feelings. By reminding the family to continue its respect for the clan, the therapists also obscured their intention to separate the family of four from their kinfolk.

In addition to such specific strategies, the Milan team also engages in a careful and consistent self-monitoring which is based on their understanding of systems. They consider themselves part of the family systems they work with, they regard negative feedback to treatment maneuvers as evidence that their strategies are misguided, or at least mistimed. Many therapists blame the family when something goes wrong in the course of treatment, and accuse it of "regression," "resistance," "acting out," and "scapegoating." The Milan team considers setbacks a valuable form of negative feedback, allowing them to recognize their errors. Every feedback is an output of the therapists' interventions, and is used as a guide to future interventions.

From beginning to end there is a gamelike quality to Selvini Palazzoli's approach to families. So impressed is she with the complexity of the pathological family's functioning that she makes every effort to avoid being drawn into declared combat, and also to avoid feeling discouraged or defeated when the family outwits her. She takes responsibility for the conduct of therapy, but she never completely accepts the responsibility for change. Instead she pursues her work with seriousness and dedication, but also with resignation that she can only do her best. This attitude as well as the remarkable cohesiveness of her team enables them all to persevere in very trying therapy with severely disturbed families without being defeated by setbacks.

EVALUATING THERAPY THEORY AND RESULTS

Strategic therapists have reported a number of clinical case studies demonstrating the effectiveness of their techniques (Hare-Mustin, 1975; Selvini Palazzoli, *et al.,* 1974; deShazer, 1975). Such reports illustrate their methods and provide anecdotal support for their efficacy. Watzlawick and his colleagues at the Brief Therapy Center have attempted a more systematic clinical evaluation of their results (Watzlawick, *et al.,* 1974). A cohort of all patients seen during the period of study had followup interviews approximately three months after their treatment was terminated. Interviewers asked the patients if their behavior had changed as planned, and whether their complaints were relieved. The interviewers also asked if the patients had sought additional treatment elsewhere, and, to check for possible symptom substitution, they asked if any new problems had developed. To minimize the possibility that patients might exaggerate the benefits of treatment to please their therapists, all interviews were conducted by members of the team who were not involved in treatment.

Outcomes were classified into three categories: complete relief; considerable but not complete relief; and little or no change. The total sample consisted of 97 cases, who were seen for an average of seven sessions. Thirty-nine (40 percent) were said to have achieved complete relief; 31 (32 percent) were said to have achieved considerable relief; and 27 (28 percent) were said to have made no change. In no cases where complaints were resolved was there any sign of symptom substitution.

Haley, who is interested in family structure as well as problem behavior, has said that evaluations should be based not just on the presence or absence of symptoms, but also on changes in the system (Haley, 1976). This point of view is consistent with the mainstream of thinking in the family therapy movement, but was sharply criticized by Richard Fisch, Director of the Brief Therapy Center at MRI. Fisch rebuked Haley for using what he considers a variant of the old psychoanalytic "iceberg" formulation—a symptom is merely a manifestation of a deeper, underlying disturbance, and unless the basic conflict is altered the symptom will reappear or be displaced (Fisch, 1978).

There are a few reports of the outcome of other family therapies that are based on, or similar to, the methods of strategic therapy. Langsley, Machotka, and Flomenhaft (1971) studied the effectiveness of their family crisis therapy, which is similar to the brief therapy model practiced at MRI. Patients who were seen as needing hospitalization were randomly assigned to either a psychiatric hospital or to crisis family therapy on an outpatient basis. Eighteen months later, the group who received family therapy had spent less than half the number of days in the hospital than the group who had previously been hospitalized. Furthermore the cost of treatment during this period was six times as high for the hospitalized group.

In another, very carefully controlled study, Alexander and Parsons found behaviorally-oriented family therapy to be more effective in treating a group of delinquents than a client-centered family approach, an eclectic-dynamic approach, or a no-treatment control group (Parsons and Alexander, 1973). Recidivism was cut in half by the systems approach, in contrast to the other three goups which did not differ significantly from each other. Furthermore, a three-year followup showed that the incidence of problems in the siblings was significantly lower for the family systems treatment. This work strongly supports strategic therapy because the treatment was adapted from the systems approach described by Haley and by Watzlawick.

Finally, Stanton has convincingly demonstrated the effectiveness of an approach combining Minuchin's structural approach with Haley's strategic one for treating drug addicts (Stanton and Todd, 1979). Stanton's approach, like Haley's, uses strategic techniques as tactics to augment an over-all strategy dictated by structural theory. The results of Stanton's study are particularly impressive, because family therapy resulted in twice as many days of abstinence from heroin than a methadone maintenance program.

Despite the indirect empirical support from these few studies, strategic family therapy remains a promising but unproven approach to treating psychologcal problems. The same lack of convincing research support, of course, applies to most therapies, except those behavioral ones developed and studied in academic settings. Meanwhile, clinical observation and anecdotal reports of effectiveness continue to generate a great deal of enthusiasm for the strategic models.

SUMMARY

With a background in communications and cybernetic systems theory, and influenced by Milton Erickson's therapeutic techniques, strategic therapists have developed a body of powerful procedures for treating psychological problems. Problems are explained in terms of behavioral sequences and their social context.

Strategic approaches vary somewhat in the specifics of theory and technique, but they share a problem-centered, pragmatic focus. Insight and understanding are eschewed in favor of directives which are designed to change the way family members relate to each other. Directives may be straightforward, but are more often paradoxical, reflecting the belief that effective solutions may appear illogical to those with problems.

Strategic therapists begin by setting specific goals and consistently focusing on the presenting problem throughout the course of treatment. They think that problems are exacerbated by the usual solutions people attempt, and therefore design therapeutic interventions to change the solutions. A premium is placed on careful observation of interactions, and most strategists work with a team of observers. They also take full responsibility for the outcome of therapy and generally adopt a directive stance.

Although there are now many strategic therapists, the most influential groups are the Brief Therapy Center group at MRI, Jay Haley and Cloe Madanes, and Mara Selvini Palazzoli. The MRI group emphasizes that problems are maintained by attempts to solve them, and they concentrate on interdicting these problem-maintaining solutions.

Jay Haley sees problems as maintained by recurrent sequences of interaction among family members, and so intervenes to change these sequences. Haley also sees family structure and hierarchy as important factors in family life, and believes that successful treatment requires structural change and the establishment of appropriate hierarchies, in addition to resolving presenting symptoms.

Selvini Palazzoli and her collaborators treat families as systems that are maintaining their cohesion and stability at the expense of one or more symptomatic members. Pathology is perpetuated by an overly rigid set of family rules. Their interventions, which usually take the form of written paradoxical directives, are designed to force changes in the rules.

The Milan Associates use of "positive connotation" is an important and original contribution which has influenced other members of the strategic school. Ascribing positive motives to families circumvents resistance which is mobilized when therapists blame and criticize. Addressing patients with respect and understanding of their ambivalence to change is an effective way to disarm their opposition to therapy—particularly when the therapists actually believe that their clients are doing the best they can.

Tactics to outwit resistance are the very essence of strategic therapy; they are both its greatest contribution and the object of the strongest criticism. Paradoxical strategies are a form of indirection that automatically assumes great resistance to change. No doubt, many people do seek professional treatment only after failing to resolve their problems with commonsense approaches; but reflexly rejecting straightforward solutions is almost an article of faith among strategic therapists. It is a stance which is sometimes not necessary. When families come to therapy with high motivation and low resistance, there is no need to resort to paradox. It may be true that insight and reason will not solve entrenched family problems, but many families *will* respond to straightforward directives, tasks, and suggestions. Paradoxical strategies may at times be necessary; but when a more direct approach is possible it should be tried. The straightforward approach is not only more economic, but also more likely to teach the family how to cope with problems in the future.

These approaches are notable for their powerful, often paradoxical, techniques. Techniques are carefully developed to fit each case based on the therapist's clear understanding of the family's dynamics. Haley is the most explicit in stressing the need to understand family structure before trying to resolve symptoms, but the others too are very careful students of family systems. There is a danger, however, in using strategic techniques if there is no understanding how families work. To be effective and do no harm, techniques must be tailored to fit each family's particular circumstances and dynamics. Interventions should be based on a clear understanding and careful observation of particular families, not simply upon general rules, hypotheses, or opinions.

REFERENCES

Bowen, M. The use of family theory in clinical practice. *Comprehensive Psychiatry,* 1966, *7,* 345–374.

Bross, A. (Ed.), *Family therapy: Principles of strategic practice.* New york: Guilford, 1983.

deShazer, S. Brief therapy: Two's company. *Family Process,* 1975, *14,* 79–93.

Fisch, R. Review of *Problem-solving therapy,* by Jay Haley. *Family Process,* 1978, *17,* 107–110.

Fisch, R., Weakland, J.H. & Segal, L. *The tactics of change: Doing therapy briefly.* San Francisco: Jossey-Bass, 1982.

Frankl, V. Paradoxical intention. *American Journal of Psychotherapy,* 1960, *14,* 520–535.

Haley, J. *Strategies of psychotherapy.* New York: Grune & Stratton, 1963.

Haley, J. (Ed.), *Advanced techniques of hypnosis and therapy: Selected papers of Milton H. Erickson, M.D.* New York: Grune & Stratton, 1967.

Haley, J. *Uncommon therapy.* New York: Norton, 1973.

Haley, J. *Problem-solving therapy.* San Francisco: Jossey-Bass, 1976.

Haley, J. *Leaving home.* New York: McGraw-Hill, 1980.

Hare-Mustin, R.T. Treatment of temper tantrums by a paradoxical intervention. *Family Process,* 1975, *14,* 481–485.

Hoffman, L. Breaking the homeostatic cycle. In P.J. Guerin (Ed.), *Family therapy: Theory and practice.* New York: Gardner Press, 1976.

Hoffman, L. *Foundations of family therapy.* New York: Basic Books, 1981.

Jackson, D.D. The myth of normality. *Medical Opinion and Review,* 1967, *3,* (5), 28–33.

Langsley, D., Machotka, P. & Flomenhaft, K. Avoiding mental hospital admission: A follow-up study. *American Journal of Psychiatry,* 1971, *127,* 1391–1394.

Madanes, C. *Strategic family therapy.* San Francisco: Jossey-Bass, 1981.

Minuchin, S. *Families and family therapy.* Cambridge, Mass.: Harvard University Press, 1974.

Parsons, B. & Alexander, J. Short-term family intervention: A therapy outcome study. *Journal of Consulting and Clinical Psychology,* 1973, *41,* 195–201.

Rabkin, R. *Strategic psychotherapy.* New York: Basic Books, 1977.

Riskin, J. & McCorkle, M.E. "Nontherapy" family research and change in families: A brief clinical research communication. *Family Process,* 1979, *18,* 161–162.

Rohrbaugh, M., Tennen, H., Press, S., White, L., Raskin, P. & Pickering, M.R. *Paradoxical strategies in psychotherapy.* Symposium presented at the American Psychological Association convention, San Francisco, 1977.

Satir, V. *Conjoint family therapy.* Palo Alto: Science and Behavior Books, 1964.

Selvini Palazzoli, M., Boscolo, L., Cecchin, G. & Prata, G. The treatment of children through the brief therapy of their parents. *Family Process,* 1974, *13,* 429–442.

Selvini Palazzoli, M., Boscolo, L., Cecchin, G. & Prata, G. *Paradox and counterparadox.* New York: Jason Aronson, 1978.

Sifneos, P.E. *Short-term dynamic psychotherapy.* New York: Plenum, 1979.

Sluzki, C.E. Marital therapy from a systems theory perspective. In T.J. Paolino & B.S. McCrady (Eds.), *Marriage and marital therapy.* New York: Brunner/Mazel, 1978.

Stanton, A. & Schwartz, M. *The mental hospital.* New York: Basic Books, 1954.

Stanton, M.D. & Todd, T.C. Structural family therapy with drug addicts. In E. Kaufman & P. Kaufmann (Eds.), *Family therapy of drug and alcohol abuse.* New York: Gardner Press, 1979.

Watzlawick, P., Beavin, J.H. & Jackson, D.D. *Pragmatics of human communication.* New York: Norton, 1967.

Watzlawick, P., Weakland, J. & Fisch, R. *Change: Principles of problem formation and problem resolution.* New York: Norton, 1974.

Weakland, J. Communication theory and clinical change. In P.J. Guerin (Ed.), *Family therapy: Theory and practice.* New York: Gardner Press, 1976.

Weakland, J., Fisch, R., Watzlawick, P. & Bodin, A.M. Brief therapy: Focused problem resolution. *Family Process, 1974, 13,* 141–168.

Wolpe, J. *Psychotherapy by reciprocal inhibition.* Stanford: Stanford University Press, 1958.

Zuk, G.H. *Family therapy: A triadic-based approach.* New York: Behavioral Publications, 1971.

11

Structural
Family
Therapy

INTRODUCTION

i

n the 1970s structural family therapy emerged as one of the most popular and influential approaches in the field. The main reason for its success is that it describes families as having an underlying organization in terms that provide clear guidelines for diagnosis and treatment.

One of the reasons family therapy is so complex is that families often appear as collections of individuals who affect each other in powerful but unpredictable ways. Beginning therapists are usually puzzled by the complex transactions that make up family life. Structural family therapy offers a clear framework that brings order and meaning to those transactions. The consistent, repetitive, organized, and predictable modes of family behavior are what allow us to consider that they have a structure, although of course only in a functional sense. The emotional boundaries and coalitions that make up family structure are abstractions; nevertheless, using the concept

469

of family structure enables therapists to intervene in a systematic and organized fashion.

Salvador Minuchin was not among the first wave of family therapists; he first started seeing families only about 1960. Known initially as a clinician rather than as a theoretician, he established a reputation in dramatic and compelling teaching demonstrations which are extraordinarily effective. Minuchin developed a theory of family structure and a set of guidelines for treatment to organize his therapeutic techniques. Families who come for treatment are seen as stuck for lack of alternatives. Therapy is designed to unfreeze them from rigid habits, creating the opportunity for new structures to emerge. This approach was so successful that it captivated the field of family therapy. Minuchin helped build the Philadelphia Child Guidance Clinic into a world-famous complex, where thousands of family therapists have been trained in structural family therapy.

SKETCHES OF LEADING FIGURES

Minuchin was born and raised in Argentina. He served as a physician in the Israeli army, then came to the United States, where he trained in child psychiatry at the Jewish Board of Guardians in New York City and studied psychoanalysis at the William Alanson White Institute. After completing his studies, Minuchin returned to Israel to work with displaced children; during this time he became interested in families. When he moved back to the United States and took a job at the Wiltwyck School for delinquent boys, he suggested to his colleagues that they start seeing families. Other family therapists at this period, such as Nathan Ackerman and Don Jackson, were working with middle-class families; their approaches hardly seemed suitable to multiproblem, poor families with children at Wiltwyck. Therefore Minuchin had to develop new concepts and techniques applicable to these families, one of which was the idea of *enactment*—that is, bringing problematic sequences into the treatment room by having families act them out so that the therapist can observe and change them. Most of Minuchin's techniques were concrete and action-oriented, developments that have continued to characterize structural family therapy ever since.

The clinical and conceptual success of Minuchin's work with the families at Wiltwyck led to a book, *Families of the Slums,* written with Montalvo, Guerney, Rosman, and Schumer. Minuchin's reputation as a practitioner of family therapy grew, and he became the Director of the Philadelphia Child

Guidance Clinic in 1965. The Clinic, located in the heart of Philadelphia's black ghetto, then consisted of less than a dozen staff members. From this modest beginning Minuchin created one of the largest and most prestigous child guidance clinics in the world. When he stepped down ten years later, there were nearly 300 people on the staff and the clinic had become part of an elaborate modern complex along with the Children's Hospital of Philadelphia adjacent to the University of Pennsylvania campus.

Among Minuchin's colleagues were Braulio Montalvo, Jay Haley, Bernice Rosman, Harry Aponte, Marianne Walters, and Stephen Greenstein, all of whom have had an important role in shaping structural family therapy. Many other therapists associated with the Philadelphia Child Guidance Clinic as students and staff members have also influenced structural family therapy with their own ideas and styles; these second-generation structuralists are now dispersed throughout the country. By the late 1970s, structural family therapy had become perhaps the most influential and widely practiced of all systems of family therapy.

THEORETICAL FORMULATIONS

The prominence of structural family therapy is due in part to Minuchin's renown as a clinician, and to the excellent training programs offered at the Philadelphia Child Guidance Clinic, but also to the fact that Minuchin's theory is both simple and practical.

Many clinicians are impatient with theories. They see them as abstractions, which they are eager to bypass in order to learn techniques. But all the specific techniques and clever interventions that one can pick up from books and supervisors are nothing but tactical maneuvers. Without a map you are lost: caught up in the detailed content of family discussions with no overall plan. This often occurs in individual therapy, where we become experts at passivity. You can sit back and listen impassively, week after week, as Mr. Jones harangues about his wife. As long as he gets some relief from just complaining, there's no need to do much but listen and nod sympathetically. In family work it's harder to be passive. Family members aren't confirmed into the status of patienthood and they won't put up with a passive therapist. They want action! They want solutions! They want a therapist to solve their problems. Families present problem after problem, crisis after crisis, and demand to be told what to do.

Beginners tend to get caught up in the content of these problems because they don't have a theory to help them see the process of family dynamics. Structural family therapy is a blueprint for analyzing the process of family interactions. As such it provides a basis for consistent strategies of treatment, which obviates the need to have a specific technique—usually someone else's—for every occasion.

Three constructs are the essential components of structural family theory: *structure, subsystems,* and *boundaries.*

Family structure, the organized pattern in which family members interact, is a deterministic concept. It does not prescribe or legislate behavior; it does describe sequences that are predictable. When they are repeated, family transactions establish enduring patterns. These repeated patterns determine how, when, and to whom family members relate. When a mother tells her daughter to pick up the toys and the daughter refuses until the father shouts at her, an interactional pattern is initiated. If it is repeated it creates a structure in which father is competent as a disciplinarian, mother is incompetent. In addition, mother is likely to be more affectionate to her daughter, while father, the disciplinarian, remains on the outside.

Family structure involves a set of covert rules which govern transactions in the family. For example, a rule such as "family members must always protect one another" will be manifested in various ways depending on context and which family members are involved. If an adolescent son has to be up early for school, mother wakes him; father does all the shopping if driving makes the mother nervous; the kids intervene to diffuse conflict between the parents; and the parents' preoccupation with the kids' problems keeps the couple from spending time together. All of these sequences are isomorphic; they are structured. Changing any of them may or may not affect the underlying structure, but altering the basic structure will have ripple effects on all family transactions.

Family structure is shaped partly by universal and partly by idiosyncratic constraints. For example, all families have some kind of hierarchical structure, with parents and children having different amounts of authority. Family members also tend to have reciprocal and complementary functions. If one parent is supercompetent and responsible, the other will be less so; if the supercompetent one gets "sick" or less competent in some other way, the other will need to take over.

Other aspects of family structure depend upon the unique history of each family. Transactional patterns foster expectations that determine future patterns. Often these become so ingrained that their origin is forgotten, and they are presumed necessary rather than optional. If a young mother, burdened by the demands of her infant, gets upset and complains to her husband, he may respond in various ways. Perhaps he will move closer toward her and share the heavy demands of childrearing. This creates a united parental team. On the other hand, if he decides, and his wife concurs, that she is "neurotic," she may be sent into psychotherapy to get the emotional support she needs. This creates a structure where the mother remains distant from her husband, and learns to turn outside the family for emotional support. Whatever the chosen pattern, it tends to be self-perpetuating and resistant to change. Although alternatives are available, families are unlikely to consider them until changing circumstances produce stress and dysfunction in the system.

Family structure is not easily discerned. Two things are necessary: a theoretical system that explains structure, and seeing the family in action. The facts are not enough. Knowing that a family is a single-parent family with three children, or that two parents are having trouble with a middle child does not tell you what the family structure is. It only becomes evident when you observe the actual interactions among family members over time. Single interactions are affected by specific circumstances; it is the repeated sequences that reveal structural patterns.

Consider the following example. A mother calls the clinic to complain of misbehavior in her 17-year-old son. She is asked to bring her husband, son, and their three other children to the first session. When they arrive, the mother begins to describe a series of minor ways in which the son is disobedient around the house. He responds angrily, saying nobody understands him and he never gets any sympathy from his mother. This spontaneous dialogue between mother and son reveals an intense involvement between them—an involvement no less real or intense simply because it is conflictual. This dyadic sequence does not reveal the whole family structure, however, because it doesn't include the father or the other three children. They must be engaged in interaction to observe their role in the family structure. If the father sides with his son against his wife, a cross-generational coalition is revealed. If father sides with his wife, but seems unconcerned, then it may be that the mother's preoccupation with her son is related to her husband's lack of involvement. Further, if the three younger children tend to agree with their mother and describe their brother as bad, then it becomes clear that all the children are close to the mother—close and obedient up to a point, then close and disobedient.

Families are differentiated into *subsystems* of members who join together to perform various functions. Every individual is a subsystem, and dyads or larger groups make up other subsystems, determined by generation, gender, or common interests. Obvious groupings such as the parents or the teenagers are sometimes less significant than covert coalitions. A mother and her youngest child may form such a tightly bonded system that others are excluded. Another family may be split into two camps, with mom and the boys on one side, and dad and the girls on the other. Though certain patterns are common, the possibilities for subgrouping are endless.

Every family member plays many roles in several subgroups. Mary may be a wife, a mother, a daughter, and a niece. In each of these roles she will be required to behave differently and exercise a variety of interpersonal options. If she is mature and flexible she will be able to vary her behavior to fit the different subgroups in which she functions. Scolding may be okay from a mother, but it causes problems from a wife or a daughter.

Individuals, subsystems, and whole families are demarcated by interpersonal *boundaries*. Boundaries are invisible barriers which surround individuals and subsystems, regulating the amount of contact with others. They serve to protect the separateness and autonomy of the family and its subsystems. A rule forbidding phone calls at dinner time establishes a boundary which protects the family from outside intrusion. When small children are permitted to freely interrupt their parents' conversation at dinner, the boundary separating the parents from the children is minimal. Subsystems which are not adequately protected by boundaries limit the development of interpersonal skills achievable in these subsystems. If parents always step in to settle arguments between their children, the children won't learn to fight their own battles and will be impaired in their dealings with peers.

Interpersonal boundaries vary from being rigid to diffuse (Figure 1). Rigid boundaries are overly restrictive and permit little contact with outside systems, resulting in *disengagement*. Disengaged individuals or subsystems are relatively isolated and autonomous. On the positive side, this permits independence, growth, and mastery. If parents don't hover over their children, telling them what to do and fighting their battles, then the children will be forced to develop their own resources. On the other hand, disengagement

Figure 11-1
Interpersonal Boundaries

Rigid Boundary	Clear Boundary	Diffuse Boundary
———————	– – – – – – – – –	· · · · · · · · · ·
Disengagement	Normal Range	Enmeshment

limits warmth, affection, and nurturance, and disengaged families must be under extreme stress before they can mobilize mutual support. If parents keep their children at a distance, affection is minimized, and the parents will be slow to notice when the children need support and guidance.

Enmeshed subsystems offer a heightened sense of mutual support, but at the expense of independence and autonomy. Enmeshed parents are loving and considerate; they spend a lot of time with their kids and do a lot for them. However, children enmeshed with their parents learn to rely on the parents and tend to be dependent. They're less comfortable by themselves, and may have trouble relating to people outside the family.

Minuchin describes some of the features of family subsystems in his most accessible work, *Families and Family Therapy* (Minuchin, 1974). Families begin when two people join together to form a spouse subsystem. Two people in love agree to share their lives and futures and expectations, but a period of often difficult adjustment is required before they can complete the transition from courtship to a functional spouse subsystem. They must learn to accommodate to each other's needs and preferred styles of interaction. In a normal couple each gives and gets. He learns to accommodate to her wish to be kissed hello and goodbye. She learns to leave him alone with his paper and morning coffee. These little arrangements, multiplied a thousand times, may be accomplished easily or only after intense struggle. Whatever the case, this process of accommodation cements the couple into a unit.

The couple must also develop complementary patterns of mutual support. Some patterns are transitory and may later be reversed—perhaps, for instance, one works while the other completes school. Other patterns are more stable and lasting. Traditional sex role stereotypes may allow couples to achieve complementarity, but at the expense of fully rounded functioning for each spouse. A traditional woman may not have to open doors, earn a living, or mow the lawn; on the other hand, she may have to deny her own intelligence, submerge her independence, and live in the shadow of her husband. A traditional husband may get to make all the decisions, not have to change dirty diapers, and be waited on hand and foot around the house; however, the price for these "masculine" perogatives may be that he's not allowed to cry, never learns the pleasure of cooking a special meal, and does not fully share the joy of caring for his children.

Exaggerated complementary roles can detract from individual growth; moderate complementarity enables spouses to divide functions, and support and enrich each other. When one has the flu and feels lousy, the other takes over. One's permissiveness with children may be balanced by the other's strictness. One's fiery disposition may help to melt the other's icy reserve.

Complementary patterns, such as pursuer-distancer, active-passive, dominant-submissive, exist in most couples. They become pathological when they are so exaggerated that they create a dysfunctional subsystem. Therapists must learn to accept those structural patterns that work, and challenge only those that do not.

The spouse subsystem must also have a boundary which separates it from parents, from children, and from the outside world. All too often, husband and wife give up the space they need for supporting each other when children are born. A rigid boundary around the couple deprives the children of the support they need; but in our child-centered culture, usually the boundary separating parents and children is extremely diffuse.

The birth of a child instantly transforms the family structure; the pattern of interaction between the parental and child subsystems must be worked out and then modified to fit changing circumstances. A clear boundary enables the children to interact with their parents but excludes them from the spouse subsystem. Parents and children eat together, play together, and share much of each others' lives. But there are some spouse functions which need not be shared. Husband and wife are sustained as a loving couple and enhanced as parents if they have time to be alone together—alone to talk, alone to go out to dinner occasionally, alone to fight, and alone to make love. Unhappily, the demands of small children often make parents lose sight of their need to maintain a boundary.

In addition to maintaining some privacy for the couple, a clear boundary establishes a hierarchical structure in which the parents exercise a position of leadership. All too often this hierarchy is disrupted by a child-centered ethos which influences family therapists as well as parents. Parents enmeshed with their children tend to argue with them about who is in charge, and misguidedly share—or shirk—the responsibility for making parental decisions. Offering a child the choice in picking out clothes or choosing friends is respectful and flexible. Asking children whether they want to go to school, or trying to convince a toddler to agree that it's dangerous to play in the street simply blurs the line of authority.

NORMAL FAMILY DEVELOPMENT

The prevailing view is that normal family life is harmonious and problem free. This is an idealized myth. Normal families are constantly struggling with problems in living. What distinguishes a normal from an abnormal family is not the absence of problems, but a functional family structure. Normal husbands and wives must learn to adjust to each other, rear their children, deal with their parents, cope with their jobs, and fit into their community. The nature of these struggles changes with developmental stages and situational crises. Normal family life is neither static nor problem free. Nevertheless, as Minuchin put it, "the myth of placid normality endures, supported by hours of two-dimensional television characters" (1974, p. 50).

When two people marry, the structural requirements for the new union are *accommodation* and *boundary making*. The first priority is mutual accommodation to manage the myriad details of everyday living. Each spouse tries to organize the relationship along familiar lines and pressures the other to accommodate. Each must adjust to the other's expectations and wants. They must agree on major issues, such as where to live and if and when to have children; less obvious but equally important they must coordinate daily rituals, like what to watch on television, what to eat for supper, when to go to bed, and what to do there. Often the little things are the most irksome and problematic, and the couple may argue heatedly about who will take out the garbage, or wash the clothes.

In accommodating to each other the couple also must negotiate the nature of the boundary between them as well as the boundary separating them from the outside. A vague, diffuse boundary exists between the couple if they call each other at work frequently; if neither has separate friends or outside independent activities; and if they come to view themselves only as a pair rather than also as two separate personalities. On the other hand, they have established a rigid boundary between them if they spend little time doing things together; have separate bedrooms, take separate vacations, have different checking accounts; and each is considerably more invested in careers or outside relationships than in the marriage. While none of these markers by itself defines enmeshment or disengagement, each of them suggests the pattern that will develop.

Typically spouses come from families with differing degrees of enmeshment or disengagement. Each spouse tends to be more comfortable with the sort of proximity that existed in the family of origin. Since these expectations differ, a struggle ensues that may be the most difficult aspect of a new marriage. He wants to go play poker with the boys; she feels deserted. She wants to hold hands and whisper in the movies; he wants to concentrate on the picture. His major attention is on his career; her major attention is on the marriage. Each thinks the other wrong, unreasonable, and terribly hurtful.

Couples must also define a boundary separating them from their original families. Rather suddenly the families that each grew up in must take second place to the new marriage. This too is a difficult adjustment, both for newlyweds and their parents. Families of origin vary in the ease with which they accept and support the new union.

The addition of children transforms the structure of the new family into an executive parental subsystem and a sibling subsystem. It is typical for spouses to have different patterns of commitment to the babies. A woman's commitment to a unit of three is likely to begin with pregnancy, since the child inside her belly is an unavoidable reality. Her husband, on the other hand, may only begin to feel like a father when the child is born. Many men don't accept the role of father until the infants are old enough to begin to respond to them. Thus even in normal families a child brings with it great potential for stress and conflict. The woman's life is usually more radically transformed than the man's. She sacrifices a great deal and typically needs more support from her husband. The husband, meanwhile, continues his job, and the new baby is far less of a disruption. Though he may try to support his wife, he's likely to resent some of her demands as inordinate and unreasonable.

The family takes care of the psychosocial needs of the children and transmits the culture to them. Children develop a dual identity within the family: a sense of belongingness and a sense of being separate. John Smith is both a Smith and also John, part of the family, yet a unique person.

Children require different styles of parenting at different ages. Infants primarily need nurturance and support. Older children need guidance and control; and adolescents need independence and responsibility. What is good parenting for a two-year-old may be totally inadequate for a five-year-old or a fourteen-year-old. Normal parents adjust to these developmental challenges. The family modifies its structure to adapt to new additions, to the children's growth and development, and to changes in the external environment.

Minuchin (1974) warns family therapists not to mistake family growing pains for pathology. The normal family experiences anxiety and disruption as its members adapt to growth and change. Many families seek help at transitional stages, when the therapist must keep in mind that they are in the process of modifying their structure to accommodate to new circumstances.

All families face situations which stress the system. Although no clear dividing line exists between normal and abnormal families, we can say that normal families tend to modify their structure to accommodate to changed circumstances; and pathological families tend to increase the rigidity of a structure which is no longer functional.

DEVELOPMENT OF BEHAVIOR DISORDERS

Family systems must be stable enough to insure continuity, but flexible enough to accommodate to changing circumstances. Behavior disorders arise when inflexible family structures cannot adjust adequately to maturational or situational challenges. Adaptive changes in structure are required when the family or one of its members faces external stress and when transitional points of growth are reached.

Structural family therapists use a few simple symbols to diagram structural problems, and these diagrams usually make it clear what changes are required. Figure 11-2 shows some of the symbols used to diagram family structure.

Figure 11-2
Symbols for Family Structure

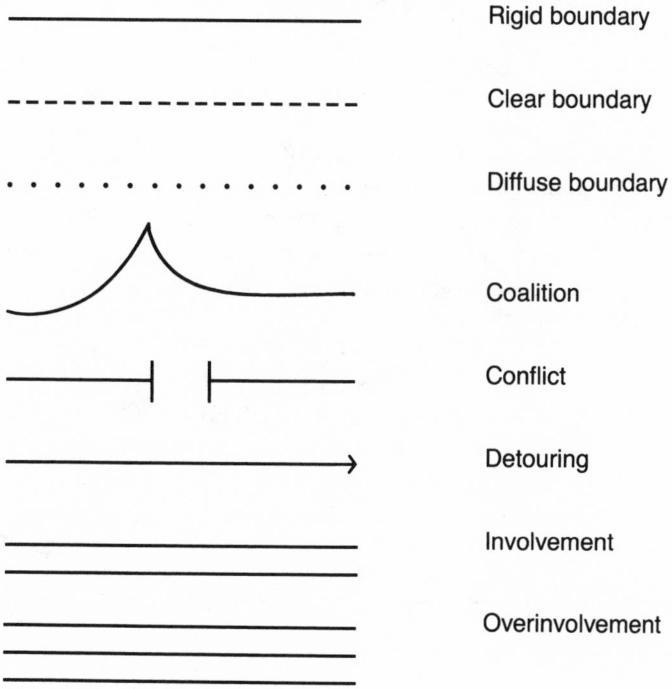

————————	Rigid boundary
– – – – – – – – –	Clear boundary
· · · · · · · · · ·	Diffuse boundary
	Coalition
	Conflict
———————→	Detouring
	Involvement
	Overinvolvement

One problem often seen by family therapists arises when parents who are unable to resolve the conflicts between them divert the focus of concern on to a child. Such parents may feel that the birth of the child has simply provided a new focus for their concerns. Instead of worrying about each other, they worry about the child; see Figure 11-3. Although this reduces the strain on father (F) and mother (M), it victimizes the child (C) and is therefore dysfunctional.

Figure 11-3
Scapegoating As A Means Of
Detouring Conflict

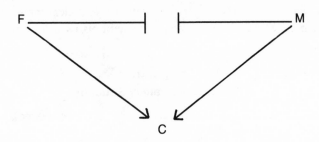

An alternate but equally common pattern is for the parents to continue to argue through the children. Father says mother is too permissive; she says he is too strict. He may withdraw, causing her to criticize his handling of the child, which in turn causes further withdrawal. The result is a cross-generational coalition between mother and child, which excludes the father (Figure 11-4).

Figure 11-4
Mother-Child Coalition

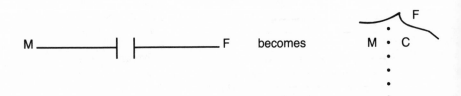

Some families function quite well when the children are small, but are unable to adjust to a growing child's needs for discipline and control. Parents may be particularly solicitous of children if they have had reason to worry about the children's health, if they had to wait a long time before they had them, or if they have few interests outside the family to give meaning to their lives. Parents who are unable to have children of their own, and finally decide to adopt, may find it very difficult to set appropriate limits. They are too invested and enmeshed with their children to be able to exercise appropriate control (Figure 11-5).

Figure 11-5
Parents Enmeshed with Children

F   M
. . . .

children

Infants in enmeshed families receive wonderful care: their parents hug them, love them, and give them lots of stimulation. Although such parents may be too tired from caring for the children to have much time for each other or for outside interests, the system may be moderately successful. However, if these doting parents do not teach the children to obey rules and respect adult authority, the children may be unprepared to successfully negotiate their entrance into school. Used to getting their own way, they may be unruly and disruptive. Several possible consequences of this situation may bring the family into treatment. The children may be afraid to go to school, for instance, and their fears may be covertly reinforced by "understanding" parents who permit them to remain at home (Figure 11-6).

Figure 11-6
School Phobia

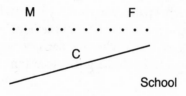

Such a case may be labeled as school phobia, and may become entrenched if the parents permit the children to remain at home for more than a few days.

The children of such a family may go to school; but since they have not learned to accommodate to others they may be rejected by their schoolmates. These children are often presented as depressed and withdrawn. In other cases, children enmeshed with their parents become discipline problems at school, and the school authorities may initiate contact with the clinic.

A major change in family composition that requires structural adjustment occurs when divorced or widowed spouses remarry. Such "blended families" either readjust their boundaries or soon experience transitional conflicts. When a woman divorces, she and the children must first learn to readjust to a structure that establishes a clear boundary separating the divorced spouse but still permitting contact between father and children; then if she remarries, the family must readjust to functioning with a new husband and stepfather (Figure 11-7).

Figure 11-7
Divorce and Remarriage

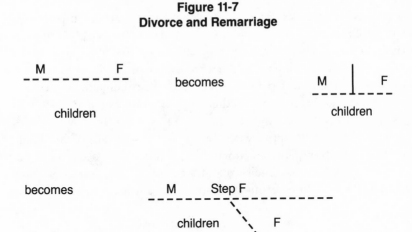

Sometimes it is hard for the mother and children to allow the stepfather to participate as an equal partner in the new parental subsystem. Mother and children have long since established transactional rules and have learned to accommodate to each other. The new parent may be treated as an outsider who is supposed to learn the "right" (accustomed) way of doing things, rather than a new partner who will give as well as receive ideas about child rearing (Figure 11-8).

Figure 11-8
Failure to Accept a Stepparent

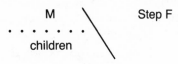

The more mother and children insist on maintaining their familiar patterns without adjusting to the modifications required to absorb the stepfather, the more frustrated and angry he will become. The result may lead to child abuse or chronic arguing between the parents. The sooner such families enter treatment the easier it is to help them adjust to the transition. The longer they wait the more entrenched the structural problems become.

An important aspect of structural family problems is that symptoms in one member reflect not only that person's relationships with others, but also the fact that those relationships are a function of still other relationships in the family. If Johnny, aged sixteen, is depressed, it is helpful to know that he is enmeshed with his mother. Discovering that she demands absolute obedience from him and refuses to let him develop his own thinking or outside relationships helps to explain his depression (Figure 11-9).

Figure 11-9

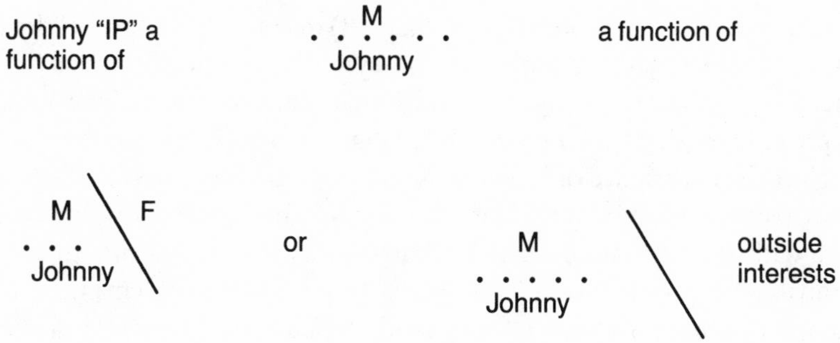

Johnny "IP" a
function of

M
. . . . . .
Johnny

a function of

M
. . .
Johnny

or

M
. . . . .
Johnny

F

outside
interests

But it is only a partial view of the family system, and therefore an incomplete guide to treatment.

Why is the mother enmeshed with her son? Perhaps she is disengaged from her husband; perhaps she is a widow who hasn't found new friends, a career, or any other outside interests. Helping Johnny resolve his depression may best be accomplished by helping his mother to satisfy her needs for closeness with her husband or friends.

Because problems are a function of the entire family structure, it is important to include the whole group for assessment. For example, if a father complains of a child's misbehavior, seeing the child alone won't help the father to state rules clearly and enforce them effectively. Nor will seeing the father and child together do anything to stop the mother from undercutting the father's authority. Only by seeing the whole family interacting is it possible to get a complete picture of their structure.

Sometimes even seeing the whole family is not enough. Structural family therapy is based on recognition of the importance of the context of the social system. The family may not be the complete or most relevant context. If one of the parents is having an affair, that relationship is a crucial part of the family's context. It may not be advisable to invite the lover to the family sessions, but it is crucial to recognize the structural implications of the extramarital relationship.

In some cases the family may not be the context most relevant to the presenting problem. A mother's depression may be due more to her relationships at work than at home. A son's problems at school may be due more to the structural context at school than to the one in the family. In such instances, structural family therapists work with the more relevant context, to alleviate the presenting problems.

Finally, some problems may be treated as problems of the individual. As Minuchin has written, "Pathology may be inside the patient, in his social context, or in the feedback between them" (1974, p. 9). Elsewhere Minuchin (Minuchin, Rosman, and Baker, 1978, p. 91) refers to the danger of "denying the individual while enthroning the system." Family therapists should therefore not overlook the possibility that some problems may be most appropriately dealt with on this individual basis. The therapist must not neglect the experience of individuals, although this is easy to do, especially with young children. While interviewing a family to see how the parents deal with their children, a careful clinician may notice that one child has a neurological problem or a learning disability. These problems need to be identified and appropriate referrals made. Usually when a child has trouble in school, there is a problem in the family or school context. Sometimes, however, there is a problem in the child.

GOALS OF THERAPY

Structural family therapists believe that problems are maintained by dysfunctional family structures. Therefore therapy is directed at altering family structure so that the family can solve the problems. The goal of therapy is structural change; problem-solving is a byproduct of this systemic goal.

The structural family therapist joins the family system in order to help its members change their structure. By altering boundaries and realigning subsystems, the therapist changes the behavior and experience of each of the family members. The therapist doesn't solve problems; that's the family's job. The therapist helps modify the family's functioning so that family members can solve their own problems. Thus structural family therapy is like dynamic psychotherapy—symptom-resolution is sought, not as an end in itself, but as a result of lasting structural change. The analyst modifies the structure of the patient's mind; the structural family therapist modifies the structure of the patient's family.

Symptomatic change and enhanced family functioning are seen as inextricably interrelated goals. The most effective way to change symptoms is to change the family patterns that maintain them. An effectively functioning family is a system that supports its members. The goal of structural family therapy is to facilitate the growth of the system in order to resolve symptoms and encourage growth in individuals, while also preserving the mutual support of the family.

Short-range goals may be to alleviate symptoms, especially life-threatening symptoms such as anorexia nervosa (Minuchin, Rosman, and Baker, 1978). At times behavioral techniques, suggestion, or manipulation may be used to provide temporary surcease. However, unless structural change in the family system is achieved, short-term symptom-resolution may collapse.

The goals for each family are dictated by the problems they present with and by the assessment of their structural dysfunction. Although every family is unique, there are common problems and typical structural goals; some aspects of family structure are thought to be generally important for all families.

Most important of the general goals for families is the creation of an effective hierarchical structure. Parents are expected to be in charge, not to relate as equals to their children. A general goal is to help parents function together as a cohesive executive subsystem. When only one parent is present, or when there are several children, one or more of the oldest children may be encouraged to be an assistant.

With enmeshed families the goal is to differentiate individuals and subsystems by strengthening the boundaries around them. With disengaged families the goal is to increase interaction by making boundaries more permeable.

CONDITIONS FOR BEHAVIOR CHANGE

Structural family therapy changes behavior by opening alternative patterns of family interaction which can modify family structure. It is not a matter of creating new structures, but of activating dormant ones. If, once activated, the dormant sequences are functional, they will be reinforcing; and family structure will be transformed. When new transactional patterns become regularly repeated and predictably effective, they will stabilize the new and more functional structure.

The therapist produces change by joining the family, probing for areas of possible flexibility and change, and then activating dormant structural alternatives. Joining gets the therapist into the family; accommodating to their accustomed style gives him or her leverage; and restructuring interventions transform the family structure. If the therapist remains an outsider or uses interventions that are too dystonic, the family will reject him or her. If the therapist becomes too much a part of the family or uses interventions that are too syntonic, the family will assimilate the interventions into previous transactional patterns. In either case there will be no structural change.

For change to occur the family must first accept the therapist, and then respond to his or her interventions as though to a novel situation. This increases stress which in turn unbalances family homeostasis, and thus opens the way for structural transformation.

Joining and accommodating to the family is considered prerequisite to restructuring. To join the family the therapist must convey acceptance of family members and respect for their way of doing things. Minuchin (1974) likens the family therapist to an anthropologist who must first join a culture in order to study it.

To join the family's culture the therapist makes accommodating over-tures—the sort of thing that we usually do unthinkingly, although often unsuccessfully. If the parents come for help with a child's problems, the therapist does not begin by asking for the child's views. This conveys a lack of respect for the parents and may lead them to reject the therapist.

Only after the therapist has successfully joined with a family is it fruitful to attempt restructuring—the often dramatic confrontations that challenge families and force them to change.

Structural family therapy changes behavior by reframing the family's presentation of their problems into a systemic model. Families define problems as a function of individuals or outside forces; structural family therapists redefine these problems as a function of the family's structure. The first task is to understand the family's view of their problems. The therapist does this by tracking their formulation, in the content they use to explain it, and in the sequence they use to demonstrate it. Then the family therapist reframes their formulation into one based on an understanding of family structure.

In fact, all psychotherapies use reframing. Patients, whether individuals or families, come with their own views as to the cause of their problems —views that usually haven't helped them solve the problems—and the therapist offers them a new and potentially more constructive view of these same problems. What makes structural family therapy unique is that it uses enactments within therapy sessions to make the reframing happen. This is the *sine qua non* of structural family therapy: observing and modifying the structure of family transactions within the immediate context of the session. Although this sounds simple, it has important implications for treatment. Structural family therapists work with what they see going on in the session, not what family members describe about what happens outside, nor with the content of family discussions. Action in the session, family dynamics in process, is what the structural family therapist deals with.

There are two types of live, in-session material on which structural family therapy focuses—*enactments* and *spontaneous behavior sequences*. An enactment occurs when the therapist stimulates the family to demonstrate how they handle a particular type of problem. Enactments commonly begin when the therapist suggests that specific subgroups begin to discuss a particular problem. As they do so, the therapist observes the family process. Working with enactments requires three operations. First the therapist defines or recognizes a sequence. For example, the therapist observes that when mother talks to her daughter they talk as peers, and little brother gets left out. Then the therapist enacts a transaction. For example, the therapist might say to the mother, "Talk this over with your kids." Third and most important, the therapist must guide the family to modify the enactment. If mother talks to her kids in such a way that she does not assume appropriate responsibility for major decisions, the therapist must guide her to do so as the family continues the enactment. All the therapist's moves should create new options for the family, options for new behavior sequences. A common mistake made by many family therapists is to simply criticize what they see by labeling it, without offering options for change.

In addition to working with enacted sequences, structural family therapists are alert to observe and modify spontaneous sequences of behavior that are the illustrative processes of family structure. Creating enactments is like directing a play; working with spontaneous sequences is like focusing a spotlight on action that occurs without direction. In fact, by observing and modifying such sequences very early in therapy sessions the therapist avoids getting bogged down in the family's usual nonproductive ways of doing business. Dealing with problematic behavior as soon as it occurs in the first session enables the therapist to organize the session, to underscore the process, and to modify it.

An experienced therapist can develop formulations about probable family structure even before the first interview. For example, if the therapist knows nothing more than that a family is coming to the clinic because of a "hyperactive" child, it is possible to guess something about the family structure and something about sequences that may occur as the session begins, since "hyperactive" behavior is often a function of the child's enmeshment with the mother. Mother's relationship with the child may be a product of a lack of hierarchical differentiation within the family; that is, parents and children relate to each other as peers, not as members of different generations. Furthermore, mother's overinvolvement with the "hyperactive" child is likely to be both a result of and a cause of emotional distance from her husband. Knowing that this is a common pattern, the therapist can anticipate that early in the first session the "hyperactive" child will begin to misbehave, and that the mother will be inadequate to deal with this misbehavior. Armed with this informed guess the therapist can spotlight (rather than enact) such a sequence, as soon as it occurs, and modify it. If the "hyperactive" child begins to run around the room, and the mother protests but does nothing effective, the therapist might say, "I can't believe you're going to let your child disobey like that!" This powerful confrontation may force the mother to behave in a more competent manner. The therapist may have to push further, saying, "Come on now, do something about it." Once such a theme is focused on, the therapist needs to pursue it relentlessly.

TECHNIQUES

Those who claim that psychotherapy is a science maintain that its techniques are specifiable and teachable. Those who contend that it is an art insist that theories are teachable, but techniques are not. Minuchin believes that implementing the specific techniques of therapy is an art, and that therapists must discover and create techniques that fit each family's transactional style and therapist's personality. Since every therapeutic session has idiosyncratic features, there can be no interpersonal immediacy if the specific context is ignored. Imitating someone else's technique is stifling and ineffective—stifling because it doesn't fit the therapist, ineffective because it doesn't fit the family.

Although the details of therapy are a matter of personal style, Minuchin believes that the large movements of therapeutic strategy can be specified and taught.

In *Families and Family Therapy* Minuchin (1974) lists three overlapping phases in the process of structural family therapy. 1) The therapist joins the family in a position of leadership; 2) maps their underlying structure; and 3) intervenes to transform this structure. This program is simple in the sense that it follows a clear and specifiable plan, but immensely complicated because it is difficult to accomplish these tasks, and furthermore because there is an endless variety of family patterns.

The three phases listed by Minuchin are conceptually comprehensive, but the specific techniques that structural family therapists employ must be clarified. Any scheme of techniques is necessarily a simplification and therefore incomplete; in what follows the techniques of structural family therapy will be subsumed under a six-part strategy.

Observed in practice, structural family therapy is an organic whole, created out of the very real human interaction of therapist and family. If they are to be genuine and effective, the therapist's moves cannot be preplanned or rehearsed. Competent family therapists are more than technicians. The strategy of therapy, on the other hand, must be thoughtfully planned. In general, the strategy of structural family therapy follows these steps:

1. Joining and accommodating
2. Working with interaction
3. Diagnosing
4. Highlighting and modifying interactions
5. Boundary making
6. Adding cognitive constructions

The first three strategies comprise the opening phase of treatment. Without carefully planning and skillfully accomplishing the critical opening moves, therapy usually fails. When we begin we're often too anxious or eager to consider opening wisely. Only after we get started and the jitters calm down, do we look around, assess the situation and then act accordingly. Unfortunately this sort of catch-up strategy results in the loss of much valuable ground. The therapist who neglects the opening moves of treatment may lose all chance of having a significant impact.

Genuine preparation and an effective opening must be distinguished from obsessional rituals which do nothing but bind anxiety and use up energy. Habitually arriving ten minutes early for sessions, arranging and rearranging the furniture, and endlessly reading charts or books on technique — as many of us do — should not be confused with careful planning.

Joining and Accommodating. Because families have firmly established homeostatic patterns, effective family therapy requires strong challenge and confrontation. But assaults on a family's habitual style will be dismissed unless they are made from a position of leverage. Family therapists earn this leverage by performing competently, and by demonstrating acceptance and understanding of family members.

The need for leverage is even more important in family treatment than in individual therapy. Individual patients generally enter treatment already predisposed to accept the therapist's authority. By seeking therapy, the individual tacitly acknowledges suffering, need for help, and willingness to trust the therapist. So familiar is the doctor-patient model that most patients accept its assumptions; many even welcome it. Not so with families.

The family outnumbers the therapist, and they have mutually agreed upon and long-practiced ways of seeing and doing things. Their set is to treat the family therapist as an unwelcome outsider. After all, why did the therapist insist on seeing the whole family rather than just the official patient? They expect to be told that they're doing things all wrong, and they're prepared to defend themselves. The family is thus a group of nonpatients who feel guilty and anxious; their set is to resist, not to cooperate.

First the family therapist must disarm their defenses and ease their anxiety. This is done by generously conveying understanding and acceptance to every single member of the family. The therapist greets each person by name and makes some kind of friendly contact.

These initial greetings convey respect, not only for the individuals in the family, but also for their hierarchical structure and organization. The therapist shows respect for the parents by taking their authority for granted. They, not their children, are asked first to describe the problems. If a family elects the mother as their speaker, the therapist notes this but does not initially challenge it.

Children also have special concerns and capacities. They should be greeted gently and asked simple, concrete questions. "Hi, I'm so-and-so; what's your name? Oh, Johnny, that's a nice name. Where do you go to school, Johnny?" Those who wish to remain silent should be "allowed" to do so. They will anyway, but the therapist who reflects their feelings of fear or anger and conveys acceptance of their reticence will have made a valuable step toward keeping them involved. "And what's your view of the problem? I see, you don't feel like saying anything right now? That's fine, perhaps you may have something to say later."

Failure to join and accommodate produces tense resistance, which is often blamed on the family. It may be comforting to blame others when things don't go well, but it doesn't improve matters. Family members can be called negative, rebellious, resistant, or defiant, and seen as unmotivated; but it is more useful to make an extra effort to connect with them.

It is particularly important to join powerful family members, as well as angry ones. Special pains must be taken to accept the point of view of the father who thinks therapy is hooey, or of the angry teenager who feels like a hunted criminal. It is also important to reconnect with such people at frequent intervals, particularly as things begin to heat up in later sessions.

A useful beginning is to greet the family and then ask for each person's view of the problems. Listen carefully, and acknowledge each person's position by reflecting what you hear. "I see, Mrs. Jones, you think Sally must be depressed about something that happened at school." "So Mr. Jones, you see some of the same things your wife sees, but you're not convinced it's a serious problem. Is that right?"

Working with Interaction. Family structure is manifest in the way family members interact. It cannot be inferred from their descriptions, nor from reconstructing previous discussions. Therefore, asking questions like, "Who's in charge?" "Do you two agree?" or "Can you recreate yesterday's argument?" tend to be unproductive. Families generally describe themselves more as they think they should be than as they are.

Family dynamics are what happens when the family is in action, not what they *say* happens, or what the therapist *imagines* must happen. They have to talk among themselves for the dynamics to emerge. When they do, the therapist observes, who talks to whom? when? in what way?

Structural family therapists work with two sorts of interactions, enactments and spontaneous sequences. Getting family members to talk among themselves runs counter to their expectations, and they resist doing it. They expect to present their case to an expert, and then be told what to do. If asked to discuss something in the session, they'll say: "We've talked about this many times"; or "It won't do any good, he (or she) doesn't listen"; or, "But you're supposed to be the expert."

If the therapist begins by giving each person a chance to speak, usually one will say something about another which can be responded to as a springboard for an enactment. When, for example, one parent says that the other is too strict, the therapist can develop an enactment by saying: "She says you're too strict. Can you answer her?" Picking a specific point for response is more likely to stimulate dialogue than a vague request, such as "Why don't you two talk things over?"

Once an enactment is begun, the therapist can discover many things about the family's structure. How long can the two people talk without being interrupted—that is, how clear is the boundary? Does one attack, the other defend—that is, who is central, who peripheral? Do parents bring children into their discussions—that is, are they enmeshed?

In addition to creating enactments, structural therapists also work with spontaneous sequences of behavior. In the first instance they are like theatrical directors, telling the actors what to do. In the second case, they are like lighting experts, focusing the spotlight of attention on some particular action.

Families may demonstrate enmeshment by frequently interrupting each other; speaking for other family members; doing things for children that they can do for themselves; or by constantly arguing. In disengaged families one may see a husband sitting impassively while his wife cries; a total absence of conflict; a surprising ignorance of important information about the children; a lack of concern for each other's interests.

If, as soon as the first session starts, the kids begin running wildly around the room while the parents protest ineffectually, the therapist doesn't need to hear descriptions of what goes on at home to see the executive incompetence. If a mother and daughter rant and rave at each other while the father sits silently in the corner, it isn't necessary to ask how involved he is at home. In fact, asking may yield a less accurate picture than the one revealed spontaneously.

Diagnosing. It is necessary to have a formulation to organize strategies of change. Clinicians must steer a course between the Scylla of unorganized experience and the Charybdis of rigid characterizations which don't capture the reality of the family's experience. Structural diagnostic categories organize what otherwise may be a confusing welter of impressions, without arbitrarily distorting the dynamic aspects of family interaction.

Families usually conceive of problems as located in the identified patient and as determined by events from the past. They hope the therapist will change the identified patient with as little disruption as possible to the family homeostasis. Family therapists regard the identified patient's symptoms as an expression of dysfunctional transactional patterns affecting the whole family. A family therapist's diagnosis broadens the problem beyond individuals to family systems, and moves the focus from discrete events in the past to ongoing transactions in the present. A family diagnosis is predicated on the goal of transforming the family in a way that benefits all of its members.

Even many family therapists categorize families with constructs that apply more to individuals than to systems. "The problem in this family is that the mother is smothering the kids," or "These parents are defiant," or "He's a placater." Structural family therapists diagnose in such a way as to describe the systemic interrelationships of all family members. Using the concepts of boundaries and subsystems, the structure of the whole system is described in a way that points to desired changes.

These diagnoses are based on observed interactions that take place in the first session. In later sessions the formulations are refined and revised so that they are increasingly more accurate. Although there is some danger of bending families to fit categories when they're applied early, the greater danger is waiting too long.

We see people with the greatest clarity and freshness during the initial contact. Later as we come to know them better we get used to their idiosyncracies and soon no longer notice them. Families quickly induct therapists into their culture. A family that initially appears to be chaotic and enmeshed soon comes to be just the familiar Jones family. For this reason, it is critical to make structural formulations as quickly as possible.

In fact, it is helpful to make some guesses about family structure even before the first session. This starts a process of active thinking which sets the stage for observing the family. For example, suppose you are about to see a family consisting of a mother, a sixteen-year-old daughter and a stepfather. The mother called to complain of her daughter's misbehavior. What do you imagine the structure might be, and how would you test your hypothesis? A good guess might be that mother and daughter are enmeshed, excluding the stepfather. This can be tested by seeing if mother and daughter tend to talk mostly about each other in the session—whether positively or negatively. The stepfather's disengagement would be confirmed if he and the girl are unable to converse without the mother's intrusion.

The structural diagnosis takes into account both the problem that the family presents and the structural dynamics that they display. And it includes all family members. In this instance, knowing that the mother and daughter are enmeshed is not enough; you also have to know what role the stepfather plays. If he is reasonably close with his wife but distant from the daughter, finding mutually enjoyable activities for stepfather and stepdaughter will help increase the girl's independence from her mother. On the other hand, if the mother's proximity to her daughter appears to be a function of her distance from her husband, then the marital pair may be the most productive focus.

Without a diagnostic formulation and a plan, the therapist is defensive and passive. Instead of knowing where to go and moving forcefully, the therapist lays back and tries to cope with the family, put out brush fires, and help them through a succession of incidents. Consistent awareness of the family's structure and focus on one or two structural changes helps the therapist see behind the various content issues that family members bring up.

Highlighting and Modifying Interactions. Once families begin to interact, problematic transactions emerge. Noticing them demands focus on process, not content. Nothing about structure is revealed by hearing who is in favor of punishment or who says nice things about others. Family structure is revealed by who says what to whom, and in what way.

Perhaps a husband complains, "We have a communication problem. My wife just won't talk to me; she never expresses her feelings." The therapist then stimulates an interaction to see what actually does happen. "Your husband says it's a communication problem; can you talk it over with him?" If, when they talk, the husband becomes domineering and critical while the wife grows increasingly silent and withdrawn, then the therapist sees what goes wrong. The problem is not that she doesn't talk, which is a linear explanation. Nor is the problem that he nags, also a linear explanation. The problem is that the more he nags, the more she withdraws, *and* the more she withdraws, the more he nags.

The trick is to highlight and modify this pattern of interaction. This requires forceful intervening. It is usually necessary to use therapeutic dynamite to break families loose from their patterns of equilibrium. Structural therapists use *intensity* to make these interventions.

Minuchin himself frequently speaks to families with dramatic and forceful impact. He regulates the intensity of his messages to exceed the threshold that family members have for not hearing challenges to the way they perceive reality. When Minuchin speaks, families listen.

Minuchin is forceful, but his intensity is not a function of his personality; it reflects his clarity of purpose. Knowledge of family structure and a serious commitment to help families change make powerful interventions possible. Families will usually respond to messages delivered with the kind of intensity that comes from being clear about the goal.

Structural therapists achieve intensity by selective regulation of affect, repetition, and duration. Tone, volume, pacing, and choice of words can be used to raise the affective intensity of statements. It helps if you know what you want to say. Here is an example of a nonforceful statement. "People are always concerned with themselves, kind of seeing themselves as the center of attention and just looking for whatever they can get. Wouldn't it be nice for a change if everybody started thinking about what they could do for others? I mean, thinking about other people and the country before themselves." Compare that with, "Ask not what your country can do for you—ask what you can do for your country." John Kennedy's words had impact because they were carefully chosen and clearly put. Family therapists don't need to make speeches or be clever phrase-makers, but they do occasionally have to speak forcefully to get through.

Affective intensity is not simply a matter of crisp phrasing. You have to know how and when to be provocative. For example, I was recently working with a family in which a twenty-nine-year-old woman with anorexia nervosa was the identified patient. Although the family maintained a facade of togetherness, it was rigidly structured; the mother and her anorectic daughter were enmeshed, while the father was excluded. In this family, the father was the only one to express anger openly, and this was part of the official rationale for why he was excluded. His daughter was afraid of his anger, which she freely admitted. What was less clear, however, is that the mother had covertly taught the daughter to avoid him, because she, the mother, couldn't deal with his anger. Consequently, the daughter grew up afraid of her father and of men in general.

At one point the father described how isolated he felt from his daughter; he said he thought it was because she feared his anger. The daughter agreed,

"It's his fault all right." I asked the mother what she thought, and she replied, "It isn't his fault." I said, "You're right." She went on, denying her real feelings to avoid conflict, "It's no one's fault." I answered in a way that got her attention, "Like hell it isn't!" Startled, she asked what I meant. "It's *your* fault!" I said.

This level of intensity was necessary to interrupt a rigid pattern of conflict avoidance that sustained a pathogenic alliance between mother and daughter. The content—who really is afraid of anger—is less important than the structural goal: freeing the daughter from her position of overinvolvement with her mother.

Therapists too often dilute their interventions by overqualifying, apologizing, or rambling. This is less of a problem in individual therapy, where it is often best to elicit interpretations from the patient. Families are more like the farmer's proverbial mule—you sometimes have to hit them over the head to get their attention.

Intensity can also be achieved by extending the duration of a sequence beyond the point where the dysfunctional homeostasis is reinstated. A common example is the management of severe temper tantrums. Temper tantrums are maintained by parents who give in. Most parents try not to give in; they just don't try long enough. Recently, a four-year-old girl began to scream bloody murder when her sister left the room. She wanted to go with her sister. Her screaming was almost unbearable, and the parents soon were ready to back down. However, the therapist demanded that they not allow themselves to be defeated, and suggested that they hold her to "show her who's in charge" until she calmed down. She screamed for one solid hour! Everyone in the room was frazzled. But the little girl finally realized that this time she was not going to get her way, and so she calmed down. Subsequently, the parents were able to use the same intensity of duration to break her of this highly destructive habit.

Sometimes intensity requires frequent repetition of one theme in a variety of contexts. Infantalizing parents may have to be told not to hang up their child's coat, not to speak for her, not to take her to the bathroom, and not to do many other things that she is able to do for herself.

Shaping competence is another method of modifying interactions, and it is a hallmark of structural family therapy. Intensity is generally used to block the stream of interactions. Shaping competence is like altering the direction of the flow. By highlighting and shaping the positive, structural therapists help family members use functional alternatives that are already in their repertoire.

A common mistake made by beginning family therapists is to attempt to foster competent performance by pointing out mistakes. This is an example of focusing on content without due regard for process. Telling parents that they're doing something wrong, or suggesting they do something different has the effect of criticizing their competence. However well-intentioned, it is still a put-down. While this kind of intervention cannot be completely avoided, a more effective approach is to point out what they're doing right. Generous praise for competent performance uses both content and process to boost confidence and effectiveness.

Even when people do most things ineffectively, it is usually possible to pick out something that they're doing successfully. A sense of timing helps the therapist punctuate sequences while they're going well. For example, in a large, chaotic family the parents were extremely ineffective at controlling the children. At one point the therapist turned to the mother and said, "It's too noisy in here; would you quiet the kids?" Knowing how much difficulty the woman had controlling her children, the therapist was poised to comment immediately on any step in the direction of effective management. The mother had to yell "Quiet!" a couple of times before the children momentarily stopped what they were doing. Quickly—before the children returned to their usual uproar—the therapist complimented the mother for "loving her kids enough to be firm with them." Thus the message delivered was "You're a competent person, you know how to be firm." If the therapist had waited until the chaos resumed before telling the mother she should be firm, the message would be "You're an incompetent parent, you need to be more firm."

Wherever possible, structural therapists avoid doing things for family members that they are capable of doing themselves. Here too the message is "You are competent, you can do it." Some therapists justify taking over the family's functions by calling it "modeling." Whatever it's called it has the impact of telling family members that they are inadequate. Recently, a young mother confessed that she hadn't known how to tell her children that they were coming to see a family therapist and so had simply said she was taking them for a ride. Thinking to be helpful, the therapist then explained to the children that "Mommy told me there were some problems in the family, so we're all here to talk things over to see if we can improve things." This lovely explanation tells the kids why they came, but confirms the mother as incompetent to do so. If instead the therapist had suggested to the mother, "Why don't you tell them now?" then the mother, not the therapist, would have had to perform as an effective parent.

Boundary Making. Dysfunctional family dynamics are developed from and sustained by overly rigid or diffuse boundaries separating subsystems in the family. Structural therapists intervene to realign the boundaries by increasing either the proximity or distance between family subsystems.

In highly enmeshed families the therapist's interventions are designed to strengthen the boundaries between subsystems and to increase the independence of individuals. Family members are urged to speak for themselves, interruptions are blocked, and dyads are helped to finish conversations without intrusion from others. A therapist who wishes to support the sibling system and protect it from unnecessary parental intervention may say, "Susie and John, talk this over, and everyone else will listen carefully." If children frequently interrupt their parents, a therapist might challenge the parents to strengthen the hierarchical boundary by saying, "I can't believe you let them horn in on your conversation! Why don't you get them to butt out so that you two grownups can settle this?"

Although structural family therapy is begun with the total family group, subsequent sessions may be held with individuals or subgroups to strengthen the boundaries surrounding them. A teenager who is overprotected by her mother is supported as a separate person with individual needs by participating in some separate sessions. Parents so enmeshed with their children that they never have private conversations may begin to learn how if they meet separately with a therapist.

When a forty-year-old woman called the clinic for help with depression, she was asked to come in with the rest of the family. It soon became apparent that this woman was overburdened by her four children, and received little support from her husband, either as a husband or a father. The therapist's strategy was to strengthen the boundary between the mother and the children, and help the parents move closer toward each other. This was done in a series of stages. First the therapist joined with the oldest child, a sixteen-year-old girl, and supported her competence as a potential helper for her mother. Once this was done, the girl was able to assume a good deal of responsibility for her younger siblings, both in the sessions and at home.

Freed from some of the preoccupation with the children, the parents now had the opportunity to talk more with each other. They had very little to say to each other, however. This was not the result of hidden conflict or anger, but instead it reflected the marriage of a relatively nonverbal husband and wife, with different interests. After several sessions of trying to get the pair to enjoy talking with each other, the therapist realized that while talking may be fun for some people, it may not be for others. So to support the bond between the couple the therapist asked them to plan a special trip together. They chose a boatride on a nearby lake. When they returned for the next session, the spouses were beaming. They reported having had a wonderful time, being away from the kids and enjoying each other's company. Subsequently, they decided to spend a little time out together each week.

Disengaged families tend to avoid or detour conflict, and thus minimize interaction. The structural therapist intervenes to challenge conflict avoidance, and to block detouring in order to help disengaged members increase contact with each other. The therapist creates boundaries in the session which permit family members to discuss their conflicts without being interrupted. In addition, the therapist prevents escape or avoidance, so that the disagreements can be resolved.

Without acting as judge or referee, the structural therapist creates conditions in which family members can face each other squarely and struggle with the difficulties between them. When beginners see disengagement, they tend to think first of ways to increase positive interaction. In fact, disengagement is usually maintained as a way of avoiding arguments. Therefore, spouses isolated from each other usually need to fight before they can become more loving.

Most people underestimate the degree to which their own behavior influences and regulates the behavior of those around them. This is particularly true in disengaged families. Problems are usually seen as the result of what someone else is doing, and solutions are thought to require that the others change. The following complaints are typical. "We have a communication problem. He won't tell me what he's feeling." "He just doesn't care about us. All he cares about is that damn job of his." "Our sex life is lousy. My wife's frigid." "Who can talk to her? All she does is complain about the kids." Each of these statements suggest that the power to change rests solely with the other person. This is the almost universally perceived view of linear causality (Chapter 3).

Whereas most people see things this way, family therapists see the inherent circularity in systems interaction. He doesn't tell his wife what he's feeling, because she nags and criticizes; *and* she nags and criticizes because he doesn't tell her what he's feeling.

Structural therapists move family discussions from linear to circular causality by stressing the complementarity of family relations. The mother who complains that her son is naughty is taught to consider what she is doing to stimulate or maintain his behavior. The one who asks for change must learn to change his or her way of trying to get it. The wife who nags her husband to spend more time with her must learn to make increased involvement more attractive. The husband who complains that his wife never listens to him may have to listen to her more, before she's willing to reciprocate.

Minuchin emphasizes complementarity by asking family members to help each other change. When positive changes are reported he is liable to congratulate others, underscoring family interrelatedness.

Adding Cognitive Constructions. Although structural family therapy is not primarily a verbal or cognitive treatment, its practitioners use words and concepts to alter the way family members perceive reality. Reality, Minuchin says, is a perspective. Changing the way family members relate to each other offers alternative views of reality. The converse is also true: changing the way family members view reality enables them to change the way they relate to each other.

Structural family therapists have a more flexible and functional view of reality than those who believe in immaculate perception. Cognitive constructions may be veridical interpretations, pragmatic fictions, or paradoxes.

Sometimes, the structural family therapist acts as a teacher, offering information and advice based on training and experience. Information may be imparted to reassure anxious family members, to help them behave more competently, or to restructure their interactions. When family members feel embarrassed because they fight over little things, it may be helpful to tell them that most people do. Sometimes young parents will profit from a simple suggestion that they hire a babysitter and get out once in a while.

Minuchin occasionally teaches families about structure. Doing so is likely to be a restructuring maneuver and must be done in a way that minimizes resistance. He does this by delivering first a "stroke," then a "kick." In order to avoid direct challenge and attack which might produce resistance, interpretations are phrased to acknowledge the good that people are trying to do (the "stroke") before pointing to needed changes (the "kick"). If Minuchin were dealing with a family in which the mother speaks for her children, he might say to her, "You are very helpful" (stroke). But to the child, "Mommy takes away your voice. You can speak for yourself" (kick). Thus mother is defined as helpful, but intrusive (one stroke and one kick).

Structural therapists also use constructions, which are pragmatic fictions, to provide family members with a different framework for experiencing. The aim is not to educate or to deceive, but to offer a pronouncement which will help the family to change. For instance, telling children that they are behaving in a way that is consistent with being younger than they are is a very effective means of getting them to change. "How old are you?" "Seven." "Oh, I thought you were younger, because when you really get to be seven, you won't need Mommy to take you to school anymore."

Paradoxes are cognitive constructions which frustrate or confuse family members into a search for alternatives. Minuchin himself makes little use of paradox, but it can be an effective means of stimulating new transactional patterns (Chapter 10).

EVALUATING THERAPY THEORY AND RESULTS

While he was Director of the Philadelphia Child Guidance Clinic, Minuchin developed a highly pragmatic commitment to research. As an administrator he learned that research demonstrating effective outcomes is the best argument for the legitimacy of family therapy. Both his studies of psychosomatic children and Stanton's studies of drug addicts show very clearly how effective structural family therapy can be.

In *Families of the Slums*, Minuchin and his colleagues (1967) at Wiltwyck described the structural characteristics of low socioeconomic families, and demonstrated the effectiveness of family therapy with this population. Prior to treatment, mothers in patient families were found to be either over- or undercontrolling; either way their children were more disruptive than those in control families. These observations were the basis of Minuchin's classification of families as either *enmeshed* or *disengaged*. After treatment, mothers used less coercive control, yet were clearer and more firm. Treatment was found to be more successful with enmeshed than with disengaged families.

Studies demonstrating the effectiveness of structural family therapy with severely ill psychosomatic children are convincing because of the physiological measures employed, and dramatic because of the life-threatening nature of the problems. Minuchin, Rosman, and Baker (1978) reported one study which clearly demonstrated how family conflict can precipitate ketoacidosis crises in psychosomatic-type diabetic children. The investigators compared three groups of families—psychosomatic, behavior disorder, and normal—in terms of their response to a sequence of stress interviews. In the baseline interview parents discussed family problems with their children absent. Normal spouses showed the highest levels of confrontation, while psychosomatic spouses exhibited a wide range of conflict-avoidance maneuvers. Next, a therapist pressed the parents to increase the level of their conflict, while their children observed behind a one-way mirror. As the parents argued, only the psychosomatic children seemed to be really upset.

Moreover, these children's manifest distress was accompanied by dramatic increases in free fatty acid levels of the blood, a measure which is related to ketoacidosis. In the third stage of these interviews, the patients joined their parents. Normal and behavior-disorder parents continued as before, but the psychosomatic parents detoured their conflict, either by drawing their children into their discussions or by switching the subject from themselves to the children. When this happened, the free fatty acid levels of the parents fell, while the children's levels continued to rise. This study provided strong confirmation of the clinical observation that psychosomatic children are used (and let themselves be used) to regulate the stress between their parents.

The first outcome study of structural family therapy was conducted at Wiltwyck by Minuchin and his colleagues (1967). In this study, seven of eleven families were judged to be improved after six months to a year of family therapy. Although no control group was used, the authors compared their results favorably to the usual 50 percent rate of successful treatment at Wiltwyck. The authors also noted that none of the families rated as disengaged improved.

By far the strongest empirical support for structural family therapy comes from a series of studies with psychosomatic children and adult drug addicts. Minuchin, Rosman, and Baker (1978) summarized the results of treating 53 cases of anorexia nervosa with structural family therapy. After a course of treatment which included hospitalization followed by family therapy on an outpatient basis, 43 of these anorectic children were "greatly improved," two were "improved," three showed "no change," two were "worse," and three had dropped out. Although ethical considerations precluded using a control treatment with these seriously ill children, the 90 percent improvement rate is extremely impressive, especially when compared with the usual 30 percent mortality rate for this disorder. Moreover, the positive results at termination have been maintained at follow-up intervals of up to several years. Structural family therapy has also been shown to be extremely effective in treating psychosomatic asthmatics and psychosomatically-complicated cases of diabetes (Minuchin, Baker, Rosman, Liebman, Milman, and Todd, 1975).

Finally, Duke Stanton has shown that structural family therapy can be an effective form of treatment for drug addicts and their families. In a well-controlled study, Stanton and Todd (1979) compared family therapy with a family placebo condition and individual therapy. Symptom reduction was significant with structural family therapy; the level of positive change was more than double that achieved in the other conditions, and these positive effects persisted at follow-ups of six and twelve months.

SUMMARY

Minuchin may be best known for the artistry of his clinical technique, yet his structural family theory has become one of the most widely used conceptual models in the field. The reason that his theory is popular is that it is simple, inclusive, and practical. The basic structural concepts—boundaries, subsystems, alignments, and power—are easily grasped and applied; they take into account the individual, family, and social context; and the model provides a clear organizing framework for understanding and treating families.

Minuchin first developed his technique while working with disorganized families from inner city slums. In order to gain entrance to these families he developed techniques of joining, and in order to change them he developed concrete and powerful restructuring techniques. It is a therapy of action, directed at the here-and-now interactions of families, but designed to alter the basic structure underlying those interactions.

The single most important tenet of this approach is that every family has a structure, and that this structure is revealed only when the family is in action. According to this view, therapists who fail to consider the entire family's structure, and intervene in only one subsystem are unlikely to effect lasting change. If a mother's overinvolvement with her son is part of a structure that includes distance from her husband, no amount of therapy for the mother and son is likely to change the family.

Subsystems are units of the family based on function. If the leadership of a family is taken over by a father and daughter, then they are the executive subsystem, not the husband and wife. Subsystems are circumscribed and regulated by emotional boundaries. In normal families boundaries are clear enough to protect the separateness and autonomy of individuals and subsystems, and permeable enough to insure mutual support and affection. Enmeshed families are characterized by diffuse boundaries; disengaged families have very rigid boundaries.

Structural family therapy is designed to resolve the presenting problem by reorganizing the family structure. Assessment, therefore, requires the presence of the whole family, so that the therapist can observe the structure underlying the family's interactions. In the process, therapists should distinguish between dysfunctional and functional structures. Families with growing pains should not be treated as pathological. Where structural problems do exist, the goal is to create an effective hierarchical structure. This means activating dormant structures, not creating new ones.

Structural family therapists work quickly to avoid being inducted as members of the families they work with. They begin by making concerted efforts to accommodate to the family's accustomed ways of behaving, in order to circumvent resistance. Once they have gained a family's trust, structural therapists promote family interaction, while they assume a decentralized role. From this position they can watch what goes on in the family and make a diagnosis, which includes the problem and the structure that supports it. These diagnoses are framed in terms of boundaries and subsystems, which are easily conceptualized as two-dimensional maps that can be used to suggest avenues for change.

Once they have successfully joined and diagnosed a family, structural therapists proceed to activate dormant structures using techniques that alter alignments, and shift the power within and between subsystems. These restructuring techniques are concrete, forceful, and often highly dramatic. However, their success depends as much on the joining and assessment as on the power of the techniques themselves.

Structural family therapy's popularity is based on its theory and techniques of treatment; its central position in the field has been augmented by its research and training programs. There is now a substantial body of research which lends considerable empirical support to this school's approach. Moreover, the training programs at the Philadelphia Child Guidance Clinic have influenced an enormous number of family therapy practitioners throughout the world.

REFERENCES

Minuchin, S. *Families and family therapy.* Cambridge: Harvard University Press, 1974.

Minuchin, S., Montalvo, B., Guerney, B., Rosman, B. & Schumer, F. *Families of the slums.* New York: Basic Books, 1967.

Minuchin, S., Baker, L., Rosman, B., Liebman, R., Milman, L. & Todd, T.C. A conceptual model of psychosomatic illness in children. *Archives of General Psychiatry,* 1975, *32,* 1031–1038.

Minuchin, S., Rosman, B. & Baker, L. *Psychosomatic families: Anorexia nervosa in context.* Cambridge: Harvard University Press, 1978.

Minuchin, S. & Fishman, H.C. *Family therapy techniques.* Cambridge: Harvard University Press, 1981.

Stanton, M.D. & Todd, T.C. Structural family therapy with drug addicts. In E. Kaufman & P. Kaufmann (Eds.), *The family therapy of drug and alcohol abuse.* New York: Gardner Press, 1979.

12 Comparative Analysis

INTRODUCTION

t he exponential growth of family therapy has crowded the field with competing schools, every one of which has made important contributions. This diversity has produced a rich and varied literature, which bears witness to the vitality of the field. But these different approaches also constitute a confusing array of concepts and techniques, creating a dilemma: with the bewildering variety of family therapies, how is one to choose among them?

A therapist's theoretical orientation is no accident. The choice is overdetermined and rooted in personal experience. For some the choice of which approach to follow is dictated by what is available from their teachers and supervisors. Others pick and choose concepts and techniques from here and there, hoping to mold their own eclectic approach. Unfortunately, with no anchor to insure coherence, this strategy may be intellectually satisfying but clinically ineffective. Finally, there are those who pledge allegiance to a single approach; this provides them with a unified but often incomplete model.

In this chapter, I will offer a comparative analysis of systems of family therapy to sharpen the reader's appreciation of the separate approaches and to serve as a guide to understanding the similarities and differences among the systems. Each system proclaims a set of "truths," yet despite some overlap there are notable conflicts among these "truths." This chapter will highlight the conflicts and examine the competing positions.

My aim is to examine different solutions to some of the most significant problems of family therapy. This is somewhat different from the aim of the classification schemes presented in Chapter 2. There the goal was to organize the rival schools; here the focus is more on concepts and techniques than on the schools themselves. Therefore, some of the ideas in this chapter will be relevant only to a subset of the eight schools; schools that have an important position on those variables will be considered.

Theoretical Purity and Technical Eclecticism. Systems of family therapy are most clearly distinguished by their conceptual positions. Whether they claim to be based entirely on theory (behavioral family therapy) or to be atheoretical (experiential family therapy), each of the systems is supported by a set of beliefs about families and how to change them. Moreover, these theories relate to practice in a circular and mutually reinforcing manner. Practice generally precedes theory; thereafter progress in theory and practice proceeds in leapfrog fashion. Developments in one lead to developments in the other, in a continuing process.

The systematizers of family therapy are methodologists first, theoreticians second. The facts of their clinical observations and experience come before the hypotheses and speculations of their theories. Originally these theories were like maps drawn by explorers of new territories. But for those who came afterwards, students and colleagues, the theories offered preset guidelines for viewing the terrain.

Because they offer a preset way of looking at clinical data, theories have a biasing effect on observation. Students undoubtedly "see" what the theories they have studied prepare them to see. This is easily demonstrated by showing a videotape of the opening minutes of a family therapy session to a group of students. Even if the family conducts itself in a perfectly unremarkable fashion, students will "see" evidence of pathology, phrased in terms of whatever concepts they have learned.

Theories can bias observation and stultify creative thinking; but they also bring order out of chaos. They enable us to organize our observations, and to make sense out of what families are doing. Instead of seeing a "blooming, buzzing confusion," we begin to see patterns of interaction. Moreover, these patterns are organized in conceptual categories that are directly relevant to therapeutic intervention.

Theories also serve a political purpose. They demarcate one system of family therapy from the others and announce the unique point of view of that system. For this reason, theoretical positions tend to be stated in pure terms that maximize their distinctions. While this makes interesting reading, it is somewhat misleading. The truth is that the different systems of family therapy are more alike in practice than their theories suggest. Moreover, each new approach tends to become more eclectic over time. Practitioners start out as relative purists, but eventually discover the validity of theoretical concepts from other approaches and the usefulness of other people's techniques. The result is that, with increasing experience, most family therapists gradually become more eclectic.

Practice is the expected consequence of theory, but it doesn't always work out that way. Theory is molded by the requirements of logical consistency and elegance, and often reflects a desire to be seen as original and clever. Practice is molded in the pragmatic arena of clinical treatment; it is shaped by encounters with real people, who often turn out to be more complicated than abstract models. Clinicians trained in one school are often forced by the complexity of the task to incorporate methods from other schools. In everyday practice, the schools of family therapy tend to become synthetic and integrative. Therapists from technique-oriented schools, that focus on small sequences of interaction (behaviorists and strategists), have begun to adopt the organizing frameworks of schools with more comprehensive understanding of family dynamics (Bowenian and structural). At the same time, certain techniques that have proven their potency have been adopted by many of the schools of family therapy. Family therapists of all persuasions are now likely to clarify communications, direct enactments, and prescribe resistance, no matter what their approach.

Family Therapist—Artist or Scientist? Theories are modified in practice to suit the personal qualities of therapists as well as the practical needs of families. Expertise requires a body of operative knowledge, but it is not synonymous with expertness. Accomplished therapists begin with a grounding in theory; beyond that they must learn to extemporize. The therapist is not the system; just because Minuchin cures anorexia nervosa does not mean that any structural family therapist can.

The phrase, "the art and science of psychotherapy," implies that the therapist assumes a dual role, that of artist and scientist (Jasnow, 1978). On the surface, this seems innocuous—even banal. We all agree that a practitioner is first required to master the general principles and proven techniques in the field. Later, these principles and techniques must be applied skillfully in a way that is appropriate to each case and in a manner that is congruent with the therapist's personality. However, there is much room for disagreement about the degree to which the family therapist is more like an artist or more like a scientist.

Techniques alone do not make a family therapist. The therapist's personal qualities, respect for patients, and reverence for life are also important. Techniques are the tools, but human qualities are the supreme qualification of the good psychotherapist. Compassion—a deeply felt understanding of other people's sufferings—and sensitivity—an appreciation of people's inner world—can be lost in preoccupation with theoretical concepts. Without understanding and respect for individuals, family therapy remains a technical operation, instead of becoming a living human experience.

Behavioral and strategic therapists emphasize the scientific role of the therapist, while experiential and group family therapists stress the artistic side of the person. I believe that the best way to become an effective family therapist is to first learn to be a "scientist" and then become an "artist." A beginner should concentrate on learning theory and technique, and subject himself or herself to a tutorial program of supervision. During this training it is reasonable, even wise, to adopt or copy outright technique, style, and even language from one's mentors. Furthermore, it may be necessary to identify and modify or subdue certain types of responses that come naturally.

Mr. C. was a straight-A student in a psychiatric social work program, who came to a well-known family therapy institute with very strong references. His previous supervisors rated him as an outstanding young therapist, and stressed his warmth and ability to empathize with clients. When he began to see families it was immediately apparent that he had a natural gift for understanding and communicating his acceptance of people. His families liked him and they tended to remain in treatment with him.

Unhappily, his natural warmth and compassion for people made him respond to family problems by expressing sympathy and then by taking over. Although many of his families were happy to become dependent upon him, they failed to learn how to solve their own problems. Moreover, since they experienced no pressure to resolve their own problems, the therapist was left with very little leverage to change them in significant ways.

In supervision, Mr. C. was helped to recognize and restrain his well-meaning but counterproductive tendency to rescue his clients. The immediate result was a long and painful period of self-imposed restraint, but this eventually enabled him to become a better therapist.

Most young therapists come equipped not only with some innately helpful qualities, but also with a number of nontherapeutic impulses. Common among these are: assuming an overly central and controlling position with families; paying more attention to family members' feelings (or behavior, or thinking) than to other aspects of their experience; taking on the families' dilemmas as problems to be solved by the therapist; getting angry at resistant families; and identifying only with adolescents (or small children, or parents). Because most of these tendencies (chronic counter-transferences) tend to be characterological, it is unlikely that young therapists will be able to identify them without supervision. The only other way to detect chronic countertransference is to recognize repeated failures or stalemates with certain types of families. Once these clues to problems in the therapist are identified, self-analysis, consultation, or supervision will help to determine if the problem stems from inadequate therapeutic skill or from unrecognized countertransference.

THEORETICAL FORMULATIONS

All schools of family therapy have theories. Some are elaborate (psycho-analytic), some simple (experiential); some are developed from other disci-plines (behavioral), others are developed directly from family work (structural, strategic). Theories are ideas abstracted from experience and observation. Their purpose is to simplify and order the raw data of family life as an aid to understanding. In this chapter I will evaluate theories for their pragmatic function—understanding families in order to better treat them. The schools of family therapy will be compared on the basis of their theoretical positions on a sample of key conceptual dimensions: families as systems; stability and change; past or present; communication; content/process; monadic, dyadic, or triadic points of view; the nuclear family in context; and boundaries.

Families as Systems. Communications family therapists introduced the idea that families are systems. More than the sum of their parts, systems are the parts *and* the way they function together. Family group therapists also treat families as more than collections of individuals; but their idea of a superordinate group process is a more limited concept that refers to some-thing that happens when a group of people interact, rather than to an organizing principle that governs their entire lives.

All family therapists now accept the idea that families are systems; not believing in systems theory is a bit like not believing in the flag, apple pie, and motherhood. Schools of family therapy vary, however, in the degree to which they actually incorporate systems thinking in their practice. At one extreme, behavioral family therapists say very little about systems, and treat individuals as separate entities who influence each other only by acting as stimuli and reinforcers. At the other extreme, Bowenian, communications, strategic, and structural therapists base their approach to families on systems thinking.

Stability and Change. Communications theorists describe families as rule-governed systems with a tendency toward stability or homeostasis (Jackson, 1965). If a member of the family deviates from the family's rules, this constitutes negative feedback and the family reacts to force that person to change back. Families, like other living systems, maintain their interactions within a relatively fixed range in order to remain stable in the face of normal environmental stresses. In structural family theory the same point is made by saying that families have a relatively stable structure which enables them to function effectively as a system, with various subsystems each fulfilling part of the family's overall task.

Families must also change to adapt to changing circumstances. To do so they must be capable of revising their rules, and modifying their structure. Dysfunctional families are distinguished by their rigidity and inflexibility; when circumstances change, they do not.

The dual nature of families—homeostatic and changing—is best appreciated by family therapists from the communications, structural, and strategic schools; they expect families to come to treatment because they failed to adapt to changing circumstances. They do not presume that the families they see are inherently pathological.

Anyone who ignores this principle runs the risk of placing an undue emphasis on pathology. If a therapist sees a family that is having trouble, but fails to consider that they may be stuck at a transitional impasse, then he or she is apt to think that they need an overhaul, when a tuneup might do. The therapies that emphasize long-range goals are all susceptible to this therapeutic overkill. Although they emphasize growth, rather than pathology, psychoanalytic, experiential, and extended family practitioners are inclined to assume that the families they see are basically flawed and need fundamental reorganization. Since they have the equipment for major surgery—long-term therapy—they tend to see the patient as needing it. Sometimes the patient does not.

Past or Present. When it was inaugurated, family therapy was heralded as a treatment which emphasizes the present, in contrast to individual therapies which emphasize the past. Psychoanalysis was the chief whipping boy of family therapists eager to define themselves as different in every way. Psychoanalysis was portrayed as a monadic theory which focused on past traumas as the cause of problems, and directed treatment to cure people by helping them remember the past. While this picture accurately describes Freud's treatment in 1895, modern psychoanalysis is quite a bit more complicated.

That people are influenced by past experiences is an unarguable fact. The question is, how necessary is it to think about the past in order to understand the present? All family therapists work in the here-and-now; some see residues of the past, others do not.

Emphasis on the past is correlated with concern for individuals. Psychoanalytic practitioners view the determinants of behavior as resting with individuals. Theirs is a personality-trait model, in which family life is seen as a product of enduring dispositions, internalized from early object relations. This viewpoint affects practice, but not in the obvious way. Psychoanalytic therapists use their knowledge of past influences to inform their understanding of the present. They do not concentrate on helping people remember the past; instead they use psychoanalytic theory to help them understand what is going on in the present. The present may be understood in terms of transference and projection from the past, but it is still the present.

Surprisingly, the therapists who spend the most time talking with their patients about the past are the very ones who accentuate the here-and-now in their writings. Experiential therapists believe that unfinished business from the past interferes with full experiencing in the present. For this reason, they spend a lot of time talking with patients about old preoccupations in order to help them let go of the past (Pierce, Nichols, and DuBrin, 1983). An example of this approach is Paul's (1967) technique of *operational mourning*.

The past also plays a prominent role in Bowenian theory. Present family relationships are assumed to be products of relationships within the original family. Problems with a child, for example, are presumed to result from the parents' unresolved conflicts with their own parents. Unlike psychoanalytic therapists, who deal with the residuals of those relationships by pointing out their influence in the current family, Bowenian therapists send patients back to their families. Is this a return to the past? In practice, that is impossible; conceptually it is a return to the past.

The schools of family therapy that view the determinants of behavior as being outside—that is, between—individuals stress the present, in theory and practice. Family group therapists, communicationists, strategists, and structuralists have little to say about the past. They are less interested in history than in current development. They often see families as stuck in transition between one developmental phase and another, but their concern is with the progressive unfolding of function, not with events fixed in time.

Behavior therapists once explained all behavior as a result of past learning history. Pavlov's dogs salivated at the sound of a bell because they had been conditioned to do so; parents had trouble with their children because they had trained them improperly. Today, behavior therapists rely on operant conditioning as the model to explain most human behavior. According to this model, behavior is maintained by its consequences. Parents have trouble with their children because of the way they respond to them in the present. Therapy derived from this model deals with how people currently reinforce maladaptive behavior. The classical conditioning model is still used to explain certain anxiety disorders, especially sexual dysfunction, but treatment is designed to relax anxiety in the present.

Communication. Working with communication no longer distinguishes one school of family therapy from the others. All behavior is communicative, and all family therapists deal with verbal and nonverbal behavior. Although they all think about communication, they do so in very different ways.

Family group therapists have the most straightforward and simple view of communication. For them, communication is the medium of exchange through which members of families interact. Their treatment is to help transform blocked, incomplete, and covert communication into clear and open expression. They take what is conscious but unexpressed (except perhaps nonverbally), and bring it out into the open.

Behaviorists also think of communication in simple terms; for them communication is a skill that can be taught. In addition, they understand something less obvious about communication, namely that the message received may not be the one intended. They distinguish reinforcement from aversive control, and have, for example, pointed out that yelling at a child may be reinforcing, even though it is intended to be punishing. On the other hand, shouting what you want from your spouse may be more punishing than informing.

In psychoanalytic psychotherapy, communication is taken as metaphor, with the manifest content conveying derivatives of hidden needs and feelings. The therapist's job is to decode these latent meanings in order to help patients better understand themselves. In psychoanalytic family therapy the therapist not only brings these hidden meanings to light, but also helps family members express their latent emotions to each other. The therapist uses a knowledge of defenses, especially displacement and symbolization, to understand the unconscious content of family members' communications, and a knowledge of family dynamics to help complete these communications in the family.

Communications therapists also deal with communication on two levels, but instead of conscious and unconscious content, they deal with content and intent. Every communication is treated as conveying not only a message but also a statement about the relationship. For communications therapists this second communication, or metacommunication, is the more significant because it is less obvious.

Structural and strategic therapy both may be considered offshoots of communications theory (Madanes and Haley, 1977), and each emphasizes a particular aspect of communications in family relations. According to structural family theory, patterns of communication are what create family structure. Family organization develops from repeated sequences of interaction — communication; therapists detect the family's underlying structure by observing who speaks to whom and in what way. If a mother complains that she "cannot communicate" to her teenaged daughter, the structural therapist will enact a sequence where they try to talk to each other in the session. If they talk for only a few moments before breaking off, the therapist will conclude that they are disengaged; if they argue back and forth like peers or siblings, the therapist may conclude that there is no hierarchical distinction and that they are enmeshed; or if their conversation is repeatedly interrupted by the father, the therapist may conclude that interpersonal boundaries are blurred, and that the communication problem between mother and daughter is a product of the father's enmeshment.

In strategic therapy the main purpose of metacommunication is seen as a struggle for power in interpersonal relationships. From this point of view, symptoms are perceived as communications designed to manipulate other family members. For instance, a child's phobic fear of going to school may be a covert way to communicate that he is afraid that his parents might separate; the symptom serves to keep them together to take care of him. Family members' responses to problems are thought to create symptoms. In this case the parents' decision to stay home to take care of the child only makes matters worse. A strategic therapist would not try to help the family understand the meaning of these symptoms, but would instead try to provoke them to relate — communicate — in a way that makes the symptoms unnecessary. If the parents, together, took the child to school and, together, helped him with his homework, the improvement of the child could be divorced from whether or not the parents stay together.

The experientialists' interest in communication is also two-layered; what they consider important are unexpressed feelings, lying beneath the surface content of family members' communications. Like psychoanalytic therapists, they consider it important to reduce defenses so that people can communicate what is really on their minds; unlike psychoanalysts, they look in the present for relatively conscious feelings. Instead of interpreting defenses, they confront them in order to help people break out of their inhibitions. Because they work with families, they are concerned not only with uncovering feelings, but also with helping family members communicate their feelings honestly and openly within the family.

Extended family systems therapists foster communication as a vehicle for opening up relationships with the wider kinship group. In emotional cutoffs there is a breakdown in communication; in emotional reactivity communication comes from an undifferentiated stance in which people lose sight of their own thoughts and feelings; and in triangulated relationships communication is diverted from unresolved conflict in a dyad to a third person. Therapy is designed to help people re-establish communication with extended family members, teach them to communicate I-position statements, and redirect communication from a triangulated third party to the person for whom it was originally intended.

Content/Process. A system is the parts of a whole plus the way they function; process is the way families and groups function. Family and group therapists learn to attend to process and attempt to change it. When a mother and her teenaged daughter discuss the daughter's curfew, the mother and daughter are interested in *what* the other one says; the mother listens to when the daughter wants to come home and the daughter listens to her mother's response. A family therapist, listening to the same conversation, will be more interested in *how* the mother and daughter talk to each other. Does each state her point of view directly? Do they listen to each other? Is the mother clearly in charge? These questions have to do with the process of the conversation; they may not determine when the daughter comes home, but they reveal how the dyad functions.

When families come for treatment, they are usually focused on a content issue: a husband wants a divorce, a child refuses to go to school, a wife is depressed, and so on. The family therapist talks with the family about the content of the problem, but thinks about the process by which they try to solve it. While the family discusses what to do about a child's refusal to go to school, for instance, the therapist notices whether the parents seem to be in charge and if they support each other. If the therapist tells the parents to solve the problem by making the child go to school, then he or she is working with content, not process. The child may go to school, but the parents will not have improved the process of their decision-making.

All schools of family therapy have a theoretical commitment to working with the process of family interaction. Psychoanalytic and experiential clinicians try to reduce defensiveness and foster open expression of thoughts and feelings; family group and communications therapists increase the flow of interactions and help family members reduce the incongruence between different levels of communication; Bowenians block triangulation and encourage family members to take differentiated, I-position stances; strategic therapists ferret out and interdict problem-maintaining sequences of interaction; behaviorists teach parents to use positive control, and couples to eliminate coercive communication; structural therapists realign emotional boundaries and strengthen hierarchical organization.

Despite their theoretical commitment to process concepts, family therapists sometimes get distracted by content issues. Once in a while this does no harm. But to the extent that therapists focus exclusively on content, they are unlikely to help families change to become better functioning systems. Psychoanalytic therapists sometimes lose sight of process when they concentrate on individual family members and their memories of the past. Similarly, experientialists are prone to becoming overly central, while working with individual family members to help them overcome emotional defensiveness. The danger is that by so doing therapists will neglect the interactional processes in the family that effect individual expression.

Behavioral family therapists generally neglect process in favor of content. They do so when they isolate a particular behavioral sequence from its context in the family, ignoring the process that maintains it. They also interfere with the process of family interaction by assuming a directive, teaching role. As long as the teacher stands in front of a class and lectures, there is little opportunity to observe how the students behave on their own.

Process concepts are so central to extended family systems therapy that there is little danger that therapists in this school will forget them. Only naive misunderstanding of Bowenian therapy would lead someone to think merely of re-establishing family ties, without also being aware of processes of triangulation, fusion, and differentiation. The same is true of structural family therapy, family group therapy, and communications therapy; process issues are always at center stage.

Strategic family therapists have a dual focus—their goals are content-oriented, but their interventions are directed at process. As in behavioral therapy, the goal is in terms of content—solving the presenting problem. To understand what maintains the problem, however, strategic therapists shift their attention to process. Usually this involves discrete sequences of inter-action, which they try to block by using directives. The goal, though, is not to improve the process of family functioning, but merely to interdict a particular sequence in order to resolve the content of the presenting problem.

Monadic, Dyadic, or Triadic Model. Family therapy was initiated when clinicians recognized that the identified patient's behavior is a function of the whole family; all family practitioners now subscribe to this systems viewpoint. In practice, however, family therapists sometimes think in terms of units of one, two, or three persons. Some clinicians think of one person in the family as the patient, and bring in the family to help cure the patient. When these therapists work with families they emphasize the individual's thoughts and feelings. Their aim is to help family members become more aware of how they feel about and deal with each other.

Psychoanalytic therapists tend to think about individual dynamics, whether they meet with people alone or with their families. They see current family relations as a product of internalized relationships with the previous family, and they are often more concerned with these mental ghosts than with flesh and blood families. Child behavior therapists use a monadic model when they accept a family's definition that their symptomatic child is the problem, and set about teaching the parents to change the child's behavior. Experiential therapists also work with individuals to help them uncover and express their feelings.

The chief advantage of the monadic model is that it permits greater depth of analysis. The progression from monadic, to dyadic, to triadic models carries less depth but greater leverage for achieving change in a short span of time. Is it better to study something with a microscope or to take a wide-angle view? The answer is that both procedures are useful, depending on the purpose of the investigation. For a family therapist interested in helping people solve their problems, a triadic model is useful; for one interested in personal understanding and growth, a monadic model is also useful.

Actually, no living thing can adequately be understood in monadic terms. A bird's egg may be the closest thing in nature to a self-contained monad. The fetus is locked away inside its shell with all the nutrients it needs to survive. Even this view is incomplete, however, for there is an exchange of heat between the egg and the surrounding environment. Without the mother's warmth, the baby bird will die.

A dyadic model is necessary to understand the fact that people are always in relationships. Even the psychoanalytic patient, free associating on the couch, is filtering memories and dreams through reactions to the analyst. Most of the time family therapists operate with a dyadic model; they usually work on relationships between two people at a time. Even when a large family is in treatment, the focus is usually on various pairs of family members, considered in sequence.

Helping two people learn to relate better does not always mean that the therapist thinks in dyadic terms. Behavioral couples therapists work with two spouses, but treat them as separate individuals, each of whom is deficient in the art of communicating. A true dyadic model is based on the understanding that two people in a relationship are not separate monads interacting with each other; they each define the other. Using this model, a wife's agoraphobia would be understood as a reaction to her husband and as a means of influencing him. Likewise, his decision to send her for behavior modification reflects his refusal to accept his relationship to the symptom.

Family therapists of all schools use some dyadic concepts: unconscious need complementarity, expressive/instrumental, projective identification, symbiosis, intimacy, quid pro quo, double-bind, symmetrical, complementary, pursuer/distancer, and behavioral contract. Some terms are based on dyadic thinking even though they may involve more than two people: compliant (referring to a family's relationship to a therapist), or defiant; some seem to involve only one: countertransference, dominant, and supercompetent. Still other concepts are capable of encompassing units of three or more, but are often used to refer to units of two: boundary, coalition, fusion, and disengagement.

Most of the time family therapists think in dyadic terms, and most schools of family therapy do not take triadic relationships into account. Murray Bowen introduced the concept of emotional triangles into the family therapy literature, and has done more than anyone else to point out that human behavior is always a function of triadic relationships. Structural family therapists have also consistently been aware that enmeshment or disengagement between two people is always a function of a reciprocal relationship with a third. Communications therapists wrote about triadic relationships, but tended to think in terms of units of two. The same is true of most strategic therapists, although Selvini Palazzoli and Lynn Hoffman are consistently aware of triadic relationships.

The advantage of triadic thinking is that it permits a more complete understanding of behavior in context. If a boy misbehaves when his mother does not use firm discipline, teaching her to be firm will not work if her behavior is a function of her relationship with her husband. Perhaps she subtly encourages her child to misbehave as a way of undermining her husband's authority; or she and her husband may have worked out a relationship where her incompetence reassures him that he is the strong one.

The fact that triadic thinking permits a more complete understanding does not mean that family therapists must always include all parties in treatment. The issue is not how many people are in treatment, but whether or not the therapist considers problems in their full context.

The Nuclear Family in Context. Just as all family therapists espouse the ideas of systems theory, they also all regard families as open systems. The family is open in that its members interact, not only with each other, but also with extrafamilial systems in a constant exchange of information, energy, and material. Family therapy is a treatment of people in context; the most significant context for most people may be the nuclear family, but even to understand the nuclear family properly it is necessary to consider its context.

Communications family therapists introduced the concept of open systems to family therapy, but actually treated families as though they were closed systems. They paid little attention to sources of stress outside the family and rarely considered the impact of friends or extended family on the nuclear unit. The first clinicians to take the extrafamilial into account (and into treatment) were Murray Bowen and Ross Speck. Bowen has always stressed the critical role of extended family relationships, and Speck mobilized the patient's network of family and friends to aid in treatment.

Bowenian therapists and network therapists virtually always include people outside the nuclear family in treatment; psychoanalytic, group-oriented, behavioral, and communications therapists almost never do. Among experientialists, Whitaker has begun to routinely include members of the extended family in treatment for one or two sessions. Including extended family members or friends in treatment is often useful and sometimes essential. It is not, however, the same thing as thinking of the family as an open system. An open system is not a larger system, it is a system that interacts with its environment.

Nowhere is the idea of families as open systems better articulated than in Minuchin's (1974) *Families and Family Therapy.* Writing about "Man in His Context," Minuchin contrasts family therapy with psychodynamic theory. The latter, he says, draws upon the concept of man as a hero, remaining himself in spite of the circumstances. On the other hand, "The theory of family therapy is predicated on the fact that man is not an isolate. He is an acting and reacting member of social groups" (p. 2). He credits Gregory Bateson with erasing the boundary between inner and outer space, and goes on to say that just as the boundary separating the individual from the family is artificial, so is the boundary separating the family from the social environment. "Theories and techniques of family therapy lend themselves readily to work with the individual in contexts other than the family" (p. 4).

Structural family therapists recognize that families are embedded in a social context, and they often include teachers, school administrators, and other social agents in family diagnosis and treatment. If a single mother is enmeshed with her children, a structural family therapist might help her get more involved with friends or community activities as a way of helping her loosen her grip on the children.

Strategic family therapists may not treat families as open systems, but they do not confine their search for problem-maintaining sequences to the nuclear family. Selvini Palazzoli's work illustrates that in close-knit Italian families grandparents are often directly involved in sequences of behavior that support symptoms; and members of the MRI group often work with problem-maintaining sequences that involve someone outside the family, like a supervisor at work or a neighbor. Routinely including grandparents or friends in family therapy is useful but not essential; however, to gain a full understanding of families you must consider the forces outside the family acting and interacting with them.

Boundaries. Family practitioners study and treat people in context —individuals in context of their families, and families in context of their extended families and communities. One of the most useful concepts in family therapy is that of boundaries, a concept that applies to the relationship of all of these systems within systems in terms of the nature of their interface. The individuality and autonomy of each subsystem (individual, siblings, parents, nuclear family) is maintained by a semipermeable boundary between it and the suprasystem.

The clearest and most useful concepts of interpersonal boundaries are in the works of Murray Bowen and Salvador Minuchin. Bowen is best at describing the boundaries between individuals and their families; Minuchin is best at describing the boundaries between various subsystems within the family. In Bowen's terms, individuals vary on a continuum from fusion to differentiation, and Minuchin describes boundaries as diffuse or rigid, with resultant enmeshment or disengagement.

Bowen's thinking reflects psychoanalytic sources. Psychoanalytic theory emphasizes the development of interpersonal boundaries while describing how individuals emerge from the context of their families. Beginning with the separation and individuation from symbiosis with the mother that characterizes the psychological birth of the human infant (Mahler, Pine, and Bergman, 1975), psychoanalytic clinicians describe repeated and progressive separations that culminate first in the resolution of oedipal attachments and then eventually in leaving home.

Bowen's thinking about boundaries continues the somewhat one-sided emphasis on poorly defined boundaries between self and other. He pays little attention to the problems of emotional isolation stemming from rigid boundaries, and describes this as an artifact—a defense against—a basic lack of psychological separateness. Bowen uses a variety of terms—togetherness, fusion, undifferentiation, emotional reactivity—all of which refer to the danger that he is most concerned with, that people will lose themselves in relationships.

Minuchin offers a more balanced view of boundaries, describing the problems that result when they are either too rigid or too diffuse. Diffuse boundaries allow outside interference into the functioning of a subsystem; rigid boundaries interfere with communication, support, and affection between different segments of the family. Bowen describes only one boundary problem—fusion; and only one goal—differentiation; Minuchin speaks of two possibilities—enmeshment or disengagement—and his therapy is designed to fit the specific case.

Minuchin (1974) explains the function of boundaries, their reciprocal relationship, and how a knowledge of boundaries can be used to plan therapy. Boundaries protect individuals and subsystems from intrusion so that they can function autonomously. Newlyweds, for instance, need to establish a clear boundary between themselves and their parents in order to work out their own independent relationship. A diffuse boundary will leave them overly reliant on their parents, preventing them from developing their own autonomy and intimacy. If a wife calls her mother whenever she is upset, she will not learn to work things out with her husband; if she borrows money from her father whenever she wants to make a large purchase, she will not develop her own potential to earn a living.

In Bowenian theory, people tend to be either emotionally fused or differentiated. Fusion is like a disease—you can have a bad case or a mild one. In structural family theory the enmeshment-disengagement distinction plays two roles. Some families are described as either enmeshed or disengaged; but more often families are described as made up of different subsystems with the enmeshment of some producing the disengagement of others. For example, a mother and child may be described as enmeshed (Bowen would say fused); this will be seen not in isolation but as a product of the woman's disengaged relationship with her husband. Using this understanding of the interlocking nature of subsystem boundaries, it is possible to design therapy to fit a specific family and to co-ordinate change among its subsystems.

Bowen's "fusion" and Minuchin's "enmeshment" both deal with the consequences of blurred boundaries, but they are not alternate vocabularies for the same thing. Fusion is a quality of individuals and it is the counterpart of the psychoanalytic concept of individuation. Both are intrapsychic concepts for a person's *psychological* embeddedness—undifferentiation—within a relationship context. The dynamics of fusion have an impact on other relationships (especially in the form of triangulation), but fusion is *within* the person. Enmeshment is strictly a social systems concept; enmeshment is *between* people. These conceptual differences are also related to differences in treatment. Bowen coaches individuals to stay in contact and maintain an I-position; success is measured in individual differentiation. Minuchin joins the system and realigns coalitions by strengthening *or* weakening boundaries; success is measured by change in the whole system. Bowen's conceptualization may lead to lasting individual personality change, which may affect the whole family system; Minuchin's conceptualization permits greater leverage and quicker change. The difference is between working with individuals to change the system, and working with the system to change individuals.

NORMAL FAMILY DEVELOPMENT

As a rule family therapists have less to say about developmental issues than do individual psychotherapists. One of the distinguishing characteristics of family therapy is its focus on the here-and-now interactions that maintain family problems. Normal family development involves the past and what is healthy, and therefore has been underemphasized.

Many family therapists have pointed out that normality and abnormality are not discrete, that there is a wide range of functional and dysfuctional behavior (Watzlawick, Beavin, and Jackson, 1967; Minuchin, 1974). This point is well taken, but it has been made often enough; it is no longer a valid excuse for failing to develop models of normal, or functional, family behavior.

Most therapists do have implicit models about what is normal, and these assumptions influence their clinical assessment and treatment. The problem is that these unarticulated models are based largely on personal experience; as long as these remain unexamined they are apt to reflect personal bias.

Many people assume that healthy families are just like their own—or just the opposite. However, the fact that a therapist comes from a relatively disengaged, upwardly striving, intact nuclear family does not make this the only, or the best, model of family life. When it comes to setting goals for family treatment, the choice is not between using a model of normality or having no model, but between using a model that has been spelled out and examined, or operating on the basis of ill-defined and personal standards.

Among family therapists, those concerned with the past, especially members of Bowenian and psychoanalytic schools, have had the most to say about normal development. These two schools share an evolutionary, developmental perspective. Whereas most other family therapists explain problems in terms of ongoing interactional difficulties, Bowen and the psychoanalysts are interested in the developmental history of problems. Although their main interest in development is to understand how problems arise, their analyses also describe normal development.

Whereas most schools of family therapy are not concerned with how families get started, the Bowenian and psychoanalytic schools have a great deal to say about marital choice. Bowen speaks about differentiation, fusion, and triangles, while the psychoanalytic writers speak of unconscious need-complementarity, projective identification, and idealization; but they seem to be using different terms to describe similar phenomena. Psychodynamic therapists speak of marital choice as an object of transference from the family of origin, and of people as choosing partners with the same level of maturity; Bowen says that people pick partners who replicate familiar patterns of family interaction, and select mates at the same level of differentiation as in the family of origin.

These are descriptions of significant ways in which people marry partners with similar underlying personality dynamics. Both of these schools also discuss ways in which people choose mates who appear to be different—at least on the surface—in ways that are exciting and that seem to make up for deficiencies in the self. Obsessives tend to marry hysterics, and according to Bowen togetherness-oriented people often marry distancers. This brings up another way in which the Bowenian and psychodynamic schools are similar to each other and different from the others. Both have an appreciation of depth psychology; both recognize that personalities have different strata. Both think that the success of a marital relationship depends not only on the partner's shared interests and values, but also on the nature of their internal, introjected object images. Spouses will perceive and relate to each other in terms of their inner (unconscious) object worlds.

Psychoanalysts emphasize the critical importance of good object relations in early childhood. The infant's ability to develop a cohesive self-image and good internal objects depends upon "good-enough mothering" in an "average expectable environment." With a cohesive sense of self the child will grow up able to be with others and be independent; without a coherent self, being with others may feel like being engulfed, and being alone may feel like being abandoned. Early object relations are not just memories, they actually form psychic structures of the mind which preserve early experiences in the form of self-images and object-images. These internalized object-images, in turn, determine how people in the environment will later be experienced. Thus, the child's future—and the future of his or her family development—is laid down at a very early age.

Bowen's description of normal family development is also highly deterministic. Parents transmit their immaturity and lack of differentiation to their children; emotional fusion is passed on in a multigenerational transmission process. A family's fate is a product of relationships worked out in preceding generations.

Bowenian and psychoanalytic therapists also describe the triangular relationship between mother, father, and child as a crucial determinant of all later development. The psychoanalytic writers describe this oedipal situation in terms of conflicting drives, and believe that their resolution affects all future relationships. Bowenians describe this triangle in terms of stabilizing unresolved emotional tension in the marital dyad, and see it as the prototype of all subsequent relationships.

Clinicians are most likely to see people from families in which the triangular family romance was not resolved, but these theories include the possibility of successful resolution. Both theories, Bowenian and psychoanalytic, hold up visions of ideal functioning toward which people can strive but which they can never fully achieve. The result can be either a utopian model which condemns patients to dissatisfaction with their lives, or a standard used to guide people toward an enriched but not perfect life.

The clearest statement of such a standard is Bowen's (1966) description of families with "moderate to good differentiation." In these families the marriage is a functioning partnership in which spouses can be intimate without losing their autonomy. They permit their children to develop autonomous selves without becoming unduly anxious or trying to mold the children to their own images. Everyone in these families is responsible for himself or herself and neither credits others for personal success, or blames them for failure. They are able to function well with other people or to be alone, as the situation requires. Their intellectual functioning is not infused with emotionality at times of stress; they are adaptable, flexible, independent, and able to cope with good times and bad.

While they do not emphasize the past, most of the other schools of family therapy have a few isolated concepts for describing processes of normal family development. For example, communicationists speak of the *quid pro quos* (Jackson, 1965) which are exchanged in normal marriages. The behaviorists describe the same phenomenon in terms of social exchange theory (Thibaut and Kelley, 1959).

Although all family therapists have a few concepts for dealing with normal family development, Minuchin is one of the few (other than Bowen and the psychodynamic therapists) who says that it is important to know what is normal in order to recognize what is abnormal. According to Minuchin (1974), clinicians need to have both an intellectual and emotional appreciation of the facts of ordinary family life in order to become effective family therapists. First, it is necessary to recognize that normal family life is not a bed of roses. When two people marry they must learn to accommodate to each other; each succeeding transition in the family life cycle requires further modifications of the family structure. Clinicians need to be aware of this, and able to distinguish functional from dysfunctional structures, as well as pathological structures from structures that are simply in a transitional process. Moreover, Minuchin adds, it is hard to be a truly effective therapist without having personally experienced some of the problems that families in treatment are struggling with. This is a point that older and more experienced therapists are more sympathetic with than are young ones.

Because structural family therapy begins by measuring the adequacy of the client family's structure, it sometimes appears to have an ideal standard. In fact, however, normality is defined in terms of functional accomplishment, and structural family therapists recognize that diverse patterns may be functional. Functional families may be somewhat enmeshed or disengaged. The clarity of subsystem boundaries is far more important than the composition of the subsystem. For example, a parental subsystem made up of a father and oldest child can function effectively if the lines of responsibility and authority are clearly drawn. Patterns of enmeshment and disengagement are viewed as preferred styles, not necessarily as indications of abnormality.

The other schools of family therapy describe concepts of normality by mentioning specific mechanisms that are missing in dysfunctional families. Strategic therapists, for example, portray dysfunctional families as creating symptoms out of normal problems by failing to adjust their functioning to meet the demands of changing circumstances, and then trying to solve the problem by doggedly doing more of the same.

Bowenian and psychoanalytic family clinicians have developed elaborate models of normal development partly because they have an intrinsic interest in theory building. Both schools value understanding for its own sake. But what are the practical consequences of building models of normal family development? To begin with, it is important to realize that the goals of these two approaches are different from the goals of most other family therapies. They are designed not merely for solving problems, but for life-long structural reorganization—intrapsychic and interpersonal. To reorganize the dynamic residues of a family's past it is necessary to have a model of how the past was—and should be—organized.

Most family therapists do not think in terms of restructuring the past, and therefore believe they have little need for models of normal family development. Instead, they intervene around specific sequences of problem-maintaining behavior, which are conceptualized in terms of function. The sequences they observe are dysfunctional, and therefore, by implication, what is functional must be just the opposite. Communication therapists use discrete concepts of family functioning, like rules and metarules. That is what they think about, that is what they see, and that is what they intervene to alter.

While it may not be necessary to have a way of understanding a family's past in order to help them, it is necessary to have a way of understanding the family's organization of the present, using a model of normal behavior to set goals for treatment. Such a model should include a design for the present and for change over time. Among the ideas presented in this book the ones most useful for a basic model of normal family functioning include structural hierarchy, effective communication, and family life cycle development.

DEVELOPMENT OF BEHAVIOR DISORDERS

In the early days of family therapy, patients were seen as scapegoats on whom families projected their conflicts and whose deviance maintained family stability. Much of the literature emphasized how parents with serious but covert conflict unite in concern for their emotionally disturbed child, who then becomes the identified patient. This was a theory of how family conflict causes behavior disorders in children. Many of the concepts put forward at that time were about dysfunctional ways of keeping the peace: scapegoating, pseudomutuality, rubber fence, family projection process, double-bind, disqualification, mystification, and so on. These mechanisms may have driven young people crazy, but they helped keep their families together.

Initially, the patterns of disturbed function observed in schizophrenic families were thought to cause schizophrenia. Eventually, etiological models gave way to transactional ones. Instead of causing schizophrenia, these disturbed family interactions came to be seen as patterns of family relationship in which schizophrenia is embedded. Neither the family nor the symptomatic member is the locus of the problem—the problem is not *within* people, it is *between* them.

Today, family therapists do not think about what causes problems, they think about how families unwittingly maintain their problems. Each of the systems of family therapy have unique ideas about how pathological families fit together, but the following themes are useful to define some of the important differences of opinion in the field: inflexible systems, function of symptoms, underlying dynamics, and pathological triangles.

Inflexible Systems. Inflexibility is the characteristic of pathological family systems most frequently indicted. Chronic inflexibility is a striking feature of families with disturbed members; these families are so rigid that it is virtually impossible to grow up in them healthy and normal. Acute inflexibility explains why other families become dysfunctional at transitions in the life cycle; disorder breaks out in these families when they fail to modify their organization in response to growth or stress.

Early observers of schizophrenic family interactions emphasized the rigid inflexibility of these families. Wynne coined the term *rubber fence* to dramatize how psychotic families resist outside influence, and *pseudomutuality* to describe their rigid facade of harmony. R.D. Laing showed how parents, unable to tolerate their children's healthy strivings, used *mystification* to deny and distort their experience. Communications theorists thought that the most striking disturbance in schizophrenic families was the extreme inflexibility of their rules. According to this systems analysis, these families were unable to adapt to the environment because they had no mechanisms for changing their rules; they were rigidly programmed to negative feedback, treating novelty and change as deviations to be resisted. Forces of homeostasis overpower forces of change, leaving these families stable but chronically disturbed.

Explaining family pathology in terms of rigid homeostatic functioning is today one of the cornerstones of the strategic school. Strategists describe dysfunctional families as responding to problems within a limited range of solutions. Even when the attempted solutions do not work, these families rigidly keep trying; thus the attempted solutions, rather than the symptoms, are the problem. Behavorists use a similar idea when they explain symptomatic behavior as a result of faulty efforts to change behavior. Often when parents think they are punishing their children, they are actually reinforcing them with attention.

Psychoanalytic and experiential clinicians have identified pathological inflexibility in individuals and couples, as well as in whole families. According to these two schools, intrapsychic rigidity, in the forms of conflict, developmental arrest, and emotional suppression, are the individual's contribution to family pathology. Psychoanalysts consider pathological families as closed systems that resist change. According to this line of thought, symptomatic families are rigid in that they treat the present as though it were the past. When faced with a need to change, dysfunctional families regress to earlier levels of development where unresolved conflicts left them fixated.

Experientialists often describe pathological families as chronically resistant to growth. The symptom-bearer is seen to be signaling a family pattern of opposition to life forces. Unfortunately this model makes the family the villain, and the individual the victim. The experiential model of inflexibility is fairly simple, and is primarily useful with minor forms of psychic difficulty.

Structural family therapists locate the inflexibility of dysfunctional families in the boundaries between subsystems. Disturbed families tend to be either markedly enmeshed or markedly disengaged. Young therapists who have trouble diagnosing family structure are at first happily surprised when confronted with a profoundly disturbed family. The structure is so easy to see. Unfortunately, families with an unmistakably clear structure are extremely deviant and very difficult to change.

Structural family therapy also identifies acute inflexibility in symptomatic families. Minuchin (1974) stresses that otherwise normal families will develop problems if they are unable to modify a previously functional structure to cope with an environmental or developmental crisis. Family therapists should be very clear on this point: symptomatic families are often basically sound, they simply need help adjusting to a change in circumstances.

The Function of Symptoms. Early family therapists described the identified patient as serving a critical function in disturbed families, detouring conflict and thus stabilizing the family. Vogel and Bell (1960) portrayed emotionally disturbed children as family scapegoats, singled out as objects of parental projection on the basis of traits which set them apart from other members of the family. Thereafter, their deviance promotes cohesion. Communications theorists thought that symptoms were fraught with meaning —functioning as messages—and with consequences—controlling other family members.

Today, many family therapists deny that symptoms have either meaning or function. Behavioral and strategic therapists do not assume that symptoms are necessary to maintain family stability, and so they intervene to block the symptom without being concerned about restructuring the family. Behaviorists have always argued against the idea that symptoms are a sign of underlying pathology or that they serve any important function. Behavioral family therapists treat problems as the uncomplicated result of faulty efforts to change behavior and lack of skills. Restricting their focus to symptoms is one of the reasons why they are successful in discovering the contingencies that reinforce them; it is also one of the reasons why they are not very successful with cases where a child's behavior problems function to stabilize a conflicted marriage, or where a couple's arguments protect them from dealing with unresolved personal problems. Strategic family therapists recognize that symptoms may serve a purpose, but deny that it is necessary to consider that purpose when planning therapy. Instead of trying to figure out what function may be served by symptoms, they concentrate on understanding how the pieces of the system fit together in a coherent fashion. Members of this school take the modest position that if they help to free families from their symptoms, then the families can take care of themselves.

Some of the other schools of family therapy continue to believe that symptoms signal deeper problems and that they function to maintain family stability. In families that cannot tolerate open conflict, a symptomatic member serves as a smokescreen and a diversion. Just as symptomatic behavior preserves the balances of the nuclear family, so may problems in the nuclear family preserve the balance in the extended family. In psychoanalytic, Bowenian, and structural formulations, a couple's inability to form an intimate bond may be ascribed to the fact that one or both of them are still being used to mediate the relationship between their parents. In this way, symptomatic behavior is transmitted across generations, and functions to stabilize the multigenerational family system.

Many times it is possible to see how symptoms function to arouse a depressed or disengaged parent to become more involved with the family. Two examples will illustrate this frequent observation. The first is from Jay Haley's (1976) *Problem-Solving Therapy*. According to Haley, a child's misbehavior is often part of a repetitive cycle that serves to keep the parents involved. In a typical sequence, father becomes unhappy and withdraws; the child misbehaves; mother fails to discipline the child; father steps in, reinvolving himself with the mother through the child. The second example is from an interview conducted by Harry Aponte (a noted structural family therapist), quoted in Hoffman (1981, p. 83).

> The interview is with a poor black family that fully answers to the description "multiproblem." Everybody—the mother, six grown or nearly grown children, and two grandchildren—is at risk, from breakdown, illness, nerves, violence, accident or a combination of all these factors. In addition, the family members are noisy, disruptive, and hard to control.
>
> At a certain point Aponte asks the mother, "How do you handle all this?" The mother, who has been apathetic and seemingly unconcerned as the therapist tries to talk with the children, says, "I put on my gorilla suit." The children laugh as they describe just how terrible their mother is when she puts on her gorilla suit.
>
> An incident occurs shortly after this conversation which suggests that a circular causal sequence is at work, one of those redundancies that may have to do with family balance. Mother is still apathetic and looks tired, and the therapist begins to ask about her nerves. At first the children are somewhat quiet, listening. As she begins to admit that she has had bad nerves and that she is taking pills, they begin to act up. One boy pokes the baby; another boy tries to restrain the baby from kicking back; the baby starts to yell. The therapists asks the twenty-year-old daughter (the baby's mother) if she can control him; she says no. At this point the mother gets up and smacks her daughter's baby with a rolled-up newspaper, rising out of her lethargy like some sleeping giant bothered by a gnat. She sits the baby down with a bump, and he makes no further trouble. During this sequence the rest of the children jump and shriek with joy, causing their mother to reprimand them, after which they calm down and the mother sits back, more watchful now and definitely in control.

Here a mother overwhelmed by stress becomes depressed; as she describes her depression the children become anxious and misbehave; the misbehavior triggers a reaction in the mother, rousing her from withdrawal to control the chaos. The children's symptomatic misbehavior functions as cause and cure of the mother's depression, in a recurring cycle.

Underlying Dynamics. The idea that there are hidden dynamics underlying observable behavior is reminiscent of the individual psychodynamic theory that family therapy developed in opposition to. In the 1950s, family therapists challenged the psychoanalytic belief that symptoms are only surface phenomena and that the real problems are inside. Instead, they showed how observations limited to the surface of family interactions were sufficient to understand and treat behavioral problems.

Today there are still many family therapists who deny that it is necessary or valid to look for underlying dynamics in order to explain or treat symptomatic behavior. These clinicians believe that it is sufficient to observe patterns of interaction in the family. Some strategic therapists, like the MRI group, confine the field of focus to interactions surrounding symptomatic behavior; others, like the Milan group, take a broader view of the whole family. Behaviorists maintain that in order to account for unwanted behavior it is necessary only to observe its reinforcing consequences.

Despite the family therapy tradition of explaining problem behavior without bringing in underlying dynamics, many family therapists believe that neither the presenting symptoms nor surrounding interactions are the real problem; the real problem is some form of underlying family pathology. When families come in, these therapists look beneath—or beyond— behavioral sequences for some hypothesized basic flaw in the family. Minuchin's concept of family structure is the leading example of such a concept. Structural family therapists listen to families describe problem behavior, but they look for underlying structural pathology to explain and resolve these problems.

Structural pathology is conceptually different from the intrapsychic conflict in psychodynamic theory. Intrapsychic conflict is an *inferred* psychological concept, structural pathology is an *observed* interactional concept. Nevertheless, in practice, structural family therapists shift their attention from the family's complaints to a different level of analysis.

Family structure is now one of the central concepts in family therapy, and the field can be divided into those who include structure in their analyses and those who do not. Haley (1980) does, and for this reason many people consider him a structuralist as much as a strategist. Selvini Palazzoli and Lynn Hoffman bring in structural concepts in terms of systemic conflict and "too richly cross-joined systems" (Hoffman, 1981). John Weakland of the MRI group emphatically denies the need to include structural concepts in family assessment, and he considers doing so a species of discredited psychodynamic theorizing. Others in the family field, including behaviorists (Patterson) and some experientialists (Whitaker), accept the utility of structural concepts; their doing so shows a growing convergence among competing systems.

Neither psychoanalytic nor Bowenian therapists use Minuchin's structural family theory, but both schools have their own concepts of underlying dynamics. Psychoanalysts originated the idea of underlying dynamics; present-day psychoanalytic family practitioners use this idea in concepts of intrapsychic structural conflict (id, ego, superego); developmental arrest; internal object relations; and interlocking psychopathological structures among family members. According to the psychoanalytic model, problems may develop in interactions, but it is the interacting individuals who have the basic flaws.

In Bowen's theory, fusion, family projection process, and interlocking triangles are the major concepts of underlying family dynamics. So much are these underlying issues emphasized that Bowenians probably spend less time than anyone else dealing directly with presenting symptoms or even with symptom-bearers.

Bowenian theory uses a *diathesis-stress* model of mental disorder. This is a model from genetic research in which a person develops a disorder when a genetic weakness is sufficiently stressed by an event in the environment. In Bowenian theory, people who develop symptoms in the face of anxiety-arousing stress have low levels of differentiation and are emotionally cut off from support systems, especially in the extended family. The diathesis may not be genetic, but it is passed on from one generation to the next.

Pathological Triangles. The double-bind theory was a landmark in the shift from an individual to a systems unit in the analysis of the development of behavior disorder. Current concepts of pathology sometimes refer to individuals—fusion of emotion and intellect, repressed affect, developmental arrest; and sometimes to dyads—fusion in a relationship, mystification, unresolved symbiotic attachment. However, the most sophisticated thinking in the field is triadic.

Pathological triangles are at the heart of several family therapy explanations of behavior disorder. Among these, Bowen's theory is perhaps the most elegant and well-known. Bowen explains how when two people are in conflict, the one who experiences the most anxiety will triangle in a third person. This model not only provides a beautiful explanation of systems pathology, but also serves warning to therapists. As long as a therapist remains fused with one party to an emotional conflict, then he or she is part of the problem, not part of the solution.

In psychoanalytic theory, oedipal conflicts are the root of neurosis. Here the triangle is stimulated by family interactions, but formed and maintained in the individual psyche. Mother's tenderness may be seductive and father's jealousy threatening, but the wish to destroy the father and possess the mother is a figment of fantasy. Pathological fixation of this conflict may be caused by developments in the outer space of the family, but the conflict is harbored in the inner space of the mind.

The psychoanalytic model of the individual is that of a divided self at war within. But psychoanalytic family practitioners treat family problems as disorders in relationships. The cause of the problem may be a function of individual personalities, but the result is in the interaction. *Pathological need complementarity* is the core psychoanalytic concept of interlocking pathology of family relationships. A person with a strong need to be submissive, for instance, will marry someone with a strong need to be dominant. These needs are based on early identifications and introjections. The husband who has a sense of himself as a victim has internalized pathogenic introjections that revolve around aggressive conflicts, but his needs are acted out in pathological relationships—that is, his unconscious need for an aggressor will lead him to select a mate who can act this role, allowing him to project his repressed or split off aggression onto his wife. Divided selves thus become divided spouses.

Structural family theory of disorder is based on triangular configurations where a dysfunctional boundary between two people or subsystems is a reciprocal product of a boundary with a third. Father-and-son's enmeshment reflects father-and-mother's disengagement; a single mother's disengagement from her children is the counterpart of her overinvolvement outside the family. Structural family theory also uses the concept of pathological triangles to explain *conflict-detouring triads,* where parents divert their conflict onto a child. Minuchin, Rosman, and Baker (1978) have even demonstrated physiological changes that occur when parents in conflict transfer their stress to a psychosomatic child. Using this model, therapy is designed to disengage the child from the parents' struggle and to help the parents work out their conflicts directly.

Most strategic family therapists work with a dyadic model—one person's symptoms are maintained by others' (taken as a single group) efforts to resolve them. Haley and Selvini Palazzoli, however, use a triangular model in the form of *cross-generational coalitions.* These "perverse triangles," as Haley (1977) calls them, occur when a parent and child, or a grandparent and child, collude to form a bastion of covert opposition to another adult. Failure to recognize these cross-generational coalitions dooms to failure any attempt to help parents resolve "their" problems with a symptomatic child. For this reason, behavioral parent training probably will not work when there is significant unrecognized conflict between the parents. Teaching a father how to reward respectful behavior from his son will not get very far if mother subtly reinforces the son's disrespect.

GOALS OF THERAPY

The goal of all psychological treatment is to help people change in order to relieve their distress. This is true of individual therapy, group therapy, and family therapy. Why then is so much written about the different goals of various schools of therapy? Some of it has to do with differing ideas about how people change; some of it merely has to do with alternate vocabularies for describing change. When Bowenians speak of "differentiation of self" and psychoanalytic therapists speak of "increased ego strength," they mean pretty much the same thing.

If we strip away the semantic differences, there are two major dimensions of goals on which the schools of family therapy vary. First, the schools differ with respect to their mediate goals; they seek change through different aspects of personal and family functioning. Second, the schools differ in terms of how much change they seek. Some are content with symptom resolution, others aspire to transform the whole family system.

The variations in mediate goals among the systems are based upon theoretical differences about which aspects of personal and family functioning it is most necessary to change. One of the goals of experiential family therapy is to help families become more emotionally expressive. Experientialists believe that emotional stagnation is a primary problem, and that increased expressiveness will make people more alive and happy. To a large extent, therefore, the differences in mediate goals among different schools reflects theoretical differences of opinion about how behavior change is best accomplished. I will discuss these distinctions more fully below in *Conditions for Behavior Change*.

The second difference in goals—how much change—has to do with how the schools differ with respect to their aims about the resolution of presenting problems or the overhauling of family systems. All family therapists are interested in resolving problems and decreasing symptomatology. But they vary along a continuum from being exclusively concerned with symptom resolution to being more concerned with ultimately changing the entire family system. Strategic and behavioral therapists are least concerned with changing the whole system; psychoanalytic and Bowenian therapists are most concerned with systems change. In addition, psychoanalysts and Bowenians are particularly interested in fundamental changes in individual personalities (intrapsychic structural change or differentiation), and they are unique among family therapists in this respect.

The goal of structural family therapy is both symptom resolution and structural change. But the structural change sought has the modest aim of reorganizing that particular part of the family structure which has become dysfunctional and problematic by failing to change to meet changing circumstances. Structural family therapists do not have the more ambitious goal of remaking the whole family. Group, communications, and experiential family therapists also aim midway between symptomatic improvement and systematic family reorganization. Practitioners from these schools focus neither on presenting complaints nor on the overall family system. Instead they pay special attention to discrete processes which they think underlie symptoms: group dynamics, patterns of communication, and emotional expressivity. Improvements in these processes are thought to resolve symptoms and promote growth and health, but neither symptom resolution alone nor systems change per se is the goal.

In this writer's view, one goal of family therapy must be to resolve the problems that clients come in with. If a family asks for help with a specific problem and the therapist helps them express their feelings better, but does not help them solve the problem, then he or she has failed the family in an important way. One of the virtues of the behavioral and strategic approaches that focus narrowly on presenting complaints is that they do not fool themselves or their clients about whether or not these problems get solved. Some of the other approaches with grander aspirations run the risk of losing sight of this first responsibility of family therapists. For example, if a mother complains that her small daughter is disobedient and does not do well in school, and a therapist bypasses these problems to get to "the real issues," which may be defined as the woman's relationship with her parents or conflicts with her husband, there is a real danger of the therapist's failing the family. If success is defined as accepting the therapist's point of view and working toward his or her conceptual goal, then therapy becomes a power struggle or an indoctrination. To some extent this happens in all therapies, but it is justified only when achieving the therapist's conceptual goals also meets the family's goals.

The advantages of working toward symptom change is that it is directly responsive to the family's request and eliminates much obfuscation about whether or not therapy is successful. The disadvantage is that working only at the level of symptomatic or symptom-maintaining behavior may produce changes that do not last. This fundamental debate about the effects of symptomatic improvement must ultimately be answered empirically. In the meanwhile, it seems clear that changing symptom-maintaining behavior —even without worrying much about underlying family dynamics—can produce a positive spiral, or "runaway," increasing change that leads to increasingly satisfactory family functioning. On the other hand, there is the danger that symptom resolution will succeed but not last, especially when interventions are designed to effect monadic or dyadic change without taking into account how individuals or pairs are affected by the whole family context.

I do not agree with psychoanalysts who say that without insight into unconscious motivation, behavioral changes will not last, or with Bowenians who say that problems in the nuclear family will not change until relationships with the extended family are repaired. But it does seem that to insure symptom resolution will last, successful interventions must take into account triangular patterns of relationship in the nuclear family.

CONDITIONS FOR BEHAVIOR CHANGE

Once it was necessary to contrast family therapy with individual therapy in order to establish family treatment as a distinct and legitimate approach. Family therapists used to emphasize their differences with individual therapists; today they emphasize differences among themselves. Now that family therapy is an established force in the helping field, family therapists are competing among themselves for recognition and patronage.

The various family therapies share a consensus about broad principles of change, but differ on many specific issues. The core principle of family therapy is treating people in their natural environment. What divides the field into competing camps are differences of opinion about how best to bring about change. In this section, I will compare and contrast the different systems of family therapy in terms of action or insight; change in the session or change at home; duration of treatment; resistance; family-therapist relationship; and paradox.

Action or Insight. One of the early distinctions between family therapy and individual therapy had to do with action and insight. Individual therapists stressed intellectual and emotional insight; family therapists stressed action. Although they emphasized action in their writing, many of the techniques of early family therapists were designed to change action through understanding. Actually, since people think, feel, and act, no form of therapy can succeed without affecting all three of these aspects of the human personality. Different approaches may concentrate on different modes of experience, but they inevitably deal with the total—thinking, feeling, and acting—person.

Action and insight are the primary vehicles of change in family therapy. Most family therapists use both mechanisms, but some schools emphasize either action (strategic) or insight (psychoanalytic).

The case for action is based on the observation that people often do not change even though they understand why and how they should. The truth of this is familiar to anyone who has ever tried and failed to lose weight, stop smoking, or spend more time with the kids. Behaviorists make the case for action by pointing out that behavior is often reinforced unwittingly; explanations, they say, do not change behavior, reinforcement does. Parents are taught to change their children's behavior by rewarding desired actions and ignoring or punishing undesirable actions. Likewise, married couples are taught that actions speak louder than words; it does not matter so much what you tell your spouse, what matters is that you reward pleasing behavior. Behavioral family therapists do not, however, practice what they preach. They tell clients that reinforcement is the way to change behavior, but they rely on simple explanations to bring about those changes. Action may be the message, but understanding is the medium.

Like behaviorists, strategic therapists focus on behavior, and are not concerned with insight. However, they differ from behaviorists in one important respect—behaviorists rely on the power of rational instruction, strategic therapists eschew understanding altogether. They do not believe in insight and they do not believe in teaching; instead they believe that the way to change behavior is through manipulation. They box families into a corner, from which the only way out is to change.

The case for insight is based on the belief that if people understand themselves they will be free to act in their own best interests. Psychoanalytic clinicians believe that people are blind to their real motives and feelings. Without insight into hidden conflicts, they believe, action is self-defeating, even dangerous. Unexamined action is considered self-defeating because symptomatic relief without insight fosters denial and repression; it is considered dangerous when repressed impulses are acted on precipitously.

Many actions are regarded in this school as symptomatic—that is, such actions are protective devices designed to bind the anxiety that signals impulses whose expression might lead to punishment. Only by understanding their impulses and the dangers involved in expressing them can people change. Moreover, since the most important conflicts are unconscious, only methodical interpretation of the unconscious brings about lasting change. In psychoanalytic therapy, unanalyzed action initiated by families is called "acting out"; unanalyzed action initiated by therapists is considered manipulation. Insight can only be achieved if families verbalize their thoughts and feelings rather than act on them, and if therapists interpret unconscious meaning rather than suggest or manipulate action.

Discussions of insight are often divisive, because *insight* is a buzzword; proponents extol it, opponents ridicule it. Advocates of insight use the concept as a pseudomedical idea—insight, like medicine, cures. Actually, insight does not cure anything; it is something through which cure occurs. To say that a family acquires insight means that family members learn what they intend by their actions, and also what they want from each other; how they act on their insight is up to them.

Do people change when they are propelled into action, or when they develop understanding? Both. People change for a variety of reasons; the same person may change one day because of being forced into action, and another day because of some new understanding. Some individuals may be more or less responsive to either action or insight, and these people will be more or less successful in therapies that emphasize insight or action. People change when they are ready *and* when the right stimulus is applied.

In contrast to the polar positions taken by these three schools, the other systems work with action *and* insight. In structural family therapy, change is initiated in action and then supported by understanding. According to Minuchin (Minuchin and Fishman, 1981), family structure and family beliefs support and reinforce each other; the only way to achieve lasting change is to challenge both. Action comes first, because it leads to new experiences which then make insight possible. In Bowenian theory, interventions also affect both levels—action and understanding; but the order of effect is reversed. Bowenians begin by calming people down, so that they will be receptive to learning extended family systems theory. Once family members are armed with this new understanding, they are sent into action —back to their families to re-establish ties based on differentiation of self.

Change in the Session or Change at Home. All family therapists aim to transform interactions among family members, but they differ as to where they expect these transformations to take place. In structural family therapy, transformation occurs in the session, in the present, and in the presence of the therapist. Action is brought into the consulting room in the form of enactments, and change is sought then and there. The same is true in experiential family therapy; emotional breakthrough comes in the session, in response to the therapist's provocations. In both of these therapies, changes wrought in the session are believed to transfer to the family's life outside.

Other family therapists promote change that they expect to occur, not in the session but at home. Strategic therapists are relatively inactive in the session. They listen and observe, but do not say much; instead they silently formulate interventions which they deliver in the form of directives to be carried out at home. Bowenians also plan changes that will take place outside the consultation room. Family members are encouraged to return to their families of origin, and coached to respond in new and more productive ways. Most forms of behavior therapy are planned to influence interactions that take place at home. Parents are sent home to reward their children's positive behavior, and spouses are taught to please each other, or have sex without anxiety, at home. Some behaviorists, however, supervise parents playing with and disciplining their children in the session, usually behind a one-way mirror.

The goal of family therapy is to solve problems so that people can live better. The ultimate test of success comes at home after therapy is over. But since therapists take on the job of creating change, utilizing the context of the session first to promote interactions and then to observe and change them gives maximum impact. Just as live supervision is preferred because it teaches therapists what to do while they do it, so supervised change in the session seems more effective than unsupervised change at home.

Duration of Treatment. Most family therapy is brief. Families generally seek treatment at a time of crisis and are motivated only to solve their immediate problems. Usually they only reluctantly agree to come in as a family, and generally they are not interested in personal growth. Because family therapists only have the leverage necessary to work with families as long as they are in distress, family treatment tends to be pragmatic and symptom-focused. This is especially true in strategic family therapy.

Strategic therapists limit treatment to about ten sessions, and announce this at the outset as a means of motivating families to work for change. Haley (1976) says that change occurs in stages and he plans therapy accordingly, but most strategic therapists believe that change occurs in sudden shifts (Hoffman, 1981; Rabkin, 1977). Strategists do not reason with families, they give them a sudden jolt. These jolts—usually paradoxical directives —provoke families stuck in dysfunctional homeostasis to change with or without their willing co-operation. Success in this operation requires that lasting change be achieved on the basis of one impact, and that it can occur without any understanding on the part of the family.

Other schools of family therapy believe that lasting change requires understanding, and that it occurs gradually over the course of several months of treatment. The duration of therapy is related both to the goal of treatment and the question of who is considered to be responsible for change. Strategists and behaviorists limit their goals to solving the presenting problem, and they assume responsibility for change. Psychoanalytic and experiential practitioners seek profound personal changes in their clients and they place the responsibility for change with the clients. These therapists take responsibility only for providing a therapeutic atmosphere in their sessions; change is up to the clients.

Structural family therapists are interested in solving problems, not in personal growth; however, the problems that they are concerned with are structural. They believe that it is necessary to restructure dysfunctional families for lasting benefit to occur. Strategic therapists on the other hand say that it is not necessary to change the whole family; all that is required is to interrupt the vicious feedback cycles that maintain presenting symptoms.

Bowenian therapy can be a life-long enterprise. The goal is personal growth *and* change in the entire extended family system. Since change is the responsibility of the client and occurs during visits home, the process may take years.

If the family's goal is growth and enrichment, then therapy must be protracted; but if the goal is relief, then therapy should be brief. Problems arise when therapists try to hold on to families. The motives for doing so are many and complex, including pursuit of utopian goals, money, guilt over not having done more, and unresolved emotional attachments. For some mental health professionals being in therapy is a way of life. These therapists may convey exaggerated expectations of improvement, with the result that family members are bound to suffer disillusionment. Fortunately, therapy is expensive, time-consuming, and stressful; this puts pressure on families to get it over with and get on with their lives.

In brief prescriptive therapy, termination is initiated by the therapist when there is a change in the presenting problem or when the agreed-upon number of sessions is up. With compliant families, strategic therapists acknowledge progress and give the family credit for success; with defiant families, they express skepticism and predict a relapse. (The idea of giving families credit for success may have a hollow ring, when families have no idea what they did to bring it about.) In longer, elicitory therapy, termination is initiated by the clients, either directly or indirectly. It is time to consider termination when family living becomes more enjoyable, when family members run out of things to talk about in therapy, or when they begin to complain about competing obligations. Part of successful termination is helping families accept the inevitability of the normal problems of everyday life. Successful therapy partly changes behavior and partly changes expectations. Therapy *can* go on forever, but by keeping it brief, therapists prevent families from becoming dependent on outside help and teach them to rely on their own resources.

Resistance. Families are notoriously resistant to change. In addition to the combined resistances of individual family members, the system itself resists change. Where there is resistance, therapy cannot succeed without overcoming it. Behavior therapists minimize the importance of resistance and succeed only where their clients are willing and able to follow instructions. The other schools of family therapy consider resistance *the* major obstacle to treatment, and have devised various ways to overcome it.

Psychoanalytic practitioners believe that resistance is motivated by unconscious defenses, which first must be made manifest and then resolved through interpretation. This is an intrapsychic model, but does not ignore conscious and interactional resistances. Instead, psychoanalytic therapists believe that interactional problems—among family members or between the family and therapist—have their roots in unconscious resistance to basic drives. Experiential therapists have a similar model; they see resistance to emotional expression, and they blast away at it using personal confrontations and emotive exercises. Experientialists believe that breeching defenses automatically releases natural, healthy strivings; change occurs from the inside out.

People do avoid knowing painful things about themselves, but even more strenuously conceal painful truths from other members of the family. It is one thing to tell a therapist that you are angry at your spouse; it is another thing to tell your spouse. Therapies that are more interactive and systems-oriented focus on conscious withholding and on the system's resistance to changing its rules.

Minuchin's solution to the problem of resistance is straightforward: he wins families over by joining and accommodating to them. This gives him the leverage to utilize powerful confrontations designed to restructure the pattern of family interactions. Resistance is seen as a product of the interaction between therapist and family; change is accomplished by alternately challenging the family and then rejoining them to repair breaches in the therapeutic relationship.

Strategic family therapists expect resistance, but avoid power struggles by going with resistance rather than opposing it head on. They assume that families do not understand their own behavior and will oppose attempts to change it. In response, strategic practitioners try to gain control by provoking families to resist. Once the family begins to respond in opposition to therapeutic directives, the therapists can manipulate them to change in the desired direction. In practice, this can result in either doggedly pursuing reverse psychology, or in a creative form of therapeutic jujitsu. The creative response to resistance is illustrated by the Milan group, who, for example, routinely ask a third person to describe interactions between two others in order to minimize defensiveness.

Finally, under the heading of resistance, we should consider the phenomenon of *induction*. Induction is what happens when a therapist is drawn into the family system. When this happens the therapist becomes just another member of the family; this may stabilize the system, but it reduces therapeutic mobility and prevents systems change. A therapist is inducted when he or she is sucked in to fulfill a missing family function—disciplining children when the parents do not or cannot, sympathizing with a husband whose wife does not, or coaxing a reticent teenager to open up to the therapist instead of to his parents.

Minuchin describes the danger of induction, and teaches structural family therapists how to recognize and avoid it (Minuchin and Fishman, 1981). Working with colleagues helps to avoid induction, either with cotherapists (Whitaker) or with a team (Selvini Palazzoli). Bowenians avoid induction by remaining calm and objective; they stay in contact but keep themselves detriangled and outside of the family projection system.

Induction is so subtle that it is hard to see, so seductive that it is hard to resist. As helpers and healers, therapists are especially prone to take over for people, doing for them what they do not do for themselves. But taking over—being inducted—precludes real change. As long as families have someone to do for them, they do not have to learn to do for themselves.

Family-Therapist Relationship. Individual psychotherapists have argued that the fundamental pillar of treatment is the patient-therapist relationship. Carl Rogers even claimed that certain qualities of the therapist are necessary and sufficient to produce successful outcomes. Family therapists tend to be more technically-oriented and they de-emphasize the therapeutic relationship in their writing. Systems thinkers run the risk of losing sight of the individuals that make up the system. Furthermore, whether or not they consider the human qualities of the participants in therapy, all family therapists have an implicit model of patient-therapist relationship.

The variations of patient-therapist relationships—including subject-object, interpersonal, phenomenological, and encounter—are a function of individual practitioners, but they also tend to characterize different schools of treatment. The hallmark of the *subject-object* paradigm is the therapist's objective observation of the family. In this model the therapist is a natural scientist, who makes observations and carefully tailored interventions. Personal and emotional reactions are regarded as confounding intrusions. The assumption is that therapists and family are separate entities. This is not an attractive description, and few family therapists would describe themselves in these terms; nevertheless there are aspects of behavioral, psychoanalytic, and strategic therapy that fit this model.

Behavioral family therapists think of themselves as objective observers and rational scientists; without a doubt they fit this paradigm. Psychoanalytic practitioners operate within this model when they think of themselves as neutral and objective, as blank screens upon whom patients project their distorted perceptions and fantasies. Although many psychoanalytic clinicians still maintain this assumption, it is not consistent with the best and latest psychoanalytic thinking. No therapist is neutral and objective; the blank screen is a metaphor and a myth. Therapists reveal themselves in a thousand ways, and patients' reactions are always influenced by the reality of the therapist's behavior as well as by personal distortions. The strategic school has produced some of the most sophisticated concepts of the intricate relationship between therapists and families (Hoffman, 1981). The subject-object paradigm is not a basic feature of this school, but it creeps in when therapists think of themselves as outsiders, locked in contest with families. The adversarial stance of some therapists in this system assumes that the therapist and family can and should be separate.

The *interpersonal* paradigm treats therapy as a two-way interaction. This model acknowledges that therapists and families are related and that they constantly influence each other. Psychoanalytic clinicians employ this idea in their concepts of transference/countertransference, projective identification, and introjection; the model of influence here is interactive and transversal. In fact, this paradigm describes most family therapists most of the time.

The *phenomenological* paradigm is one in which the therapist tries to adopt the patient's frame of reference. It is what happens when psychoanalytic practitioners try to identify with their patients, when structuralists join families, and when therapists of any persuasion try to understand and accept that families are doing the best they can. Stanton (1981) uses this concept in his technique of "ascribing noble intention" to families. This tactic fits the phenomenological model when it is done sincerely; it does not when it is used merely as a strategic ploy—for example, in most reframing. Selvini Palazzoli's positive connotation is probably done with sincerity; Boszormenyi-

Nagy's recognition that symptomatic behavior is an act of unconscious loyalty to the family is definitely sincere. Experientialists speak of accepting the patient's frame of reference, but they do not. Instead, they follow an encounter paradigm, in which they loudly proclaim their own honest feelings and challenge families to do the same.

The *encounter* paradigm is an encounter between the therapist's total personality and the client's. It involves mutual sharing, honesty, openness, and self-disclosure, and its use in family therapy is primarily restricted to experientialists. During an encounter the therapist becomes a full participant, which is something that most family therapists do not let happen. However, it is possible to let yourself go and confront a family if you do so with clear therapeutic indications and not simply because you feel like it. Minuchin engages in genuine encounters from time to time, but he shows good timing and the ability to recover his professional objectivity. Honest encounters are perhaps useful when done occasionally, for a good reason, and by someone with enough experience and insight to keep from losing perspective.

Paradox. The use of paradox is a central and controversial topic in family therapy. Paradoxical instructions encourage rather than attack symptoms and objectionable behavior. They are designed to block or change dysfunctional sequences using indirect and seemingly illogical means. Paradoxical interventions are used instead of direct attempts to introduce change by therapists who assume that families cannot or will not comply with advice or persuasion.

Paradoxical interventions are associated with the newer strategic forms of therapy, but they are not confined to this group and they are not new. Behavior therapists have used paradoxical interventions for over fifty years, as negative practice or conditioned inhibition. Dunlap (1928) advised patients who wished to get rid of certain undesirable habits to practice them. He called this "negative practice," and reported success with tics, typing errors, stammering, and thumb sucking. Learning theorists believe that negative practice works through "conditioned inhibition," which has been described as fatigue induced by mass practice (Kendrick, 1960).

Frankl's (1960) "paradoxical intention" was an early version of what communications family therapists later called "prescribing the symptom." In all of these applications the idea is the same: if you deliberately practice a symptom, it will go away. The Bateson group reasoned that since family pathology was a function of paradoxical communication, it could be cured by "therapeutic double-binds." According to Haley (1963), the person with a symptom gains power by controlling those around him or her. He interpreted the effectiveness of paradoxical directives as a result of the therapist's gaining control over the symptoms by ordering them to occur on command. If symptoms are a tactic in interpersonal power struggles, the therapist can take control by prescribing them. Rabkin (1977) suggests that while some symptoms serve such devious purposes, others are simply habits reinforced by trying too hard not to do something and anxiously worrying about it. For example, worrying about being self-confident and trying too hard to be it, may cause a lack of self-confidence. When a therapist prescribes the symptom, however, the patient may stop worrying about the problem and family members may stop trying to solve it.

Strategic therapists use paradox in two ways: as directives and as reframing, which is really interpretation and subtle direction. Reframing not only gives a new label for behavior, it also acts as an indirect message to change. Strategic therapists think of symptoms as part of self-reinforcing sequences; symptoms are maintained by attempts to suppress them. Paradoxical directives provoke change by altering the attempted solutions and thus resolving the symptoms. Hoffman (1981) cites an example of a wife whose constant jealous questioning of her husband only reinforced his reticence, which in turn reinforced her jealousy. The strategy to disrupt this sequence was to use a paradoxical directive to the wife to redouble her jealous questioning. The expected result was that the wife rebelled against the task and so solved the problem. Strategic therapists claim that it is usually unnecessary to look at the context or history of a symptom in order to resolve it.

There are two problems with provoking people to change by telling them not to. The first is obvious. This paradoxical device implies that families are oppositional; many are, but many are not. The second problem is that intervening only around a symptom neglects the broader family context. Ignoring the family context is like going to London without an umbrella; you won't get wet unless it rains. Symptoms may be maintained by attempts to suppress them, but many symptoms also serve a purpose in the family structure. Among strategic therapists, Haley and Selvini Palazzoli are the most aware that symptoms fit into the larger field of the family.

Minuchin's structural concepts have been carried into the strategic camp by Jay Haley, whose approach is now a hybrid of structural and strategic methods. Haley (1976) recognizes that problem-maintaining sequences may be rooted in the family's dysfunctional structure. He has also gotten away from using paradoxical directives and has become more concerned with shifting triadic sequences and with establishing appropriate hierarchical structure in families.

Selvini Palazzoli and her Milan cohorts rely on paradox as an explanatory concept and a treatment device, but they also look beyond symptom-maintaining sequences to the context of the whole family. Since disturbed families sustain their pathology through an intricate network of paradoxes, Selvini Palazzoli (1980) reasons that the best way to break these pathological networks is through therapeutic counterparadox. The Milan group not only prescribes the problem behavior, but also the whole configuration of interactions surrounding it. Usually this takes the combined form of positive connotation and assignment of a paradoxical family ritual. In this way, they deal with the problem *and* its larger context at the same time. This seems to me the best and most appropriate use of therapeutic paradox. Best, because it deals with the family structure as well as with the symptom; and most appropriate, because the Milan group works with severely disturbed families. Paradoxical interventions keep the therapist distanced from the family; it's not a technique for therapists who need to be liked, but it does help to avoid the suction of families with seriously disturbed members.

Paradoxical directives can break a fixed family pattern, but why should such changes last? They will if the change also effects a change in the total family structure. Many examples of paradoxical instructions are insulting. (Madanes' (1980) pretend techniques avoid this insulting quality, and allow the therapist to avoid emotionally distancing himself or herself from the family.) Hoffman (1981), for example, describes a therapist's telling a depressed wife to become more subservient to her husband. Not surprisingly, the woman rebels to defy the therapist. According to Hoffman, this technique worked because the paradoxical directive unbalanced a complementary balance, which then became symmetrical. Previously, the husband and wife were balanced in a relationship where he was one-up and she was one-down. By trying to push her further down, the therapist provoked a rebellion and the couple then established a relationship based on equality. Why that should happen is not at all clear. Why don't they simply re-establish the same complementarity they had before?

Paradoxical techniques are so appealing that they seem like a magic solution to entrenched family problems. Actually, the way to resolve problems is to understand their context. In structural terms, this means understanding the family's dysfunctional structure; in systemic terms, it means understanding the circular patterns and relational context. The real key is the understanding; whether the therapist intervenes directly or indirectly is far less important.

TECHNIQUES

Comparing techniques by reading about them is difficult because clinicians often describe techniques as abstract concepts rather than as concrete actions. Modeling, for example, is a concept invoked by behaviorists for telling or showing parents how to speak to their children; by experientialists for talking about their own feelings; and by structural family therapists for speaking sharply to children who interrupt their parents. Are all these techniques modeling? Actually, modeling is not a technique; it is a hypothetical construct to explain how people learn through observation. Often, techniques are described in the jargon of a particular school—restructuring, therapeutic double-binds, differentiating—and it is not clear precisely what is meant. In this section, I will treat issues of technique as a series of practical questions about how to conduct therapy, and I will describe techniques as specific actions.

Much of what is written about the techniques of family therapy is about the middle game of treatment. This reflects a tendency among family practitioners to differentiate among themselves by describing their definitive and unique interventions; and it caters to the reader's wish to get on with therapy and get to the problem-solving part. Families come for treatment anxious and eager for direction, and they communicate their anxiety to the therapist. "Help us," they say, and in so doing they pass some of their anxiety on to the practitioner. Because they are the most anxious, young therapists are the most eager to discharge it by acting—by doing something definitive. Although family therapy is a therapy of action, the way must be prepared for the action to be effective. Before a therapist can know what is wrong with a particular family and gain the leverage to change it, he or she must make emotional contact and establish a therapeutic climate within which the family will be receptive to treatment. This involves such practical considerations as: who to invite to the first session? what kind of treatment team to use? how to enter into the family system? what sort of therapeutic stance to take? and how to assess the family?

Who to Invite. Most family therapists invite everyone living under the same roof to the first session. This reflects the belief that everyone in the family is involved in any problem, even if it is manifest in only one member.

It also reflects the principle that in order to change the presenting symptom it is necessry to change the family interactions that create or sustain it.

Inviting the whole family to the first consultation is a powerful restructuring and reframing move. Whether or not it is explicitly stated or openly acknowledged, the presence of the whole family in the assessment of a psychological problem implies that they are all involved. In many cases, the act of assembling the entire family to discuss a problem is the single most effective step toward solving it. Most experienced family practitioners are convinced of this, and they do not waste much time worrying about how to get the family in. They are positive that it is essential; they know that it is how they work; and so they calmly state this to the family. When the request that the whole family attend is put in a straightforward, matter-of-fact way to families, most comply. Occasionally it is necessary to explain that the therapist would like everyone to attend in order to get all their points of view, but if the therapist is comfortable with the idea most families will also accept it.

Sometimes, however, one or two family members will not attend the consultation. When this happens most family therapists work with whomever is available. In such cases the failure of key family members to participate in treatment seems like a problem; it may be *the* problem. If a father, for instance, refuses to participate in treatment designed to help his daughter overcome her shyness, his absence from treatment is a sign that his unavailability is a significant element in the problem. Working with the mother and children to get him involved may be the most important step in solving the presenting problem. On this matter, family therapists can learn from psychoanalysts to consider resistance not as an impediment to treatment, but as the object of treatment.

Members of some schools of family therapy do not insist upon seeing the entire family. Practitioners of behavioral parent training focus on teaching the parents—usually the mother—how to deal with the identified patient. For this reason, some invite only the parents and child to the first session, while others (Gordon and Davidson, 1981) recommend interviewing both parents in the child's absence. Strategic family therapists vary in whom they include in the first session. Haley (1976) recommends seeing the whole family, but many of his colleagues will see individuals, parents, or couples alone as the situation seems to require. This determination is based on who in the family asks for help and who seems to be unhappy enough to do something about the problems. Milton Erickson favored this approach, and it is now followed by Richard Rabkin and members of the MRI group.

Bowenian therapists usually work with individuals or couples. If a child is presented as the problem, members of this school see the parents; if a couple complains of marital problems, Bowenian therapists will see them together; and if only one person is willing to attend, the Bowenian therapist will see that person.

Finally, most family therapists (whether they specialize in couples therapy or not) will see a marital couple without their children if the couple complains of problems in their relationship. This is not, however, universally true. Structural, experiential, psychoanalytic therapists often ask that the children attend the first session, and exclude them only if and when the couple needs to discuss private matters, such as their sexual relationship.

Instead of seeing less than the whole family, some therapists insist on seeing more. Network therapists convene large groups of family and friends; some therapists try to include grandparents as well as the nuclear family. Inviting members of the extended family is a practice that cuts across the different schools. Many family therapists invite the grandparents in if they live in the nuclear family's household or if they seem particularly involved; some—for example, Whitaker and Selvini Palazzoli—invite grandparents as a matter of course. Another variant on the composition of therapy is seeing several families or couples together in a group. In my opinion, the only possible justification for this procedure is economic. Group therapy with individuals who are strangers is a useful method because it creates a naturalistic imitation of life. In family therapy, there is no need to imitate life; convening the family brings life into the treatment room.

Although each of these variations on who is initially invited into treatment is supported by a rationale, I believe that the best practice is to include all members of the same household in the initial meeting. Later there may be good reasons for meeting with a subset of the family, but at the outset it is best to see everyone. Deviations from this format may be due more often to anxiety than to good clinical judgment. Families are anxious about meeting together and airing their problems and so, naturally, many are reluctant to come as a whole group. This is understandable, and should be dealt with calmly by insisting that everyone attend. Therapists, too, are anxious about convening families, particularly when the family indicates that one of its members does not want to come. The therapist's anxiety is sometimes the real reason for meeting with less than the whole family; in other words, some of the variations in composition of family meetings are probably due more to countertransference than to sound principles of family treatment.

Treatment Team. Family therapists tend to work in groups, either with a cotherapist or with a team of observers. Family interactions are so complex that it is difficult for one person working alone to see all that goes on.

Moreover, the emotional pull on therapists who work with families is so strong that it is easy to be drawn in, to take sides, and to lose balance and objectivity. Working with colleagues helps because it provides additional observations and makes any loss of perspective obvious. In general, cotherapy seems to be favored by those schools of family therapy that emphasize intense emotional involvement (especially the experiential school); observation teams are favored by those schools that emphasize tactical planning (strategic, structural).

Whitaker has taken a strong position in favor of co-therapy; Minuchin and Haley take the opposite point of view. Whitaker's brand of experiential therapy is intensely personal and interactive. Because of this, he advocates (Whitaker and Keith, 1981) using cotherapists to counterbalance one another; while one is actively involved in a free-wheeling interchange with the family, the other acts to limit partiality and to counteract the intrusion of countertransference-based interventions.

Minuchin and Haley have both argued that a solo therapist is more able to act decisively and is therefore preferable to cotherapists. Haley's position is consistent with his directive style, and it is shared by most strategic therapists (with the notable exception of Selvini Palazzoli). Minuchin, on the other hand, is controlling but less central and directive than most strategic therapists. His goal is to change families by manipulating their interactions with each other in the session. To this end he uses family members as his cotherapists. If a small child is shy, Minuchin will prod someone in the family to draw the child out; if a teenager is disobedient, Minuchin will goad the parents to become disciplinarians. By using family members as cotherapists, structural family practitioners avoid being induced to take over a function that is missing in the family.

None of the other schools of family therapy take as clear a stand about cotherapy. Those who advocate cotherapy teams frequently cite the desire to provide male and female role models or advocates; this is especially true for sex therapists. Psychoanalytic therapists emphasize privacy and tend to work alone, as do Bowenian therapists. Network therapists work in teams of four or more simply as a matter of practical necessity, since they have to manage large groups. Behavioral therapists tend to work in cotherapy pairs while they are graduate students, and then work alone after they finish their training.

Most uses of cotherapy are probably based on economic and teaching considerations. In training settings, where there are more trainees than families, cotherapy may be a way to give everyone a chance to act as therapist. Beginners are often asked to work together as a way of helping each other. Although having a co-therapist may ease a beginner's initial anxiety, it seems to me that it does more harm than good because it leads to confusion about who is in charge and where to go.

A better solution and one more favored by family clinicians is to work alone backed up by a team of observers behind a one-way mirror. For research and training this method is invaluable; for everyday clinical practice it is a useful adjunct to the therapist's powers of observation. Teams of observers are most commonly used by structural and strategic therapists; the observers comment after a session is over, and also may enter or consult while the session is in progress. This is done programmatically by the MRI group and by the Milan Associates. The advantages of this format are that observers can provide additional information, advice, and feedback. By contacting the family either by entering and speaking directly to them, or by sending a message through the therapist, observers can say something that is provocative or critical without the therapist's having to share responsibility for their statements.

The use of videotape adds another dimension to the treatment team. It enhances the observers' ability to see small movements and repetitive patterns, and it enables the therapist to observe him or herself interacting with the family. Videotaping equipment is expensive and not usually found outside of training clinics; its use is thus more an economic than a theoretical or technical issue. The same is true of one-way mirrors, observers, and co-therapists, which are usually used more often in clinics and training centers than in private practice. Co-therapy is, however, common among private practitioners, and its use may be partly a way of assuaging loneliness. To some extent, then, co-therapy is a little like a marriage: it works well if the partners are well-matched and flexible, but if they are not, it can be a disaster.

Entering the Family System. Family clinicians think of the family in terms of a system—a collection of parts interacting as a single entity. Whether they realize it or not, therapists themselves are part of a larger system, one that includes the family and the therapist. This is true for therapists who keep their emotional distance (Bowenian, behavioral) as well as for those who become emotionally involved (experiential). All schools of family therapy have a more or less consistent style of making contact with families and of maintaining a particular therapeutic stance.

In structural family therapy the process of entering families is considered a critical determinant of therapeutic success, and it has been described more fully by this school than by any other. Minuchin (1974) uses the terms *joining* and *accommodation* to describe how the therapist relates to a family and adjusts to accept the family's organization and style. Most families come to treatment anxious and mistrustful; they expect their viewpoint to be challenged and they expect to be blamed for causing their own problems. Fearing criticism and worried about having to change, they are set to resist. Recognizing this, structural family clinicians begin by trying to put the family at ease: they greet each member of the family separately; ask each for his or her point of view; and accept what they have to offer, even if at first it is only angry silence. "Okay, right now you're angry and don't want to talk."

The restructuring moves that come later—often as dramatic and forceful confrontations—require a great deal of leverage; this is achieved by joining. From a structural point of view, some of the other schools that emphasize the resistant properties of families (especially the strategic school) probably do an inadequate job of joining. In addition to joining, therapists gain leverage by establishing their status as experts. Minuchin does not emphasize this point in writing, but when he introduces himself as Director of the Clinic he immediately establishes himself as an expert and a figure of authority. Not all therapists have impressive sounding titles, but most make some effort to establish themselves as authorities, whether it is by hanging diplomas on the wall or by demonstrating competence through their actions.

Among strategic therapists, Haley has written the most about the process of entering the family system. His position (Haley, 1976) is similar to Minuchin's; he describes the therapist as a host who must make the family comfortable and put them at ease, while at the same time maintaining a businesslike demeanor. He also uses the idea of accommodating to the family's organization by suggesting that therapists speak first to the parents; but his recommendation that the less involved parent be addressed first is not consistent with accommodating, and it is the first clue to Haley's stance as a therapist.

Like most strategic therapists, Haley is an expert manipulator. Members of this school relate to families from an emotionally distant position; they do not say what they really think and feel, but speak only for a calculated effect—going with resistance. Whether they take a one-up or one-down position, their stance is that of experts who coolly assess family problems and prescribe solutions. Perhaps the best illustration of this stance is the way the Milan Associates consult with their observers and return to present the family with a written prescription. Members of the MRI group usually adopt a one-down position; they demonstrate humility, confusion, and pessimism in order to avoid provoking resistance with optimistic pressure to change. To be successful with this strategy, therapists must be able to forgo the need to look good or be seen as in command.

In sharp contrast to the strategic approach, experiential family therapists enter fully into the emotional life of the family and work from a stance that is open and close. Experientialists begin by greeting families and getting acquainted. In the process, they are likely to speak of their own feelings and attitudes, and to develop a warm, empathic relationship. Such intimate emotional engagement makes it difficult to be objective; it is hard to understand the patterns in the whole family system when you are actively engaged in emotional dialogues with individual family members. This is one of the reasons why Whitaker insists upon working with a cotherapist.

Psychoanalytic practitioners scrupulously refrain from active involvement with their clients. They do so by design, to avoid directing or becoming actors in a drama that they believe should unfold spontaneously. In psychoanalytic psychotherapy, the therapist's stance is the most important ingredient in the method. Not interpretation, not analysis of the unconscious, but silent observation is the key to getting at hidden issues in the family.

The father of psychoanalytic family therapy, the late Nathan Ackerman, was an exception; he engaged in active dialogue with families, aggressively confronting them, "tickling their defenses," and even sharing some of his own feelings. He did so in part because he was more of a psychoanalyst inventing family therapy than a practitioner of psychoanalytic therapy with families. He followed the dictates of his own style and personality as much as he did his training. Perhaps this is a good place to make the point that the way that therapists relate to families—whether they are more or less active, more or less emotionally close—reflects their personality styles and personal preferences as well as the stance favored by the systems they follow. All therapists learn that using an approach that is congenial to personal style avoids unnecessary conflict.It is also true, however, that practitioners of the various schools tend to have similar stances.

Bowenian therapists take a position midway between the emotional intimacy of experientialists and the controlled technical mastery of strategists. Their byword is objectivity; their goal is to make contact with families but to remain detriangled. Learning is thought to occur in a calm atmosphere, so the Bowenian therapist tries to reduce anxiety and create a climate of rational understanding. He or she begins by inquiring about the symptoms and their clinical course. Once this is done the therapist begins to act as a teacher, explaining family systems theory, and as a coach, encouraging family members to make contact with the rest of the family and to work toward defining a self.

Behavioral therapists take over in the role of expert. Their stance is that of teachers; they take a central position, ask questions, explain principles, and assign homework. Their centrality, activity, and directiveness make it difficult for them to observe the natural and spontaneous interactions of the families they work with. It is an approach that controls and limits the field of observation. They can thus bring a great deal of technical expertise to dealing with part of the problem, but they run the risk of isolating that part from the whole family context.

Those who treat families as though they were conducting therapy groups vary in the intensity of their emotional engagement. Some, following the Tavistock model, are disengaged observers; others, influenced by the human potential movement, are active and interactive. Whether engaged or detached, family group therapists treat families as collections of individuals; they do not join families, they conduct family meetings.

When communications family therapy began, the family was treated as an opposing team—a confused and confusing opponent whose power to destroy meaning had to be controlled from the outset. Members of this school paid a great deal of attention to the structure and management of sessions; they were afraid to let things unfold naturally, because they thought that they would never be able to regain control. They began with explicit statements of their belief that the whole family was involved in the patient's symptoms, and they laid down the rules for how therapy would be conducted: "Speak for yourself"; "Don't interrupt."

As they gained experience, communications therapists realized that families tend to resist so direct an approach. They began to use more indirect means of establishing control, largely through paradoxical interventions, and so changed communications therapy into strategic therapy. But the general model is still a cerebral attempt to outwit families. Therapists are considered to be well-motivated and rational; families are treated as resistant and irrational. The result is an emotionally-distanced stance and a treatment imposed on families for their own good.

Assessment. Systems of family therapy vary in their emphasis on assessment and in the methods they use to make assessments. Each school has a theory about families that determines where they look for problems and what they see. Some look at the whole family (structural, Bowenian); some look at individuals and dyads (psychoanalytic, experiential); and some focus narrowly on sequences that maintain symptoms (strategic, behavioral). Strategic therapists think small to keep their clients from being overwhelmed, and to help them achieve immediate success.

Behavioral family therapists place the greatest importance on assessment and use the most formal and standardized procedures. In this approach assessment is separated from treatment and is the first order of business. Behaviorists also assess the effectiveness of their interventions, so it is more proper to say that their initial diagnostic assessment is separate from treatment. The great advantage of the behavioral emphasis on assessment is that it provides clear data, definite goals, and a reliable way to determine whether or not therapy succeeds. The disadvantage is that by using standardized interviews and questionnaires, behaviorists do not see the family in natural interaction. By looking only at a part of the family (mother and child, or marital couple), they miss the total context; by structuring the assessment, they see only how the family reacts to the therapists.

Strategic family therapists also make careful assessments, but they do so in a more naturalistic fashion. They begin by inquiring about problems, and then listen to discover how the problems are maintained by attempted solutions. The critical questions in this approach are: What is the problem? Who is involved? and, What are they doing to make a symptom out of a problem? These questions are answered by what the family says, and what the therapist concludes; there is less emphasis on observing actual interactions than in the experiential or structural schools. On the other hand, strategic practitioners are quite sensitive to the interactions between themselves and families, and they take these interactions into account as part of their evaluation. They frequently give directives in the first session to discover whether families are compliant or resistant. This emphasis is consistent with the centrality of the patient-therapist relationship and with the limited utilization of in-session interactions among family members.

Structural family therapists also emphasize assessment, but their evaluations are based on observation of family members interacting among themselves. These interactions take place either spontaneously or at the therapist's direction. Enactments give the therapist a chance to observe patterns of enmeshment and disengagement, which are the principal components in a structural family diagnosis. The positive aspects of this school's assessment procedure are that it utilizes the family's patterns of interaction among themselves, it includes the entire family, and it is organized in simple terms that point directly to desired changes. If the therapist enacts a discussion between two parents, but they are frequently interrupted by their child, the structural family evaluation would be that they are disengaged from each other and the child is enmeshed. The goal of therapy in such a case would be to increase the parents' involvement with each other, while strengthening the boundary between the parents and the child. A potential disadvantage to structural assessment is that it *may* lose sight of individuals while focusing on their roles in the family. This does not necessarily happen, but it is an error made by many beginning family clinicians.

The Bowenian school also does an excellent job of considering the whole family in its assessment procedure. Unlike structuralists, however, Bowenians rely on what they are told instead of what they see, and they are interested in the past as well as the present. Their evaluations consist of extensive clinical interrogatories, which are guided by Bowenian theory. The theory says that symptoms are a function of anxiety-provoking stressors, the level of differentiation of family members, and the degree of emotional cutoff from support systems, especially the extended family.

An extended family systems assessment begins with a description and history of the presenting problem. Exact dates are noted and later checked for their relationship to events in the extended family life cycle. Next comes a history of the nuclear family, including information about when the parents met, what their courtship was like, their marriage, and childrearing. Particular attention is also paid to where the family lived and when they moved, especially in relation to where their extended families live. The next part of the evaluation is devoted to the history of both spouses' extended family systems. The therapist asks about each spouse's birth, sibling position, significant facts of childhood, and about the past and current functioning of their parents. All of this information is recorded on a genogram, covering at least three generations. This assessment provides a panoramic view of the whole family and its history; it also provides detailed information about the individuals in the family.

The psychoanalytic and experiential schools also pay a good deal of attention to individuals. Their assessments focus on individual family members and their dyadic relationships within the family. Evaluations in these two schools are unstructured and take place in the ongoing process of treatment. An exception to this rule is that some psychoanalytic clinicians (Nadelson, 1978) meet with each spouse separately before proceeding to evaluate the family together. As in other approaches, the data that psychoanalytic and experiential therapists examine are not always the same as those that they are ultimately interested in. Behaviorists are interested in behavior, but they accept verbal reports; psychoanalysts are interested in latent ideas and experientialists are interested in latent feelings, but they both look carefully at behavior in the sessions for clues as to what is being withheld.

Although the form of evaluation is similar in psychoanalytic and experiential therapy, the content is quite different. These two schools occupy extreme ends on a continuum of the elaborateness of theory; psychoanalytic theory is extensive and complex, experiential theory is limited and simple. The breadth of psychoanalytic theory enables practitioners in this school to theorize well ahead of their data; a little information suggests a great deal. The advantage is that the theory organizes the data and provides valuable leads to uncovering hidden meanings. The danger is that the theory may distort the data, leading the clinician to see what is not there. Experientialists do not have these advantages or disadvantages. Their evaluations are guided by a simple theory about feelings and how they are suppressed; they tend not to uncover much that is hidden, but they also tend not to see things that are not there.

Just as there are many ways to conduct therapy, there are many assessment procedures; what works in one system may not work in another. I believe, however, that there are two general principles of assessment that are valid for all family therapists. First, it is best not to rely on formal, structured evaluation procedures. The introduction of this much structure early in treatment produces an artificial atmosphere; instead of learning how the family behaves naturally, the clinician who makes a formal assessment learns what they say and how they interact with him or her. Moreover, once a therapist becomes a formal evaluator, it is difficult to move into a decentralized position and become an observer of family dynamics. Furthermore, once a family is treated with the structure of a formal assessment, they will forever resist freely interacting in therapy.

Although it seems to contradict my first point, I also believe that most family practitioners pay too little attention to assessment. There is a tendency to treat all families the same, especially by therapists with powerful techniques but limited conceptual schemes. For example, paradoxical directives are useful, but not with compliant, well-motivated families. "Speak for yourself" is a good suggestion for enmeshed families, but not for disengaged ones. Quid-pro-quo contracts may not be appropriate for couples with a complementary structure. Using pet techniques unguided by an assessment of the whole family may do some good; but without an evaluation of the family's structure such techniques are unlikely to change the basic configuration that creates and maintains family problems.

Once a therapist has assembled the family, joined with them, established a therapeutic stance, and assessed their structure and functioning, the stage is set for the powerful techniques that constitute the decisive interventions of family therapy.

Decisive Interventions. Members of every school of family therapy use a wide variety of techniques; some are dictated by the approach, others by the therapist's personality and experience. Even if we limit our attention to the techniques common to all members of each of the schools, the list would be long and confusing. Some techniques are used by virtually everyone who practices family therapy—reflecting feelings, clarifying communication; this common list has been growing as the different approaches have become more integrated. Each approach, however, relies on one or two techniques that are relatively unique and decisive. In this section, I will highlight and compare these definitive interventions.

In psychoanalytic family therapy there are two decisive techniques. The first of these, *interpretation,* is well known, but not well understood. Properly used, *interpretation* refers to elucidating unconscious meaning. It does not mean statements of opinion—"You need to express your feelings to each other, before you can really be close"; advice—"As long as you continue writing to him, the affair isn't over"; theory—"Some of the reasons you were attracted to him are based on unconscious needs"; or confrontations —"You said you didn't care, but you were really angry." Interpretations are explicit statements of the therapist's conjectures about the unconscious meaning of certain behaviors or utterances. "You've been talking about your son's unpleasant habit of arguing with you all the time. Based on what you've said previously, I think that some of this anger is deflected from your husband. He does the same thing, but you are afraid to tell him so, and that's why you get so mad at your son."

By refraining from asking questions, giving advice, or directing what people should talk about, the psychoanalytic practitioner maintains a consistent stance of listening and fostering understanding. By limiting his or her interventions to interpretations, the therapist makes it clear that treatment is designed for learning; whether families take advantage of this atmosphere and whether they change their behavior as a result of what they learn is up to them.

The second decisive technique in psychoanalytic family treatment is *silence.* The therapist's use of silence permits him or her to discover what is on the patients' minds and to test the family's resources; it also lends force to the eventual interpretations. When the therapist is silent, family members talk, following their own thoughts rather than responding to the therapist's interests. If they know that the therapist will not often interrupt, they react and respond to each other. This produces a wealth of information that would not otherwise emerge. If a father begins the first session by saying, "The problem is my depression," and the therapist asks, "How long have you been depressed?" he or she may not discover what thoughts are associated in the man's mind with his depression, or how the man's wife responds to his complaint.

The therapist's silence tends to prolong the dialogues among family members. This enables the therapist to learn more about how they talk, and it forces the family members to find constructive ways to resolve their own interactional impasses. With an active therapist, families get in the habit of waiting for suggestions when they get stuck; with a silent therapist, they struggle to get themselves unstuck. The therapist's silence also enhances the impact of his or her interventions. Words weigh more when they are punctuated by long silences.

Many family group therapists use a number of active and manipulative techniques, including giving advice and making suggestions. The essence of this approach, however, is encouraging free and open discussions so that family members will improve their ability to communicate and learn to solve their own problems. The decisive technique in this approach is *confrontation:* family group therapists confront quiet family members and prod them to open up; they confront domineering members and encourage them to be quiet and listen.

Confrontation is also a decisive technique in experiential family therapy. In this school, confrontations are designed to provoke emotional reactions and they are often aggressively blunt. It is not unusual for experiential therapists to tell clients to shut up, or to ridicule people for expressing themselves insincerely. Confrontations are often combined with *personal disclosure* from the therapist, which is the second major technique of this school. Experientialists use themselves as spontaneous, emotionally expressive, free-wheeling models. Finally, most experiential therapists make use of a number of *structured exercises*. These include roleplaying, psychodrama, sculpting, and family drawing. The rationale for these techniques is that they are a quick way to provoke emotional experiencing in the session; their obvious drawback is that, because these gimmicks are artificial, the reactions they provoke are divorced from ordinary family experience. Family members may get something off their chests in a structured exercise, but they are unlikely to transfer this to their everyday interactions at home.

Most people associate reinforcement with behavioral therapy, but reinforcement is not a technique used in behavioral family therapy; *observation* and *teaching* are the major techniques in this approach. Behavioral family practitioners begin by observing very carefully the contingencies of reinforcement in the families they work with. Their aim is to discover the antecedents and consequences of problem behavior. Once they have completed a functional analysis of behavior, they become teachers, teaching families how they inadvertently reinforce undesirable behavior. As teachers, their most useful lesson is how to use positive control. They teach parents that it is more effective to reward children for good behavior than to punish them for bad behavior; they teach married couples to substitute being nice to each other for their usual bickering.

Positive control—rewarding desirable behavior—is one of the most useful principles in family therapy. It is a valuable lesson for families *and* therapists. Therapists, like parents, tend to chide their charges for mistakes; unfortunately, if you are told that you are suppressing your feelings, spoiling your children, or using coercive control, you are most often apt to feel stupid and inadequate. Although it may be necessary to point out people's mistakes, it is more effective to concentrate on praising the positive aspects of their behavior. Among practicing family therapists this point seems to be best understood by structuralists, who speak of working with the family's strengths, and by strategists, who use positive connotation to support families' efforts to do the right thing.

Extended family therapists are also teachers, but they follow a different curriculum. They teach people to be responsible for themselves, and how by doing so they can transform their entire family systems. Being responsible for yourself means getting clear about what you think and feel—not what your mother says or what you read in the *New York Times,* but what you *really* believe—and then being true to your beliefs in your interactions with other people. You do not have to change others or even wish they were different; you do have to speak for yourself and maintain your own values. The power of this position is tremendous. If you can accept that you are you, and that other people are different and themselves, then you no longer have to approach relationships with the idea that either you or the other person has to change. This enables you to be in contact with people without becoming unduly upset or emotionally reactive.

In addition to teaching differentiation, Bowenian therapists have two corollary lessons—avoiding triangulation and reopening cut-off family relationships. Taken together, these three lessons enable a single person to transform the whole network of his or her family system. If your spouse nags, if your kids are disobedient, if your mother never comes to visit, *you* can create a change. Other schools of therapy exert leverage for change by including the entire family in treatment sessions; Bowenians teach individuals to be themselves, to make contact with others, and to resolve conflicts with the people they are in conflict with. This lesson gives a person leverage for change that is more portable and lasting than family therapy sessions.

Communications family clinicians contributed so much to the theoretical base of the family therapy movement that it is difficult to separate out their techniques or to single out their principal interventions. Perhaps their greatest achievement was to point out that communication is multilayered and that often the most important things being said are said covertly. Therapy was designed to make the covert overt. Initially this was done by pointing out hidden messages; when this direct approach met with resistance, therapists began using directives to make the rules of family functioning explicit, and to provoke changes in the rules.

Strategic therapy is an offshoot of communications theory, and the techniques used by strategists are refinements of those used by communicationists. Principal among these are *reframing, directives,* and *positive connotation.* Strategic practitioners begin by getting detailed descriptions of problems and attempts to solve them. In the process, they pay particular attention to the family's language and expectations. They try to grasp the family's point of view and acknowledge it, which is positive connotation; then they use reframing to shift the family's point of view, and directives to interrupt their problem-maintaining behavior. Using this general outline, members of this school plan on a general method; but as many others do, they tailor their interventions to fit each case.

In every case, the single most powerful intervention is probably the use of a directive. These directives are designed to break up rigid patterns of homeostasis; they are assigned to be carried out when the family is at home; and they are usually paradoxical. Although strategic therapists emphasize fitting the treatment to the patient, they consistently assume that indirect interventions are necessary to outwit resistance. This is sometimes, but not always necessary. It is not so much that some families are resistant and others are not, but that resistance is not a property *in* families; it is a quality of interaction between therapist and family. A therapist who proceeds on the assumption that families are unable and unwilling to follow advice is likely to encounter the expected resistance.

Structural family therapy is also a therapy of action, but in this approach the action occurs in the session. The decisive technique in this system is *altering the boundaries* between family members while they are in the process of interacting. Rigid boundaries are softened when the therapist gets people to talk with each other and blocks attempts to detour or interrupt them. Likewise, diffuse boundaries are strengthened when the therapist works to realign boundaries in the whole family. Blocking a parent's intrusion into the children's functioning will not last unless that parent is helped to get more involved with the spouse.

CONTEXT AND APPLICABILITY OF THE SCHOOLS OF FAMILY THERAPY

The predominant influence of social context, emphasized in family therapy, also applies to family therapists themselves and to the systems of treatment they develop. The pioneers of family therapy worked in different settings and with different patient populations. They did not set out to invent family therapy. They were working on other problems—analyzing communication, discovering the etiology of schizophrenia, treating delinquent children—and family therapy turned out to be part of the solution. But, as we have seen, "family therapy" is not one approach, it is many. The variations in setting, population, and intent of the developers combined to influence the nature of the various family therapies, and also helps to determine the type of patients that each method is most suited to. In this section I will briefly examine the contexts from which the different sects of family treatment emerged, and then consider which approaches are best for which problems.

The contextual roots of psychoanalytic family therapy are less easy to locate than those of the other systems. Ackerman was certainly the originator of this approach, but his death in 1971 left this school without a leader. Since then, contributing influences to psychoanalytic family therapy have come from many different quarters. Until recently most of the major figures in this school, including Ackerman himself, have been psychoanalytically-trained clinicians who abandoned psychoanalysis for family therapy; their analytic training was reflected in their theoretical papers, but not in their clinical methods. These early psychoanalytic family practitioners worked in a variety of settings—child guidance, social welfare, and marriage and family clinics; but for the most part, the families they worked with were members of the middle class with mild to moderate problems.

Today, more and more psychoanalytically-trained clinicians are practicing family therapy using methods that are consistent with their training (Nadelson, 1978). These practitioners tend to work in the same settings and with similar patients as do individual psychoanalytic therapists, namely, medical school outpatient clinics and private practices, with verbal, intelligent, middle-class patients who are not seriously disturbed. Psychoanalytic treatment—individual or family—is a method of self-discovery that relies heavily on words; and it works best with verbal patients who are motivated to learn about themselves. The more educated and sophisticated, the more readily they accept this approach.

The specific methods of family group therapy were developed by John E. Bell, but the general model of group therapy was used by most practitioners who treated families before family systems models of treatment were available. For this reason it is not possible to describe a specific context of family treatment in which this approach was developed. On the contrary, since this approach was developed for treating groups of strangers, it is probably more applicable to such groups than to families.

Carl Whitaker, the most prominent experiential family therapist, worked with delinquents and schizophrenics early in his career; later, he shifted toward less seriously disturbed patients. This transition, from more to less serious psychopathology, tends to come with success as a psychotherapist. Poverty and problems seem to go together. The most seriously troubled people are often poor and are usually treated by young clinicians in public clinics.

The concepts and methods of experiential psychotherapy were developed in the human potential movement to treat people with normal problems of everyday life. The cathartic techniques of this approach may be out of place for people struggling with serious psychopathology or situational stress, but for repressed neurotics these techniques are like an elixir that infuses new life into their days of anxiety and apathy.

Behavioral marriage therapy was developed in university departments of psychology and applied primarily to members of the academic community. These couples tend to be young, educated professionals, whose relationships are symmetrical and whose problems are not severe. They are usually well-motivated and willing to follow instructions in an educational format. Behavioral parent training was also developed in academic training centers, but has been applied to seriously disturbed children in institutions as well as to mildly disturbed children in university clinics. The concrete symptomatic focus of this treatment makes it a popular approach for dealing with severely symptomatic children. For this reason, behavior therapy is often used as an adjunct to other forms of treatment for hospitalized children (Minuchin, Rosman, and Baker, 1978). In hospital settings, behavioral treatment is usually applied not by the parents but by the staff; most behavioral parent training is conducted by graduate students in university counseling centers and psychological training clinics.

Murray Bowen developed his ideas about family therapy while he was at NIMH, studying middle-class families that had a psychotic member. This may help to account for two of the main emphases in his work: differentiation of self, and working with extended families. In psychotic families there is often a blurring of psychological boundaries—what Bowen called the undifferentiated family ego mass. These families exhibit an intense clinging interdependence, in which individual identities get diffused in an amorphous family togetherness. Bowen concluded that this lack of differentiation, or fusion, is the major source of pathology in all families. The goal of his treatment is to help family members differentiate themselves, which in turn will have a beneficial effect on the entire system. The process of differentiation begins with the therapist, who must remain emotionally neutral and avoid being drawn into the emotional quicksand of the undifferentiated family. This stance must have been necessary to avoid being engulfed by the psychotic families that Bowen started out with.

Bowen distinguishes between differentiation and emotional cutoff, which is common in the middle-class suburban families he studied in Washington, D.C. Emotional cutoff is a reactive flight from fusion, masquerading as genuine independence.

Although he first developed his ideas about families while studying a psychotic population, Bowen was more successful at understanding these families than he was at treating them. He no longer believes that family therapy is effective with schizophrenic families, and most of his work now is with middle-class professional families. Bowenian therapy may be most useful for young couples who have not yet successfully separated from their original families, including not only those who are obviously still dependent on their parents, but also those whose pseudoindependence is based on reactive distance. While Bowenian therapy may be ideally suited for middle-class couples in their twenties and thirties, its applicability is certainly not limited to this group. Bowen has an exquisite appreciation of triangular processes, and his therapeutic concepts are useful in any situation where two people form a coalition against a third.

Communications family therapists were scientists first, healers second. Their original intent was to study communication in schizophrenic families; only later did they decide to treat these unhappy people. At first they saw patients as victims of a family conspiracy to keep them sick, and tried to protect identified patients from the scapegoating of their relatives. Later they realized that in schizophrenia there are no victims and victimizers; the whole family is sick.

The feature of family life that captured their attention was the strange and puzzling ways schizophrenic families communicate. Conversation in these families is permeated with paradoxes, disqualifications, and double-binds. Analyses of these patterns of pathological communication were illuminating, and the findings cast doubt on traditional views of mental illness. Having discovered the family's role in creating and perpetuating psychological disorders, communications theorists began to criticize traditional individual psychotherapy. Jay Haley was the most outspoken critic, and his writing helped prepare the way for a new form of treatment based on the family's role in mental illness.

Among these theorists, Jackson, Haley, and Satir were the most interested in healing, and they were the pioneers of communications family treatment. It is a tribute to their optimism that they thought that schizophrenia could be cured by bringing together patients with their families and somehow talking them out of their strange and destructive patterns of communication. When they found that the direct approach did not work, they developed an indirect one. In place of interpretation they began to use manipulation. When communications therapists became strategists, they took a more emotionally distanced position, conducting therapy like generals outside the fray.

Jackson and Haley were the pivotal figures in the transition from communications theory to strategic therapy. Haley took the core concept of communications theory—that messages cannot be taken at face value, because they are always qualified by other messages on different levels—and derived the notion that all communication is part of a struggle for power in relationships. This position reflects Haley's personality and the context he was working in. Haley is an intellectual and an outsider; his major contributions have been critiques and attacks against psychoanalysis, the human potential movement, and experiential family therapy. His therapy is about power and control—how to wrest power in order to gain control of families through ingenious manipulation. Psychiatric symptoms are seen as perversions of the normal struggle for control. Instead of openly fighting for control, psychiatric patients deny that there is any conflict. They do not honestly refuse to participate; they "can't" because they are "sick." Strategic therapy forces patients into a corner, from which they can escape only by giving up their symptoms.

Emotional distance, struggle for power, and manipulation—none of these sounds very nice. To understand how these positions were developed it is necessary to consider where they were developed. Communications therapists worked with acute schizophrenics whose families were capable of driving people crazy with baffling responses and maddening double-binds. Perhaps conducting therapy from a distance is the only way to avoid getting completely entangled in such families. Perhaps if therapists do not struggle for power, they will be defeated by these families; and if they do not use manipulation, there will be no way to help. Today's strategic therapists still work with seriously disturbed cases, many of whom have tried and failed with other more straightforward approaches.

Structural family therapy was first developed with families of delinquents from the inner-city slums. These families are poor and often disorganized. Some are enmeshed—chaotic and tightly interconnected; others are disengaged—isolated and seemingly unrelated. Both types lack clear hierarchical structures. Creating functional structures by differentiating subsystems and realigning their boundaries is the object of structural family therapy.

Another characteristic of the ghetto families that Minuchin worked with at Wiltwyck is that they are outside the mainstream of American culture and feel alien in relation to middle-class helping professionals. In order to work with these families it is first necessary to get their attention and then to gain their confidence; this helps to account for Minuchin's active, directive style, and his emphasis on joining.

Structural family therapy's focus on the whole family is different from some of the other approaches that tend to work with subsets of the family. Strategic and Bowenian practitioners, for instance, move quickly to the adults, even when the presenting problem is about a child. Minuchin, however, was trained as a child psychiatrist and he has always believed that it is important to include children in treatment.

Understanding the contexts in which the different systems of family therapy were developed makes it easier to see why they have the form that they do. However, it does not tell us which therapy to use with which problem. There is no hard evidence that one system is more effective than the others, nor do we know which is best with any particular problem. There are, however, a few problems that seem particularly amenable to certain approaches.

Seriously disturbed patients—schizophrenics, borderlines, antisocial personalities—are obsessed with their own inner versions of reality; they need therapies that confront them and help them get involved in real life. Psychoanalytic and experiential family therapies are not the best choices. Strategic or structural family therapy practiced by someone who has experience in treating seriously disturbed families is more likely to be successful.

Psychoanalytic and experiential approaches are most effective with a verbal, educated, and sophisticated clientele. It is not that their conceptual models are narrowly applicable to this group; their techniques fit bright families and practitioners in these schools tend to work best with such people. Because these two approaches emphasize individual growth and enrichment, they are most suitable for people interested in long-term and fundamental personal change; they are least suited to people in crisis, whose major motivation is to solve an immediate problem.

The more pressing the situational problems, the less suitable are exploratory and reconstructive approaches. Bowenian therapy works best with well-motivated, minimally anxious people. This approach also has the advantage of being applicable if only one member of a family is willing to seek help.

Anxiety and motivation are important variables that affect whether a family is best served by action or understanding. High motivation and low anxiety make it possible to profit from approaches that focus on growth and understanding, like the psychoanalytic, experiential, and Bowenian schools. Families with high anxiety or low motivation do better with action-oriented approaches—structural or strategic.

Because they do not deal well with resistance, behavioral family therapists do best with families who want action, want to be told what to do, and will follow direction. In fact, families capable of profiting from this approach are often minimally distressed. Some of them could do as well by reading about the principles of positive control. The one group ideally served by behavioral treatment is made up of people experiencing sexual problems, minimally complicated by other relationship problems.

In the final analysis, the best treatment is given by the best therapist. If the best therapist in town is an experientialist, the best therapy in town is experiential.

SELECTION OF A THEORETICAL POSITION: RATIONAL AND IRRATIONAL FACTORS

How do students go about selecting a therapeutic orientation, and how should they? Deliberate choice probably exerts less influence than the personality and values of the student, or the training milieu. Having selected and been selected by a graduate program, students are pressured to conform to the models offered by their teachers and supervisors. While the idea of conformity may not be appealing, it is probably a good idea to embrace the model offered by your teachers. Learning whatever you can from every teacher or supervisor does not destroy your independence any more than rejecting and arguing protects it.

Except in the most homogeneous settings, students are liable to be exposed to a variety of different approaches during their graduate education; their interests are based on a series of fluid identifications with faculty members. While this may be confusing, it helps inoculate beginning clinicians against dogmatic thinking. Moreover, it provides the necessary breadth of information upon which to base an informed choice of a specialty. Once you leave academic course work to begin practical training, it is too late to shop around. During your clinical training, you should concentrate on learning one method well—that is, becoming thoroughly immersed in it. It may seem more creative to blend elements from a variety of systems in a personal integration, but this is better done after you master one single approach.

Selecting a system of family therapy to specialize in is not simply a question of which one is best. For one thing, there are still no data that identify which is the best form of treatment (Halleck, 1978). The choice depends upon what is available, what suits your clientele, and what suits you. The methods and techniques of therapy are never wholly separate from the qualities of the person applying them. Therefore, it is wise to choose an approach that is congruent with your style as a person.

Far too many people discontinue their training before they have mastered their craft. Training can be expensive, job offers beckon, and nobody wants to be a student forever. Because most people discontinue their training before they become expert, the field is filled with many so-called family therapists who are equipped with little more than a basic understanding of systems theory and a rudimentary knowledge of techniques.

After training (whether it is pursued to conclusion or prematurely terminated), there is a transition from student to full-fledged therapist. This can be a very gratifying time. Freed from the constraints of a beginner's status and removed from the watchful eyes of supervisors, practicing therapists become more spontaneous and fluid. Instead of being anxious about following the model or pleasing a supervisor, the therapist is free to get more involved with families and incorporate some of his or her natural style along with techniques that by now have become almost second nature. After you have gained experience in applying your model of therapy to the treatment of families, you are liable to experience the limitations of the model or your skill as therapist, or both. Many people then take refresher courses or look for workshops in new treatment approaches. Although I do believe strongly in mastering one particular model of therapy, I do not think it matters whether an experienced practitioner returns for a brushup in the original model or seeks out some new ideas. Experienced practitioners will be able to—will have to—integrate whatever they learn with their personal styles.

However, being able to integrate a variety of family therapy models with your own personality only works for those people who have a thorough background of training and supervision in some form of family therapy. Therapists who substitute periodic attendance at workshops and training conferences for a protracted period of indoctrination and training in one

·particular school of family therapy tend not to be competent family therapists. A series of workshops can stimulate and enhance the skills of experienced practitioners, but cannot substitute for the necessary apprenticeship.

SUMMARY

Each of the rival systems of family therapy proclaims its unique way of understanding and treating families. However, as we have seen, the differences are more sharply drawn in theory than in practice. The success of new developments in one school often leads to their adoption by others, shrinking the gaps among the various therapeutic orientations. The trend toward convergence is illustrated by Haley's incorporation of structural concepts into strategic therapy; by behaviorists who are increasingly taking into account nonobservable experience—cognition, affect, attitudes, motivation; and by the widespread use of certain techniques, including clarifying communication, reframing, and paradoxical directives.

Theories of family functioning have both a scientific and a practical purpose. The most useful theories treat families as systems; have concepts to describe forces for stability and change; consider the past, but concentrate on the present; treat communication as multileveled and complex; recognize the process underlying the content of family discussions; recognize the triadic nature of human relationships; remember to consider the context of the nuclear family, rather than viewing it a closed system isolated from its environment; and recognize the critical function of boundaries in protecting the cohesiveness of individuals, subgroups, and families.

Clinicians are more concerned with pathology and change than with normality, but it is useful to have a model of normal family functioning, both to mold treatment goals and to distinguish what is pathological and needs changing from what is normal and does not. Some of the most useful concepts of normal family functioning are: Minuchin's structural model of families as open systems in transformation; the communications theory model of direct, specific, and honest communication in a family system with rules clear enough to insure stability and flexible enough to allow change; the behavioral model of equitable exchange of interpersonal costs and benefits, the use of positive control instead of coercion, and mutual and reciprocal reinforcement between spouses; the family group theory which points out that groups function best when they are cohesive, when there is a free flow of communication, and when members' roles are clearly defined and appropriate to their needs; the strategic model of systemic flexibility, which allows adjustment to changing circumstances and the ability to find new solutions when old ones don't work; and the Bowenian model which explains how differentiation of self enables people to be independent at times, intimate at others.

Most family therapy concepts of behavior disorder focus on systems and interactions, but the psychoanalytic, Bowenian, and experiential models add intrapersonal depth to the interactional view, bridging the gap between private, inner experience and outward public behavior. The clinical observation that many divorced people repeat the mistakes of their first marriages supports these schools' position that some of what goes on in families is a product of individual character. Some of the most valuable concepts of personality dysfunction in families are: Bowen's concept of fusion; the experiential concepts of repressed affect and stifled growth; and psychoanalytic concepts of developmental arrest, internal object relations, and instinctual conflict. These concepts of individual psychopathology are useful adjuncts, but the guiding ideas in the field explain behavior disorder in terms of systems theory. The most influential of these are about inflexible systems, too rigid to accommodate to individual strivings or to adjust to changes in circumstances; symptomatic family members promoting cohesion by stabilizing the nuclear and extended families; inadequate hierarchical structure; families that are too tightly or too loosely structured; and pathological triangles.

The broad goals of family therapy are to solve presenting problems and to reorganize families. Behaviorists and strategists aim for the former, Bowenians and psychoanalysts aim for the latter; most of the other schools aim for both. As we have seen, some family practitioners expect therapy to be prolonged, while others keep it brief. These diverse strategies reflect differences of opinion about how much change families need to accomplish. In my opinion, that question should be left to the family. Therapists should accept the family's goal to solve their immediate problems, and design therapy to reorganize only that aspect of the family that has become dysfunctional. If families want more, they should say so.

Some of the specific goals of family therapy are practically universal — clarifying communication, solving problems, promoting individual autonomy — and some are unique. Some of the schools take the presenting problem at face value, while others treat it as a metaphor and a sign. In either case, goals should not be so broad as to neglect symptom resolution, or too narrow to insure the stability of symptom resolution. Incidentally, values are seldom discussed in the family therapy literature. The one exception is

Boszormenyi-Nagy, but he considers the ethical dimension only in terms of the patient. There is too little consideration of the practicing therapist's ethical responsibilities, including the possibility of conflicting responsibilities to individuals, families, and the larger community.

Some of the major differences among family therapists about how behavior is changed are focused on the following issues: action or insight; change in the session or change at home; duration of treatment; resistance; family-therapist relationship; and paradox. Even though there is a general consensus about some of the issues—for example, most family therapists believe that action is primary and insight is useful but secondary—there are divergent opinions on every one of these points. Strategic therapists, for example, flatly deny that insight is necessary or useful.

I have discussed some of the major methodological issues and tried to separate out the decisive techniques of the different systems. As is always the case when a number of variables are involved in a final result, it is not easy to know to what degree each variable contributes to that result, or how important each one is. Furthermore, the more we talk about techniques, the greater the danger of seeing family therapy as a purely technological enterprise. Studying families is like solving a riddle; the art of treating them is to relieve suffering and anguish. The job of the theoretician is to decode or decipher; it requires theory and ingenuity. The job of the therapist is to cure; it requires theory, but also power, perseverance, and caring. Treating families is not only an act of science and technology; it is also an act of love.

REFERENCES

Bowen, M. The use of family theory in clinical practice. *Comprehensive Psychiatry,* 1966, *7,* 345–374.

Dunlap, K. A revision of the fundamental law of habit formation. *Science,* 1928, *67,* 360–362.

Frankl, V. Paradoxical intention: A logotherapeutic technique. *American Journal of Psychotherapy,* 1960, *14,* 520–535.

Gordon, S.B. & Davidson, N. Behavioral parent training. In A.S. Gurman & D.P. Kniskern (Eds.), *Handbook of family therapy.* New York: Brunner/Mazel, 1981.

Haley, J. *Strategies of psychotherapy.* New York: Grune & Stratton, 1963.

Haley, J. *Problem-solving therapy.* San Francisco: Jossey-Bass, 1976.

Haley, J. Toward a theory of pathological systems. In P. Watzlawick & J. Weakland (Eds.), *The interactional view.* New York: Norton, 1977.

Haley, J. *Leaving home: The therapy of disturbed young people*. New York: McGraw-Hill, 1980.

Halleck, S. *The treatment of emotional disorders*. New York: Jason Aronson, 1978.

Hoffman, L. *Foundations of family therapy*. New York: Basic Books, 1981.

Jackson, D.D. Family rules: The marital quid pro quo. *Archives of General Psychiatry*, 1965, *12*, 589–594.

Jasnow, A. The psychotherapist–artist and/or scientist? *Psychotherapy: Theory, Research and Practice*, 1978, *15*, 318–322.

Kendrick, D.D. The theory of "conditioned inhibition" as an explanation of negative practice effects: An experimental analysis. In H.J. Eysenck (Ed.), *Behavior therapy and the neuroses*. New York: Pergamon, 1960.

Luborsky, L. Research cannot yet influence clinical practice. In A.E. Bergin & H.H. Strupp (Eds.), *Changing frontiers in the science of psychotherapy*. New York: Aldine-Atherton, 1972.

Madanes, C. Protection, paradox and pretending. *Family Process*, 1980, *19*, 73–85.

Madanes, C. & Haley, J. Dimensions of family therapy. *Journal of Nervous and Mental Disease*, 1977, *165*, 88–98.

Mahler, M.S., Pine, F. & Bergman, A. *The psychological birth of the human infant*. New York: Basic Books, 1975.

Matarazzo, J.D. Interview: J.D. Matarazzo. In A.E. Bergin & H.H. Strupp (Eds.), *Changing frontiers in the science of psychotherapy*. New York: Aldine-Atherton, 1972.

Minuchin, S. *Families and family therapy*. Cambridge: Harvard University Press, 1974.

Minuchin, S., Rosman, B. & Baker, L. *Psychosomatic families: Anorexia nervosa in context*. Cambridge: Harvard University Press, 1978.

Minuchin, S. & Fishman, H.C. *Family therapy techniques*. Cambridge: Harvard University Press, 1981.

Nadelson, C.C. Marital therapy from a psychoanalytic perspective. In T.J. Paolino & B.S. McCrady (Eds.), *Marriage and marital therapy: Psychoanalytic, behavioral and systems theory perspectives*. New York: Brunner/Mazel, 1978.

Paul, W.L. The use of empathy in the resolution of grief. *Perspectives in Biology and Medicine*, 1967, *11*, 153–169.

Pierce, R., Nichols, M.P. & DuBrin, J. *Emotional expression in psychotherapy*. New York: Gardner Press, 1983.

Rabkin, R. *Strategic psychotherapy*. New York: Basic Books, 1977.

Rogers, C.R. The necessary and sufficient conditions of therapeutic personality change. *Journal of Consulting Psychology*, 1957, *21*, 95–103.

Selvini Palazzoli, M., Bascolo, G., Cecchin, G. & Prata, G. Hypothesizing-circularity-neutrality: Three guidelines for the conductor of family interviews. *Family Process*, 1980, *19*, 3–12.

Stanton, M.D., Todd, T.C. & Associates. *The family therapy of drug addiction*. New York: Guilford, 1981.

Thibaut, J.W. & Kelley, H.H. *The social psychology of groups*. New York: Wiley, 1959.

Vogel, E.F. & Bell, N.W. The emotionally disturbed child as the family scapegoat. In

N.W. Bell & E.F. Vogel (Eds.), *The family.* Glencoe, Ill.: Free Press, 1960.

Watzlawick, P., Beavin, J. & Jackson, D.D. *Pragmatics of human communication.* New York: Norton, 1967.

Whitaker, C.A. & Keith, D.V. Symbolic-experiential family therapy. In A.S. Gurman & D.P. Kniskern (Eds.), *Handbook of family therapy.* New York: Brunner/Mazel, 1981.

APPENDIX A
RECOMMENDED READINGS

1. The Historical Context of Family Therapy

Ackerman, N.W. & Sobel, R. Family diagnosis: An approach to the preschool child. *American Journal of Orthopsychiatry*, 1950, *20*, 744–753.

Boszormenyi-Nagy, I. The concept of schizophrenia from the point of view of family treatment. *Family Process*, 1962, *1*, 103–113.

Bowen, M. A family concept of schizophrenia. In D.D. Jackson (Ed.), *The etiology of schizophrenia*. New York: Basic Books, 1960.

Guerin, P.J. Family therapy: The first twenty-five years. In P.J. Guerin (Ed.), *Family therapy: Theory and practice*. New York: Gardner Press, 1976.

Haley, J. The family of the schizophrenic. *American Journal of Nervous and Mental Diseases*, 1959, *129*, 357–374.

Haley, J. & Hoffman, L. (Eds.), *Techniques of family therapy*. New York: Basic Books, 1968.

Jackson, D.D. The question of family homeostasis. *The Psychiatric Quarterly Supplement*, 1957, *31*, 79–90.

Jackson, D.D. Family rules: Marital quid pro quo. *Archives of General Psychiatry*, 1965, *12*, 589–594.

Lidz, T., Cornelison, A., Fleck, S. & Terry, D. Intrafamilial environment of schizophrenic patients. II: Marital schism and marital skew. *American Journal of Psychiatry*, 1957, *20*, 241–248.

Weakland, J.H. The "double bind" hypothesis of schizophrenia and three-party interaction. In D.D. Jackson (Ed.), *The etiology of schizophrenia*. New York: Basic Books, 1960.

Whitaker, C.A. Psychotherapy with couples. *American Journal of Psychotherapy*, 1958, *12*, 18–23.

Wynne, L.C., Ryckoff, I., Day, J. & Hirsch, S.I. Pseudo-mutuality in the family relationships of schizophrenics. *Psychiatry*, 1958, *21*, 205–220.

2. The Contemporary Context of Family Therapy

Beels, C.C. & Ferber, A. Family therapy: A view. *Family Process*, 1969, *8*, 280–332.

Bloch, D.A. & Weiss, H.M. Training facilities in marital and family therapy. *Family Process*, 1981, *20*, 133–146.

Foley, V.D. *An introduction to family therapy*. New York: Grune & Stratton, 1974.

Group for the Advancement of Psychiatry. *Treatment of families in conflict: The clinical study of family process*. New York: Jason Aronson, 1970.

Guerin, P.J. *Family therapy: Theory and practice*. New York: Gardner Press, 1976.

Gurman, A.S. & Kniskern, D.P. Research on marital and family therapy: Progress, perspective and prospect. In S. Garfield & A. Bergin (Eds.), *Handbook of psychotherapy and behavior change*, Second edition. New York: Wiley, 1978.

Olson, D.H. Marital and family therapy: Integrative review and critique. *Journal of Marriage and the Family*, 1970, *32*, 501–538.

Sluzki, C. Interview on the state of the art. *Family Therapy Networker*, 1983, *7*, (1), 24.

3. The Theoretical Context of Family Therapy

Barnhill, L.R. & Longo, D. Fixation and regression on the family life cycle. *Family Process*, 1978, *17*, 469–478.

von Bertalanffy, L. *Robots, men and minds*. New York: George Braziller, 1967.

Carter, E.A. & McGoldrick, M. The family life cycle and family therapy: An overview. In E.A. Carter & M. McGoldrick (Eds.), *The family life cycle: A framework for family therapy*. New York: Gardner Press, 1980.

Eiduson, B.T. Emergent families of the 1970s: Values, practices, and impact on children. In D. Reiss & H. Hoffman (Eds.), *The American family: Dying or developing*. New York: Plenum Press, 1979.

Erikson, E.H. *Childhood and society*. New York: Norton, 1950.

Hill, R. Contemporary developments in family theory. *Journal of Marriage and the Family*, 1966, *28*, 10–26.

Levinson, D.J. *The seasons of a man's life*. New York: Ballantine Books, 1978.

Lidz, T. *The person*. New York: Basic Books, 1976.

McGoldrick, M. The joining of families through marriage: The new couple. In E.A. Carter & M. McGoldrick (Eds.), *The family life cycle: A framework for family therapy*. New York: Gardner Press, 1980.

Parson, T. & Bales, R.F. *Family socialization and interaction processes.* Glencoe, Ill.: Free Press, 1955.

Piaget, J. *The origins of intelligence in children.* New York: Norton, 1963.

Walsh, F. (Ed.), *Normal family processes.* New York: Guilford, 1982.

Weiner, N. *Cybernetics or control and communication in the animal and the machine.* Cambridge, Mass.: Technology Press, 1948.

Whitaker, C.A. The hindrance of theory in clinical work. In P.J. Guerin (Ed.), *Family therapy: Theory and practice.* New York: Gardner Press, 1976.

4. Psychoanalytic Family Therapy

Ackerman, N.W. *The psychodynamics of family life.* New York: Basic Books, 1958.

Ackerman, N.W. *Treating the troubled family.* New York: Basic Books, 1966.

Boszormenyi-Nagy, I. Loyalty implications of the transference model in psychotherapy. *Archives of General Psychiatry,* 1972, *27,* 374–380.

Boszormenyi-Nagy, I. & Framo, J. (Eds.), *Intensive family therapy: Theoretical and practical aspects.* New York: Harper & Row, 1965.

Boszormenyi-Nagy, I. & Spark, G. *Invisible loyalties: Reciprocity in intergenerational family therapy.* New York: Harper & Row, 1973.

Dicks, H.V. *Marital tensions.* New York: Basic Books, 1967.

Meissner, W.W. The conceptualization of marriage and family dynamics from a psychoanalytic perspective. In T.J. Paolino & B.S. McCrady (Eds.), *Marriage and marital therapy.* New York: Brunner/Mazel, 1978.

Nadelson, C.C. Marital therapy from a psychoanalytic perspective. In T.J. Paolino & B.S. McCrady (Eds.), *Marriage and marital therapy.* New York: Brunner/Mazel, 1978.

Skynner, A.R.C. *Systems of family and marital psychotherapy.* New York: Brunner/Mazel, 1976.

Vogel, E.F. & Bell, N.W. The emotionally disturbed child as the family scapegoat. In N.W. Bell & E.F. Vogel (Eds.), *The family.* Glencoe, Ill.: Free Press, 1960.

Zinner, J. & Shapiro, R. Projective identification as a mode of perception and behavior in families of adolescents. *International Journal of Psychoanalysis.* 1972, *53,* 523–530.

5. Family Group Therapy

Bell, J.E. *Family group therapy.* Public Health Monograph N. 64. Washington, D.C.: U.S. Government Printing Office, 1961.

Bell, J.E. *Family therapy.* New York: Jason Aronson, 1975.

Bion, W.R. *Experience in groups.* London: Tavistock Publications, 1961.

Lewin, K. *Field theory in social science.* New York: McGraw-Hill, 1957.

Shaw, M.E. *Group dynamics: The psychology of small group behavior.* New York: McGraw-Hill, 1981.

Yalom, I.D. *The theory and practice of group psychotherapy.* New York: Basic Books, 1970.

6. Experiential Family Therapy

Duhl, B.S. & Duhl, F.J. Integrative family therapy. In A.S. Gurman & D.P. Kniskern (Eds.), *Handbook of family therapy.* New York: Brunner/Mazel, 1981.

Duhl, F.J., Kantor, D. & Duhl, B.S. Learning, space and action in family therapy: A primer of sculpture. In D.A. Bloch (Ed.), *Techniques of family therapy.* New York: Grune & Stratton, 1973.

Kaplan, M.L. & Kaplan, N.R. Individual and family growth: A Gestalt approach. *Family Process,* 1978, *17,* 195–205.

Keith, D.V. & Whitaker, C.A. The divorce labyrinth. In P. Papp (Ed.), *Family therapy: Full length case studies.* New York: Gardner Press, 1977.

Kempler, W. *Experiential psychotherapy within families.* New York: Brunner/Mazel, 1981.

Laing, R.D. & Esterson, A. *Sanity, madness and the family.* Baltimore: Penguin Books, 1970.

Napier, A.Y. & Whitaker, C.A. *The family crucible.* New York: Harper & Row, 1978.

Neil, J.R. & Kniskern, D.P. (Eds.), *From psyche to system: The evolving therapy of Carl Whitaker.* New York: Guilford, 1982.

Satir, V. *Peoplemaking.* Palo Alto, Calif.: Science and Behavior Books, 1972.

Whitaker, C.A. The growing edge. In J. Haley & L. Hoffman (Eds.), *Techniques of family therapy.* New York: Basic Books, 1967.

Whitaker, C.A. & Keith, D.V. Symbolic-experiential family therapy. In A.S. Gurman & D.P. Kniskern (Eds.), *Handbook of family therapy.* New York: Brunner/Mazel, 1981.

7. Behavioral Family Therapy

Alexander, J.F. & Barton, C. Behavioral systems therapy with families. In D.H. Olson (Ed.), *Treating relationships.* Lake Mills, Iowa: Graphic Publishing, 1976.

Gordon, S.B. & Davidson, N. Behavioral parent training. In A.S. Gurman & D.P. Kniskern (Eds.), *Handbook of family therapy.* New York: Brunner/Mazel, 1981.

Graziano, A.M. Parents as behavior therapists. In M. Hersen, R.M. Eisler & P.M. Miller (Eds.), *Progress in behavior modification.* New York: Academic Press, 1977.

Jacobson, N.S. & Margolin, G. *Marital therapy: Strategies based on social learning and behavior exchange principles.* New York: Brunner/Mazel, 1979.

Kaplan, H.S. *The new sex therapy: Active treatment of sexual dysfunctions.* New York: Brunner/Mazel, 1974.

Liberman, R.P. Behavioral approaches to family and couple therapy. In C.J. Sager & H.S. Kaplan (Eds.), *Progress in group and family therapy*. New York: Brunner/Mazel, 1972.

Masters, W.H. & Johnson, V.E. *Human sexual inadequacy*. Boston: Little Brown, 1970.

O'Leary, K.D. & Turkewitz, J. Marital therapy from a behavioral perspective. In T.J. Paolino & B.S. McCrady (Eds.), *Marriage and marital therapy*. New York: Brunner/Mazel, 1978.

Patterson, G.R. *Families: Application of social learning theory to family life*. Champaign, Illinois: Research Press, 1971.

Weiss, R.L. The conceptualization of marriage from a behavioral perspective. In T.J. Paolino & B.S. McCrady (Eds.), *Marriage and marital therapy*. Brunner/Mazel, 1978.

8. Extended Family Systems Therapy

Anonymous. Differentiation of self in one's family. In J. Framo (Ed.), *Family interaction*. New York: Springer, 1972.

Bowen, M. *Family therapy in clinical practice*. New York: Jason Aronson, 1978.

Carter, E. & Orfanidis, M.M. Family therapy with one person and the family therapist's own family. In P.J. Guerin (Ed.), *Family therapy: Theory and practice*. New York: Gardner Press, 1976.

Fogarty, T.F. Systems concepts and the dimensions of self. In P.J. Guerin (Ed.), *Family therapy: Theory and practice*. New York: Gardner Press, 1976.

Fogarty, T.F. Marital crisis. In P.J. Guerin (Ed.), *Family therapy: Theory and practice*. New York: Gardner Press, 1976.

Guerin, P.J. & Pendagast, E.G. Evaluation of family system and genogram. In P.J. Guerin (Ed.), *Family therapy: Theory and practice*. New York: Gardner Press, 1976.

Laqueur, H.P. Mechanisms of change in multiple family therapy. In C.J. Sager & H.S. Kaplan (Eds.), *Progress in group and family therapy*. New York: Brunner/Mazel, 1972.

Speck, R. & Attneave, C. *Family networks: Rehabilitation and healing*. New York: Pantheon, 1973.

Ruevini, U. Network intervention with a family in crisis. *Family Process*, 1975, *14*, 193–203.

9. Communications Family Therapy

von Bertalanffy, L. An outline of General System Theory. *British Journal of the Philosophy of Science*, 1950, *1*, 134–165.

Haley, J. *Strategies of psychotherapy*. New York: Grune & Stratton, 1963.

Hoffman, L. Deviation-amplifying processes in natural groups. In J. Haley (Ed.), *Changing families*. New York: Grune & Stratton, 1971.

Jackson, D.D. Interactional psychotherapy. In M.T. Stein (Ed.), *Contemporary psychotherapies*. New York: Free Press of Glencoe, 1961.

Lederer, W. & Jackson, D.D. *Mirages of marriage*. New York: Norton, 1968.

Satir, V. *Conjoint family therapy*. Palo Alto: Science and Behavior, 1967.

Scheflen, A.E. Human communication: Behavioral programs and their integration in interaction. *Behavioral Science*, 1968, *13*, 86–102.

Sluzki, C.E. Marital therapy from a systems theory perspective. In T.J. Paolino & B.S. McCrady (Eds.), *Marriage and marital therapy*. New York: Brunner/Mazel, 1978.

Watzlawick, P., Beavin, J.H. & Jackson, D.D. *Pragmatics of human communication*. New York: Norton, 1967.

Wynne, L.C. Communication disorders and the quest for relatedness in families of schizophrenics. *American Journal of Psychoanalysis*, 1970, *30*, 100–114.

10. Strategic Family Therapy

Fisch, R., Weakland, J.H. & Segal, L. *The tactics of change: Doing therapy briefly*. San Francisco: Jossey-Bass, 1982.

Haley, J. *Uncommon therapy*. New York: Norton, 1973.

Haley, J. *Problem-solving therapy*. San Francisco: Jossey-Bass, 1976.

Haley, J. *Leaving home*. New York: McGraw-Hill, 1980.

Hoffman, L. Breaking the homeostatic cycle. In P.J. Guerin (Ed.), *Family therapy: Theory and practice*. New York: Gardner Press, 1976.

Madanes, C. *Strategic family therapy*. San Francisco: Jossey-Bass, 1981.

Rabkin, R. *Strategic psychotherapy*. New York: Basic Books, 1972.

Selvini Palazzoli, M., Boscolo, L., Cecchin, G. & Prata, G. *Paradox and counterparadox*. New York: Jason Aronson, 1978.

Watzlawick, P., Weakland, J. & Fisch, R. *Change: Principles of problem formation and problem resolution*. New York: Norton, 1974.

11. Structural Family Therapy

Minuchin, S. *Families and family therapy*. Cambridge: Harvard University Press, 1974.

Minuchin, S., Baker, L., Rosman, B., Liebman, R., Milman, L. & Todd, T.C. A conceptual model of psychosomatic illness in children. *Archives of General Psychiatry*, 1975, *32*, 1031–1038.

Minuchin, S. & Fishman, H.C. *Family therapy techniques*. Cambridge: Harvard University Press, 1981.

Minuchin, S., Montalvo, B., Guerney, B., Rosman, B. & Schumer, F. *Families of the slums*. New York: Basic Books, 1967.

Minuchin, S., Rosman, B.L. & Baker, L. *Psychosomatic families: Anorexia nervosa in context*. Cambridge: Harvard University Press, 1978.
Stanton, M.D. & Todd, T.C. Structural family therapy with drug addicts. In E. Kaufman & P. Kaufmann (Eds.), *The family therapy of drug and alcohol abuse*. New York: Gardner Press, 1979.

12. Comparative Analysis

Gurman, A.S. Contemporary marital therapies: A critique and comparative analysis of psychoanalytic, behavioral and systems theory approaches. In T.J. Paolino & B.S. McCrady (Eds.), *Marriage and marital therapy*. New York: Brunner/Mazel, 1978.
Hoffman, L. *Foundations of family therapy*. New York: Basic Books, 1981.
Madanes, C. & Haley, J. Dimensions of family therapy. *Journal of Nervous and Mental Disease*, 1977, *165*, 88–98.

Appendix B
Glossary

anorexia nervosa. Self-starvation leading to loss of 25 percent or more of body weight, hyperactivity, hypothermia, and amenorrhea (in females).

aversive control. Using punishment and criticism to eliminate undesirable responses; commonly used in dysfunctional families.

basic assumption theory. Bion's concept that group members become diverted from the group task to pursue unconscious patterns of *fight-flight, dependency,* or *pairing.*

behavior exchange theory. Explanation of behavior in relationships as maintained by a ratio of costs to benefits.

blended families. Separate families united by marriage; stepfamilies.

boundary. A concept used in structural family therapy to describe emotional barriers that protect and enhance the integrity of individuals, subsystems, and families.

circular causality. The idea that events are related through a series of interacting loops or repeating cycles.

classical conditioning. A form of respondant learning in which an unconditioned stimulus (UCS), such as food, which leads to an unconditioned response (UCR), such as salivation, is paired with a conditioned stimulus (CS), such as a bell, the result of which is that the CS begins to evoke the same response; used in the behavioral treatment of anxiety disorders.

communications theory. The study of relationships in terms of the exchange of verbal and nonverbal messages.

complementary. Relationships based on differences which fit together, where qualities of one make up for lacks in the other; one is one-up, while the other is one-down.

concurrent therapy. Treatment of two or more persons, seen separately, usually by different therapists.

conjoint therapy. Treatment of two or more persons in sessions together.

contingency contracting. A behavior-therapy technique whereby agreements are made between family members to exchange rewards for desired behavior.

countertransference. Emotional reaction, usually unconscious and often distorted, on the part of the therapist to a patient or member of a family in treatment.

cross-generational coalition. An inappropriate alliance between a parent and child, who side together against a third member of the family.

cybernetics. The study of control processes in systems, especially analysis of the flow of information in closed systems.

differentiation. Psychological separation of intellect and emotions, and independence of self from others; opposite of fusion.

disengagement. Minuchin's term for psychological isolation that results from overly rigid boundaries around individuals and subsystems in a family.

double-bind. A conflict created when a person receives contradictory messages on different levels of abstraction in an important relationship, and cannot leave or comment.

dyadic model. Explanations based on the interactions between two persons or objects: Johnny shoplifts to get his mother's attention.

emotional cutoff. Bowen's term for flight from an unresolved emotional attachment.

enactment. An interaction stimulated in structural family therapy in order to observe and then change transactions which make up family structure.

enmeshment. Minuchin's term for loss of autonomy due to a blurring of psychological boundaries.

expressive role. Serving social and emotional functions; in traditional families, the wife's role.

extended family. All the descendants of a set of grandparents.

extinction. Eliminating behavior by not reinforcing it.

family drawing. An experiential therapy technique where family members are asked to draw their ideas about how the family is organized.

family group therapy. Family treatment based on the group therapy model.

family homeostasis. Tendency of families to resist change in order to maintain a steady state.

family life cycle. Stages of family life from separation from one's parents, to marriage, having children, growing older, retirement, and finally death.

family structure. The functional organization of families that determines how family members interact.

family myths. A set of beliefs based on a distortion of historical reality and shared by all family members that help shape the rules governing family functioning.

family of origin. A person's parents and siblings; usually refers to the original nuclear family of an adult.

family projection process. In Bowenian theory, the mechanism by which parental conflicts are projected onto the children or a spouse.

family ritual. Technique used by Selvini Palazzoli and her Milan Associates that prescribes a specific act for family members to perform, which is designed to change the family system's rules.

family rules. A descriptive term for redundant behavioral patterns.

family sculpting. A nonverbal experiential technique in which family members position themselves in a tableau that reveals significant aspects of their perceptions and feelings.

feedback. The return of a portion of the output of a system, especially when used to maintain the output within predetermined limits (negative feedback), or to signal a need to modify the system (positive feedback).

first order change. Superficial change in a system which itself stays invariant.

functional analysis of behavior. In operant behavior therapy, a study of a particular behavior, what elicits it, and what reinforces it.

fusion. A blurring of psychological boundaries between self and others, and a contamination of emotional and intellectual functioning; opposite of differentiation.

general systems theory. A biological model of living systems as whole entities which maintain themselves through continuous input and output from the environment; developed by Ludwig von Bertalanffy.

genogram. A schematic diagram of the family system, using squares to represent men, circles to indicate women, horizontal lines for marriages, and vertical lines to indicate children.

group dynamics. Interactions among group members that emerge as a result of properties of the group rather than merely their individual personalities.

hierarchical structure. Family functioning based on clear generational boundaries, where the parents maintain control and authority.

homeostasis. A balanced steady state of equilibrium.

identified patient. The symptom bearer or official patient as identified by the family.

instrumental role. Decision-making and task functions; in traditional families, the husband's role.

intensity. Minuchin's term for changing maladaptive transactions by using strong affect, repeated intervention, or prolonged pressure.

introjection. A primitive form of identification; taking in aspects of other people, which then become part of the self-image.

invisible loyalties. Boszormenyi-Nagy's term for unconscious commitments that children take on to help their families.

joining. A structural family therapy term for accepting and accommodating to families in order to win their confidence and circumvent resistance.

linear causality. The idea that one event is the cause and another is the effect; in behavior, the idea that one behavior is a stimulus, the other a response.

live supervision. Technique of teaching therapy whereby the supervisor observes sessions in progress and contacts the therapist to suggest different strategies and techniques.

marital schism. Lidz's term for pathological overt marital conflict.

marital skew. Lidz's term for a pathological marriage in which one spouse dominates the other.

metacommunication. Every message has two levels, report and command; metacommunication is the implied command or qualifying message.

modeling. Observational learning.

monadic model. Explanations based on properties of a single person or object: Johnny shoplifts because he is rebellious.

multigenerational transmission process. Murray Bowen's concept for the projection of varying degrees of immaturity to different children in the same family; the child who is most involved in the family emotional process emerges with the lowest level of differentiation, and passes problems on to succeeding generations.

multiple family therapy. Treatment of several families at once in a group therapy format; pioneered by Peter Laqueur and Murray Bowen.

multiple impact therapy. An intensive, crisis-oriented form of family therapy developed by Robert MacGregor; family members are treated in
various subgroups by a team of therapists.

mystification. Laing's concept that many families distort their children's
experience by denying or relabeling it.

network therapy. A treatment devised by Ross Speck in which a large
number of family and friends are assembled to help resolve a patient's
problems.

nuclear family. Parents and their children.

object relations. Internalized images of self and others based on early
parent-child interactions which determine a person's mode of relationship to other people.

object relations theory. Psychoanalytic theory derived from Melanie Klein
and developed by the British School (Bion, Fairbairn, Guntrip,
Winnicott) which emphasizes the object-seeking propensity of the
infant, instead of focusing exclusively on libidinal and aggressive
drives.

operant conditioning. A form of learning whereby a person or animal is
rewarded for performing certain behaviors; the major approach in
most forms of behavior therapy.

paradox. A self-contradictory statement based on a valid deduction from
acceptable premises.

paradoxical directive. A technique used in strategic therapy whereby the
therapist directs family members to continue their symptomatic behavior. If they conform, they admit control and expose secondary gain; if
they rebel, they give up their symptoms.

parental child. A child who has been allocated power to take care of younger
siblings; adaptive when done deliberately in large or single parent
families; maladaptive when it results from unplanned abdication of
parental responsibility.

Premack principle. Using high probability behavior (preferred activities)
to reinforce low probability behavior (nonpreferred activities).

prescribing the symptom. A paradoxical technique which forces a patient
to either give up a symptom or admit that it is under voluntary
control.

positive connotation. Selvini Palazzoli's technique of ascribing positive
motives to family behavior in order to promote family cohesion and
avoid resistance to therapy.

pretend techniques. Madanes's playful paradoxical intervention in which family members are asked to pretend to engage in symptomatic behavior. The paradox is, if they are pretending to have a symptom, the symptom cannot be real.

process/content. Distinction between how members of a family or group relate and what they talk about.

projective identification. A defense mechanism that operates unconsciously whereby unwanted aspects of the self are attributed to another person and that person is induced to behave in accordance with these projected attitudes and feelings.

pseudohostility. Wynne's term for superficial bickering which masks pathological alignments in schizophrenic families.

pseudomutuality. Wynne's term for the façade of family harmony that characterizes many schizophrenic families.

quid pro quo. Literally, "something for something," an equal exchange or substitution.

reframing. Relabeling a family's description of behavior to make it more amenable to therapeutic change; for example, describing someone as "lazy" rather than "depressed."

regression. Return to a less mature level of functioning in the face of stress.

reinforcement. An event, behavior, or object that increases the rate of a particular response. A positive reinforcer is an event whose contingent presentation increases the rate of responding; a negative reinforcer is an event whose contingent withdrawal increases the rate of responding.

reinforcement reciprocity. Exchanging rewarding behaviors between family members.

resistance. Anything that patients or families do to oppose or retard the progress of therapy.

restraining. A strategic technique for overcoming resistance by suggesting that a family not change.

roleplaying. Acting out the parts of important characters to dramatize feelings and practice new ways of relating.

rubber fence. Wynne's term for the rigid boundary surrounding many schizophrenic families, which allows only minimal contact with the surrounding community.

scapegoat. A member of the family, usually the identified patient, who is the object of displaced conflict or criticism.

schizophrenogenic mother. Fromm-Reichmann's term for aggressive, domineering mothers thought to precipitate schizophrenia in their offspring.

second order change. Basic change in the structure and functioning of a system.

separation-individuation. Process whereby the infant begins, at about 2 months, to draw apart from the symbiotic bond with mother and develop his or her own autonomous functioning.

shaping. Reinforcing change in small steps.

social learning theory. Understanding and treating behavior using principles from social and developmental psychology as well as from learning theory.

structured family interview. An assessment procedure, introduced by Watzlawick, in which families are given a series of tasks for discussion, and their interactions are observed and coded.

subsystem. Smaller units in families, determined by generation, sex, or function.

symmetrical. In relationships, equality or parallel form.

systems, closed. A functionally related group of elements regarded as forming a collective entity that does not interact with the surrounding environment.

systems, open. A set of interrelated elements that exchange information, energy, and material with the surrounding environment.

systems theory. A generic term for studying a group of related elements that interact as a whole entity; encompasses general systems theory and cybernetics.

theory of logical types. Bertrand Russell's theory of hierarchical levels of abstraction; a class is a different logical type than a member of the class.

three generational hypothesis of schizophrenia. Bowen's concept that schizophrenia is the end result of low levels of differentiation passed on and amplified across three succeeding generations.

token economy. A system of rewards using points, which can be accumulated and exchanged for reinforcing items or behaviors.

transference. Psychoanalytic term for distorted emotional reactions to present relationships based on unresolved, early family relations.

triadic model. Explanations based on the interactions among three people or objects: Johnny shoplifts because his father covertly encourages him to defy his mother.

triangle. A three-person system; according to Bowen, the smallest stable unit of human relations.

triangulation. Detouring conflict between two people by involving a third person, stabilizing the relationship between the original pair.

unconscious. Psychoanalytic term for memories, feelings, and impulses of which a person is unaware. Often used as a noun, but more appropriately limited to use as an adjective.

undifferentiated family ego mass. Bowen's early term for emotional "stuck-togetherness" or fusion in the family, especially prominent in schizophrenic families.

Name Index

Subject Index

ABOUT THE AUTHOR

Michael P. Nichols, Ph.D. is Associate Professor and Director of Outpatient Psychiatry at Albany Medical College. A graduate of the University of Rochester, he has received training from several of the leading family therapists in the country. In addition to teaching and practicing family therapy, Dr. Nichols is also interested in emotional expression and individual psychotherapy. Among his other books are *Catharsis in Psychotherapy* (Gardner Press), with Melvin Zax and *Emotional Expression in Psychotherapy* (Gardner Press) with Robert Pierce and Joyce DuBrin.